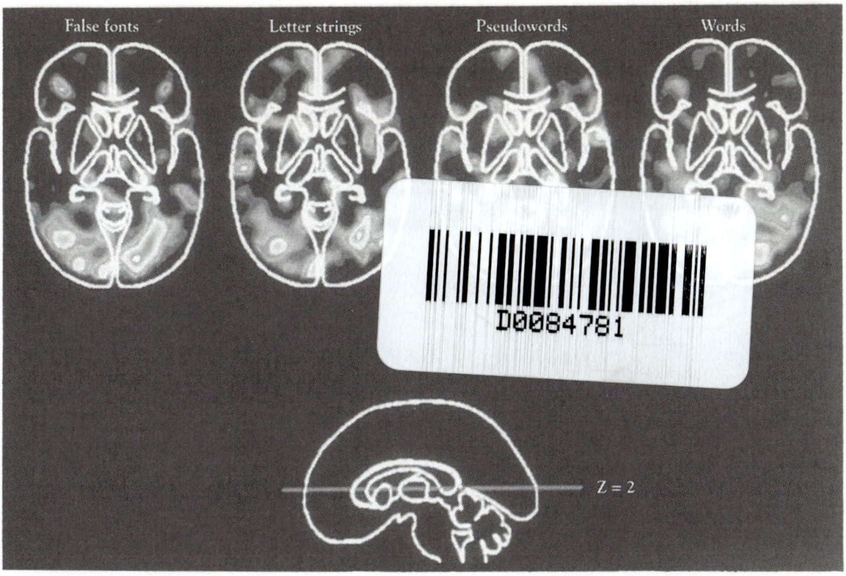

Color Plate 3. Passive viewing of four types of visual stimuli produce different patterns of brain activation. All four types activate the primary visual cortex. But only words and pseudowords, which both follow the orthographic rules of English, activate other areas laying along the inner surface of the left cerebral hemisphere.

SOURCE: From *Images of Mind* by Posner and Raichle (1994, pp. 79, 80). Copyright © 1994 by Scientific American Library. Used with permission of W. H. Freeman and Company.

Example of the Four Types of Visual Stimuli

Words	Pseudowords	Letterstrings	False Fonts
ANT	GEEL	VSFFHT	AH3
RAZOR	IOB	TBBL	JqJN
DUST	RELD	TSTFS	NO?N
FURNACE	BLERCE	JBTT	⊢ΓOΠ
MOTHER	CHELDINABE	STB	NNЯJ3
FARM	ALDOBER	FFPW	ƘAON

PREPUBLICATION COPY

4-color diagrams appear in student copies

COGNITIVE
PSYCHOLOGY

ADVANCED PSYCHOLOGY TEXTS

Lyle E. Bourne, Jr.
Series Editor

Advanced Psychology Texts (APT) is a series of intermediate but highly readable textbooks and monographs in the core areas of psychology. The primary objective of the series is to give undergraduate student majors and beginning graduate students in psychology a basis for evaluating the state of the science and a springboard into further guided or independent scholarship in a particular area. Each volume will center on the current issues and the basic concepts of a core content area of psychology. Students who use these books are expected to have some general background in the field. The textbooks take advantage of that background, building it into a sophisticated contemporary understanding of the facts and of the important yet-to-be answered questions. Each text focuses on recent developments and the implication of those developments for future research. Although the emphasis is on psychology as an evolving systematic scientific discipline, applications of basic research findings are also included. Authors have been asked to present clearly and thoughtfully what it is that each sub-area of psychology has to contribute to human knowledge and welfare.

Volume 1 Skill Acquisition and Human Performance
Robert W. Proctor and Addie Dutta

Volume 2 Cognitive Psychology
Ronald T. Kellogg

COGNITIVE PSYCHOLOGY

RONALD T. KELLOGG

 ADVANCED PSYCHOLOGY TEXTS

 **SAGE Publications**
International Educational and Professional Publisher
Thousand Oaks   London   New Delhi

For information address:

 SAGE Publications, Inc.
2455 Teller Road
Thousand Oaks, California 91320
E-mail: order@sagepub.com

SAGE Publications Ltd.
6 Bonhill Street
London EC2A 4PU
United Kingdom

SAGE Publications India Pvt. Ltd.
M-32 Market
Greater Kailash I
New Delhi 110 048 India

Printed in the United States of America

Library of Congress Cataloging-in-Publication Data

Kellogg, Ronald Thomas.
    Cognitive psychology / Ronald T. Kellogg.
       p. cm. — (Advanced psychology texts ; v. 2)
    Includes bibliographical references and indexes.
    ISBN 0-8039-5329-1 (alk. paper)
    1. Cognitive psychology. I. Title. II. Series.
BF201.K45 1995
153—dc20   95-11732

This book is printed on acid-free paper.

95 96 97 98 99 10 9 8 7 6 5 4 3 2 1

Production Editor: Astrid Virding   Typesetter: Christina Hill

To Alicia and Kristin

▣ Brief Contents

▣ Contents

PART V: THINKING SKILLS AND INTELLIGENCE

11. Problem Solving   329

12. Reasoning and Decision Making   363

PART VI: THE PAST AND FUTURE

▣ Preface

Cognitive psychology has evolved over the past 40 years to become the dominant approach to virtually all aspects of human psychology. Its influence is strong in clinical, assessment, developmental, social, comparative, and physiological psychology, among other areas. Alternative approaches such as psychoanalysis, behaviorism, and humanistic psychology carry less force not only in psychology but in related fields. Linguistics, computer science, philosophy, anthropology, and the other sister disciplines of cognitive psychology are part of a remarkable and exciting enterprise known as cognitive science. The cognitive approach promises to dominate the scientific study of mind and behavior well into the twenty-first century.

This book presents a survey of cognitive psychology designed for students from the sister disciplines as well as traditional psychology students. It is appropriate for both undergraduates and graduate students, with the latter able to explore topics in greater depth through the recommended readings. The book assumes that the reader has a solid background in general psychology. For instance, material on neurocognitive psychology is written at a level accessible to those who have studied the brain in a general psychology course.

I sought to provide a synthesis of cognitive psychology at its best rather than a chronicle of its arguments and conflicts. Certainly, the difficult struggle of cognitive approaches in psychology during the past 100 years deserves coverage, as do the many disagreements in contemporary theories and findings. But controversy can easily be overdone to the point of befuddling students. Graduate students, however, will want to dip deeper into the many controversies in the field by consulting the primary sources cited throughout the text and by doing the recommended reading.

For similar reasons, I have avoided extensive discussions of the experimental methods on which findings are based. Although the methods are vitally important for researchers, too much focus on how an experiment was conducted can obscure the main point for students. Upper level undergraduates and certainly graduate students should supplement this text with readings in the primary literature. The original journal articles detail experimental designs, procedures, and materials.

I also sought to encapsulate the relevant background, theory, and research within each chapter. Details about brain structure, for example, are discussed when needed to understand a point about, say, language use. As another example, details about the development of language, memory, or perception are covered in their respective chapters rather than being culled and packaged as cognitive development.

Given that entire books are written on cognitive development and neuroscience, it strikes me as inappropriate to summarize these areas under separate chapters that can readily be ignored by teachers and students. One can argue for separate chapters to enable teachers to customize their course by omitting all references to these. But the state of the art no longer makes that tenable. Because development and neuroscience contribute vitally to current cognitive psychology, the material must be integrated in a way that will be read, understood, and remembered.

The book is divided into six sections. The first part introduces the discipline of cognitive psychology in the opening chapter. I turn to the basic cognitive operations of perception, attention, and memory in the next part. The third part addresses acquiring and using knowledge and skill. The fourth part covers language, its nature, and its use. The fifth part explores thinking skills and intelligence. The final part, and final chapter, is devoted to consciousness.

An instructor using the text for a sophomore-level introduction to cognitive psychology would probably want to sample chapters from the third, fourth, and fifth parts. All of the first two parts probably should be included. The final part could be omitted or included depending on the instructor's preference. For advanced courses in cognitive psychology for undergraduates and for graduate students in psychology and related fields, all chapters should be assigned.

No author composes a book alone. I am indebted to many individuals in the writing of this one, but assume full responsibility for the form that the final product has taken. I thank my editor C. Deborah Laughton and her colleagues, Janet Brown and Astrid Virding, at Sage Publications for their guidance and assistance throughout the writing and production phases of the work. I gained many useful ideas from the critical readings provided by James Chumbley and Ira Fischler and other, anonymous reviewers. Lyle E. Bourne Jr., the Series Editor, provided not only many suggestions for improvement but also encouragement to press forward. I thank him for both. Ramona Taylor, Cara Saling, and Robin Hilbert provided vital secretarial assistance, and Chris Maxfield and Rob Donnelly aided with the graphics. Finally, I am indebted to my spouse, Carol, and children, Alicia and Kristin, for their support and tolerance during the course of this project.

PART I

Introduction

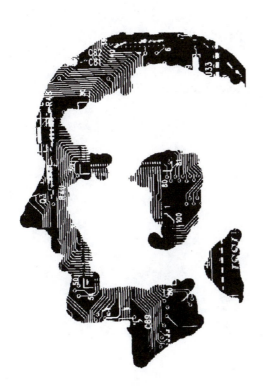

CHAPTER 1

▣ The Discipline

Introduction to Cognitive Psychology

Cognitive psychology, and its more inclusive partner cognitive science, have come of age. They have come to exert a strong influence on psychology as a whole and promise a scientific understanding of the human mind in all its complexity and significance. The discipline that you will study in this book concerns itself with the science of mental life, as defined by contemporary research methods, theories, and findings. Though the questions raised by cognitive psychology typically have ancient roots, the answers provided by the discipline are recent and undergoing continual refinement. Here you will learn how far we have come in one of science's grandest quests: the mind seeking to understand itself.

The time and place of cognitive psychology today both contribute to its vibrancy. The 1990s have been declared the "Decade of the Brain" by the U.S. Congress. Cognitive psychology, neuroscience, evolutionary biology, anthropology, linguistics, philosophy, artificial intelligence (AI), and other research programs that comprise the broad interdisciplinary field of cognitive science are thriving. The congressional declaration symbolizes the hope that the mysteries of brain, mind, and behavior are within our grasp. Discoveries beckon in understanding how human beings perceive, remember, imagine, think, and create. The despair of a child who struggles with reading because of dyslexia or the anguish of an elderly victim of the confusion and memory loss of Alzheimer's disease may eventually find relief through applications of these basic discoveries.

The place as well as the time of cognitive psychology attracts students of both the sciences and the humanities. If you were to imagine a map of psychology and related fields, then you would find cognitive psychology centrally located and bordering numerous neighbors. The shortest path from, say, evolutionary biology to linguistics or from computer science to neuroscience cuts through the territory of cognitive psychology. The territory you will explore in this book has been crossed by many students of human nature.

Definitions of the Discipline

Cognitive psychology may be defined as the study of human mental processes and their role in thinking, feeling, and behaving. Perception, memory, acquisition of knowledge and expertise, comprehension and production of language, problem solving, creativity, decision making, and reasoning are some of the broad categories of such study. Experimentation lies at the heart of cognitive psychology, although, as we will see, mathematical models and computer simulations also play a role.

The discipline portrays the human mind as, first, a processor of information; it computes answers to problems in a manner analogous to a computer. A digital computer represents an arithmetic problem, such as 21 + 14, in a symbolic code of zeros and ones according to an agreed upon convention. Then, a software program processes those symbols according to the rules of addition, yielding the correct answer, 35. Similarly, as you read this problem and verified the answer, your mind represented the numbers symbolically and processed the information. The analogy between mental processes and computation has proven extremely fruitful and provides the basis for much of what follows in this book.

But the human mind does more than process information. *Information* technically refers to a reduction in uncertainty about events. For instance, if I flip a penny and determine that it came up heads, then uncertainty about the event has been reduced (one bit of information has been transmitted, to be mathematically precise). Information is transmitted in this example but the event is meaningless. Now, suppose I flip the penny again but this time heads means I owe you $500 and tails means you owe me. Are you ready for the toss? The outcome again reduces un-

Table 1.1 Demonstration of Meaning

Trigrams	Words
WZT	PIG
BTC	LIP
LPK	CUP
RMZ	BAT
QBZ	MAP
LNT	CAP
DKM	TAG
PHX	RIB
GFM	CAT
FRB	LOG

certainty by one bit, but more important it refers to other events that are significant to you as a human being. Meaning, not information in the mathematical sense, provides the focus of human mental life (Bruner, 1990).

Throughout our study in this book, the fundamental importance of meaningfulness will be plain. A simple illustration concerns your ability to remember the items from two different lists. The first list in Table 1.1 contains meaningless trigrams; each set of three letters carries little if any natural associations (unless I happened to pick your initials by accident). The second list contains three-letter words, each of which refers to an object that you have experienced in the world and know well. Study the trigram list for 30 seconds and then try to recall the items without looking. Then do the same with the word list. No doubt, you will find the meaningful list much easier to memorize.

The mind lives and breathes through meaning. Our use of symbols to refer to objects, events, and other experiences, our efforts to understand why experiences occur as they do, and ultimately our longing to comprehend the significance of our own existence all reflect the human longing for meaning.

Finally, the discipline of cognitive psychology assumes that the mind and brain are biological systems that emerged through evolution. They have adaptive functions that enable us to succeed as reproducing organisms. The structures of mind and brain must be related to these adaptive functions, just as the opposable thumb of primates is related to their ability to grasp objects. Systems for perceiving, remembering, and thinking have evolved in a manner that allows us to adapt to our environment. Understanding these systems in the context of neurophysiology and evolutionary biology provides another driving force in the discipline. The functions and structures of the mind have not emerged from the spotless laboratory of a computer scientist but from the messy forces of biological development and survival.

Relation to Cognitive Science

Cognitive science may be defined as the study of the relationships among and integration of cognitive psychology, biology, anthropology, computer science, linguistics, and philosophy (Hunt, 1989). It represents an interdisciplinary effort to address basically the same issues that confront cognitive psychology. How is knowledge represented? How does an individual acquire new knowledge? How does the visual system organize sensory experiences into meaningful objects and events? How does memory work? As shown in Figure 1.1, these are among the problems that cognitive science attempts to understand in terms that make sense to scholars from diverse backgrounds.

Cognitive science is not a coherent discipline in and of itself but is a perspective on several disciplines and their associated questions (Hunt, 1989). A survey of cognitive science takes one into topics that find little if any coverage here, such as the details of computer simulation models. Researchers who regard themselves as cognitive scientists typically have educational backgrounds in at most one or two of the contributing disciplines. Further, they approach the issues of mind and brain with research methods unique to their disciplines. As Stillings et al. (1987), an interdisciplinary team of coauthors, explained in their pioneering text in cognitive science:

> Psychologists emphasize controlled laboratory experiments and detailed, systematic observations of naturally occurring behaviors. Linguists test hypotheses about grammatical structure by analyzing speaker's intuitions about grammatical and ungrammatical sentences or by observing children's errors in speech. Researchers in AI test their theories by writing programs that exhibit intelligent behavior and observing where they break down. Philosophers probe the conceptual coherence of cognitive scientific theories and formulate general constraints that good theories must satisfy. Neuroscientists study the physiological basis of information processing in the brain. (p. 13)

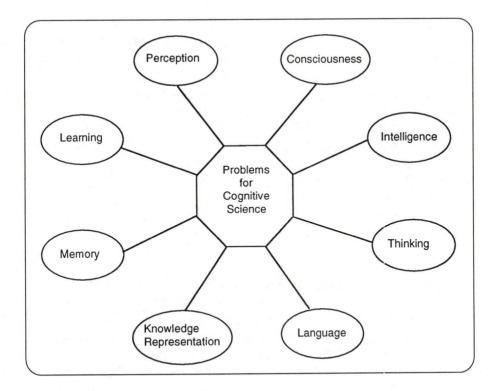

Figure 1.1. Eight critical areas of research in cognitive science and cognitive psychology.

The present textbook focuses on the theories, methods, and results of cognitive psychology. On occasion we will encounter in passing arguments and evidence that might constitute an entire section or chapter in a text of another branch of cognitive science. I hope to provide you with enough context to grasp the matter at hand, without assuming that you have had a course in, say, neuroscience and without elaborating to the point of distraction.

History of Cognitive Psychology

With these definitions in hand, it is time to turn to a closer look at the field of cognitive psychology per se. We begin with a historical overview to show how the field arrived where it is today; the major influences are summarized in Figure 1.2. The history of particular topics, such as mem-

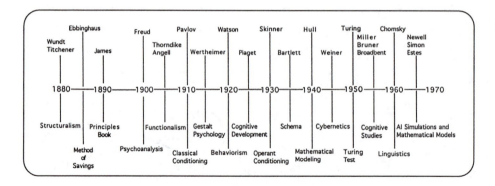

Figure 1.2. The major historical influences on the development of contemporary cognitive psychology.

ory, is woven into the fabric of later chapters. After following the discipline's history to the present, we will step back and examine the contemporary scene.

William James (1890) defined the whole of psychology as "the science of mental life, both of its phenomena and their conditions" (p. 1). Over a century ago, then, the entire enterprise of psychology could be equated with what we now call cognitive psychology. The psychology of the late nineteenth and early twentieth centuries touched on many of the research problems that confront cognitive psychologists today. Moreover, the cognitive approach in recent years pervades all areas of psychology and even some of its neighbors. The term surfaces often, as in *cognitive development, social cognition, cognitive therapy,* and *cognitive anthropology.* Yet, for much of the twentieth century, psychologists scarcely whispered the term *cognition.* Let us examine why.

Structuralism

Wilheim Wundt, as every student of psychology has memorized, founded the first psychological laboratory in 1879 in Leipzig, Germany. The Englishman Edward Bradford Titchener brought the Wundtian approach to psychology to America in 1892. Titchener established the school of structural psychology, which concerned what the mind is as opposed to what the mind is for. **Structuralism** aimed to describe the elemental components of consciousness, specifically, sensations, images, and feelings. Titchener borrowed introspection from Wundt's laboratory as the method of choice for scientific psychology.

Selbst-beobachtung, or self-observation, became known in English as **introspection** and consisted of a carefully controlled technique of looking inward and reporting mental experiences. Their research participants undertook rigorous training to learn how to report accurately the contents of their conscious experience. They attended carefully to the stimulus presented in the experimental situation and verbalized only their immediate conscious experiences. Intrusions of memory fouled the observations. They repeated each stimulus many times to improve the reliability of their descriptions.

Structuralism encountered several difficulties. One concerned the reliability of introspection as the only valid scientific method. Different observers too often gave different introspective reports in the experimental conditions arranged by Wundt, Titchener, and their followers. Another difficulty was that certain activities failed to register any image or sensation. An especially well-known experiment on imageless thought showed that the judgment of which of two weights is heavier occurs unconsciously. As the individual lifts each weight, the individual is conscious of numerous sensations. But the judgment itself falls outside the scope of consciousness (Boring, 1957).

Functionalism

An alternative to structuralism arose in a functionalist approach to the mind. **Functionalism** addressed what the mind is for rather than what it is. Functional psychologists, such as James Angell, studied mental processes that mediated between the environment and the organism. Angell investigated the nature of mental operations rather than mental elements, the focus of the structuralists. He and others aimed to understand, from a biological point of view, the utilities of consciousness in adapting to the demands of the environment (Boring, 1957). James's *Principles of Psychology*, first published in 1890, provided the backdrop for the functionalist school. James followed a Darwinian line of thinking to question what purpose consciousness served, to ask why it evolved. James's work influenced many American students, including Angell and Thorndike. It was Angell who brought functionalism to center stage in his 1906 presidential address to the American Psychological Association (Hilgard, 1987). Angell focused attention on mental operations as opposed to mental structures. The functionalist school sought to understand how mental operations served the needs of organisms in adapting to their environment. Thorndike's classic laws of learning developed directly from studies of how animals adapt to the "situations" posed by their environment.

James's 1890 masterpiece influenced more than the functionalists. Many of the topics covered in cognitive psychology today find their roots in his book, along with the methods used to study them. For example, James cited the findings of Hermann Ebbinghaus (1885), who pioneered the study of memory without relying on introspection. Ebbinghaus memorized lists of meaningless verbal material—nonsense syllables—to the point of mastery, recording the time required in seconds. Then, at later dates, he returned to the same lists and relearned them to a criterion of perfect recitation. He noted that fewer seconds were required to relearn the lists than to learn them originally and took the time saved as an index of memory. This method of savings and variations on it are among the methods used to study memory today.

Gestalt Psychology

While functionalism thrived in America, in Germany another movement arose in opposition to structuralism. **Gestalt psychologists** emphasized the meaning and organization of objects and events. They opposed the use of Wundt's introspection because it analyzed a stimulus into separate sensations that inherently exist as an organized whole. The term *Gestalt* means form or shape and was used by these psychologists to emphasize that experience enters the mind as structured forms. As Boring (1957) tells us: "In perceiving a melody you get the melodic form, not a string of notes, a unitary whole that is something more than the total list of its parts or even the serial pattern of them" (p. 588). We will return later to the Gestalt grouping principles in the chapter on perception. For now the key point is that Gestalt psychology provided yet another approach to the study of mind that strongly influenced psychology in Europe beginning with Max Wertheimer's 1912 publication on movement perception, and infiltrated American psychology by the 1920s (Boring, 1957). Gestalt psychologists not only challenged existing approaches to perception, they opened the door to the study of higher mental processes in their extensive work on problem solving. In this arena, too, they emphasized the holistic phenomenon of gaining insight into the solution of a problem. As a person struggles with the parts of a problem, the parts reorganize and fit together in a new way that solves the problem.

Psychoanalysis

Still another perspective on the nature of mind and consciousness came from a medical doctor from Vienna. Through the analysis of his own thoughts, dreams, and physical symptoms as well as those of his patients, Sigmund Freud created a unique theory of the human mind. The profound influence of Freud's theory on early twentieth-century Western culture is an accomplishment that cognitive psychologists dream to match as the century closes. The Freudians may still interpret those dreams, but their theories attract little interest today.

Freud published *The Interpretation of Dreams* in 1900 in which he first described the Oedipus complex and provided a guide to the symbolic processes of the mind that emerge in dreams. Each dream held a symbolic meaning, the latent content, that revealed unconscious desires and conflicts. The symbols of dreams at times are unique to the individual and at other times universal, according to Freud. Gardens and doors universally signify the female, and candles and serpents the male genitals; falling in a dream means surrender to erotic desires while flying means sexual conquest (Schultz & Schultz, 1992). *The Interpretation of Dreams* proved so popular that it was reprinted eight times in Freud's lifetime.

All students of psychology are familiar with the basic tenets of **psychoanalysis,** the distinctions between the conscious and unconscious aspects of mental life and the dynamic tensions among them. The id, ego, superego, pleasure principle, and reality principle are the standard fare of general psychology. These concepts firmly established the notion of the unconscious in psychology and throughout popular culture as well. As we will see, though, contemporary cognitive psychologists describe unconscious processes differently than Freud.

Behaviorism

Given the diversity of introspective psychology, it should surprise no one that some longed for an alternative. John B. Watson launched **behaviorism** in 1913 with his paper "Psychology as the Behaviorist Views It" in an effort to establish a purely objective psychology. Watson's answer to the problems of introspection and consciousness was to throw both out of court. He envisioned an objective science of psychology based on a description of observable, repeatable behavior.

The Russian physiologist Ivan Pavlov was a well-known figure in Watson's time. Pavlov won a Nobel prize in 1904 for his work on digestion and then turned to the development of what became known as classical conditioning. Pavlov's work on the learned or conditional reflex showed that purely objective measures of glandular secretions and muscle movements could be fruitfully studied instead of the subjective measures of introspection. This appealed greatly to the young Watson, who found introspection with human subjects difficult and preferred biological research with animals (Schultz & Schultz, 1992).

Watson pursued a science of behavior, not a science of mental life. He tried to translate the mental contents and processes of the structuralists and functionalists into behavioral terms. Imagery and thinking, for instance, consisted of minute movements of the vocal tract and elsewhere. Human beings, as every other animal, adapted to their environment using the tools provided by their genetic and learning histories. By knowing enough about these histories, Watson believed that the response of an organism to any given stimulus could be accurately predicted. Stimulus-response psychology thus began.

Behaviorism profoundly influenced the direction of psychology in America. From the 1920s to the mid-1950s, the dominant approach to psychology was behaviorism in one form or another. The mathematical learning theory of Clark Hull advanced the cause of behaviorism by sticking to objective measurement and rigorous theoretical development. The task of psychology, in Hull's view, was to develop models of behavior expressed as mathematical equations. Hull believed that machines could learn and think, and he set about trying to build them in 1929 (Leahey, 1987). This idea, as we will see, is very much alive today.

By far the most influential behaviorist both in academic circles and in American culture was B. F. Skinner. From *The Behavior of Organisms* (1938) to *Verbal Behavior* (1957) to *Beyond Freedom and Dignity* (1971), Skinner articulated the principles of operant conditioning and their applications to societal problems. Information processing psychology clashed with behaviorism over the past four decades, as we will soon see. Skinner fought back literally to the end of his life. Only days before his death, he received the Distinguished Lifetime Achievement Award from the American Psychological Association. In his final remarks to the association, he derisively called cognitive psychologists the "creationists" of behavioral science. In the heat of the battle, cognitive psychologists have too often painted behaviorism as a wasted effort that blocked the advance of psychology. Such a view, however, overlooks the reasons behaviorism was launched in the first place and the legacy of careful, experimental procedures that behaviorism left in its wake.

Information Processing

World War II transformed the face of psychology in many ways. Testing and training recruits, designing tanks, aircraft, and other equipment that people could use effectively, and treating battle fatigue raised important psychological questions. The mental as well as behavioral abilities of human beings simply could not be ignored in designing, say, the cockpit of an aircraft that would fly in combat. Further, mathematicians and early computer scientists sought to eliminate human beings from harm's way by mechanically controlling missiles and other weapons. This effort led to the development of cybernetics, or the theory of informational feedback, by Norbert Weiner and others. When a missile was off target, feedback to the control mechanism allowed it to take corrective steps.

The birth of the modern digital computer followed quickly. A. M. Turing led the way in formulating computational theory during the war and in 1950 published a paper titled "Computing Machinery and Intelligence." This paper appeared in a journal titled *Mind* and set the agenda for the future of artificial intelligence and cognitive science (Leahey, 1987). It picked up on Hull's earlier speculations about the possibility of thinking machines. To decide whether machines can think, Turing proposed an "imitation game" in which a person using a keyboard asks questions of two respondents, a human being and a computer. The person poses questions that help her to decide which respondent is the computer and which is the human being. If the computer can fool the person into believing that it is the human being, then we conclude that the computer is truly intelligent and able to think. The **Turing test** is still debated in cognitive science, as to whether it captures the essence of intelligence and thinking.

By the mid-1950s the split from behaviorism was well under way and information processing psychology came into its own (Leahey, 1987). This became known as the cognitive revolution against the tyranny of behaviorism. George Miller and Jerome Bruner at Harvard founded the Center for Cognitive Studies and revitalized interest in thinking and memory. In England, Donald Broadbent pioneered the study of attention and memory from the perspective of information processing. The too often ignored work on cognitive development by Jean Piaget began to receive attention. Numerous verbal learning researchers revived the pioneering work on memory of Ebbinghaus and Sir Frederic Bartlett. The notion that knowledge is represented in a dynamic mental structure called a schema evolved from the work of Piaget and Bartlett. Further, the linguist Noam Chomsky wrote a devastating critique of Skinner's book on verbal behavior, showing the serious inadequacies of explaining human language in behaviorist terms. In the early 1960s, Allen Newell and Herbert Simon explored computer simulations of intelligent behavior, while William Estes developed the role of mathematical models in the discipline.

The **information processing** approach to psychology argues for the existence of mental representations and for processes that modify these representations in a series of stages (Massaro & Cowan, 1993). One influential version of information processing identifies with what Nobel prize winner Herbert Simon (1990) called the **Physical Symbol System Hypothesis,** which asserts that

> a system will be capable of intelligent behavior if and only if it is a physical symbol system . . . capable of inputting, outputting, storing, and modifying symbol structures, and of carrying out some of these actions in response to the symbols themselves. (p. 3)

The input, output, storage, and processing capabilities of the digital computer provided an explicit analogy for understanding the human mind. Information processing formed the trunk of cognitive psychology, the modern scientific study of mental life, whose roots extend back over a century.

Contemporary Cognitive Psychology

Context

The contemporary scene of cognitive psychology draws upon enduring ideas from mathematics, the humanities, and the life sciences. The full scope of cognitive psychology cannot be appreciated without recognition of all these links. After briefly discussing the context of the discipline, we will turn to some major themes of cognitive psychology and to the research methods used today.

Mathematics. Mathematics shapes cognitive psychology in several ways, especially the branch known as computational theory and computer science. This can be seen clearly in the Physical Symbol System Hypothesis, which assumes that the brain and mind of human beings are (at least) physical symbol systems that take in, store, process, and act upon information. Computational theory makes important statements about the power and limitations of physical symbol or information processing systems. The most powerful system, a **universal Turing machine,** can compute the solution to any problem that can be solved by an algorithm—a deterministic rule such as the rules of addition and subtraction.

The universal Turing machine is elegantly simple. It consists of an infinitely long tape of symbols (e.g., 0 or 1), a device that can read each location on the tape and determine the symbol residing there, and a means for advancing the tape, in either direction to any location. The initial symbols on the tape provide the program or instructions regarding the operations to be done on the remaining symbols, including symbols that might be added to new locations on the infinitely long tape. The tape serves as an input and output device as well as a dynamic memory in that it can move in either direction and store any number of intermediate symbol manipulations or computations along the way. Because the tape is infinitely long, any new symbol resulting from a computation can be stored without erasing any of the tape's current contents (Hunt, 1975).

Where can we find a Turing machine? Any computer existing today meets the essential requirements; even though there is no infinitely long tape inside a computer, the hardware and software design allows it to mimic the requirements laid down for a Turing machine. Similarly, the practitioners of cognitive science, including many psychologists, would argue that the human mind also fits the requirements. Even though the "software" representations of the mind and "hardware" of the neural circuits of the brain show little if any resemblance to computers or long tapes of symbols, at an abstract level, one can think of the mind as a universal Turing machine. This philosophical equation of minds with machines is not accepted by all cognitive psychologists, however. Some contend that the mind is very much a product of exclusively neural operations and cannot be meaningfully compared with an abstract machine (Hill, 1991).

Humanities. Historians, linguists, literary theorists, and philosophers, to name only a few scholars in the humanities, also shape the contemporary look of cognitive psychology. The humanities have focused attention on language as being a graced path to understanding the human mind. Language is an immensely rich system of symbols and operations. The more cognitive psychologists learn about how we create, comprehend, and use language, the more awesome the human mind appears.

It was a linguist, Noam Chomsky (1959), who highlighted the problems that language poses for behaviorism. For example, only a theory based on mental representations of the rules for generating sentences would suffice in trying to explain human language use. Specifying the linguistic abilities of even a 5-year-old child demanded sophisticated theories of mental representations and structures. By focusing attention on language, cognitive theories flourished.

More recently, the humanities have pointed to narratives, a special form of language use, as another clear window on the mind. As every historian and novelist knows, if you want to engage a person's mind, then tell him a good story. Sarbin (1986) noted the intimate connection between narrative and cognition this way:

> Present two or three pictures, or descriptive phrases, to a person and he or she will connect them to form a story, an account that relates the pictures or the meanings of the phrases in some patterned way. On reflection, we discover that the pictures or meanings are held together by the implicit or explicit use of plot. When the stimulus materials depict people, the story will reflect recognizable human sentiments, goals, purposes, valuations, and judgments. The plot will influence the flow of action of the constructed narrative figures. (pp. 8-9)

The mental representation of narratives is an area of great interest in contemporary cognitive psychology. So, too, is the use of stories in our culture. Jerome Bruner (1990), one of the founders of cognitive psychology, now pioneers the study of how people create meaning through participation and immersion in the shared stories of their culture. The use of autobiographies and oral histories, long-standing tools of the humanities, are critical in such studies.

Life sciences. The relation of mind and brain is now not only a matter of intense philosophical debate, it is also a scientific research program. The era when psychologists cared little about brain structures and when neurophysiologists cared even less about cognitive structures is ended. Today efforts are under way to understand how findings about the brain set constraints on theories of mental representations and processes; conversely, cognitive theories provide clues about how the brain might be structured to carry out mental functions. **Connectionist models** exemplify this approach by taking a very large number of simulated neurons (computer elements) and interconnecting them in a manner that parallels the neuronal connections of the brain.

The breadth of evolutionary theory in particular offers much to cognitive psychology. The astonishingly rapid development of language skill in children must be seen in light of the adaptive advantages provided by speaking. Similarly, the hemispheric specialization that underlies human language can be viewed in terms of evolutionary biology. Through natural selection, cognitive as well as physical traits endure to the extent that they provide successful adaptation to an organism's environment. The survival and reproduction of an individual's genes are ultimately what matter from an evolutionary point of view (Goldsmith, 1991).

Themes

Resource limits. Simon (1990) observed that computational resource limits, such as time and processing capacity, impose strict constraints on what we can solve. For example, playing a perfect game of chess theoretically could be achieved using a particular algorithm called minimaxing. This algorithm could, in theory, be run on a universal Turing machine. But it calls for checking on more chess positions than there are molecules in the universe; the time and effort required rule out such an approach to computation in practice if not in theory. Simon (1990) made clear the implications in what follows:

> If the game of chess, limited to its 64 squares and six kinds of pieces, is beyond exact computation, then we may expect the same of almost any real-world problem, including almost any problem of everyday life. . . . Because of the limits on their computing speeds and power, intelligent systems must use approximate methods to handle most tasks. Their rationality is bounded. (pp. 5-6)

Throughout this book we will encounter theories that assume people are limited in their ability to process information and solve problems. Bounded rationality, as Simon calls it, is a central theme of what we know about attention, learning, memory, problem solving, reasoning, decision making, and other topics.

Components of cognition. Another recurring theme in cognitive psychology is that human performance can be understood in terms of components that are used frequently across a wide variety of situations (Massaro & Cowan, 1993). The mind viewed as an information processing system can be decomposed into smaller systems, such as working, or short-term,

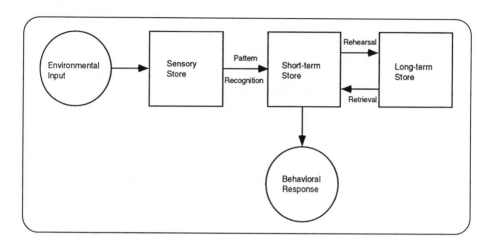

Figure 1.3. A three store model of human memory.
SOURCE: Adapted from Atkinson and Shiffrin (1971).

memory and long-term memory. These subsystems in turn can be analyzed into still smaller units, such as the visual scratch pad of working
memory that we will examine in later chapters. The architecture of cognition, then, assumes a hierarchical arrangement of components that can
be analyzed and studied in isolation (Simon, 1969).

Although the notion of cognitive components is a central theme, substantial disagreements arise in identifying just how many cognitive components there are and their precise characteristics. For example, an
influential model of human memory proposed a sensory, a short-term,
and a long-term store (Atkinson & Shiffrin, 1971). As shown in Figure 1.3,
perception of environmental input involves recognizing the pattern of
information held briefly in sensory memory. The recognized patterns
transfer to short-term memory, where they are held for many seconds. If
rehearsed properly, then the newly learned information is transferred to
long-term memory for permanent storage and later retrieval. Responses
to the environment occur following decisions made on the basis of information currently held in the short-term store. This includes both perceived information and information retrieved from the long-term store.
In the next section of the book, we will consider the characteristics of these
three components and the controversies over whether these are too many
or too few in number to account for human memory performance.

Automatic and conscious processes. Automatic mental operations proceed without drawing on limited attentional resources. They provide a background level of cognitive activity in that they operate independently and in parallel with other ongoing processes. Once initiated, automatic processes proceed to completion in a ballistic fashion, without intentional control and often without awareness. In contrast, controlled or conscious mental operations require substantial attention, so much so that they proceed only one at a time in serial fashion. Conscious processes proceed only under intentional control. They typically proceed slowly and with awareness (Shiffrin & Schneider, 1977).

Time and again in this book, the distinction between automatic and conscious processes arises. The old debates over imageless thought, the workings of the cognitive unconscious, and the functions of consciousness are still with us and many new ones have emerged. For example, we will encounter debates over whether a particular mental operation is automatic or consciously controlled. The interplay of conscious and unconscious processes in perception, learning, and memory continues to challenge researchers. Related to this matter is the question of whether particular mental functions, such as perception and language, exist as separate modules in the brain that work automatically and independently of other cognitive systems (Fodor, 1983).

Constructive cognition. One theme that distinguished cognitive psychology from behaviorism is the notion that people actively process information. Stimulus-response psychology portrayed the organism as passive and reactive, not active and constructive. The cognitive approach revived two long-standing and related ideas. Herman von Helmholtz contended in the nineteenth century that we unconsciously construct perceptions of reality, and Immanuel Kant argued in the eighteenth century that we experience a world mediated through mental representations.

In current theory, knowledge is represented mentally in a dynamic structure called a **schema.** These structures allow one to build mental models of the physical world. They also allow one to think about, reflect on, or imagine actual situations, possible situations, or even frankly impossible situations of pure fantasy. Some schemata or schemas universally appear to develop shortly after birth partly through the guidance of a genetic program (e.g., the motor schema for sucking), whereas most develop purely as a consequence of learning about our environments (e.g., the schema for restaurants). Schemas provide us with expectations about our environment and continually undergo modification through maturation and learning. Schemas direct the construction of all conscious experience in perceiving, remembering, imagining, and thinking. As you read the words on this page, you bring expectations about everything from the shapes of the letters to the meaning of the text and you actively construct your understanding of each word, sentence, and paragraph.

Methods

Laboratory experiments form the methodological backbone of cognitive psychology. Researchers typically isolate a particular component of cognition that they wish to investigate, such as working memory. They design a laboratory task that allows them to study the characteristics of this component by manipulating independent variables. For example, the digit span task calls for a research participant or subject to recall a list of digits, such as 1-6-4-8-3-9-2, immediately after their presentation. The number of digits presented is an independent variable.

The independent variable causes changes in a dependent variable or measurement of performance in the chosen task. By manipulating the independent variable and measuring its effects, clear causal relationships may be established. In our example, the percentage of digits correctly recalled is the dependent variable. The percentage correctly recalled decreases once the number of digits exceeds about seven. Studies of this type will be considered in Chapter 4 on working memory. As we will see, researchers commonly manipulate more than one independent variable at a time. For example, the researcher might vary both the number of digits presented and whether they are heard or seen by the subject.

Typical dependent variables in cognitive psychology measure the speed and accuracy of human performance. **Reaction time,** the number of milliseconds required to carry out a particular process, provides a sensitive measure in many cognitive tasks. The rate of correct responding or, conversely, the **error rate** provides another widely employed measure. The faster the reaction time in a task, usually the higher the error rate: There is a trade-off of speed and accuracy. Finally, **verbal protocols** or tape recordings of a person thinking aloud while she carries out a task are the contemporary version of introspection and provide a rich record of conscious processing.

One problem with laboratory experiments is that they may lack **ecological validity.** This means that the task designed to study, say, working memory fails to reflect the way this component is used in everyday ac-tivities. Researchers design laboratory experiments precisely so that they can carefully control influences on their measurements and establish causal relations between independent and dependent variables. These requirements can rarely be met outside the laboratory in real-world situations. On the one hand, the control of the laboratory is needed to establish a truly generalizable, scientific effect (Banaji & Crowder, 1989). On the other hand, the laboratory may be so artificial that the essential characteristics of interest are lost (Neisser, 1976).

To ensure ecological validity, researchers may select tasks that model the essential characteristics of everyday cognition. For example, one could experimentally study in the laboratory an employee carrying out a task done on the job every day that demands the use of working memory (e.g., an air traffic controller remembering aircraft positions when the computer system fails momentarily). Researchers may also turn to natu-ralistic studies based on field observations, interviews, and other assessment methods that are not experimentally based. For example, a case study of a controller actually on the job directing air traffic could point to the importance of working memory. Similarly, correlational studies based on psychological tests, questionnaires, and field observations are useful. For example, air traffic controllers might be tested for their span of working memory and observed on the job. A correlation between span size and success on the job would be an ecologically valid finding about working memory. The naturalistic observations can highlight interesting relationships for experimentalists to bring under laboratory control (Roediger, 1991).

AI simulations of human cognitive processes by computer programs are another fundamental research method of cognitive psychologists. These simulations aim to duplicate the pattern of errors and correct responses made by a human being in a particular information processing task. If the simulation produces results comparable to those of the person, then we infer that the processes used by the AI program provide a potentially valid model of human cognition. Closely related to simulations is the use of mathematical models of any kind. Again, correct responses, errors, and also reaction times are predicted by a mathematical model in a particular task. The data produced by human beings are then fit to the predictions to test the assumptions of the model. Simulations and mathematical models that successfully fit the human data narrow the range of plausible theories, but they are not proof that human beings use exactly the same processes.

Finally, the methods of neuroscience are increasingly used in experiments, case studies, and correlational studies to understand brain functioning. In human research, three techniques are particularly pertinent. The electroencephlagram (EEG) provides a record of the continuous electrical activity of the brain by measuring the voltage changes generated by large numbers of neurons below an electrode placed on the scalp. **Event related potentials** are EEG changes in response to a specific stimulus. Neurometric profiles can be developed that show how various stimuli and tasks evoke activities in different regions of the brain.

Posner and his colleagues have developed a geodesic sensor net containing 64 electrodes, shown in Figure 1.4 (Posner & Raichle, 1994). Each electrode, in the form of a tube containing saline solution, rests on a small sponge that makes contact with a carefully calibrated spot on the person's head. By averaging together the voltage changes that occur following the presentation of a stimulus, a waveform can be plotted at each of the locations. Figure 1.5 illustrates the waveforms obtained at the sites activated by the visual presentation of a meaningful word.

Positron emission tomography (PET) scans provide another picture of the areas of the brain that are especially active during specific cognitive tasks. Figure 1.6 shows a PET scanner, which as you can see encircles the subject's head. She receives a small dose of water laced with a radioactive isotope. During the next minute, the water accumulates in the brain in smaller or greater amounts, depending on the degree of blood flow to various regions. The radioactive isotope emits positrons, which are the antimatter equivalent of electrons. When they come to rest in brain tissue, the positrons are attracted to the negative charge of electrons. A positron-electron pair is annihilated, creating what are called annihilation photons. These photons are then detected by the scanner. In this way, the scanner can track the relative blood flow to each region of the brain.

The more active a region is during a given cognitive task, the greater the blood flow. The blood is needed in higher concentrations in a highly active area of the brain to provide the metabolic fuel for the neural activity. Researchers construct color-coded photographs that depict the relative blood flow, allowing a remarkable picture of the living brain as it carries out cognitive processes. The highest degree of blood flow is coded white, followed by red, orange, yellow, and green. Lower and lower degrees of blood flow are coded by darker and darker blues, with purple anchoring the scale at the bottom.

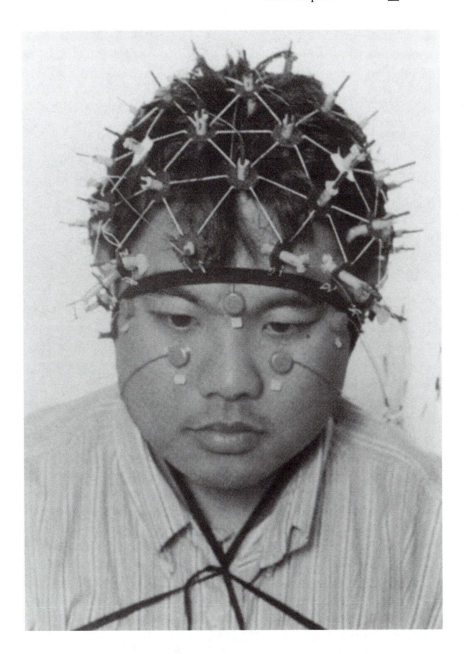

Figure 1.4. A geodesic sensor net of 64 electrodes for EEG recordings.
SOURCE: From *Images of Mind* by Posner and Raichle (1994, p. 135). Copyright © 1994 by Scientific American Library. Used with permission of M. E. Raichle.

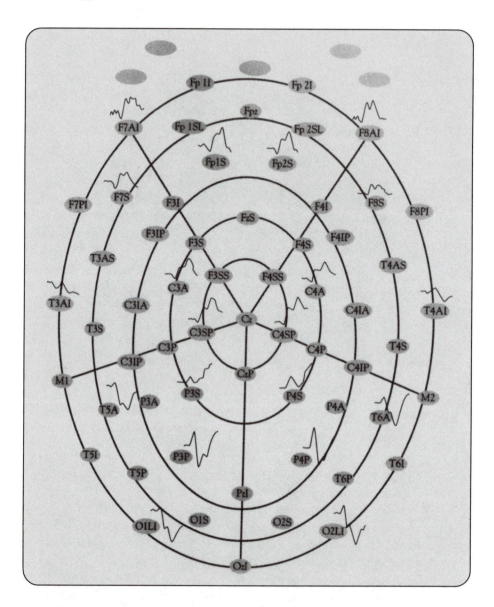

Figure 1.5. The average waveform recorded at selected electrode sites, following the presentation of a visual word.

SOURCE: From *Images of Mind* by Posner and Raichle (1994, p. 136). Copyright © 1994 by Scientific American Library. Used with permission of M. I. Posner.

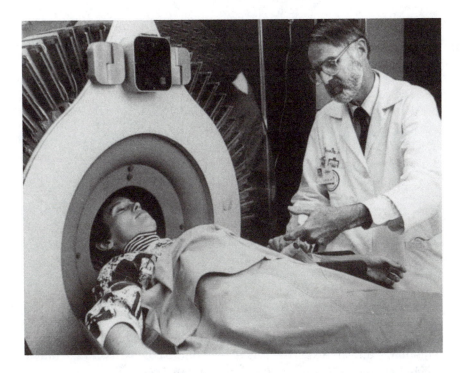

Figure 1.6. A PET scanner at the Washington University laboratory in St. Louis.
SOURCE: From *Images of Mind* by Posner and Raichle (1994, p. 61). Copyright © 1994 by
Scientific American Library. Used with permission of M. E. Raichle.

Color Plate 1 [on the cover page at the front of your book] shows the
results of PET scans obtained when people used language in different
ways (Peterson, Fox, Posner, Mintun, & Raichle, 1989). Participants in the
study processed familiar nouns, presented one at a time. For example, in
the upper left pet scan, they simply viewed the word, such as *hammer*. As
you can see, the regions toward the rear of the brain showed high levels
of blood flow during passive viewing. In the upper right pet scan, they
heard rather than saw the same words. An entirely different area then
showed high levels of activity.

In the lower left scan, participants spoke aloud the word as soon as
they viewed it visually. Speaking activated yet a third localized region of
the brain. In the final scan, the participants spoke aloud a verb that went

with the noun. In the case of *hammer,* they might have responded *pound.* Generating the verb elicited still another unique pattern of activation. Thus the PET scan can provide valuable insights into how the brain carries out particular cognitive operations.

The final neurological method of research with human beings is to test people who have suffered a lesion or damaged area of the brain as a consequence of a stroke, tumor, or accident. By studying how the lesion affects their cognitive abilities, as measured by psychological tests and clinical observations, the researcher gains further insight.

Overview of the Text

Following this introductory section, we will examine the basic cognitive operations in Part II of the book. Chapters 2, 3, and 4 cover perception, attention, and memory, respectively. The third part of the book continues the examination of memory and considers how we use what we know in skilled performance. Learning, memory, knowledge representation, skill, and expertise raise many of the core issues of cognitive psychology today. We turn to these in Chapters 5, 6, and 7.

Part IV presents research on how we create and use symbols. Our art, dance, and music all depend on symbols but here we will focus on language, perhaps the most intricate form of symbol use and certainly the most studied. Chapter 8 covers the nature of language and its role in human thought. Chapters 9 and 10 detail our production and comprehension of language in speaking, listening, writing, and reading. We will then move to the application of language, memory, and other cognitive components of thinking and intelligence in Part V. Chapters 11, 12, and 13 cover problem solving, decision making, reasoning, and intelligence. Many examples of AI research enter into the discussion throughout this section.

In the final part of the book, Chapter 14 addresses contemporary approaches to consciousness. Drawing on our knowledge of cognitive psychology, neuroscience, and philosophy, we will examine the psychology of consciousness today. The recent advances made on this ancient intellectual puzzle conclude the book. The final section brings us full circle to the introductory section. We have seen in Chapter 1 the early history of scientific theories of consciousness; Chapter 14 foreshadows the direction of research in the twenty-first century.

▣ SUMMARY ▣

1. After more than 100 years of laboratory-based research, the beginnings of a scientific understanding of the human mind are taking shape in the fields of cognitive psychology and cognitive science. These fields connect with numerous areas of inquiry, as one would expect of a science of mental life.

2. Cognitive psychology is the study of human mental processes and their role in thinking, feeling, and behaving. Cognitive science takes a mathematical perspective of the mind or brain as a computational device and draws insights and methods from psychology, biology, anthropology, linguistics, philosophy, and computer science.

3. The laboratory investigation of the human mind began in 1879. Structuralism, functionalism, Gestalt psychology, and psychoanalysis all relied on various forms of introspection to reveal properties of conscious and unconscious mental activities and contents. Behaviorism rejected introspection in an effort to establish an objective psychology. The development of information processing systems led to a "cognitive revolution" against behaviorism.

4. Contemporary cognitive psychology draws on mathematics in portraying the sense in which minds, brains, and computers are equivalent. It further draws on the humanities in showing how language provides a key to unlocking the nature of mind. Finally, it draws on the life sciences in seeing how brain structures and cognitive functions are related and products of evolutionary development.

5. There are resource limits on human information processing ability. Theorists attempt to describe the components of cognition and their hierarchical structure. Some component processes operate automatically, unconsciously, and in parallel whereas others operate intentionally, consciously, and in serial fashion. Cognitive processes construct representations of reality in perception, memory, and imagination. These ideas surface as themes throughout the book.

6. The primary method of research is laboratory experimentation because it allows one to establish causal relationships between independent and dependent variables. However, concerns about the ecological validity of laboratory studies prompt the use of other standard psychological research methods, such as surveys, field observations, and case studies. Also, recent advances in neuropsychological assessment offer new techniques for studying how brain structures and cognitive functions relate.

Key Terms

cognitive science	psychoanalysis
Physical Symbol System Hypothesis	verbal protocols
introspection	behaviorism
connectionist models	ecological validity
structuralism	information processing
schema	AI simulations
functionalism	Turing test
reaction time	event related potentials
Gestalt psychologists	universal Turing machine
error rate	PET scans

Recommended Readings

In addition to the references cited in this chapter, students seeking more information will want to consult some of the following sources. The history of cognitive psychology and its contemporary flavor are portrayed in Gardner's (1985) book titled *The Mind's New Science: A History of the Cognitive Revolution* and in Baars's (1986) *Cognitive Revolution in Psychology.* Bruner, Goodnow, and Austin's (1956) *A Study of Thinking* and Broadbent's (1958) *Perception and Communication* are early research monographs that still merit reading. Neisser's (1967) *Cognitive Psychology* is generally recognized as the first textbook in the field.

Mandler's (1985) *Cognitive Psychology: An Essay in Cognitive Science* provides an insightful analysis of the past, present, and, most significant, future of cognitive psychology as the flagship of psychology as a whole. Posner's (1989) *Foundations of Cognitive Science* surveys for students the broad research program of cognitive science. Those seeking a popular account written for the general public will find Hunt's (1982) *The Universe Within* interesting reading.

The technical journals in cognitive psychology are many and the number is growing. References to specific articles will be made throughout the text. Details about why research was done, how it was done, what was found, and what was concluded can be obtained from these references. Also, the *Annual Review of Psychology* provides useful summaries of research topics.

PART II

Basic Cognitive Operations

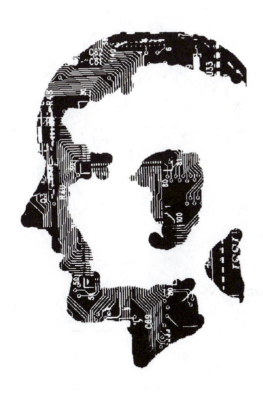

CHAPTER **2**

🔲 Sensation and Perception

We come to know our world through sensing and perceiving the environment. As the three store model of information processing showed in the last chapter (Figure 1.3), input from the environment first enters **sensory memory,** where it is held briefly. Sensory registration, or *sensation,* refers to the transduction of physical energy, such as sound waves or electromagnetic radiation, into a preliminary neural code that can be further processed and transformed over time. Perceptual processes and transformations operate from the moment of sensory registration—it is not possible to draw a line where sensation ends and perception begins.

All that we see, hear, taste, smell, and feel are internal neural representations—images of the mind—of external stimuli. As we will see in this chapter, the sensory and perceptual systems of the brain actively construct these psychological representations from the physical energy available to them. If the frequencies of sound waves are too high or too low, falling outside the range detectible by the ear and auditory system, then we remain unaware of their existence. The family dog might notice the high-pitched whistle or the very low-pitched early rumblings of an earthquake that we miss altogether.

Perception works through orchestrated stages of information processing and complex computations. Sensory registration is the beginning point of numerous processes that transform and store the initial internal representation of a stimulus input. **Pattern recognition** refers to the processes responsible for identifying the stimulus. When you recognize the book in front of you, the desk on which the book rests, and the contents of the room (perhaps) in which you are reading this, then pattern recognition has succeeded. The initial mental representation has been transformed into a more elaborate representation that involves such attributes as color, location, size, brightness, and name. The short-term store provides a record of mental representations that you have recognized as familiar patterns and attended to consciously. *Perception* refers to these multifaceted processes of pattern recognition and attention that result in conscious awareness of an environmental input. When you see your mother smile, hear Beethoven's Fifth Symphony, smell a fragrant rose, taste a grilled steak, or feel a lover's kiss, you have perceived sensations, interpreting them in meaningful ways.

Sensation and perception dominated the early history of psychology. It allowed the experimenter to manipulate physical properties of the stimulus in careful laboratory settings and then measure the psychological result. In this chapter, we will begin with a brief look at the classic controversy regarding the constructive nature of perception. Next, we will turn to psychophysical concepts of sensory thresholds and signal detection theory as well as more recent work on the persistence of sensations. Then we will examine the nature of pattern recognition in general. Finally, we will consider in some detail the nature of visual pattern recognition in object and event perception. We will see that the Gestalt psychologists and their intellectual descendants have strongly shaped our current understanding of perception (Banks & Krajicek, 1991).

Perception as Informed Construction

The gifted physicist of the nineteenth century, Hermann von Helmholtz, argued that perception involved unconscious inferences; the mind registers elementary sensations—such as brightness, color, and direction of movement in the case of vision—and then constructs, without awareness, a mental representation of the environment from these sensory cues. In this century a gifted psychologist, James Gibson, took strong issue with the constructive view of perception. He argued persuasively that perception is direct in the sense that the informational structure of an object or event determines entirely what it is that a person will see or hear (Gibson, 1966, 1979). Rather than starting with elementary sensations, Gibson sought to describe the "higher order" invariant structure that the perceiver may "pick up" directly through interacting with the environment. The Gibsonian strategy, then, is to describe carefully the information provided by the physical stimulus energy available in the environment as a way of understanding the process of perception.

Rather than sink you in controversy, I summarize in this chapter the key contributions of researchers who take diverse perspectives on perception. We must draw upon advocates of direct perception and advocates of constructive perception alike. I prefer to think of perception as an act of informed construction. Certainly, to understand perception, we must understand the structure of the information available in the physical energy that stimulates our senses. But we also must understand how this information is actively represented and transformed by the nervous system. This is particularly true when the amount of sensory information exceeds the limits of our ability to pick it up or, conversely, when darkness, brief exposures, and other conditions severely limit the available information (Shepard, 1984, 1990). Constructive activity not only begins in perception, it dominates the cognitive functions of memory, imagination, and thinking.

The human nervous system, and that of other species, has evolved to provide the perceptual information needed for successful adaptation to the environment. The visual system, for instance, extracts relevant physical energy and constructs from that energy internal representations that inform us accurately about our world. The frequencies of visible light allow us to identify the creatures, objects, events, and physical layout of our environment that clearly have consequences for our survival and reproduction. The frequencies of gamma rays, X rays, radar, and perhaps especially radio and television are less vital and require that we invent technologies to detect them. As you scan your immediate environment, you perceive meaningful objects, colors, and a three-dimensional scene. All these are constructions in your mind, built from the electromagnetic waves entering your eyes. Standing at the top of a flight of stairs, you accurately perceive what could prove to be a very dangerous or even fatal drop-off. This happens only because your visual system can pick up cues from the environment that allow the construction of an internal model that correctly represents depth relations of three-dimensional space.

Figure 2.1 illustrates the constructive nature of perception with a case in which the depth cues lead the mind astray. The upper right creature appears larger than the lower left creature. Yet, if you take a moment to measure them, you will find them to be equal in size. Under normal circumstances, the environment provides texture gradients—like the lines in Figure 2.1—that inform us about the distance of objects. As units of texture gradient grow smaller, they signal greater distance from the viewer. Two objects of equal size should also appear to differ in size depending on their distance, in accordance with the information conveyed by texture gradients. For example, as a friend walks away from you, he or she will appear to shrink, looking small indeed at 100 yards away.

That the two creatures in Figure 2.1 look different in size vividly demonstrates how perceptual processes *construct* a model of the world by picking up and using the *informational structure* provided to the senses. The informational structure of texture gradients informs us that the upper right creature ought to look smaller as well as further away. Because the eyes sense that it is no different in actual size, the perceptual processes of the brain correct for the discrepancy by inflating the mental image of the upper right creature. Unconsciously and automatically, the brain concludes that the upper right creature must be indeed quite large for it to look as it does that far away.

It is important to stress that we do not live in a world of illusions. Our perceptual systems have evolved, through natural selection, so as to pick up the informational structure of the environment that is pertinent to survival. The shape, position, color, and movement of an object are biologically relevant; the mental models that we construct of objects inform us accurately about the environment. The phenomenon of **shape constancy** makes this point well, as shown in Figure 2.2. The shapes of the circle and square are perceived by a viewer examining them at an angle as a circle and a square. The objects are seen as their correct shapes despite the distortions introduced by angular viewing. Without perceptual processes constructing a mental model of the circle and square, the viewer would perceive an ellipse and a trapezoid. Perceptual systems that failed to process information in a manner that missed the true shape of objects in the environment would be at a severe disadvantage in the struggle for survival. Clearly, they would be selected against.

Figure 2.1. An illustration of the constructive nature of perception.

SOURCE: From *Mind Sights* by Shepard (1990). Copyright © 1990 by Roger N. Shepard. Used with permission of W. H. Freeman and Company.

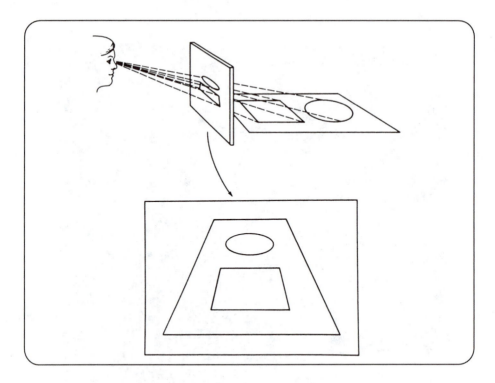

Figure 2.2. The phenomenon of shape constancy.
SOURCE: From Levine and Shefner (1981). Copyright © 1981 by Addison-Wesley Publishing Company. Reprinted by permission.

Sensory Registration

Thresholds

The Weber-Fechner Law. Predating the establishment of Wundt's program of research, two physiologists at the University of Leipzig began to explore sensory registration. Ernst Weber questioned how small a change in physical energy could be made by an experimenter and still be noticed by an observer. A **just noticeable difference** refers to the smallest difference between two stimuli that can be reliably detected. Weber selected weight discrimination to study this question. An observer lifted a standard weight and a comparison weight and reported whether one felt heavier than the other. Through systematic experimentation, he discovered that the absolute difference between the two weights was not the crucial factor. An observer could easily judge that a 2-gram weight was heavier than a 1-gram weight. But an 81-gram weight felt the same as an 80-gram weight.

Instead of the absolute difference, Weber found that the ratio of the stimulus magnitudes defined a just noticeable difference. In the case of weight discrimination, the constant ratio equaled 1:40. The observer could distinguish a 41-gram weight from a 40-gram standard, and an 82-gram weight from an 80-gram standard. The greater the weight of the standard, the greater the difference in weight needed for a just noticeable difference.

To model these data, Gustav Fechner proposed the following mathematical equation:

$$S = K \log R$$

where S is the degree of experienced sensation, K is a constant that varies with the sense involved, and R is the magnitude of the stimulus. This elegantly captures Weber's experimental observations and shows that as the magnitude of the stimulus gets larger and larger, the sensation experienced increases less and less. In short, to notice a difference between two large stimulus magnitudes, they must be very different indeed. This law pioneered the use of mathematical models in psychology.

The differential threshold tells us how great a difference between two weights, sounds, lights, and so on is needed for an observer to perceive that the pair differs. But what about our ability to register that a stimulus has occurred at all? The **absolute threshold,** or *limen,* refers to the minimum degree of stimulus energy needed for an observer to sense it. Imagine an experiment in which a faint light is presented to an observer in a darkened room. The experimenter carefully controls the intensity of light from levels that fail to register at all in the visual system of the observer to levels that the observer senses easily.

It is difficult to specify the precise intensity below which the person never reports seeing the light and above which he always sees it. Typically, the probability of detecting the light increases as the intensity increases. Researchers commonly define the absolute threshold as the stimulus energy that produces detection 50% of the time for a given observer, but other criteria may be used.

People differ in their sensitivity to stimulus energy. For example, the threshold for hearing a high-frequency tone (say, 10,000 hertz or cycles per second) increases with age. Part of this loss of sensitivity is due to normal aging of the sensory system and part of it is due to the negative effects of exposure to high levels of noise in our workplaces, cities, cars, homes, and places of leisure.

Even so, our sensory systems have evolved to an extraordinary degree of sensitivity. Calculations have been made of the absolute threshold for an ideal observer—one suffering no hearing loss and tested in a special soundproof chamber. Air pressure changes so slight that they would deflect the key structure in the inner ear (the basilar membrane) a mere 0.001 nanometers (billionth of a meter) could be detected; this distance is markedly less than the diameter of a single hydrogen atom (Levine & Shefner, 1981). Human vision is no less astonishing. An ideal observer, based on theoretical calculations, could detect as few as 10 quanta of light simultaneously striking 10 receptors on the retina. A single quantum, a vanishingly small degree of physical energy, activates each receptor (Hecht, Schlaer, & Pirenne, 1942).

Signal detection theory. Imagine that you are having your hearing tested using a device that presents a tone of a particular frequency and intensity on each trial and you, the observer, report whether you heard it or not. On some trials, imagine the intensity is zero—no tone is presented at all. It turns out that some of us are quite cautious in our willingness to report hearing the tone; such individuals respond yes only when the sensation that they experience is strong and clear. In contrast, others are biased to report hearing a tone when there is only the slightest hint of an auditory sensation. These biases clearly complicate the determination of absolute thresholds. It is necessary to take into account not only a person's **sensitivity** to stimulus energy but also his **response criterion or bias. Signal detection theory** achieves both.

Figure 2.3 presents a graphical representation of the signal detection task. The theory assumes that all sensations represent either noise in the nervous system or a combination of noise plus the signal. Imagine the sensations that a person experiences in the auditory nervous system as ranging from very weak to very strong. Many of the very weak signals are likely nothing more than the normal noise that always is present in the auditory system. Most of the very strong signals, on the other hand, represent a combination of both a signal plus noise.

A "hit" refers to the observer correctly saying yes when a signal is present. A "false alarm" refers to incorrectly saying yes when only noise

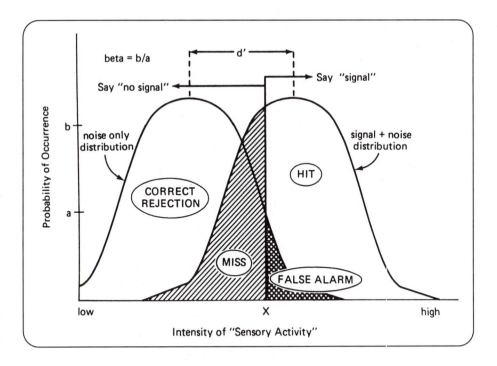

Figure 2.3. Signal detection theory.
SOURCE: From Sanders, M. S., & McCormick, E. J. (1993) *Human factors in engineering and design* (7th ed.). New York: McGraw-Hill. Copyright © 1993 by McGraw-Hill, Inc. Reprinted by permission.

is present. The complements of these two cases are the "miss" and the "correct rejection" as shown in Figure 2.3. Notice that an extremely cautious observer who reports only very strong sensations will generate a high rate of correct rejection, which is good, but unhappily will miss many signals at the same time. In Figure 2.3, such an observer could be modeled in the context of signal detection theory by moving the response criterion from point x to the right, to high-intensity sensory activity. The daring observer who reports even very weak sensations will generate a high hit rate, but only at the cost of many false alarms.

Signal detection theory allows one to separate the sensitivity of an observer to a signal from the response bias, whether cautious, daring, or in between (Green & Swets, 1966). The theory is based on the mathematical model shown in Figure 2.3.

Two probability distributions are plotted on a scale of the strength of sensation experienced by the observer. The theory assumes that the distributions are normally distributed as bell-shaped curves. The noise distribution is centered on relatively weak sensations whereas the mean of the signal plus noise distribution equals a relatively strong sensation value. You can see that the distributions overlap. This means that the physical intensity of tones being presented is fairly low; the strength of the sensations they generate in the nervous system could, with some probability, be caused by noise alone or by a signal plus noise.

The vertical line represents the response criterion. The position of this line can be determined by how many hits, and false alarms, the person generates. The area under the two distributions corresponds to the probabilities of the possibilities as shown. Notice that our cautious observer would have a response criterion positioned far to the right—only a very strong sensation prompts a yes response. Notice also that, given the degree of overlap between the two distributions, the response criterion shown in Figure 2.3 is ideal for an observer trying to maximize her hit rate while at the same time minimizing her false alarm rate.

By collecting data in an experiment on tone detection or any other type of signal, we can model an individual's performance by calculating two parameters from the hit and false alarm rates. Beta is the response criterion used by the observer and d' is the sensitivity shown by the observer to the physical signal intensities used in the experiment. Thus d' represents a pure measure of an individual's threshold for sensing a tone of a particular intensity; it is untainted by the response criterion that the individual happens to choose. The difference between the mean values of the two distributions defines d'. A large value of d' means high sensitivity: The signal plus noise distributions overlap little with the noise distribution. Beta is defined by the position of the vertical line shown in Figure 2.3. More precisely, if we let a and b represent the height of the signal plus noise and noise-only distributions, respectively, then beta = b/a. Beta is the relative height of distributions at the criterion point.

Signal detection theory has played an important role in memory as well as perception research. From time to time throughout the book, we will encounter the terminology of the theory. One interesting illustration concerns the so-called phenomenon of extrasensory perception or psi, as explained in Box 2.1.

BOX 2.1: Extrasensory Perception?

Extrasensory perception (ESP or psi) refers to perception that allegedly occurs by some process unknown to psychologists and physicists. Telepathy, the perception of a thought or image by a receiver that was sent mentally by a sender, is one example of psi. About two thirds of psychologists deny that psi exists (Wagner & Monnet, 1979). Of those extensively trained in the experimental methods of cognitive psychology, the number of skeptics is no doubt far greater. Such psychologists are trained to demand carefully collected and properly analyzed experimental data before accepting any phenomenon, especially one as bizarre as psi. Anecdotal evidence just will not do. Second, psychologists, or scientists of any stripe, are skeptical of phenomena that defy any rational explanation. Whereas laypersons lump together hypnosis, déjà vu, psi, and other mysterious psychological phenomena, psychologists regard psi as uniquely incomprehensible, because no known theory provides an adequate explanation (Bem & Honorton, 1994). Parapsychologists who investigate psi have tried to design rigorously controlled experiments, but to date their efforts have failed. As Hyman (1994) explained:

> Since the beginnings of psychical research in the mid-nineteenth century, its investigators have believed that they have scientific evidence sufficiently strong to place before the general scientific community. . . . The particular evidence put forward has changed from generation to generation. What a previous generation of parapsychologists considered to be a solid case for psi was abandoned by later generations in favor of a more current candidate. This shifting database for parapsychology's best case may be why parapsychology still has not achieved the recognition it desires from the general scientific community. (p. 19)

The latest case for psi has turned to the Ganzfeld method, a form of sensory deprivation (Bem & Honorton, 1994). The halves of a ping-pong ball are taped over the eyes, a red floodlight creates a uniform visual field, and headphones with white noise create a comparable auditory field. While a sender concentrates on a target picture or film clip, the receiver provides a verbal protocol of all images and thoughts. After the transmission period, the receiver examines four stimuli and rates the degree to which each matches the imagery experienced earlier. In some studies, the experimenter interacts with the receiver while the ratings are done, but the experimenter does not know which of the four stimuli is the correct target. The selection of targets is automated by computer (hence, the name autoganzfeld) and the sender and receiver are isolated in soundproof, electrically shielded chambers.

In a literature review, Bem and Honorton concluded that the hit rate—when the receiver describes images and thoughts that match the targets—was reliably higher than would be expected by chance. They suggested a signal detection explanation in which "psi-mediated information is conceptualized as a weak signal that is normally masked by internal somatic and external sensory 'noise' " (p. 5). Ganzfeld reduces external sensory input and thus may raise the signal-to-noise ratio, improving perception as a result.

Hyman (1985, 1994), however, questioned whether the randomization procedures used in such studies were adequate. Within any finite number of trials, the frequency of occurrence of specific targets would vary. If the experimenter actively prompted the receivers in any way while making their judgments, the experimenter's response bias may have distorted the true hit rate. It turned out that in more than half of the autoganzfeld studies, active prompting by the experimenter took place. Now, suppose that the experimenter's bias was to encourage selection of the targets that just happened to occur most often in the sequence of trials. This would artificially elevate the hit rate, even though the experimenter was blind to which items were targets. Hyman's (1994) analysis of the autoganzfeld studies led him to conclude that just such a failure of adequate randomization and coincidence was responsible for the greater than chance hit rate. Cognitive psychologists remain rightfully skeptical of psi because of such methodological problems.

Sensory Memory

Once a stimulus has been initially registered, the processes of pattern recognition establish its properties, such as location, color, shape, and name in the case of vision. *Sensory memory* refers to the persistence of the stimulus in the early phases of processing that allows the complete perceptual processing to take place. If there were no sensory storage or if the information stored there were to decay away before pattern recognition processes completed their work, then the stimulus information would be lost to the observer.

Iconic storage. The best known investigation of a brief visual persistence, or **iconic storage,** comes from Sperling (1960). An observer saw an array of nine letters presented for only 50 milliseconds using a device called a tachistoscope. Here is a sample array:

J	M	C
R	G	B
T	X	L

When immediately asked to recall as many letters as possible, the typical participant managed to report four or five. This Sperling called the whole report condition. He suspected, however, that all the letters persisted briefly in iconic storage, but that as the letters were located in space, their shapes specified, and their names recognized, information gradually was lost. By the time the observer named four or five, the others had faded from storage and were no longer available for processing.

To test his hypothesis, Sperling arranged a partial report condition, in which the observer had to report only the letters from a single row but did not know in advance which row. A high-pitched tone occurred after the 50-millisecond presentation to indicate that only the letters *JMC* needed to be reported. Similarly, a medium-pitched tone cued the middle row, and a low-pitched tone, the bottom row. He reasoned that if the observer could report all three letters from a single row without knowing in advance which row would be cued, then the true number of letters available in iconic memory equaled three times the number given under partial report. Sperling then delayed the onset of partial report cue systematically from zero to 1 second to examine how quickly the iconic storage was lost.

Figure 2.4 presents the results. The line graph shows the percent correct recall of the letters in the partial report condition. With an immediate cue, the observer recalled on average about 2.5 letters, implying that nearly all 9 letters persisted in iconic storage. But within about 200 to 300 milliseconds, the estimated number of letters available dropped to 4 or 5, no different than the number obtained in the whole report condition (shown as a bar graph).

Several later experiments by others suggest that iconic storage holds most if not all sensations registered by the retina for a brief period of time (e.g., Averbach & Coriell, 1961). Much less certain is the format of the information and the location in the nervous system of iconic storage.

For example, Sperling (1960) concluded that the format of iconic storage was precategorical. That is to say, only preliminary pattern recognition processes had operated on the information, allowing one to locate items in space but not to name them or identify them as members of a category. Sperling (1960) argued this position on the basis of studies that included a matrix with half letters and half numbers. The observer failed to show any advantage with a partial report cue to name only, say, the letters, whereas the location cue of top, middle, or bottom row resulted in nearly perfect recall. However, Merikle (1980) later showed that the haphazard arrangement of the letters and numbers forced the observer

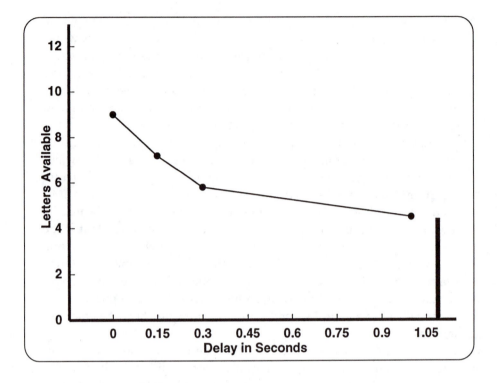

Figure 2.4. Results on iconic memory.
SOURCE: Adapted from Sperling (1960).

to process them one at a time. By carefully arranging the format and spacing of the display, Merikle (1980) demonstrated that either locational or categorical cuing were equally effective. He concluded that we recognize different properties of a stimulus, such as location and identity, at different rates.

Precisely where iconic storage takes place in the nervous system has also been contested. Sakitt (1976) concluded on the basis of a series of experiments that persistence of photoreceptor activity at the retinal level accounts for iconic storage. It is, in other words, a cousin of the much stronger afterimages that are known to involve continued retinal stimulation. Coltheart (1980), on the other hand, distinguished between visible persistence at a retinal level and iconic storage, which presumably takes place deeper in the brain structures underlying vision.

A likely resolution of these disagreements comes from Merikle's (1980) suggestion that the rate at which stimulus properties are recognized in the nervous systems varies. Typically, within 500 milliseconds a physical stimulus gives rise to a meaningful conscious perception (Libet, 1978). As that half second unfolds, various properties are identified, probably starting with the physical attributes of location and ending with the categorical attributes of naming or identity. The processes progressively involve first the retina, later higher levels of visual system, and eventually many other brain structures including those responsible for naming and categorization.

Echoic storage. The auditory system also stores sensations briefly in a component dubbed **echoic storage** by Neisser (1967). He noted that

> sound is an intrinsically temporal event. Auditory information is always spread out in time; no single millisecond contains enough information to be very useful. . . . Therefore, we must assume that some "buffer," some medium for temporary storage, is available in the auditory cognitive system. (pp. 199-200)

Experiments parallel to Sperling's partial report study have been conducted to test the capacity and duration of echoic storage (Darwin, Turvey, & Crowder, 1972; Moray, Bates, & Barnett, 1965). Using stereo headphones, Darwin et al. presented three separate sequences of stimuli to an individual—one to the left ear, one to the right, and one dichotically (both ears) that is perceived in the center of the head. For example, consider the following sequences.

Left	Center	Right
X	2	B
5	6	R
K	F	4

In a single second, the individual heard all nine stimuli and then immediately tried to remember all of them in the whole report condition. Typically, the person would report about four items correctly. A visual cue was used in the partial report condition, signaling recall of only the left, right, or center sequence. For immediate partial report, the estimated number of stimuli available (the number recalled times three) was reliably greater than four. As the experimenter delayed the partial report cue up to 2 seconds, the estimated number dropped to the level seen in the whole report condition.

Darwin et al. concluded that echoic memory persists for about 2 seconds. Notice that such a duration is an order of magnitude greater than that observed for iconic memory. Some investigators have concluded that echoic storage may last as long as 20 seconds (Watkins & Watkins, 1980). On the one hand, such a duration looks suspiciously like another component of memory—the classic short-term store introduced in Chapter 1. On the other hand, a good case can be made that we need a longer lasting sensory memory to handle auditory stimuli. The spatial information in the optic array presented to the eye typically remains available to us to sample again and again, whereas the temporal information in the auditory array necessarily comes and goes.

The ability to hold auditory information, especially speech, for several seconds is advantageous if one cannot attend to the information right away. Perhaps you have had the experience of ignoring what your friend or spouse just said to you while you were engrossed in reading or watching television. Notice that if the "intruder" demands a response to his or her statement soon enough—perhaps with a sharp elbow to the ribs—you can retrieve the lingering voice from echoic storage and manage a response.

Crowder and his colleagues developed the theme that auditory sensory memory, what they called **precategorical acoustic storage,** or PAS, is a critical component in the recognition of speech. In their experiments, people tried to recall a list of nine digits that had been rapidly presented in one of several ways. The silent vocalization participants viewed the digits, reading them silently. The active vocalization participants spoke the digits aloud. The passive vocalization participants heard a tape recording that named the digits as they viewed them.

The key outcome was that the people who heard the digits, either through active or passive vocalization, recalled the very last digit almost without error. In sharp contrast, those who read the digits silently made an error on the last digit about half of the time. Visual presentation proved inferior to auditory presentation. This **modality effect,** as Crowder and Morton (1969) called it, seemed to show how a brief "echo" of the last digit allowed virtually flawless recall.

Another line of research examined recall of a list of items when a final "zero" is tacked on at the end that the learners are supposed to ignore

(Crowder, 1978). The **suffix effect** refers to the decline in recall of the final list item when this extra, irrelevant item is added. The suffix item—though not relevant to the recall task—interferes with the final list item in PAS. Because PAS is precategorical, the suffix should interfere whenever it is acoustically similar to the final list item. However, it turns out that a given sound can act as an effective suffix, depressing recall, when the learner thinks of it as human speech, but when exactly the same sound is regarded as a musical sound (Ayres, Jonides, Reitman, Egan, & Howard, 1979) or an animal sound (Neath, Surprenant, & Crowder, 1993), the suffix effect vanishes. The suffix must be categorized as human speech for it to impair recall of the final item. Thus PAS cannot serve as a wholly adequate model of echoic memory.

Cowan (1988) concluded in his review of relevant research that so-called echoic memory actually contains two phases. The first one is clearly sensory in nature and persists for about 250 milliseconds, comparable to the duration of iconic sensory memory (e.g., Massaro, 1970). The second phase lasts much longer, at least 3 or 4 seconds (Crowder, 1982a). Auditory stimuli persisting for several seconds probably have undergone extensive processing; not only have sensory features been identified such as pitch and location but also categorical or semantic features that allow one to name the stimuli or to categorize them as human speech. This longer lasting, more extensively processed and meaningful form of memory can also be identified in the visual system, as we will see in the next chapter. The longer lasting component is probably identical with auditory and visual forms of short-term memory. From this perspective the modality effect—the superiority of auditory presentation—reflects properties of short-term memory, not PAS or a fleeting echoic store (Penney, 1989).

In conclusion, the initial registration of information in both vision and audition produces a record that persists only briefly. Yet, with 250 milliseconds or so to work with, perceptual processes have more than enough time to begin identifying all the needed properties of the stimulus. Within 500 milliseconds, pattern recognition is generally complete.

Pattern Recognition Processes

The term *pattern recognition* refers to the step between initial sensory registration of a stimulus and identification of the stimulus as a whole, meaningful object or event. Conscious perception of the environment—

what we see and hear, for example—occurs only as a result of pattern recognition processes. In this section, we will consider the interactive nature of pattern recognition, the role of parallel processes, and models of how perceptual patterns are stored in long-term memory.

The Cycle of Perception

Perception, as with all other cognitive functions, is situated in the environment. That is, the perceiver must interact extensively and continuously with the environment to construct and maintain an accurate internal model of external objects and events. Neisser (1976) described this interaction as the **cycle of perception** (Figure 2.5).

Recall from Chapter 1 that the term *schema* refers to a mental representation of knowledge about the world. Imagine for a moment the room in which you attend cognitive psychology class. In forming a mental picture of this particular environment, you activate a schema that represents what you know about classrooms in general and their relations to other types of rooms. A schema that captures knowledge about the layout of our physical environment typically is called a frame in cognitive psychology (Minsky, 1977). The classroom frame includes various objects, such as tables, chairs, lectern, and chalkboard. In imagining each of these objects, you activate another type of schema—a natural concept—that represents what you know about the general characteristics of a category of objects, say, tables. Schemas are hierarchically organized, in other words, with a given frame containing several natural concepts. The concepts that occur virtually all the time in a particular scene are called the default values of the frame.

The cycle of perception begins with numerous schemas providing expectations about what one will encounter in the environment. As you walk into the building on campus containing your classroom, your mind unconsciously begins to anticipate the objects and events that will soon be seen and heard. These anticipations play a vital role in directing exploration of the environment. The steps you take, the way you turn your head, the objects you reach for and grasp, and the eye movements you make are directed by your expectations. The eyes can explore the environment in vision just as the hands do in haptic perception—the sense of touch.

The purpose of exploring the environment is to sample features that allow us to identify scenes and objects. The optical information available

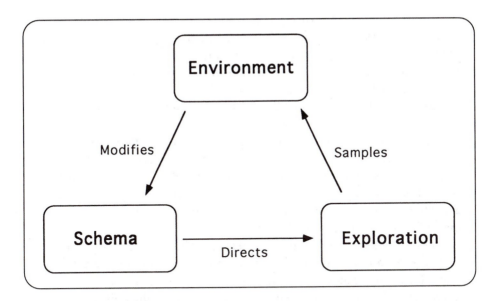

Figure 2.5. The cycle of perception.
SOURCE: From Ronald Kellogg, *The Psychology of Writing.* Copyright © 1994 by Oxford University Press. Reprinted by permission.

to the viewer contains features that may be picked up through exploration. Recordings of eye movements made by an individual in looking at a picture under different instructional conditions give insight into the active and directed nature of this exploration (Yarbus, 1967). The eyes dart about the picture extensively, fixating on the key features that enable recognition and understanding. With Yarbus's pictures, the fixations occurred most often on the people and the relations among the people. Further, the particular pattern of exploration changed in accordance with the viewer's purpose. For example, in one case the instructions called for estimating how long the visitor had not seen his family. Presumably, this instruction activates schemas concerned with personal relationships and emotions as well as the people and objects in the picture. The schemas directed the fixations to sample carefully the facial expressions of the characters.

The contents of the environment complete one revolution of the cycle by updating or modifying the schemas, which in turn initiate more exploration. The sampled information feeds back to the schemas and it may confirm the perceiver's expectations, deviate from them slightly, or deviate from them radically when something surprising happens. In all cases the information from the environment modifies what the perceiver needs to look for next. If all expectations are met, then eye fixations can be directed elsewhere. If expectations are violated, particularly in the case of surprising information, then clearly more sampling of the environment is in order.

Returning to our classroom example, your eye and body movements typically sample information that confirms your expectations about the people, objects, and events that you will encounter. But suppose that a student brings his pet boa constrictor to class one day. This violation of expectations at the concept level would no doubt direct eye fixations at the snake and quite reasonably bodily movements out the door.

Less extreme violations have been studied in the laboratory and eye movements carefully monitored. Friedman (1979) presented line drawings of various scenes. The frame activated by each scene, such as a kitchen, led the viewer to anticipate certain concepts, the default values, such as a stove. In Friedman's study, these were high-likelihood items. She also included medium- (e.g., dishes) and low- (e.g., plants) likelihood kitchen items as well. The eye fixation data revealed that the unexpected objects, such as the plants, received markedly greater exploration than the default values on the initial fixation. The eye first turns to the unusual features of the environment. The difference lessened on the second and subsequent fixations, as the viewer explored all the objects present in the picture.

Top-Down and Bottom-Up Processes

The anticipations of active schemas in long-term memory direct the pattern recognition process in a sense from the top down. At the same time, as a result of exploring the environment, information enters sensory memory from the bottom up. **Top-down** (or conceptually driven) **processes** reduce the need to sample all the information available in the environment by providing the perceiver with a hypothesis. Simultaneously, **bottom-up** (or data-driven) **processes** are analyzing the edges, lines, areas of light and dark, colors, sounds, and other physical features available briefly in sensory memory. These processes pick up the features needed to verify the hypothesis or, in cases that violate expectations, to reject the hypothesis and activate alternative schemas with alternative hypotheses. Through such simultaneous processing from both the bottom up and the top down, people can perceive the features of the environment with remarkable quickness and accuracy.

Tulving, Mandler, and Baumal (1964) investigated the accuracy of correct identifications of a single word. They examined the role of top-down processing by varying the context in which the target word appeared, either with no context (0 words), as the last word of a phrase (4 words), or as the last word of a sentence (8 words). The more context provided, the more conceptually driven processes should aid recognition of the target. As shown below, the participant first read the context, if given, and then briefly viewed a target word, such as *opponent:*

opponent

challenged by a dangerous opponent

The political leader was challenged by a dangerous opponent

Tulving et al. varied the exposure duration of the final word, *opponent,* from zero to 140 milliseconds. The longer the exposure, the more data-driven processes should aid recognition. Note that in the zero condition only conceptually driven processes are at work, allowing perhaps a correct guess about the target word. As can be seen in Figure 2.6, with 8 words of context, the proportion of correct recognition averaged nearly .20. The systematic increases with longer exposure durations show the role of making more data available from the bottom up. The differences among the 8-, 4-, and 0-words curves show the role of more precise expectations from the top down.

A major finding in reading research documents is the importance of conceptually driven processes in word perception. In Reicher's (1969) pioneering experiment, an observer received a word (WORK), a nonword (ORWK), or a single letter (K) as a stimulus. A mask (####) then appeared that stopped processing of the original stimulus by filling the contents of iconic memory with irrelevant visual elements. Probe letters also appeared above (D) and below the fourth element of the mask (K). The observer then guessed which of these had occurred earlier. Noticeably, the letter K was correctly identified more often when it appeared in the word then when it appeared in isolation. This is called the **word superiority effect** and has been replicated dozens of times by numerous researchers (e.g., Baron & Thurston, 1973; Carr, Davidson, & Hawkins, 1978;

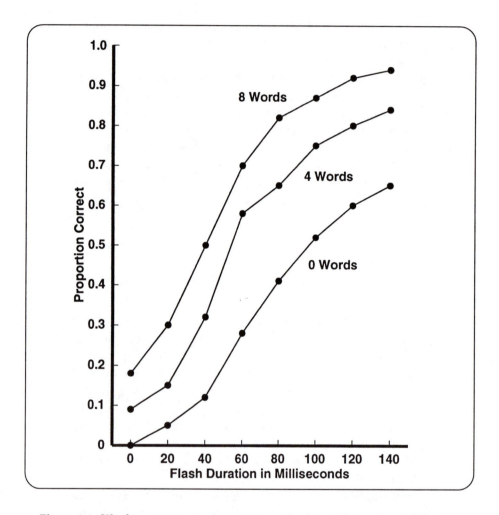

Figure 2.6. Word recognition varies with the amount of context provided.
SOURCE: From Tulving, Mandler, and Baumel (1964). Copyright © 1964. Canadian Psychological Association. Reprinted with permission.

Wheeler, 1970). The word activates conceptually driven processes that ease the recognition of each individual letter. The nonword stimulus fails to activate these processes and so supports the same level of identification accuracy as the single letter.

Several other experiments have shown that the speed as well as the accuracy with which a person can identify an object depends on the context in which it occurs (Biederman, Glass, & Stacy, 1973; Palmer, 1975). We expect to see a cow in a farm scene or a fireplug in a city street scene. Putting the cow and the fireplug in the wrong scene measurably slows recognition of them, by pitting top-down processes against bottom-up processes. Preventing the activation of a schema or frame—by removing or scrambling the context so that it looks incoherent—also hinders pattern recognition by requiring that all the work be done from the bottom up.

Patterns in Long-Term Memory

We have seen that schemas in long-term memory guide the search for data in the environment. But can we specify the details of what is activated in memory and what is picked up in the environment? Answers to these questions can be divided into four proposals.

Templates. The simplest approach assumes that every pattern in the environment has an exact counterpart—a **template**—stored in memory. Pattern recognition, then, is a matter of template matching. Optical character recognition machines of the sort used in a bank to read account numbers or in a store to read prices of items use template matching. As long as all possible variations of patterns in the environment can be specified, template matching offers a viable approach to pattern recognition.

The difficulty lies in the immense number of possible variations. Consider a template for recognizing a capital letter A. One would need a different template for each possible size of this one letter. Depending on the height and width of the letter and the distance at which it is viewed, the size would of course vary. Moreover, suppose the orientation of the letter was not perpendicular. Rotating the letter through 360 degrees necessitates multiple templates, one for each distinguishable orientation.

To deal with these problems, template vision systems must proceed in two stages (Ullman, 1989). First, the sensory input must be "cleaned up" by adjusting its size and orientation. Then the transformed stimulus is matched with templates in memory. Of interest, Jolicoeur (1988) has found that time needed to recognize a natural object increases to the extent that its orientation differs from a standard upright orientation stored in memory. This outcome fits well with a template theory in which the object is first rotated to an upright position.

Size and orientation are not the only difficulties facing a template approach, however. Consider that the letter A might appear in any of numerous type fonts, each one of which calls for a new template. Even worse, if the letter is handwritten, the number of possible variations of the letter A explodes. Despite the best efforts of our handwriting teachers in grade school, individuals differ substantially in how they shape each letter. Even the same person shows variations in handwriting, depending on speed, mental state, age, and other factors. Despite all these variations, I can decipher virtually any handwritten text, with the unfortunate exception of my mother-in-law's hand. How can you and I recognize handwritten letters that vary so widely? Template theory has proved to be a very useful basis for machine vision (Ullman, 1989). But no computer system to date is any match for the perceptual skills of people, with handwriting recognition being only one of many examples.

Feature analysis. A solution to the problems faced by template theory is to look for smaller units that may be combined to generate the innumerable variations of a pattern. The second proposal assumes that the frames, concepts, and other schemas are stored in memory in the form of component features. In vision, we then pick up information about the presence or absence of features that match a particular schema. For example, the features of printed text include lines at various angles and curves with varying degrees of closure. Some features may be redundant in the sense of being repeated cyclicly or symmetrically (e.g., E or M). Further, some are continuous (e.g., O or C) whereas as others show discontinuities (e.g., T or F). A list of this relatively small number of **distinctive features** allows a complete specification of the printed alphabet (Gibson, 1969).

There is powerful evidence that the visual cortex of mammals is organized to detect the presence or absence of simple features. Hubel and Wiesel (1959, 1963) presented an edge, a slit of light, or a darkened bar at different orientations to the eyes of a cat or monkey. At the same time, they recorded the neural activity in single nerve cells in the occipital lobe of the lightly anesthetized animal. Hubel and Wiesel discovered that the cells were tuned to respond maximally to bars of a particular orientation. For instance, some cells fired rapidly to a vertical bar whereas others preferred a horizontal bar. Hubel (1963) summarized their Noble prize winning research in the following way:

> For each stimulus—each area of the retina stimulated, each type of line (edge, slit, or bar) and each orientation of the stimulus—there

is a particular set of simple cortical cells that will respond; changing any of the stimulus arrangements will cause a whole new population of cells to respond. The number of populations responding successively as the eye watches a slowly rotating propeller is scarcely imaginable. (pp. 60-61)

In human vision, evidence for feature detection can be seen in visual search tasks. Neisser (1963) asked participants to search for a particular letter among a long list of lines of printed letters. In one condition the letter shared many features with the distractors, such as searching for Z among T, L, K, M, V, and other letters with straight lines. In another condition the target letter, for example, Z, stood out clearly from the distractors, such as O, Q, P, B, D, and other rounded letters. The more rapid search times obtained by Neisser in the second condition, in which the target stood out, suggest that the human visual cortex analyzes stimuli in terms of simple component features. Note that if people compared each letter with a unique template in memory, then their search time ought to be the same for the straight and rounded distractors. This is one of several experimental results at odds with template theory (Hummel & Biederman, 1992).

One problem with feature theory is that not all visual stimuli can be so easily decomposed into a set of distinctive features, as can printed text (Pinker, 1984b). For example, in the scenes noted earlier of a farm or a city street, just what are the fundamental lines, angles, and so on that distinguish the objects from the background or one object from another? It is not clear-cut.

Structural descriptions. Another serious deficiency with a theory based on lists of distinctive features is that the relations among features are as important to recognition as the features themselves. A letter Z is not simply three independent lines at certain angles. The lines must be structured in accordance with the rules for constructing the letter Z. A face, for instance, is not simply a collection of features positioned haphazardly, an eye here, a nose there, a mouth over there. The relations among features must conform to the rules that define the structure of the face. In other words, the whole object is not simply a list of independent features; the relations among features are equally important. One also needs a grammar or set of rules for how to put the features together properly (Reed, 1973; Sutherland, 1968).

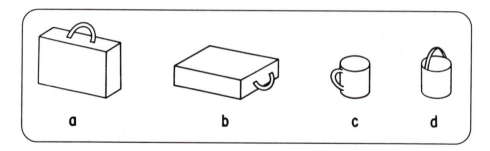

Figure 2.7. A demonstration of the importance of structural relations.
SOURCE: From Biederman (1985). Copyright © 1985 by Academic Press, Inc. Reprinted by permission.

The importance of such relations to perception can be seen in Figure 2.7. Notice that the objects labeled (a) and (b) contain the same features. But the structural relations among these features differ and our perception differs accordingly. In the same way, objects (c) and (d) are seen as a cup and as a pail only by virtue of their structural relations among the same features (Biederman, 1985). Several other studies have shown that people process the relations among features in perception (Hummel & Biederman, 1992; Reed, 1974; Reed & Johnsen, 1975).

Relational information is not only needed, it may be more critical to perception than the features themselves. Biederman (1985) deleted 65% of the contours (features) from drawings of common objects, such as the cups shown in Figure 2.8. The cup in the middle keeps the vertices so that an observer can pick up the relations among the remaining contours. The cup on the right destroys this relational information by removing contours from the vertices. After a brief, 100-millisecond exposure, Biederman found that observers could accurately identify the left-hand cup 70% of the time compared with only 50% for the right-hand cup.

Prototypes. A **prototype** refers to the best or ideal example of a given concept, frame, or other schema. For example, the concept of bird appears to be best represented by the robin (at least for inhabitants of North America). The robin captures many of the features and relations among features of birds that are commonly encountered. The prototype includes

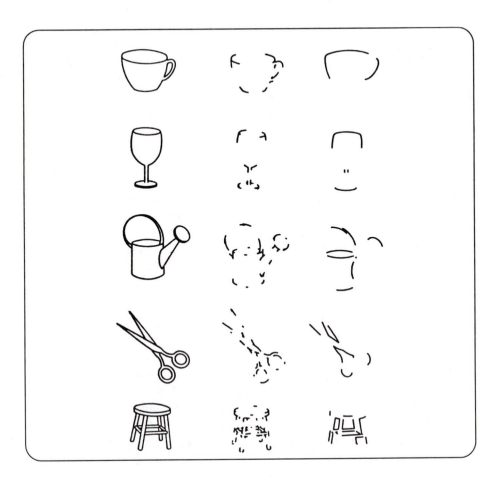

Figure 2.8. Perception of the object depends on the availability of structural relations at the vertices.
SOURCE: From Biederman (1985). Copyright © 1985 by Academic Press, Inc. Reprinted by permission.

the most commonly occurring features or those that represent the average of all features on a given dimension (e.g., the size of a robin is typical or average for birds in general). Prototype theory assumes that we represent in memory a set of transformations or acceptable variations in features and relations along with the ideal example (Franks & Bransford, 1971; Reed, 1972).

There are many studies supporting the notion that prototypes play an important role in perception, memory, and other cognitive functions. For example, the time needed to decide whether an object belongs to a category depends on how closely the object matches the prototype (Rosch, 1975). A canary resembles the prototype robin more so than a turkey and therefore is more rapidly recognized as a bird. This is an example of a typicality effect, which we will encounter time and again in later chapters.

Prototype theory blends the ideas of templates, feature lists, and structural descriptions. One can think of the prototype as being the best possible template for matching as many possible related patterns. However, it also includes a specification of all the variations in features and relations among features that are acceptable. As Attneave (1957) explained, a prototype approach to representing a schema for, say, birds requires information about dimensions along which birds vary (e.g., size, color, shape of wings, and so on). It also includes information about the range of feature values on these dimensions (e.g., Just how big can a bird get anyway?) and the values that typically occur (e.g., What is the typical or average size of a bird?).

The chief drawback to such a theoretical approach is its complexity. The manner in which prototypes and their transformations are learned and stored in memory is far from clear, as we will see in a discussion of relevant research later in the book. Even so, the complexity of human pattern recognition abilities may well call for some approach that combines the power of feature lists, structural descriptions, and prototypes in some fashion.

Perceiving Objects in Scenes

Thus far we have examined the registration of sensory information, the cyclic nature of picking up stimulus information and modifying schema-based expectations, and some views of how schemas may represent patterns as templates, feature lists, structural descriptions, or prototypes. We conclude this chapter with a more detailed look at object perception, to integrate the themes of the chapter. We will examine speech perception in a later chapter, echoing again many of the same themes. Depth perception, motion perception, speech perception, or music perception, to name just a few, are equally worthy topics that fall beyond the scope of this chapter.

Gestalt Principles of Organization

The perceiver picks up information about the structure of an object from the optical array available to the eyes. We have seen evidence that the visual system detects features such as edges, slits, and bars at various orientations. Moreover, the structural relations among these features are picked up, allowing one to construct whole objects. The term **Gestalt** refers to the perception of a meaningful whole pattern that is different than simply a summation of parts. The Gestalt psychologists explored the complex types of information that our perceptual systems pick up from the environment in the process of making it meaningful to us.

Figure-ground relationships are one example of such complex information. To perceive an object, one must segregate it from the other visual information available in a scene that composes the background of the figure. Whenever the visual system detects a boundary between adjacent areas, it must select a distinct shape with well-defined edges as the figure, leaving all else as background. The faces-vase drawing in Figure 2.9 illustrates this selection process. Unlike typical stimuli in the real world, this drawing affords two possible Gestalts that actively compete for your attention. At one moment, you might see as the figure the vase in the center, but in the next moment the faces on each side are perceived and the center area slips into the background.

The specific principles by which elementary features are related structurally in forming a whole object are called Gestalt **grouping principles.** Many such principles have been identified and empirically supported as the means by which the human visual system segments visual stimuli (Levine & Shefner, 1981). To illustrate their nature, consider Figure 2.10. Most people describe panel (a) as three sets of parallel lines, grouping them on the basis of proximity. Close features belong together. The surfaces of a coherent object are connected together, a fact that even infants are able to pick up about their environment (Spelke, 1990). In (b), most people describe a group of Xs and a group of Os; similarity, not proximity, dictates perception. At the boundaries between one object and another, the principle of similarity allows one to distinguish the two objects (assuming they contain dissimilar elements).

Figure 2.9. A demonstration of figure-ground in visual perception.
SOURCE: From Levine and Shefner (1981).

In (c), most people see two line segments, one from A to B and the other from C to D. Alternative organizations with angles, such as A to D or D to B, violate the principle of good continuation. In (d), most people see the circle on the right occluding one on the left. The mind closes the left-hand circle even though it is not visible. Moreover, the mind assumes the missing part takes the form of a circle, rather than, say, an attached rectangular "beak" or perhaps a jagged, broken edge. Panel (d), then, illustrates the principles of closure and of good form.

Scene Analysis

The Gestalt principles segment visual scenes in predictable ways. A scene segments into multiple objects. Each object in turn segments into subobjects. Biederman (1987) proposed 36 basic categories of subobjects—which he called "geons," or geometric icons—that allow construc-

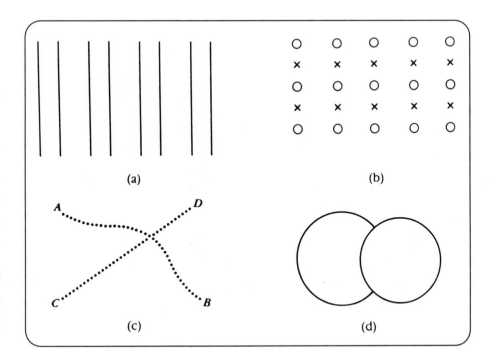

Figure 2.10. Examples of Gestalt grouping principles: (a) the principle of proximity, (b) the principle of similarity, (c) the principle of good continuation, (d) the principle of closure.
SOURCE: From *Cognitive Psychology and Its Implications* (3rd. ed.) by Anderson (1990). Copyright © 1990 by W. H. Freeman and Company. Used with permission.

tion of any whole object. Figure 2.11 shows some sample geons. The geons serve as letters of the alphabet in a sense. When related appropriately, they provide the outlines of any natural object.

An interesting prediction of Biederman's theory is that the edges constitute the critical information that the visual system must pick up in object perception. Color, texture, and other details that add such richness to our perceptual experience may be irrelevant to object recognition. Biederman and Ju (1988) found that schematic line drawings are indeed recognized as quickly as color photographs of objects. This result is but one of many suggesting that the recognition of objects in visual scenes involves the picking up of features and the relationships among features (Hummel & Biederman, 1992).

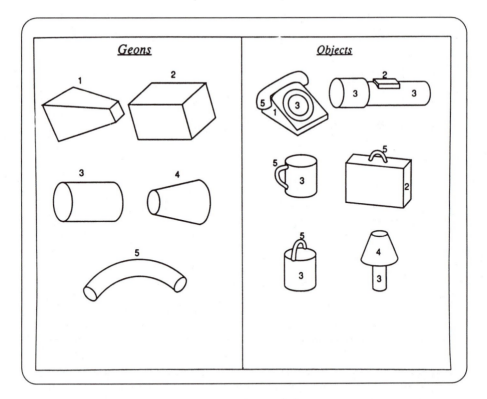

Figure 2.11. Examples of geons, basic subobjects involved in scene perception. SOURCE: From Biederman (1985). Copyright © 1985 by Academic Press, Inc. Reprinted by permission.

Although the theorist can identify the geons, subparts, or features that constitute the whole stimulus, an observer may perceive only the meaningful Gestalt. Several factors control the extent to which perception is dominated by the whole versus the parts, including the type of stimuli presented to and the task required of the observer (Treisman, 1987). For example, it seems that faces are typically perceived holistically. An intriguing demonstration of this fact comes from an illusion that occurs when the normal orientation of facial features is inverted (Bartlett & Searcy, 1993; Valentine, 1988).

First, study the pair of faces in Figure 2.12 in the normal orientation. In the face on the left, the eyes and mouth have been turned upside down.

BOX 2.2: Misperceiving Objects

Although the features and relations that provide the outline of an object may be critical in recognizing objects, they alone are not sufficient when brain damage limits the perceiver. Oliver Sacks, the noted neurologist and author of *Awakenings*, described a man identified as Dr. P who suffered from a massive brain tumor or degenerative disease that destroyed portions of his occipital cortex. Dr. P taught music at a local school and appeared to Dr. Sacks as a cultivated man with great charm, humor, and imagination, certainly not someone suffering terribly from a serious brain disorder. However, upon closer examination, it became clear that Dr. P suffered from a form of visual agnosia, specifically an inability to recognize objects clearly from their shapes. For example, during a neurological examination, Dr. P had removed his shoe as part of a reflex test. When asked to put his shoe back on, Dr. P seemed baffled as he stared intently at his foot, put his hand to it, and said, "This is my shoe, no?" Stunned, Dr. Sacks replied, "No, it is not. That is your foot. There is your shoe." "Ah!" exclaimed Dr. P, "I thought that was my foot" (Sacks, 1970, p. 9). The damage to Dr. P's brain had impaired his ability to pick up the concrete textures and other details of visual experience. Because the outline of his foot matched the outline of his shoe, he could not distinguish the two. Although Dr. P could see in a limited sense, his visual world consisted of mere abstractions, not real objects and scenes. This particular neurological case provided the title for Sacks's (1970) book, *The Man Who Mistook His Wife for a Hat*. It seems that as Dr. P prepared to leave the examining room, he "reached out his hand, and took hold of his wife's head, tried to lift it off, to put it on." "He had apparently mistaken his wife for a hat! His wife looked as if she was used to such things" (p. 10).

As you can see, the face takes on a grotesque appearance as a consequence. Now turn the book upside down and study the two faces again. Notice that when viewing the faces in an unusual orientation, the grotesqueness disappears! Both faces take on a normal appearance. This demonstrates that in the normal orientation, holistic processing heavily influences face perception. By rearranging the normal relations among the eyes, nose, mouth, and eyebrows, the face looks grotesque. But the holistic processing of the face can be disrupted by inverting the face 180°,

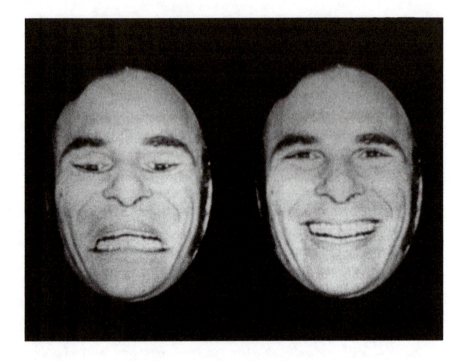

Figure 2.12. A demonstration of holistic processing of faces.
SOURCE: From Bartlett and Searcy (1993). Copyright © 1993 by Academic Press, Inc.
Reprinted by permission.

a position that we rarely encounter in everyday perception. The face as a whole no longer dominates perception; the individual parts of the faces are taken on their own terms and appear perfectly normal to the eye.

◉ SUMMARY ◉

1. Perception begins with the transduction of the physical energy of a stimulus into an initial neural representation of the stimulus. The initial representation of a stimulus persists briefly, allowing further processing of the stimulus. To consciously perceive the stimulus, pattern recognition processes must match the incoming stimulus with schemas or knowledge representations stored in long-term memory.

The absolute threshold defines the minimum physical energy of a stimulus that can be consciously detected.

2. Sensory memory is defined as persistence of an initial neural representation of incoming stimuli. This initial sensory representation is transformed or recoded into meaningful representation as pattern recognition processes unfold. The capacity of sensory memory is large, allowing all stimuli registered by the nervous system to persist. *Iconic sensory memory* refers to the persistence of visual stimuli for about 250 milliseconds. *Echoic sensory memory* refers to the persistence of auditory stimuli for at least 250 milliseconds and possibly much longer.

3. Perceiving stimuli in the environment involves extensive interaction with that environment in what is called the cycle of perception. Schemas generate expectations about the objects and events that will be encountered. These expectations direct exploration of the environment in the form of eye movements and other bodily movements that pick up the available information. The sampled information either confirms or modifies the original expectations, which in turn leads to renewed exploration.

4. *Top-down or conceptually driven pattern recognition* refers to the use of expectations to ease the process of finding a match between incoming stimuli and schemas that store our knowledge about the world in long-term memory. *Bottom-up or data-driven pattern recognition* refers to the use of the features picked up from the environment. Both the data and the expectations play a critical role in rapid, accurate, and hence adaptive perception.

5. The information stored in schemas theoretically takes the form of templates, feature lists, structural descriptions, or prototypes. Templates are too rigid given the variability required by perception. Feature lists avoid the problem of rigidity and enjoy strong empirical support. However, it is clear that the relations among features must also be specified, as structural descriptions do. Prototypes in effect combine these approaches. The prototype can be viewed as the template that best represents all related objects and events. Acceptable variations in the features and relations among the features of the prototype are also represented in memory.

6. Object recognition begins with separating the figure from the background and with the grouping of sensory features in accordance

with the principles of Gestalt psychology. Proximity, similarity, good continuation, closure, and goodness of figure illustrate these principles. Theoretically, a relatively small number of features allow the construction of all perceivable objects.

Key Terms

sensory memory	modality effect
pattern recognition	top-down processes
shape constancy	suffix effect
Weber-Fechner Law	bottom-up processes
just noticeable difference	cycle of perception
absolute threshold	word superiority effect
signal detection theory	template
sensitivity	distinctive features
response criterion or bias	prototype
iconic storage	Gestalt
echoic storage	figure-ground relationships
precategorical acoustic storage (PAS)	grouping principles

Recommended Readings

For a full discussion of the ways in which perception is constructive, on the one hand, and directly informed by the structure of stimuli, on the other, pursue the following sources. Gibson's *The Senses Considered as Perceptual Systems* (1966) and *The Ecological Approach to Visual Perception* (1979), Neisser's (1976) *Cognition and Reality*, and Shepard's (1984) article in the *Psychological Review* and his (1994) article in the *Psychonomic Bulletin & Review* are all informative. Perception has been covered in the *Annual Review of Psychology* by Banks and Krajicek (1991) and by Kolers (1983).

For a detailed discussion of the physiology and psychophysics of visual and auditory perception, I refer the reader to Cornsweet's (1970) *Visual Perception* and to Gulick's (1971) *Hearing: Physiology and Psychophyics*. Reed's (1973) *Psychological Processes in Pattern Recognition* offers a detailed look at templates, feature lists, prototypes, and structural descriptions. Goldstein's (1989) textbook titled *Sensation and Perception* covers sensing touch, temperature, pain, smell, and taste as well as vision and hearing. The information processing approach to the study of perception is well represented by Marr's (1982) *Vision* and by Hummel and Biederman's (1992) *Psychological Review* article.

The links among art, music, and perception can be explored in Arnheim's (1986) *New Essays on the Psychology of Art*, Shepard's (1990) *Mind Sights*, Deutsch's (1982) *The Psychology of Music*, and Dowling and Harwood's (1986) *Music Cognition*.

CHAPTER 3

Attention

Of all the stimuli that impinge on our senses and find their way into sensory memory, only some register consciously, enter into memory, and engage other cognitive functions. **Attention** refers to the process of selecting only certain stimuli and concentrating cognitive processes on them. As William James (1890) told us over a century ago:

> Everyone knows what attention is. It is the taking possession by the mind, in clear and vivid form, of one out of what seem several simultaneously possible trains of thought. Focalization, concentration, of consciousness are of its essence. (pp. 403-404)

Attention allows us to focus on what is important at the moment and to ignore the rest. Without attention, the world would overwhelm us with sensory information. Perception, without attention, would be a swirl of confusion as the mind tried to comprehend everything stimulating the senses at once. The disordered perception and thought of schizophrenia appear to be in part related to a breakdown in the normal process of selective attention (David, 1993; Place & Gilmore, 1980).

Many of James's observations on attention can still be found embedded in modern theories of attention (LaBerge, 1990). First, we will examine these theoretical explanations of attention, which no doubt are foreign territory for most readers. These theories divide into two major camps. One camp assumes that attention operates as a filter that blocks the processing of some stimuli and allows the processing of others. This camp addresses at what point in the processing of information selection takes place. The other camp assumes that the person actively chooses stimuli for further processing by allocating a portion of one or more limited pools of attentional capacity. This camp addresses how the concentration of cognitive processes on particular stimuli takes place. Filter theories and capacity theories have spawned impressive research on the nature of attention and we will consider each class in turn. A full understanding of selectivity and concentration benefits from both theoretical approaches. In the remainder of the chapter, we will consider automatic versus consciously controlled processes in detail. This distinction, recall, is a recurring theme of the discipline. We will close with a close look at visual attention.

Filter Theories

Early Selection

The advent of information processing models and the cognitive revolution can be traced to the late 1950s, as discussed in Chapter 1. Broadbent's (1957, 1958) mechanical model of attention heralded these events. The model aimed to explain the results of experiments in which two streams or channels of information must be processed simultaneously, such as in dichotic listening when both ears receive stimuli in synchrony. The **shadowing** technique, a widely used experimental procedure, requires a person to listen to a series of words in one ear and repeat them aloud while a second series arrives simultaneously in the other ear.

A classic study by Cherry (1953) found that people noticed and remembered little about the second, unattended series. Specifically, they seemed oblivious to the meanings of unattended words, failing even to notice that on occasion the material shifted from English to German. In contrast to missing the meaningful or semantic features, they did notice changes in physical or sensory features, such as when a low-pitched male voice changed to a higher pitched female voice.

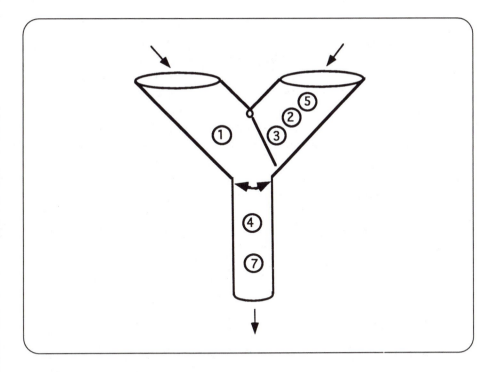

Figure 3.1. The early selection model of attention.
SOURCE: From Broadbent (1957).

Broadbent (1957) examined how well a series of digits could be recalled under dichotic listening conditions. For example, suppose the
series 7-4-1 arrived at the left ear perfectly synchronized with the series
3-2-5 at the right ear, each pair separated by only 500 milliseconds. When
allowed to recall the digits in any order, the participants successfully
recalled nearly two thirds of the digits. Of interest, their successes came
when they reported first from one ear and then the other (e.g., 741325).
However, when instructed to recall the digits in the order of their arrival
(e.g., 734215), they correctly reported less than a fifth of the digits on
average.

Broadbent (1957) proposed an **early selection model** of attention to
account for such findings, as illustrated in Figure 3.1. The upper branches
of the Y-shaped tube represented a large capacity sensory memory for
each auditory channel. Many digits or other stimuli could be held briefly
in the echoic memory of each ear, as discussed in the previous chapter.

The narrow central stem represented a limited capacity perceptual channel that could process only a single stimulus at a time. The swinging gate represented an early selection filter that allowed stimuli from one sensory memory store to proceed forth for additional perceptual processing. At a given instant, only one channel or the other undergoes full pattern recognition, leading to meaningful identification of the stimuli.

Broadbent's model captured Cherry's findings in that only the shadowed channel benefited from full perceptual analysis at the deep level of semantic features. Shifts in languages should go unnoticed, despite German being unintelligible to the English-speaking participants in the experiments. However, a sensory feature such as pitch should be identifiable at a very early stage of processing, in echoic storage, even on the unattended channel. Identifying the pitch and storing it in echoic memory should occur simultaneously in both channels before the selective filter operates. Similarly, the model explained Broadbent's findings by assuming that with only 500 milliseconds between each dichotic pair of digits, the gate cannot be swung back and forth quickly enough to allow a correct report of digits in their order of arrival. Successful recall should occur only by leaving the gate in one position until all three digits from one ear moved through the perceptual channel, followed by those from the other ear. Note that this assumes that echoic memory persists for more than a second or two, an assumption that we called into question in the previous chapter (Cowan, 1988).

Attenuation

Moreover, other experimental results from dichotic listening showed that the early selection model overly simplified human attention. It turned out that if the participant's name occurred on the unattended channel, then it sometimes received semantic processing and was reported (Moray, 1959). Moray's finding can readily be observed firsthand in any crowded, conversation-filled room. While engaged in one conversation, the words of other conversations are ignored—unless our name happens to crop up in a supposedly ignored conversation!

Another problematic finding also showed that unattended words seem to undergo analysis for meaning. If a word from the unattended channel best fit the meaning of a sentence being shadowed on the attended channel, then the unattended word would intrude, causing an error in shadowing (Treisman, 1960). One example Treisman gave of such intrusions is the following. The instructions called for shadowing the words on the left ear, while ignoring the right. The italicized words were those actually reported by the individual. Notice that the semantically appropriate *table* was perceived instead of the correct response of *three*.

> Left: . . . *sitting at the mahogany* three *possibilities* . . .
> Right: . . . let us look at these *table* with her head . . .

Such findings violated the assumptions of the early selection model. Processing the meaning of any item on the nonshadowed material should not occur if the filter selects only the shadowed items for complete pattern recognition. Perceiving *table* in Treisman's or one's name in Moray's experiment refutes this claim. Clearly we need an alternative theory to handle such results.

One alternative to Broadbent's model again placed a filter early in the sequence of information processing, before pattern recognition. Instead of an all-or-none filter that allows only a single channel to undergo pattern recognition at a time, Treisman (1970) suggested a filter that attenuates the unattended channel. You can think of attenuation as lowering the strength of the signals coming in on the rejected channel, making them less likely to be heard.

Figure 3.2 shows Treisman's **attenuation model.** The intensity or subjective loudness of the signals from the shadowed ear are stronger, penetrating more deeply into the pattern recognition system labeled here as the "dictionary." Treisman assumed that recognition of a word required that its intensity exceed its threshold. Words differed in terms of their threshold depending on how important the word was or how expected it was in a particular context. Thus even the attenuated signal intensity of one's name on the unattended channel should exceed the low threshold. Similarly, because top-down pattern recognition processes build an expectation for the word *table* to follow the word *mahogany*, it too could exceed its temporarily low threshold. Note that without that expectation, the threshold for *table* would normally be too high for recognition on anything but the shadowed ear, as shown in Figure 3.2.

Late Selection

Another alternative to Broadbent's model retains an all-or-none filter but moves its location. Instead of assuming that selection occurs prior to full pattern recognition, the **late selection model** designed by Deutsch

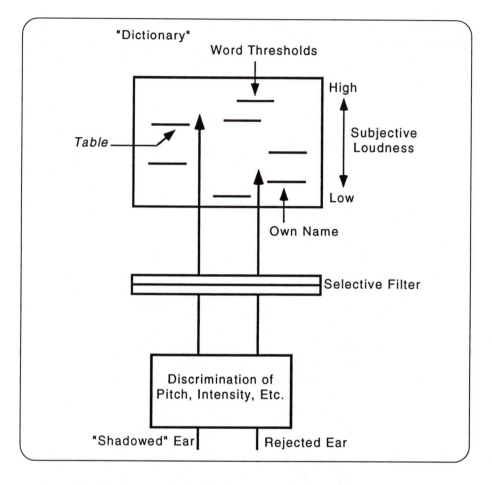

Figure 3.2. The attenuation model of selective attention.
SOURCE: From Anne Treisman (1970). Copyright © 1970. Reprinted by permission of the
Quarterly Journal of Experimental Psychology.

and Deutsch (1963) and refined by Norman (1968) placed the filter after
recognition. Perhaps the words on both channels receive full semantic
analysis. Then, just prior to the listener responding aloud, the words are
selected on the basis of their importance or pertinence. Figure 3.3 illustrates the idea.

Here the term *memory* is analogous to the dictionary of Treisman's
model and represents the pattern recognition processes responsible for
identifying the meaning of stimuli. The words represented by i, j, and k
best match the data-driven processes sending information up the system
from sensory inputs. At the same time, the words represented by g, h, and

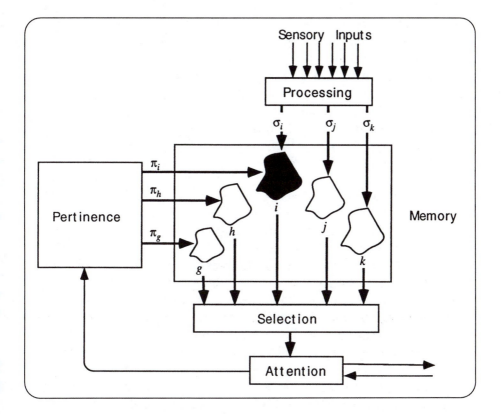

Figure 3.3. The late selection model of attention.
SOURCE: From Norman, D. A. (1968). Toward a theory of memory and attention. *Psychological Review, 75,* 522-536. Copyright © 1968 by the American Psychological Association. Reprinted by permission.

i are activated by conceptually driven processes because of their pertinence to the individual at the moment. Norman (1968) assumed that the word with the greatest sum of pertinence and sensory input would be selected for responding, such as repeating it aloud in a shadowing task.

Notice that the late selection model requires that all stimuli receive full analysis from pattern recognition processes. Nothing is saved in terms of perceptual processing, unlike the case with the early selection and attenuation models. The only purpose for the filter in the late selection model is to provide a focus of attention for further processing beyond pattern recognition. In addition to naming a stimulus, one could focus attention on, say, rehearsing it for storage in memory or using it to think and reason.

The late selection model accounts for the same findings as Treisman's attenuation model. Perceiving one's name or repeating an anticipated word from the unattended channel occurred because of the high pertinence values, not because only the name or word received full semantic analysis owing to its low threshold. The only way to distinguish which model best explains attention is to try to tell whether stimuli that are unattended and unselected for further processing actually receive full semantic analysis. Some experiments suggest that they do.

For example, MacKay (1973) had the person shadow a sentence such as the following in one ear: "They were standing near the bank." In the other ear, MacKay presented either the word *river* or the word *money* at the same time. The results showed the unattended and unselected word successfully biased the individual's interpretation of the sentence as referring to a "river bank" or a "financial bank."

Marcel (1983) adopted a very different methodology—backward masking—but reached the same conclusion. If a word is presented very briefly and quickly followed by another visual stimulus, the original word is masked backward in time such that the observer fails to perceive it consciously. Thus the word is both unattended and unselected for further processing. Even so, Marcel found that the word primes the observer in a way that confirms the word has undergone semantic analysis. Specifically, the time it takes to decide whether a subsequent string of letters is a word or not is speeded reliably if the original masked item is related in meaning. Lexical decision time, as it is called, is faster for, say, the word *ship* if the masked prime was *boat* compared with *book*. Remember the observer claims no awareness of the prime itself, whether it is *boat* or *book*. It seems as if the prime is perceived unconsciously.

Results of the type reported by MacKay (1973) and Marcel (1983) hardly settled the matter in favor of a late selection model. First, some questioned whether the unreportable words fell totally outside the scope of attention and awareness (Cheesman & Merikle, 1984; Holender, 1986). Whether unconscious perception is possible continues to draw great interest among researchers and to spur the development of new experimental techniques (Debner & Jacoby, 1994; Jacoby & Whitehouse, 1989; Merikle & Reingold, 1992). Second, compelling evidence could be marshaled for either an early or a late location of the filter or bottleneck in information processing (Johnston & Heinz, 1978). It was as if the filter could move depending on the task at hand. Third, an alternative theoretical approach took hold that showed that filter theories of any sort fail to capture the full complexity of human attention.

BOX 3.1: Unconscious Perceptual Defense

Freud's psychoanalytic theory strongly influenced the fields of abnormal and clinical psychology throughout the first half of this century. During the second half, Freud's influence waned in all areas of psychology. Of interest, one of the most controversial issues in the history of cognitive psychology stemmed from psychoanalytic theory (Erdelyi & Goldberg, 1979).

Unconscious sexual or aggressive impulses theoretically cause tremendous anxiety if allowed direct entry into the conscious ego. Studies examined whether people were less likely to perceive a sexually related word embedded in a list of control words. At issue was whether the absolute threshold for sexually related terms was abnormally high for some individuals, a phenomenon called **perceptual defense** (Erdelyi, 1974). One criticism of studies purporting to show that some people failed to perceive sexually related terms as readily was that it all came down to a response bias. Out of embarrassment, the participants may have adopted a criterion of responding only when they were absolutely certain about their perceptions. However, signal detection analyses revealed that perceptual defense in fact arose from a lessened sensitivity to the sexual terms (Erdelyi & Goldberg, 1979). Indeed, certain individuals displayed a heightened sensitivity to such terms, a phenomenon called **perceptual vigilance.**

Blum and Barbour (1979) avoided the response bias criticism by using nonsexual terms. They trained participants under hypnosis to associate neutral words with cartoons that, in theory, aroused castration anxiety in men and penis envy in women. The cartoons were tailored to each participant. Blum and Barbour then gave a word perception test, in which each of the key words plus control words appeared in a tachistoscope for only 33 milliseconds. Compared with control words, the participants failed to correctly recognize the key words much less often.

Capacity Theories

Single Capacity

Kahneman (1973) proposed that attention is limited in overall capacity and that our ability to carry out simultaneous tasks depends in part on how much capacity the tasks require. The capacity approach conceives of attention as mental effort. The more a task requires of a limited pool of available capacity, the more mental effort the person exerts. For instance, try these two mental arithmetic problems:

(a) $6 \times 6 = ?$ versus (b) $32 \times 12 = ?$

Clearly, problem b demands more **mental effort,** more of the capacity you have available for carrying out the task.

The central idea can be readily grasped by considering the dual task method of measuring mental effort. Suppose that while you carry out a series of either easy (a) or hard (b) mental multiplication problems presented over headphones, you are given a secondary task of detecting the random appearance of a light on a panel in front of you. I instruct you to focus attention on the primary multiplication task, but to respond to the light with, say, a button press as rapidly as you can without disrupting primary task performance. The more effortful the primary task, the less capacity you will have available for rapidly detecting the light. I can then compare your dual task reaction times with a simple reaction time, when light detection is the only demand on your limited attentional capacity. The more dual task reaction time increases over simple reaction time, the more effortful the primary task must be. In this case, I would expect the hard problems would slow you down markedly more than would the easy problems in detecting the lights.

Kahneman's model is pictured in Figure 3.4. The amount of available capacity achieves a peak when an individual is moderately aroused in terms of activation of the sympathetic nervous system (e.g., moderate heart rate and moderate levels of cortisol and other stress hormones may be detected). Insufficient arousal decreases capacity, as when a student dozes off while reading a textbook. Of interest, too much arousal does as well, as when a student has an impossible deadline to meet because of an unfair professor or perhaps procrastination. That performance is best at moderate levels of arousal has long been recognized in the Yerkes-Dodson (1908) law.

Enduring dispositions, momentary intentions, and evaluation of current demands on capacity shape the allocation policy. For example, in navigating a car on an interstate highway at, say, 65 miles per hour, the driver may be predisposed to direct attentional capacity to listening to a favorite song on the radio, reducing the capacity available for driving. Or, in a moment, the driver may intentionally speak to a companion in the front seat or scream at the kids in the backseat, again reducing capacity. If something unexpected happens on the road ahead—a tractor-trailer begins to swerve into the driver's lane—a quick evaluation of demands may rapidly force all available capacity to steering and braking.

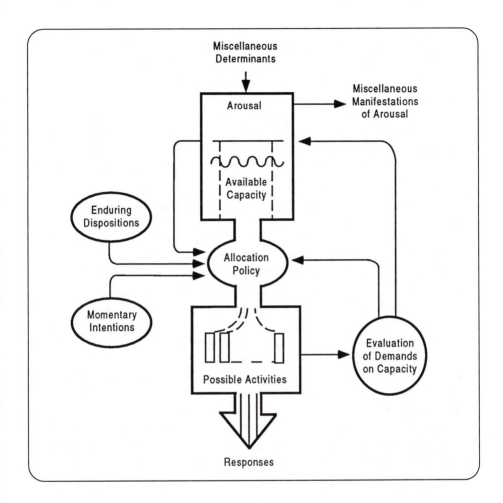

Figure 3.4. The single capacity model of attention.
SOURCE: From Kahneman, Daniel, *Attention and Effort*, © 1973, p. 47. Reprinted by permission of Prentice-Hall, Inc., Englewood Cliffs, N.J.

Of course, if the driver is too distracted by other demands or if his available capacity is insufficient because of drowsiness or panic, then an accident may well be in the making.

    Kahneman (1973) advanced the notion of a limited pool of capacity as an addition rather than replacement of the bottleneck idea of filter theories. He retained the idea that two activities using exactly the same cognitive structures or processes will indeed interfere with one another. For example, in the shadowing task, both channels of information require higher level auditory processes and speech recognition mechanisms despite the fact that two ears are involved. Kahneman referred to this as structural interference. Yet even when two tasks do not require the same structures, they still can interfere with each other to the extent that they compete for a limited pool of available capacity.

Tasks engendering both specific structural interference and general capacity interference should show greater performance decrements than one showing only capacity interference. Allport, Antonis, and Reynolds (1972) found exactly this by checking memory for unattended words either spoken or printed in a shadowing task. When the unattended words were auditory, presented dichotically, participants remembered them much more poorly than when they were visually presented during the shadowing task. Presenting them without the demands of shadowing resulted in the best memory of all. Thus the shadowing task takes general capacity away from the processes of learning the words, but when structural interference also enters in, memory is especially poor.

Johnston and Heinz (1978) extended capacity theory to account for the conflicting conclusions about whether the structural filter comes early or late in information processing. They proposed that, depending on the demands of the task, a person can flexibly employ either early or late selection, though the semantic processing of late selection comes at the cost of greater capacity usage. The researchers studied dichotic listening in which the shadowed message could be identified by a sensory feature of pitch (male versus female voice) or only by a semantic analysis (same voice but different categories, such as cities versus occupations). They measured secondary task reaction times to detect a light during shadowing.

It took about 120 milliseconds longer to respond to the light while simultaneously shadowing using an early selection mode based on pitch relative to simply detecting the light alone. Yet, it took more than 170 milliseconds longer when shadowing required a late selection mode based on meaning. It would surely have been even longer had the participants managed to maintain accurate performance in the late selection case. As it happened, their error rate quadrupled when semantic analysis was needed! Thus a capacity theory can subsume the findings of filter theories and explain further the nuances of human attention.

Multiple Resources

Further research has shown that a full accounting of the complexities of human attention require that still finer distinctions be drawn than those seen in Kahneman's capacity theory (Navon & Gopher, 1979). Multiple resource theories account for how two simultaneous tasks will interfere with each other depending on the level of resource or capacity demands they make and on the specific structures, processes, or resources they require. This approach elaborates the distinction that Kahneman drew between general capacity interference and specific structural interference.

For example, Wickens (1980) proposed three dimensions of resources. First, he distinguished auditory versus visual perceptual modalities, as Kahneman did in his notion of structural interference. Second, he distinguished perceptual-cognitive resources, consumed by the demands of tasks such as reading or mentally calculating, and response resources, consumed by speaking or moving the hand. Third, he distinguished verbal versus spatial processing codes. Speech or text illustrate verbal codes whereas pictures or diagrams illustrate spatial codes.

Multiple resource theories attempt to explain how well two tasks can be done concurrently by specifying the capacity or effort demands, on the one hand, and the types of resources needed, on the other. For instance, attending simultaneously to speech and pictures should be more manageable than processing two channels of speech (recall the results of Allport et al., 1972). Further, attending to two channels of speech should be easiest when the capacity demands of the task are low, as when the shadowed message can be identified by pitch, than when the demands are high, as in semantic analysis (recall the results of Johnston & Heinz, 1978).

An alternative multiple resource theory identifies the left and right cerebral hemispheres as independent resource types (Friedman & Polson, 1981; Polson & Friedman, 1988). These researchers identified specific neurological components corresponding to resources, arguing that their hemispheric model can better predict task interference than Wickens's dimensions of resources. While that claim remains to be verified, we will see later in the chapter that neurological identification of attentional systems is clearly the direction in which the field is moving.

Conclusion

To summarize, filter theories evolved to explain the selective nature of attention. Experiments designed to test these theories showed the validity of assuming structural bottlenecks in the flow of information processing. However, they also showed the difficulty of specifying the exact location of these bottlenecks. Capacity theories build upon the idea of bottlenecks while recognizing that the location of the bottleneck from early to late stages in perception and cognition can vary. Specifically, an individual can adopt either mode of selectivity in response to the demands of the current situation. Capacity theories also recognized that various dimensions of structural interference exist, such as the distinction between structures that process verbal versus spatial information. Finally, and most important, capacity theories recognized the mental effort aspect of attention as well as the selective aspect. The degree of attentional resources demanded by a task became a focal point of research.

Automatic Processes

It has long been known that perceptual, cognitive, and motor processes may unfold effortlessly. Stroop (1935) devised an ingenious and somewhat diabolical test to show that reading of familiar color terms occurs automatically and effortlessly. The color terms (e.g., red, green, blue, yellow) are printed in an incompatible color of ink. The word *red* appears in green ink, the word *green* appears in yellow ink, and so on. The task is to say aloud the color of the ink while ignoring the meaning of the word itself.

The identification of words—one aspect of fluent reading—occurs automatically. That is, it is exceedingly difficult to ignore the meaning of the word *red* when it appears in green ink. The correct response of *green* competes with the habitual response of *red*. Errors and delays in responding are the usual result. For more than 50 years now, the **Stroop effect** and variations on it have challenged theorists to account for the detailed patterns of errors and delays observed in experiments (MacLeod, 1991).

Word recognition illustrates one of many processes that have become automatic because of extensive practice, maturation, and skill development. Walking, running, riding a bicycle, typing on a keyboard are among the many motor skills that people automatize. Perceptual and cognitive skills also become automatic. Depth and object perception, as seen in the previous chapter, occur effortlessly despite the intensive computations that they require. Speech recognition, as we will discuss later in the book, is one of the most complex perceptual tasks that we undertake. Yet by age 5 the child effortlessly deciphers and comprehends the speech stream.

Criteria of Automaticity

Posner and Snyder (1974, 1975) categorized a process as automatic if it met three criteria. First, an automatic process occurs unintentionally, as the Stroop effect demonstrates so well. Try as you might, *red* pops into mind even when the correct ink color is green. Second, the process occurs unconsciously, outside the scope of even peripheral awareness. We will return to the difficult matters of consciousness and gradations of awareness in the final chapter. For now, suffice it to say that automatic processes unfold without our awareness as well as without our intention. Third, the process operates without depleting attentional resources. The automatic process can carry on without interfering with processes that demand attentional resources. Hence we need to distinguish between conscious, **controlled processes,** on the one hand, and **automatic processes,** on the other (Hasher & Zacks, 1979; Schneider & Shiffrin, 1977).

Some mental operations can be classified as automatic versus consciously controlled by examining performance in priming tasks. **Priming** refers to the presentation of a stimulus that either facilitates or inhibits the processing of a subsequent stimulus. The prime precedes the target and has consequences for how well the target is processed.

For example, Posner and Snyder (1975) presented one of three kinds of primes in a task calling for participants to decide whether pairs of letters were physically identical to one another. The pair AA called for a yes response whereas Aa called for a no response in this task. Just prior to presenting the letter pair, a prime appeared that was relevant to the decision to be made (A), irrelevant to the decision (B), or neutral (+). Posner and Snyder theorized that the relevant prime would facilitate or speed the time needed to respond yes or no, because it primed the representation of A in memory in advance. This facilitation was measured relative to the reaction time obtained in the neutral condition. In fact, they found a facilitation effect of 85 milliseconds. In contrast, the irrelevant prime inhibited the processing of the letter pairs, slowing the decision times by 36 milliseconds relative to the neutral prime.

In a follow-up experiment, Posner and Snyder varied the stimulus onset asynchrony: the delay interval between presentation of the prime (+, A, or B) and the target letters (e.g., AA or Aa, BB or Bb). In 80% of the trials, the prime was relevant to the target letters, encouraging participants to form conscious expectations of the target letters to follow. Plotted in Figure 3.5 are the degrees of facilitation and inhibition observed at various delay intervals ranging from zero to 500 milliseconds. Zero on

BOX 3.2: Automaticity in Behavior

Our social behavior seems to be especially susceptible to automatic processes. Langer (1989) aptly referred to such behavior as mindless. She illustrated mindlessness with the following anecdote:

> Once, in a small department store, I gave a cashier a new credit card. Noticing that I hadn't signed it, she handed it back to me to sign. Then she took my card, passed it through her machine, handed me the resulting form, and asked me to sign it. I did as I was told. The cashier then held the form next to the newly signed card to see if the signatures matched. (pp. 12-13)

Langer studied such mindless social actions by sending an interdepartmental memo to various university offices, identical in appearance to routine memoranda. The sole content of the message was one of these two statements: (a) "Please return this immediately to Room 247" or (b) "This memo is to be returned to Room 247." Now surely it should have occurred to mindful recipients of such messages that if the senders had really wanted the memo in Room 247, they would have sent it there in the first place. A mindful person would pitch such nonsense in the trash. But that did not happen. Instead, 90% of the recipients returned the memo as requested (Langer, 1989, p. 15).

Langer pointed out that the mindlessness of social behavior can play into the hands of con artists. A Los Angeles newspaper ran the following ad: "It's not too late to send $1 to _ ." The name and address appeared in the blank. Nothing more was stated; nothing was promised in return. Astonishingly, many people actually sent the person their dollar, earning the con artist a tidy sum. Other theorists have implicated automatic processes in a wide range of social and antisocial behaviors (Bargh, 1989), including drug and alcohol addiction (Tiffany, 1990).

the y-axis refers to no difference from the neutral prime. Notice first that the degree of facilitation rapidly rises over the first 200 milliseconds. Processing of the target letters quickened in direct relation to the amount of time available to process the prime, at least up to 200 milliseconds. In sharp contrast, the irrelevant prime produced no reliable degree of inhibition until 300 milliseconds was allowed for processing the prime before the target letters appeared.

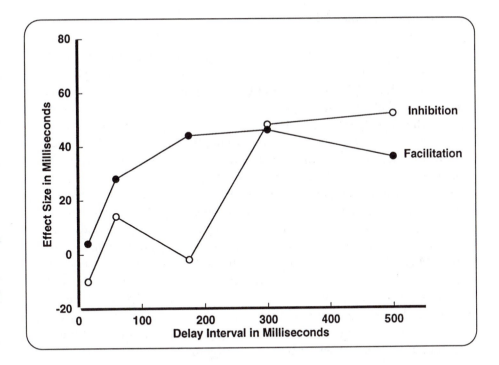

Figure 3.5. Facilitation and inhibition in a physical identity task.
SOURCE: From Posner and Snyder (1975). Copyright © 1975 by Academic Press, Inc. Reprinted by permission.

Posner and Snyder interpreted the different time courses of facilitation and inhibition as distinguishing the automatic and conscious aspects of their task. The presence of facilitation only early on represents the automatic processing of the prime that immediately occurs, long before conscious awareness of the prime enters the picture. Presumably an irrelevant prime (e.g., B given the target Aa) has no automatic effect on making a decision about the target letters. But later, after the prime has been consciously processed, the participant consciously expects the occurrence of target letters related to the prime (Bb or Bb for the prime B). This expectation developed because the prime was indeed related to the target letters 80% of the time. The presence of both facilitation and inhibition at the longer delay intervals represents conscious processing in Posner and Snyder's experiment.

Practice and Automaticity

Typically, a process or a set of processes used in a particular skill, such as typing, becomes automatic only after extensive practice. Shiffrin and Schneider (1977) investigated the development of automaticity in a search task that has been extensively investigated by cognitive psychologists. The participants viewed a series of frames on a computer screen containing letters and digits. Their task entailed visually searching each frame for a target item, while ignoring distractor items. The participants memorized the target items at the beginning of each series. Figure 3.6 shows two sample sequences for positive trials that contained a target. In the top case, the memory set consisted of two target items, the letters J and D. After memorizing the targets, a sequence of frames rapidly appeared on the screen, with one of the target items (J) occurring toward the middle of the sequence on positive trials. In addition to target items, the frames contained either distractor items or nonmeaningful masks (dot patterns). The number of items in the memory set and the number in each frame of the sequence varied. The observer pressed a button as quickly as possible upon detecting a target. On negative trials, in which targets did not appear, the observer pressed a different button at the end of the sequence.

Schneider and Shiffrin (1977) examined two types of sequences, called varied mapping and consistent mapping. With varied mapping, the letters or numbers that served as targets on one sequence of frames could turn up as distractors on another sequence. These were letter-letter (or number-number) trials, because in one sequence the observer might be looking for a particular memory set of letters while ignoring the distractor letters. Then, on a latter sequence, he or she might be looking for the very letters that earlier had been distractors. Thus, to identify the targets accurately, the observer must carefully search each frame of the visual display and compare the items with the memory set on that trial. With consistent mapping, the memory set of numbers, say, remained the same from one trial sequence to the next (see the bottom case in Figure 3.6). These number-letter trials allowed the observer to look consistently for only the numbers and ignore all the letters. In fact, the appearance of any number at all was by definition a target, meaning that a close check as to whether the number was one of the memory set was not necessary.

The participants practiced the search task for 10 hours beforehand and received further practice during the experiments. Schneider and Shiffrin (1977) manipulated the number of items in the memory set (1, 2,

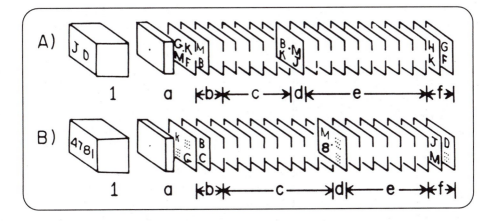

Figure 3.6. A visual search task for studying automatic and consciously controlled processing.
SOURCE: From Schneider, W., & Shiffrin, R. M. (1977). Controlled and automatic human information processing: Detection, search, and attention. *Psychological Review, 84,* 1-66. Copyright © 1977 by the American Psychological Association. Reprinted by permission.

or 4) and the number in each frame of the sequence (1, 2, or 4). The results in Figure 3.7 reveal that, with varied mapping, reaction time to identify the targets increased systematically with the number of items in the frame. This occurred for both positive trials containing a target (open circles) and negative trials containing only distractors. This increase in reaction time was much steeper when there were more items in the memory set. Varied mapping produced an effortful, controlled search process. The observer had to consciously and deliberately match each item detected in a frame against each item held in short-term memory to decide if a target appeared.

In sharp contrast, the reaction times with consistent mapping remained flat as frame size increased. (Note that only memory set sizes of 1 and 4 were tested in the consistent mapping condition.) Remarkably, the observer could detect targets on the positive trials (closed triangles) just as fast when there were four items held in memory and four items to search in the frame as when there was only one item in memory and in the frame. Notice, too, how much faster the observers responded in the consistent mapping conditions. Thus after extensive practice the observer performed the search task automatically and effortlessly. The effortful controlled process seen with varied mapping was replaced by an effortless automatic process with consistent mapping.

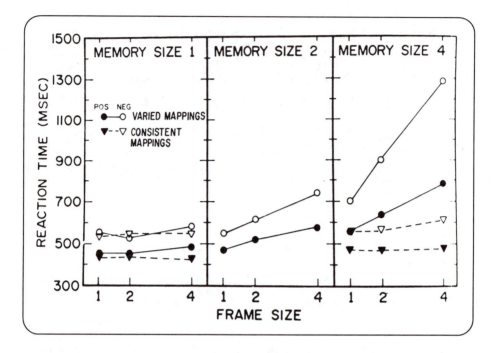

Figure 3.7. Automatic search is observed with consistent mapping and controlled search with varied mapping.
SOURCE: From Schneider, W., & Shiffrin, R. M. (1977). Controlled and automatic human information processing: Detection, search, and attention. *Psychological Review, 84*, 1-66. Copyright © 1977 by the American Psychological Association. Reprinted by permission.

Spelke, Hirst, and Neisser (1976) reported that with extensive practice even tasks that theoretically demand high levels of attentional capacity can be performed without interfering with each other. They trained two individuals to read short stories while simultaneously writing down words dictated by the experimenter. Their procedure harks back to work done at the turn of the century in William James's laboratory at Harvard. The writer Gertrude Stein was interested in automatic writing under hypnosis. At that time, automatic writing was popularly practiced as a way to channel the voices of spirits (Ellenberger, 1970), a practice that lingers in some circles today. Solomans and Stein (1896) reported that they both learned to read stories while automatically and unconsciously writing at dictation. They had no recall of the words they had written, despite being aware that they had indeed written something. Gertrude Stein later developed her famous stream of consciousness style from her experiences with automatic writing.

Eschewing hypnosis and spirits for hard work and practice, Spelke et al. managed to train their participants to take dictation of short sentences, which should require highly effortful semantic processing, while simultaneously reading. After massive practice, they found people could accurately transcribe while reading with full comprehension. Hirst et al. suggested that neither automaticity nor rapid alternation of attention accounted for the results. They contended that people split attention and simultaneously attended to both reading and dictation. Perhaps so, but it seems equally plausible that at least some of the component processes in reading, taking dictation, or both became automatized. The remaining component processes could have then been consciously controlled by a rapid alternation of attention.

Logan (1988) provided one explanation of how changes in the way a task is performed through practice leads to automaticity. Specifically, if a task can be restructured so that performance depends on retrieval from long-term memory, then automaticity occurs. Taking our example from earlier in the chapter, if you multiple 6×6, you do not need to carry out the algorithm because you can retrieve the answer 36 from a memorized multiplication table stored in your long-term memory. The process is fast, effortless, and, most important, here it is different in nature than the alternative. If you must multiply 18×32, the only route available is to calculate the answer, unless perhaps you performed the same problem just a few minutes before. Thus, as we learn to do a task automatically, it may be that the underlying processes change qualitatively by relying more on direct retrieval from memory.

Genetics and Maturation

Certain processes may be so basic for human learning and survival that they are genetically programmed to operate through maturation and interaction with the environment. Motor skills exemplify processes that achieve automaticity through genetic programming in addition to practice. Learning to crawl, walk, and run is not simply a matter of practice. At birth a reflex is present to move the arms and legs in a crawling movement. This reflex typically disappears around the third or fourth month with the ability to crawl appearing later, at around 7 months (Gallahue, 1989). Whereas some species are programmed to walk moments after birth to ensure their survival, our species adopts a more leisurely pace, with the infant wholly dependent on mother and father for survival. The effortlessness and automaticity that we see in the motor skills of an older child running at play is only partly due to practice.

Basic cognitive processes may also be genetically programmed or hard-wired in the nervous system (Flavell, Miller, & Miller, 1993). These should appear early in development and require relatively little learning to become fully operational. Moreover, individual differences in the functioning of these processes should be minimal if they are species-specific processes. Age, culture, intelligence, educational attainment, and other factors that strongly influence consciously controlled processes ought to be unimportant for innate automatic processes.

Hasher and Zacks (1979, 1984) proposed that humans innately and automatically process the frequency of occurrence of environmental features and events. They reported evidence that young children keep track of stimulus frequencies as well as adults, suggesting that the process undergoes little if any cognitive development. Individual differences in frequency processing also are minimal. Numerous studies have challenged the conclusion that frequency processing is fully automatic. At times intention to keep track of frequency helps performance, and heavy concurrent demands on attention hurts performance. Even so, the evidence strongly supports the conclusion that frequency processing operates automatically and innately, albeit less than optimally at times (Sanders, Gonzalez, Murphy, Liddle, & Vitina, 1987).

Visual Attention: A Closer Look

Let us turn to visual attention to illustrate some details regarding the dovetailing of automatic and controlled processes, the focusing of attention, and the switching of attention. Along the way we will consider some of the neurological components associated with these phenomena. Kinchla (1992) noted that visual attention can be overt, such as when we orient our eyes toward one object rather than another, and covert, such as when we attend to an object in peripheral vision rather than foveal vision without moving our eyes. We will concern ourselves primarily with the mechanisms involved in overt attending.

Automatic and Controlled Processes

Treisman and her colleagues have proposed a **feature integration theory** of vision that entails both automatic or preattentive processes dovetailed with controlled or focused attentional processes. An observer first scans a visual field preattentively, allowing the simultaneous, parallel recognition of basic stimulus dimensions such as color and shape. A

BOX 3.3: Subliminal Influences

Subliminal perception refers to the automatic, unconscious processing of information that has some impact on subsequent behavior. Advertisers have long looked to subliminal perception as a potential hook for catching unsuspecting customers.

Subliminal information can be visually presented too briefly for conscious recognition, embedded in the background of a picture such that attention fails to focus on the information, aurally presented in the presence of high levels of noise, or aurally embedded in music by presenting the information backward (e.g., lyrics in rock music). The latter technique in particular has drawn public outcry, as evidenced by the debate in the 1980s in the California legislature over the subliminal influence of rock music on teenagers.

Vokey and Read (1985) tested listeners' ability to identify the meaning of backward statements. Each statement fits one of five categories: nursery rhymes, Christian, satanic, pornographic, or advertising. The listeners simply had to identify the correct category, giving them a 20% chance of being correct through random guessing. Their listeners performed at this chance level (19%), indicating they had not analyzed the meaning of the backward speech. Moreover, studies on attention and memory show that little if any unattended information is stored such that it can be explicitly recalled or recognized several minutes later (Carlson & Dulany, 1985; Fisk & Schneider, 1984; Kellogg, 1980).

However, perhaps subliminal information affects not cognition, but emotion. For example, researchers have found that subliminally presented information slightly alters our future emotional responses to the material, despite our not being able to explicitly remember it (Kunst-Wilson & Zajonc, 1980; Seamon, Marsh, & Brody, 1984). We are more inclined to like a stimulus somewhat more if it has been previously presented in a subliminal manner. Coren (1984) concluded that subliminal advertising, if it works at all, operates solely at this level of emotional response. The meaning of the message need not be understood or remembered explicitly for such emotional changes.

further stage of processing requiring focused attention is then needed to integrate the specific stimulus features into a unitary object. To test their theory, they required observers to detect a target that differed from distractor items in terms of one dimension, such as color.

Following the logic of the set size effects discussed earlier, Treisman predicted that the number of distractor items should be irrelevant to speed of detection if the observer could automatically recognize the dimensions of all stimuli in the display in parallel. For example, finding a red X in a display with nothing but blue Xs and blue Os should be automatic. Indeed, she found observers could detect such targets as fast in a display with 30 items as in one with only 3 items (Treisman & Gelade, 1980; Treisman & Sato, 1990).

When they required the observer to search for a unique conjunction of color and form, Treisman expected that focal attention would be needed to integrate the two features. For example, finding a red X in a display that includes red Os and blue Xs demands focused attention. In this case, she expected and found a strong set size effect; the more distractors, the longer it took to find the target.

Treisman's work provides details on how an automatic and a controlled process work together in perceptual search. Her suggestion that features are first identified automatically and then conjoined with attentional effort is consistent with neurological evidence as well. Livingston and Hubel (1987) have found specialized neural channels or populations of neurons devoted to identifying a single stimulus dimension. They reported separate channels for color, form, motion, and depth.

Focusing Attention

Visual attention often has been likened to a spotlight that shines onto a portion of the visual field (Posner, 1980). The focus of attention equates with the illuminated area. Stimuli falling outside the focus must be processed automatically if at all.

The spotlight metaphor is an attractive one. However, in using the metaphor, we must keep in mind two facts about visual attention. First, the diameter of the spotlight can change, from a highly focused to a highly diffuse beam of light. Numerous experiments calling for an observer to focus attention on a centrally presented target letter reveal "flanker effects," in which adjacent letters influence the time to name the target (Murphy & Eriksen, 1987). The logic of these experiments borrows from the Stroop effect. If the adjacent letters are associated with a wrong or different response than the target, then reaction time to the target slows down, just like in the Stroop effect. Alternatively, the response to the target is faster if the adjacent letters are associated with the same response.

Murphy and Eriksen (1987) found that if the observer knew exactly where to focus attention, then the spotlight beam was concentrated. Any letter more than about one letter away from the target had no impact on response time. In contrast, if a target could occur anywhere, then the spotlight was more diffuse. Adjacent letters often affected response times in this case.

The findings of LaBerge, Brown, Carter, Bash, and Hartley (1991) suggest that the size of the spotlight beam also contracts as the load on attentional capacity increases. The harder it is to identify the target letter, the less likely it is that adjacent letters will affect response time. They discovered this by presenting a digit at the same spot as the target letter. The observer received instructions to name the target letter only on trials when the digit was a 7. They increased the attentional demands of the task by shortening the exposure duration of the digit from 250 milliseconds to only 50 milliseconds. The less time available to identify the digit, the more momentary cognitive effort the task required. The flanker effects gradually disappeared as the digit recognition task became more difficult.

Attention Switching

The manner in which attention shifts from one area of the visual environment to another has also been investigated. By precuing the observer as to the location of the next target, one can monitor the shift. If the time between the cue and target is very brief—too fast for an overt movement of the eyes—then one can monitor a covert shift of attention. It turns out that attention can be shifted to the periphery of the visual field while simultaneously fixating the eyes on a central target; sophisticated mathematical models of covert attention shifts have been developed (Reeves & Sperling, 1986).

Kinchla (1992) summarized the research in this area: Attention does not shift from one area to another in an all-or-none fashion. Instead, about 50 milliseconds after the cue, attention begins to build up gradually at the cued location, not reaching full strength until 200 milliseconds have elapsed. To quote Kinchla (1992): "In terms of the spotlight metaphor, it is as if the spotlight went off at one point and then gradually came on again at the target location" (p. 726).

One way to study covert attention shifts entailed briefly presenting a cue in a peripheral location just before a target stimulus appeared; the observer pressed a key upon detecting the target. In 80% of the trials the cue drew attention to the correct location, whereas on the remaining trials the cue was invalid. The results showed a faster response time to the target, a facilitation effect, relative to a control condition (Posner & Cohen, 1984). In other experiments the cue appeared in a peripheral location *opposite* the location where the target most often appeared. Of interest, people briefly shifted attention to the cue location, facilitating responses on those occasions when the target actually appeared there (Posner,

Cohen, & Rafal, 1982). But then they rapidly shifted attention back to the location where the target generally occurred, again as seen by a facilitation effect. The cue seemed to compel a quick covert shift of attention followed by a shift back to the expected target location. Despite the complexity of the system governing such covert shifts of attention, Johnson, Posner, and Rothbart (1994) have demonstrated that even infants 4 months of age can be trained to covertly shift attention in this manner. Plainly, the system develops early in life.

Neuroanatomical Systems

Recall from our discussion of feature detectors in the previous chapter that a neuron in the visual or occipital lobe (lower, rear area of the neocortex) is tuned to, say, a specific orientation of a line. Moreover, the line must stimulate a specific area in the retina of the eye, which defines the receptive field for the neuron in question. A group of cells in the retina—the **receptive field**—all map onto a specific neuron in the cortex that is "looking for" the feature to which it is tuned. Animal studies done on one of the areas in the occipital cortex—called V4—revealed what seems to be the operation of an attentional spotlight narrowing in on relevant stimuli while ignoring others.

For example, the size of a receptive field apparently contracts so as to include a stimulus relevant to the task at hand while excluding an irrelevant stimulus. This occurs when both stimuli fall within the range of the original receptive field (Moran & Desimone, 1985). Further, when the task requires a finer discrimination between, say, the orientation of two lines, the response of a neuron to a specific orientation becomes still more specific, more finely tuned (Spitzer, Desimone, & Moran, 1988). Thus Kinchla (1992) noted that "the contraction of receptive fields and the sharpening of tuning curves would seem to serve a selective or 'attentional' function" (p. 734).

The control of these changes in receptive fields seems to lie in the thalamus, a structure deep in the midbrain that serves as a crossroad for an extremely large number of sensory pathways. PET scans with human beings have revealed increased blood flow—implying increased neural activity—in a portion of the thalamus called the **pulvinar thalamic nucleus** when observers receive instructions to ignore an irrelevant but clearly visible stimulus (LaBerge & Buchsbaum, 1990). Equally telling is clinical evidence with patients suffering damage to the pulvinar thalamic nucleus. Lesions in this area are associated with difficulties in directing visual attention (Rafal & Posner, 1987).

The pulvinar thalamic nucleus certainly is not the only control mechanism for attention in the human brain. Posner and Peterson (1990) concluded from the relevant evidence that different areas turn the attentional spotlight off from its present focus and move it to a new focal point. The pulvinar thalamic nucleus, in their view, then reads out the information available in the new focus of attention. A breakdown in this system may cause a disorder called **spatial neglect**, characterized by a failure to attend to both the left and the right sides of an object. Spatial neglect can be seen in patients who read only the words on the right side of a paragraph presented to them or in those who draw only the right half of a picture they are asked to copy (McCarthy & Warrington, 1990). These patients seem to have trouble in voluntarily shifting the attentional spotlight to the neglected side (Posner et al., 1982).

🔲 SUMMARY 🔲

1. *Attention* refers to the selection of certain stimuli for processing to the exclusion of others. It also refers to the concentration of mental resources on a particular process. Two broad classes of theories have developed to explain attention. Filter theories address the selective nature of attention, whereas capacity theories address the allocation of resources to specific mental processes. Filter theories postulated a bottleneck in the flow of information from initial sensory processing to registration in conscious awareness. Capacity theories recognized that one or more bottlenecks exist, but added the assumption that mental processes compete for limited resources as well.

2. Early selection theory placed a bottleneck or filter immediately after sensory memory. Pattern recognition of attended material proceeded, while unattended material faded rapidly from sensory memory because it failed to pass the selective filter. Attenuation theory also placed the bottleneck after sensory registration but it assumed that the filter merely lessened or attenuated the signal strength of unattended material. If the threshold for pattern recognition for a given stimulus, such as one's name, was sufficiently low, then even the weak unattended signals might undergo pattern recognition. Late selection theory placed the filter after all pattern recognition of attended and unattended stimuli has taken place. This view held that all stimuli are fully analyzed for their meaning. Yet the filter excludes all but the attended stimuli from entering conscious awareness and memory systems.

3. Single capacity theory assumed that mental processes compete for a general pool of attentional resources. Two tasks can also interfere with each other if they both demand a high level of general resources. The general pool is always limited, though the exact amount of available capacity fluctuates with arousal and other factors. The percentage of available capacity used by a process defines the degree of mental effort involved. Multiple capacity theory assumes that pools of resources can be defined in terms of several independent dimensions. Auditory versus visual resources is one such dimension, while verbal versus spatial resources is another. If two tasks both demand, say, verbal capacity, then performance suffers. If one draws on verbal capacity while the other taps spatial capacity, then dual task performance can proceed without interference. Multiple capacity theory therefore integrates the insights of filter theories and single capacity theory to provide a comprehensive and detailed description of attention.

4. Automatic processes require little if any mental effort. Moreover, they occur without intentional control; even when an individual attempts to stop an automatic process from operation, it unfolds anyway, as demonstrated by the Stroop effect. Finally, automatic processes operate outside the scope of conscious awareness. Processes develop automaticity either through genetic programming or as the result of extensive practice. Obtaining proficiency in a skill often entails developing automaticity of underlying processes through practice. Controlled processes contrast with automatic processes on each point. They demand extensive mental effort, they require intentional control to operate, and they enter conscious awareness.

5. The feature integration theory of visual attention contends that feature detectors operate preattentively or automatically, allowing the identification of shape, color, and other properties. Effortful controlled processing must then conjoin the features to complete the pattern recognition process. The focus of controlled processing in vision can be likened to a spotlight. The beam of spotlight varies in size, being more diffuse when attentional demands are light and contracting to a narrow beam when demands are heavy. Even when no eye movements are involved, it takes as long as 200 milliseconds to turn the beam off in one location and to bring it back to full strength in another.

6. The neuroanatomical basis for visual attentional systems is only beginning to be understood. The facts to date suggest that the pulvinar nucleus in the thalamus serves the function of filtering irrelevant stimuli. It does so by controlling how sharply tuned a neuron in

the neocortex is to a specific stimulus feature and by altering the size of a neuron's receptive field from the receptor cells in the eye. Other areas of the brain appear to turn off the attentional spotlight in one location and move it to a new location in space.

Key Terms

attention	automatic processes
shadowing	controlled processes
early selection model	Stroop effect
attenuation model	priming
late selection model	subliminal perception
perceptual defense	feature integration theory
perceptual vigilance	receptive field
single capacity	pulvinar thalamic nucleus
mental effort	spatial neglect
multiple resources	

Recommended Readings

Broadbent's (1958) *Perception and Communication* is the classic reference on filter theory whereas Kahneman's (1973) *Attention and Effort* holds this distinction for capacity theory. For detailed information on the complexities of multiple capacity theory, the reader should turn to Navon and Gopher's (1979) *Psychological Review* article and to an edited volume titled *Varieties of Attention* by Parasuraman and Davies (1984). For the latest research on attention, the reader should consult the Attention and Performance book series published by Elsevier Press.

For those who ignored my advice from the previous chapter to read Neisser's (1976) *Cognition and Reality*, I repeat it here. Neisser argued that neither filter theories nor capacity theories can account for the nature of human attention. Further, he critiqued the entire notions of automaticity and limited attentional abilities. His arguments certainly challenge the orthodox theories discussed here.

Kinchla (1992) provided the most recent installment on the attentional literature in the *Annual Review of Psychology*. Posner and Peterson's (1990) article in the *Annual Review of Neuroscience* and Näätänen's (1992) *Attention and Brain Function* offer details on the neuropsychology of human attention.

CHAPTER 4

▣ Memory

T he final chapter on the basic components of human cognition covers what are perhaps the most fundamental questions in the discipline. Certainly, the study of memory has attracted the most attention from researchers, dating from the pioneering work of Ebbinghaus in the nineteenth century to the burgeoning mass of memory work going on today. We will repeatedly encounter questions related to memory throughout the remainder of the book. The next three chapters in particular address aspects of memory. Chapter 5 covers fundamental questions about learning and forgetting specific events or episodes in life. Chapter 6 turns to questions about how general knowledge about the world is represented and used. Chapter 7 examines questions about the high levels of learning and skill observed in an expert. By examining the principles that characterize expert performance in cognitive tasks, we can see clearly how the fundamental issue of memory lies at the heart of cognitive psychology. Moreover, later chapters on language, speech, reading, writing, problem solving, reasoning, and decision making draw heavily on the concepts from theories of memory as well as those proposed for perception and attention.

The intense interest in memory is hardly mysterious. The life of an individual has meaning only because of memory. Our immediate and distant past defines who we are, what we believe, what we can do, and what we feel. Try to imagine what your life would be like if you lost all memory. Imagine no recollection of where you were born, where you grew up, what you did in school, and where you work, whom you live with, what you look like, and even what you thought or did just moments ago. The loss of perception or attention would be tragic, but one would still possess a sense of identity as long as memory remained intact. The loss of memory, in contrast, would rob one of one's very life and person-hood.

In this chapter, we will begin with a consideration of the classic distinction between short-term or working memory and long-term memory. The reasons for drawing the short-term versus long-term distinction will be considered first, followed by revisions of it. Then, we will consider the structure of long-term memory in greater detail. Specifically, we will examine the evidence both for and against the proposal that multiple long-term systems must be distinguished.

Short-Term Versus Long-Term Memory

All of us have had the experience of looking up a novel telephone number in the directory and then repeating it silently until we reach for the telephone and dial the number successfully. Without silent rehearsal, the meaningless sequence of digits is easily lost from memory if we wait too long to dial or we are interrupted. Subjectively, the number seems available only temporarily, in a short-term store. Our experience is quite different with the automatic, well-learned recall of our own telephone number. Unlike the fragile short-term memory, our own number seems locked permanently in a long-term store from which it can be retrieved with ease. Other numbers, less often used, such as a friend not called for years, can sometimes also be retrieved from a seemingly permanent form of memory though only with great effort.

Introspection along these lines has suggested a distinction between short-term and long-term memory from the time of James's *Principles of Psychology* in 1890. He referred to immediate memory of events currently attended to as primary memory and all other memory as secondary. Waugh and Norman (1965) formalized the distinction in their model of separate primary and secondary memories. Atkinson and Shiffrin (1968) added a sensory store and provided us with the modern labels of short- and long-term stores. Their model, shown in Figure 4.1, became perhaps

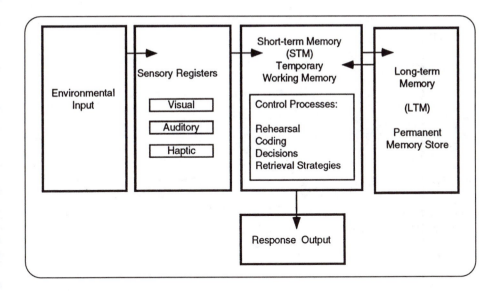

Figure 4.1. The multistore model of human memory.
SOURCE: Illustration by Allen Beechel from "The Control of Short-Term Memory," by Richard C. Atkinson & Richard M. Shiffrin, August 1971. Copyright © 1971 by Scientific American, Inc. Reprinted by permission.

the most influential theory in the field of cognitive psychology. It is called the **multistore model** in reference to the separate boxes for sensory, short-term, and long-term memory. In this chapter, we will focus on the short-term versus long-term distinction.

The Serial Position Effect

Suppose that I read you a list of 20 words and then ask you to recall them in whatever order you like. The classic outcome of this free recall procedure is known as the **serial position effect** and is illustrated in Figure 4.2 with the curve labeled zero. As we shall see, the effect has historically been regarded as central to the distinction between short- and long-term memory. The initial words on the list are recalled reasonably well, a phenomenon called the **primacy effect**. The words in the middle of the list are typically forgotten. Finally, the words at the end of the list are also remembered well; in fact, these are the words most likely to be recalled first. This high level of recall is aptly labeled the **recency effect.**

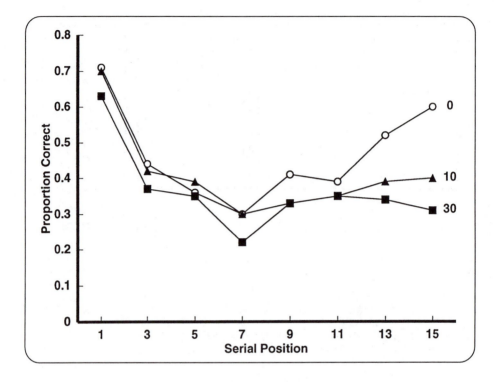

Figure 4.2. The serial position effect.
SOURCE: From Glanzer and Cunitz (1966). Copyright © 1966 by Academic Press, Inc. Reprinted by permission.

The data in Figure 4.2 are from an experiment by Glanzer and Cunitz (1966). They allowed one group of participants to recall the words immediately (Condition 0) whereas others counted backward by sevens from a number given by the experimenter (e.g., 93, 86, 79, 72, 65 . . .) for either 10 or 30 seconds. Notice that the attention demanding task of counting backward eliminated the recency effect but left the primacy effect unscathed.

The serial position effect can readily be accounted for in terms of the Atkinson and Shiffrin model and related mathematical models (Murdock, 1974). Because the words were all attended to and pattern recognized, they all presumably passed from the echoic sensory memory into the short-term store. If you repeated silently or in some other manner rehearsed a given word, then it may be transferred into the long-term store. Successfully recalling a word from a particular serial position, then, could reflect retrieval from either the short- or the long-term store. Atkinson and Shiffrin assumed that the capacity of the short-term store was limited to about five words. They further assumed that transfer into long-term memory varied as a function of the person's learning ability and the number of seconds the word remained in the short-term store before being bumped by a new incoming word. Atkinson and Shiffrin (1968) could closely fit a person's serial position curve by adjusting for the individual's capacity size and learning rate.

The primacy effect follows naturally from the assumptions of their model. First, the beginning words on the list are likely to remain in the short-term store for a longer period of time than later words because the short-term store has yet to fill to capacity. Remember that once the short-term store fills, a new word may enter only by displacing a previous word. Thus the initial words are more likely to be stored and successfully retrieved from the long-term store.

The recency effect, on the other hand, reflects retrieval from the short-term store. The last words on the list still reside in the short-term store and can be readily retrieved as long as recall is immediate (Condition 0). In Condition 30 of Figure 4.2, the recency effect disappeared completely, because all words had been flushed from the short-term store after 30 seconds of counting backward.

The process responsible for transfer presumably is rehearsal, such as repeating the words silently. To establish a direct link between rehearsal and the primacy effect, Rundus (1971) asked people to say aloud any words from the list that they wished during a 5-second interval between each word presentation. Rundus found that the initial items of the list received far more rehearsals than later items. People tended to repeat aloud the first words many times, but then as the short-term store filled to capacity, they had more words competing for rehearsal than could be handled. Rundus thus established a compelling explanation of the primacy effect in terms of rehearsal.

Neuropsychological Evidence

Another reason for distinguishing short-term memory and long-term memory came from the study of amnesia, specifically **anterograde amnesia.** This refers to difficulty in remembering events that occur after the onset of amnesia. **Retrograde amnesia**, on the other hand, refers to the loss of memory for events that occurred prior to the onset of the illness. Organic amnesia, in which the brain has been damaged from a tumor, accident, or stroke, offers insights into memory theory. A famous case, a patient known by his initials H. M., suffered from untreatable epilepsy. He finally found relief from violent seizures following the bilateral surgical removal of the medial temporal lobe. But H. M. suffered severe anterograde amnesia as a consequence.

Milner (1966) described his memory loss in the following words:

> He could no longer recognize the hospital staff, apart from Dr. Scoville himself, whom he had known for many years; he did not remember and could not relearn the way to the bathroom, and he seemed to retain nothing of the day-to-day happenings in the hospital. . . . A year later, H.M. had not yet learned the new address, nor could he be trusted to find his home . . . He is unable to learn where objects are usually kept. (p. 113)

Milner and her colleagues used several tests to document in detail the nature of H. M.'s loss of memory. They found that he showed profound deficits in learning and remembering both verbal material such as word lists and nonverbal material such as faces or sequences of lights. Of interest, H. M. scored well above average on a standard IQ test (Wechsler Bellvue Scale, IQ 112), which shows that the brain lesion selectively impaired a particular aspect of memory only. Specifically, Milner concluded that such anterograde amnesia reflected a failure to transfer information from short-term into long-term memory.

A study of six other patients suffering from anterograde amnesia provided convincing support for Milner's conclusion. Baddeley and Warrington (1970) assessed free recall of a list of 10 words, either immediately after their presentation or after 30 seconds of distraction. For immediate recall, the amnesia patients showed a strong recency effect much like the control patients in the experiment. This implied that short-term memory per se suffered no deficit. However, the amnesia patients showed no primacy effect at all and recall from the middle of the list was also well below the level shown by the controls. Baddeley and Warrington interpreted these differences as showing that transfer into long-term memory failed for the amnesia patients. Consistent with this interpretation, recall performance after a 30-second delay was virtually nil for the amnesia patients, in sharp contrast to the controls, who showed the normal pattern (see Condition 30 in Figure 4.2).

Mounting evidence points to the hippocampus as the essential structure responsible for anterograde amnesia (Squire, 1992). Damage to the hippocampus from a stroke prevents the learning of new events information (Zola-Morgan, Squire, & Amaral, 1986). Additional evidence comes from the use of magnetic resonance imaging. This method for examining the living brain has revealed a smaller than normal hippocampus in four patients with severe anterograde amnesia (Squire, Amaral, & Press, 1990). Squire (1992) theorized that the hippocampus binds together the various places in the neocortex that process different features of a new event, such as shape, color, and location. In primates, these areas of neocortex project to the hippocampus. If this binding and other learning processes, such as rehearsal, are successful, then presumably the hippocampus is no longer used in retrieving the event from long-term memory.

Further neuropsychological evidence on the separation of short- and long-term memory comes from cases with impaired immediate recall. Warrington and Shallice (1972) first documented what seems to be a defect in short-term memory per se in the patient K. F. The normal span of short-term memory is about seven items. However, K. F. and others like him show a dramatically smaller short-term memory, particularly when auditory rather than visual presentation is used. K. F. could correctly repeat a single letter even after a 60-second delay. But a mere two letters spoken to him were rapidly forgotten. Three letters showed still greater loss over time, even for those presented visually.

Differences in Memory Stores

The characteristics of sensory, short-term, and long-term stores are summarized in Table 4.1. Several criteria for distinguishing these forms of memory have been proposed, though not all have fared well. Here we will review the evidence on each criterion and then move on to revisions in the multistore model. In a nutshell, the multistore model contends that sensory memory briefly stores a large number of incoming sensations. Short-term memory, in sharp contrast, holds only about seven recognizable items, but can do so for 20 to 30 seconds without rehearsal. Long-term memory, in turn, appears to be virtually unlimited in capacity, capable of storing the experiences, factual knowledge, and skills of an entire lifetime.

Capacity. A classic paper in the discipline carried the title "The Magical Number Seven, Plus or Minus Two: Some Limits on Our Capacity for

Table 4.1 Characteristics of Memory Stores

			Characteristic		
Store	*Duration*	*Capacity*	*Forgetting*	*Coding*	*Retrieval*
Sensory	250 milli-seconds	large	decay masking	sensory	parallel search
Short term	20 seconds	7 ± 2	decay interference displacement organic	sensory semantic	serial exhaustive search
Long term	years	unlimited	decay interference cue dependent organic	sensory semantic	parallel search

Processing Information" (Miller, 1956). The span of short-term memory for digits is limited to about seven items. Cover the digit sets given below with a piece of paper and then uncover one set at a time. Read the set quickly, look away, and try to recall it correctly by writing the set down on another sheet of paper.

> 6 4 8 2
>
> 5 9 3 1 7
>
> 2 7 4 3 1 9
>
> 4 9 5 2 8 7 6
>
> 3 5 2 9 6 8 4 7
>
> 1 8 3 5 6 2 9 4 7
>
> 9 8 7 6 5 4 3 2 1

Although five or six items can be recalled fairly easily, eight or nine digits burden short-term memory. Few people can correctly recall more than nine items, as required by the next to the last digit set. But what about the final set? Although it also contains nine items, all nine are easily recallable.

Miller (1956) recognized that the capacity limitation of short-term memory is a very real biological constraint. However, Miller further recognized that a nonbiological, cultural process can overcome this limitation. He called the process **chunking**. It is easy to remember the final set of digits because they constitute a single chunk: the descending order of single digit numbers. Meaningful patterns of information, often those grounded in the cultural tool of language, allow a person to remember far more than seven individual items. By grouping meaningful information together, we form a coherent chunk of information.

The capacity of short-term memory is limited to about seven chunks, though the amount of information per chunk can be quite large. To illustrate, try to recall the following sequences of digits and letters.

$$1 \quad 4 \quad 9 \quad 2 \quad 1 \quad 7 \quad 7 \quad 6 \quad 1 \quad 9 \quad 4 \quad 5 \quad 1 \quad 9 \quad 6 \quad 3$$

Although the set contains 16 digits, one can remember them readily by chunking each subset of four digits as a familiar date in American history.

Other theorists place the capacity of short-term memory at only three to five chunks (Broadbent, 1975; Schneider & Detweiler, 1987). The precise capacity of short-term memory varies depending on the task used to estimate and the materials used in the task (Cavanagh, 1972). The essential point is that short-term memory capacity is severely limited. Of interest, this limitation turns out to be highly adaptive for an organism that depends as heavily on memory as humans do. MacGregor (1987) provided mathematical proofs that a range of three to six items, depending on the memory search strategy employed, is actually optimal for retrieving information from long-term memory.

The capacity of long-term memory stands in stark contrast to the meager limits of short-term memory. The truth is that no one really knows how much information the human brain can retain, but the consensus is that its capacity is astronomical in proportion. It is useful to reflect on the complexity of the cerebral cortex alone in this regard. It contains on the order of 55,000,000,000 neurons (Mountcastle, 1979). Each neuron connects to hundreds, thousands, or even 10,000 other neurons! The storage capabilities of a neural network of this magnitude are awesome indeed. It is doubtful that most human beings even come close to learning and experiencing so much in life that they push the limits of long-term memory capacity. Forgetting, as we will see, certainly occurs, but it is unlikely to be necessary as a way of making room for new information, as is surely the case with short-term memory.

Duration. As we noted at the beginning of the chapter, you can retain a telephone number long enough to dial it by rehearsing the number silently. But what if someone interrupts the rehearsal or another task at hand distracts you from dialing? How long will the digits of the telephone number persevere? The answer appears to be about 20 seconds. Depending on the specific task and materials used to assess the duration, estimates range from as brief as 10 seconds to as long as 30 seconds (Cowan, 1988). The classic method is called the Brown-Peterson procedure after the pioneering research by Brown (1958) and Peterson and Peterson (1959).

In this task, an individual listens to a series of three random consonants—a trigram—followed by the presentation of a three digit number. As a distracting activity, the person counts backward by threes, speaking aloud to the pace of a metronome that clicks every half second. The counting continues for various unpredictable intervals ranging from 3 to 18 seconds; immediate recall without the intervening distraction also is tested at times. The outcome of such an experiment is shown in Figure 4.3. The researchers clearly showed that information in short-term memory is lost over time, even when it consisted of only three chunks, well below the capacity limits.

The duration of long-term memory must be measured in terms of years, not seconds. Once material is stored in long-term memory, it may well persist for a lifetime. Because of the difficulties of measuring such durations, a precise estimate cannot be given. We do know from the remarkable studies by Bahrick and his colleagues that the duration of long-term memory is at least 50 years (Bahrick, 1983, 1984; Bahrick, Bahrick, & Wittlinger, 1975). Memory for information acquired in high school or college was assessed many years after graduation. For example, the names and faces of classmates, foreign language vocabulary, and locations of buildings on a college campus were checked. Although much of the information was forgotten, Bahrick found clear evidence of apparently permanent storage even 50 years after graduation. For example, after 46 years, students could recall the names of campus buildings and correctly place them on a map of the campus (Bahrick, 1983).

Conway, Cohen, and Stanhope (1991) measured what students remembered about their cognitive psychology class over a period of about 10 years. They tested their participants for the names of researchers and

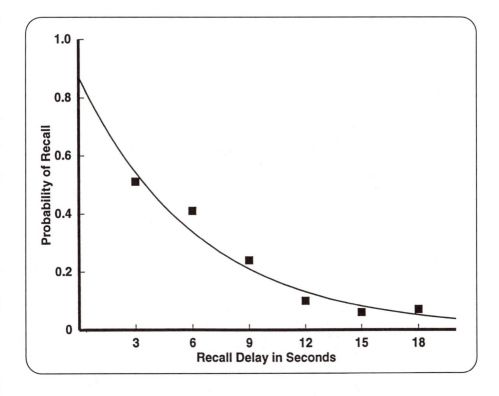

Figure 4.3. The duration of short-term memory as shown by its rate of forgetting. SOURCE: Peterson and Peterson (1959).

for concepts acquired by the students. Conway et al. controlled for the differences in the degree of original learning of the material by taking the grade received in the course into account. Accurate recognition of both names and concepts declined quickly over the first 40 months or so, but then stabilized. It remained well above chance even 125 months later. It will not come as a surprise to any student that free recall of the same information showed more forgetting. As I will discuss later, recognition is typically easier than recall. Still, even on the recall measure, Conway et al. found retention of about a third of the material after 10 years (see Figure 4.4). These results may surprise you, because it often seems that course material is forgotten within minutes after the final exam. But remember that the forgetting curve eventually stabilizes after many months and years, so that further forgetting does not occur.

BOX 4.1: Early Childhood Memories

Although long-term memory can retain information for decades, our earliest experiences in life are virtually always forgotten. Most people suffer from infantile amnesia, meaning they cannot recall the events of their first 2 or 3 years (Howe & Courage, 1993; Spear, 1979). The reason for such amnesia is still unclear. Traditionally, theorists have explained infantile amnesia either in terms of unretrievable, though permanently stored, experiences or in terms of failure to store such events adequately in the first place.

Freud (1905/1953b) held the former view in his theory of psychoanalysis. Repression of unsettling early childhood experiences was taken by Freud to be the source of neurosis in adulthood. These experiences were clearly available in long-term storage, but their retrieval was actively avoided by means of the defense mechanism of repression. Only by successfully retrieving autobiographical information from childhood could therapy proceed effectively. Freud used free association to unlock early memories. Another technique for doing so is hypnotic age regression, in which an individual presumably assumes the personality held at an earlier age (Nash, 1987). Repression is not the only reason for retrieval failure; perhaps the events are coded by the infant very differently than the way an adult, with fully developed cognitive systems, including language, would go about trying to cue the lost memories.

Other theorists question the permanence of early childhood memories (Kail, 1984; Loftus & Loftus, 1980). Maybe we cannot retrieve them simply because they do not exist. One reason for this impermanence is that the attentional and perceptual systems of the infant may not have been sufficiently developed to encode the events properly in the first place. Another possibility is that they were encoded and could be retrieved for a brief period of time, but then the events decayed from memory.

Research on the phenomenon has demonstrated even 2-year-olds can recall events that happened 3 or even 6 months in the past (Fivush, Gray, & Fromhoff, 1987). Moreover, Perris, Myers, and Clifton (1990) reported that children aged $2\frac{1}{2}$ years could recall a single experience in a psychology laboratory that occurred when they were $6\frac{1}{2}$ months old! That attests either to the remarkable memory of young children or to the bizarreness of psychology laboratories.

Yet Howe and Courage (1993) pointed out that the nature of these recollections by preschoolers are very fragmentary. These theorists contended that until a child develops a concept of the self, which takes place about the age of 18 months, he or she cannot possibly organize memories autobiographically. Shortly thereafter at about 22 months, children acquire the pronouns of *I* and *you*. Language acquisition provides an enormously powerful tool for organizing memory as an autobiographical narrative (Nelson, 1990). The source of infantile amnesia most likely lies either in the initial absence of a self-concept or in the absence of language needed to support memory for experiences.

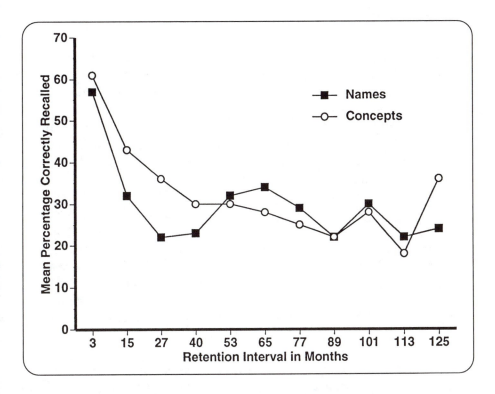

Figure 4.4. Long-term retention of facts about cognitive psychology.
SOURCE: From Conway, M. A., Cohen, G., & Stanhope, N. (1991). On the very long-term retention of knowledge acquired through formal education: Twelve years of cognitive psychology. *Journal of Experimental Psychology: General, 120,* 395-409. Copyright © 1991 by the American Psychological Association. Reprinted by permission.

Coding. Although researchers at first thought the other criteria would prove equally clear-cut, they turned out not to be. The code or type of information stored is probably sensory or precategorical in the case of sensory memory, but as we saw in the last chapter, some evidence suggests otherwise. The short-term and long-term stores draw on the same codes, ranging from perceptual representations such as acoustic and visual images to abstract semantic representations such as propositions of meaning.

Initially, short-term memory appeared to be based on an **acoustic-articulatory code.** Errors in immediate recall typically reflected confusions in stimuli that sound alike or that are enunciated in similar ways (Conrad, 1964). People often confused two letters if they sounded alike— such as B and V—in tests of short-term memory. Confusions based on a visual code of how letters looked rarely occurred. The letters F and E differ by only a single distinctive feature in visual coding, yet Conrad's participants failed to confuse them. The acoustic alphabet (e.g., "Alpha," "Bravo," "Charlie," . . . "Victor") used by the military and others avoids such acoustic errors by assigning a name for each letter that is unique in terms of the acoustic-articulatory code.

Thus, in processing verbal material for later recall, we rely on an acoustic-articulatory code. But short-term memory could hardly be limited to such a code. We can plainly daydream in visual images and sometimes rely on images in certain tasks, such as planning a route across town. Not only can short-term memory involve visual codes (Brooks, 1968; Penney, 1975, 1989), it can also employ semantic codes (Wickens, 1972).

Wickens's experiments introduce a central concept in forgetting— interference—and so warrant a close look. **Proactive interference** means that past learning interferes with the ability to learn and remember new information. For example, first learning a list of words (List A) would interfere with learning and recall of a second list B. Imagine an experiment in which we presented list A, then list B, and then tested list B. Proactive interference is defined as poorer recall of list B relative to a condition that first rests, then receives list B, then is tested on list B. **Retroactive interference** refers to recent learning interfering with the recall of previous learning. That is, receive list A; receive list B; recall list A (which goes more poorly than when receiving list A; rest; recall list A). Thus learning list B interferes backward in time on the recall of list A.

Wickens, Dalezman, and Eggemeier (1976) presented four trials of a Brown-Peterson task, wherein on each trial a triad of three words occurred followed by backward counting to prevent their rehearsal. Each triad of words came from the same semantic category (types of fruit) on the first three trials. The researchers expected recall of the triads to get progressively worse as proactive interference built up across the first three trials, confusing the person about which fruits they heard on the current trial. On trial four, the researchers shifted the category in the experimental condition to vegetables, fruits, or professions. The control condition received another triad of fruits.

The results appear in Figure 4.5. Recall in the experimental groups improved on trial four, a phenomenon known as release from PI (proactive inhibition). By shifting the category, recall improves substantially because there is less confusion about the triad presented on the current trial. The key point here is the systematic pattern of release obtained. The

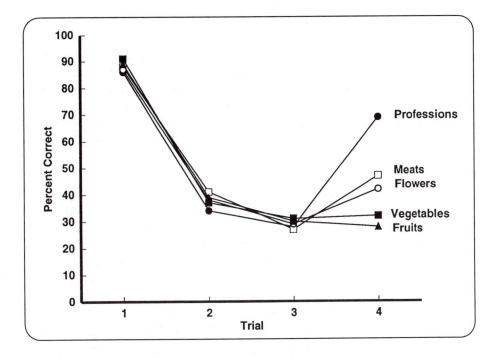

Figure 4.5. Release from PI showing semantic coding in short-term memory.
SOURCE: From Wickens, D. D., Dalezman, R. E., & Eggemeier, F. T. (1976). Multiple encoding of word attributes in memory. *Memory & Cognition, 4,* 307-310. Copyright © 1976. Reprinted by permission of the Psychonomic Society, Inc.

further apart the categories are in meaning, the greater the release. This outcome convincingly shows that the semantic code of each triad is stored in short-term memory. Similar semantic codes show less release from PI than dissimilar codes.

Retrieval. In considering the retrieval of information from memory, we must begin with some theoretical distinctions in how memory is searched. A **serial search** means that the items in memory are somehow ordered and are examined one at a time, starting with the first item and proceeding to the next. A **parallel search**, in contrast, means that all items in memory are examined simultaneously, not serially. Obviously, a parallel search process would result in much more efficient retrieval of information, especially when the amount of information that must be searched is large, as is the case in long-term memory.

Another distinction concerns when the search terminates. A **self-terminating search** refers to one that stops as soon as the item being sought is found. Thus, in a serial self-terminating search for the letter K among the letters ordered in memory D B K X M, the search would end after examining the third letter. In contrast, an **exhaustive search** refers to one that continues to examine all items in memory even after the target item has been found. In our example, a serial exhaustive search would look at all five letters one at a time. It would not stop at the third position even though the target was found.

Sternberg (1966) explored the nature of retrieval in short-term memory using a simple probe task. On each trial, the person memorized a short list of letters. The number of letters in the memory set varied from one to six, within the capacity of short-term memory. Next, Sternberg presented a probe letter. Using our example above, we have a memory set size of five and the letter K as our probe. The person then pushed a "yes" button or a "no" button as rapidly as possible to indicate whether the probe could be found in the memory set. In our example, K brings a yes response whereas, say, L brings a no.

If all items in memory are searched in parallel, then the set size should not affect retrieval time. Furthermore, a negative trial in which the probe could not be found would be no slower than a positive trial in which the probe matched one of the items. If a serial search is used, in contrast, then reaction time should increase linearly as a function of set size. Each additional letter should add a constant number of milliseconds to the search time. An exhaustive serial search implies that the negative trials and positive trials should take exactly the same amount of time per item; their slopes should be equal. That is, the search does not stop just because a target is found on the positive trials. In contrast, a self-terminating serial search should reveal an advantage, a less steep slope, for the positive trials, because the search stops as soon as the target is found.

Sternberg's results are shown in Figure 4.6 and they clearly indicate that retrieval from short-term memory involves a serial exhaustive search. The search time increased linearly with set size, and both positive and negative trials showed identical search times per item. This outcome is counterintuitive in that a self-terminating search seems more logical. Why bother searching all items in memory, even after the target has been found? The answer may be related to the extremely rapid rate at which we search our short-term memory. The slope of the function in Panel A is only 38 milliseconds, the time needed to examine each additional letter in the memory set.

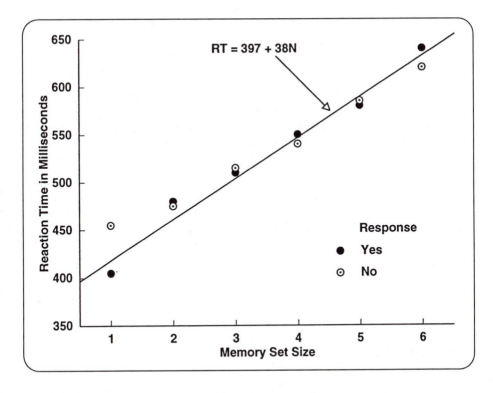

Figure 4.6. Evidence for a serial exhaustive search of short-term memory.
SOURCE: Reprinted with permission from Sternberg, S. (1966). High-speed scanning in human memory. *Science, 153,* 652-654. Copyright © 1966 by the American Association for the Advancement of Science.

Given the rapid speed of the search process itself, there is little cost to searching all the items as long as the capacity of memory is small. Clearly, if we were dealing with millions of items to search, as we find in long-term memory, then a serial exhaustive search would be highly maladaptive. Remembering anything could easily take all day. Given the relative ease with which we retrieve events, knowledge, and skills, the retrieval of information from long-term memory is assumed to be a parallel, self-terminating process.

Forgetting. The causes of forgetting also show some differences, but also similarities, across the three stores. Masking or replacing all the contents of sensory memory with new information is a unique mode of forgetting. In the case of short-term memory, new information displaces a portion of the old information, nudging out one item but leaving others intact. The decay of information with the passage of time, in the absence of new information, affects sensory memory and possibly short-term memory. Another common means of forgetting in short-term memory is interference. Several studies examined whether decay or interference best explained short-term forgetting.

Peterson and Peterson (1959) initially attributed forgetting in short-term memory to the decay of information with the passage of time. In fact, these scholars specifically chose a distractor task of counting backward to minimize the extent to which the numbers might cause interference at the time of recall. Keppel and Underwood (1962), however, observed that on the first trial, when there is no proactive interference from other items, there is also no forgetting even though counting backward took time.

Waugh and Norman (1965) contrasted the interference and decay explanations in a clever experiment. Participants heard a long sequence of digits followed by a probe digit, which prompted them to recall the digit that had followed the probe earlier in the list. The probe occurred after either one or several intervening digits. This allowed an assessment of whether recall declined with increases in the amount of retroactive interference. The digits came at a fast rate in one condition and a slow rate in another; thus the time that passed before the probe occurred was longer in the slow rate condition. If decay over time is an important source of forgetting, then recall should be poorer in the slow condition than in the fast condition. Waugh and Norman found that recall decreased with the amount of interference the probe caused, yet the rate of presentation had no reliable impact on recall. Decay that occurs across time failed to decrease recall. Interference, then, seemed to fully explain forgetting from short-term memory. Later research suggested some role for decay, however (Baddeley & Scott, 1971; Reitman, 1974).

Another means by which forgetting occurs in short-term memory is displacement. Because the capacity is limited to about seven chunks, trying to remember an eighth chunk likely will displace another. Finally, brain lesions and other organic problems can cause short-term forgetting (recall patient K. F., discussed earlier).

Displacement can hardly be taken seriously in the case of long-term memory, because its capacity is so large, virtually unlimited. It will not do to claim that you cannot learn the facts of this textbook because you know so much already and fear displacing valuable information. In fact, as will be discussed in the next chapter, prior knowledge aids learning and remembering.

Decay from long-term memory is certainly possible and, given retention intervals of decades, perhaps inevitable. Assuming that a memory representation of an event occurring at, say, age 10 has rarely if ever been retrieved over the course of a lifetime, the passage of time, say, a half century, may result in loss through decay. The key implication of decay theory is that forgotten information is no longer available in memory. Theoretically, one might plot the half-life of the memory record of an event, as one would other biological and physical processes. In practice, however, the picture clouds quickly. We know that retrieving a memory serves as a form of rehearsal, producing better recall (Roediger & Payne, 1982). A memory that lasts 50 years may have benefited from recalling the event deliberately or even in fantasies or dreams.

Moreover, seemingly unavailable events may only be *inaccessible* to retrieval. Penfield (1959) found in the course of conducting brain surgery that electrical stimulation of the brain occasionally elicited episodic recall. After exposing the brain using general anesthesia, surgeons may maintain the patient using only local anesthetic in a conscious, alert state. Repeated stimulation of a particular site in the auditory cortex caused a small number of patients to experience a memory, such as the sounds of a musical tune long forgotten. Loftus and Loftus (1980) noted, however, that one cannot say whether the patient's experience exactly matched a prior experience from years in the past. As we will see in the next chapter, it is possible that such memories were distorted reconstructions of the original experiences. Also, Penfield's observations have not been replicated.

More convincing is Erdelyi and Becker's (1974) discovery that after viewing pictures of common objects, people show cumulative gains in recall over successive attempts at remembering. Pictures inaccessible at one point in time became accessible at a later point in time, after further efforts to recall them. As more time passes with each successive test, recall astonishingly improves. They called this reversal of the usual forgetting curve **hypermnesia,** to contrast it with amnesia. Of interest, successive attempts at the recall of words often do not show this phenomenon. Payne (1987) concluded that the visual coding of pictures and deliberate attempts to recall produce the phenomenon. The point here is that seemingly forgotten information can be made accessible under the right conditions.

Why, then, does information become inaccessible over time, even though it remains available? The classic answer is interference (McGeoch, 1942). Learning theorists in the 1940s and verbal learning researchers in the 1950s developed detailed models of how forgetting takes place through wrong responses interfering with right ones. Earlier we saw how material proactively interferes with recall in short-term memory.

Contemporary theory stresses the cue dependent nature of forgetting from long-term memory. Recognizing or recalling a past event depends on reactivating the contextual cues associated with the event at the time of encoding (Tulving, 1983). A retrieval cue will be effective if and only if it was initially encoded with the target event, allowing the cue to guide reconstruction of the target (Tulving, 1983). Cue dependent forgetting occurs when the cues that a person encounters or otherwise thinks about at the time of retrieval are not the ones associated with the original event. More about cue dependent forgetting will come in the next chapter when the topic of retrieval is treated in detail. Future work may well find that short-term memory is also susceptible to similar failures in the retrieval process (Shiffrin, 1993).

To summarize, the theory that long-term and short-term memory are distinct has fueled major advances in our understanding of human memory. The multistore theorist tried to assign unique characteristics to sensory, short-term, and long-term stores. As we have seen, this has not been entirely successful. Now let us turn to some of the theoretical alternatives that have been proposed.

Revisions to the Multistore Model

Fuzzy Criteria

Craik and Lockhart (1972) mounted the first serious challenge to the multistore model. They pointed out the difficulties of assigning unique characteristics to the different stores. For example, if short-term memory uses visual and semantic codes as well as acoustic codes, just as does long-term memory, then they ought not be viewed as separate systems. Craik and Lockhart argued against a structural view of memory and in favor of a process view. Specifically, they suggested that memory representations are linked to the perceptual and higher order cognitive processes that operate on stimuli. As we will see in the next chapter, their focus on the processes involved in long-term memory have strongly affected the direction of research over the past 20 years.

The Problem With Recency

Other research showed that recency effects are not necessarily the result of recall from short-term memory. Bjork and Whitten (1974) modified the usual task by distracting the learner after each pair of words were presented. The distracting task should have prevented recall of the last pair of words from short-term memory, as found by Glanzer and Cunitz (1966). Instead, a recency effect persisted, despite that the recall of the recent words must have come from long-term memory. This recency effect remained even when highly effortful distracting tasks were used, ensuring that the learners could not have been simultaneously rehearsing the final items (Glenberg et al., 1980).

Roediger and Crowder (1976) even found a recency effect when people recalled from long-term memory the names of U.S. presidents. The early presidents and the most recent presidents were recalled most often. As Greene (1986) concluded in his review of such findings, recency effects can no longer be explained as recall from short-term, as opposed to, long-term memory.

Crowder (1982b) advanced the case that long- and short-term memory are indeed one and the same system. The problem with recency is one of the arguments he used. If there is one way to explain why recency effects occur both after short delays and after long delays since learning took place, then why distinguish the two? One strong candidate assumes that the time when learning occurs—temporal coding—is relied upon to retrieve information from memory. More recent temporal codes may stand out as more distinctive and hence more effective as retrieval aids. Such a line of reasoning applies equally well in long-term and short-term memory tasks (Glenberg, 1987).

Activated Memory

A less extreme revision of the multistore model regards short-term memory as the currently active subset of long-term memory (Cowan, 1988, 1993). One version of this perspective is shown in Figure 4.7. It incorporates many of the phenomena discussed here and in earlier chapters regarding sensory memory, attention, and controlled versus automatic behaviors. Here our interest is in the hierarchical organization of

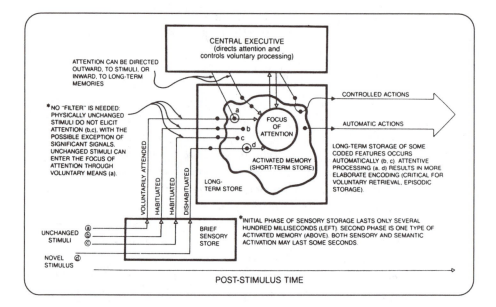

Figure 4.7. A revised model of the relation between sensory, short-term, and long-term memory.

SOURCE: From Cowan, N. (1988). Evolving conceptions of memory storage, selective attention, and their mutual constraints within the human information-processing system. *Psychological Bulletin, 104,* 163-191. Copyright © 1988 by the American Psychological Association. Reprinted by permission.

long-term memory, short-term memory, and attention. The current focus of attention represents only a small subset of all information activated in short-term memory, which in turn represents a very small subset of all that is stored in long-term memory. Because short-term memory is indeed part of long-term memory, it should not be surprising that both employ the same types of memory codes and the same mechanisms of forgetting.

The process view of memory has been highly influential, as we will see in the next chapter, and healthy debate persists over the value of the activated memory idea (Cowan, Wood, & Borne, 1994; Crowder, 1989, 1993). Yet, the basic distinction between short- and long-term memory has been remarkably enduring (Estes, 1988) and several contemporary models assume that short-term memory reflects sustained neural activation of information (e.g., Schneider & Detweiler, 1987). The focus of much current research has shifted to the question of how such temporary activation is used in learning, comprehending, and other cognitive tasks. The term **working memory** is used to emphasize that activated memory does more than store a list of items for later recall; it is used to accomplish cognitive work.

A Model of Working Memory

Baddeley (1986) has developed a multicomponent model of working memory in an effort to study how activated memory is used in reading, listening, reasoning, and problem solving. Baddeley distinguished between an articulatory rehearsal loop and a visual-spatial scratch pad. The rehearsal loop allows one to maintain verbal information over time by repeating it covertly—mentally articulating the letters or words. The visual-spatial scratch pad allows one to imagine events in the mind's eye. Learning information by visualizing it, solving a problem by imaging a solution, or even daydreaming idly make use of the scratch pad.

The third component is an executive control system. It draws upon a central pool of attentional resources in carrying out its operations. The executive system directs attention, initiates decisions, and handles the essential tasks of learning, comprehending language, and reasoning, among others. The articulatory rehearsal loop and the visual-spatial scratch pad are so-called slave systems with their own separate resources. Once initiated by the executive, each of these components can operate independently without using the central resources, at least as long as the resources of the slave systems are not overloaded. If given too much to handle, then either performance will suffer or the slave systems can draw on the resources of the executive system to help with the overload. Thus Baddeley combines a short-term memory theory with a multiple capacity theory of attention to understand how activated memory handles the work of high-level cognitive tasks. We will make use of the working memory idea throughout the remainder of the book.

Types of Long-Term Memory

A growing body of evidence points to the conclusion that long-term memory is not a monolithic storehouse but instead involves **multiple memory systems,** each with their own special functions. The criteria for distinguishing one long-term memory system from another are hotly contested and a consensus has not yet been reached on precisely how many systems are involved.

The debate concerning multiple systems of memory highlights the mutual influences of mathematics and biology on the discipline. Mathematical models and computer simulations of memory begin with the assumption that the fewer systems of memory the better. Not only is a single long-term store a more parsimonious explanation of memory phenomena, it assuredly is easier to model with the necessary precision of mathematics (Hintzman, 1990). From the perspective of evolutionary biology, however, fewer and better need not coincide at all. Different systems evolve precisely because they afford successful adaptations to the challenges posed by the environment. Just as with other characteristics of an organism, a novel system of memory shown by a subpopulation of a species will come to dominate if it aids, in some fashion, survival and reproduction. A separate memory system evolves when the functions of existing systems fail to meet the demands of a new environmental challenge (Sherry & Schacter, 1987).

The danger with the biological perspective lies in strewing our theories needlessly with a separate memory system for each seemingly separate memory phenomenon. The danger with the mathematical perspective is in overlooking the messy nature of biological organisms in the search for an elegant computer simulation. Ideally, both perspectives must be accommodated. Here I try to give you a flavor of the still raging debate over multiple long-term systems.

Declarative Versus Procedural Memory

Philosophers have distinguished between declarative and procedural knowledge, knowing *what* versus knowing *how*. Knowing, say, the rules and traditions of baseball is not the same as being able to play baseball. Knowing how is often tacit or unconscious, whereas knowing what is explicit or conscious. Memory theorists have proposed that declarative memory and nondeclarative or procedural memory are distinct systems (e.g., Tulving, 1985; Zola-Morgan & Squire, 1990). **Declarative memory** refers to events, facts, and concepts—knowing *what*. **Procedural memory** refers to skills and related behaviors—knowing *how*.

For example, Squire and his colleagues have identified several kinds of procedural or nondeclarative knowledge. As seen in Figure 4.8, these include skills, classical conditioning, dispositions, and nonassociative forms of learning. Motor skills, such as running or typing, are familiar to all. Bear in mind that skills also may be perceptual, such as reading, or cognitive, such as problem solving. The basic learning of associations through classical conditioning, priming, and the nonassociative process

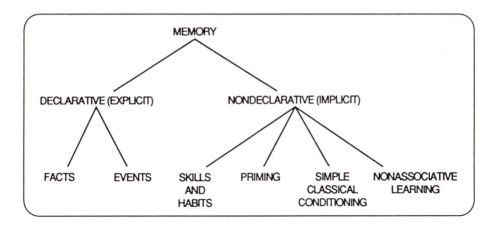

Figure 4.8. Classification of memory.
SOURCE: . Reprinted with permission from Squire, L. R., & Zola-Morgan, S. (1991). The medial temporal lobe memory system. *Science, 253,* 1380-1386. Copyright © 1990 by the American Association for the Advancement of Science.

of habituation are other forms of nondeclarative knowledge. We habituate when we show less and less of a response to a repetitive, ongoing stimulus.

A **priming effect** refers to increases in the accuracy, probability, or speed of a response to a stimulus as a consequence of prior exposure to the stimulus. Priming effects have been extremely important in studies that try to distinguish between procedural memory and declarative memory, as we will soon see. Priming can take several forms. For example, perceptual priming occurs when the speed of recognizing a stimulus increases because the same stimulus had been processed earlier (chair . . . chair). Pattern recognition takes less time for an old item, the second occurrence of chair, than for a new one. Lexical decision priming occurs when the speed of deciding whether a stimulus is a word or not increases because of prior exposure. It is important to note that priming can occur even when the person has no conscious recollection of having perceived the prime.

Declarative memory—knowing what—takes two forms (Tulving, 1972, 1985). **Episodic memory** refers to a specifically dated occurrence of an event in a particular context. Such a memory is tagged with both a time and a place. **Semantic memory** refers to factual and conceptual knowledge about the world, including our knowledge of language. Such memory makes no reference to specific episodes in time and space. Suppose you spot a bicycle on campus. If you begin to recall the bicycle you received on your sixth birthday, then you are using episodic memory. The specific memories you have of learning to ride it and the accidents you had with it are episodic memories. If instead you begin to think about the properties of bicycles in general (e.g., they have two wheels, a seat, and handlebars), then you are using semantic memory. You can think about bicycles in general, without making reference to a particular episode in your life. Of course, if instead you hop on and ride the bicycle, then you are engaging the motor skills of procedural memory.

The Argument for Multiple Systems

The argument for multiple systems of long-term memory stems from results obtained with different kinds of memory tests. **Explicit or direct tests** require the conscious recollection of information, as when a person recognizes or recalls a past event. **Implicit or indirect tests** require the use of information stored in long-term memory to improve performance, but not its conscious recollection (Richardson-Klavehn & Bjork, 1988; Schacter, 1987). The perceptual priming task discussed earlier illustrates this kind of test. A prior occurrence of the prime (chair) increases the likelihood of later perceiving a very brief exposure to the same word (Jacoby, 1983a; Jacoby & Dallas, 1981). One can use the prior occurrence of the prime to enhance perceptual processing without consciously recalling or recognizing the prime.

Tulving and Schacter (1990) argued that dissociations on implicit and explicit tests support the multiple system viewpoint. A **dissociation** means that a variable affects performance on an explicit test differently than on an implicit test.

To illustrate, one variable is the use of normal versus amnesic subjects. Amnesic patients forget recent or past episodic events, yet they still show priming effects right along with normal individuals (Graf, Squire, & Mandler, 1984; Shimamura, 1986). Warrington and Weiskrantz (1970) pioneered the use of a word completion test to reveal normal priming effects in amnesiacs. They first presented a printed list of words and tested the ability of amnesic and normal individuals to recall and recognize them correctly. They also asked the participants to complete a word fragment (cha__) with the first English word that came to mind. If *chair* appeared on the original study list and the individual completed the fragment as *chair*, then priming occurred. Whereas recall and recognition failed badly for the amnesic patients, priming on word completion showed no decrement.

Milner (1965) discovered that H. M. could learn how to trace the outline of a shape while looking in a mirror rather than at the shape. Such motor skill learning remained intact despite the anterograde amnesia for episodic events caused by H. M.'s brain surgery. Learning of perceptual skills also may be preserved in amnesic patients (Moscovitch, 1982) as can learning of a classically conditioned response (Weiskrantz & Warrington, 1979). By pairing a flash of light just prior to the onset of a puff of air to the eye, both normal and amnesic patients acquire a conditioned eye blink response to the presentation of the light alone. Although the amnesic patients retained the conditioned response on a test 24 hours later, they had no conscious recollection of having gone through the conditioning experiment only 10 minutes after it was completed!

Drug-induced dissociations between implicit and explicit memory tests have also been documented. Drugs such as alcohol and scopolamine can produce amnesia for episodes that occurred during the altered state of consciousness. Despite this amnesia, the drugs leave unimpaired performance on tests of procedural memory (Hashtroudi, Parker, DeLisi, Wyatt, & Mutter, 1984; Nissen, Knopman, & Schacter, 1987).

There is even evidence that patients unconscious from general anesthesia register a list of words read to them! Most of us assume that under general anesthesia there is no perception and memory storage of events in the environment. As far as explicit memory tests are concerned, this appears to be the case. However, implicit memory tests can reveal that some events were in fact registered. Specifically, patients read a list of target words during surgery displayed a priming effect on a free association test administered up to two weeks after surgery. The target words were neither recalled nor recognized after surgery. Yet when the patients were asked to say the first word that came to mind in response to a cue word, they often responded with the targets (Kihlstrom, Schacter, Cork, Hunt, & Behr, 1990).

Other variables also reveal dissociations. As I will explain in the next chapter, the degree to which the meaning of a word is processed relates positively and substantially to explicit recognition. However, the degree of semantic encoding has little if any impact on perceptual priming effects (Schacter & Graf, 1986). Also, implicit priming effects follow different forgetting curves than do explicit recall and recognition. Priming persists even after recognition shows marked forgetting (Jacoby, 1983a; Jacoby & Dallas, 1981).

Findings such as these have led some scholars to conclude that explicit, conscious recollection is supported by a declarative memory system. In contrast, a separate procedural system mediates performance on implicit tests of memory (Squire & Cohen, 1984). Other versions of multiple memory systems have also been proposed (Schacter, 1987). Other scholars, however, contend that multiple systems are unnecessary to account for the findings to date.

The Argument Against Multiple Systems

The dissociations in variables affecting different kinds of memory tasks are not clear-cut. Whereas one variable might affect only one kind of test, another may affect both in the same fashion (Schacter, 1987). For example, the number of repetitions of an item in a list increases *both* later recognition performance and the degree of perceptual priming (Jacoby & Dallas, 1981).

Moreover, the dissociations that are observed may be explained without recourse to multiple systems of memory (Hintzman, 1990; Jacoby, 1983b; Johnson & Hasher, 1987; Roediger, 1984). It may be that the two tasks require different sets of processes that operate in the context of the same structural system.

In Chapter 2, we distinguished between conceptually driven processes of pattern recognition and data-driven processes. This distinction can readily be extended to processes involved in the storage of information in long-term memory (Roediger & Blaxton, 1987). Top-down or conceptually driven processes are initiated by the learner, such as focusing on ways of organizing new information. Bottom-up or data-driven processes are forced by the stimuli or data themselves, such as whether the modality of presentation was auditory or visual. Implicit tests such as perceptual priming are more affected by data-driven processes. Explicit tests are more affected by conceptually driven processes.

The principle of **transfer appropriate processing** holds that test performance hinges on engaging in a process at encoding that is compatible with the demands of the test (Morris, Bransford, & Franks, 1977). For example, different kinds of studying may be called for depending on the nature of the test. Practice at generating and organizing ideas would be highly appropriate as a way to prepare for an essay test, but such preparation may transfer less well to a multiple choice test. Roediger and Blaxton contended that the principle of transfer appropriate processing could explain the dissociations seen on implicit/explicit tasks. It is not necessary, in their view, to hypothesize separate memory systems on the basis of such dissociations. Even so, it may be fruitful to develop theories

BOX 4.2: Social Cognition

The field of social psychology has always been interested in cognition, even when behaviorism ruled the day in the rest of psychology (Fiske & Taylor, 1991). But over the past 20 years or so, research on social cognition has exploded on numerous fronts. All the classics in social psychology—attribution theory, stereotypes, prejudice, attitude change, impression management, and social inference—are now steeped in the concepts and language of cognitive psychology. This influence can be seen in bold relief in work on social memory of the self and of others.

We can retrieve from long-term memory numerous pieces of information about the personality traits, behaviors, and appearances of other people (Fiske & Taylor, 1991). Memory for appearance, in fact, often serves as the basis for social inferences about personality. For example, if one recalls another person as physically attractive, then an inference is made that the person is highly sociable, competent, and likable (Kalick, 1988).

Memory for facial appearance in particular is often remarkably accurate (Bahrick et al., 1975). Even over long periods of time, facial recognition can approach perfection. Two exceptions to this generalization do occur, however. First, cross-race facial recognition is much less accurate than own-race recognition. It seems we process the faces of our own race more carefully than those of other races (Chance & Goldstein, 1981). Second, eyewitnesses to crimes can make mistakes in their identifications during standard lineup procedures (Loftus, 1979; Ross, Read, & Toglia, 1994). The unexpected and rapid nature of the events in a crime conspire against accurate identifications.

Ross (1989) argued that we rely on implicit theories when recalling attributes about ourselves and others. For instance, suppose that you are asked to remember what your attitude was toward capital punishment 5 years ago. Ross presumes that long-term memory includes schemas that organize our beliefs about ourselves. These implicit theories, as he calls them, include predictions about changes in attitudes, behaviors, appearances, and abilities over time. Often these theories predict no changes, but at times they lead us to expect changes, such as gains in ability to play a musical instrument with experience versus losses in physical strength with age. The recall process proceeds in two steps, as explained below.

> The individual begins by noting his or her status on the attribute in question. The present serves as a benchmark because it is generally more salient and available than a person's earlier standing on an attribute. As a result, construction of the past may consist, in large part, of characterizing the past as different than or the same as the present. To determine their attitude toward capital punishment, individuals might ask themselves: Is there any reason to believe that I felt differently than I do now? As a second step in the recall process, people may invoke an implicit theory of stability or change to guide their construction of the past. Implicit

theories include specific beliefs regarding the inherent stability of an attribute, as well as a set of general principles concerning the conditions likely to promote personal change or stability. These theories are implicit in that they encompass rarely discussed, but strongly held, beliefs (Ross, 1989, p. 342)

that accommodate both multiple systems and transfer appropriate processing (Hayman & Tulving, 1989).

We can expect further debate over the status of multiple memory systems. It is clear that multiple kinds of knowledge, such as procedural versus declarative, are represented in long-term memory. It is still unclear whether these various kinds of knowledge can be stored within a unitary system of long-term memory.

▣ SUMMARY ▣

1. The multistore model of memory distinguishes among sensory, short-term, and long-term stores. This highly influential model sought to identify unique characteristics with each store. The efforts proved relatively successful with regard to capacity, duration, and retrieval but less so with coding and forgetting.

2. Current revisions of the multistore model contend that short-term memory represents the subset of long-term memory that is currently activated. Thus it is not surprising that both stores employ the same codes and lose information to forgetting in similar ways. The focus of attention at the moment in turn represents but a small subset of activated or short-term memory. Sensory memory, on the other hand, exists as a separate register associated with perceptual systems.

3. The activated subset of long-term memory works through the hippocampus to consolidate and permanently store new information. The **hippocampus,** a structure in the **medial temporal lobe** of the brain, binds together neural activity from locations distributed across the neocortex during learning. Neuropsychological evidence with patients suffering amnesia strongly implicates the hippocampus in short-term memory and learning.

4. Short-term memory supports higher levels of cognition such as language use, problem solving, reasoning, and decision making. It serves as an active workspace for thinking. An influential model of short-term or working memory distinguishes an executive component and two slave components. One of these, the articulatory rehearsal loop, holds verbal information in the form of an acoustic-articulatory code. The other, the visual-spatial scratch pad, supports imaginal processes and codes information visually. The model adopts the assumptions of a multiple resource theory of attention, and assumes that the slave systems plus the resources of the executive system are used when cognitive demands are high.

5. It is necessary to distinguish different types of information or knowledge in long-term memory. A central division is between declarative and procedural long-term memory. The former encompasses both memory for specific episodes that are coded in terms of dates and places of occurrence (episodic memory) and general knowledge of facts and concepts (semantic memory). Nondeclarative or procedural memory includes skill learning, priming, conditioning, and habituation. It is possible, but by no means certain, that separate memory systems have evolved to process particular types of information.

Key Terms

multistore model	retrograde amnesia
chunking	medial temporal lobe
acoustic-articulatory code	hippocampus
proactive interference	multiple memory systems
retroactive interference	declarative memory
serial search	procedural memory
parallel search	priming effect
self-terminating search	episodic memory
exhaustive search	semantic memory
serial position effect	explicit or direct test
primacy effect	implicit or indirect test
recency effect	dissociation
working memory	transfer appropriate
hypermnesia	processing
anterograde amnesia	

Recommended Readings

There is no shortage of outstanding books available on human memory. For a broad overview of the contemporary scene of memory research, I recommend Parkin's (1993) *Memory: Phenomena, Experiment, and Theory*. It includes excellent chapters on the development of memory during infancy and childhood and on the effects of aging on memory. For a single chapter summary of memory, Potter's (1990) contribution to *Thinking: An Invitation to Cognitive Science* (Volume 3) fills the bill. Both of these sources are relevant to the following two chapters as well as the present one.

Squire, Knowlton, and Musen (1993) discuss contemporary views of the structure of memory in the *Annual Review of Psychology*. They present in detail the psychological and neuropsychological evidence supporting the view that long-term memory consists of declarative and procedural components. Also, the reader should consult Lewandowsky, Dunn, and Kirsner's (1989) edited volume titled *Implicit Memory: Theoretical Issues*. An edited volume by Roediger and Craik (1989) covers some of the same territory from a variety of perspectives. Its title, *Varieties of Memory and Consciousness: Essays in Honour of Endel Tulving*, testifies to the stature of one explorer of human memory. Of Tulving's many writings, I recommend his 1983 classic titled *Elements of Episodic Memory*. For more on anaesthesia, consult *Memory and Awareness in Anaesthesia* edited by Bonke, Fitch, and Millar (1990).

Baddeley's (1986) book, *Working Memory*, is essential reading on the topic of short-term memory; so too is the entire March 1993 issue of *Memory & Cognition*. It contains articles by leading researchers on the question: "Short-term memory: Where do we stand?"

PART III

Acquiring and Using Knowledge and Skill

Encoding and Storing Events

Retrieval Processes

Schemas and Memory

Summary

Key Terms

Recommended Readings

CHAPTER 5

□ Learning, Remembering,
and Forgetting

In this chapter, we will turn to the three core processes of memory. The logical place to begin is with a discussion of learning, which involves encoding and storing events in long-term memory. Encoding begins with the perceptual operations that lead to the entry of information into short-term memory and ends with deeper or higher order processes that store the information in long-term memory. Much is known about the operations that support the learning of new events and we will examine the relevant studies here.

Second, we will consider the processes involved in retrieving or failing to retrieve events from long-term memory. The focus will be the learning and retrieval of episodic information that can be identified as the time and place of its occurrence. A discussion of how we learn and retrieve semantic information will be postponed until the next chapter, because it takes us off into an extensive literature on how conceptual and factual knowledge is acquired and represented in long-term memory. Here we will also consider how retrieval cues are used to remember already learned events. Forgetting occurs when the available retrieval cues fail to activate available, but inaccessible, information. We will also examine how schemas play a crucial role by guiding encoding processes and a reconstructive process of retrieval.

Encoding and Storing Events

Attention

As noted in Chapter 3, perceptual processing is limited without the power of attention. Attended information is much better remembered than unattended. In fact, attention has been regarded as necessary for memory (Shiffrin & Schneider, 1977) and early recall experiments supported this view. Moray (1959) reported that words repeated 35 times on the unattended channel in a dichotic listening experiment could not be recalled by the listener! This lack of recall is remarkable given the usual benefits of repetition and the evidence that even unattended information receives at least a degraded analysis at a semantic as well as a sensory level (Cherry, 1953; Mackay, 1973; Marcel, 1983).

Other studies have found that immediate recognition of unattended input lies well above chance levels of guessing, but that forgetting rapidly occurs (Cowan, Lichty, & Grove, 1990; Norman, 1969). At the very best, long-term recognition of unattended material hovers just above or at the level of chance responding (Fisk & Schneider, 1984; Kellogg, 1980). Moreover, the degree of attended or controlled processing of allocated stimuli affects both recognition and judgments regarding the frequency of occurrence of stimuli (Fisk & Schneider, 1984). Fisk and Schneider extensively trained people to categorize words according to their meaning in a consistent mapping task (see Chapter 3) to the point of automaticity. Even when people had unconsciously categorized the same word up to 20 times, they failed to recognize it. Without attention at encoding, little if anything persists beyond the short term.

Individuals suffering from depression frequently report difficulties in remembering. One possible reason for their difficulties is that depression carries with it a decrease in available attentional capacity (Ellis, Thomas, & Rodriguez, 1984). With diminished capacity, depressed individuals may fail to engage in the kinds of effortful strategies that support memory. We will look at some of those shortly. Another possibility is that depressed individuals have sufficient capacity available but lack the initiative to engage in effortful but successful encoding processes (Hertel & Hardin, 1990). In any case, it is clear that the availability or deployment of attention plays a major role in the episodic memory problems of depressed people (Johnson & Magaro, 1987).

Rehearsal

Rehearsal refers to practicing, whether it involves a motor skill such as gymnastics or declarative learning of facts or events. The rehearsal can be overt, such as doing work on the parallel bars or side horse, or covert, such as imagining the same movements. Remarkably, mental rehearsal of athletic skills has a useful role in training. However, it is not quite as effective as actual physical practice (Druckman & Bjork, 1991).

Spacing effect. In the case of storing a new event in memory, *rehearsal* refers to mentally processing the event. To begin, we know that the number of repetitions or rehearsals of an event relates directly to the probability of successful storage (Rundus, 1971), as discussed in the previous chapter. Further, we know that the distribution of repetitions over time matters also. Consecutive repetitions of the same event yield poorer learning than distributed or spaced practice in which a repetition is preceded and followed by different items for study. This advantage is called the distributed practice or **spacing effect** (Melton, 1970). Practice is generally more effective when it is distributed over multiple brief sessions relative to a single long session (Payne & Wenger, 1992). For example, in studying a chapter of this book for 3 hours, you are better off studying it in three separate sessions of 1 hour each than in cramming all 3 hours into a single session.

Types of rehearsal. The nature of the rehearsal processes plays a critical role, regardless of spacing. Craik and Lockhart (1972) distinguished between Type I or **maintenance rehearsal,** which involves recycling information within short-term memory using the articulatory rehearsal loop, and Type II or **elaborative rehearsal,** which involves linking the information with items already stored in long-term memory. Elaborative rehearsal can take many forms. In a typical experiment of learning a list of words or reading and remembering a short story, imaging the words or story serves as a type of elaborative rehearsal. Imagery draws on the visual-spatial scratch pad as the learner forms an image of the to-be-learned information in the mind's eye. Imagery works especially well for familiar, concrete objects that can readily be visualized. Forming images clearly elaborates the words or story events and links them with other images in long-term memory (Bower, 1972; McDaniel & Pressley, 1987).

Craik and Lockhart (1972) made the strong claim that only elaborative rehearsal results in permanent long-term learning because of the necessity to analyze broadly and deeply the features of the stimulus. Maintenance rehearsal merely recycles the perceptual processes used to bring the stimulus into awareness but fails to enrich the mental representation by associating it with other information in long-term memory. Because their claim conflicted with the multistore model and several experimental findings, a wave of research followed. Craik and Watkins (1973) indeed failed to find any increase in the probability of free recall of words as the time spent in maintenance rehearsal increased. However, other studies did detect such an increase in recall (e.g., Darley & Glass, 1975). Moreover, recognition tests, which are more sensitive to the availability of information in long-term memory, have consistently and unequivocally found that maintenance rehearsal produces long-term storage (Greene, 1987).

Still, an overwhelming body of evidence indicates that elaborative rehearsal in all its forms produces superior long-term retention relative to maintenance rehearsal. Much of the remainder of this section and later discussions of mnemonic devices in the chapter on expertise reveal the nature of elaborative rehearsal and its effectiveness. This advantage for elaborative rehearsal may surprise you. People often repeat a series of items in an effort to learn them. Rote repetition in schools remains common as a means of learning. Yet, this popular and commonsense way to learn turns out to be a weak strategy.

Levels of Processing

In Chapter 2, we examined how sensory and semantic features are analyzed during pattern recognition. Data-driven and conceptually driven processes rapidly and accurately identify the objects, events, and symbols of our environment. These perceptual processes operate automatically when attention is devoted to a stimulus and occur to some degree even when the stimulus is unattended. In memory research, the effect of **levels or depth of processing** refers to a superiority for information attentively processed at a semantic level compared with a sensory level.

The usual procedure directs a person to attend carefully to either sensory-level features (e.g., Is the word in capital letters? or Does the word rhyme with blue?) or to semantic features (Does the word fit the sentence? "He slipped on his _____ "). In answering these orienting questions about the word *shoe*, the focus of attention would be physical, acoustic, or semantic features. These three conditions reflected increasing levels or depths of processing.

The results showed that sensory processing, as illustrated in the case and rhyme orienting tasks in the experiment by Craik and Tulving (1975), supported only low probabilities of recognition on a test given after processing a list of questions and words. The target words appeared for only 200 milliseconds. Craik and Tulving interpreted these levels of processing difference in terms of elaborative rehearsal. They argued that the case questions prompted only a superficial analysis of the target words; attention focused only on the shapes and sizes of the letters. The rhyme orienting task prompted a slightly more elaborate encoding process, in that attention focused on the whole word, albeit only on its acoustic features. The sentence condition, however, prompted a much more elaborate analysis based on the semantic features of the target. This elaborate semantic processing yielded recognition two or three times better than the impoverished sensory processing.

The principle of transfer appropriate processing, introduced in the previous chapter, must be kept in mind when interpreting the levels effect (Morris et al., 1977). Semantic encoding is only superior to sensory encoding on an explicit recognition or recall test. A test that requires the learner to make use of rhyme or acoustic information would reveal the best performance for the rhyme encoding condition. In this case, the semantic orienting task would steer the learner's attention away from the very information most appropriate for the coming test. We will return to the importance of considering the retrieval requirements in conjunction with encoding later in the chapter.

Self-reference effect. Is there an orienting task that produces maximal elaboration and memory? Some research suggests that processing the information in relation to our own self-concepts is superior, a finding called the **self-reference effect.** Rogers, Kuiper, and Kirker (1977) found that when people asked whether a word applied to themselves (e.g., ambitious?), later recall rose above that obtained for even the semantic orienting task. The recall results for physical, acoustic, semantic, and self-reference levels of processing are shown in Figure 5.1.

Of interest, the same outcome occurs when people make judgments about consumer products shown in advertisements (D'Ydewalle,

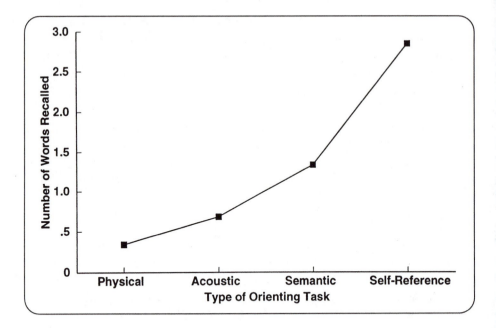

Figure 5.1. Recall as a function of the level of processing.
SOURCE: Adapted from Rogers, Kuiper, and Kirker (1977).

Delhaye, & Goessens, 1985). Answering the question, "Have you ever used this product?" supported greater recall of brand names than a semantic orienting task. Other evidence indicates the key ingredient in this effect involves relating the information to a highly developed schema in long-term memory, providing many links with well-ingrained information (Bellezza, 1986). Bower and Gilligan (1979), for example, asked different groups of people to decide whether a list of personality traits applied to themselves, to their mother, or to Walter Cronkite, the newscaster. They found that the self and mother conditions were both highly but equally effective. Cronkite did not fare well in this comparison.

Distinctiveness

Plainly, the extent to which we store information in an elaborate manner predicts how well it will be remembered. But why should elaboration have this effect? A compelling line of research indicates that the **distinct-**

iveness of the resulting memory representation is the answer. Elaborative rehearsal processes establish a highly distinctive representation in long-term memory, one that can be discriminated easily in a search for the representation at the time of retrieval. The better information is specified in long-term memory, the easier it is to find.

Suppose you are asked to memorize a list of nonsense syllables and one odd item: a number. People rarely forget the isolated, distinctive number, an effect named after its German discoverer, von Restorff (1933), and described in English by the famous Gestalt psychologist, Koffka (1935). The role of distinctiveness can be seen in the levels of processing effect. Eysenck (1979) compared sensory versus semantic orienting tasks. The sensory task entailed attending to the sounds of words. In a distinctive encoding condition, Eysenck used unusual pronunciations of the words designed to produce a highly distinctive albeit sensory level of processing. Because the unique pronunciations stood out in memory, they were remembered just as well as the words processed with a semantic focus. Typically, semantic encoding produces greater elaboration, which in turn increases the likelihood of storing a distinctive code. Eysenck's finding shows that it is distinctiveness per se that ultimately matters.

Picture memory. It has long been known that people can recognize with a high degree of accuracy a long series of complex pictures that they have viewed for only a few seconds each. People can discriminate old from new pictures almost perfectly, when there are hundreds (Shepard, 1967) or even thousands of pictures (Standing, 1973). The reason seems to be that the pictures used in these studies contained many highly distinctive features, allowing one to discriminate one from another. However, suppose you must discriminate a picture of a particular $20 bill from a thousand such pictures. When the pictures all relate to the same schema, there is no distinctiveness and recognition suffers (Mandler & Ritchey, 1977; Nickerson & Adams, 1979). We will return to this point when we discuss the role of schemas in retrieval.

Flashbulb memories. An especially intriguing phenomenon may also shed light on the power of distinctiveness. A **flashbulb memory** is a vivid recollection of some autobiographical event that carries with it strong emotional reactions (Brown & Kulik, 1977; Pillemer, 1984). Depending on your age, you might be able to recall clearly exactly what you were doing, seeing, hearing, and feeling upon receiving the news that President Kennedy was assassinated in 1963, or that an attempt was made on the life of President Reagan in 1981, or that the space shuttle *Challenger* exploded in 1986. As Pillemer (1984) noted: "Images of only a tiny subset of specific episodes—death of a loved one, landing a first job, getting married, hearing about public tragedies—persist over a lifetime, with little subjectively experienced loss of clarity" (p. 64).

Some researchers have challenged whether a so-called flashbulb memory is really more accurate than normal memories (e.g., Neisser & Harsch, 1992). Others, however, have confirmed that flashbulb memories can indeed be real for many people, as long as the precipitating event had a strong, personal impact on them (Conway et al., 1994).

One explanation for the phenomenon is that a special flashbulb memory system has evolved to capture highly important, emotionally charged events. Brown and Kulik pondered the adaptive value of such a system for a primitive human being who just witnessed an attack on the group leader. A flashbulb recollection of where the attack occurred, who did the attacking, and whether the attack succeeded would offer a survival advantage. Others have questioned the need for such a special mechanism, given that distinctiveness plays an important role in memory (McCloskey, Wible, & Cohen, 1988). The flashbulb recollection may simply be a highly distinctive event because of its emotionally charged nature. Further research is needed to settle this controversy, however (Schmidt & Bohannon, 1988).

Organization

Category cues. Tulving and Pearlstone (1966) showed the power of organization in their comparison of free and cued recall. The participants studied a list of 48 words that came from several categories, such as tools, fruits, vehicles, and so on. The words occurred in a random order, but the learner noticed the organization of the items nonetheless (see Bousfield, 1953). When asked to recall as many words as possible with no hints or cues (free recall), the investigators found that the participants clustered related items together, for example, apples, oranges, and grapes. Of greater interest, if the person remembered a single item from a category, then she likely remembered most of the others. Conversely, if an item was forgotten—say, truck—then the other examples of vehicles also were forgotten. The category, in other words, served to organize recall.

But only about a third of the words were remembered in free recall. Tulving and Pearlstone also provided some participants with the category names as retrieval cues. Remarkably, the cues roughly doubled the number of words successfully recalled. This result for cued recall shows the powerful effect of organization as an aid to retrieval. It also shows that events may be available in memory, but inaccessible to recollection without the right retrieval cues. More will be said about retrieval cues later in the chapter.

Subjective organization. The tendency to cluster items from the same semantic category is perhaps not surprising. Yet organization plays a critical role in recall even when a clear basis for it is lacking. Tulving (1962) presented people with lists of unrelated words and tracked their *free recall* over a series of trials. Over a series of trials of studying the words and attempting to recall them in whatever order they wished, each participant adopted a consistent pattern of output. That is, each person imposed a **subjective organization** on the words, recalling clusters of items in the same manner trial after trial, even though the clusters themselves were purely idiosyncratic. This finding, perhaps more than any other, indicates the importance if not the necessity of organization in long-term episodic memory.

The power of subjective organization is apparent in tests of recognition as well as recall. On immediate tests, this is not apparent, but as the retention interval increases, recognition performance comes to depend more and more on subjective organization. Mandler, Pearlstone, and Koopmans (1969) gave participants sets of unrelated words and instructed them to sort the words into as many or as few categories as they wished. They then administered a recognition or a recall test at varying retention intervals. As it happens, the more categories the learner used, the better he remembered the words on either type of test. For recall, this dependence on the number of categories used was seen on an immediate test and one given 5 weeks later. For recognition, in contrast, this dependence did not appear until a test given 2 weeks later and was still more prominent on the 5-week test.

Organization, that is, encoding the relations among events and prior knowledge, benefits both learning and remembering. First, the events may be chunked together during their storage (G. Mandler, 1979). Just as finding meaningful groupings increases learning on tests of short-term memory, the same effect may be seen in long-term memory. Second, organization provides retrieval cues that are vital to remembering (Tulving & Pearlstone, 1966). The categories imposed by the materials or by the learner serve as highly effective retrieval cues. Mnemonic techniques take advantage of both benefits of organization as discussed in Box 5.1.

BOX 5.1: Mnemonic Techniques

Imagery has been recognized as crucial to memory from the time of the ancient Greeks. Cicero recounted a story about the Greek poet, Simonides, who delivered a long poem at a Roman banquet. Upon finishing, Simonides left the building just moments before catastrophe struck. The building collapsed, killing all who remained buried in the rubble. According to the legend, Simonides was able to survey the ruins and recall the names of the mutilated dead by first imaging where they had been seated. The method of loci, or places, developed from such imagery. The method consists of identifying a sequence of familiar locations and then forming an image of each item to be remembered at each of the locations. Once a clear image is formed, then the locations provide a plan for retrieving the items. By imagining a walk to each of the locations in the sequence, the items are remembered (Bower, 1970).

To illustrate, first picture a sequence of 10 locations at home or on campus that you know well. Now, try to form an image with each of the following grocery items, placing one item at each location in order. For example, for the first item you might imagine a banana peel on the front steps of your home. Try to create a distinctive image for each item and location:

bananas, lettuce, crackers, bacon, milk, olives, bread, hamburger, tuna, mayonnaise

Now close the book and try to recall the items by taking a mental walk to each of the 10 locations. Most people find it much easier to remember the 10 items using this imaginal technique than trying to simply rehearse the items repetitively. Recall from the previous chapter how difficult it was to retain more than seven or so chunks of information. Yet most people find it easy to recall all 10 items using the method of loci.

Bellezza (1986) showed that even the abstract terminology of psychology could be better remembered by associating each term with a distinctive location on a picture. For example, the learners saw a picture of a truck and a cue word *drive*. By associating the cue word with the truck, they could recall the other words that had been imaged at various locations on the truck (*hunger, thirst, sex, incentives, Lorenz,* and *instinct*).

One reason for the superior recall produced by the method of loci and related techniques centers on the power of imagery. Paivio (1971, 1983) hypothesized that mental images provided a second code for the memory system to use in storing and retrieving information. Without forming a mental image of the words to be remembered, one was left with only a verbal code. The combination of a verbal plus an imaginal code provided the advantage. Further investigation of imagery and mnemonics suggests that the imagery makes an event in memory stand out as more distinctive, and hence easier to recall (Marschark, Richman, Yuille, & Hunt, 1987; McDaniel & Einstein, 1986).

The second reason for the power of mnemonics is that a set of retrieval cues are provided that match the cues encoded with the to-be-remembered material (Bower, 1970). Taking a mental walk with the method of loci is a retrieval plan as well as an encoding plan. Each location visited at the time of retrieval allows one to reconstruct the event originally stored there with relative ease.

The recall of an event depends on successful encoding of both distinctive features and relational features (Hunt & Einstein, 1981; Hunt & McDaniel, 1993). That is, one must know how the information may be distinguished from other memory representations and how it is organized with other information in memory. To illustrate, Hunt and Einstein found that sorting *unrelated* items into subjectively defined categories produces superior recall than rating the same items for "pleasantness," a task that encourages the processing of distinctive features. Because the unrelated items already were distinctive by their very nature, the task that forced the learners to focus on relationships and organization proved superior. In learning a list of *related* items, whose organization was apparent, the pleasantness task that focused attention on distinctive features proved superior.

Retrieval Processes

In the previous chapter, we considered how forgetting in long-term memory may relate to the decay or lack of availability of information, on the one hand. On the other hand, such forgetting may reflect the temporary or even permanent lack of accessibility of information. This could arise because of interference between similar, competing information stored in memory or because of a failure to activate the retrieval cues associated with the forgotten information. Contemporary research has focused on the cue dependent nature of remembering and forgetting. It has emphasized how the context and knowledge related to material in memory play pivotal roles in successful retrieval.

To illustrate, recalling an event from episodic memory, such as one's tenth birthday party, requires retrieval of the time, the place, and the circumstances of stored information. Retrieval can be an active process of reimagining the perceptions, feelings, and possibly thoughts about the event and its context. Being provided with a cue, such as a photograph taken at the party, can trigger a chain of recollections that at first seemed lost from memory. The cue activates related knowledge in long-term memory that eventually allows one to retrieve or perhaps reconstruct the needed information. What one knows about birthday parties in general affects both how one's tenth party was encoded and how it will be later retrieved.

Encoding Specificity

Tulving (1983) proposed that remembering depends on activating precisely the same cues at retrieval that were originally encoded with the event in question. Tulving's principle of **encoding specificity** asserts that "specific encoding operations performed on what is perceived determines what retrieval cues are effective in producing access to what is stored" (Tulving & Thomson, 1973, p. 369). The interaction between encoding and retrieval conditions is the key to high levels of recall and recognition.

For instance, Light and Carter-Sobell (1970) presented people with a cue and a target word to study, such as *strawberry jam*. Later they tried to recognize whether the target word (jam) had appeared during study. If on the test the cue word was switched (traffic jam), they had a harder time recognizing the target than if the retrieval cue matched the encoding cue. Further, when encodings are highly distinctive and retrieval cues are available that match precisely the encoding cues, recall performance can be dazzlingly accurate. Mantyla (1986) obtained better than 90% accuracy in cued recall for a list of 600 words!

Recall of unrecognizable events. If one studies a list of words and later tries to remember them on a recognition versus a recall test, then performance is often better on the recognition test (Kintsch, 1970). Cued recall tests generally yield better performance than free recall tests, in which no retrieval cues are provided. But cued recall still fails to come close to the accuracy typically observed on a recognition test. This makes sense if you think of the word on the recognition test as the perfect retrieval cue—it is an exact copy. Not only is the word familiar, it allows one to retrieve the context in which the word was originally seen in the experiment (Mandler, 1980).

Suppose you see someone at a party who looks familiar. Recognition requires not only a judgment about familiarity but an identification of the context in which you have encountered the person before (oh yes, I've seen her at the grocery store). This identification is much easier when looking at the person than when given a weakly related cue (think of shopping) or given no cues at all.

In a clever experiment, Tulving and Thomson (1973) arranged a situation in which the encoding specificity principle counterintuitively predicted accurate recall of an unrecognizable word. They presented a list of to-be-remembered target words (e.g., black) along with encoding cues that were weak associates of the targets (e.g., train). After presentation of the list, the participants were given strong semantic associates of the target words (e.g., white) and were asked to think of related words. Not surprising, target items (black) were often generated. Next, the participants were asked to examine all the words that they generated and to indicate which if any had originally been presented as targets. Finally, a cued recall test was given in which the encoding context (train) served as the retrieval cue.

Tulving and Thomson found that the participants successfully recognized the targets only a quarter of the time. But when given the proper cue (train), they recalled the targets a stunning two thirds of the time. What is so striking about this is that the retrieval cue is only a weak associate of the target. Yet, because it had been encoded with the word initially, it was the ideal cue for recall. This phenomenon of recall of unrecognizable words strongly supports the principle of encoding specificity.

Tip of the tongue states. Surely you have seen a familiar face that you could not quite place or perhaps you could not retrieve the person's name. People often experience a feeling of knowing or familiarity in which some name, word, date, or other information cannot be retrieved despite a certainty that it is available in memory. When such feelings become particularly intense, psychologists refer to the experience as a TOT or **tip of tongue state.** Brown and McNeill (1966) studied such TOT states for words by giving people definitions of rare words and asking them to recall the words. Strikingly, when people experienced a TOT, they could correctly identify the number of syllables in a forgotten word over 60% of the time. Further investigations showed that

TOTs (a) are a nearly universal experience, (b) occur about once a week, (c) increase with age, (d) are frequently elicited by proper names, (e) often enable access to the target word's first letter, (f) are often accompanied by words related to the target, and (g) are resolved during the experience about half of the time. (Brown, 1991, p. 204)

TOT states suggest that information may be available, but inaccessible, in memory. The forgetting seems to be clearly caused by a failure to find the right retrieval cue. Sometimes we can successfully recall the forgotten information by stumbling upon a thought or perception that triggers the memory. The principle of encoding specificity explains this as another example of cue dependent forgetting. Numerous other experiments have documented the principle that the specific cues associated with an event during learning provide the key to later recall (e.g., Begg & White, 1985; Jacoby, 1974).

Environmental cues. Smith, Glenberg, and Bjork (1978) had people learn a list of words in a particular room and then later try to recall them in the same room or in one very different in appearance. The environmental context affected recall in the direction one would expect. The same room provided the right retrieval cues and supported superior performance.

Psychological states. The emotional state of the individual also may serve as an effective retrieval cue. A **mood congruence effect** may be studied by inducing people into a happy mood or an unhappy mood by thinking about positive or negative life events. Bower (1981) found that the best learning occurs when the material being learned fits with the induced mood. Thus depressing information is best learned when in a sad mood (Blaney, 1986).

State dependent learning is sometimes observed when a person's mood or state of consciousness (e.g., sober or intoxicated) is directly manipulated during learning and retrieval. State dependency for mood has not been convincingly documented, according to Blaney's (1986) review of this literature. That is, recall performance when one's mood at retrieval matches mood at the time of learning is not reliably better than when the moods do not match.

However, several drugs, including alcohol, amphetamines, barbiturates, and marijuana, have shown state dependency effects (Eich, 1989; Overton, 1971) when dosages are sufficiently large to produce clear signs of intoxication, such as slurred speech (Eich, 1980). Information learned in a sober state is better retained when later recalled in a sober state, whereas learning in an intoxicated state is better retained when tested while intoxicated. As one would expect from what we know about the importance of cognitive effort and elaboration during study, recall is by far the best during sober learning and sober test. Also, there is an asymmetry in the relationship (Eich, 1989). A shift from intoxication to sobriety produces a larger deficit in recall than a shift from sobriety to intoxication.

Schemas and Memory

Reconstructive Retrieval

We have seen in Chapter 2 how schemas play a critical role in perception by providing expectations. They play a similar crucial role in memory. The schemas of long-term memory represent everything that we know. These schemas are intricately organized in a complex web of relations. The concepts and facts of semantic memory and the specific autobiographical events of episodic memory are linked in countless ways.

Imagine a scenario of a cat prowling for mice. Where might the cat find mice? In a barn on a farm, of course. Immediately related images might come to mind about farms. You might recall the farm you grew up on or one you visited as a child or one you saw in a movie last week. In turn, images of cows, pigs, horses, and other farm animals might then come to mind. The thought of a horse would perhaps bring to mind the time you went horseback riding with friends. More images pop into mind, as you reflect on each of the friends on the trip. The possibilities of such free association are endless because the schemas of long-term memory are massively interconnected. Virtually any thought, through some chain of associations, can lead to any other thought as a result of such organization.

Much, if not all, of what we learn and retrieve from memory passes through the organizational web. The schemas provide expectations that help us to learn, but also to miss on occasion events that do not fit with these expectations. The schemas help us to remember, but also at times to distort memories so as to conform to momentary expectations. The key point here is that schemas enable us to fabricate how past events most likely unfolded. The term **reconstructive memory** refers to the manner in which schemas guide explicit memory when an episode is retrieved from the long-term system.

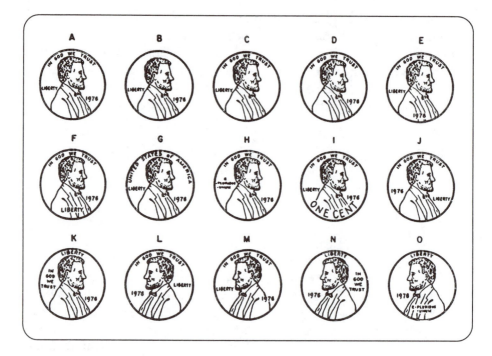

Figure 5.2. Fifteen alternative drawings of a U.S. penny.
SOURCE: From Nickerson and Adams (1979). Copyright © 1979 by Academic Press, Inc. Reprinted by permission.

Earlier we saw that the excellent recognition memory for distinctive pictures depends on their activating numerous diverse schemas. When the pictures all relate to the same schema, they are difficult to distinguish. A remarkable illustration of this is shown in Figure 5.2. Which of these drawings accurately depicts a U.S. penny? Can you identify the error contained in the remaining 15 drawings? The hundreds if not thousands of times we have seen a penny seem to blur together into a schematic representation. Instead of recalling the details of a specific penny, we reconstruct how a penny ought to look from a sketchy representation.

Nickerson and Adams (1979) found that fewer than half of the participants in their experiments correctly identified drawing A. Further, very few of the participants could confidently reject many of the drawings as incorrect. When asked to draw a penny from memory, the reconstructive nature of retrieval was especially apparent. The participants tried to imagine what a penny ought to look like based on their schema for pennies. Nearly two thirds of the time a feature was either omitted or mislocated. Omissions alone accounted for one third of the errors.

Many experiments have documented that recall may at times be driven by a schema-based, reconstructive process. For instance, Brewer and Treyens (1981) showed how our recollections of places are schema based. After waiting in an experimenter's office for 35 seconds, people were taken to another room and asked to recall the office. Virtually everyone recalled that the office had a chair, a desk, and walls, but only about one out of four recalled unexpected items, such as a skull. Moreover, items that fit preconceptions about a psychologist's office, such as books, were falsely recalled by some participants.

The role of schemas in text comprehension and memory is particularly well researched (Bower, Black, & Turner, 1979; Dooling & Christiaansen, 1977; Spiro, 1980). These and numerous related experiments took as their starting point the classic work by Bartlett (1932) on schemas and reconstruction. Particularly well known are Bartlett's studies in which participants tried to recall a folk tale of North American Indians—the War of the Ghosts. Several features of his results indicated that recall took place through an attempt to fabricate or reconstruct the original story. Within 15 minutes of reading the story, people recalled an abstracted, summarized version. Details were lost, leveling the story to a shorter version. In particular, unfamiliar terms and ideas were omitted. Other ideas were assimilated or rationalized to fit with preconceived notions about how a story should go. At times, certain details were sharpened or elaborated, including the addition of erroneous details. Again these were in keeping with the expectations of the reader, not with what the story actually said. Over hours, weeks, months, and years, repeated attempts to recall the story magnified all these distortions.

Encoding Distortions

In addition to reconstructive retrieval, schemas sometimes constructively distort memory during encoding in multiple ways. The strength and generality of these effects are in dispute (Alba & Hasher, 1983; Mandler, 1984). So we will focus on three that are reasonably well supported to illustrate constructive effects: selection, interpretation, and integration.

Selection. The selective encoding of information that fits with prior knowledge defines **selection.** This idea is well illustrated in an experiment by Bransford and Johnson (1972). They presented people with the following obscure text:

> The procedure is actually quite simple. First you arrange items into different groups. Of course one pile may be sufficient depending on how much there is to do. If you have to go somewhere else due to lack of facilities that is the next step; otherwise, you are pretty well set. It is important not to overdo things. That is, it is better to do too few things at once than too many. In the short run this may not seem important but complications can easily arise. A mistake can be expensive as well. At first, the whole procedure will seem complicated. Soon, however, it will become just another facet of life. It is difficult to foresee any end to the necessity for this task in the immediate future, but then, one never can tell. After the procedure is completed one arranges the materials into different groups again. Then they can be put into their appropriate places. Eventually they will be used once more and the whole cycle will then have to be repeated. However, that is part of life. (p. 722)

When first reading this, you no doubt felt what Bartlett (1932) called an "effort after meaning" as various schemas actively struggled to shape the sentences into a comprehensible pattern. Without knowing the title or topic of the text in advance to select the sentences to fit into a preconceived schema, comprehension is poor and so is subsequent recall. The data from Bransford and Johnson's experiment show this plainly in the first column of Table 5.1. However, when given the topic of "washing clothes" before reading, both ratings of comprehension and recall scores improved greatly. Notice that receiving the topic after reading failed to help. The schema must be active to select details at the time of learning.

Interpretation. Inferences and suppositions are made to conform new material to activated schemas; these define **interpretation.** Prior knowledge provides a basis for interpreting the meaning of events and these interpretations become part of memory. Johnson, Bransford, and Solomon's (1973) results illustrate interpretation well. Consider these two versions of statements based on the brief passages presented to different groups of people:

1. John was trying to fix the bird house. He was pounding the nail when his father came out to watch him and to help him do the work.

Table 5.1 Comprehension and Recall Scores for the "Washing Clothes" Passage

	No Topic	Topic After	Topic Before	Maximum Score
Comprehension ratings	2.29	2.12	4.50	7.00
Number of idea units recalled	2.82	2.65	5.83	18.00

SOURCE: From Bransford and Johnson (1972). Copyright © 1972 by Academic Press, Inc. Reprinted by permission.

2. John was trying to fix the bird house. He was looking for the nail when his father came out to watch him and to help him do the work.

The passages were the same but for a minor change. Johnson et al. later gave a recognition test that included the following novel sentence:

3. John was using the hammer to fix the bird house when his father came out to watch him and to help him do the work.

The researchers found that the group of individuals who had read passage 1 were much more likely to say that they had previously seen passage 3 in the experiment. The false recognition of passage 3 indicates that these individuals inferred that John was using a hammer, an assumption that fits well with the expectations of schemas activated by the passage.

Integration. The third type of encoding distortion, **integration,** refers to the melding together of numerous ideas into a unified schematic structure. As a result of integration, we remember the main idea or gist of events rather than the details of their occurrence. Bransford and Franks (1971) investigated integration by presenting people with a long list of sentences. In Table 5.2, you can read a sample of these sentences. Answer the question after each one to ensure that you comprehended each sentence.

Table 5.2 A Memory Experiment: Part 1

Instructions: Read each sentence, count to five, answer the question, and go on to the next sentence.

The girl broke the window on the porch.	Broke what?
The tree in the front yard shaded the man who was smoking his pipe.	Where?
The hill was steep.	What was?
The cat, running from the barking dog, jumped on the table.	From what?
The tree was tall.	Was what?
The old car climbed the hill.	What did?
The cat running from the dog jumped on the table.	Where?
The girl who lives next door broke the window on the porch.	Lives where?
The car pulled the trailer.	Did what?
The scared cat was running from the barking dog.	What was?
The girl lives next door.	Who does?
The tree shaded the man who was smoking his pipe.	What did?
The scared cat jumped on the table.	What did?
The girl who lives next door broke the large window.	Broke what?
The man was smoking his pipe.	Who was?
The old car climbed the steep hill.	The what?
The large window was on the porch.	Where?
The tall tree was in the front yard.	What was?
The car pulling the trailer climbed the steep hill.	Did what?
The cat jumped on the table.	Where?
The tall tree in the front yard shaded the man.	Did what?
The car pulling the trailer climbed the hill.	Which car?
The dog was barking.	Was what?
The window was large.	What was?

STOP. Cover the preceding sentences. Now read each sentence in Table 5.3 and decide if it is a sentence from the list given above.

SOURCE: From Jenkins, J. J. (1974). Remember that old theory of memory? Well, forget it! *American Psychologist, 29*, 785-795. Copyright © 1974 by the American Psychological Association. Reprinted by permission.

Now take a moment to decide whether the sentences in Table 5.3 are old sentences that appeared earlier in the list that you read or are new sentences. Check old or new for each one before reading further in the text. After finishing the recognition test, count the number of items that you checked as old sentences.

Typically, people indicate that well more than half of the 30 sentences in Table 5.3 are old sentences. In fact, none of the test sentences occurred earlier in Table 5.2. The test sentences, however, represent plausible sentences based on the schemas that were activated in reading the original sentences. The individual ideas of the original sentences become integrated into larger, organized ideas. The integration is so compelling that people actually are more confident that they saw a sentence that contains all related ideas than they are about sentences containing fewer ideas. This is exactly opposite to what one would expect if we stored the individual sentences in memory verbatim.

Bransford and Franks's results are plotted in Figure 5.3. The number of ideas in the test sentence increased from one to four. Noncase sentences were totally novel and unrelated to the schemas activated during reading. They were readily rejected as new sentences. As you can see, the participants falsely recognized new sentences that contained more than one idea, and their confidence increased with each additional idea. The same result occurred for actual old sentences. These results plainly show how integration can distort memory by giving us the gist of the original events.

Eyewitness Testimony

Researchers are keenly interested in how constructive and reconstructive processes influence the accuracy of eyewitness testimony. Neisser (1981) analyzed the testimony of John Dean regarding meetings Dean had with President Nixon during the Watergate scandal. Commentators found Dean's memory quite remarkable, given the many details he confidently offered in his testimony. Yet, by comparing Dean's sworn testimony with the transcripts of President Nixon's tapes of those meetings, Neisser could identify the errors in Dean's testimony.

On the whole, Dean did very well in recalling the gist of what President Nixon had said. Dean integrated information about different meetings and conversations into broad themes. Yet, he also added faulty details. Regarding the September 15 meeting that had taken place 9 months before Dean's testimony, Neisser observed:

Table 5.3 A Memory Experiment: Part 2

Instructions: Decide whether each sentence is old or new.

1. The car climbed the hill.	(old _____ , new _____)
2. The girl who lives next door broke the window.	(old _____ , new _____)
3. The old man who was smoking his pipe climbed the steep hill.	(old _____ , new _____)
4. The tree was in the front yard.	(old _____ , new _____)
5. The scared cat, running from the barking dog, jumped on the table.	(old _____ , new _____)
6. The window was on the porch.	(old _____ , new _____)
7. The barking dog jumped on the old car in the front yard.	(old _____ , new _____)
8. The tree in the front yard shaded the man.	(old _____ , new _____)
9. The cat was running from the dog.	(old _____ , new _____)
10. The old car pulled the trailer.	(old _____ , new _____)
11. The tall tree in the front yard shaded the old car.	(old _____ , new _____)
12. The tall tree shaded the man who was smoking his pipe.	(old _____ , new _____)
13. The scared cat was running from the dog.	(old _____ , new _____)
14. The old car, pulling the trailer, climbed the hill.	(old _____ , new _____)
15. The girl who lives next door broke the large window on the porch.	(old _____ , new _____)
16. The tall tree shaded the man.	(old _____ , new _____)
17. The cat was running from the barking dog.	(old _____ , new _____)
18. The car was old.	(old _____ , new _____)
19. The girl broke the large window.	(old _____ , new _____)
20. The scared cat ran from the barking dog that jumped on the table.	(old _____ , new _____)
21. The scared cat, running from the dog, jumped on the table.	(old _____ , new _____)
22. The old car pulling the trailer climbed the steep hill.	(old _____ , new _____)
23. The girl broke the large window on the porch.	(old _____ , new _____)
24. The scared cat which broke the window on the porch climbed the tree.	(old _____ , new _____)
25. The tree shaded the man.	(old _____ , new _____)
26. The car climbed the steep hill.	(old _____ , new _____)
27. The girl broke the window.	(old _____ , new _____)
28. The man who lives next door broke the large window on the porch.	(old _____ , new _____)
29. The tall tree in the front yard shaded the man who was smoking the pipe.	(old _____ , new _____)
30. The cat was scared.	(old _____ , new _____)

STOP. Count the number of sentences judged "old."

SOURCE: From Jenkins, J. J. (1974). Remember that old theory of memory? Well, forget it! *American Psychologist, 29,* 785-795. Copyright © 1974 by the American Psychological Association. Reprinted by permission.

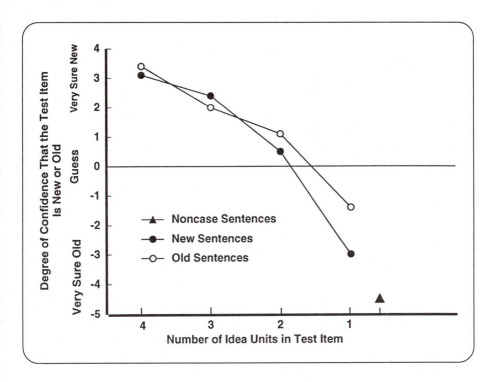

Figure 5.3. Confidence in recognition judgments for both old and new sentences varies with the number of idea units expressed.
SOURCE: From Bransford and Franks (1971). Copyright © 1971 by Academic Press, Inc. Reprinted by permission.

Comparison with the transcript shows that hardly a word of Dean's account is true. Nixon did not say *any* of the things attributed to him here: He didn't ask Dean to sit down, he didn't say Haldeman had kept him posted, . . . he didn't say anything about Liddy or the indictments. Nor had Dean himself said the things he later describes himself as saying. (p. 9)

These faulty details were all reconstructions of what Dean believed he must have heard, said, and done. Schemas most likely generated these details as Dean reconstructed the original events for his testimony.

Attorneys in criminal trials are well aware that the testimony of an eyewitness exerts a powerful influence on jurors. The members of a jury typically believe that eyewitness reports are accurate, unless for some reason deliberate lying by the witness is suspected. In reality, eyewitnesses can fall victim to distortions of memory, because of both inaccurate encoding and inaccurate retrieving of episodes (Loftus, 1979). Errors can and do occur even when witnesses are confident that their testimony is accurate, leading in turn to wrongful convictions. According to some estimates, roughly 8,500 such miscarriages of justice occur each year in the United States alone, with as many as half attributable to incorrect eyewitness testimony (Loftus, 1986). Explanations of errors have focused on selective encoding and misinformation effects.

Selective encoding. The scene of a crime may not be plainly visible because of poor lighting and fleeting glimpses of the perpetrator (Buckhout, 1974). Moreover, eyewitnesses to violent crimes, particularly when they are the victims, may experience tremendous stress that diminishes their ability to encode the event adequately. Even less severe stressors can distort memory through selective encoding. For example, the social anxiety of being the next in line to give a public address can lower subsequent recall of the speech given just before ours (Bond & Omar, 1990). Perhaps you have experienced this while waiting to give a presentation in class. You may remember earlier and later speakers much better than the person just ahead of you.

Not all scholars agree that emotional duress weakens encoding, however. Recall here our earlier discussion of the controversy over flashbulb memories. The literature on eyewitness reports of crimes is similarly open to multiple interpretations. For example, Christianson (1992) concluded that only the peripheral details of a crime tend to be lost under high levels of stress. The central features of the event at times are remembered especially well, through effects of selective attention, elaboration, and distinctiveness. Thus most errors in eyewitness testimony may be caused by factors other than selective encoding.

The misinformation effect. Work by Loftus and her colleagues has shown that the questions asked of eyewitnesses after an event can potentially influence their memory. When the questions contain misleading information, they may distort memory, a finding called the **misinformation effect.** For example, Loftus and Palmer (1974) presented people with a film of a traffic accident and then questioned them, as might an investigator or an attorney, about what they had witnessed. One of several questions asked was, "How fast were the cars going when they *hit* each other?"

Table 5.4 Speed Estimates for Critical Questions with Various Verbs After Watching Film Strip of Car Accident

Verb	Mean Speed Estimate in Miles per Hour
Smashed	40.8
Collided	39.3
Bumped	38.1
Hit	34.0
Contacted	31.8

SOURCE: From Loftus and Palmer (1974). Copyright © 1974 by Academic Press, Inc. Reprinted by permission.

In the various conditions of the experiment, the verb *hit* was replaced by more or less violent words, as shown in Table 5.4. Later on in the experiment, the participants gave estimates of how fast the cars were traveling when they collided. As you can see in the table, the average speed estimate varied in direct relation to the wording of the question. By using the word *smashed*, the questioner altered the memory of the accident, causing people to give a reliably higher estimate of vehicle speed.

Moreover, a week later new questions were posed, for example, "Did you see broken glass?" In fact, no broken glass appeared in the film and 80% of the participants correctly answered no to this question. Yet, most of those who answered yes were in the condition that had been asked about the cars smashing into each other. As time wore on, the leading question continued to shape the nature of the recollection.

The misinformation effect can be strikingly large. Loftus, Miller, and Burns (1978) showed people a series of slides portraying an accident in which a red car stops at an intersection, turns the corner, and hits a pedestrian. Some participants saw a yield sign at the intersection but were asked either 20 minutes or a week later whether a second car passed the red car "while it was stopped at the stop sign." Loftus et al. administered a recognition test after providing the misleading information, which required participants to say which of a pair of slides had been part of the accident series. The key pair showed the red car at either a stop sign or a yield sign. When the misinformation occurred 20 minutes after the accident, about 60% of the time the participants incorrectly picked the stop sign. This rose to 80% when the misleading question occurred after a week, presumably because the participants forgot the details of the original accident and were more susceptible to a misleading question.

The misleading information effect seems to show that memory for the original event is either unavailable or inaccessible (Christiaansen & Ochalek, 1983; Loftus et al., 1978). Memory impairment is not the only explanation of the effect, however. Critics have countered that response bias best accounts for the findings (McCloskey & Zaragoza, 1985; Zaragoza, McCloskey, & Jamis, 1987). Adopting a signal detection approach, these researchers deny a loss of memory for the original event *caused by the misleading question*. That is, the witnesses were no less sensitive to the correct information (the yield sign). Rather, they were biased to pick the stop sign because the details of the original event were forgotten over time *before* the experimenter introduced the misleading question. Without a clear recollection of the yield sign, the misleading question could bias the witnesses. After all, they had no reason to doubt the wording of the question about the stop sign and it was one of the two choices on the test.

But suppose the test pitted the stop sign against, say, a deer crossing sign. Would people forget they had seen the stop sign? McCloskey and Zaragoza (1985) modified the recognition test to include an item unrelated to the misleading question and found that the witnesses correctly recognized the original event, as predicted by the response-bias hypothesis. Loftus, Schooler, and Wagenaar (1985) doubted whether such results definitively rule out the hypothesis of true memory impairment, however.

Recovered memories. Research on eyewitness testimony is ongoing and unsettled at this point in time (Ross et al., 1994). Interest in resolving the key issues has intensified in recent years because of an eruption of cases of alleged child abuse. The victims in these cases have recovered memories of abuse that took place months, years, and even decades earlier. Therapists working with these individuals typically have attributed their forgetting to repression. Psychoanalytic **repression** refers to the prevention of unpleasant memories from entering consciousness in an effort to protect the ego.

Another possibility suggested by memory researchers and, of interest, by Freud himself is that memories of sexual and other abuse are false

BOX 5.2: Memories of Abuse

A stunning application of research on reconstructive memory concerns charges of child abuse. In some cases, the eyewitness testimony of a child is the primary source of evidence. A major problem with this is the possibility that children are especially suggestible. Through the questions that are asked and the way they are asked, children may come to falsely remember abuse that in fact never happened.

Ceci and Bruck (1993) reviewed the extensive literature on the suggestibility of children. They concluded that preschool-aged children are especially vulnerable to suggestion compared with older children and adults. But clinical psychologists who specialize in working with abused children contend that such findings do not apply to important actions, particularly those involving a personal bodily experience. It is common for experts in clinical psychology, social work, and psychiatry to testify in court that children do not lie about events as traumatic as bodily abuse and could not be falsely led through suggestion to believe abuse occurred.

Ceci, Leichtman, Putnick, and Nightingale (1993), however, reported that a false memory of having been kissed during a bath can indeed be planted in the minds of a young child. In an anatomical doll study, nearly a quarter to a third of 3-year-olds inaccurately answered abuse questions, such as the following: "Did he touch your private parts?" or "How many times did he spank you?" (Goodman & Aman, 1990). Such findings may imply that suggestion has led to a false memory, but Ceci and Bruck noted that children might also lie for social reasons (e.g., avoiding punishment, game playing, or personal gain).

Forgotten memories of abuse sometimes have surfaced years later, while an adult is in therapy for severe emotional distress and an inability to cope with daily life (Olio, 1989). The therapeutic techniques used to help the individual often include memory work; the individual regresses to an earlier age under hypnosis, receives sexually suggestive questions or dream interpretations from the therapist, or tries to remember childhood events while drugged with sodium amytal. These techniques presumably work against Freudian repression. Freud contended that repression automatically protected the ego by keeping unpleasant memories out of consciousness. Abuse as a child is horribly traumatic and so repression or even conscious denial are anticipated by therapists (Olio, 1989). Yet, sound empirical evidence that adults can forget traumatic events for years and then recover them accurately is sorely lacking (Loftus, 1993). Hypnosis and other techniques of recovered memory therapy have the strong potential of convincingly suggesting events that may never have taken place. Normally, adults can monitor reality so as to draw a clear line between events stemming from memory and those generated in fantasy (Johnson, 1988). But this line may be tragically erased in so-called recovered memory cases by the methods of therapy itself (Loftus, 1993).

The stakes are obviously high here. Abusers must not go free, but the innocent must not be falsely accused and wrongly convicted. The debate between clinicians and cognitive researchers rages on in scholarly articles (e.g., Loftus, 1994; Olio, 1994). The debate is also heard in the courtroom, as our legal system weighs the evidence in abuse cases. Perhaps the most famous case concerned the accusation by Eileen Franklin that her father, George, not only sexually abused her and her sisters but also abused and murdered her best friend (MacLean, 1993). The prosecution called a clinician, Dr. Terr, to testify that Eileen had recovered a repressed memory of the murder 20 years after its occurrence. Dr. Terr's extensive work with victims of trauma convinced her that Eileen's recollection was accurate, despite the 20 years of repression.

The defense called Dr. Loftus, who cited her laboratory evidence that misleading questions and other factors can cause distortions in memory. Dr. Loftus testified that the murder recollection was a classic case of false memory. MacLean's account of the tragic story leaves plenty of room for wondering whether Eileen's testimony was true or false. The jury, which has the critical say, convicted George Franklin of murder.

---

memories. They may reflect the reconstructive processes of schemas, leading one to recall vividly events that never transpired. Suggestions from therapists and others may serve as misleading information, prompting the reconstruction of false memories. These issues, as we will see in Box 5.2, are hotly debated by researchers, therapists, and jurists alike.

▣ SUMMARY ▣

1. Encoding and storage of episodic information in long-term memory depends on attention and effort. Unattended, automatic encoding fails to support explicit memory. However, merely attending is insufficient as well for good recall and recognition. Elaborative rehearsal in which links are established between new information and information already stored is important. Simply recycling information through attention and short-term storage, what is called maintenance rehearsal, is far less effective.

2. The level of processing also affects learning success, with deep semantic processing supporting better memory than shallow sensory processing. This probably reflects the importance of establishing a distinctive memory representation that can be easily retrieved in the future. Finally, the organization of newly learned information is necessary for both successful recognition and recall.

3. Encoding processes are important, but they cannot be considered apart from retrieval processes. The encoding specificity principle asserts that events are recognized or recalled only when retrieval cues at the time of the test match the encoding cues present at the time of learning. The retrieval cues allow one to activate the to-be-remembered episode and its context. From this perspective, forgetting represents a failure to access an episode because the retrieval cues are inadequate.

4. Schemas shape both what is stored and what is retrieved. They establish expectations that result in selection of the features of events that are encoded in the first place. Schemas also constructively guide the encoding of events through processes of interpretation and integration. Finally, schemas reconstructively guide the retrieval process, enabling us to fabricate how events must have originally happened.

5. The constructive and reconstructive properties of human memory have important implications for our legal system. Currently, there is fierce debate over the reliability of eyewitness testimony, based on laboratory evidence that selective encoding and misleading information can produce false memories. The suggestibility and credibility of young children as witnesses or adults who have recovered a repressed memory are issues at the center of the still unresolved debate.

Key Terms

spacing effect	tip of the tongue state
maintenance rehearsal	mood congruence effect
elaborative rehearsal	state dependent learning
levels or depth of processing	reconstructive memory

self-reference effect	selection
distinctiveness	interpretation
flashbulb memory	integration
subjective organization	repression
encoding specificity	misinformation effect

Recommended Readings

For further information on attention and explicit and implicit memory, I refer the reader to Lewandowsky, Dunn, and Kirsner's (1989) *Implicit Memory: Theoretical Issues*. Richardson-Klavehn and Bjork (1988) reviewed related issues in the *Annual Review of Psychology*. Cermak and Craik's (1979) *Levels of Processing in Human Memory* provides important perspectives on encoding processes.

With regard to forgetting, I recommend Kihlstrom and Evans's (1979) *Functional Disorders of Memory*. Also Loftus's (1979) book titled *Eyewitness Testimony* provides an introduction to forgetting in real-world settings. Another valuable resource on everyday forgetting and the implications of such forgetting in the eyes of the law is an edited volume by Ceci, Ross, and Toglia (1989) titled *Perspectives on Children's Testimony*. More recently, Ross, Read, and Toglia (1994) edited a collection titled *Adult Eyewitness Testimony: Current Trends and Developments*. The entire August 1994 issue of *Applied Cognitive Psychology* concerns reported memories of childhood sexual abuse.

Flashbulb memories, the antithesis of forgetting, are well covered in Winograd and Neisser's (1992) *Affect and Accuracy in Recall: Studies of "Flashbulb" Memories*. An earlier volume by Neisser (1982) covers both forgetting and remembering (*Memory Observed: Remembering in Natural Contexts*).

As for mnemonic methods, I suggest further readings in McDaniel and Pressley's (1987) volume titled *Imagery and Related Mnemonic Processes*. Hayes's (1981) *The Complete Problem Solver* explains how to use several mnemonic techniques, as does Yates's (1966) *The Art of Memory*. Baddeley (1982) also provides practical advice on memory in his book titled *Your Memory: A User's Guide*.

Mathematical models of remembering have adopted the encoding specificity principle as a key assumption. Two examples are CHARM and SAM. The composite holographic associative recall model (CHARM) is described in Eich's (1982) article in *Psychological Review* and the search of associate memory (SAM) model is described in Raaijmakers and Shiffrin's (1981) article in the same journal. These models can simulate many of the empirical findings discussed in this chapter. Readers interested in these models should also examine Murdock's (1982) paper in *Psychological Review.*

CHAPTER **6**

▣ Knowledge Representation and Use

Factual and conceptual knowledge constitutes a key ingredient in speaking and listening, reading and writing, problem solving and thinking. Without an ability to acquire, represent, and use knowledge about the world and its meaningful symbols, high-level forms of human cognition would not be possible. It is through semantic memory that we categorize the world, allowing us to ignore the details, to see a specific object as a general kind. Lakoff (1987) aptly underscored the importance of categorization as follows:

> There is nothing more basic than categorization to our thought, perception, action, and speech. Every time we see something as a *kind* of thing, for example, a tree, we are categorizing. Whenever we reason about *kinds* of things—chairs, nations, illnesses, emotions, any kind of thing at all—we are employing categories. Whenever we intentionally perform any *kind* of action, say something as mundane as writing with a pencil, hammering with a hammer, or ironing clothes, we are using categories. The particular action we perform on that occasion is a *kind* of motor activity. . . . They are never done in exactly the same way . . . yet . . . we know how to make move-

ments of that kind. Any time we either produce or understand any utterance of any reasonable length, we are employing dozens if not hundreds of categories: categories of speech sounds, of words, or phrases and clauses, as well as conceptual categories. Without the ability to categorize, we could not function at all, whether in the physical world or in our social and intellectual lives. (pp. 5-6)

In this chapter, we will examine the fundamental questions about semantic memory. First, we will consider the nature of schemas in greater detail than in past chapters. Similarities and differences among various concepts, frames, and scripts require our attention. Second, we will consider the processes by which schemas are learned in the first place. Third, we will consider the debate regarding the codes used to represent knowledge in long-term memory. One view holds that all semantic representations must take the form of abstract propositions, whereas another view allows concrete images as well as propositions. Finally, we will consider the models that account for how we use knowledge representations to answer conceptual and factual questions about the world.

Schemas

Knowledge representations are variously described in the literature as schemas, mental models, categories, classes, concepts, scripts, and frames. In this book the term *schema* generically refers to these representations of knowledge. We will begin with a definition of the general term *schema* and outline its chief characteristics. Then we will turn to the more specific meanings of terms such as *scripts*.

As briefly noted earlier in the book, a schema is a dynamic mental representation of a type of object or event that describes only the general characteristics that define the type; the details of the specific tokens of the type in question are irrelevant and identified as variables in the schema that assume different values (Stillings et al., 1987). Schemas for trees and birds, for example, allow for considerable variations in the individual tokens or examples that fit the general idea. A tree schema includes a set of variables or slots, such as the types of roots, trunks, branches, and leaves, that may be instantiated in a large number of ways. Many unique trees all fit the general schema.

The standard definition must be broadened to encompass more than simply knowledge of physical objects and events. Knowledge of mathematical ideas (e.g., the square root of minus one), philosophical beliefs (e.g., free will), and psychological states (e.g., depression) illustrate schemas of a nonphysical nature.

Chafe (1990) explained that schemas are "prepackaged expectations and ways of interpreting" (p. 80) that largely are supplied by learning, through immersion in a given culture. We learn by doing, observing, and communicating. J. M. Mandler (1979) noted that a schema "is formed on the basis of past experience with objects, scenes, or events and consists of a set of (usually unconscious) expectations about what things look like and/or the order in which they occur" (p. 263).

The schema, then, provides an abstract representation of knowledge that allows us to categorize objects and events as *kinds* of things. It is important to note here that not all categorization depends on the use of schemas. Theorists have recognized that categorization can also take place by drawing analogies between a novel object, say, and a specific, well-remembered object. For example, you might categorize a never-before-seen dog by drawing an analogy to the family dog. Such categorization would depend on memory for specific instances, not on an abstract schema (Hintzman, 1986; Medin & Schaffer, 1978).

Characteristics of Schemas

A schema summarizes or represents numerous objects, events, or ideas that differ in one or more ways. The schema groups these and allows a person to categorize them as the same. For example, there are a dizzying number and range of examples that fit one's schema for bird. The variety of birds in the Amazon River basin of South America alone challenges any cognitive structure that tries to represent them. As Attneave (1957) explained, the schema for bird includes information about the dimensions along which birds differ from one another (e.g., size, color, shape of wings, and so on). It also includes information about the range of values on these dimensions and the values that occur quite frequently (e.g., just how big a bird can get, on the one hand, and the typical or average size of a bird, on the other).

Generally, schemas have fuzzy or flexible boundaries (Rosch, 1973). Such schemas are ill-defined in that it is difficult to decide whether a particular poor example falls within the legitimate range of membership or not. Good examples, in contrast, are easily seen. From the most typical instance of a schema—the prototype—there is a gradient of membership. At least for residents of North America, the robin assumes the role of prototype for the bird schema. The turkey lies far out on the gradient from the prototype and the penguin just about falls off the gradient altogether. A crow falls in between these extreme cases. People show substantial agreement in their ratings of the typicality of such examples (Rosch & Mervis, 1975). Also, the speed with which people categorize an example varies with how close or far it is from the prototype, the **typicality effect** in classification. One can correctly categorize a robin as a bird faster than a crow, which in turn proceeds faster than a turkey (Rosch, 1975). As we will see, prototypes and ill-defined boundaries of membership are important properties of virtually all schemas.

The fuzzy boundary of class membership can be readily seen from the results of Labov (1973), who presented people with the cuplike objects seen in Figure 6.1. Exactly at what point does an object cease to be a cup and become a bowl, a glass, or a mug? For instance, the first four items varied in terms of the ratio of the width of the cup to its depth. In the context of thinking about food, Labov's results showed that the probability of calling the object a bowl increased gradually, not abruptly, as this ratio increased. Similarly, the probability of calling it a cup gradually decreased, but for middle ratios both responses often occurred, reflecting the fuzzy boundary of membership. In a neutral context, the cup response became less likely, but people were more reluctant to call items 3 and 4 a bowl. This difference in judgment with context shows the flexible nature of schemas; boundaries of membership shift depending on what other schema are currently active.

In addition, a schema is coherent in that it relates well to other schemas; it is embedded in and consistent with people's background knowledge or naive theories about the world (Keil, 1989; Murphy & Medin, 1985). For example, a person's knowledge and intuitions about biology dovetail with the bird schema. If a person believes that birds breathe, eat, and reproduce, then these abstract theoretical constraints would lead one to reject a robotic robin as not really being a robin. It may look and act exactly like a robin, but if the person knows it is not a biological organism then it fails to fit the schema. In other words, similarity to perceptual and functional properties provides only a surface-level means of organizing categories. Deeper, less accessible, theory-based properties (e.g., the genetic structure of a bird) constrain our categorizations as well as surface properties (Keil, 1989).

Schemas may be organized hierarchically in some cases. The hierarchy of subordinate (robin), basic (bird), and superordinate categories

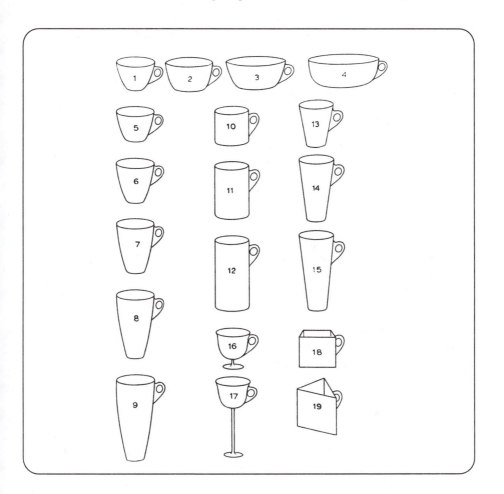

Figure 6.1. The boundary of the natural concept of *cup* is fuzzy.
SOURCE: From Labov (1973). Copyright © 1973 by Georgetown University Press. Reprinted by permission.

(animal) is one example (Rosch, Mervis, Gray, Johnson, & Boyes-Braem, 1976). The basic level of categorization is learned earlier by children and allows a more rapid response in tasks that require people to name the category to which a stimulus object belongs. For example, if shown a picture of a robin or a turkey, people can most quickly categorize the objects as birds. The subordinate and superordinate classifications take more time. Basic-level schemas carve the world into groups that provide the optimal amount of information (Murphy & Smith, 1982; Rosch et al., 1976). All examples that fit the same basic-level category share many common features. This is not true at the superordinate level. At the same time, the basic level carves the world into far fewer groupings than the subordinate level. Thus, by first learning and thinking in terms of basic-level categories, one can deal with the environment most adaptively.

Types of Schemas

Frames and scripts. **Frames** are schemas that represent the physical structure of the environment. Minsky (1977) proposed the term in his theoretical analysis of the perception of complex visual scenes, such as a room or the office considered in the previous chapter. In addition to perception, frames are used in generating mental maps of the environment and other forms of remembering and imagining. The essence of a frame is a detailed structural description, which specifies the features and relations among features that define the physical setting.

Scripts are schemas that represent routine activities (Abelson, 1981; Mandler, 1984). They are usually sequential in nature and often involve social interactions. Schank and Abelson (1977) described the restaurant script to illustrate this class. Each script specifies a theme (eating in a restaurant), typical roles (customer and waiter), entry conditions (hungry customer), and a sequence of scenes and actions within scenes (ordering, which involves getting a menu, reading a menu, and so on). Cantor, Mischel, and Schwartz (1982) studied common social situations and found they are organized in a stereotypical manner. People can readily describe a prototypical blind date or job interview, for instance.

The sequential nature of many scripts affects their use in perception and memory. Barsalou and Sewell (1985) asked people to recall scenes from a script or examples from a natural concept in order of typicality, from the most representative to the least representative. In the case of a script (how to write a letter), recall proceeded at a steady rate, as if the people searched memory in an orderly, sequential fashion. In contrast, in the case of a natural concept (tool), recall started at a rapid rate, as people quickly retrieved prototypical examples, and then slowed progressively.

Some theorists have proposed that scripts are best thought of as memory organization packets (MOPs) that describe in an abstract manner the order in which events occur in a given scene (Schank, 1982; Seifert, McKoon, Abelson, & Ratcliff, 1986). For example, entering always comes before ordering. By keeping the scene description abstract and not tied to a particular script, such as a restaurant MOP, the same scene can operate in a different script, such as a mail order MOP. A single scene may appear in numerous scripts or MOPS.

Concepts. All other types of schemas are generally referred to as concepts or categories. Two major branches of concepts are **identity categories** versus **equivalence categories** (Bruner et al., 1956). Identity involves categorization of different forms of the same thing.

For example, an identity schema allows one to identify an individual across a life span of changes in appearance due to aging. Such a schema represents the transformations that occur through aging, a remarkable feat given the complexities involved (Shaw & Pittenger, 1977). Recall that Bahrick et al. (1975) found that people could recognize the faces of their high school classmates (though not necessarily their names) with 90% accuracy after 34 years since high school. The self-schema also illustrates an identity concept. In addition to work on the self-reference effect in memory, the self-schema has played an important role in understanding social relations and how people explain their behavior in social settings (Markus & Wurf, 1987).

In equivalence classes, in which different stimuli evoke a common response, three important types must be distinguished. **Rule-governed concepts** specify the features and relations that define membership in the class on an all or none basis (Bourne, 1966; Bruner et al., 1956). The definitions of real numbers, gravity, and grand larceny can be specified formally. Such rule-based, formal concepts lie at the heart of mathematics, science, law, and other disciplines of human thought. It is only these abstract creations of the human mind that fail to show the fuzzy boundary characteristic of other schemas. Nevertheless, they still show gradients of within the rule-governed boundaries (Bourne, 1982). Hampton (1982) found that abstract concepts such as a crime, a science, and a just decision show a gradient of membership falling away from a prototypical example.

The study of such concepts in the laboratory has employed logical rules that relate two defining features (Bourne, 1970). Consider a set of stimuli that vary in terms of color (red, green, or blue), shape (square, triangle, or hexagon), size (small, medium, or large), and number (one,

Table 6.1 Logical Rules Relating Two Defining Features (Red, Square)

Rule	Relation	Description
Conjunction	AND	All red and square patterns are examples
Disjunction	OR	All patterns that are red or square or both are examples
Conditional	IF, THEN	If a pattern is red then it must also be square to be an example
Biconditional	IF AND ONLY IF, THEN	Red patterns are examples if and only if they are also square

SOURCE: Adapted from Bourne (1970).

two, or three patterns). Depending on the defining features selected and the logical rule relating the defining features, the stimuli can be grouped in various ways.

For example, suppose that red and square are selected as the defining features and a **conjunctive rule** is used. Any pattern that is both red and square is a positive example of the concept. All patterns that are neither red nor square, red but not square, or square but not red are negative examples. The size of the pattern makes no difference, nor does the number of patterns; size and number are irrelevant dimensions. The conjunctive, disjunctive, conditional, and biconditional rules are shown in Table 6.1 (Bourne, 1970).

Haygood and Bourne (1965) informed people which pair of features defined the concept to be learned. They left the rule unspecified. On each trial, the participant guessed whether a pattern was a positive or a negative instance and then received feedback as to whether he or she classified it correctly. The number of trials needed to learn the rule involved varied substantially with the logical complexity of the rule. The conjunction was easiest followed by the disjunction. The conditional rule was substantially harder to learn than the disjunction. The biconditional rule was the hardest of all.

Natural concepts represent objects and events in the real world. They are characterized by a family resemblance structure in which no set of features and relations constitutes a sharp category boundary. Rosch and Mervis (1975) asked people to rapidly list all the features they could think of for a variety of common objects. The objects fit the categories of furniture (e.g., chair, piano, telephone), vehicle (e.g., car, tractor, elevator), fruit (e.g., orange, grapefruit, olive), weapon (e.g., gun, tank, screwdriver), vegetable (e.g., peas, lettuce, rice), or clothing (e.g., pants, pajamas, necklace). Twenty objects per category were used and they clearly varied in typicality, as can be seen from the examples.

The key outcome was that few attributes applied to all 20 objects. Those few that were common to all failed to distinguish the category from numerous other natural categories (e.g., "you eat it" was listed for all fruits; yet this applies to all foodstuffs). What defined the category was not a small set of defining features but a large number of features that applied to some, but not all, instances. Rosch and Mervis referred to this as the **family resemblance** structure of natural concepts.

The researchers computed a family resemblance score, which reflected the sum of the frequency with which features applied to all instances. They found that this family resemblance score correlated strongly with ratings of typicality. Thus an orange and apple achieve high typicality ratings in the fruit category, because they exhibit features that occur frequently among all members of the category. Tomato and olive are given low typicality ratings because their features are not characteristic of most fruits.

Ad hoc concepts are groupings of objects and events that satisfy some specific task requirement at hand (Barsalou, 1983; Bruner et al., 1956). For example, "things to take on a picnic" or "things for killing that huge spider in the corner" are ad hoc concepts. These are generated on the spot to meet some need. Ad hoc concepts also reveal a gradient of typicality. Bringing sandwiches on a picnic is more typical than bringing caviar. However, this gradient can shift and adapt to the specific conceptual requirements at hand (Barsalou, 1987), illustrating especially well

BOX 6.1: Defining Natural Concepts

Rosch's work on prototype theory and family resemblance overturned long-held beliefs about the nature of human categorization. From the time of Aristotle to Wittgenstein's philosophical analysis of language, categories were all regarded as rule governed. The conjunction of features held in common by all members of a category were taken as the defining features. The classical view of a concept assumed the existence of common, defining features and the presence of a clear boundary separating members from nonmembers.

Wittgenstein was the first to articulate that some linguistic categories seemed to defy the classical description by lacking defining features. For instance, take the concept of a *game*. As Lakoff (1987) observed:

> Some games involve mere amusement, like ring around the rosy. Here there is no competition—no winning or losing—though in other games there is. Some games involve luck, like board games where a throw of the dice determines each move. Others, like chess, involve skill. Still others, like gin rummy involve both. (p. 16)

Games do involve a family resemblance to one another. Each member shares some features in common with other members, but no set of defining features are common to all. Rather, what makes games a category is that the examples show similarities to one another in a wide variety of ways.

Lakoff (1987) titled his book *Women, Fire, and Dangerous Things* to illustrate the unusual categories that may be conceived by the human mind under the principle of family resemblance. An aboriginal language of Australia, Dyirbal, classifies all objects into four categories. When referring to an object, the Dyirbal speaker must use the right classifier before each noun. One of these classifiers, *Bayi,* refers to human males and to all animals. Another, *Balan,* refers to human females, water, fire, and fighting. To the Dyirbal way of viewing the world, women, fire, and dangerous things exhibit a family resemblance to one another. Women, bandicoots, dogs, some snakes, scorpions, some spears, the sun and stars, and all things connected with water and fire are grouped together through family resemblance. So too do men and nondangerous animals share a family resemblance. Men, kangaroos, most fishes, most insects, the moon, storms, and rainbows are grouped together.

the dynamic and fluid nature of schemas. Schemas change to adapt to current needs, including fashioning a new, momentary schema in an ad hoc manner.

Schema Modification and Acquisition

Frames, scripts, natural concepts, and so on are acquired and modified throughout the life span. Certainly, we come into the world with fundamental and rudimentary schemas that initiate the cycle of perception and learning discussed in Chapter 2. A long-standing philosophical debate surrounds the nature and extent of "innate ideas," and theories of cognitive development, such as Piaget's work, address the relevant issues in detail.

From the moment of birth and perhaps in utero, the human infant explores the environment, as guided by particular genetically determined schemas, and the schemas accommodate to new experiences. Piagetian theory identifies a sucking schema, for example, that immediately guides the newborn's interaction with the environment. The biological imperative for finding nourishment through nursing begins a process of exploration and accommodation. Although initially specialized for nursing, the sucking schema generalizes rapidly. As any parent knows, the infant comes to put his fingers, toys, and virtually any other object within reach into his mouth as a way of exploring it, further modifying the scheme.

Forms of Accommodation

Rumelhart and Norman (1978) differentiated three forms of modifying schemas. **Tuning** refers to slight adjustments in schemas that are made on a temporary basis to meet a transient problem. The schemas metaphorically stretch and shape themselves for a moment to accommodate to the novel situation. Tuning continually alters schemas to meet the new demands of the environment. To illustrate, suppose that as an American student you visit Australia and encounter for the first time a Tasmanian wolf, a leadbeater's possum, or perhaps a rabbit bandicoot. You would no doubt tune your schema for the wolf, the squirrel, or the rabbit familiar to North Americans. Your perception and memory of these creatures would depend on simply fine-tuning preexisting schemas.

Over long periods of time, another form of accommodation operates. **Accretion** gradually and permanently modifies a schema as new information is added through repeated explorations of the environment. Each time a schema accommodates to a novel object, event, or situation, it registers the results. Slowly, but surely, the shape and complexity of the schema modify themselves to the requirements of the environment. For example, if you moved to Australia permanently, it is likely that your schemas for wolves, squirrels, and rabbits would accommodate, through slow accretion, to the novel environment.

Finally, another permanent change in schemas is abrupt and massive, not cumulative and small. A sudden insight can prompt a major reorganization of existing knowledge structures. Rumelhart and Norman labeled this seismic process **restructuring.** Such major changes in the representations of knowledge may come about spontaneously after enough exposure to discrepant experiences, through conscious reflection on one's experience, or through active efforts to reorganize what one knows. The last case includes, of course, formal education in which teachers try to impose schemas. If one took a course in evolutionary biology, then schemas for the wolf, squirrel, and rabbit would be restructured to include two parallel branches of evolution, two paths for different continents. The leadbeater's possum, for example, evolved to fit the same ecological niche as the gray squirrel.

Hypothesis Testing Theory

The acquisition of novel schemas involves two distinct types of learning processes. One of these, **hypothesis testing,** provides the means by which the defining features of a schema are selectively isolated from among all irrelevant features. The study of this process has focused on formal concepts in which the defining features and the logical rule governing their relations may be specified. The process could also be used to identify the highly characteristic or less than perfect defining features of natural concepts and other schemas (e.g., birds have wings, feathers, and fly).

The theory holds that people actively test hypotheses about the defining features of a concept. All possible features constitute the pool of available hypotheses. The learner samples one or more of the features and then tries to classify examples of the concept based on the current hypothesis.

If feedback provided to the learner is positive, meaning the way the learner classified the examples was correct, then the current hypothesis is retained. If feedback is negative, then the hypothesis is rejected and a new hypothesis is sampled. This is termed the win-stay, lose-shift assumption. A critical feature of hypothesis theory is that learning to classify correctly can occur suddenly and dramatically. If the defining feature is hypothesized, then correct classification follows. Complete learning takes place, then, in a single classification trial.

The patterns used earlier to describe the structure of formal concepts help to illustrate the theory. Recall that the patterns varied in terms of color, shape, size, and number. Suppose that a conjunctive rule defines the concept and the defining features are red and square. In concept identification tasks, people are told the nature of the rule, but they must discover the relevant features. On each trial of the task, the experimenter presents a stimulus pattern, the learner classifies it as a positive or negative instance of the concept, and the experimenter provides feedback by indicating whether the classification was correct or wrong. According to hypothesis testing theory, the learner eventually can successfully classify all patterns correctly by selectively attending to a hypothesis, testing whether it works, and proceeding until the right hypothesis is sampled.

To study the thinking strategies that people use to test hypotheses, Bruner et al. (1956) provided the learner with all patterns and identified one positive instance. The person then selected patterns, one at a time, and received feedback as to whether each was a positive or negative instance of the concept. To illustrate, suppose the experimenter identified one small red square as a positive instance. Using a systematic and conservative strategy, the learner would start by hypothesizing all four features of the positive instance and then change only one dimension at a time so as to narrow the hypothesis.

For instance, the learner might then select one large red square, changing only the size dimension. The learner gains new information regardless of whether the feedback is positive or negative by changing only a single dimension at a time. If the feedback is positive, then the changed feature, large, can be dropped from the pool, which leaves only three remaining features. Suppose, on the other hand, the learner changes the color, selecting one large green square. In this case, the feedback would be negative, allowing the learner to infer that the color red must be one of the defining features.

Bruner et al. called the above strategy conservative focusing. Notice that it hones in on the defining features in a systematic manner. The advantage is that the learner need only retain the current hypothesis in working memory, and eventually the strategy will succeed. The disadvantage is the tedious nature of the process—a quick lucky guess would work much faster. Of interest, fewer than 20% of the participants adopted conservative focusing. Other riskier strategies were more common.

For example, in focus gambling, the learner again hypothesizes all four features of the first positive instance but then changes two or more dimensions of the next selected pattern. If the feedback is positive, the learner quickly identifies the defining features. Negative feedback, on the other hand, provides little useful information: Which of the several dimensions changed caused the negative feedback? Another risky strategy, scanning, involved hypothesizing only two features. Through sheer luck the learner might select the correct pair. More probably the learner had to repeatedly try out various pairs over the course of many trials and at best store in working memory all the pairs that had already been tried unsuccessfully.

In another variant of the concept identification task, the experimenter selects the stimulus patterns to be shown to the learner. Levine (1966, 1975) devised a way to track the size of the hypothesis pool as learning proceeded. In a series of elegant experiments, Levine contrasted theoretical predictions about how learners modified the size of the hypothesis pool from trial to trial. In these experiments, the patterns varied on four binary dimensions: color (black or white), shape (X or T), size (small or large), and position (left or right). The concept to be learned was defined by the presence of only a single feature, for example, large. Levine arranged a series of trials with feedback that allowed the logical deduction of the identifying feature. On each feedback trial, two patterns are shown, the learner guesses which one is the positive instance, and then the experimenter provides feedback. The pairs are chosen by the experimenter so that the pool decreases from eight to four features after trial 1, from four to two after trial 2, and from two to one after trial 3.

Using a special procedure with blank or no feedback trials, Levine monitored the hypothesis currently in use by the learner. According to a **global focusing strategy**, the learner must process the feedback trials correctly and reduce the hypothesis pool by half on each trial. The predicted outcome is shown in Figure 6.2. In this task, global focusing implies that the learner can remember perfectly which of the hypotheses are still viable or in the pool and which have been rejected. At the opposite extreme, **sampling with replacement** assumes that the learner stores nothing in working memory from the feedback trials. That is, if the learner hypothesized the feature to be large on trial one and the feedback showed it was wrong, it entered right back into the hypothesis pool and could be randomly hypothesized again on the next trial. Only by guessing the correct hypothesis and staying with it if it leads to correct feedback

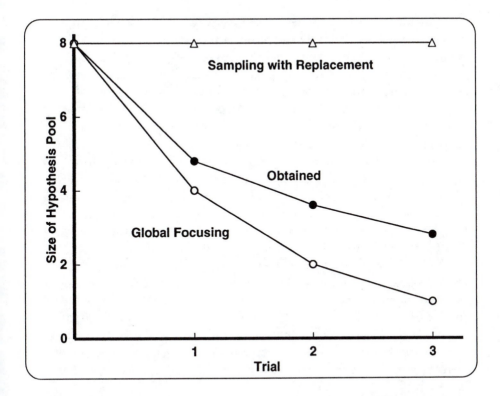

Figure 6.2. The size of the hypothesis pool expected with a global focusing strategy in concept identification.
SOURCE: From Levine, M. (1966). Hypothesis behavior by humans during discrimination learning. *Journal of Experimental Psychology, 71,* 331-338. Copyright © 1966 by the American Psychological Association. Reprinted by permission.

can the learner succeed. The actual estimate of the hypothesis pool decreased over the three trials, as shown in Figure 6.2. Certainly the learner processed the feedback and stored with some but not perfect accuracy a record of still viable hypotheses.

Automatic Learning

Concept identification. Hypothesis testing is an active, controlled process that demands selective attention to stimulus features and the resources of working memory. It has long been recognized that another unconscious, automatic process also may play a role in schema acquisition. Study of this alternative mode of learning dates back to Hull (1920), who investigated how people could learn to associate a particular nonsense syllable response to a category of Chinese characters. A particular feature of the characters, called a radical, defined each category of characters. The radical was a stroke that appeared in each of the category members; it was the only stroke common to all the members. The other strokes in the characters were irrelevant features. The learner received multiple lists of the Chinese characters paired with the name. They tried to learn the correct name for each character presented. Hull found that performance improved from list to list, increasing from only about 30% correct on list 1 to about 60% correct on list 6.

The interesting outcome in Hull's experiments was that the learners could not consciously identify and verbalize the defining feature, the radical. Rather, they found it easier to learn the correct nonsense syllable on later lists but did not know why. Hull interpreted his findings in terms of an unconscious buildup of associative strength of all the features of the Chinese characters and the nonsense syllables with which they were paired. Over the lists, the strength of the relevant feature would increase because it consistently occurred on every list. The irrelevant features occurred less frequently across lists, resulting in less associative strength.

Bourne and Restle (1959) refined associative strength theory to include a buildup of strength for the defining feature and a decline in strength of irrelevant features. Their mathematical model provided a detailed account of some of the basic findings regarding the concept identification task. For example, the number of errors made increased as more irrelevant dimensions were added. Moreover, feature frequency or strength information can accurately account for the order of difficulty of learning conjunctive, disjunctive, conditional, and biconditional rules (Bourne et al., 1976).

As discussed in Chapter 3, human beings from a very early age can compile the frequency of occurrence of environmental features and events without intention or cognitive effort (Hasher & Zacks, 1979, 1984). Associative strength may build up through a process of frequency compilation, even though the counting process is by no means perfectly accurate. As long as one attentively encodes an object, perceiving it consciously, a record of the past frequency of the object and its features may be updated.

Numerous experiments have followed in the path of Hull's pioneering work to show that people can learn schemas in the apparent absence or failure of active hypothesis testing. For example, one set of experiments directly probed working memory for retention of the hypothesis used on the previous trial in a concept identification task (Kellogg, Robbins, & Bourne, 1978). Noticeably, recognition of the hypothesis provided by the learner on the immediately preceding trial was poor, contrary to the predictions of hypothesis testing theory. Recognition of the exact features of the stimulus also was poor. Despite the poor hypothesis memory and stimulus memory, the participants learned to classify the patterns without error. One explanation of these results is that the learners automatically compiled feature frequency information. Because of the many demands placed on working memory in the task, hypothesis testing apparently failed as a useful strategy.

Implicit learning. In a similar vein, hypothesis testing appears not to underlie the learning of very complex rules. This is referred to in the literature as implicit learning (Seger, 1994). Unlike the concept identification task, implicit learning tasks involve many stimulus features that are related in highly complex ways. For example, researchers have studied the acquisition of artificial grammars (e.g., Knowlton, Ramus, & Squire, 1992; Reber, 1989; Reber & Allen, 1978). Participants study a set of letter strings that conform to detailed rules governing which letters are permitted to follow which other letters. Strings that violate the rules are noninstances or ungrammatical strings.

Here are grammatical strings taken from a set of rules used by Knowlton et al.: BFZBZ, LBF, LLBL, BZB. One rule allowed an F to follow a B and another specified that a Z could follow a B. However, the Z could follow B only if the B had been preceded by another Z or an L. Thus FBZ was an ungrammatical string. There were several other such rules, meaning there were many types of ungrammatical strings, including BB, ZZB, and LFZBZF. As you can imagine, it would be challenging to try to identify all the rules involved by means of hypothesis testing. Yet, after studying a couple dozen examples, people can distinguish grammatical from ungrammatical strings at well above chance levels and are unable to verbalize the rules of the grammar. It appears that they have implicitly learned the rules by adopting a passive, unconscious mode of acquisition.

Alternative explanations have been proposed and tested with some success. One straightforward explanation is that the learners successfully tested hypotheses that allowed them to identify some, though not all, of the rules. With an incomplete, but adequate, set of hypothesized rules, the participants may have been able to discriminate between grammatical and ungrammatical strings at better than chance levels (Dulany, Carlson, & Dewey, 1984; Perruchet & Pacteau, 1990). One difficulty with this explanation is that learners instructed to test hypotheses actually show poorer classification performance than those not so instructed (Reber & Allen, 1978; Reber, Kassin, Lewis, & Cantor, 1980).

Another explanation is that participants compared test strings with a specific grammatical string, one of those initially studied. They may have classified test strings by analogy with specific examples rather than implicitly acquiring the complex rule system (Hintzman, 1986; Medin & Schaffer, 1978). One argument against this alternative is that amnesic patients perform as well as normal individuals in learning to distinguish grammatical and ungrammatical strings. Yet, the amnesic patients could not store and recognize the specific examples presented to them for study (Knowlton et al., 1992).

Moreover, other studies have continued to accumulate that show what seems to be learning without conscious awareness and without testing of hypotheses using other kinds of rules and tests (Curran & Keele, 1993; Lewicki, Czyzewska, & Hoffman, 1987; Stadler, 1993). The debate over whether implicit learning entails automatic processes is far from settled (Nissen & Bullemer, 1987; Seger, 1994). Even if implicit learning is automatic, it is unclear whether the specific process involves the compilation of frequency information or a more complex operation. However, the studies reviewed here on concept identification as well as implicit learning suggest that two modes of schema acquisition ought to be distinguished. One mode relies on conscious, controlled hypothesis testing, while the other is automatic and unconscious (Hayes & Broadbent, 1988).

Representational Codes

Earlier we discussed evidence that short-term memory, as the activated subset of long-term memory, involves sensory codes as well as semantic codes. This implies that the schemas of semantic memory and the representations of specific events in episodic memory also involve both kinds of codes. Paivio (1971) theorized that long-term memory representations include both images and verbal symbols. The dual code view is now generally accepted. But identifying precisely how visual and auditory imagery is represented by the brain has been an ongoing and difficult challenge to scholars (Kolers, 1983).

On the one hand, Pylyshyn (1973, 1981) and others have argued that all visual images, for example, are not really pictures in the mind's eye at all. Rather, they are generated by abstract or verbal symbols known as propositions. The experience of an image is different than the deep psychological processes giving rise to the image, in Pylyshyn's view. The processes operate in the realm of propositions, but these are cognitively impenetrable. We do not have conscious access to them.

On the other hand, Kosslyn and Pomerantz (1977) and Finke (1980) argued for the reality of mental images. Such images presumably are independent of propositional representations and manipulable through psychological processes in their own right. The key distinction is that images possess a spatial or analog quality that cannot in principle be explained in terms of an abstract, propositional, or verbal representation. Thus these researchers reaffirmed Paivio's original proposal that long-term memory includes both images and verbal representations.

The essential point for our purposes is to grasp the distinction between propositional and imaginal representations. Anderson (1978) argued that Pylyshyn's claim could not be decided without neurological evidence. Without looking into the neurophysiology of the brain, how could one determine whether images were in fact reducible to propositions? Some evidence based on cerebral blood flow and EEG studies in fact shows that brain activity during imagery is localized in the areas known to be used in vision (Farah, 1988). In any case, we will examine the respective natures of propositions and images, going on the assumption that we need to understand both as important forms of mental representation.

The Nature of Propositions

As we will see later in this chapter and in the chapter on language, verbal knowledge is coded in terms of abstract representations called propositions. A **proposition** refers to the smallest unit of knowledge that one can sensibly judge as true or false. "Fred is tall" is a proposition; "tall" or "is tall" are not. A proposition is an assertion that may be understood and evaluated. It is an abstract representation of the meaning conveyed by language, by all words, phrases, sentences, paragraphs, and whole speeches and documents.

One way to show the elements of a proposition is in a list format (Kintsch, 1974). The list begins with a **relation** followed by a set of **arguments.** Verbs, adjectives, and other phrases that convey a relationship are listed first. The arguments follow in a specified order; they define the agent of an action (e.g., Who does X?), the object of the action (Does X to what?), the time of the action, and other elements of a meaningful assertion. To illustrate, consider a few of the sentences like those that Bransford and Franks (1971) presented to participants in their memory experiment. The propositional lists needed to express the smallest units of meaning follow each sentence.

1. The jelly was sweet.
   (Sweet, Jelly, Past)

2. The ants in the kitchen ate the jelly.
   (Eat, Ants, Jelly, Past)
   (In, Ants, Kitchen, Past)

3. The ants ate the sweet jelly which was on the table.
   (Sweet, Jelly, Past)
   (Eat, Ants, Jelly, Past)
   (In, Ants, Kitchen, Past)
   (On, Jelly, Table, Past)

Propositions provide, then, an abstract and elemental representation of the meaning of verbal information. They provide the mental code for language, judging from a voluminous body of research (e.g., Kintsch, 1974). The outcome of Bransford and Franks's study illustrates this point well. Recall from the previous chapter that they tested recognition memory for sentences of the type seen above. Their recognition test included actual old sentences (The ants in the kitchen ate the jelly), new sentences that included novel propositions (The ants ate the jelly beside the woods), and new sentences comprising propositions previously used in related sentences (The ants ate the sweet jelly).

They found that people correctly rejected the new sentences with novel propositions (noncases). But new sentences with familiar propositions were falsely recognized as readily as actual old sentences were correctly recognized. In fact, if the new sentence contained all the familiar propositions (The ants in the kitchen ate the sweet jelly which was on the table), then virtually all participants falsely believed they had seen it before. It represented the prototype, comprising the frequently occurring propositions.

The Nature of Images

Shepard and his colleagues pioneered the study of visual images with an extensive series of experiments on mental rotation (Metzler & Shepard, 1974; Shepard & Cooper, 1983; Shepard & Metzler, 1971). The researchers presented people with pictures of three-dimensional objects such as those shown in Figure 6.3. They presented a pair of objects and asked the viewers to decide whether the objects were identical, except for their orientation.

For example, the first pair in Panel A are the same, with the object on the right rotated 80 degrees in the plane of the picture. Verify this by mentally rotating the object on the left and matching it to the one on the right. Now compare the objects in Panels B and C, deciding whether they are the same or different. In Panel B, the objects are again identical, but this time you must rotate the object on the left 80 degrees in depth, rotating into the page. In Panel C, the object on the left cannot be rotated so that it looks the same as the one on the right. They are different objects.

Shepard and his colleagues systematically varied the angle of rotation required to determine that the pair of objects is the same. They also tested rotations in the picture and depth planes. If mental images are like real objects in the mind's eye, then, they reasoned, the time required to make a same-different decision ought to increase as a linear function of the angle of rotation. If instead the decision is based on a propositional representation of the objects, a rotation of 180 degrees should be no slower than one of 80 or even 10 degrees. In each case, the degrees of rotation would simply be a variable in one of the propositional arguments (e.g., left object, clockwise rotation, picture plane, 180). In addition, the researchers argued that picture-plane and depth rotations should take equal amounts of time, if in fact the mental image were represented as three dimensional in the mind's eye. Just like an object in the real world, it could be rotated just as readily in either plane.

Their results are presented in Figure 6.4 (from Shepard & Metzler, 1971). Plainly, decision times increased as a linear function of the angle of rotation. The function in Panel A is for objects rotated in the picture

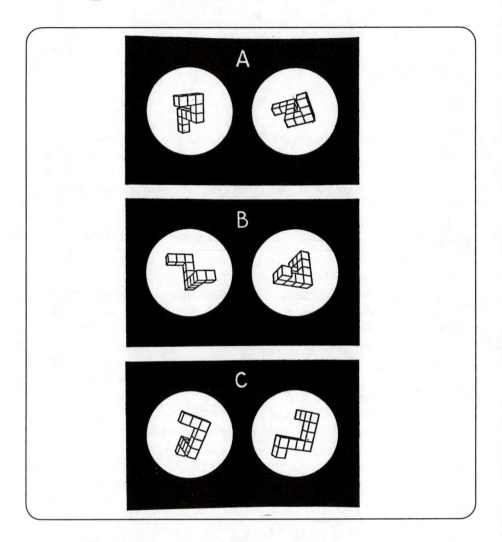

Figure 6.3. Try to rotate mentally the left object of each pair so that it matches the right object.

SOURCE: Reprinted with permission from Shepard, R. N., & Metzler, J. (1971). Mental rotation of three-dimensional objects. *Science, 171,* 701-703. Copyright © 1971 by the American Association for the Advancement of Science.

plane, whereas the one in Panel B is for depth rotations. As you can see, the linear functions are virtually identical. Thus there is a striking resemblance between rotating a real object and rotating a mental representation

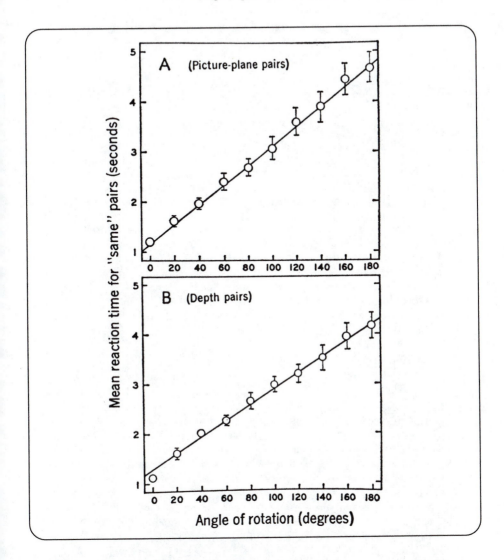

Figure 6.4. Mental rotation time increases with the degrees of rotation required to judge the objects as the same. Results for pairs involving rotation in the picture plane (A) and in the depth plane (B).

SOURCE: Reprinted with permission from Shepard, R. N., & Metzler, J. (1971). Mental rotation of three-dimensional objects. *Science, 171,* 701-703. Copyright © 1971 by the American Association for the Advancement of Science.

of that object. Shepard and Chipman (1970) called this a **second-order isomorphism.** Although an image is not identical to an object (first-order

BOX 6.2: Mental Maps

One common use of imagery is to construct spatial mental models. As Tversky (1991) explained:

> There are many simple, everyday tasks, such as following road directions, using instructions to assemble a bicycle, reading a novel, or helping to solve your child's geometry homework, that seem to entail constructing a spatial mental model from a description. In order to comprehend *Go straight till the first light, then turn left, go down about three blocks to Oak, and make a right* it is useful to have a spatial representation. (p. 109)

The spatial mental models we construct reveal our beliefs about our environments. Which city is farther west, San Diego, California, or Reno, Nevada? Which city is further north, Rome or Philadelphia? The mental map that most people generate places San Diego further west (Stevens & Coupe, 1978). After all, California is west of Nevada, so surely San Diego must be further west. In turns out not to be. Similarly, most people regard Philadelphia as further north than Rome (Tversky, 1981). The opposite is actually the case. (You may wish to check a map or globe at this point.)

The distortions in our mental maps reflect our beliefs about how the world is organized. Tversky (1981) argued that we simplify these beliefs and associated images by using two heuristics, or rules of thumb. One is the alignment heuristic. The odd shapes of the United States and Europe are difficult to image exactly. So we tend to align their shapes at the same latitude. Doing so would definitely place Rome at a southern location relative to Philadelphia. But in reality, Europe lies at a more northern latitude relative to the United States.

We also use a rotation heuristic, according to Tversky. This suggests that states or countries that are tilted in reality are visualized as more vertical than they really are. They are rotated to the perpendicular in other words. This explains the San Diego error. California is imaged in the mind's eye as more or less vertical, forming the western boundary of much of the United States. In fact, California is rotated such that San Diego lies much further east than most people realize. Reno, sitting on the border of California and Nevada, actually lies slightly west of San Diego. Because of the rotation heuristic, we conceive mental maps at odds with this reality.

isomorphism), the images behave in the same fashion as objects. The images act as analogues of the real objects.

Kosslyn and his colleagues explored the analog aspect of mental imagery in detail (Kosslyn, 1973, 1975, 1980, 1981). For example, Kosslyn

(1973) showed that the time to scan a mental image depended on "how far" one must scan. Participants memorized a picture of an object, such as a speedboat, and then visualized it. They looked at the stern, or rear, of the boat in their imagination and then answered a question about the memorized image (e.g., "Does the boat have a porthole?" or "Does the boat have a flag on the front?"). The flag question took longer to answer than the porthole question, because a greater scanning distance was required (all the way to the front of the boat).

If images are analogous to real objects, then it stands to reason that a small image ought to be harder to see clearly than a large image. Kosslyn (1975) instructed people to imagine a target animal, such as a rabbit, next to a small (a fly) or a large (an elephant) animal. Try this yourself. Most people report visualizing a very small image for a rabbit when next to an elephant, and a much larger image of a rabbit next to a fly. When then asked to search for a property of the target (the rabbit's ears), people take about 200 milliseconds longer when looking at the small image compared with the large image. Because the image is an analogue of the real rabbit, a small image is harder to see clearly ("Now where are those ears . . . ?").

Using Semantic Memory

In this final section, we study alternative models of how people retrieve factual and conceptual knowledge to answer simple questions. As explained in the previous section, we have good reason to believe that schemas in some fashion represent both propositional and imaginal codes in long-term memory. Theorists have devoted much effort to understanding the way in which the propositional codes are organized. The studies bearing on this issue serve to integrate a number of theoretical concepts advanced in this chapter and earlier in the book. Also, the experiments designed to test these ideas illustrate especially well the manner in which the careful design of materials and tasks can yield significant insights into human cognition.

Network Theories

A propositional code for semantic memory can be easily presented as a network of relations. Figure 6.5 illustrates a small portion of what you know about the natural concept of animals, with level 0 representing the subordinate, level 1 the basic, and level 2 the superordinate level.

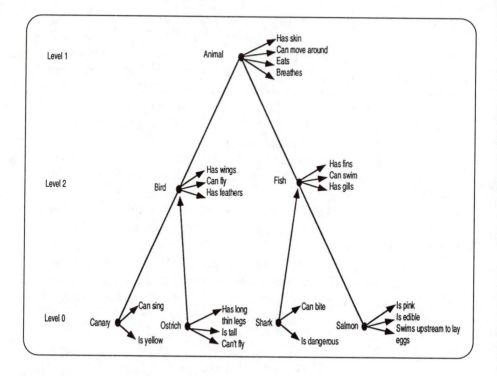

Figure 6.5. A hierarchical network theory of semantic memory.
SOURCE: From Collins and Quillian (1969). Copyright © 1969 by Academic Press, Inc.
Reprinted by permission.

Collins and Quillian (1969) proposed that retrieving information from
this network involves working through the various levels as demanded
by the task. For example, to verify that a canary can sing involves entering
the network at level 0 and searching the propositions attached to the
canary node. But to verify that a canary can fly requires moving through
the network to level 1. Still more mental travel time is required to answer
that a canary has skin, for this property applies to all animals, a superordinate or level 2 property.

Notice that this hierarchical representation of properties saves space
in long-term memory. It is not necessary, theoretically, to store that a
canary can fly and has skin, because these facts can be deduced from the
hierarchical structure of memory. Collins and Quillian referred to this as
the **cognitive economy assumption.** Though it may take more time to
use semantic memory organized in this manner, less storage space is re-

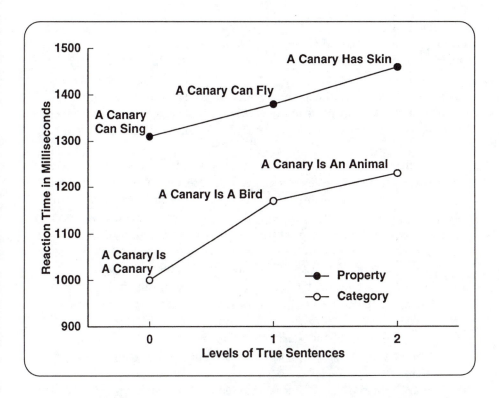

Figure 6.6. Time required to categorize a noun and to verify its properties.
SOURCE: From Collins and Quillian (1969). Copyright © 1969 by Academic Press, Inc.
Reprinted by permission.

quired than if properties were stored redundantly at all levels of the network.

Collins and Quillian examined how quickly people verified both
property questions, of the sort discussed above, and category questions
(see Figure 6.6). Notice that, as predicted, the time needed to answer
property questions increased as a function of property level. In addition,
verifying that a canary is a canary (an identity class judgment) is faster
than verifying that a canary is a bird (a basic-level categorization). The
most time was needed to verify membership in a superordinate category,
a canary is an animal. Note that almost a tenth of second is needed to
move from one level to another in answering the category questions. Also
note that searching the properties associated with a particular level of
category requires about 200 milliseconds more.

Subsequent research muddied the waters, however. To begin, Rips, Shoben, and Smith (1973) reported that the hierarchical structure of the network was not consistent. If it were, then one should verify that a "collie is a mammal" faster than a "collie is an animal." The class of mammals is a subset of all animals; therefore, strictly speaking, it ought to be searched faster than the superordinate class. The results did not show this, suggesting that people did not represent clearly a strict hierarchy of class relations.

Further, the assumption of cognitive economy also encountered problems. The associative strength or frequency with which a property occurred proved more important than the level of hierarchy. Conrad (1972) reported that strong associations (e.g., An orange is edible) can be quickly answered even though the property "edible" ought to require moving to a higher level in the network. Moreover, Conrad failed to find differences where Collins and Quillian expected them. For instance, the verification time remained the same for these types of statements: A shark can move, a fish can move, and an animal can move. In other words, if one selects a high-level property, theoretically it should take more time to move back down the network to the fish and animal levels (the reverse direction of the Collins and Quillian experiment). The results indicated no difference.

Finally, the typicality effect discussed earlier finds no place in a network model. Why should it be faster to verify that a robin is a bird relative to a canary? Obviously, the network model proposed by Collins and Quillian failed to capture the necessary phenomena. However, the network approach to modeling semantic memory has definite advantages (Collins & Loftus, 1975). Particularly as connectionist or neural networks have grown in popularity, network models have proliferated. Another line of research, using a feature list approach, resulted in answers to some of the basic problems with the Collins and Quillian model.

The Feature-Comparison Model

Smith, Shoben, and Rips (1974) borrowed from the literature on pattern recognition in formulating their model of how people query semantic memory. They assumed that every concept or schema included two types of information. **Characteristic features** referred to those that applied to most but not all instances. Birds characteristically are small and fly, but counterexamples are not difficult to find (e.g., the ostrich or the

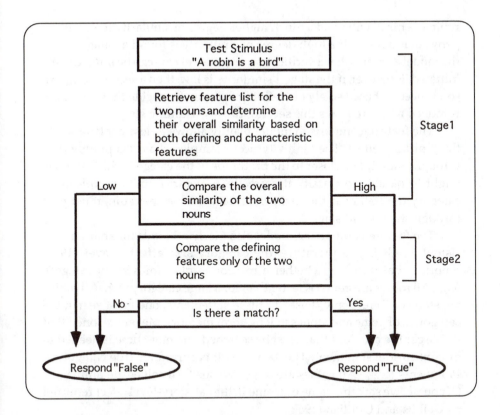

Figure 6.7. The feature-comparison model of categorization.

SOURCE: From Smith, E. E., Shoben, E. J., & Rips, L. J. (1974). Structure and process in semantic memory: A featural model for semantic decisions. *Psychological Review, 81,* 214-241. Copyright © 1974 by the American Psychological Association. Reprinted by permission.

penguin). **Defining features** refers to those that theoretically applied to all instances. For example, all birds live and have feathers. These define the category, though, as noted earlier, it is difficult to enumerate a list of truly defining features for natural concepts, features that apply entirely and uniquely to the class.

The model for retrieving information from semantic memory, based on a comparison of features, is shown in Figure 6.7. In stage 1 of the comparisons, one determines the degree of similarity between the subject and predicate of the sentence or proposition. At stage 1, both defining and characteristic features are taken into account. Thus the sentence "A robin is a bird" will yield a much higher degree of similarity than will "A penguin is a bird." If a high degree of similarity is found at stage 1, then the model assumes that a verification response of true can be immediately initiated. However, if the stage 1 similarity is low, then a second comparison is needed based solely on defining features. To decide that a penguin is indeed a bird requires this second, time-consuming stage.

The feature-comparison model plainly allows a clear explanation of the typicality effect. The highly typical examples of a concept only pass through stage 1. The closer to the prototype of the category, the faster one ought to be able to classify it correctly. In contrast, the examples of a category that fall near the fuzzy boundary, such as penguin, must pass through stage 1 and stage 2.

The feature-comparison model also nicely accounts for another consistent result in the literature, the **category size effect.** Meyer (1970) reported that deciding whether a relation applies for a small category (e.g., All robins are gems) is faster than for a large category (e.g., All robins are stones). To respond "false" to these statements, one must search the categories of gems and stones in long-term memory. Meyer reasoned that the larger the category that must be searched, the more time is needed to disconfirm the statement. The same result occurred for true categorical statements (e.g., "All collies are dogs" versus "All collies are animals"). Of course, we saw this same outcome in the category-level effect reported by Collins and Quillian (1969).

The feature-comparison model explains the category size effect by noting that stage 2 processing would be needed only for large categories. For instance, to decide that a robin is a bird, the initial comparison of all features would yield a high degree of similarity. An immediate true response would be possible. Yet, to decide that a robin is an animal would demand the extra step of comparing defining features alone. Perhaps the unusual violation of the category size effect noted earlier might stem from featural similarity. Recall that people can judge "A dog is an animal" faster than "A dog is a mammal." The overall similarity of dog and animal might be quite high, leading to an immediate response after stage 1 processing. Because the term *mammal* is less familiar to most people than *animal*, a second stage of processing the defining features may be needed.

In sum, the feature-comparison model accounts for most of the major results in the literature on semantic memory. However, it too has problems (Chang, 1986). One empirical problem is that false statements involving concepts that are highly similar ought to require stage 2 pro-

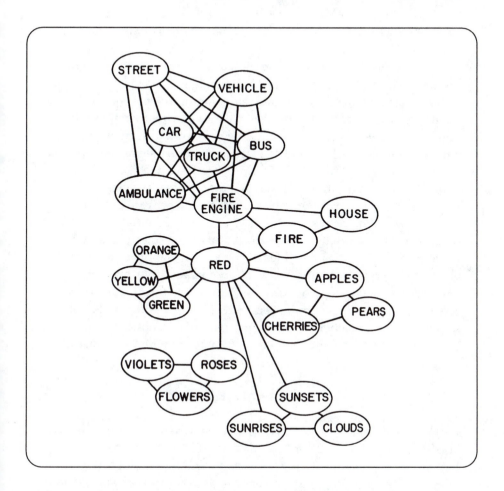

Figure 6.8. A revised network model of semantic memory with spreading activation among nodes.

SOURCE: From Collins, A. M., & Loftus, E. F. (1975). A spreading activation theory of semantic processing. *Psychological Review, 82,* 407-428. Copyright © 1975 by the American Psychological Association. Reprinted by permission.

cessing, thus taking extra time to answer. For example, "All dogs are cats" should take more time to disconfirm than "All animals are birds." The latter statement should be disconfirmed after stage 1 only. Yet, Glass and Holyoak (1975) found that the highly similar concepts, such as dogs and cats, are disconfirmed fastest. Another problem lies in the assumption that defining features can be listed. As seen earlier, natural concepts and most other schemas are best thought of in terms of a family resemblance structure.

Finally, network models have the virtue of being readily simulated on computers. Collins and Loftus (1975) substantially revised the original Collins and Quillian network model, abandoning assumptions that could not be verified but retaining the essential idea of network representation. Figure 6.8 shows a small segment of their network of semantic memory. Note that two concepts are linked extensively if they share many properties in common. Collins and Loftus proposed that when a node is activated, the activation spreads to surrounding nodes. The closer together two nodes are in the network, the more they will activate each other.

The spreading-activation theory of Collins and Loftus does not lend itself to rigorous predictions as do the other theories discussed here (Chang, 1986). Yet, their core idea of semantic memory as a richly interconnected network in which activation spreads from one concept to another is widely adopted today. As will be seen in the next chapter, researchers attempting to build comprehensive computer models of cognition turned to network representations of semantic memory and spreading activation (Anderson, 1983; Rumelhart & McClelland, 1986).

▣ SUMMARY ▣

1. A schema is a dynamic mental representation of what one knows about objects, events, and ideas. The schema treats objects that differ as the same, if they fall within the boundary of the schema. The membership boundary of schema are often fuzzy and flexible. The schema also specifies the dimensions along which members differ from one another and orders the members in terms of typicality. The prototype represents the best example of a given schema. A schema is also coherent in the sense that it relates in a deep theoretical manner to other schemas, other representations of world knowledge.

2. The types of schemas include frames, scripts, and equivalence classes or concepts. Frames represent the physical environment, such as a room. Scripts represent routine situations, often social in nature and typically involving a sequence of events (e.g., the restaurant script). There are three major subtypes of concepts. Formal concepts specify a fixed membership boundary based on a set of defining features and a logical rule relating these features (e.g., the legal defi-

nition of grand larceny). Natural concepts, in contrast, exhibit a family resemblance structure in which characteristic features vary in their frequency of occurrence, but no one of which defines the concept. Ad hoc or functional concepts are generated in response to the needs of the moment (e.g., things to take on a picnic).

3. New schemas are learned and modified through exploration of the environment and accommodation of preexisting schemas. *Tuning* refers to fine adjustments, *accretion* refers to slow cumulative modifications in the structures of schemas, and *restructuring* refers to sudden major modifications in schemas. Learning processes include active hypothesis testing, which is used to identify the defining features of concepts and other schemas. Strategies for testing hypotheses typically place demands on attention and working memory. Automatic processes of learning also play a role, as seen in studies of concept identification and the implicit learning of complex rules.

4. Schemas code our knowledge of factual and conceptual information by means of abstract propositions. A proposition is the smallest unit of knowledge that can stand on its own, that is, can be judged sensibly as true or false. In addition, schemas may code perceptual properties in an analog format as an image. The image behaves in much the same manner as the object it represents, displaying second-degree isomorphism. For example, the time needed to rotate a mental image increases linearly with the angle of rotation, just as the time needed to rotate the object itself.

5. Two of the major models of how we retrieve information from semantic memory were presented. Network theory assumes that knowledge is represented hierarchically and that features connected at a superordinate level are not redundantly represented at lower levels. Retrieving a fact involves working through the various levels of the network and searching the relevant nodes for feature information. Feature-comparison theory assumes that each concept or schema includes a list of characteristic and defining features. Retrieving a fact first involves a comparison of overall similarity based on both feature types. If similarity is low, then a second stage of comparison is needed based on defining features only. The feature-comparison model best handles experimental results; however, contemporary thinking about semantic memory assumes a richly interconnected network of schemas in which activation spreads from one schema to related schemas.

Key Terms

typicality effect

frames

scripts

identity categories

equivalence categories

rule-governed concepts

conjunctive rule

natural concepts

family resemblance

ad hoc concepts

tuning

accretion

restructuring

hypothesis testing

global focusing strategy

sampling with replacement

proposition

relation

arguments

second-order isomorphism

cognitive economy
   assumption

characteristic features

defining features

category size effect

Recommended Readings

Rosch and Lloyd (1978) covered ideas of family resemblance and ill-defined concepts in their *Cognition and Categorization*. Keil (1989) addresses the nature of natural concepts in a developmental context in *Concepts, Kinds, and Cognitive Development*. I also recommend *Categories and Concepts* by Smith and Medin (1981) as well as Medin and Smith's 1984 chapter in the *Annual Review of Psychology*. More recently, Oden (1987) examined the relations among concepts, knowledge, and thought in the *Annual Review of Psychology*. Also, Komatsu's (1992) article on conceptual structures in the *Psychological Bulletin* offers an excellent review.

Levine's (1975) *A Cognitive Theory of Learning* is a classic treatment of learning processes in concept identification. Bruner, Goodnow, and Austin's (1956) *A Study of Thinking* is still worth reading not only for its insights into concept learning but for its historical significance. It marked the beginnings of the cognitive revolution in the 1950s. Unconscious learning is well covered in Reber's (1993) *Implicit Learning and Tacit Knowledge: An Essay on the Cognitive Unconscious*. For a developmental account of concept learning, I recommend Wellman and Gelman's (1992) chapter in the *Annual Review of Psychology*.

An excellent book on the nature of mental imagery is Kosslyn's (1983) *Ghosts in the Mind's Machine*. Pinker's (1985) book titled *Visual Cog-*

nition is another valuable source. Kolers's (1983) chapter in the *Annual Review of Psychology* provides a useful perspective on the imagery versus proposition debate.

Smith's (1978) chapter in the *Handbook of Learning and Cognitive Processes* provides an overview of the theories of semantic memory. Tulving (1972) specified the difference between semantic and episodic memory in a book titled the *Organization of Memory*. Kintsch (1980) also comprehensively reviewed the field of semantic memory in his chapter of *Attention and Performance VIII*.

CHAPTER 7

◉ Expertise

We complete our discussion of learning and memory with a consideration of expertise and computer models of skilled performance. Cognitive psychologists have turned to comparisons of novices versus experts as a way to shed light on several fundamental issues. As a person learns more and becomes more skillful within a particular domain of knowledge, the structure and processes of memory are altered and refined. By studying an expert, new insights are gained into the nature of automaticity, chunking, reconstructive retrieval, and other issues introduced in earlier chapters. Moreover, the study of expertise offers insights into an important area of applied psychology. After all, one goal of education and training is to produce experts who can perform at high levels of proficiency. Cognitive research has shed light on the characteristics of expert performance, a subject of interest to virtually all organizations and sectors of the economy.

We will begin with an overview of the characteristics of expert performance and learning. The next section will provide a close-up look at expertise in two different domains: memory and problem solving. Each of these domains has been the focus of extensive cognitive research. Not only will you come away with concrete illustrations of the principles raised in the opening section, you may also gain insight into improving your own memory and problem-solving abilities. In the final section, we will consider computer models of human expertise. Some of the systems developed by computer scientists and cognitive psychologists serve as aids to human beings in reasoning and decision making. Others simulate human thinking processes to advance our theoretical understanding of expertise.

Characteristics of Expertise

The Mnemonic Encoding Principle

The study of chess masters launched our modern understanding of cognitive expertise (Chase & Simon, 1973; de Groot, 1965). Through years of practice and study, skilled chess players develop extensive schemas related to the game. Simon and his colleagues have estimated that a chess master must store about 50,000 facts regarding specific patterns of pieces and the actions to take when faced with these patterns (Newell & Simon, 1972; Simon & Gilmartin, 1973).

With the exception of the degree of knowledge about the specific domain of chess, the experts were no different than the less experienced players (de Groot, 1965). Their general memory and other intellectual skills failed to differ at all. Even more intriguing, the experts considered slightly fewer moves than the novices. The exceptional performance of the grand master did not derive from his being able to ponder a large number of moves in a very rapid manner. There was one striking difference, however.

When presented for 5 seconds with valid chess positions, pieces arranged in a manner that makes sense in terms of established strategies for winning the game, the master player could recall and reproduce the position readily. Whereas the novice could reproduce only fewer than five pieces, the master could manage more than twenty. The master succeeded by chunking the positions into meaningful clusters of four or five pieces. The chunking process, as we have seen, overcomes the limitation of short-term memory.

The reason the expert, but not the novice, could chunk the positions so effectively stemmed from his chess knowledge. Schemas in long-term memory, specific to the domain of chess, guided the chunking process. When the pieces were arranged haphazardly in ways inconsistent with the expert's schemas, the expert as well as the novice remembered only four or five pieces. The **principle of mnemonic encoding** refers to using the organization of long-term memory to guide the encoding of information into meaningful chunks (Chase & Ericsson, 1982).

Charness (1976) compared master and novice players in a Brown-Peterson short-term task. When using the standard letter trigrams as stimuli, both groups showed the typical forgetting function discussed earlier over a 30-second period in which rehearsal was prevented. Yet, when using meaningful chess positions, the experts showed no loss over the interval. The phenomenon that experts easily retain meaningful chunks is not unique to chess. Other research has extended this basic finding in other domains, including other games (Charness, 1979; Reitman, 1976), computer programming (Schneiderman, 1976), and electronic circuit diagrams (Egan & Schwartz, 1979).

The superior performance of experts in a domain is no doubt linked to their ability to perceive and think in terms of meaningful chunks. For instance, in pondering the next move in chess, the expert can retrieve a move consistent with the particular tactics and strategy adopted from the start. The expert need not evaluate a large number of moves, because most alternatives make no sense under the plan being pursued. The novice, in contrast, cannot draw on such tactics and strategy for lack of the necessary schemas. The novice considers about the same number of alternatives, within the limits of working memory, but the specific moves evaluated may well be nonsensical.

Principle of Retrieval Structure

As we will examine more closely later, studies of memory experts have yielded significant insights into the nature of expertise in general. Specifically, these studies have shown that effective retrieval of domain knowledge is every bit as important as effective organization during encoding. The **principle of retrieval structure** refers to the highly specialized means used by experts to gain access to what they know (Chase & Ericsson, 1982). The development of retrieval structures also allows experts to anticipate what they need to remember and to encode the relevant information in a format that ensures later retrieval.

Chase and Ericsson (1981, 1982) trained an undergraduate with average intelligence and memory to excel on the digit span test. The training consisted of massive practice, about an hour a day, 2 to 5 days a week for a duration of 2 years. The student (SF) began with a typical memory span

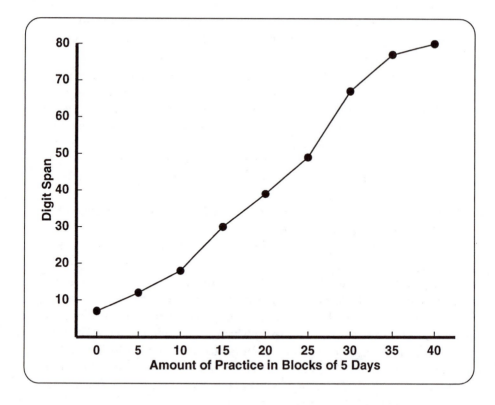

Figure 7.1. Mnemonic practice greatly increases memory span for SF. Each day in the 5-day block corresponds to an hour of practice. The 43 blocks shown here correspond to about 215 hours of practice.

SOURCE: From Chase, W. G., & Ericsson, K. A. (1981). Skilled memory. In J. R. Anderson (Ed.), *Cognitive skills and their acquisition* (pp. 141-189). Hillsdale, NJ: Lawrence Erlbaum. Copyright © 1981 by Lawrence Erlbaum Associates. Reprinted by permission.

of seven digits. As shown in Figure 7.1, after about 215 hours of practice, his memory span rose to a remarkable 80 digits!

Just as chess experts show exceptional memory only for chess positions, SF succeeded only with digits, because they were what he practiced exclusively. When tested with random letters, for instance, his span remained normal. Thus SF did not exercise his working memory to the point that his capacity somehow increased for all materials. The gains were limited to a specific domain. Ericsson and Kintsch (1995) suggested that experts effectively extend the capacity of working memory by storing relevant information in long-term memory in a highly accessible form. The methods they use for such storage and retrieval are dependent on the domain of expertise.

At the end of each practice session, SF tried to recall all the digits presented during the course of the hour. At first, he recalled little if anything about the digits. But slowly his recall began to increase, paralleling the gains obtained in his memory span. That is, as he learned to become a mnemonic expert, his long-term retention of all digits presented during a session increased to an accuracy of 90% as the short-term span increased to 80 digits.

One explanation of these facts lies in the mnemonic encoding principle. SF started by coding the digits phonemically and repeating them silently. With practice, he replaced this relatively ineffective method of maintenance rehearsal with elaborative rehearsal. Specifically, he began to code the numbers in terms of running times. As a long distance runner who knew much about the sport, he was able to draw on schemas to chunk the digits.

For example, on hearing the digits 3492 as part of a sequence, he labeled the number a running time, either a mile or a 10,000-meter time, after the first two digits. Then, after hearing 9, he recognized the sequence as a near world record in the mile. Here are some excerpts from his verbal protocol, describing the chunking process for other sequences (Chase & Ericsson, 1981):

> 9462 Then I remembered the nine forty-six point . . . two!
> It's definitely point two, two mile. I said, so I said to myself, "what did you run it in?" I ran it in nine forty-six point two. Nine-forty six point two. Right.
> 4131 It's four thirteen point one mile . . . I made the four thirteen point one a mile time. (pp. 148-149)

When SF heard another time close to one already encoded, he organized them together in memory and then differentiated the sequences, making each code unique. For example, "3492 is 1/10 second faster than, say 3493" (p. 165). These larger groups of related times invariably were remembered as clusters when recalled at the end of a session, revealing this subjective organization.

The mnemonic coding allowed SF to recall seven chunks, where each chunk involved three or four digits. This permitted accurate recall of 20 or so digits. To achieve a still greater memory span, SF devised a special retrieval structure. He started out by separating three chunks from the

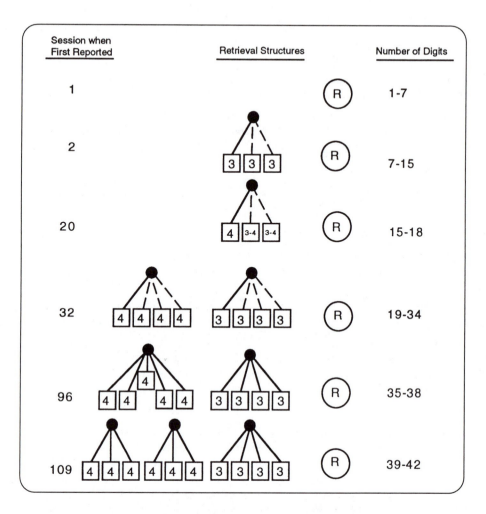

Figure 7.2. The development of SF's retrieval structure. Each square is a digit group; the circled R is the rehearsal group recalled by rote after the digits in the retrieval structures. By session 109, SF recalled 39-42 digits using the bottom retrieval structure.

SOURCE: From Chase, W. G., & Ericsson, K. A. (1981). Skilled memory. In J. R. Anderson (Ed.), *Cognitive skills and their acquisition* (pp. 141-189). Hillsdale, NJ: Lawrence Erlbaum. Copyright © 1981 by Lawrence Erlbaum Associates. Reprinted by permission.

remaining digits, which he rehearsed by rote. As shown in Figure 7.2, the rehearsal group (R) was retrieved after recalling each of the three chunks. By adding up to four digits per chunk, plus a rehearsal group of four to six digits, SF attained a digit span up to 18. Next, he devised a hierarchical structure. The first major branch contained four chunks each with four digits. Next he retrieved the second major branch, which contained four chunks each with three digits; last came the rehearsal group. Figure 7.2 illustrates how this retrieval structure developed with practice. Further development, with added hierarchical layers, apparently allowed SF to handle 80 digits.

Speedup Principle

It has long been known that speed of performance increases with practice. Chase and Ericsson (1982) called this the **speedup principle.** Within their specific domain, experts perceive, remember, think, and behave faster than do novices. The relation governing performance and practice is a power function (Logan, 1988), which may be described as follows:

$$RT = a + bN^{-c}$$

RT is reaction time and a is the asymptote, the minimum value that reaction time may take in the particular task; N is the amount of practice; b and the exponent c vary from task to task and control the exact shape of the curve.

A stunning range of tasks fit the power law (Logan, 1988). From motor skills such as typing to cognitive skills such as solving geometry problems, one finds the power law. Figure 7.3 illustrates the law with data from Neves and Anderson (1981) on learning how to justify proofs in geometry problems. When plotted on a normal scale, the amount of time needed to justify the proofs dropped rapidly with practice initially and then leveled off with higher levels of practice.

PET scans have revealed changes in the brain structures that are active as one practices at a task (Posner & Raichle, 1994). In Chapter 1, we examined PET scans for four tasks: viewing words, listening to words, speaking words, and generating verbs. In the generation task, the participant named a verb that is associated with the noun presented on a trial (hammer . . . hit). This is more complicated than speaking the noun (hammer) or listening to or viewing it passively. Without any practice (the naive condition), the generation task demanded controlled, effortful processes. Posner and Raichle identified activation in several brain struc-

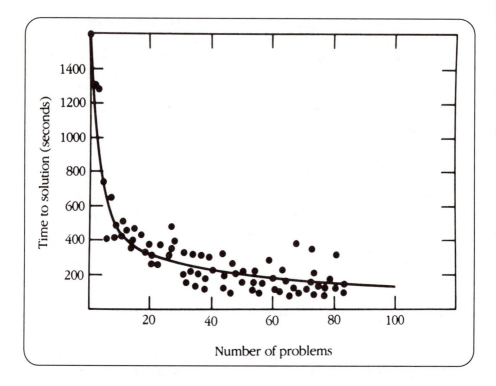

Figure 7.3. Time to solve geometry problems decreased with practice according to a power function.

SOURCE: From *Cognitive Psychology and Its Implications* 3/E by Anderson. Copyright © 1990 by W. H. Freeman and Company. Used with permission.

tures as shown in Color Plate 2 [at the front of your text]. The anterior cingulate (top row), left frontal and temporal cortex (middle row), and right cerebellum (bottom row) are all strongly activated.

After 15 minutes of practice in generating the same verb to each of 40 nouns used in the experiment, the pattern of activation changed dramatically. None of the structures seen in the naive PET scans showed strong activation. As the individual gained expertise with practice, automatic processes took over the task. This pattern was then reversed by giving a novel list of 40 words as shown in the final column of Color Plate 2. You can see the renewed activation of the anterior cingulate, the frontal and temporal lobes, and the right cerebellum.

Principle of Flow

Experts in a domain frequently lose themselves in their work. Their attention is fully engaged in the task at hand, yet they describe the work as effortless and enjoyable. Csikszentmihalyi (1990) described this experience as a **flow state**. Again, across a wide range of tasks and skills, this flow state may be observed, from rock climbers and artists to surgeons and writers. Theoretically, the state occurs only when there is an optimum match between the demands of the task and the skills of the performance. If task demands exceed skill level, then anxiety ensues. If, on the other hand, task demands fall short of skill level, then boredom is the likely result.

Other researchers have also noted that experts generally can rely on automatic processes to a far greater degree and can perform with much greater ease than novices (Holyoak, 1991). In any challenging form of work or play, novices must endure a period of frustration and anxiety as they gradually learn the necessary skills. Only by simplifying the task somehow would a novice be able to enjoy the flow state described by Csikszentmihalyi (1990).

The flow state itself appears to be essential for experts to attain a peak level of performance. Highly trained musicians and athletes, for example, perform at world-class level when they are able to relax and become totally absorbed in their skill. The enjoyable emotions experienced during such flow states can be addicting, as seen in workaholics who would rather do nothing else. Csikszentmihalyi (1990) interviewed surgeons, for example, who admitted an addiction to their work and felt that "anything that takes them away from the hospital—a Caribbean vacation, a night at the opera—feels like a waste of time" (p. 155).

Principle of Deliberate Practice

Highly skilled performance may invoke the enjoyable state of flow, but the learning process itself is best characterized by effort. Ericsson, Krampé, and Tesch-Römer (1993) define **deliberate practice** as a regimen of effortful activities, typically begun in childhood, that lead to extraordinary performance. Ericsson et al. begin with the observation that research designed to uncover genetic reasons for exceptional levels of talent has not succeeded. For example, intelligence as measured by IQ tests is known to be partly inherited; most psychologists would agree that the heritability of IQ is as high as 50%. Yet IQ does not correlate very strongly with exceptional levels of performance in many areas including music and chess.

A virtuoso on the concert stage, a grand master in a world-chess tournament, a major league slugger in baseball, or an Olympic skating star need not exhibit a high IQ at all. The average correlation between aptitude test scores and later occupational success is a meager .19 (Ghiselli, 1966). This means that less than 4% of the variation in on-the-job success can be predicted in advance through aptitude tests, which presumably tap one's suitability, including innate preparedness, for a line of work. The only domain in which heritable characteristics play a clear role in attaining eminence is sports, where an obvious physical characteristic such as height or weight has a bearing. For example, to succeed in professional basketball today, it certainly does not hurt to be nearly 7 feet tall and weigh more than 250 pounds.

Even in sports, however, it is obvious that we must look beyond genetics alone to understand exceptional performance. Human behavior virtually always arises from the interaction of genetic and environmental factors (Plomin, DeFries, & McClearn, 1990). A survey of literature on acquiring expertise points to practice as playing a much larger role in the equation than most psychologists previously believed (Chi, Glaser, & Farr, 1988). This does not mean that anyone could become a world-class performer in any chosen field, given appropriate training and practice. Such a claim contains an echo of Watson's bragging that through rewards and other tools of behaviorist theory, he could turn any infant into a surgeon, banker, or whatever. Rather, the point is that attaining expertise requires extensive and intensive practice. Advancing to world-class level requires going beyond the achievements of all other experts in the given field.

Ericsson et al. offered substantial evidence that practice must be deliberate. First, a person must practice many hours a week for a bare minimum of 10 years in his or her chosen field. Studies have examined the preparation time required across a broad range of fields, including music, mathematics, tennis, swimming, long-distance running, writing, scientific discovery, and medical diagnosis. As a concrete example, Ericsson et al. found that professional violinists, along with the very best violin students, practiced 7 hours per week by the age of 12. They steadily increased their practice time as they matured, reaching more than 30 hours per week by the age of 20. Calculating from age 3 to 20, these individuals averaged more than 10,000 hours of cumulative practice! Talent comes from persistent, deliberate practice, a conclusion that may come as a surprise to those readers who thought that outstanding performers came by their skill naturally and easily, through some innate giftedness.

The myth of giftedness is particularly strong in music and other fields characterized by child prodigies. Yet, Hayes (1981) concluded that a minimum of 10 years and more likely 20 years of practice is needed before an individual composes a truly outstanding musical piece. Even Mozart, one of the world's greatest prodigies, fit this pattern. By playing the harpsichord at age 4 and composing at age 5, Mozart reached eminence by his twenties, a fortunate occurrence for Western civilization given his early death at 35.

Second, the person must be highly motivated to spend time on the task and to devote high levels of cognitive effort to improvement. As we have seen, with enough time and effort given to practice, performance improves in accordance with the power law. For this practice to be effective, a learner must understand the nature of the task and must receive immediate feedback or knowledge on the results of his or her effort (Bower & Hilgard, 1981).

Third, the individual must discover the best methods or receive direct instruction on them by teachers and coaches. Adopting correct methods or strategies has turned up as essential in cognitive tasks such as mnemonic skill and mental calculation, in motor skills, and in job performance (Ericsson et al., 1993). Teachers and coaches design practice activities that focus on the proven methods. Given the importance of picking up the right methods, it is obviously important for children to have access to teachers, training facilities, and parental support and encouragement to study and practice.

The Principle of Metacognitive Control

Metacognition refers to cognition about cognition, to thinking about thinking. Metacognition is a central feature of human consciousness. To be aware of, to monitor, and to control mental processes adds a vital dimension of flexibility and adaptiveness to our behavior. Developmental psychologists have charted the emergence of metacognition through early and late childhood. This form of cognitive development is essential to skill in problem solving, strategy selection, and modification in memory, language use, and social cognition, among others (Flavell et al., 1993).

For example, young children and at times older children and adults fail to comprehend instructions. However, young children are unaware that they do not comprehend (Markman, 1977). Whereas older children and adults monitor their comprehension and are usually able to detect that they do not understand, young children remain unaware of what they do not understand. Further, children must learn how and when to use maintenance rehearsal, elaborative rehearsal, and organizational strategies in learning and remembering (Brown, Bransford, Ferrara, & Campione, 1983). It simply does not occur to a 5-year-old that to remember a list of words it would help to rehearse them deeply. Awareness of memory processes takes maturation and development. Until one gains awareness of cognitive processes, it is not possible to monitor how well things are going. Until one can monitor progress, it is not possible to control how things are going.

The power of metacognitive control can be seen perhaps nowhere better than in the skill of experts. Glaser and Chi (1988) noted two characteristics of experts that reflect metacognitive abilities. First, experts think through problems carefully and consciously before taking any steps toward solving them. Novices impulsively jump right in, committing themselves to a course of action, a strategy, or a plan far too soon. Experts bide their time and reflect on matters, allowing them to ponder several courses, strategies, and plans. We will see examples of this in the next section on problem-solving expertise.

In addition, experts show more self-monitoring skills than do novices. Just as young children show less self-monitoring than older children in basic learning and problem-solving tasks, novices are inferior to experts in their specialties. For example, experts in chess can better predict than novices how often they must look at a chess board to remember the locations of the pieces (Chi, 1978). Experts' awareness of their encoding processes, as related to chess, is superior. Further, gaining expertise in a discipline brings with it the ability to monitor comprehension of information in the specialty. Chi, Bassok, Lewis, Reimann, and Glaser (1989) found that physics students who excelled at solving the problems in the course also were aware of when they failed to comprehend a line in a textbook example. Poor solvers seemed unaware of their lack of comprehension, a finding reminiscent of young children's unawareness of comprehension failure (Markman, 1977). The poor solvers generally thought that they understood all the textbook examples presented. The good solvers knew when they failed to comprehend, knew which specific point eluded them, and asked questions about the troublesome point.

BOX 7.1: Oddities of Expertise

Holyoak (1991) summarized the findings on expertise and noted several interesting exceptions to the typical outcomes. In general, experts perform difficult tasks within their domain far better than novices. But on occasion experts achieve only mediocre performances. For instance, physicians who are experts in their specialty are very good at generating hypotheses and sifting among the evidence bearing on possible diagnoses. They are far more efficient in reaching their decisions than less experienced practitioners. Yet their accuracy in diagnosis is far less impressive and at times is no better than what one would expect from a simple statistical decision model (Camerer & Johnson, 1991). We will cover decision making in detail in Chapter 12.

Expertise generally involves automatic processing. The expert therefore typically expends less cognitive effort to carry out a task than a novice. Scardamalia and Bereiter (1991) pointed out a blatant exception to the rule in the domain of writing. In their words, "expert writers generally are found to work harder at the same assigned tasks than nonexperts, engaging in more planning and problem solving, more revision of goals and methods and in general more agonizing over the task" (p. 172). In writing and other creative endeavors, a novel problem can spur the expert to engage him- or herself fully in the task. Deep engagement of cognitive effort can be highly pleasurable for the expert when the demands of the task match the expert's capabilities. This is the flow state discussed earlier.

Typically, experts have better memory for information in their domain. However, several dissociations between expert performance and memory have been observed. Adelson (1984) reported that novice computer programmers actually remembered the specific code used in a program better than the expert. The code itself was irrelevant to the expert, who focused on goals and methods for achieving goals. Patel and Groen (1991) found that recollection of specific clinical cases was not superior for experts in medical diagnosis. To the expert in medicine, the key is knowing the right diagnosis for a given set of symptoms, not the recall of specific past cases.

Illustrations of Expertise

Mnemonic Skill

Exceptional skill at remembering has long been recognized in the field of psychology, going back nearly to the time of Ebbinghaus's pioneering work in 1885 on the classic forgetting curve. Binet investigated the phenomenal memory skills of chess masters and of mental calculators who specialized in number memorization. For example, the calculators could memorize a large matrix of numbers after only a brief presentation, far exceeding the usual limitations of short-term memory. Further, they could perform complex arithmetic (e.g., 57892×63475) entirely in their heads, without any external aid such as paper and pencil. As if they had a "photographic memory," the calculators reported hearing or seeing the digits as clear auditory or visual images (Ericsson & Chase, 1982). In the electronic age, a century after Binet's work, such an ability is stunning; with ready access to a calculator, performing five-digit multiplication on paper, let alone mentally, is onerous.

A. C. Aitken, a professor of mathematics at the University of Edinburgh, astonished psychologists on tests of his memory and calculation skills (Hunter, 1962, 1964). Presented with a list of 25 words in 1933, Aitken recalled them all, through repeated attempts, 27 years later! He also showed virtually flawless recollection of Bartlett's "War of the Ghosts" tale that he had memorized 27 years earlier. As a mathematician, he quickly understood the equivalencies of numerical expressions. For example, he immediately apprehended that 37×53, $40^2 + 19^2$, and 1961 are equivalent. Of interest, deliberate practice can enable bright, motivated (and paid) college students to greatly enhance their abilities as mental calculators. Staszewski (1988) reported that after 300 hours of practice on simple (e.g., 7×4382) and complex (e.g., 78×41275) multiplication, an undergraduate attained the speed and accuracy of a world-class mental calculator.

Photographic memory, known technically as **eidetic imagery,** refers to the ability to examine a visual stimulus for only a few seconds and to retain it as an exact, high-fidelity copy or image. A stringent test for eidetic imagery is the ability to superimpose one pictorial image upon another to form a third, novel picture. Stromeyer and Psotka (1970) reported that at least one eidetiker could even carry out such superimposition with two random dot patterns, presented one to each eye. When viewed separately, the 10,000 dots in a pattern looked random, signifying nothing. When viewed stereoscopically, that is, with the unique patterns to the left and right eye presented simultaneously, they merged to form a recognizable object, such as the letter T.

Stromeyer (1982) described Elizabeth, an instructor and artist at Harvard University who retained eidetic imagery into adulthood.

Perhaps she did so because of its relevance to her work. As Stromeyer noted:

> She has a talent that most painters don't have. At will, she can mentally project an exact image of a picture or scene onto her canvas or onto another surface. This hallucinated image appears to contain all of the detailed texture and color of the original. Once the image is formed, it remains still and Elizabeth can move her eyes about to inspect the details. (p. 76)

Stromeyer and Psotka (1970) presented Elizabeth with a 10,000-dot pattern for 1 minute to her right eye. Following a 10-second rest, she viewed with her left eye the accompanying 10,000-dot pattern and, when asked to superimpose the two, immediately reported seeing the letter T coming at her. She then looked at both patterns through a stereoscope and confirmed that her eidetic image of the T appeared exactly as it should. Note that this implies the ability to retain in memory the precise location of 10,000 random dots! Further tests showed that she could retain the right eye image for up to 24 hours before superimposing upon it the left eye pattern. Even an extraordinary million-dot image was successfully retained for up to 4 hours.

Elizabeth appeared to transfer iconic memory into short-term and even long-term storage without loss or other alteration of details. Such a powerful demonstration of eidetic imagery has never been duplicated by other investigators, however. Elizabeth's exceptional ability to superimpose images is probably extremely rare. Eidetic imagery most often has been claimed in children rather than adults (Haber, 1979), though it is difficult even to find children who qualify (Gummerman & Gray, 1982).

Perhaps less remarkable examples of detailed, though not flawless, visual and auditory memory are more common, but we have only anecdotes by which to judge. The most common example seems to be the alleged ability to recall images of specific pages of books that have been studied, a talent that would serve one well as a college student. Do not be alarmed should you lack this ability. Neisser (1982) noted that such individuals typically report losing their knack for this by the end of adolescence.

The best known example of extraordinary memory ability in this century is the case of S. V. Shereshevskii (S) documented by the famous Russian psychologist Luria (1968). Over a period of 20 years, Luria studied the memory abilities of this individual. He tested his memory span for variety of materials and found it remarkable, seemingly without limit. In Luria's words:

> I gave S. a series of words, then numbers, then letters, reading them to him slowly or presenting them in written form. He read or listened attentively and then repeated the material exactly as it had been presented. I increased the number of elements in each series giving him as many as thirty, fifty, or even seventy words or numbers, but this, too, presented no problem to him. . . .
>
> The experiment indicated that he could reproduce a series in reverse order—from the end to the beginning—just as simply as from start to finish; that he could readily tell me which word followed another in a series, or reproduce the word which happened to precede the one I'd name. He would pause for a minute, as though searching for the word, but immediately after would be able to answer my question and generally made no mistakes. . . . It was of no consequence to him whether the series I gave him contained meaning words or nonsense syllables, numbers or sounds; whether they were presented orally or in writing. . . .
>
> As the experimenter, I soon found myself in a state verging on utter confusion. An increase in the length of the series led to no noticeable increase in difficulty for S., and I simply had to admit that the capacity of his memory *had no distinct limits;* that I had been unable to perform what one would think was the simplest task a psychologist can do: measure the capacity of an individual's memory. (pp. 9-11)

Further testing only compounded Luria's confusion, for it turned out that the duration of S's memory, as well as its capacity, seemed to have no limit. Some tests revealed error-free recall of word lists presented 15 years previously! Moreover, S could recall the context in which list had been presented, describing the place in which Luria had read him the words, the chair in which Luria sat, and even the clothes Luria had worn.

S put his skill to work by performing mnemonic feats for audiences. He thus practiced often. The source of his exceptional memory appeared to lie elsewhere. From early childhood, S experienced **synesthesia,** or cross-talk among sensory modalities, such that sounds, for example, are experienced visually as well as aurally. Normal individuals experience mild degrees of synesthesia in that colors are reliably associated with specific pitches of sounds (Marks, 1987). The bright colors of yellow and white elicit high pitches while the dark colors of black and brown echo low pitches. But S experienced an extreme form in which tones and noises would be apprehended as "puffs" and "splashes" of color. He would perceive the "color" of a speaker's voice and each speech sound assumed a visual "form" with its own "color" and "taste." Plainly, these images added a unique code to memory and we have seen the importance of distinctiveness in Chapter 5. This illustrates, albeit in a bizarre fashion, the principle of mnemonic encoding discussed earlier.

Further, S exhibited the principle of retrieval structure. He distributed the images for a given list of items to be remembered along a street that he visualized. For instance, he might select Gorky Street in Moscow, begin at Mayakovsky Square, and walk slowly down the street in his mind's eye, "distributing" his images at houses, gates, and store windows. By repeating his walk later, he could "see" the image of the item in a particular location and scan the images on either side of it. Hence his ability to remember in forward or reverse order and his ability to name items preceding or following a particular item derived from this retrieval structure. Recall from Chapter 5 that the idea of using geographic locations as a retrieval scheme is old, going back to the ancient Greeks.

The strange sensory experiences of S enabled him to succeed as a professional mnemonist, but they interfered with normal abstract thinking. For S, every thought quickly provoked an image, which in turn led to another image. The concrete image replaced the abstract thought. As Neisser (1982) observed, however, most mnemonists studied by psychologists have not suffered in abstract thinking or experienced such extreme synesthesia.

Hunt and Love (1982) reported the case of VP. In tests of short-term memory capacity, VP showed an average digit span of 21 for nonrepeating sequences. His recall of Bartlett's "War of the Ghosts" tale amply demonstrated his remarkable long-term memory ability. VP recalled nearly 60% of the story in a verbatim fashion a full year after originally reading it. VP showed far less loss of detail than normal individuals. He excelled in memory tasks without experiencing synesthesia and certainly without imagery dominating his thinking processes. He possessed a high IQ (136 on the Wechsler-Bellevue Adult Scale), spoke eight languages, and read widely. VP therefore had a well-developed system of long-term memory, enabling him to encode material elaborately. His quick perception of the details of stimuli also served him well in the encoding process. Finally, VP was encouraged and rewarded by his family and teachers to excel at memory. He thus had the type of support needed to practice learning and remembering in a deliberate fashion.

S and VP showed excellent memory skill across a variety of situations. Mnemonic skill can also be acquired in more limited domains, as seen by the undergraduate SF, who practiced the digit span test in the laboratory (Chase & Ericsson, 1981). In a more natural setting, a waiter, JC, learned to recall orders in a restaurant flawlessly. Ericsson and Polson (1988) brought JC into their laboratory analogue of a restaurant to study the basis for his skill. They challenged JC and control participants, who were not waiters or waitresses, to recall dinner orders given by a table of three, five, or eight people. Each dinner included an entrée, instructions for cooking the entrée (e.g., make my steak rare), type of salad dressing, and vegetable. Each dimension included three to seven choices. The number of errors made by untrained participants climbed steeply as more needed to be remembered, whereas JC had no difficulties (see Figure 7.4).

Analyses of JC thinking aloud while taking orders revealed two familiar principles of expertise. JC encoded the orders mnemonically. For instance, the first letter of each salad dressing uniquely coded that dimension (B for bleu cheese). He attended carefully to each customer and generated associations between the order and features of the customer.

JC also used a hierarchical retrieval structure. This entailed encoding the orders in groups of four. Before moving to the next group of four, he rehearsed and consolidated the orders taken thus far. His could then recall an entire table of eight by dealing with two branches, each with only four customers, which in turn contained the four items for each order. Having acquired an ability to encode mnemonically and to use a retrieval structure in a restaurant job, JC could generalize to remembering lists of words unrelated to foods to only a limited extent. He could not match his performance with food items. Recall that the retrieval structure developed by SF for remembering sequences of digits also could not be generalized to other types of materials. Experts extend working memory capacity only within the domain of their expertise (Ericsson & Kintsch, 1995).

Problem Solving

Partly because of the intense interest in improving education in mathematics and the physical sciences, researchers have explored in detail how experts and novices solve physics problems. Problems are chosen that are within the range of skill of novices, defined as undergraduates with only a background in high school physics and a semester or so of college-level physics. One such problem is finding the velocity of

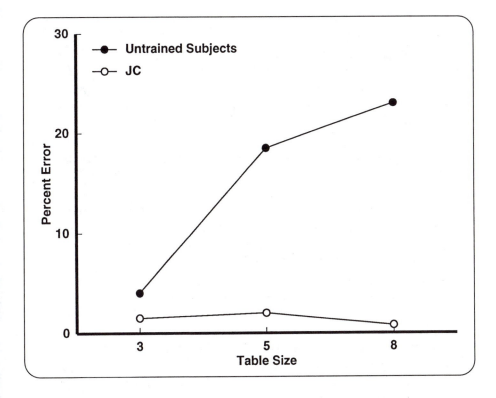

Figure 7.4. Errors for untrained waiters and a mnemonically experienced waiter (JC).
SOURCE: Adapted from Ericsson and Polson (1988).

an object sliding down an incline plane at the point that it reaches the bottom. Often story problems are presented that require one to read a paragraph and identify the given information and the information that must be calculated. Verbal protocols are collected as novices and experts work through problems of this sort. Experts are defined as those with doctorates in physics, who solve physics problems regularly as part of their research and teaching professions. Analyses of the protocols reveal a number of interesting features that reflect the principles of expertise.

First, experts think through the problem before putting down a single formula (Glaser & Chi, 1988). They prefer to study the problem and ponder alternatives, no doubt in part because their knowledge representations are so much richer and offer so many more possible approaches relative to the novice. The delay reflects more than greater knowledge, however. It reflects the principle of metacognitive control. One interesting illustration is the tendency for the expert to produce a simple qualitative diagram, involving no mathematics, after reflecting on the problem initially. The expert consciously selects a strategy of simplifying the problem to the barest qualitative elements. In that way, alternative approaches can be monitored before investing time and effort in calculations.

Second, the expert has mnemonically encoded theories, formulas, facts, and principles and has developed appropriate strategies for structuring them when required. The knowledge schemas of the expert are naturally both richer and better organized than those of the novice. One consequence of this better organization is that the expert perceives the problem differently than the novice (Chi et al., 1981). In reading a problem description, the expert, but not the novice, very quickly triggers the appropriate schema for solution.

Chi et al. asked experts and novices to categorize physics problems to study the role of knowledge organization. When novices are asked to categorize problems, they group them on the basis of their physical features, such as problems involving inclined planes versus springs versus objects in free fall. The novice perceives the problem at a relatively superficial or shallow level of analysis. To illustrate, the diagrams of two problems grouped together by novices in a study by Chi et al. are shown in Figure 7.5. As you can see, the problems certainly appear to be related in that both involve an inclined plane. But in fact the similarity lies in appearances only; the procedures needed to solve the two problems are quite different.

Experts, on the other hand, perceive the problems at a deeper, theoretical level, characterized by principles and laws. Newton's three laws of motion each encompass a class of problems whose members on the surface appear quite different, for example. As another example, consider the two problems shown in Figure 7.6, which can be solved by applying the law of conservation of energy. Chi et al. found that experts readily categorized these problems as related, despite that one involved an inclined plane and the other a spring. What mattered to the experts was theoretical principle, not superficial appearance.

Another consequence of highly organized schemas is that experts adopt a different reasoning strategy than do novices (Larkin, McDermott, Simon, & Simon, 1980). The novices are likely to begin with the unknown quantity in the problem, such as the velocity of the block at the bottom

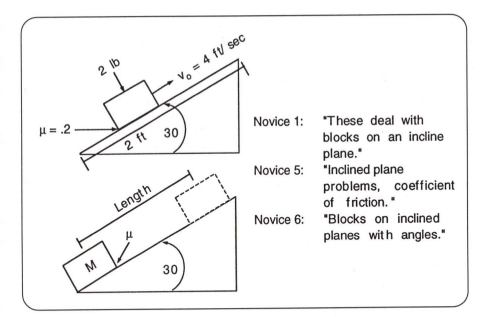

Figure 7.5. Diagrams of two problems grouped together by novices in physics, along with sample explanations.
SOURCE: From Chi, Feltovich, and Glaser (1981). Copyright © 1981 by Ablex Publishing Corporation. Reprinted by permission.

of the inclined plane. From that unknown, they attempt to work backward to the quantities that are given in the problem. They seek an equation that contains the unknown. If that equation also contains another unknown, they then look for yet another equation that will bridge the gap. This procedure, called **backward chaining,** continues until they find an equation with the given information in the problem.

The expert proceeds in a forward direction. After having reflected on the problem and perhaps drawn a qualitative diagram, the expert selects an equation that immediately uses the given information. The result of the first calculation, then, becomes a given piece of information for entry into the next formula. Such **forward chaining** advances until the unknown velocity is calculated and the problem solved. Experts use the forward chaining procedure whenever the problem strikes them as readily solvable. They are much more efficient as a result, solving the problems in less than a quarter of the time required by novices.

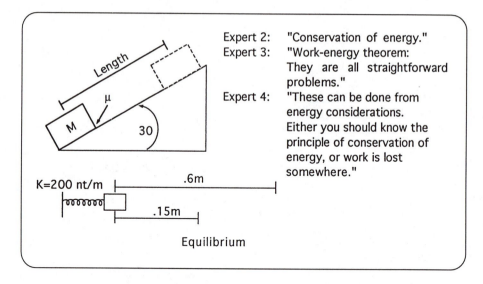

Length

μ

M

30

K=200 nt/m

.6m

.15m

Equilibrium

Expert 2:   "Conservation of energy."
Expert 3:   "Work-energy theorem:
           They are all straightforward
           problems."
Expert 4:   "These can be done from
           energy considerations.
           Either you should know the
           principle of conservation of
           energy, or work is lost
           somewhere."

Figure 7.6. Diagrams of two problems grouped together by experts in physics, along with sample explanations.
SOURCE: From Chi, Feltovich, and Glaser (1981). Copyright © 1981 by Ablex Publishing Corporation. Reprinted by permission.

Computer Models of Expertise

Expert Systems

Expert systems are computer programs with access to knowledge about a specific domain (Mishkoff, 1985). They are sometimes referred to as knowledge-based systems. Their purpose is to simulate human reasoning and decision making within their domain of expertise. They aid diagnosis, planning, instruction, management, and design (McGraw & Harbison-Briggs, 1989).

The knowledge of an expert system is often coded in the form of **production rules,** which specify how to proceed given a particular pattern of stimuli. For example, MYCIN is a medical expert system for diagnosing blood infection (Shortliffe, 1976). IF-THEN rules are used where the if condition stipulates a pattern of observations and the conclusion represents either an assertion or an action. Forsyth (1989) provided the following sample MYCIN rule:

IF
1. the infection is meningitis, and
2. the subtype of meningitis is bacterial, and
3. only circumstantial evidence is available, and
4. the patient is at least 17 years old, and
5. the patient is an alcoholic

THEN
There is suggestive evidence that Diplococcus pneumoniae is an organism causing the meningitis. (p. 11)

The conditions and conclusions in MYCIN were obtained from experts by knowledge engineers, whose task it is to elicit as much relevant knowledge from human experts as possible. Often knowledge engineers pose examples of problems to an expert who thinks aloud. The verbal protocol contains clues as to the knowledge and reasoning patterns used by the expert and these are then programmed.

In addition to a knowledge base, expert systems include problem-solving and reasoning procedures that are called an **inference engine.** One type of inference engine uses a forward chaining strategy of working from evidence, such as the symptoms in MYCIN, to a conclusion or diagnosis. The production rule just examined illustrates forward chaining because we look for matches to the IF conditions. Backward chaining is another type of inference engine that begins with a hypothesis and then seeks evidence to confirm or reject the hypothesis. In practice, most systems combine forward and backward chaining (Forsyth, 1989).

A wide range of applications for expert systems are in use today (McGraw & Harbison-Briggs, 1989). In addition to MYCIN, these include PROSPECTOR, which advises mining companies on mineral exploration; DENDRAL, which assists chemists in identifying the structure of unknown compounds; ISIS, which advises managers in job scheduling conflicts in a factory; and COMPASS, which assists telephone workers in maintaining switching systems. The growing use of such expert systems promises to spread the skills of experts to areas lacking human experts, to aid in the training of experts, and to enhance the productivity of experts on the job.

*ACT**

Other computer models of interest ambitiously attempt to simulate the full range of human cognition, as witnessed in learning, remember-

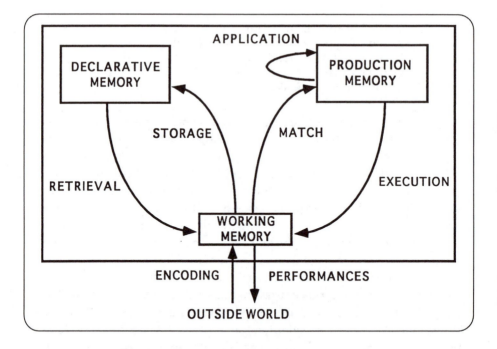

Figure 7.7. The ACT* model of human cognition and expertise.
SOURCE: Reprinted by permission of the publishers from *The Architecture of Cognition* by John R. Anderson, Cambridge, MA: Harvard University Press. Copyright © 1983 by the President and Fellows of Harvard College.

ing, and forgetting as well as problem solving and reasoning. They are AI simulations designed to test our theoretical understanding of the processes involved in skilled performance in various tasks. **ACT*** is the most recent version of a series of such AI simulations developed by Anderson (1983). It stands for the adaptive control of thought and simulates expert behavior through the use of production rules stored in a system called production memory. A related AI simulation has been described by Rosenbloom, Laird, and Newell (1993).

The basic structure or architecture of ACT* is shown in Figure 7.7. Production memory is analogous to procedural memory; it includes IF-THEN rules that embody knowledge about how to do things. Declarative memory, on the other hand, contains the factual and conceptual knowledge about the world stored in terms of propositions and spatial images. Working memory contains the subset of declarative information currently activated for use in a particular task.

The contents of working memory are checked to see whether the IF portion of a given production rule is satisfied. The set of actions specified by the THEN portion of the rule creates new representations in working memory. Once a representation is created in working memory, it may be stored in long-term memory according to a fixed probability. Working memory also holds the current intentions, plans, or goals of the system.

ACT* simulates the development of skill and expertise by starting with declarative representations relevant to the goals of a task (Anderson, 1983, 1987). The model stores a series of facts that are needed to perform the task. For example, in simulating the development of typing skill, ACT* might begin by memorizing the locations of the keys for the letters and other characters. These representations would be stored in declarative memory in the form of propositions and spatial images. Other forms of declarative knowledge would specify how to spell a particular word, giving the sequence of letters that must be used. To type a given word, the novice, as simulated by ACT*, would depend on very general rules or strategies for solving problems (e.g., take a step that moves one toward the goal). Such a strategy might direct the system to find the key for the first letter, to strike it, and then find the key for the second letter. ACT* would in essence hunt and peck its way to achieving the goal. Production rules would not yet be tailored and stored for use in typing per se.

With sufficient practice, the reliance on general strategies and declarative knowledge would give way to specific production rules, a process called **proceduralization.** Memory for where to move the fingers to find a particular letter would be converted to a procedural representation from a declarative representation. Special production rules would be developed for typing certain letter combinations (e.g., the). As typists learn to dance their fingers automatically about the keyboard, ACT* simulates the gain in expertise in terms of the development of, and reliance on, production memory. Anderson's (1983, 1987) approach to simulating expertise has been useful in understanding cognitive as well as motor skills. Solving geometry problems, programming a computer, and learning a language are among the domains of expertise to which ACT* has been applied.

◙ SUMMARY ◙

1. Experts in a particular domain are skilled at mnemonically encoding information. Often, though not always, there is a coupling

between expert performance and superior memory. The principle of *mnemonic encoding* refers to using the expert's organization of long-term memory to guide the encoding of information into meaningful chunks.

2. Experts also adopt highly effective strategies for retrieving information of use to them. As we saw earlier, memory depends not only on how well relevant information is encoded but also on how well it is retrieved. The principle of retrieval structure refers to the highly specialized means used by experts to gain access to what they know.

3. As a consequence of practice, an expert carries out a task more rapidly than a novice, a finding known as the speedup principle. The decrease in task time follows an orderly relation described by a power function. PET scans have revealed that the brain structures activated when engaged in a novel task are markedly different than those used in a well-practiced task. When experts are fully challenged by a task, they experience a state of flow, which is characterized by a total absorption of attention, a sense of effortlessness, and a feeling of enjoyment.

4. Becoming an expert requires enormous amounts of learning and practice. It has been estimated that attaining the status of expert requires a minimum of 10 years of preparation. The principle of deliberate practice refers to the regimen of effortful activities that lead to extraordinary performance. It is through deliberate practice, not genetic endowment, that one becomes an expert in virtually all fields of endeavor. Even in sports, where inherited body size makes some difference, deliberate practice is still essential for success.

5. *Metacognition* refers to cognition about cognition, or thinking about thinking. Throughout cognitive development, individuals grow in their ability to monitor their thought processes and to select strategies that are effective for the task at hand. Experts and novices in adulthood also differ greatly in their metacognitive abilities within a particular domain. Experts think through problems carefully and consciously before taking any steps toward solving them. Further, experts monitor how well problem solving or learning is going, making changes in strategies when things are not going well.

6. Expert or knowledge-based systems are computer programs with access to declarative and procedural knowledge about a specific domain. These programs simulate human reasoning and decision making and are used to help human experts in diagnosis, planning,

instruction, management, and design. A medical expert system called MYCIN has a knowledge base about blood infections based on production rules. Each rule specifics a set of observations that in turn trigger a particular assertion or action. Operating on the knowledge base is an inference engine, which directs the system in reasoning about observations and hypothesized conclusions. ACT* is a computer model that simulates human cognition in a variety of domains. At its heart lies a system of production rules that duplicate the skilled performance of an expert.

Key Terms

principle of mnemonic encoding
principle of retrieval structure
speedup principle
flow state
deliberate practice
metacognition
eidetic imagery
synesthesia

backward chaining
forward chaining
expert systems
production rules
inference engine
ACT*
proceduralization

Recommended Readings

Ericsson and Smith (1991) edited an outstanding collection of essays on expertise in a book titled *Toward a General Theory of Expertise: Prospects and Limits.* An earlier collection edited by Anderson (1981), titled *Cognitive Skills and Their Acquisition,* still warrants reading. I also recommend Chi, Glaser, and Farr's (1988) *The Nature of Expertise* and Sternberg and Kolligian's (1990) *Competence Considered.* Gardner's (1983) *Frames of Mind: The Theory of Multiple Intelligences* includes sketches of highly talented individuals in a wide range of domains, including writing, mathematics, music, and dance.

Luria's (1968) *The Mind of a Mnemonist,* Hunter's (1957) *Memory: Facts and Fallacies,* and Smith's (1983) *The Great Mental Calculators: The Psychology, Methods and Lives of Calculating Prodigies, Past and Present* are all fasinating reading. Neisser's (1982) book titled *Memory Observed: Remem-*

bering in Natural Contexts brings together work on memorists in his section on special people.

Expertise in problem solving has been well researched and I will devote all of Chapter 11 to problem solving. A chapter by Larkin in Anderson's (1981) book is an excellent source. Also, the classic work by Newell and Simon (1972) titled *Human Problem Solving* deserves mention. A contemporary account of problem solving, including a discussion of expertise, may be found in Holyoak's contribution to *An Invitation to Cognitive Science: Thinking* (Volume 3) edited by Osherson and Smith (1990).

For more information on production systems and their applications, the reader should turn to Anderson's (1983) book titled *The Architecture of Cognition* and an edited collection by Klahr, Langley, and Neches (1987) titled *Production System Models of Learning and Development*. A classic reference on production systems is Newell's chapter in *Visual Information Processing*, edited by Chase (1973).

PART IV

The Nature and Use of Language

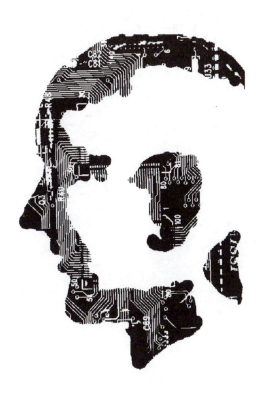

CHAPTER **8**

□ Language

One of the most remarkable and distinguishing features of our species is our use of language. Language can be thought of as a cognitive tool that sculpts the very shape of culture. Consider all the ways that you have used language today. From the first "good morning" you spoke or heard, oral communication has been an integral part of your daily activities. From the first glance at the morning paper, you have been awash in a sea of written language. The words of this sentence are among the hundreds if not thousands you have read today.

Try to imagine your world without language, without the ability to speak, listen, write, and read. Although you could perceive the objects and events surrounding you in the physical world, you could not name them. The power to name, to refer to this world by means of abstract symbols, opens the door to another universe, one of the intellect. All human endeavors, from the ancient tribal cultures of hunters and gatherers to the recent technological culture of knowledge workers, rest on the foundation of language.

Human thinking intertwines with language so intricately that some scholars have equated the two, as we shall see. This section of the book surveys the role of language in cognition. We begin our survey in this chapter by considering what is meant by the term *language*. Our discussion will take us through debates over the relation of language and thought, as well as the possibility that nonhuman animals naturally use their own languages or can learn to use ours. Then in Chapter 9 we turn to a detailed treatment of the most ancient means of using language, oral communication. The production and comprehension of speech has been intensively investigated by cognitive psychologists. The study of written language has also received substantial attention, but in an unbalanced fashion. Whereas the science of reading is well advanced, the science of writing is still in its early phases of development.

Language is a system of symbols that allow communication of ideas among two or more individuals. Ordering a hamburger at a fast-food restaurant, arguing with a friend over politics, answering a professor's question in class, professing religious beliefs in church, and praising a child's school performance are but five of an infinite number of acts of communication. In speaking, people convert their thoughts and feelings into words. In listening, others comprehend these thoughts and feelings through converting the spoken words back into the ideas of their own mental life. The success of communication hinges on the ability of both speakers and listeners to use language well. Recall your last argument with a parent, friend, or spouse over money. Were there failures to speak plainly? To listen carefully?

Cognitive psychologists have investigated three major areas regarding language (Clark & Clark, 1977). First, there are the questions of comprehension, the processes by which we hear or read, comprehend, and remember language. Second are the questions of production, the processes by which we speak or write language. Third, developmental psychologists have tackled the acquistion of language, the processes by which children learn to produce and comprehend the linguistic symbols to which they are exposed. Throughout the next three chapters, we will encounter studies concerned with comprehension, production, and acquisition of language. But first we need to examine what we mean by language as a system of symbols for communication.

Characteristics of Language

Linguistic Universals

One intriguing matter studied by linguists and philosophers for centuries is the search for **linguistic universals,** properties shared by all languages. By definition, languages must share four rudimentary properties (Clark & Clark, 1977). A language must be learnable by children; adults must be able to speak and understand it readily; it must capture the ideas that people normally communicate; and it must enable communication among groups of people in a social and cultural context. Hockett (1966) contrasted human language with the communication systems of other animals in an effort to isolate linguistic universals. His list of 16 defining features of human languages is given in Table 8.1. All human languages show these features and each is absent in at least one animal system of communication. The primary mode of human language is speech, not writing. As we will see in Chapter 10, written language is relatively recent in the evolutionary history compared with speech. Thus Hockett regarded the features of the vocal-auditory channel, broadcast transmission and directional reception, rapid fading, and total feedback as defining aspects of language. Omitting them broadens the discussion to include the written word as well as the spoken. But including them clarifies how speech operates as a system of communication, just as do radio, television, telegraph, telephone, and other electronic systems. So too does interchangeability. If you can produce a sentence, then you can also comprehend it.

Other properties go to the heart of language as a conveyer of meaning. **Semanticity** means just that: The sounds or symbols used in language refer to objects, events, beliefs, desires, feelings, and intentions. They carry meaning. In fact, the sounds of speech and the symbols of written language are specialized for this purpose. If I say to you, "I am happy," then the sounds pack meaning about my state of mind in a specific way. If instead you hear me whistling a tune while strolling across campus, the sounds may say something about my mood. On the other hand, for all you know I may whistle whenever I feel happy, angry, energetic, *or* tired. Unlike speech, whistling is not specialized to convey a clear meaning.

Arbitrariness refers to the lack of any obvious connection between the symbol and the meaning it carries. *Uno, ein, one* are arbitrary sounds referring to the same numerical concept. A single scratch in the dirt or mark on a clay tablet would be a nonarbitrary way of referring to the number one. Ten such marks would nonarbitrarily refer to ten. But the use of nonarbitrary symbols can get very cumbersome. The invention of Arabic numerals for representing numerical quantities vastly simplified the task of representing, say, 432 jars of olive oil or wine. Nonarbitrary or iconic forms of written language can be pointed to (e.g., Egyptian hiero-

Table 8.1 Linguistic Universals Distinguishing Human Language from Animal Communication Systems

1. Vocal-Auditory Channel. The channel for all linguistic communication is vocal auditory.
2. Broadcast Transmission and Directional Reception. All linguistic signals are transmitted broadcast and are received directionally. These properties are the consequences of the nature of sound, of binaural hearing, and of motility, and are thus implied by property 1.
3. Rapid Fading. All linguistic signals are evanescent.
4. Interchangeability. Adult members of any speech community are interchangeably transmitters and receivers of linguistic signals.
5. Complete Feedback. The transmitter of a linguistic signal himself receives the message.
6. Specialization. The direct-energetic consequences of linguistic signals are usually biologically trivial; only the triggering effects are important. Even the sound of a heated conversation does not raise the temperature of a room enough to benefit those in it.
7. Semanticity. Linguistic signals function in correlating and organizing the life of a community because there are associative ties between signal elements and features in the world; in short, some linguistic forms have denotations.
8. Arbitrariness. The relation between a meaningful element in language and its denotation is independent of any physical or geometrical resemblance between the two. Or, as we say, the semantic relation is *arbitrary* rather than *iconic*.
9. Discreteness. The possible messages in any language constitute a discrete repertory rather than a continuous one. Any utterance in a language must differ from any other utterance of the same length by at least a whole phonological feature.
10. Displacement. Linguistic messages may refer to things remote in time or space, or both, from the site of the communication.
11. Openness. New linguistic messages are coined freely and easily.
12. Tradition. The conventions of a language are passed down by teaching and learning, not through the germ plasm. Genes supply potentiality and probably a generalized drive, since nonhuman animals cannot learn a (human) language and people can hardly be prevented from acquiring one.
13. Duality (of Patterning). More commonly, we speak rather of the phonological and grammatical (or grammatico-lexical) subsystems of a language. . . . By virtue of duality of patterning, an enormous number of minimum semantically functional elements . . . (morphemes) can be and are mapped into arrangements of a conveniently small number of minimum meaningless but message-differentiating elements . . . (phonological components).
14. Prevarication. Linguistic messages can be false, and they can be meaningless in the logician's sense. . . . Lying seems to be extremely rare among animals.
15. Reflexiveness. In a language, one can communicate about communication.
16. Learnability. A speaker of a language can learn another language.

SOURCE: From Hockett (1966) in J. H. Greenberg (Ed.), *Universals of language* (2nd. ed., pp. 1-29). Cambridge: MIT Press. Copyright © 1966 by The MIT Press. Reprinted by permission.

glyphic, Chinese ideographs, and one form of written Japanese), but all spoken languages are essentially arbitrary. The exceptions to the rule we identify as examples of onomatopoeia, in which the words sound like the things that they describe (e.g., buzz, ding-dong, hum).

Duality concerns the use of a small set of sounds to yield multiple meanings through combination. All human languages make use of 50 or so utterances generated by our vocal apparatus. Each such utterance or phoneme, which we will define more precisely later, is a building block of words. Different patterns or structures of phonemes mean different things. The phrase *the dear old queen* certainly does not mean the same thing as *the queer old dean;* by recombining the phonetic features, new meanings emerge. Further, as we will see in detail in the next chapter, sound varies continuously in frequency and intensity across time as someone speaks. But language does not heed most of the variations. Instead, language requires discrete boundaries on these variations; within the boundaries, all variations in sound are treated as the same phoneme. Thus I might pronounce a sentence slightly differently each time that I utter it, yet listeners would ignore the insignificant variations and grasp the intended meaning, as long as the sounds fall within the phonemic boundaries.

Language also involves **displacement.** We have already examined memory and its centrality to cognition. Imagination in the sense of constructing future scenarios, feelings, and so forth also is integral to the human mind. In our use of language, we incessantly refer to events in the past as well as in the future, to objects that may or may not be present, to experiences that we fret having had or those we fear may come. Neither time nor space constrains the dominion of language and this is what we mean by displacement.

Of all the characteristics of language, two might stand as the most important, at least in setting human language apart from other forms of animal communication. One is called **openness.** By it we mean that language is infinitely novel and creative. There is no limit to the number of unique utterances or written sentences that people can generate. The other is duality. A small number of meaningless sounds or phonological components can be combined or patterned in numerous ways to create a very large number of meaningful utterances or morphemes. Hockett (1966) noted that "no animal system known to this writer shows a significant degree of duality" (p. 12).

Meaning, Structure, and Use

Semantics. Hockett's list provides us with a picture of the general territory of language, but it offers only a glimpse at the major landmarks. **Semantics,** defined as the study of meaning, is one such landmark. A theory of semantics must explain how people mentally represent the meaning of words and sentences. The expression of one's thoughts and their comprehension by listeners or readers obviously depend on these mental representations.

In our discussion of memory, we examined how meanings are represented in the form of propositions, abstract codes of the concepts, frames, scripts, and other schemas referred to in a sentence. For example, "The professor praised the industrious student" can be analyzed into two propositions. Each involves a list that starts with a relation followed by one or more arguments:

(praise, professor, student, past)
(industrious, student)

The sounds that we generate in saying a sentence must code meaning in a consistent manner so that listeners can understand our utterances. Words, or, more precisely, morphemes, achieve this coding. A **morpheme** is the smallest unit of speech used repeatedly in a language to code a specific meaning. A word is a morpheme, such as praise, but so too are prefixes and suffixes. Each morpheme signals a distinct meaning. The suffix *-ed* tells us that the act of praise took place in the past, a unit of meaning that must then be added as an argument in our abstract propositional representation.

Each morpheme consists of smaller units of speech called **phonemes,** or phonetic segments. As we will see in the next chapter, each phoneme is pronounced or articulated by our vocal apparatus in a unique manner. The /p/ of *praised* and the /b/ of *braised* are pronounced almost identically; they differ only in that the vocal cords vibrate for /b/ but not for /p/. This difference, called voicing, is also seen between /s/ and /z/. Say each aloud and you can feel with your fingers on the Adam's apple the vibration with /z/. The phonemes of a language are the building blocks of meaningful units, the morphemes. The phoneme by itself does not code meaning.

Words compose our **mental lexicon,** the dictionary of long-term memory, that we rely upon in speaking and listening, reading and writing. In particular, we are concerned in semantics with content words, the verbs and especially the nouns that refer to natural (e.g., chair) or formal (the legal definition of marriage) concepts. Function words such as articles (e.g., the) or prepositions (e.g., by) often serve a grammatical rather than a semantic role. For example, the *by* in "Jill bought groceries by the week" plays the grammatical role of starting a prepositional phrase; the entire phrase could easily be replaced by the adverb *weekly* without a change in meaning. The content words, on the other hand, each contribute to the unique meaning of the sentence.

Semantics can be approached as a problem of pattern recognition. Componential analysis attempts to describe the world to which words refer in terms of features and dimensions, sometimes called semantic primitives. Classic examples of this work come from studies of the folk taxonomies used to describe the plants, animals, diseases, and people of a particular culture. Kinship terms illustrate this well. Romney and D'Andrade (1964) examined the terms *father, mother, grandfather, grandmother, son, daughter, grandson, granddaughter, uncle, aunt, nephew, niece, brother, sister,* and *cousin*. They characterized the "semantic space" in terms of different dimensions as shown in Table 8.2. Sex (male or female), generation (two generations before or after the self, one generation before or after the self, and same generation as the self), and directness (direct ancestor or descendent versus a collateral relative) differentiate key relationships among the kinship terms. Romney and D'Andrade found that high school students judged the terms *father* and *daughter* to be less similar than either *father* and *mother* or *father* and *son*. This outcome followed from their componential analysis because, of these three comparisons, only the father-daughter comparison differs on both the dimensions of sex and generation.

Syntax. Another landmark of language is its structure. The grammatical rules defining how words, prefixes, and suffixes are arranged so as to yield acceptable sentences is defined as **syntax**. Technically, syntax is only part of the study of grammar, the complete set of rules by which people speak and write correctly (including, for example, punctuation). Here, though, we speak of a grammar as an abstract set of syntactic rules that describe how language is put together. Syntactic rules ensure that speakers and listeners, writers and readers, are all playing the same structural game with language. Because language must follow a linear order—one word after another—either in time (as occurs in speech) or in space (as occurs with text), some convention is needed to order the words.

Table 8.2 A Componential Analysis of Meaning

	Direct		Collateral	
Generation	Male	Female	Male	Female
Two before	grandfather	grandmother		
Two after	grandson	granddaughter		
One before	father	mother	uncle	aunt
One after	son	daughter	nephew	niece
Same	brother	sister	cousin	

SOURCE: Adapted from Romney and D'Andrade (1964). Used by permission of the American Anthropological Association.

In English, for instance, a declaration consists of a subject (S) followed by a verb (V) followed by an object (O). In German, the grammatical rule is SOV, not SVO as in English. The grammar of a language specifies the rules that enable one to generate all and only acceptable sentences. Nonsentences in the language fail to meet one or more of these rules. If you can speak and understand a language, then you have learned and can use its grammar, even if what you know is implicit and not available for conscious articulation. Many students learning a second language discover much, at a conscious level of analysis, about their native tongue (Just what is the pluperfect tense anyway?).

The implicit knowledge of grammar that we carry about provides us with linguistic intuitions. Being able to identify the parts of speech in a sentence, knowing what is the subject as opposed to, say, the verb is one such intuition. Another is recognizing that two different sentence structures mean the same thing (e.g., The student passed the exam. The exam was passed by the student.). Recognizing syntactic ambiguity, in which multiple structures are possible, is yet another linguistic intuition (e.g., Visiting relatives can be a pain). A very basic intuition is recognizing whether a string of words is a grammatical sentence.

To illustrate further the concepts of semantics and syntactics and the idea of linguistic intuitions, consider these three assertions:

The psychologist slept fitfully, dreaming new ideas.

Fitfully the slept new, ideas dreaming psychologist.

The new ideas slept fitfully, dreaming a psychologist.

The first assertion is an English sentence, for it conveys meaning and is syntactically correct. The second assertion is not a sentence because it violates syntactic rules. All the elements of meaning are there but in the wrong order. The third assertion violates no syntactic rules, yet it fails to make any sense. Your mental representation of the noun *ideas* does not allow them to sleep in any fashion, let alone dream about a psychologist.

Pragmatics. The third landmark is the uses or functions of language in social intercourse. **Pragmatics** is defined as the study of the social functions of language. When speakers use language to communicate with listeners, they do so to achieve particular functions or goals. Speakers may command a listener to take a particular action, on the one hand, or inform her about some state of affairs, on the other. Consider these sentences to illustrate the nature of pragmatics:

> It is hot in this room.
> Open the window!

I might utter the first sentence to inform others about how I feel about the room temperature. The second sentence I might utter to command someone to let some cool air into the room. But note that in a specific setting I might utter the first sentence to achieve the goal of the second. To take an extreme case, suppose my arm is in a cast and I utter the first sentence, in just the right way, to an able-bodied person standing next to the window. My intent would be to have the person open the window, but I seek this end indirectly. A command to do so might seem impolite; better to first try dropping a subtle hint as to what I want done.

Pragmatics addresses the various ways that speakers communicate their intentions depending on the social context. **Speech acts** refer to the types of utterances used by people. We inform, command, question, warn, thank, dare, request, and so on. A direct speech act assumes a grammatical form tailored to a particular function. For example, "Open the window!" directly commands. An indirect speech act achieves a function by assuming the guise of another type of speech act. For example, one might question ("Can you open the window?"), warn ("If you don't open the window, we'll all pass out"), threaten ("If you don't open the window, I'll shoot!"), declare ("The window really should be open"), inform ("It really is hot in here"), or even thank, in a sarcastic tone ("Thanks a lot for opening the window").

BOX 8.1: Animal Language

Pioneering work on communication in the animal kingdom was conducted by von Frisch (1950). The waggle dance of the honeybee directs other members of the hive to distant sources of nectar. The precise nature of the dance communicates the direction and distance from the hive of a source discovered by the dancing bee. Since then, a stunning array of communication systems have been documented, including the antennae and head gestures of weaver ants, the alarm calls of vervet monkeys, and the complex signaling of dolphins and whales.

However, comparisons of the characteristics of animal communication systems with human language bring out major differences between the two (Morton & Page, 1992). For example, the large vocabularies of human beings dwarf the number of different signals expressed in naturally occurring animal communication systems. A child of 6 years of age has a vocabulary on the order of 2,500 words (Dale, 1976). By adulthood, vocabulary is measured in the tens of thousands.

Some very exciting laboratory work has involved teaching American Sign Language and specially designed languages to chimpanzees, orangutans, and gorillas. Gardner and Gardner (1969, 1975), for example, raised a chimpanzee named Washoe in an environment comparable to one suitable for an American human baby. Those who raised Washoe "spoke" to the chimp using American Sign Language. They trained Washoe to use sign language to ask for what she wanted. Washoe learned more than 130 signs. When shown the picture of an object, she could make the appropriate sign. More important, Washoe occasionally improvised signs or combined them in novel ways. For example, upon first seeing a swan, Washoe gave the sign for "water" and the sign for "bird."

Terrace, Petitto, Sanders, and Bever (1979), however, doubted that what Washoe and other apes learned was really language. In particular, they doubted that the apes showed the productivity or openness of human language. Terrace and his colleagues raised Nim Chimsky, a young male chimpanzee. Like Washoe, Nim learned about 130 signs and could use these to request objects or actions that he wanted at the moment. Terrace, however, concluded from careful review of videotapes that Nim's signs were often repetitions of what his human caretaker had just signed. Terrace found little evidence that Nim could combine signs according to syntactic rules. Nim could not generate a simple sentence, in other words.

Other researchers question Terrace's strongly negative conclusion. Yet most all investigators in the field recognize that young children with small vocabularies greatly exceed trained apes in their linguistic abilities. As fascinating as it might be to "talk with the animals," using our language or their signal systems, the depth of the conversation is likely to be limited. The fact remains that language is one of the most stunning accomplishments of human evolutionary history.

Pragmatics underscores the point that language is a social tool as well as a cognitive one. Much of the discussion in cognitive psychology necessarily focuses on the role of language in thinking. Yet a text on social psychology could as easily include a major section on language. Virtually every utterance we make and every text we compose carries social consequences. Speech and writing are embedded in a **discourse community,** meaning the social organizations that collectively listen, read, comprehend, interpret, and respond to our uses of language. Granted, we may occasionally carry on a soliloquy or jot a private note, but psychologists of any stripe begin to worry about those who talk to themselves too much.

Competence Versus Performance

In oral communication, we often fail to follow the rules of grammar exactly. Words are omitted, *uhs* and *ahs* are added, sentences are garbled, often with one run right onto another. We add to our speech hand and arm gestures and point to objects and events in the immediate environment. We also pay close attention to whether our listener shows signs of comprehension, such as nodding, or of noncomprehension, such as frowning, and recast our thoughts accordingly. Because the reader is separated in space and time from the writer, syntactical rules must be adhered to more carefully for communication to be ensured.

Hesitations, omissions, repetitions, slips of the tongue are commonplace in speech, yet all speakers of a language know its grammar and are capable of uttering correct sentences. Chomsky (1968) defined **linguistic competence** as the capacity to use a language and distinguished this capacity from **linguistic performance,** the actual use of language in uttering sentences. You may recall from Chapter 1 that Noam Chomsky's work in linguistics served to hasten the turn from behaviorism to cognitive approaches in the field of psychology. The competence versus performance distinction is one of his several key contributions.

Chomsky argued that understanding competence is the task for linguists who must specify the complete grammar underlying the acceptable sentences in a given language. Understanding performance, Chomsky contended, fell to psychologists who study the mental processes actually used in applying competence through acts of speaking and listening. The field of **psycholinguistics** addresses these performance matters. Most of what we review in this and the next two chapters concerns psycholinguistics. However, we make reference in passing to issues explored by linguists, particularly in the section on grammar in this chapter.

Language Acquisition Device

Chomsky (1965) regarded linguistic universals as essential for children to learn language so readily. Natural languages, those found and learned in diverse cultures around the world, all conform to linguistic universals that simplify the learning task. These universals narrow the range of possibilities that the infant, toddler, and young child must explore in listening to the language around them. Artificial languages that violate these universals would be difficult if not impossible to learn.

Chomsky (1965) proposed that a **language acquisition device** is part of the human genetic endowment. The device drives the learning process by innately providing the possible forms that natural languages may take. To illustrate, consider the syntactic order of subject (S), verb (V), and object (O) introduced earlier. Greenberg (1966) concluded from his examination of natural languages that only four of the six possible orders are used and one of these (VOS) is quite rare. The common orders are SOV, SVO, and VSO. In theory, the developing infant would come equipped at birth with the implicit knowledge that natural languages never follow the OVS and OSV orders. Children the world over would come prepared to examine whether the language (or languages) to which they are exposed conform to one of the four possible word orders.

Languages also differ in the degree of word-order variation allowed. Russian, for example, tolerates more variation in the order of words in a sentence compared with English. Pinker (1990) hypothesized that children are programmed to assume that the grammar of their native language demands a fixed order of words. The evidence suggests that early utterances indeed follow a strict ordering, regardless of the language being learned. In the case of English, these early utterances approximate the grammatically correct order. For Russian children, however, their utterances initially fail to show the full scope of possible word orders. It appears that an innate language acquisition device guides children to try out a fixed order first.

Congenitally deaf children have never heard spoken language; some are not taught standard sign language either. Despite the absence of speech or sign input, such children invent their own gestural language that reflects properties of speech acquired by children with normal hearing (Goldin-Meadow & Mylander, 1990). For example, one-word utterances by normal children occur at about 18 months and these are later followed with two- and three-word utterances. The deaf children similarly invent one-sign gestures at 18 months, followed later by two- and three-sign gestures. Presumably, an innate language acquisition device dictates this common pattern of development.

Neural Systems

Very early in the scientific study of the brain, the localization of language was proposed. Broca reported in 1861 a patient who had lost his ability to produce meaningful speech but retained his ability to hear and comprehend speech (McCarthy & Warrington, 1990). The patient received the nickname "Tan" because he uttered only this sound. Broca observed that the muscles of the vocal apparatus were not at fault, for Tan could eat and drink without difficulty. Broca speculated that Tan suffered from damage to a specific area in his brain that controlled speech, located in the third convolution of the frontal lobe in the left hemisphere. As it turned out, Tan suffered brain damage in many areas but we still refer to this part of the brain as Broca's area in honor of his early investigations (see Figure 8.1).

In 1874 Wernicke reported on patients who could speak easily (albeit unintelligibly) but who failed to comprehend speech (McCarthy & Warrington, 1990). They tended to pronounce phonemes in a jumble, sometimes uttering novel words or neologisms. Postmortem examination of one such patient revealed a lesion in the area just behind or posterior to Broca's area (Figure 8.1).

Broca and Wernicke pointed to a path traveled by many researchers. They reached the conclusion that the left hemisphere generally controls the production and comprehension of language. We will examine speaking and listening in detail in the next chapter. For now, the essential point is that compelling evidence localizes oral language in the dominant left hemisphere.

Hemispheric dominance or brain lateralization in human beings means that one hemisphere controls key motor and cognitive functions. Approximately 90% of people reveal a left dominant hemisphere, meaning that they are right-handed. Recall that the brain shows contralateral control, such that the motor and sensory nerves of the right side of the body are controlled by the left hemisphere of the brain. Right-handedness is found universally across diverse cultures (Corballis, 1989). Moreover,

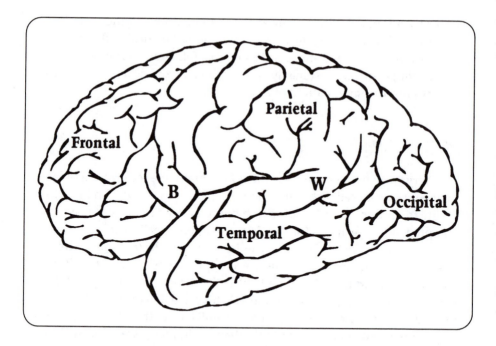

Figure 8.1. Broca's area (B) and Wernicke's area (W) in relation to the four major lobes of the left cerebral hemisphere.
SOURCE: From McCarthy and Warrington (1990). Copyright © 1990 by Academic Press, Inc. Reprinted by permission.

language is localized in the left hemisphere of virtually all right-handed individuals.

Evidence for the localization of language in the left hemisphere comes from a variety of sources. The study of **aphasia,** an acquired language dysfunction, is one such source. There are several specific types of aphasia. Broca's aphasia, for example, refers to an inability to speak, whereas Wernicke's aphasia refers to a comprehension dysfunction. Research has shown that when right-handed people suffer damage to their left hemisphere, the frequency of aphasia is high (McCarthy & Warrington, 1990). Only rarely does a right-handed individual lose language function from damage to the right hemisphere.

Further, surgeons preparing to operate on patients suffering from epilepsy have checked to determine which hemisphere controls language as a precautionary measure (Milner, 1975). They do so using a procedure developed by Wada in which a barbiturate, sodium amytal, is sent to a single hemisphere by injection in either the right or the left carotid artery (Wada & Rasmussen, 1960). By sedating only one hemisphere, the surgeon can test for whether speech and comprehension are disturbed and therefore isolated in the sedated hemisphere. Once again, right-handed individuals usually show language functions isolated in the left hemisphere.

Finally, Sperry and his colleague Gazzaniga investigated the localization of language in a remarkable series of studies involving split-brain patients (Gazzaniga, Bogen, & Sperry, 1965). These individuals suffered horrendous seizures from epilepsy, seizures that could not be controlled by the usual therapies. In the 1950s, physicians treating such severe cases successfully controlled the seizure by cutting the connective tissue between hemispheres called the corpus callosum. The epileptic seizure could be likened to an electrical storm; by severing the hemispheric bridge, the surgeons isolated the storm to one hemisphere, lessening its devastation. After recovering from the surgery, these patients behaved quite normally and revealed no cognitive deficits to a casual observer. Yet, careful testing revealed highly selective deficits.

If a right-handed, split-brain patient were given a common object such as a coin, then her ability to verbalize the name of the object depended on which hand she used. If the coin were placed in her right hand, then all information about it would be processed by the left hemisphere. This was because of contralateral control in which the left hemisphere controlled the right side of the body and the right hemisphere controlled the left side. Because of the language centers in the left hemisphere, the patient could readily name the object as a coin. But if placed in the left hand, sending the information to the right hemisphere, the patient would be unable to name the object. When pressed to do so, the patient could point to the object just placed in the left hand—but only by pointing with the left hand. This astonishing outcome showed that the right hemisphere indeed knew what the object was, but could not name it because language use depended on involving the left hemisphere.

The situation for left-handed individuals is much more complicated. It appears, from the various tests noted above, that most left-handed individuals show speech functions in both hemispheres. Some left-handers show speech localized in the left hemisphere, and few if any reveal localization in the right hemisphere (McCarthy & Warrington, 1990). As we will see in a later chapter, there are a variety of **dyslexias,** which are disorders of reading (such as confusing letters). It turns out that left-handers are highly susceptible to this form of language impairment, possibly because of the atypical pattern of localizing language in the brain.

Grammars

At the heart of linguistics lies the effort to specify the rules that govern the construction of acceptable sentences. The grammar of a language allows one to recognize strings of words that are sentences and to reject strings that are nonsentences. Linguists have proposed three classes of grammars that try to account for the regularities of all languages. These are phrase structure grammars, transformational grammars, and case grammars. Our purpose in the next section is to describe these briefly and relate them to psycholinguistic studies.

Phrase Structure Grammar

The first grammar we will examine will probably sound familiar to most readers from their memories of composition classes in primary and secondary schools. The **phrase structure** of a sentence consists of the hierarchical relations among its constituent phrases, such as noun phrases, verb phrases, and prepositional phrases. A phrase is a group of grammatically related words that function as a single part of speech; a phrase does not contain a subject and a verb. A tree diagram can be used to represent the grammatical structure of a sentence, as shown in Figure 8.2. Composition instruction has long relied on sentence diagramming exercises to teach how to construct sentences.

The sentence in Figure 8.2 provides a simple case. Indeed, linguists call it a simple sentence because it contains but one independent clause, with a subject, verb, and object. This structure is partitioned into two branches—a noun phrase and a verb phrase. The verb phrase contains a verb and another embedded noun phrase. Modifiers can of course be added to each of these grammatical elements, yet the sentence remains simple until additional clauses are added. A clause is like a phrase, but it contains both a subject and a verb. Independent clauses stand on their own as complete assertions, whereas dependent clauses must be embedded in the context of an independent clause. Consider these sentences:

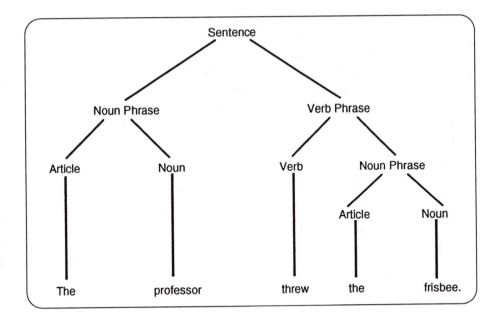

Figure 8.2. Phrase structure of a simple sentence.

The balding professor threw the frisbee poorly.

The professor, who was balding, threw the frisbee poorly.

The professor threw the frisbee and he left the picnic.

The first sentence is a simple sentence with added modifiers. The second adds a dependent clause (who was balding), making it a complex sentence. The third sentence adds another independent clause, making it a compound sentence.

Thus, as can be gleaned from these examples, a phrase structure grammar allows the linguist to determine whether a string of words is a sentence. If it can be diagrammed, following all the rules, then the words constitute a sentence. It certainly provides the means for identifying the parts of speech. These are linguistic intuitions, then, that can be accounted for by presuming that people implicitly know or store in memory a representation based on phrase structure. Put differently, human competence with phrase structure grammar can be argued plausibly.

Researchers have also examined human performance to shed light on the psychological reality of phrase structure grammar. A classic psycholinguistic experiment by Garrett, Bever, and Fodor (1966) illustrates this point. They had discovered in earlier research that the boundary between phrase structures influenced auditory perception in an interesting way. They presented listeners with a series of sentences through earphones; they superimposed on the tape recording of each sentence the sound of a click. The click occurred at various locations relative to the boundaries among the phrases in a given sentence. The listeners' task was to identify the location at which they heard the click. It turned out that the sound of the click tended to be heard at a phrase boundary, even when its actual location occurred earlier or later.

For example, the following two sentences were used by Garrett et al.:

1. (As a direct result of their new invention's influence) (the company was given an award).
2. (The retiring chairman whose methods still greatly influence the company) (was given an award).

The final words in each sentence (influence the company/was given an award) were tape recorded once and inserted into the sentences. Thus listeners heard precisely the same words, pauses, and click in both cases. Specifically, the listeners located the click during the first syllable of the word *company*. Yet in sentence 1, a phrase boundary occurs between the words *influence* and *the* as shown by the parentheses. In sentence 2, the boundary falls between the words *company* and *was*. Garrett et al. predicted that, despite the identical auditory stimulus in both cases, the click would "migrate" to different perceptual locations determined by the syntax of the sentence. They found just that. Listeners given sentence 1 heard the click much earlier relative to those given sentence 2. It was as if the listeners constructed a psychological boundary as dictated by the phrase structure grammar and then punctuated it by "hearing" the click.

Transformational Grammar

The intriguing results of Garrett et al. (1966) show that human performance can be affected by the grammar of phrase structures. Yet, remember that the linguist is interested not in performance but in competence. On this score, Chomsky and other linguists began to view phrase structure grammar as an incomplete account of language. It simply could not deal with important linguistic intuitions. For example, earlier we briefly considered the ambiguous sentence, "Visiting relatives can

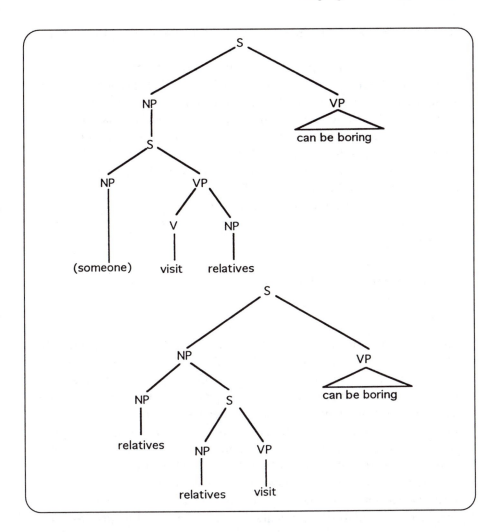

Figure 8.3. Alternative deep structures of an ambiguous sentence.
SOURCE: Reprinted by permission of the publishers from *Language Acquisition* by Jill G. de Villiers and Peter A. de Villiers, Cambridge, MA: Harvard University Press. Copyright © 1978 by the President and Fellows of Harvard College.

be boring." One meaning of this is that "visiting relatives are boring," referring to those aunts, cousins, or in-laws that one would rather not have around the house during the holidays. Another meaning is that "visiting relatives is boring," referring to the agonies of wasting a vacation trip on traveling to see relatives. The difficulty with this sentence is that it may be parsed only in one way based on the rules of phrase structure.

Chomsky (1965) proposed an alternative grammar to account for this and many other linguistic intuitions that fell outside the scope of phrase structures. Chomsky contended that the phrase structure should be viewed merely as a surface structure. The critical level of analysis in his view was the deep structure of a sentence. The **deep structure** precisely captured the intended meaning of the ambiguous sentence. Thus the above sentence with but one surface structure actually has two different deep structures, as shown in Figure 8.3.

In addition, it is quite commonly the case that a single deep structure can be embodied in two different surface structures. Consider these two sentences:

The professor threw the frisbee.

The frisbee was thrown by the professor.

Both sentences mean the same thing. This can be captured through Chomsky's grammar by assuming that both sentences can be represented by the same deep structure, despite their differing phrase structures at a surface level. Specifically, Chomsky proposed that the deep structure would take the active voice for both sentences, with *the professor* as the subject, *frisbee* as the direct object, and *throw* as the verb. Further, he proposed that a transformation operating on the deep structure could yield a surface structure that differs from the deep structure. In this case, a passive transformation produces the second version of the sentence. **Transformational grammar** contends that meaning is derived from a deep structure and the transformations create an acceptable surface structure from the deep structure. Phonetic rules then operate on the surface structure to produce a spoken sentence (see Figure 8.4).

The essential point of Chomsky's transformational grammar is that one must look to the deep structure of language to understand linguistic competence. Many linguistic intuitions in addition to the handful considered here can be understood through transformational grammar.

Some psycholinguistic evidence that examines human performance also suggests the reality of deep structure and transformational grammar. Blumenthal (1967) investigated whether the grammatical function played by a word in the deep structure of a sentence influenced human memory. Blumenthal tested memory in a cued recall test. After listening to a list of

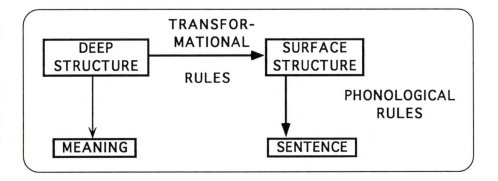

Figure 8.4. Transformational rules convert a grammatical deep structure into the surface structure of a sentence.

SOURCE: Reprinted by permission of the publishers from *Language Acquisition* by Jill G. de Villiers and Peter A. de Villiers, Cambridge, MA: Harvard University Press. Copyright © 1978 by the President and Fellows of Harvard College.

sentences, the participant tried to remember the sentences using a one-word cue for each sentence. Blumenthal varied the grammatical function of the cue word at the level of deep structure. He predicted that an important function, such as subject of the verb in the deep structure, would be a better recall cue than a minor function, such as object of the preposition.

To see the logic of Blumenthal's study, consider the diagrams in Figure 8.5. Pairs of sentences were included in the list in which each member of the pair exhibited the same surface structure but different deep structures. For instance, the surface structures of "Gloves were made by tailors" and "Tables were built by hand" are identical, as diagrammed in the top half of Figure 8.5. The deep structures shown in the bottom half of the figure differ, however. By using the last word of each sentence (*tailors* or *hand*) as the recall cue, the implications of the observed difference in deep structure could be explored. Note that, at a deep structure level, *tailors* serves the key function of subject. In contrast, *hand* serves merely as an object of the preposition. Does this difference affect recall performance?

The results are shown in Table 8.3. Nearly twice as many sentences were correctly recalled when the cue or prompt word served an important function in the deep structure compared with a minor role. This can be seen in the experimental condition in which the final word of the sentence was used as the cue. Blumenthal also included a control condition in

252

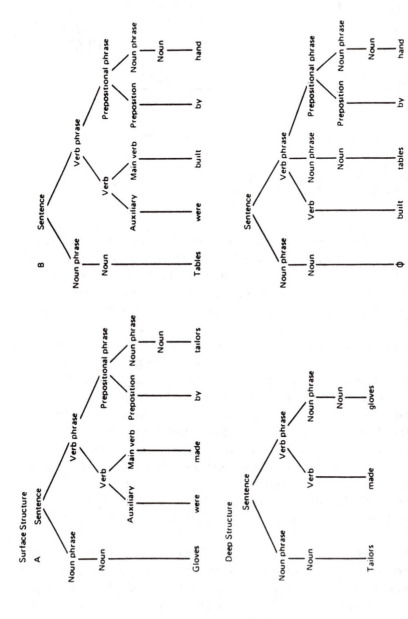

Figure 8.5. The surface structures and deep structures of two sentences used in a test of transformational grammar. SOURCE: From Bourne et al., *Cognitive Processes.* Copyright © 1986, Fig. 7-4. Reprinted by permission of Prentice-Hall, Inc., Englewood Cliffs, NJ.

Table 8.3 The Number of Sentences Recalled Varies With Deep Structure Function

Recall Cue	Deep Structure Function	
	Subject (Sentence A)	Object (Sentence B)
Final noun	7.2	3.9
Initial noun	7.1	6.9

SOURCE: Adapted from Blumenthal (1967). Used with permission from Academic Press, Inc.

which the initial word of the sentence was used as a cue. Looking back at Figure 8.5, you can see that the initial word in each case (*gloves* and *tables*) fulfilled the same role in the surface structure (namely, as the subject). But they also fulfilled the same role in the deep structure (namely, as the direct object). Therefore they were not expected to differ in their effectiveness as recall cues and, as can be seen in Table 8.3, they did not.

Case Grammar

Fillmore (1968) challenged Chomsky's theory of transformational grammar on the grounds that it ignores the semantic roles played by words in a sentence. We of course know that semantics cannot be ignored in language. Without a consideration of semantics and pragmatics, as well as syntax, our understanding of language is incomplete. Yet, Fillmore contended that the grammar underlying human linguistic competence cannot omit semantic relations. The terms of Chomsky's deep structure, such as subject, verb, and object, are purely syntactical concepts. Fillmore argued that the deep structure of a complete grammar must also specify semantic relations or "cases."

According to Fillmore, each noun in a proposition serves in one of a small number of **case roles**. These include the agentive case (who acted), the instrumental case (how the agent acted), the experiencer case (the one being affected by action), and the goal case (the result of the action). A word can play different roles in the surface structure of the sentence yet fill the same semantic case. For example, the professor is the agent in both of these surface structures.

The professor threw the frisbee.

The frisbee was thrown by the professor.

To illustrate the other cases, I have underscored the words that fill each of the following cases:

Instrumental: The child crushed the spider with a rock.

Experiencer: The spider felt the pain.

Goal: The child made certain the spider was dead.

The central thesis of Fillmore's case grammar is that the syntactic relations of Chomsky's theory are necessary but not sufficient for an adequate deep structure. Once again, linguistic intuitions provide the key evidence. Fillmore marshaled evidence of sentences like those shown above in which the semantic relation, not the syntactic relation, captured the similarity among sentences. Bourne, Dominowski, Loftus, and Healy (1986) offered three sentences that captured the difference between Fillmore's and Chomsky's position:

The congressman received a message by telegram.

A message reached the congressman by telegram.

A telegram conveyed a message to the congressman. (p. 205)

Congressman fills the goal case in each sentence. If you take a moment to analyze each sentence, you will find that *congressman* plays a different deep structure (and surface structure) role in each sentence. It is the subject of the first sentence and the direct object of the second sentence, for example. The same point can be made about *message.* It fills the experiencer case in all three variations, despite taking on differing syntactic roles. The story is similar for *telegram,* which uniformly fills the instrument case. These sentences therefore provide linguistic evidence that a complete grammar must embody not only syntactic relations but also semantic cases at the level of deep structure.

What about psycholinguistic evidence? The recall data reported by Blumenthal (1967) are relevant. Notice that in the sentences presented in Figure 8.5, the final cue word *tailors* differed from the word *hand* in semantic case. Whereas *tailors* fills the important agentive role, *hand* plays the instrumental role. One could argue that Blumenthal's findings could be explained as showing the validity of case grammar, not transformational grammar. In other words, semantic cases and deep structure syntactic roles are confounded in Blumenthal's study.

Healy and Levitt (1978) set out to separate these factors in a memory experiment. They presented people with a list of sentences with instructions to remember them. The sentences included the words *John* and *Sam*. In the semantic role condition, *John* always appeared in the experiencer case (e.g., John was sleepy by the fire) and *Sam* always appeared in the goal case (e.g., Sam was the recipient of the grant). The deep structure syntactic condition assigned these names differently. In this condition, *John* always appeared as the deep structure subject (e.g., The accident was imagined by John), whereas *Sam* appeared as the deep structure object of the preposition (e.g., The roar was deafening to Sam). Other conditions were also designed as controls, including one in which *Sam* and *John* appeared in consistent surface structure roles and one in which they appeared randomly.

Healy and Levitt measured the accuracy with which participants could remember whether *Sam* or *John* appeared in a particular sentence (e.g., Sam/John was the recipient of the grant). Their correct identification of the name varied substantially by condition. Of key importance here, participants made almost as many errors (24%) in the deep structure syntactic condition as in the random condition (28%). This implies that people do not store in memory the deep structure syntactic role played by a word terribly well. In contrast, they committed only a third as many errors in the semantic condition (8%). Plainly, the semantic role played by the words were stored in memory with reasonable accuracy.

Thought and Language

Thought and language are related intimately. Chomsky (1968) among many others regarded the study of language as essential in any program of research into the nature of the human mind. Specifying the degree and nature of the relation between thought and language has been the focus of much attention. Broadly speaking, three relations are possible. Thought and language might be identical; thought might depend on language; or language might depend on thought (Jenkins, 1969). Let us consider the evidence.

The Identity Hypothesis

The notion that thought can be equated with language has a rich history. It served as a central tenet of behaviorism throughout the first half of this century. Watson (1924/1930) proposed that thought—an unscientific concept not open to empirical study from the standpoint of behaviorism—could be addressed as **subvocal speech.** If all human activities were to be reduced to a set of responses that could be conditioned, then plainly thought must be an overt response of some kind. The most natural way to deal with thinking in terms of a behaviorist model was to regard thought and language as identical. Thus people sometimes speak aloud and sometimes they speak to themselves.

Numerous experiments set out to identify the muscular movements of the vocal tract that the behaviorists expected whenever a person engaged in thinking. Sure enough, for some people in some tasks, such subvocal speech could be measured. Reading is one example in which subvocal speech can be detected. The vocal movements involved in reading aloud can at times be detected in minute form during silent reading. Subvocal speech also plays in a role in writing, reasoning, decision making, problem solving, and other thinking tasks. However, in numerous cases, no evidence of subvocalization could be detected in tasks that called for silent thinking.

Watson tried to account for the negative results by suggesting that other muscular movements may be just as critical as vocal movements. For example, when I lecture to a class, I frequently gesture with my arms and hands. Perhaps, in thinking alone, I make minute hand and arm movements as well as on occasion vocal movements. To test this notion, Smith, Brown, Toman, and Goodman (1947) conducted a remarkable experiment. Smith agreed to be paralyzed by the drug curare, losing muscular control. Without access to his muscles, he in theory should have lost his ability to think. But the outcome proved otherwise. Smith found that he could still perceive his surroundings, recall past events, and think under the influence of curare.

Today, the notion that thought and language are identical is a straw man, a hypothesis easily refuted. But in its time, the notion deserved and most definitely received a careful hearing. Two famous contributors on the matter were the Russian psychologist Vygotsky and the American linguist Chomsky.

Vygotsky (1962) investigated what he termed **inner speech,** by which he meant the thinking that occurs in the form of word meanings. In particular, he studied the development of speech, thought, and inner speech. He concluded from his research that speech and thought have different roots in the course of cognitive development. Vygotsky pointed to a time in the life of an infant and toddler when thinking has not yet begun and a different point when speech has not yet begun. He suggested that the two follow different tracks of development but eventually merge in what he called inner speech. Yet, even in the merging of two, the behaviorist equation failed to capture the relationship in Vygotsky's view. To quote Vygotsky (1962):

> Inner speech is not the interior aspect of external speech—it is a function in itself. It still remains speech, i.e., thought connected with words. But while in external speech thought is embodied in words, in inner speech words die as they bring forth thought. Inner speech is to a large extent thinking in pure word meanings. It is a dynamic, shifting, unstable thing, fluttering between word and thought, the two more or less stable, more or less firmly delineated components of verbal thought. (p. 149)

Chomsky (1959) entered the discussion on language, thinking, and behavior in his critique of Skinner's (1957) *Verbal Behavior.* This book provided what was then a state-of-the-art, sophisticated version of Watson's view that thought is nothing but language and language is nothing but behavior. Skinner attempted to explain human language in terms of stimulus, response, and reinforcement contingencies. Chomsky charged Skinner with stretching behaviorism to the breaking point to accommodate the phenomenon of language. To illustrate, in what useful sense can one say that an uttered sentence is a specific response elicited by particular properties of a stimulus? For a sentence to be under stimulus control, there must be a specific associative link. Suppose we visit an art gallery, encounter a room full of Campbell soup cans, and I say: "These pieces are by Andy Warhol." Some knowledge of modern art combined with the stimulus in the environment could elicit this response. But I might just as easily have said: "So this is modern art," or "I'm ready for lunch." Chomsky's point was that behaviorism failed to capture the essential features of language, such as the ability to produce an infinite variety of sentences in any given situation.

The Whorfian Hypothesis

Given that thought is not identical to language, is thought dependent on language or vice versa (Jenkins, 1969)? The former view is named after Benjamin Whorf, an engineer who took up the study of North American Indian languages as an avocation. The **Whorfian, or linguistic relativity, hypothesis** holds that thought depends on language. In particular, the lexicon and the syntactic structure of a given language constrain how the native speakers of the language can think. To illustrate, consider that skiers distinguish between the wet, slushy qualities of corn snow and the dry, fluffy qualities of powder snow, for example. The linguistic relativity hypothesis would hold that skiers perceive and think about the world differently than people for whom snow is snow. Alternative words in a lexicon affect cognition in this view. Whorf and many other linguists and psychologists have searched for evidence that the way the members of a culture think can be traced to the structure of their language.

An early test of the linguistic relativity hypothesis investigated labels for colors. Languages differ markedly in the words used to identify divisions among the hues of the spectrum (Brown & Lenneberg, 1954). In English, six primary terms are used: *purple, blue, green, yellow, orange,* and *red.* In Shona, an African language, these terms are reduced to four. In another African language, Bassa, only two terms are used, with one referring to the brighter, long wavelength hues of yellow, orange, and red while the other refers to the darker, shorter wavelengths. If language determines perception, then speakers of these languages ought to see the color spectrum differently.

Brown and Lenneberg (1954) did not directly test speakers of all three languages, however. Instead, they examined only English speakers in two ways. They measured the consistency with which people provide a label for each of 24 color chips that varied in hue systematically from short to long wavelengths. It turned out that certain variations of blue, red, and other colors in between were easier to label, in the sense that everyone agreed on what to call them, compared with other colors. Next, they measured short-term recognition of specific color chips. Brown and Lenneberg found that the ease of labeling a chip correlated highly with the ease of retaining the color in memory. That is, the linguistic measure correlated with a measure that reflected perception and cognition.

Yet, as every student of psychology knows, a correlation between the two measures does not assure that language caused the variation in recognition memory. It may well be that some third factor caused both the ease of labeling and the ease of recognizing particular colors. Brown (1976) reviewed a number of findings that followed his earlier work and came to just that conclusion.

Recall that members of a natural category differ in terms of typicality, with one instance best representing all others. Rosch-Heider, a student of Brown's, first documented such typicality differences with colors (Heider, 1972). She included in her study eight color chips that English speakers identified as prototypical of a region of the spectrum (e.g., the best example of red). To this she added 21 atypical colors. Next, by measuring speed of naming, Rosch-Heider tested the ease with which a native speaker from each of 23 different languages provided a label for the color chips. As it happened, the typical colors were markedly easier to label relative to the atypical colors. This outcome occurred across all languages tested. In addition, the typical colors were better recognized in a test of short-term memory.

Rosch-Heider also tested the Whorfian hypothesis by contrasting English speakers from North America with a Stone Age tribe of New Guinea, the Dani Indians. The Dani use only two color names, corresponding roughly to bright and dark hues. To assess how individuals from the two cultures perceived color, she devised a learning task in which arbitrary, nonsense syllables were paired with segments of the spectrum. The number of errors made in learning the new names was taken as an index of the ease with which a color is perceived and cognitively processed. She found that the English speakers made the fewest errors on the prototypical colors, those taken as the best representatives of red, blue, and so on. The Dani also made the fewest errors on the same prototypical colors, even though their language had no terms for them (Rosch, 1973).

These results, then, speak against linguistic relativity. Rosch-Heider concluded that the visual system determines how human beings of any culture perceive and process prototypical colors (see de Valois & Jacobs, 1968). Indeed, many natural languages around the globe include terms or divide the color space in essentially the same manner as English. Perception, then, clearly can affect the structure of language.

Later research, however, indicated that another aspect of color cognition can be influenced by the linguistic terms used in a given culture (Kay & Kempton, 1984). Unlike English, a Mexican Indian language, Tarahumara, omits blue and green color terms. When native speakers of English viewed a prototypical green, a prototypical blue, and a greenish/ bluish test color, they consistently categorized the test color. If it was

---

BOX 8.2: Language Influences Thought

Although the strong version of the Whorfian hypothesis has not fared well, we should not overlook that language can certainly influence thought. Bilingual speakers sometimes claim that they think differently depending on the language they are using at the moment. Dreaming—a unique form of thinking—may occur only in the native tongue of a bilingual. Wierzbicka (1985) documented how her thoughts were shaped partly by whether she was speaking English or Polish.

Hunt and Agnoli (1991) argued that the weak version of the Whorfian hypothesis fares very well. Aspects of a language can indeed influence the way in which the speakers and listeners think. For example, English and Italian differ in that a given word in English may have several meanings (high polysemy) whereas in Italian it has only one or two meanings. In English, "I went out to buy the pot" demands more processing time to understand as the listener sorts out "whether the speaker spends leisure time in gardening or recreational pharmacology" (Hunt & Agnoli, 1991, p. 382). In Italian, "Uscii a comperare il vaso" unambiguously identifies a gardening pot. Italian is also less ambiguous because it relies on inflections rather than word order to assign syntactic roles. A story on the same topic regarding East Germany in 1989 published by similar Italian and American newspapers revealed a startling difference. Two English speakers "agreed that 18 of 33 sentences were potentially ambiguous out of context" (p. 384). Two Italian speakers "found that only 3 of 64 sentences were ambiguous."

Hunt and Agnoli (1991) concluded in favor of the weak version of the Whorfian hypothesis as follows:

> Every utterance in language A has a translation in language B. . . . The issue is one of cost: Are there statements that are natural in language A that are statable but unmanagable in language B? The Whorfian hypothesis is properly regarded as a psychological hypothesis about language performance and not as a linguistic hypothesis about language competence. Our review has convinced us that different languages pose different challenges for cognition and provide differential support to cognition. (p. 387)

---

closer to blue, then English speakers indicated it should be grouped with the prototypical blue. In contrast, they put the test color with green if it was closer to the prototypical green. Speakers of Tarahumara failed to categorize the test colors in a consistent manner. The nature of the language, then, influenced whether people drew a sharp boundary in their categorizations of color.

In conclusion, thought is not fully dependent on language, as is suggested by the linguistic relativity hypothesis. In fact, in some ways, language is partly influenced by the nature of our perceptual systems, as explained earlier. However, it appears that language can also influence thought, supporting a weak version of the Whorfian hypothesis. A growing body of studies, in addition to the color research discussed here, support such a weak version of linguistic relativity (Hunt & Agnoli, 1991).

▣ SUMMARY ▣

1. Language is a system of symbols that are used to communicate ideas among two or more individuals. There are 16 linguistic universals that are characteristic of all languages. Prominent among these are semanticity, arbitrariness, displacement, and openness. Animal communication systems share some but not all of the defining characteristics of human language.

2. Languages differ in terms of their semantics, syntactics, and pragmatics. Semantics concerns the use of symbols to refer to objects, events, and ideas in the world. The words used in language constitute the lexicon that must be represented mentally in fluent speakers. Syntactics concerns the rules for ordering words to construct meaningful, acceptable sentences in a language. Pragmatics concerns the use of language within social contexts. People command, inform, warn, and otherwise communicate their intentions as direct speech acts (e.g., Open the window!) or indirect speech acts (e.g., Dreadfully hot in here, don't you think?).

3. Transformational grammar distinguishes between the surface structure, the noun and verb phrases that constitute the sentence, and the deep structure. The deep structure is the phrase structure that specifies the core meaning of a sentence. Through one of several transformations, the deep structure is converted to the surface structure. Case grammar adds semantic roles to the deep structure of sentences, arguing that syntactic rules alone are insufficient.

4. Thought and language were viewed by behaviorists as identical. Thinking occurred in the form of subvocal speech. Experiments showed, however, that thinking could occur in the absence of

subvocal speech. Moreover, even the inner speech discussed by Vygotsky could not be viewed as identical with overt speech.

5. The Whorfian or linguistic relativity hypothesis holds that thought is dependent on language. An alternative view is that language depends on thought. Research on color cognition and language indicates a complex relation between language and thought. A weak version of the Whorfian hypothesis holds only that language can influence thought and on this point the evidence is clearly positive. Thoughts in one language can be more or less difficult to express in another language.

Key Terms

linguistic universals	linguistic performance
semanticity	psycholinguistics
arbitrariness	language acquisition device
displacement	aphasia
openness	dyslexias
duality	phrase structure
semantics	deep structure
morpheme	transformational grammar
phonemes	case roles
mental lexicon	subvocal speech
syntax	inner speech
pragmatics	Whorfian or linguistic
speech acts	relativity hypothesis
discourse community	linguistic competence

Recommended Readings

The present chapter illustrates well the interdisciplinary influence of the humanities, specifically linguistics, on cognitive science. For an introduction to linguistics, I recommend Akmajian, Demers, and Harnish's (1984) *Linguistics: An Introduction to Language and Communication*. Radford's (1988) book titled *Transformational Grammar: A First Course* illuminates Chomsky's work. A book by Chomsky himself is his 1986 volume titled *Knowledge of Language: Its Nature, Origin, and Use*.

An excellent review of psycholinguistics may be found in a classic text by Clark and Clark (1977) titled *Psychology and Language*. Winograd's (1983) *Language as a Cognitive Process*, Tartter's (1986) *Language Processes*, and Carroll's (1994) *Psychology of Language* offer more current overviews of the field. Foss (1988) provided a chapter on experimental psycholinguistics in the *Annual Review of Psychology*.

For more on animal language, I recommend Griffin's (1984) *Animal Thinking*. An in-depth collection of readings may be found in *"Language" and Intelligence in Monkeys and Apes: Comparative Developmental Perspectives* edited by Parker and Gibson (1990).

For reasons of space, I neglected the developmental literature on language acquisition. It is extensive. Dale's (1976) *Language Development: Structure and Function* serves as a good introduction. Further reading on the subject should include *Language Acquisition* (1978) by de Villiers and de Villiers. McLaughlin's (1978) *Second-Language Acquisition in Childhood* is also of interest.

Pinker's (1984a) *Language Learnability and Language Development* makes the case that language acquisition depends on learning processes geared specifically for this job. Other theorists counter that general learning processes can account for language development. Anderson (1983) makes this case within the context of his ACT* model in *The Architecture of Cognition*. Rumelhart and McClelland (1986) do the same from a connectionist viewpoint in their work, *Parallel Distributed Processing: Explorations in the Microstructure of Cognition*.

CHAPTER **9**

◉ Speaking and Listening

We will now delve into the details of how human beings produce and comprehend speech. Talking, listening, and conversing are aspects of human cognition that command our attention. For many of us, talking takes precedence over listening. So we will begin with the production of speech.

Speech Production

Planning and Executing Speech

Speaking involves many cognitive and motor processes (Levelt, 1989). A person first must plan what needs to be said and how it needs to be said to affect listeners in the desired manner. Then, the plans must be executed by uttering the phonemes, words, phrases, and sentences. Clark and Clark (1977) identified five distinct aspects of planning and execution. The speaker must generate discourse plans, sentence plans, and constituent plans. With these matters decided, then an articulatory program can be established followed by actually articulating the meaningful sounds. Let us examine each briefly.

Types of plans. A speaker must know the general nature of discourse in order to proceed. Storytelling brings forth one set of expectations on the part of listeners, whereas giving instructions, persuading, making small talk, or swearing to a solemn pledge call forth quite different expectations. The sentences and phrases generated must add to the development of the discourse chosen by speakers and the social situation in which they find themselves speaking.

Sentence plans address the pragmatic, syntactic, and semantic issues of language. Given a particular kind of discourse, which speech act should be used? Should the speech act be direct or indirect? What information should be the subject of a sentence, what should be included in the main clause, what should be added as a dependent clause? What meanings does the listener already take as given information and what must be provided as new information?

Constituent plans break down the sentence into its components. Each phrase must be constructed one at a time. The words that fit into each noun phrase, verb phrase, and so on must be selected, evaluated for aptness, and placed in proper syntactic order. Hitting upon just the right words and phrases is what makes speaking well a work of art.

The **articulatory program** should be viewed as a plan for the "actual phonetic segments, stresses, and intonation patterns that are to be executed at the next step" (Clark & Clark, 1977, p. 224). The sound of a sentence can vary its meaning through variations in stresses and intonation. The sentence, "You won the award," can be uttered in many different ways, for example. It could express congratulations, disbelief, or envy, depending on how the sentence is programmed and articulated. Try it yourself: Can you vary your expression so as to communicate these different meanings?

The final step of articulation, which we engage in often without a second thought, comes only after much cognitive work. Discourse plans, sentence plans, constituent plans, and the articulatory program all must be established first. Then articulation itself entails the motor commands and muscle movements of the structures of the vocal tract.

A process model. A detailed process model of how we formulate utterances has been proposed by Bock (1982). This is illustrated in Figure 9.1. The **referential arena** concerns the thoughts and ideas, coded in memory in the form of schemas, that we draw upon in speaking. This arena, then, covers the content of our speech. It includes the discourse plans discussed by Clark and Clark (1977), such as a schema or grammar for stories. We

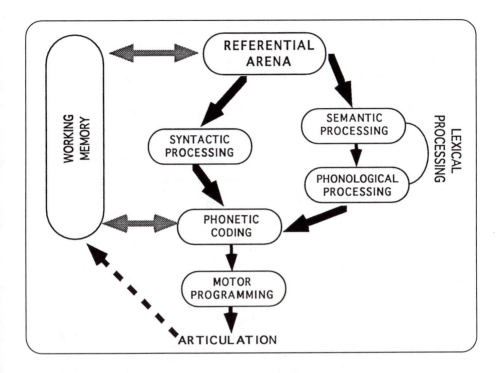

Figure 9.1. A process model of speech production.
SOURCE: From Bock, J. K. (1982). Toward a cognitive psychology of syntax: Information processing contributions to sentence formulation. *Psychological Review, 89,* 1-47. Copyright © 1982 by the American Psychological Association. Reprinted by permission.

will discuss in detail the role of story grammars in the comprehension of spoken and written language. Planning sentences and sentence constituents is represented in Bock's model in the central components. Semantic and phonological processing of individual words must be linked with the syntactic processing of constructing a sentence. The words or lexical items selected are integrated with the grammatical elements of a sentence in an automatic fashion. These components, in Bock's model, do not draw upon the limited capacity of attention and working memory. The major demand on working memory comes from the referential arena, in deciding what to say, not how to say it.

The next step in Bock's model, phonetic coding, does draw upon working memory to a small degree. **Phonetic coding** refers to the conversion, into a code for output, of the sounds of words (phonological codes) and the syntactic functions that they play in a sentence. It allows the articulation or motor programs to execute automatically to generate the correct utterance. As it happens, there is a close connection between the errors that people make in uttering words and the kinds of errors that people make in remembering words from working memory (Ellis, 1980). When phonemes sound alike (such as /b/ and /v/), people tend to confuse them when speaking, when listening, and when trying to recall them from working memory.

Both motor programming and articulation operate automatically in Bock's model. However, the utterance itself enters working memory, where it can be monitored. This is denoted by the dotted line between articulation and working memory.

Articulation

The actual production of speech sounds has been studied in great detail. Each phonetic segment in English, for example, is uttered by shaping the mouth, placing the tongue, shaping the lips, vibrating the vocal cords, and constricting or stopping the flow of air through the vocal tract in a particular way. There are 46 phonemes in the English language. They are categorized as consonants, vowels, and diphthongs, which involve gliding from the position for one vowel to that for another. Recall that a phoneme corresponds to a difference in meaning. *I till* is not the same as *I bill* by virtue of one phoneme.

Consonants and vowels differ fundamentally in their production. Consonants require constricting the mouth so that the air rushes through only partially or not at all. Vowels require opening the mouth in a particular fashion and then allowing the vocal cords to vibrate and the air to move through the mouth unimpeded. Here I will focus only on the consonants to illustrate speech production.

English consonants differ along three dimensions: place of articulation, manner of articulation, and voicing (Glucksberg & Danks, 1975). **Place of articulation** refers to the position in the mouth where there is a constriction of air flow. Bilabial consonants are those uttered with the two lips together. With labiodental consonants, the bottom lip is positioned against the upper front teeth. With dental consonants, the tongue is against the teeth. With alveolar consonants, the tongue is against the alveolar ridge of the gums, a structure just behind the upper front teeth. With platal consonants, the tongue is against the hard plate in the roof of the mouth, a structure just behind the alveolar ridge. Moving back further, with velar consonants, the tongue is against the soft palate or velum

Table 9.1 English Consonants

Manner of Articulation		Bilabial	Labiodental	Dental	Alveola	Palatal	Velar	Glottal
					Place of Articulation			
Stops	Voiceless	pat			tack		cat	
	Voiced	bat			dig		get	
Fricatives	Voiceless		fat	thin	sat	fish		hat
	Voiced		vat	then	zap	azure		
Affricatives	Voiceless					church		
	Voiced				judge			
Nasals		mat			nat		sing	
Liquids					late	rate		
Glides		win				yet		

SOURCE: From Glucksberg, S., & Danks, J. H. (1975). *Experimental psycholinguistics: An introduction*. Hillsdale, NJ: Lawrence Erlbaum. Copyright © 1975 by Lawrence Erlbaum Associates. Reprinted by permission.

in the rear of the mouth. Finally, glottal consonants involve a constriction of air flow in the glottis, which is the opening between the vocal cords in the larynx and the muscles and cartilage that initiate the air flow of speech.

The **manner of articulation,** the way sound is emitted, divides into six features. Stops involve a complete closure at the place of articulation. Fricatives involve a constriction, but not a complete closure. Affricatives involve a two-step sequence of complete closure followed by a rushing of air through a constriction, like a fricative. Nasals involve a complete closure of the mouth so that air rushes through the nose. Liquids and glides differ in how the tongue is shaped.

Table 9.1 illustrates the manner and place of articulation dimensions for English consonants. The letters within slash marks identify the consonant in each entry. For example, /m/ as in *mat* and /n/ as in *nat* are both nasal consonants, but they differ in terms of the place of articulation. Try uttering these consonants while holding your nose closed and you will hear the distortion that results, compared with /p/ as in *pat* or /k/ as in *cat*, for example.

The **voicing** dimension distinguishes consonants that allow the vocal cords to vibrate (voiced) versus those that do not (unvoiced). Table 9.1 shows pairs of consonants that differ only on this dimension. For example, /s/ as in *sat* and /z/ as in *zap* are both fricatives and the manner of articulation is alveolar. However, /s/ is unvoiced whereas /z/ is voiced. That is, /z/ involves the vibration of vocal cords whereas /s/ does not. Place your fingers on the Adam's apple of the throat and you can feel the difference. For some pairs, the difference is really a matter of the precise moment when voicing or vocal cord vibration begins. In pronouncing /b/ versus /p/, the closed lips are released, meaning the point of articulation is bilabial. But in pronouncing the syllable *ba*, the vocal cords begin to vibrate as soon as the lips release, whereas with the *pa* a delay of 60 milliseconds occurs (Clark & Clark, 1977). This delay is called **voice onset time.**

Speech Errors

Errors in articulation or **slips of the tongue** were an important window on the unconscious for Freud. According to psychodynamic theory, such slips revealed the speaker's unconscious wishes. An English clergyman, William A. Spooner, earned a spot in history for his speech slips rather than his stirring sermons (Clark & Clark, 1977). For example,

Spooner chastised a student with, "You have hissed all my mystery lectures," and warned his parishioners, "Easier for a camel to go through the knee of an idol."

According to cognitive theories, slips of the tongue reflect errors in the articulatory program or in execution. They are no different than other everyday errors that people make and they reveal much about the workings of mental schemas, not about unconscious conflicts (Norman, 1981). A spoonerism, as illustrated above, is in fact a particular type of cognitive error in which two phonetic segments are reversed. Fromkin (1973) identified this and other categories of speech errors. For example, two phonemes might be blended rather than reversed, as when the speaker meant to say *grizzly and ghastly* but came out with *grastly*. An error may occur at various levels of language structure. Reversals, for example, may occur at the level of phonetic segments. Instead of saying *Terry and Julia*, the speaker erred by saying *Derry and Chulia*. At the level of syllables, the speaker meant to say *harpsichord* but instead uttered *carpsichord*. The phonetic segments were switched across a boundary of one syllable to the next within a single word.

Speech disorders. In the previous chapter, we learned about Broca's aphasia, a disorder of speech. Modern neuropsychological research has identified two specific types of deficits in speech production (McCarthy & Warrington, 1990). The phonemic disorder characterizes patients who can produce the individual sounds of phonetic segments but who are unable to sequence the phonemes correctly. It is the most common type of aphasia. Saying *stale* instead of *snail*, or *perharst* instead of *perhaps*, or *mane* instead of *name* illustrates the disorder. Other patients can produce the sounds and program the right phonemes; they fail, however, in executing the articulatory program because of a general inability to coordinate and organize complex actions. This is referred to as a kinetic disorder and results in speech that is technically correct but sounds strange. Timing and the stressing of syllables are off the mark. Also, the rate of speech is very slow and phonemes sound "foreign" or "childlike" (McCarthy & Warrington, 1990).

A full understanding of the neuroanatomical problems that cause phonemic and kinetic disorders is not yet at hand. However, for some time now we have known the cause of a specific type of phonemic disorder, called conduction aphasia, that turns up only when words or sentences must be repeated (McCarthy & Warrington, 1990). That is, the individual speaks fluently on a spontaneous basis, but when asked to

BOX 9.1: American Sign Language

Helen Keller observed that deafness was a greater loss than blindness. "Blindness cuts people off from things," she observed. "Deafness cuts people off from people" (Dolnick, 1993, p. 37). Yet, in recent years, a movement among deaf people has denounced the view of deafness as a disability. Instead, Deaf people are a linguistic minority, those who communicate by American Sign Language (ASL). The upper case D signifies that the deaf "share a culture rather than merely a medical condition" (p. 38).

Those who share this view shun trying to speak, which is extremely difficult for those who have been deaf since infancy. To do so requires learning to articulate phonemes without any feedback, a monumental task. The Deaf culture further shuns the use of lip- or speech-reading. "Speechreading is EXHAUSTING," writes the executive director of the Northern Virginian Resource Center for Deaf and Hard of Hearing Persons; "even with peak conditions, good lighting, high energy level, and a person who articulates well, I'm still guessing at half of what I see on the lips" (p. 39).

ASL is a visual and gestural language used by Deaf communities. Many deaf children acquire ASL as a first, natural language. About a half million Americans use ASL every day (Dolnick, 1993). A sign involves a combination of a particular hand shape, a place of articulation, movement, and orientation (Stokoe, Casterline, & Croneberg, 1965). A sign is the rough equivalent of a word, but to bring a specific English word into use, finger spelling is used within ASL. Finger spelling makes use of only hand shape. ASL is regarded as a complete language, not a poor substitute for the spoken word.

As neurologist Oliver Sacks explained, ASL is "a language equally suitable for making love or speeches, for flirtation or mathematics" (Dolnick, 1993, p. 40). Correspondingly, some have argued that ASL should be the language of first choice for deaf children. However, hearing parents of deaf children are reluctant to accept this view. Such parents must communicate with their children through what is for them a foreign language. Moreover, they worry about the fact that Deaf culture, while vibrant, is not the majority culture. One solution to this dilemma is bilingual education. Students are first taught ASL and then acquire English as a second language. A wider bilingualism on the part of hearing and speaking individuals would also help considerably.

repeat even a single word, a phonemic error occurs. For example, when asked to say *wash*, the patient errs by saying *fosh*. Geschwind (1970) argued on theoretical grounds that damage to the primary neural pathways between Wernicke's area and Broca's area would cause such conduction aphasia. Recall that Wernicke's area mediates speech comprehension whereas Broca's area initiates speech. Evidence from more than two dozen studies supports Geschwind's idea (Green & Howes, 1977).

Errors and processes. The frequency of hesitations and errors provides insights into the specific processes by which sentences are produced. For some time, researchers have recognized that hesitations occur often as speakers try to formulate the grammatical components of language (Goldman-Eisler, 1968). The hesitations suggest planning processes at the levels of phrases, clauses, and multiple clauses. Garrett (1988) concluded from a variety of studies that people generally hesitate in speaking for one of three reasons. Long-range planning, which may involve multiple levels of sentences, clauses, phrases, and words, can fully occupy the speaker's attention ("Don't bother me now, I'm busy," to use Garrett's terms). Once the plan is selected, the speaker may still hesitate while preparing to execute a particular unit, such as a phrase ("Wait until the boat is loaded"). Finally, finding the right word and setting up the phonetic segments for the right words can cause hesitations within a phrase ("It's in the mail").

Recall that Bock (1982) proposed that syntactic processing operates in parallel with lexical processing, although the two interact in specific ways (see Figure 9.1). Evidence for such an interaction comes from a speech error called syntactic accommodation. Stemberger (1985) provided two examples of this: "Most cities are true of that" (when the speaker meant to say "That is true of most cities"), and "You're too good for that" (when the speaker intended, "That's too good for you"). Notice that the uttered sentence accommodated to the subject-verb agreement in number, plural in the first case and singular in the second, even though the word that appeared was not the intended subject. The process of selecting the right words to express the speaker's intended meaning went awry. Once these words were selected, they influenced syntactic processing, accommodating the number of the verb to the number of the subject just uttered.

The ways in which people monitor their speech and attempt to repair sentences also provide insights. Levelt (1989) proposed that monitoring occurs at all three stages of speech production. During conceptualization, the speaker monitors the meanings that have been conceived in the referential arena. This presumably entails monitoring preverbal representations. During formulation, the representation of inner speech must be monitored for accuracy before articulation begins. This is presumably accomplished using the same parsing processes involved in recognizing real speech, and requires 150-200 milliseconds. Finally, during articulation the speaker listens to what is actually uttered. Levelt stated that articulation requires 200-250 milliseconds to begin, allowing about 100 milliseconds for errors in the code of inner speech to be detected before utterance. Levelt further hypothesized that interruptions occur 200 milliseconds after the error is detected, usually without respect to phrase, word, or even syllable boundaries.

Evidence on the timing of repairs in spontaneous speech certainly supports the idea that monitoring takes place at multiple levels. Yet, Levelt's interruption proposal appears incorrect (Blackmer & Mitton, 1991). Nearly a fifth of the repairs observed by Blackmer and Mitton occurred immediately upon the occurrence of the error. Such 0-millisecond cutoff-to-repair times imply that "an error segment and its replacement could not have been conceptualized and formulated as a single unit, and yet the replacement can follow the error without a break" (p. 189). Planning apparently occurs in small incremental steps with correction of errors taking place all along the way.

Conversations

So far we have discussed speech production solely from the viewpoint of uttering words, phrases, and sentences. But in virtually every case, people speak so as to be heard and understood. Quite often they expect to be spoken back to by others in what may develop into a lively conversation. As noted in the previous chapter, speech is a social as well as a cognitive act. And social rules govern to a degree how we go about conversing with each other.

Turn-taking. Allowing each participant in a conversation a turn to speak is an example of a social norm. Although the rule is unwritten, participants generally perceive the need to yield the floor to others. To be sure, certain situations call for everyone talking at once (traders placing orders in the stock or commodity markets is one case in point, as is carrying on a heated argument over a family dinner). But typically only one person speaks at a time, with overlap among participants taking place only at the change of turns.

Sacks, Schegloff, and Jefferson (1974) have analyzed the process of taking turns in spontaneous conversations. The order of speakers and the amount they say are not set in advance, unlike some other settings in which speeches are given. Thus implicit social rules are needed to ensure that each person gets a turn to talk. The first rule is that the person addressed by the current speaker should go next. If that person fails to speak after a moment or two, then others may jump in, including the person who just finished.

The current speaker uses linguistic and pragmatic signals to mark the end of his or her turn. A long pause, stopping hand gestures, dropping the pitch and loudness of speech, and making direct eye contact with the next participant in line to speak illustrate these (Cook, 1977). Taking a pause in midsentence or gazing away from the other participants signal that the speaker is still thinking and has more to say. The total number of turns taken and the duration of those turns are a matter of individual personality differences (Jaffe & Feldstein, 1970) as well as a function of the topic of conversation. The social roles of the participants also affect the topics discussed and the length of turns taken by each. Two peers converse differently than a boss and employee, for example (Kemper & Thissen, 1981).

The cooperative principle. Grice (1975) proposed that when two people enter into a conversation, they in essence enter into an implicit contractual agreement. The foundation for this agreement is what Grice termed the *cooperative principle.* It simply means that the participants agree to say things that are appropriate to the conversation and to end the conversation at a mutually agreeable point. One way to understand this contractual agreement is to recall times when people have violated it. Have you ever had someone say something that makes no sense whatever in the context of the ongoing conversation or walk off abruptly, ending a conversation without warning? The cooperative principle dictates otherwise. We agree to speak audibly, to use languages that listeners understand, and to follow the rules of those languages.

In the course of cooperating with one another, participants try to follow four maxims. The maxim of quantity calls upon participants to be informative. One should tell what others need to know to understand, but avoid overloading the participants with too much information and trivial detail. Adhering to this maxim is critical for effective communication, as Clark and Clark (1977) illustrated with following exchange:

STEVEN: Wilfred is meeting a woman for dinner tonight.

SUSAN: Does his wife know about it?

STEVEN: Of course she does. The woman he is meeting is his wife. (p. 122)

Steven mislead Susan here by violating the maxim of quantity. His use of the term *a woman* failed to provide enough information. Susan inferred that the woman in question was someone other than Wilfred's wife.

The maxim of quality implies that speakers in a conversation should say things that are truthful. The maxim of relation means that contributions should be related to the thread of the conversation. The maxim of manner calls for clarity rather than obscurity and ambiguity. When speakers violate these maxims, and there certainly are times when they do, the principle of cooperation is violated.

In comprehending the utterances of the current speaker in a conversation, the other participants must frequently make inferences which Grice called **conversational implicatures.** The following example from Clark and Clark (1977) illustrates the role such inferences play in conversation:

BARBARA: I am out of gas.

PETER: There is a gas station around the corner. (p. 123)

Recall from our discussion of indirect speech acts in the previous chapter that language must be viewed as pragmatic as well as semantic and syntactic. The syntactic and semantic structure of Peter's sentence simply and briefly conveys propositions about the location of a gas station. Pragmatically, Peter is implying additional propositions, however. He assumes that Barbara will realize he is cooperating with her by following the maxim of relation. He invites her to infer that the gas station is open and has gas available for sale. These conversational implicatures need not be explicitly mentioned for communication to succeed.

By cooperating with each other in a social situation, human speech can often communicate much with little. Moreover, we can use brief phrases in nonliteral ways, trusting that others will grasp their meaning in the proper context (Clark & Wilkes-Gibbs, 1986). Imagine a group of coworkers sorting out the lunch order that just arrived from the deli. In this context, "the ham sandwich" can refer not to the food but to the worker who ordered it. The social nature of language is perhaps seen in no clearer light than in our nonliteral uses of language.

The inferences drawn in conversations and the use of nonliteral expressions raise key questions about the comprehension of language (Shapiro & Murphy, 1993). When in a stuffy room someone says, "It's awfully hot in here," how do listeners know the speaker would like the window to be opened? When at dinner someone says, "Can you pass the salt," why does the able-bodied listener next to the salt not respond, "Yes, I can," and do nothing more? The manner in which we comprehend such utterances ties into a large literature on understanding metaphors and drawing inferences while reading. We will take up that literature in the next chapter.

Conclusion

Speaking, an act that most of us take for granted as trivial, represents well the complexity of everyday human behavior. We automatically draw upon a rich storehouse of linguistic rules in conceptualizing, formulating, and articulating a single utterance. Carrying on a conversation invokes yet other rules of social interaction. The range of things that can go wrong and our ability to detect and correct these errors illuminate the intricacies of speaking. Pronunciation, syllable stress, accent, intonation, word choice, semantic roles, syntactic structures, pragmatic intentions, and conversational norms cover much territory. Yet we heed all this and more without giving it a second thought.

Speech Comprehension

Understanding how human beings produce speech is part of the challenge for the cognitive psychology of language. The flip side of the coin—perceiving and comprehending the spoken word—is, if anything, more intricate. In Chapter 2, we examined theories of pattern recognition that operate during perception. The problem of how we comprehend speech has posed major challenges to template and feature theories in particular. It turns out that the acoustic signals that arrive at the ear do not map in any simple one-to-one fashion onto the phonetic segments. Template and feature theories of pattern recognition assume that a particular pattern of acoustic energy at a given point in time must uniquely identify a given phoneme. Let us look at why this is not the case.

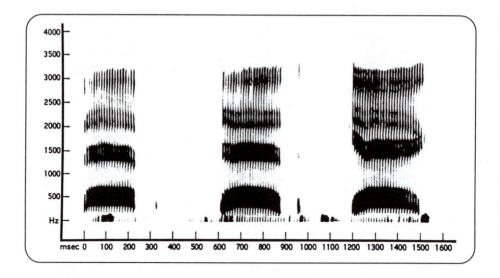

Figure 9.2. Speech spectrograms for, from left to right, "bab," "dad," and "gag," spoken with a British accent.
SOURCE: Figure from *A Course in Phonetics* by Peter Ladefoged, copyright © 1975 by Harcourt Brace & Company, reproduced by permission of the publisher.

Complexities of Speech

A **speech spectrogram** represents the physical acoustic energy of an utterance by plotting frequency in Hertz or cycles per second on the y-axis and time in milliseconds on the x-axis. Examples are shown in Figure 9.2 for "bab," "dad," and "gag," spoken with a British accent (Ladefoged, 1975). The darker the band of energy at a particular frequency, the greater is its amplitude. Notice that the energy clusters at low-, medium-, and high-level frequencies. These bands are called **formants.** The first formant is the lowest frequency band, the second formant is the next higher band, and so on. One might expect that the spectrum for, say, *gag* could be neatly divided into three time segments, with the early segment providing an invariant feature for /g/ followed by one for /a/ and then returning to the one for /g/. This is not the case.

Recall the distinctive feature approach to recognizing printed characters from Chapter 2. Primitive features consisting of lines at various orientations and segments of circles provided the building blocks for recognizing the symbols of printed language. We have seen that the relations among such features are equally important. Only a structural description approach, which takes into account both features and their relations, can begin to explain the perception of objects and events in the real world. Distinctive features alone seemed compelling as long as the domain of concern was sufficiently restricted (printed as opposed to handwritten characters). But in the case of spoken language, a distinctive feature approach fails from the outset. The acoustic segments of the speech spectrogram do not map onto the phonetic segments that we hear. The actual mapping is complicated in three ways.

Coarticulation. First, each segment of the acoustic signal provides clues about the identity of more than one phoneme (Liberman, Cooper, Shankweiler, & Studdert-Kennedy, 1967). This is called **coarticulation.** As shown in Figure 9.3, each of the three phonemes of *beg* are being transmitted simultaneously. They are not separated in time, with /b/ followed by /ae/ and then /g/. Instead, the acoustic energy corresponding to the phonetic segment of /b/ overlaps that of the other phonemes.

Phrased differently, before you have articulated /b/ the vocal track already takes shape to articulate /ae/. Notice, too, from Figure 9.3 that you begin to articulate /g/ even before finishing the articulation of /b/. The key point about coarticulation is that multiple phonetic segments are being articulated at each point in time, in parallel.

Lack of invariance. Second, the acoustic spectrum fails to reveal a distinctive feature for a particular phoneme that stays the same in all contexts (Liberman et al., 1967). This is called the lack of invariant features. The spectrogram for /di/ versus /du/ reveals different formants for the phoneme /d/ depending on whether it is followed by the phoneme of /i/ versus /u/. The first formant is the same in each case. The difference emerges in the second formant, the one with the higher frequencies. As the speaker enunciates the /d/ phoneme, a remarkable change occurs at about 200 milliseconds; the formant turns to higher frequencies when followed by /i/ and to lower frequencies when followed by /u/. Consequently, a listener could not zero in on the acoustic spectrum and identify the phonetic segment of /d/ by matching it with a distinctive feature that remains the same in all contexts.

Both coarticulation and the lack of invariance imply that listeners must process the context in which a given acoustic signal occurs. The relations among features are just as critical as the features themselves. Recall that we observed the same to be true in understanding the recognition of visual objects; only a structural descriptive theory that specifies

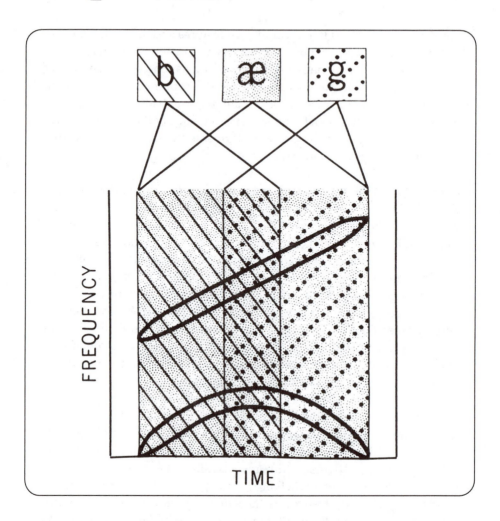

Figure 9.3. Coarticulation as parallel transmission of phonemes.
SOURCE: From Liberman, A. M., Cooper, F., Shankweiler, D., & Studdert-Kennedy, M. (1967). Perception of the speech code. *Psychological Review, 74,* 431-459. Copyright © 1967 by the American Psychological Association. Reprinted by permission.

both features and their relations proved adequate. In speech recognition a remarkably large number of features and relations must be processed in a fraction of a second simply to identify a single phoneme. Further, unlike the recognition of static visual objects, speech must be recognized over time. Both the sounds that precede a given phonetic segment and those that follow it influence perception (Salasoo & Pisoni, 1985).

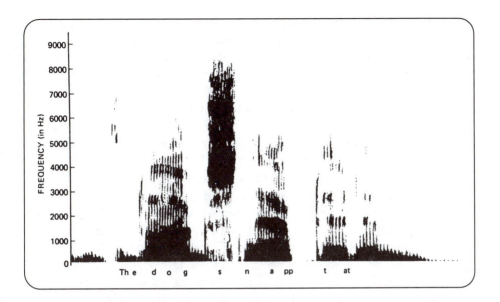

Figure 9.4. Portion of the speech spectrogram for "John said that the dog snapped at him." Pauses in acoustic energy do not make pauses heard by a listener.
SOURCE: From Foss, D. J., and Hakes, D. T., *Psycholinguistics.* Copyright © 1978, p. 77. Reprinted by permission of Prentice-Hall, Inc., Englewood Cliffs, N.J.

For example, a consonant articulated in the medial position differs depending on whether it is voiced, /b/, or unvoiced, /p/. The listener must detect this difference in discriminating words such as *pad* versus *bad*. The speaker utters the distinction by varying a single articulatory feature—voicing. But the listener must process 16 acoustic features that bear on correct identification (Lisker, 1986). The relations among these features are also processed with some occurring before, during, and after the constriction of the air flow in the vocal tract.

Continuous speech stream. Third, the acoustic signals constituting the speech stream are virtually continuous throughout a sentence (Foss & Hakes, 1978). Few pauses occur and, astonishingly, the pauses that do occur generally fall in the middle of words, not between words! Pauses mark boundaries between words less than 40% of the time (Cole & Jakimik, 1980). This phenomenon is illustrated with a portion of the speech spectrogram for the sentence, "John said that the dog snapped at him," shown in Figure 9.4.

Notice the pauses in acoustic energy between the /s/ and the /n/ and between the /p/ and /t/. The listener hears pauses between the words and phrases of the sentence, but the acoustic energy fails to provide them. They are, instead, inserted by the speech recognition processes that categorize the acoustic input; they divide the sounds into the words, phrases, clauses, and sentences through top-down or conceptually driven recognition processes. Conversely, the pauses in acoustic energy that do not signal an important linguistic unit, such as those in the word *snapped,* are not perceived by the listener.

It is easier to appreciate the role of conceptually driven processes in speech perception when listening to a foreign language. The continuous nature of the acoustic speech stream is perceived as it really is. The pauses that occur in the middle of a word are heard correctly. One word streams into another. The coarticulation effect discussed earlier applies across word boundaries as well as within word boundaries. Thus the speaker is sending acoustic clues at any given moment about the identity of phonemes that belong to adjacent words. The true complexity of the stream—if analyzed solely from bottom-up or data-driven processes— can be readily heard in listening to a native speaker of a language that is foreign to us. But when we listen to our own first language, the speech stream is heard as a sequence of neat and tidy packages of sound that specify meaning.

Categorical perception. This packaging or categorization of speech input occurs at all levels of linguistic structure. It has been extensively investigated at the phonemic level in a phenomenon known as **categorical perception.** Subtle variations in the acoustic signal are ignored unless they mark a boundary between one phoneme and another. For example, /b/ and /p/ differ in terms of the amount of time that elapses between the release of the lips and the onset of voicing. The voice onset time for /b/ is immediate, 0 seconds. For /p/, the voice onset time is 0.06 seconds. Within this narrow window of time lies the boundary between hearing one phoneme versus another.

Lisker and Abramson (1970) demonstrated the phenomenon of categorical perception by continuously varying voice onset time from –0.15 to +0.15 using computer-synthesized speech. For the 31 stimuli, the acoustic signal differed by .01 seconds in voice onset time. Yet, only two phonemes were heard. Listeners identified all sounds as /b/ over a large range of variation in the acoustic signal, from –0.15 seconds up to just over 0. As soon as the voice onset time exceeded slightly more than 0, the listeners began to hear /p/ instead of /b/ and continued to do so for all remaining stimuli. What matters then is not the degree of change in voice onset time; variations of 0.15 seconds are all heard as the same phoneme. Instead, what matters is whether the change in acoustic signal crosses a sharply defined boundary.

Although our perception of speech phonemes is categorical, it is mistaken to conclude that the auditory system cannot sense the gradual transitions in frequency. Data-driven processes plainly pick up these differences. This may be seen by designing a task that requires the listener to heed such information. For instance, Miller and Volaitis (1989) found that listeners generally report certain members of a phonemic category as more typical instances of the category than others. Of interest, the typical instances changed depending on the context in which the phoneme was perceived, again documenting the processing of contextual relations among features. In a similar vein, Repp and Liberman (1987) concluded that the boundary between two phonemic categories is flexible to a degree. Precisely where a given listener locates the boundary depends on the context provided by other stimuli.

Finally, speech as it occurs in daily settings is riddled with noise and indeterminacy (McClelland & Elman, 1986). Unless the speaker formulates complete sentences and articulates them clearly and slowly in a quiet setting, the speech signal is fragmentary. Yet we somehow manage to understand speakers who rapidly utter incomplete sentences and even distorted words in noisy environments. We also understand it when the speaker whispers a sentence, despite the alteration of not only the intensity of the acoustic signal but also its frequency in whispering.

We will return soon to some of the details regarding the intelligibility of speech. For now, the key point is that the speech signal is astonishingly complex and yet perception is generally accurate. Recall that shadowing a spoken message demands great cognitive effort, making it ideal as a primary task in studies of attention. It has been estimated that the brain must process 40,000 bits of information per second to extract phonetic segments accurately (Fodor, 1983).

Genetic Preparedness

Despite the complexity involved in extracting phonetic segments from the speech stream, infants between the ages of 1 and 4 months can detect the acoustic features that distinguish one phoneme from another. Indeed, it appears that at this age infants are prepared to identify not only

BOX 9.2: A Linguistic Genius

Learning a second language as an adult is a tremendous struggle. Unless a second, third, or fourth language is acquired in childhood, along with the first, multilingualism is unusual. At least, as all college students of foreign languages know, it is a trial to learn the basics, let alone to become fluent.

As we will see in Chapter 13, the human intellect may be highly compartmentalized. Gardner (1983) has argued that one might be a genius in one area of intelligence, such as mathematical reasoning, but poor in another area, such as language. Such a view of intelligence suggests that we should find individuals whose genius is highly circumscribed to one area. Is there any evidence for linguistic genius, the ability to learn and use multiple languages?

Hans Eberstark is such a genius (Bernstein, 1993). He can speak dozens of languages well enough to be understood by native speakers. His occupation is that of professional interpreter. Such interpreters divide their languages into three classes: A, B, and C. The A languages are those target languages that one can interpret into from some other tongue. The B languages are secondary target languages. The C languages can be understood by an interpreter. Bernstein tells us about Eberstark's abilities in the following:

> Eberstark's A languages are German and English. The latter he mastered in Shanghai, where classes were taught in it; German is his mother tongue. Eberstark's C languages (he says he has no B languages) include French, Dutch, Italian, Spanish, and Catalan. "My Portuguese would be wobbly." . . . "Then a grade below would be the Scandinavian languages—Danish, Swedish, and Norwegian. Then there is another language—I hardly ever use it in my normal interpretation, but I do speak it fairly well: Surinamese Creole, the language of Surinam. Also, but less so, Haitian Creole and Papiamentu, the language of the Netherlands Antilles." . . . "I could pass for a Swiss in Bärndütsch." . . . "I have done quite a bit of interpretation from Albanian." . . . "When I was in Ethiopia, I scratched together a basic vocabulary of Amharic. Since it is related to Hebrew, which I know, there were a number of similar word groups."

Eberstark has the remarkable ability of listening to speech in one language and simultaneously translating it in another. Listening and talking at the same time, in two languages, is an astonishing feat of attentional and linguistic ability. This was tested with a translation of Dutch to English. Eberstark appears to have a three-track mind: "He can listen to the Dutch, render the English, and think about the meaning of what is being said, all at the same time" (Bernstein, 1993, p. 96).

the phonemes of their native language but virtually all possible phonetic segments used in human languages (Eimas, Miller, & Jusczyk, 1987). Such evidence is consistent with the idea that speech is perceived by a special processing module (Eimas & Miller, 1992), one prepared for early operation by genetic factors.

Infants cannot, of course, report what they hear. Yet, by ingeniously monitoring the rate of sucking on a pacifier, developmental psychologists can infer changes in attention to a stimulus. The sucking schema is well established in a 1-month-old infant. In fact, sucking is one of a small number of reflexes present at birth. With experience in nursing, this basic sensorimotor schema develops and displaces the reflex. It turns out that infants suck faster when attending to a novel stimulus. With repeated presentations of the stimulus, the sucking rate slows down as the infant habituates to the stimulus. If the stimulus is abruptly changed in a way noticed by the infant, then dishabituation occurs, that is, the sucking rate suddenly increases. The infant's noticing the difference between preshift stimuli and postshift stimuli can be measured by the difference in rates of sucking.

Using this method, Eimas (1974) found categorical perception of speech by infants. They dishabituated when a change in the acoustic signal crossed a phonetic boundary. Subsequent research has shown that the infants can in fact discriminate among the stimuli that fall within a phonetic boundary (Miller & Eimas, 1983). Like adults, however, infants appear tuned to pick up the critical differences that separate one phoneme from another and to process the context in which the acoustic signals occur.

Further, infants are not born with full capabilities in categorizing speech. Newborns can detect differences among syllables that contain different phonemes, but their representations at this early stage of development may not be full-fledged phonetic segments (cf. Eimas & Miller, 1992). Instead, over the first month or two of life, the infant may progress from a global representation of the syllable to the specific phonemic-level representations (Bertoncini, Bijeljac-Babic, Jusczyk, Kennedy, & Mehler, 1988).

Intelligibility and Analysis by Synthesis

The intelligibility of individual phonemes and words depends on qualities of the speech signal and the linguistic context in which the signal occurs. Experiments on these factors collectively suggest that the comprehension process is active, not passive. It appears that an active construction of phonemes, words, phrases, and sentences takes place in advance. As data arrive in the form of acoustic energy, hypotheses have already been constructed as to the identity of the speech signal. This general idea has been called **analysis by synthesis.** The speech signal is correctly analyzed by synthesizing the expected language structures and then comparing the arriving data against these expectations.

Noise. When interfering background noise is more intense than the speech signal, comprehension suffers. The signal to noise ratio refers to the difference in sound pressure level, measured in decibels (dB), between the signal and the noise. Miller, Heise, and Lichten (1951) found that when the noise and signal measured the same intensity, listeners could accurately identify the presentation of 1 of 256 possible words (e.g., boat) about 70% of the time. This declined to virtually zero accuracy when the noise greatly exceeded the signal.

Predictability. Miller and his colleagues also discovered that the more predictable the words were, the greater the likelihood that they could be identified even under adverse conditions. One way to vary predictability is to restrict the number of alternative words that might occur in the experiment. Intelligibility increased systematically as the predictability of the target word increased. With only 2 alternatives instead of 256, accuracy raised from zero to nearly 80% when the background noise greatly exceeded the signal.

Miller and Isard (1963) showed that syntactic constraints strongly enhance predictability and recognition. They presented listeners with either normal sentences (e.g., Accidents kill motorists on the highways), semantically anomalous sentences (Accidents carry honey between the house), or ungrammatical sentences (Around accidents country honey the shoot). The listeners most accurately identified the words when they were presented in normal sentences regardless of background noise levels. Eliminating meaning as a cue in the anomalous sentences hampered recognition to a degree. But by far the worst performance obtained with the ungrammatical sentences. Syntactic rules therefore powerfully guide the constructive processes at work during speech perception. When these are violated, recognition often fails.

Pollack and Pickett (1964) further documented the powerful effect of context in an astonishing experiment. First, the investigators recorded a conversation among a small group of people or recorded individuals reading a passage aloud. Then, they isolated single words from such re-cordings and presented them to an observer. Remarkably, these single words were recognized accurately only about half of the time. Such poor performance occurred even when the listener heard his own speech played back as isolated words! Pollack and Pickett found that they could increase performance by adding more and more words. As the intonation of the speaker became clearer and the syntactic structure of the sentence emerged, listeners suddenly reached a threshold in which the words were plainly identifiable. The listener actively constructed hypotheses or syn-thesized speech using contextual information. As Lieberman (1967) noted: "The speech signal . . . remains unintelligible until the listener can successfully test a hypothesis. When a hypothesis is confirmed, the signal abruptly becomes intelligible" (p. 165).

Phonemic restoration. Active construction and testing of hypotheses dur-ing normal speech perception implies that a listener may perceive pho-nemes that are not actually included in the speech signal. For example, in a noisy situation the sound of a slammed door or a jack hammer may mask part of the speech signal. Or the speaker may not articulate clearly, garbling the quality of the speech signal. The listener may still perceive the speech as perfectly intelligible by constructing an illusion of a clear speech signal. Warren (1970) discovered exactly such an illusion in what he called the **phonemic restoration effect.**

A listener heard a recording of a sentence with a single phoneme deleted. For example, "The state governors met with respective legi*la-tures convening in the capital city." The asterisk marked the spot where the /s/ was removed and replaced with a cough lasting 0.12 seconds. Warren presented the recording to 20 listeners and asked them if any sounds were missing. Only one individual heard a missing sound and that person selected the wrong sound as missing. Clearly, the listeners had restored the missing phoneme. A buzz or tone yielded the same illu-sory effect of restoration, but dead silence was readily detected by all listeners. Apparently, extraneous sounds are filled in by constructive pro-cesses, whereas silence is an important feature picked up in speech rec-ognition.

In everyday situations, we comprehend speech that is often de-graded. Extraneous noises and garbled pronunciations are common, yet perception proceeds without pause. That the brain is specially tuned for speech perception should not be surprising. Speech is a uniquely human trait and one that is vital for human social interaction. The neural systems that analyze speech are remarkably powerful. In closing this section, consider that normal speech unfolds at a rate of about 12 phonetic segments per second. When the rate is artificially accelerated to 50 segments per second, the speech remains remarkably intelligible (Foulke & Sticht, 1969).

The Relation of Production and Comprehension

It has long been recognized that the processes used in perception and production overlap (Lashley, 1951). Speaking and listening plainly evolved in tandem; it would be ludicrous to assume from the outset that perception and production are separate systems. Specifically, the relation between the two may help explain how we manage to comprehend such a wide range of speakers with different voice qualities, such as dialects, impediments, and differences in speed of articulation.

Motor Theory

The **motor theory** of speech perception claims that a listener synthesizes the articulatory gestures used by a speaker (Liberman et al., 1967). In other words, the listener models the articulatory program that controls the lips, tongue, and other elements of the vocal tract. By constructing such a model, the listener can adjust for the unique characteristics of each speaker's voice.

Clark and Clark (1977) pointed out that a strong version of the motor theory cannot be correct. People do not silently say to themselves the words that are incoming. That is, at the least, no patterns of activity in the speech muscles are detectable as a person listens to speech. Further, neurological damage to the systems responsible for speech production do not impair the individual's ability to comprehend speech. Finally, people can understand speakers with foreign accents, dialects, or stuttering even though they cannot reproduce the speech themselves.

Node Structure Theory

Although the motor theory has difficulties, it may be possible to link production and perception less directly. The **node structure theory** adopts the basic assumptions of connectionism or neural networks to

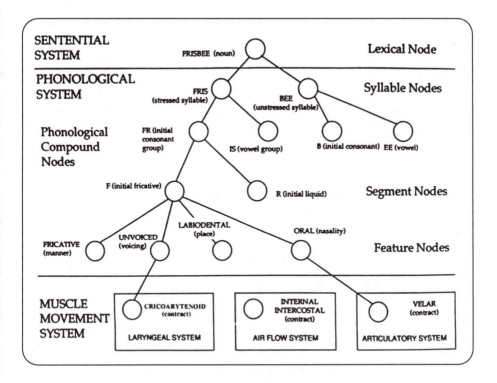

Figure 9.5. Some nodes activated in speaking "frisbee" according to node structure theory.
SOURCE: From MacKay, Wulf, Yin, and Abrams (1993). Copyright © 1993 by Academic Press, Inc. Reprinted by permission.

show how this might be done (MacKay, 1987). The units or nodes in this case are organized into hierarchical systems and subsystems that can be independently activated. Perception and comprehension use the same nodes but are linked indirectly.

For example, a few of the nodes activated in speaking the word *frisbee* are shown in Figure 9.5. Words and phrases, and their underlying concepts, are represented in the sentential system. The phonological system represents the syllables, phonetic segments, and phonetic features involved in saying or comprehending a given word. Finally, the muscle movement system controls the actual movements of the vocal track during articulation. Only two of the hundreds of muscles that are contracted in pronouncing *frisbee* are shown in the figure.

The key point to stress is the activation pattern of these subsystems. As with other neural network models, this model assumes interactive activation among the various system levels. In speaking or listening to the word *frisbee*, the node for /f/ is activated. It achieves activation by first becoming primed or excited because of its connection to other nodes in the network that already are activated. Once a node is activated, it automatically spreads its activation to prime other nodes to which it is connected. The amount of priming that occurs decreases as more and more connections are traversed until it fades altogether. For a group of related nodes (for example, alternative phonetic segments), only the most primed node in the pool becomes activated. After a node is activated, it inhibits itself for a brief period of time, reducing its priming level to below normal.

System activation. Nodes in the muscle movement system are activated only during overt speech. Internal speech, the inner speech of thought discussed in Chapter 8, invokes nodes in the phonological system but not those in the muscle movement system. Mouthing a sentence—moving lips and tongue silently—activates nodes in the articulatory subsystem, not the entire muscle movement system. The air flow and laryngeal subsystems are unaffected. Perception occurs through priming of the phonological and lexical nodes. The most primed node at a given level becomes activated. Normally, activation occurs only at the lexical level during perception in that we become aware of words but not their phonological features. The activation process in the phonological system is more critical in production. It provides the basis for sequencing phonological units in speaking and for consciously monitoring what is said (MacKay, 1987).

Verbal transformations. Empirical evidence bearing on MacKay's theory comes from a fascinating phenomenon called the **verbal transformation effect** (VTE). When a listener hears the same word repeated over and over again for several minutes, the perceptual system constructs illusions (Warren, 1968). The listener hears phonologically similar words instead of the word actually played. It may seem to lose its meaning, sounding like a nonword not contained in the perceiver's mental lexicon (this transformation is called **semantic satiation**). For example, after hearing *face* repetitively spoken on a tape recording, the listener begins to hear *space*, *base, case, lace, dace, tace,* and so on (Warren & Meyers, 1987). The number of alternatives heard increases with the number of repetitions (Warren, 1968).

Lackner (1974) explored whether such changes would occur if a person spoke the same word repetitively and listened to her own speech. In Lackner's study, VTEs occurred when observers listened to a recording of a repeated word but not when they listened to their own auditory feedback. Strikingly, this difference occurred even when they listened to the recordings of their own speech, which failed to generate VTEs at the time they were produced! The acoustic signal to the listener's ear is identical whether it comes from auditory feedback from speaking or from a recording. Thus there must be something about the production process itself that obliterates the illusions of VTEs.

Node satiation. MacKay, Wulf, Yin, and Abrams (1993) reasoned that VTEs could be explained in terms of a satiation process in their node structure theory. A lexical node that receives repeated and prolonged activation becomes satiated: It is unable to receive priming from neighboring nodes. Some satiation may result from repeated priming, but not on the order of magnitude that happens from repeated activation and its accompanying awareness. When a person overtly pronounces a word repetitively, the lexical nodes are activated from the top down as the speech is formulated and then articulated. In theory, it is this production-driven activation that provides for concurrent perception of the word, not the acoustic signal arriving at the speaker's ear a fraction of a second later. Recall that an activated node inhibits itself for a brief period of time, lowering its priming level and thus preventing immediate reactivation. The auditory feedback to the speaker, then, could not reactivate the node during this window of repetition deafness, to use MacKay's terminology. So the node could not become satiated despite the repetitive auditory input.

At the same time, MacKay and his colleagues assumed that conceptualizing a word—intending to say *face,* for instance—also primes the correct lexical entry and offsets the buildup of satiation. Such offsetting would not be possible when listening to a recording because one would not know what word was intended. Thus, for more than one reason, VTEs theoretically should occur only during repetitive perception, not repetitive production.

◙ SUMMARY ◙

1. Speaking involves conceptualizing propositions or ideas to express, formulating the sentences that capture these ideas, and articulating the sentences. Speakers must formulate plans at multiple levels of linguistic structure. Articulation involves programming the muscle commands and then actually executing the movements of the vocal tract.

2. The nature of conversations illustrates that speaking is a social as well as a cognitive act. Participants in a conversation follow implicit rules for taking turns. They also follow the cooperativeness principle; they cooperate by being sincere in what they say to ensure effective communication.

3. Comprehending speech is seriously complicated by the characteristics of articulation and the acoustic signal of speech. A speech spectrogram shows parallel transmission of more than one phoneme at each moment in time, variation in the features of a phoneme depending on the context in which it occurs, and pauses that bear little relation to individual words. Speech perception entails categorizing variations in acoustic signals as examples of a given phoneme.

4. The intelligibility of speech depends on background noise levels and characteristics of the speaker's voice. However, recognition is remarkably successful given the degraded nature of most speech. The underlying process involves an active construction or synthesis of speech that is then matched against available acoustic signals. In essence, we hear an illusion of clear and unambiguous speech through this construction.

5. A complete theory must specify the relation between production and comprehension. The motor theory of speech perception asserts that a listener recognizes a phonetic segment by silently modeling the articulatory movements of the speaker. Although such modeling does not seem to take place in speech recognition, there is evidence that both speaking and listening activate the same mental representations for words and their associated sounds.

Key Terms

articulatory program
referential arena
phonetic coding
place of articulation
manner of articulation
voicing
voice onset time
slips of the tongue
conversational implicatures
speech spectrogram

formants
coarticulation
analysis by synthesis
categorical perception
phonemic restoration effect
motor theory
node structure theory
verbal transformation effect
semantic satiation

Recommended Readings

The cognitive psychology of speech production and perception draws heavily on the specialty areas of linguistics. For instance, Ladefoged's (1975) book titled *A Course in Phonetics* is a classic reference on this topic. Key journals on phonology and phonetics are the *Journal of Speech and Hearing Disorders* and the *Journal of the Acoustical Society of America*.

Garrett's (1990) chapter in *An Invitation to Cognitive Science: Language* (Volume 1) covers both the production of sentences and their comprehension. Similarly, Cooper (1979) addressed both topics in a book titled *Speech Perception and Production: Studies in Selective Adaptation*. For a solid collection of original research articles, I suggest *Perspectives on the Study of Speech* edited by Eimas and Miller (1981).

The study of speech perception has shed light on many of the fundamental issues of perception in general. For example, Harnad's (1987) edited collection of chapters titled *Categorical Perception: The Groundwork of Cognition* illustrates this point. The chapter by Eimas (1975) in *Infant Perception* covers the developmental aspects of speech perception. For an overview of the fundamental issues in speech perception, I recommend Miller's (1990) chapter in *An Invitation to Cognitive Science: Language* (Volume 1).

CHAPTER **10**

▣ Writing and Reading

This chapter covers the production and comprehension of written, as opposed to spoken, language. The research in cognitive psychology on these topics is heavily lopsided toward reading rather than writing. One reason for this historical bias is that measuring the degree to which one writes well is a fuzzier process than measuring comprehension and memory in reading.

Reading the written word, as you are doing now, is by no means an easy problem for cognitive psychologists to tackle. As we will see in this chapter, reading invokes carefully orchestrated processes of attention, perception, memory, language, and thinking. Still, the traditional experimental approaches of cognitive psychology are well suited to understanding reading. Major advances have been made in this domain that far exceed our current understanding of writing. Before steering into the main channel of the chapter, we will begin with what little we know about writing.

For both writing and reading, the focus here will be on the high-level processes involved in formulating and understanding discourse. This focus complements our concern in the last chapter with many of the motor and perceptual processes involved in speaking and listening. The aim is to give you a survey of the research on both low- and high-level operations involved in language use.

Text Production

As a species, we have been speaking far longer than we have been writing. Casts made of the skulls of *Homo habilis,* our early ancestor from over 2 million years ago, reveal what could have been Broca's speech area (Tobias, 1987). However, the unusual shape of the human vocal tract, a necessary requirement for speech, emerged later, perhaps 150,000 to 200,000 years ago, in *Homo sapiens sapiens* (Corballis, 1989; Lieberman, 1984). By contrast, the very earliest evidence that we have of human beings using written symbols comes from the walls of caves in Europe, dating a mere 25,000 years ago. And these pictures were not writing as we know it today; the symbols were iconographs in which the object referred to was directly depicted.

Only later did the symbols come to stand for an idea, to represent something in a nonliteral fashion. Ideographs are symbols of more abstract reference and are the basis of some modern language systems. For example, each of the thousands of Chinese ideographs refers to a particular concept. Schmandt-Besserat (1988) theorized that the origins of **idiographic writing** stem from a token system developed in Sumeria (the region of modern Iran and Iraq) about 10,000 years ago to track jars of oil, grain, and other inventory. Our ancestral accountants were perhaps the first to see the need to keep written records. The Sumerian markings evolved into what is called a pictographic system for representing the many ideas needed in daily communication. From this system came the Sumerian cuneiform script about 5,000 years ago, and the well-known hieroglyphics of the Egyptians came soon after.

Most of the world languages today employ alphabets, a form of **phonetic writing** that first appeared a mere 3,500 years ago in the Sinai desert (Logan, 1986). A small number of letters (22-40, depending on the language) represent the sounds that carry meaning. By combining these letters, the writer can efficiently represent all the words possible in a language. The invention of an alphabet represented the final step in the evolution of written communication, one that serves us as well in the age of computers as it did in the age of clay tablets. With the tool of the alphabet, modern human beings carved out the cultural and intellectual life that we enjoy today.

A Model of Handwriting

Writing by hand with a pen or pencil is an important skill to understand. We have written by hand for centuries and will no doubt continue to do so even with the availability of word processors that use keyboards or voice input. Brown, McDonald, Brown, and Carr (1988) divided handwriting into stages of (a) the formulation of ideas and sentences, (b) the motor movements of behavioral output, and (c) the monitoring of output. They investigated the allocation of attention to discourse formulation, behavioral output, and monitoring. Presumably, typing or speaking into a computer differs from handwriting at the output and perhaps the monitoring stages only.

Participants in the experiments reported by Brown et al. transcribed paragraphs under instructions to write as rapidly as possible or as legibly as possible. This instructional variable affected the output stage. The paragraphs were either recalled from memory or read at the time of transcription; this variable affected the discourse formulation stage. In some cases, the writers had a concurrent listening task as another demand on their attention and working memory. The writer listened to a list of words through headphones, trying to remember either the most recent word (easy concurrent task) or the most recent two words (hard concurrent task). At random times the experimenter checked their recall accuracy.

Brown et al. found that the rate of handwriting was affected both by the instructions to write fast versus legibly and by the requirement to read or recall the paragraph. The overall performance of the system for text production could be influenced either by changes at the stage of discourse formulation or by changes at the execution/monitoring stages. In addition, the rate of handwriting slowed as the demands on attention and working memory were increased. Some of their results indicated that in the hard concurrent condition, the writers had to take resources away from execution/monitoring to protect discourse formulation. In other words, the stages draw on a common pool of cognitive resources, with formulation taking higher priority when task demands overload the writer.

A Model of Discourse Formulation

The stage of discourse formulation discussed by Brown et al. involves numerous component processes. Just as in speech production, models of writing must distinguish planning ideas from the formulation of those ideas into phrases, sentences, and texts (e.g., Bock, 1982). A highly influential model of the formulation stage of text production was proposed by Hayes and Flower (1980).

As shown in Figure 10.1, the Hayes and Flower model distinguishes three fundamental processes in the formulation of text. **Planning** refers

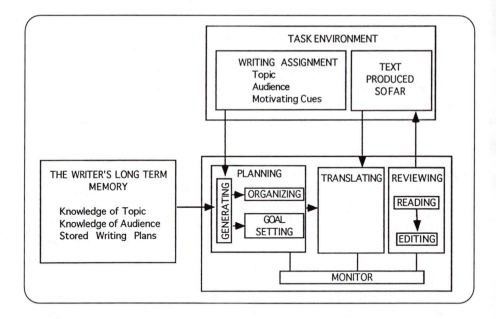

Figure 10.1. A model of discourse formulation in writing.
SOURCE: From Hayes, J. R., & Flower, L. S. (1980). Identifying the organization of writing processes. In L. W. Gregg & E. R. Steinberg (Eds.), *Cognitive processes in writing* (pp. 3-30). Hillsdale, NJ: Lawrence Erlbaum. Copyright © 1980 by Lawrence Erlbaum Associates. Reprinted by permission.

to generating ideas, organizing ideas, and setting goals to achieve during writing, such as trying to achieve the right voice or tone for a particular audience. Planning can be seen as invoking the reasoning, decision-making, problem-solving, and other high-level thinking aspects of writing.

Translating, or sentence generating, refers to the semantic, syntactic, and pragmatic operations involved in putting ideas into words. The assumption is that the thoughts of a writer—coded as propositions, phonological images of words or short phrases, or visual images of objects or events—must be translated into sentences (Flower & Hayes, 1984). The imagination of the writer and even the inner speech of the writer is not yet in the form needed for language production. Some theorists have questioned whether planning can be separated from sentence generation in the case of writing (e.g., Nystrand, 1989).

Reviewing refers to the reading of the text being produced, and evaluating and editing it. In reviewing the writer must step back from the text produced so far and take the potential reader's point of view. If the

BOX 10.1: Writer's Block

For many college students, writing assignments are a source of anxiety. Freedman (1983) surveyed college students and reported that 45% found writing painful, 61% found it difficult, and 41% lacked confidence in their ability to write. About 10% of college students experience such intense anxiety over their writing that they shirk the task altogether: They suffer from writer's block. Rose (1984) observed that these blocked writers followed highly maladaptive patterns or rules that prevented them from engaging the task successfully. For example, one blocked writer stretched prewriting activities over several days, right up to within hours of the deadline for the paper. The student then had a complex plan for the paper but with so little time left that it was impossible to translate the plan into a draft.

In Cleary's (1991) study of student writers, nearly a third reported an overloading of attention and intense frustration. Some gave up altogether. The diligent, grade-conscious students "would continue in agony when pressed by a deadline because the consequences of not completing the assignment were too great" (p. 487). Nearly two thirds of the students found their concentration broken from perceived threats in the writing environment. For example, a teacher's comment to an advanced-level writer ("You have some talent, don't lose it") combined with a C on his first paper proved threatening and disruptive. Persistent criticism from teachers sours the writing environment for many.

College students are not alone in experiencing writing apprehension and blocking. Karl Marx took 18 years, producing copious notes and plans, in writing Volume 1 of *Das Kapital*. The remaining two volumes had to be completed by his friend Friedrich Engels, after Marx died working on them for another 16 years (Myers, 1991). Van Brooks described the agony that plagued him as a professional writer in his *Opinions of Oliver Allston,* as quoted by John-Steiner (1985):

> In thirty years of writing, I have not gained an ounce of confidence. I begin each new book . . . with a sense of impotence, chaos, and desperation that cannot be overstated. I always feel that I am foredoomed to failure. Every day I begin my work with the same old feeling that I am on trial for my life and will probably not be acquitted. (p. 77)

meaning of the text does not match what the writer had intended, then further planning and sentence generation are needed.

These processes are fueled in part by the knowledge and skills stored in long-term memory. At the same time, they are constrained by the nature of the writing assignment itself and the way that the text has taken shape so far. Thus the way one plans, generates sentences, and reviews will depend on a number of factors. How much writers know about the topic at hand and in general would certainly affect the dynamics of the composing process. Planning may be extremely time consuming and rich for highly knowledgeable writers but brief and impoverished for others. A deadline to finish the assignment illustrates one motivating cue that profoundly affects how much planning and reviewing one does. If a writer engages in the usual procrastination or, worse yet, suffers from writer's block, then the deadline may force a hasty translation of poorly planned text (Rose, 1984).

By examining verbal protocols of writers, Flower and Hayes (1980) concluded that writers are trying to meet several simultaneous demands and constraints. Consider their description of the process:

> We know that when people write, they draw upon a variety of mental operations such as making plans, retrieving ideas from memory, drawing inferences, creating concepts, developing an image of the reader, testing what they've written against that image, and so on. To produce any given utterance (which is to be simultaneously correct, effective, felicitous, and true), the writer must integrate a great number of skills and meet a number of demands—more or less all at once. . . . Viewed this way, a writer in the act is a thinker on full-time cognitive overload. (p. 33)

One consequence of this view is that planning, translating, and reviewing do not occur in sequence (Hayes & Flower, 1980). Instead, the fundamental processes are highly recursive at all stages of development of a text. Planning might lead to translating and then more planning occurs. Reviewing a sentence after generating it might lead back either to planning or to more translating. All three processes are interwoven as a writer moves through the various stages of engaging in the prewriting activities of reading, taking notes, creating outlines, beginning a first draft, and modifying the draft as need and time permit.

Another consequence is that writing places heavy demands on the attentional or working memory system. As shown in Figure 10.2, remarkably high levels of cognitive effort have been observed in an essay composition task, using secondary task reaction times as the indicator of effort. Judging from secondary task reaction times measured during learning, reading, and problem-solving tasks (specifically, chess play), comparable levels of effort expenditure have been obtained only with expert-level chess play (Kellogg, 1994).

Hayes and Flower (1980) also concluded from their analysis of verbal protocols that writers cope with the demands of writing by design-

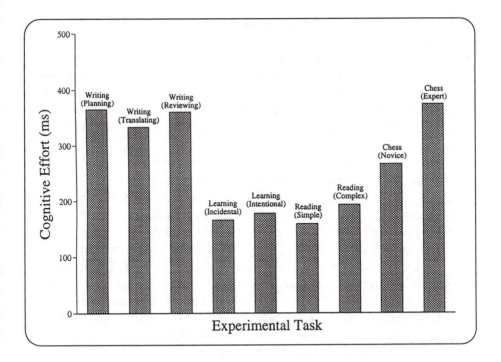

Figure 10.2. Cognitive effort expenditure for writing processes in relation to other cognitive activities
SOURCE: From Ronald Kellogg, *The Psychology of Writing*. Copyright © 1994 by Oxford University Press. Reprinted by permission.

ing plans. In their words: "Plans allow writers to reduce the level of 'cognitive strain,' that is, to reduce the number of demands being made on conscious attention" (pp. 31-32). One planning method for doing this is outlining. Creating an outline in advance of composing a short essay effectively funneled attention to the process of generating sentences (Kellogg, 1988). The writers who first outlined devoted more time to the process of translating compared with those who began a draft without outlining. By focusing attention on sentence generation to a greater degree than is possible without outlining in advance, the writers produced a superior essay.

Knowledge Transformation

In Chapter 2, we saw that cognitive activities are situated or embedded in the environment. Interactions between the individual and the environment are cyclical. In visual perception, for instance, the anticipatory schemas direct the sampling of features from the environment; features picked up in the environment in turn modify the schemas, biasing expectations as to what will be seen next (see Neisser, 1976). Writing and other high-level thinking skills also reveal cycles of interaction. An excellent illustration of this can be found in analyses of mature writers coming to grips with the problems of what to say in their texts and how to go about saying it.

Bereiter and Scardamalia (1987) noted that writers must solve two different kinds of problems. **Content problems** concern the matter of what to say. Everything that writers know about the events, facts, theories, arguments, and so on related to their topic bears on their ability to solve these problems. The term *problem space*, which we will encounter frequently in the next chapter, refers to a mental representation of the possible steps that might be taken in reaching the solution to a particular problem. **Rhetorical problems** concern the matter of how to say what needs saying. Within the rhetorical problem space, the writer struggles with the difficult issues of constructing text that is clear, persuasive, interesting, and so on. All that writers know about discourse bears on their ability to solve these problems of rhetoric.

Bereiter and Scardamalia discovered that children plan very differently than do adult writers. When given an assignment, children establish as a goal the retrieval of an idea from memory. Once they have an idea, they immediately translate it into a sentence. That done, they go back to search long-term memory again looking for another idea to write a sentence about. Children repeat this "think and then say" approach until they cannot think of anything more to say. Bereiter and Scardamalia aptly referred to this as **knowledge-telling.**

For mature writers, knowledge-telling is only one component of the overall process. Problem analysis results in the establishment of numerous goals that lie either in the content or in the rhetorical problem space. As I described earlier, mature writers are juggling many constraints at once. In doing so they engage in repeated cycles of interaction with the notes, outlines, and text that they have produced so far. By perceiving what they put down on paper or on a computer screen, writers change what they think about the topic at hand or how they think the text should be written. Their content knowledge and discourse knowledge are actively transformed as a result of sampling from the environment at hand. The mature writer engages in cycles of **knowledge transformation** as well as knowledge-telling.

Murray (1982) assembled quotations from well-known novelists that illustrate knowledge transformation. For example, John Updike noted that "writing and rewriting are a constant search for what one is saying." E. M. Forster captured the same idea in the words of one of his fictional characters: "How do I know what I think until I see what I say?" (pp. 86, 88).

Verbal protocols reveal a much richer record of planning for adult writers than for children (Bereiter & Scardamalia, 1987). The number of words in thinking-aloud protocols about equals the number of words in the essays produced by children in grades 4 and 6. The writers say little more than they actually put down on paper. Adults, on the other hand, verbalize nearly four times as many words while thinking aloud than they write, as they struggle with the content and rhetorical problems of the task.

Another experiment documenting the difference between knowledge-telling and knowledge-transforming varied the time constraints for composition (Zbrodoff, 1985). Writers were allowed different times to complete the task, ranging from 2.5 minutes to 20 minutes. Students in grades 5 and 10 began almost immediately, no matter how much time they were allowed; the mature writers took time to think through their stories. Only the adults apparently planned and reflected on their plans when sufficient time was available to do so.

Spelling

The minimal unit that carries meaning in written language is called a **grapheme.** It is the unit corresponding to a phoneme in speech. In generating a single sentence to express a proposition, speaking and writing share many common processes. One stark difference between the two, however, is the requirement to spell correctly only in writing. Unless a person is asked to spell a word orally—as in a spelling bee—the output of speech is at the phonemic and word level. **Orthography** refers to the visual characteristics of letters and contrasts with phonology, the sounds of the same letters when read aloud. In English orthography, the correct choice of graphemes cannot always be determined from the phonology or sound of a given phoneme or word.

Homophones provide a case in point. They are pairs of words that sound the same but are spelled differently and carry different meanings (*sale* versus *sail*). In another illustration, the phoneme /s/ can either take the graphemic form of /s/ or /c/. *Precede* and *presage* both contain the same phoneme but different graphemes.

The spelling process is perhaps the most extensively investigated component of writing (Badecker, Hillis, & Caramazza, 1990; Caramazza, 1991; Ellis, 1982; Shallice, 1988). Two distinct sources of knowledge are brought to bear in spelling. One is knowledge of the orthographic appearance of a whole word. Through reading, people gain lexical-orthographic knowledge. The other source is an extensive set of rules about how phonology maps onto orthography. The separate pathways are suggested by agraphia, a disorder of producing written language (Beauvois & Dérouesné, 1981; Ellis, 1982; Shallice, 1988).

Goodman and Caramazza (1986), for example, studied a patient with acquired dysgraphia, a normal individual who became agraphic following a stroke or other trauma that damages the brain. Their patient, JG, spelled nonwords as well as anyone by drawing on knowledge of the rules that map phonology to orthography. In the case of nonwords, the only path is through phonological rules. But when asked to spell real words, JG often spelled incorrectly. The nature of the errors were quite reasonable from the standpoint of phonological rules. For example, JG spelled "known" as "none." The second path for spelling that draws upon the orthography of words stored in the mental lexicon was apparently lost for JG.

Text Comprehension

As noted earlier, the study of text comprehension is an extensive area of research in cognitive psychology. Reading has long been a source of interest for psychologists and educators. Studies of literacy and disorders of reading go back to the turn of the century. Reading headed the traditional 3Rs of education: readin', 'ritin', and 'rithmetic. Reading was the first of the three areas to receive the scrutiny of cognitive psychologists in the latter half of the century as well.

Studying how people perceive the symbols of written language, extract meaning from the symbols, and store those meanings in memory has been a gold mine for cognitive psychologists. The reading task takes researchers into the depths of complex cognitive operations. Yet it offers a familiar, lighted passage using well-established methodologies of perception, comprehension, and memory research.

This section begins with the proposal that text comprehension involves the building of mental structures. The structures built by readers at the local levels of words and sentences and at the global levels of paragraphs and complete texts are then considered. Third, two pervasive aspects of text comprehension, the drawing of inferences and the interpretation of metaphors, are examined. Fourth, we step back to provide an overview by framing fluent reading as a complex skill with many component processes.

Comprehension as Structure Building

Gernsbacher (1990) captured a central theme in stating that

> the goal of comprehension is to build a coherent mental representation or "structure" of the information being comprehended. Several component processes are involved. First, comprehenders lay foundations for their mental structures. Next comprehenders develop their mental structures by mapping on information when that incoming information coheres with the previous information. However, if the incoming information is less than coherent, comprehenders engage in another cognitive process: They shift to initiate a new substructure. So, most representations comprise several branching substructures. (pp. 1-2)

Words and sentences activate representations stored in long-term memory, bringing necessary information into the limited capacity system of working memory. Mental structures are then developed moment by moment as the reader scans more text. As in building any structure, the laying of a foundation is critical in reading, according to Gernsbacher. The time and effort needed to develop mental structures that incorporate the meaning of the text provide useful information about the process. For example, the first sentence of a paragraph takes longer to read than later sentences, because the reader uses it to lay the foundation for a mental structure (Cirilo, 1981; Cirilo & Foss, 1980). This result occurs even when the topic sentence comes later in the paragraph (Kieras, 1978). So the extra time reflects foundation building, not just the time needed to process the most important or informative sentence.

A neuropsychological measure of cognitive effort used in comprehension is the N400 brain wave (Kutas & Hillyard, 1980). This is an event related potential (see Chapter 1) that reaches its peak negative amplitude 400 milliseconds after the stimulus. Kutas and Hillyard found that an unexpected word in a sentence, one that would demand considerable effort to comprehend, reliably evoked an N400. In reading a set of mundane sentences, the participants occasionally encountered one with an anomalous or a low-probability word. Here is an example of each:

He likes ice cream and sugar in his *socks*.
He likes ice cream and sugar in his *tea*.

Recording from an area in the parietal lobe, Kutas and Hillyard observed the negative component of the brain wave 400 milliseconds after *socks* or *tea* appeared. In addition, a large N400 component occurs following the first word of the sentence (He) and smaller ones after each succeeding word (Kutas, Van Petten, & Besson, 1988; Van Petten & Kutas, 1987). Taken together, these findings imply that large N400s are elicited by words receiving little if any activation from top-down processes of pattern recognition. Such words pop into place in the evolving mental structures only after substantial effort from bottom-up processes.

Structures develop at multiple levels—words, sentences, and discourse. In the 1970s and 1980s, memory researchers began to address how people remembered sentences and stories rather than lists of words, the traditional task of verbal learning. At the same time, psycholinguistics became an exciting area, following Chomsky's work on transformational grammar. A concern with the structure of sentences and still larger units of text dominated the field. Both European and North American scholars scrutinized the ways in which sentences hang together to constitute stories, conversations, expositions, and other types of discourse (e.g., Kintsch & van Dijk, 1978; Meyer, 1975; Thorndyke, 1977). By the late 1980s, the terms *comprehension, psycholinguistics, referential coherence, story grammars, macropropositions, mental models,* and *causal relations* surfaced in hundreds if not thousands of journal articles (Foss, 1988).

The upshot of the research effort has been to spell out what we mean by the term *discourse*. When does a collection of sentences constitute true discourse versus just a bunch of sentences? The answer, according to Johnson-Laird (1983), is when the references in each sentence are locally coherent with one another and when the sentences can be fit into a global framework of causes and effects. First, we consider the issue of referential coherence and then examine alternative frameworks for structuring casual relations.

Referential Coherence

When the words and phrases of one sentence in a paragraph refer unambiguously to those of other sentences in the paragraph, then the sentences possess **referential coherence**. Johnson-Laird (1983) offered the following three collections of sentences to illustrate this property of true discourse:

(1) It was the Christmas party at Heighton that was one of the turning-points in Perkins' life. The duchess had sent him a three-page wire in the hyperbolical style of her class, conveying a vague impression that she and the Duke had arranged to commit suicide together if Perkins didn't "chuck" any previous engagement he had made. And Perkins had felt in a slipshod sort of way—for at least at that period he was incapable of ordered thought—he might as well be at Heighton as anywhere. . . . (from *Perkins and Mankind* by Max Beerbohm)

(2) Scripps O'Neil had two wives. To tip or not to tip? Dawn crept over the Downs like a sinister white animal, followed by the snarling cries of a wind eating its way between the black boughs of the thorns. When I had reached my eighteenth year I was recalled by my parents to my paternal roof in Wales.

(3) The field buys a tiny rain. The rain hops. It burns the noisy sky in some throbbing belt. It buries some yellow wind under it. The throbbing belt freezes some person on it. The belt dies of it. It freezes the ridiculous field. (pp. 356-357)

Which do you judge to be true discourse? Which is the least qualified for the title? The difference between paragraphs 1 and 2 is easy to detect. The sentences in 1 hang together while those in 2 plainly do not. But what about the sentences in paragraph 3, which Johnson-Laird generated using a computer program? Although each sentence is nonsensical, the paragraph seems structured. The pronouns of one sentence seem to refer back to a previous sentence. Nouns are repeated from one sentence to the next. Words related in meaning, here words describing weather, are laced throughout. These are among the cohesive ties that a writer uses in creating true discourse (Halliday & Hasan, 1976).

Anaphora is the use of a word to substitute for a preceding word or phrase. The idea may be illustrated with these sentences, adapted from Gernsbacher (1990):

1. *Ron* was writing a book. *Ron* was having trouble thinking up enough example sentences.
2. *Ron* was writing a book. *The idiot* was having trouble thinking up enough example sentences.
3. *Ron* was writing a book. *He* was having trouble thinking up enough example sentences. (pp. 108-109)

Writers frequently use anaphora to establish referential coherence, especially anaphoric pronouns as illustrated by sentence 3. Of the 50 most common words that appear in print in the English language, nearly one third are pronouns (Kucera & Francis, 1967). But how do readers process such references in building structures in working memory?

Given-new strategy. Clark (1977) theorized that readers (and listeners) employ the **given-new strategy.** The strategy is based on the assumption that writers cooperate with readers to help make their meanings understood, just as speakers do in conversations. Specifically, writers clearly mark information that the readers already understand, the given information that provides a shared basis for communication between the writers and readers. Writers also mark what they are now making an assertion about, the new information that they want the readers to grasp.

On coming to the second sentence in example 1 above, the reader determines what is being asserted as new information (that someone is having trouble generating examples) and what is old information (the person in question is Ron). The reader next identifies a unique antecedent for the given information in working memory. The new information can then be fit into a new structure that links the predicates of both sentences to the same person.

Haviland and Clark (1974) found that the time needed to read and comprehend a sentence varied with the explicitness of the anaphora. This would be expected if readers used the given-new strategy and experienced more or less difficulty in identifying a unique antecedent for the given information. The pronoun *he* can often match more than one antecedent; so the reference in example 3 is the least explicit. Similarly, *the idiot* can, I hope, apply to people other than Ron. But in example 1, a unique referent is specified by repeating the name verbatim. In cases 2 and 3, the reader must infer a link that is not explicitly given. Haviland and Clark aptly called these **bridging inferences,** because the reader must build a bridge between two ideas to grasp their relation.

A Process Model

Kintsch and van Dijk (1978) proposed a detailed model for the processes involved in establishing referential coherence. All sentences are first broken down into their constituent propositions as defined in Chapter 8. All of the propositions comprehended by a reader form the text base, meaning simply the ideas communicated by the written text. Recall that each proposition consists of a predicate and associated arguments. For reasons that will become clear shortly, Kintsch and van Dijk referred to the constituent propositions of a sentence as **micropropositions.** If the predicate or arguments in two micropropositions overlap with each other, then the reader can link the two as a way of establishing referential coherence. In our earlier example, the repetition of *Ron* in both sentences of example 1 would readily provide the basis for such overlap. In the case of example 3, the reader would need to make a bridging inference to relate *he* back to *Ron.* The need to make such inferences makes comprehension more difficult for the reader. The basic assumption made by Kintsch and van Dijk is that referential coherence corresponds to overlap in the arguments of the propositions contained in a text.

Kintsch and van Dijk assume that the number of propositions that may be active in working memory varies across readers. On average, they assume a capacity of four propositions. Because new propositions continually enter working memory as readers proceed with a text, old propositions must be bumped from working memory to make room. In deciding what to retain at a given point in time, readers use a **leading edge strategy**, according to Kintsch and van Dijk. They keep the most recent proposition and those that overlap with it in terms of their arguments, up to the capacity limits of their working memory. As long as this strategy retains the propositions in working memory that must be matched, then referential coherence can be established. When matching fails, the reader then searches long-term memory either to reinstate a proposition processed earlier or to make an inference.

The Kintsch and van Dijk model successfully accounts for the degree of difficulty experienced in comprehending texts. The more densely a text is packed with propositions and the more often it demands bridging inferences among propositions separated in time since input, the harder it is to read (Kintsch, 1974). The number of times that previously processed propositions must be reinstated in working memory and the number of inferences that must be made when reinstatement fails are especially predictive of comprehension difficulties (Miller & Kintsch, 1980). Furthermore, the model explains which propositions later will be remembered well. The longer a proposition is held active in working memory, the more likely it will be encoded successfully into long-term memory (Kintsch & Keenan, 1973).

Global Frameworks

As noted earlier, a collection of sentences that form a chain of coreferences is still not necessarily a story, a persuasive essay, or any other type of discourse. The nonsensical sentences generated by Johnson-Laird's (1983) computer illustrated this at the outset of our discussion. Another set of perfectly decent sentences makes the same point perhaps more clearly. Even when each sentence makes sense and when the sentences are referentially coherent, something else—an organizing topic, theme, or global structure—is needed. Consider the following referentially coherent paragraph:

> My daughter works in a library in London. London is the home of a good museum of natural history. The museum is organized on the basis of cladistic theory. This theory concerns the classification of living things. Living things evolved from inanimate matter. (p. 379)

Theorists disagree on the best way to represent the global structure that characterizes true discourse. But all agree that texts are structured beyond the local level of individual micropropositions and that readers use global structures to comprehend and remember texts.

Schemas and macropropositions. Kintsch and van Dijk (1978) suggested that schemas for different types of discourse guide the construction of *macropropositions.* Telling a story, arguing a case, or recalling episodes from memory would presumably each invoke a different schema. The pertinent schema would establish certain goals for the reader and sort through which micropropositions are relevant to these goals. The schema would also generalize the form of the relevant propositions so as to make them useful as a summary of the main ideas or gist of the text. The net result is a summary of the text—a macrostructure—that guides comprehension and memory.

A related theoretical position is Graesser's (1981) schema-pointer-plus-tag model. In reading a text, memory traces are built by setting pointers to what a person knows about general world knowledge and by adding tags for specific examples and facts. To comprehend and remember a fairy tale, such as Little Red Riding Hood, the reader would set pointers to schemas about the woods, grandmother's house, and so on. Tags would differentiate typical events (e.g., the journey through the woods was long) from highly atypical events (granny's teeth were very large).

Story grammars. Another approach stems from a long tradition in the humanities to characterize the nature of narratives (Stanzel, 1984). Just what is a story? The answer to this question plainly has relevance to psychological theories of reading, at least with regard to fairy tales, short stories, novels, and other narrative genres (Mandler, 1984; Mandler & Johnson, 1977; Thorndyke, 1977).

A **story grammar** is a set of rules that allow one to generate the acceptable story. Thorndyke proposed the rules shown in Figure 10.3. The first rule states that a story consists of a setting, a theme, a plot, and a resolution. Each of these elements is in turn defined by other rules in the grammar. For instance, characters, a location, and a time constitute the setting. A theme consists of a goal, plus an optional episode (as indicated by the parentheses). An episode consists of a subgoal, one or more attempts at tackling the subgoal, and an outcome. The asterisk denotes that an attempt may be repeated. The essential idea is that a story can be understood by relying on such a grammar; it specifies all the essential elements and their relations. So, for example, the story of the Three Little Pigs can be understood as a series of episodes: the wolf blowing down the house of straw and the house of sticks and then failing with the house of bricks. The resolution entails the three pigs safely huddled in the brick house as the wolf slides down the chimney to meet his demise in a pot of boiling water.

Readers in theory use a story grammar to comprehend and remember narrative text in terms of its global structure. Evidence favoring this theory comes from studies of text recall. For example, Mandler and Johnson (1977) found that recall suffers when an ill-formed story is missing elements that are called for by a story grammar. For well-formed stories, readers recalled 88% of the ideas represented by the major elements of the grammar compared with only 66% in the fractured stories. The order in which readers recalled ideas corresponded almost perfectly with the order predicted by the grammar; a mere 2% were recalled out of order. To put this in perspective, Mandler and Johnson analyzed the story in terms of a phrase structure grammar and looked for inversions of

Rule number	Rule
(1)	STORY → SETTING + THEME + PLOT + RESOLUTION
(2)	SETTING → CHARACTERS + LOCATION + TIME
(3)	THEME → (EVENT)* + GOAL
(4)	PLOT → EPISODE*
(5)	EPISODE → SUBGOAL + ATTEMPT* + OUTCOME
(6)	ATTEMPT → $\begin{cases} \text{EVENT*} \\ \text{EPISODE} \end{cases}$
(7)	OUTCOME → $\begin{cases} \text{EVENT*} \\ \text{STATE} \end{cases}$
(8)	RESOLUTION → $\begin{cases} \text{EVENT} \\ \text{STATE} \end{cases}$
(9)	$\left. \begin{array}{r} \text{SUBGOAL} \\ \text{GOAL} \end{array} \right\}$ → DESIRED STATE
(10)	$\left. \begin{array}{r} \text{CHARACTERS} \\ \text{LOCATION} \\ \text{TIME} \end{array} \right\}$ → STATE

Figure 10.3. A story grammar.
SOURCE: From Thorndyke (1977). Copyright © 1977 by Academic Press, Inc. Reprinted by permission.

phrases in the recall data. They found seven times as many inversions of phrases as they did for nodes of the story grammar.

Causal relations. Other studies of story recall have convincingly shown that particular events are better remembered than others (Nezworski, Stein, & Trabasso, 1981; Omanson, 1982; Stein & Glenn, 1979). Virtually all the key facts about the protagonist in a story are well remembered. The time and place in which the story unfolds around the protagonist, the goals in the plot with special attention given to the major conflict between the protagonist and antagonist, and the consequences of actions taken to reach the major goal are all readily recalled. Both children and adults reveal this pattern. Intriguingly, children from diverse cultures around the world recall stories in much the same way (Mandler, Scribner, Cole, & DeForest, 1980).

These and other facts have led some theorists to propose another form of global structure based on the causal relations among events. One approach orders the events of a story into a chain of causes and effects. Events that can be fit into the sequence are recalled while all others are pruned or dropped from the memory structure (Black & Bower, 1979; Schank, 1975). Another approach recognizes that certain key events may cause multiple effects; a network can capture the multiple causal connections of these critical events, unlike a linear causal chain (Trabasso & van den Broek, 1985).

Trabasso and his colleagues have found that the story grammar, causal chain, and causal network approaches generate similar predictions. The events surrounding the protagonist assume important roles regardless of which of these formalizations of the stories are used. However, by applying the correlational method called multiple regression, it is possible to separate the influence of, say, the position in a causal chain from the position in a causal network, or the impact of being a key node in a story grammar from being a key node in a causal network. The outcome of their research suggests that network models best account for the recall data (Trabasso & van den Broek, 1985).

The central point to be made is that readers actively construct a global representation by figuring out the causal connections among events. With the story grammar approach, one gets the impression that the reader need only sort out the events according to the slots of the grammar. The process seems automatic, much like the sorting of the constituents of a sentence according to, say, a transformational grammar. The value of underscoring the active construction of global text structures was recognized by Kintsch (1988) in his updated propositional model.

Mental models. The final approach to global structure forcefully advances the theme of the reader actively constructing a representation of the relations among events in a story. Johnson-Laird (1983) proposed a comprehensive theory of cognition that distinguished procedures, propositions, and models. The models do the work of higher order cognitive processes, such as comprehension. Analyzing the propositions of a text is only the beginning of comprehension, according to Johnson-Laird. The reader must also construct a mental model that contains tokens or symbols for each of the elements of the text. The mental model provides a global structure for the text, specifying what is happening to whom and why. Foss (1988) pointed out the close similarity between mental models and the causal fields that Trabasso and his colleagues discuss in their work.

Here let us cut to the core of why models complement propositions. First, Johnson-Laird pointed out that only a model can unambiguously represent the extension or referent of an idea expressed in a text. A writer might employ diverse propositions to refer to the same entity. For example, the great white whale, the denizen of the deep, or even the diabolical demon might all refer to the same beast. Only by building a mental model that includes the sea, the ship, the captain, the whale, and so on can the reader keep these coreferential propositions straight.

Second, Johnson-Laird observed that establishing referential coherence among propositions is insufficient for comprehension. Recall the earlier paragraph about his daughter in London; it lacked a global structure despite its referential coherence. In fact, such coherence may lead to serious misunderstandings on the part of the reader. Take this other example from Johnson-Laird (1983):

> Roland's wife died in 1928. He married again in 1940. His wife now lives in Spain. (p. 380)

Here is a case in which the wife implicitly introduced in the second sentence and referred to in the third is most assuredly not the same woman of the first sentence. Yet there is nothing in the propositions themselves that makes this clear. The reader must build a global structure, a mental model, populated by two women, only one of whom is enjoying the warmth of Spain.

Suppositions, Inferences, and Interpretations

The materials with which we build mental structures include more than the actual words appearing in print. We presuppose, infer, and interpret far beyond a literal reading of the text. We examined in Chapter 5 the manner in which suppositions and inferences become part of memory for perceptual events and language. If a fact is presupposed or inferred, then it is likely to be recalled as real. In a court of law, for instance, a prosecuting attorney might fire this loaded question at the defendant: "And when, Mr. Jones, did you stop beating your wife?" The jury would presuppose and perhaps later recall that Mr. Jones in fact abused his wife.

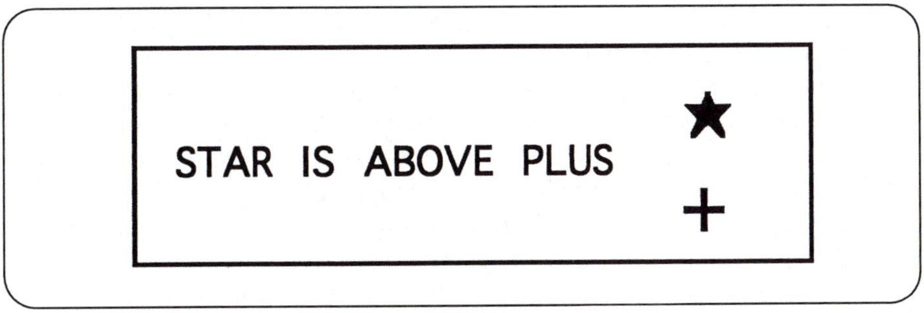

STAR IS ABOVE PLUS

Figure 10.4. A stimulus used in the study of sentence verification.
SOURCE: From Clark and Chase (1972). Copyright © 1972 by Academic Press, Inc. Reprinted by permission.

In this section, we turn to psycholinguistic studies of how we go beyond the text so as to understand it.

Suppositions. It may be that simply denying an assertion causes listeners or readers to presuppose that the assertion is true. If Mr. Jones's defense attorney objects to the above question ("I object, Your Honor, my client is not a wife-beater!"), then the jury may once again presuppose that indeed he is. Research indicates that in comprehending a negative sentence, a reader first presupposes a positive proposition and then denies it (Clark & Chase, 1972).

Clark and Chase presented readers with a picture like that shown in Figure 10.4 and one of four sentences:

1. The star is above the plus. (true affirmative)
2. The plus is above the star. (false affirmative)
3. The plus is not above the star. (true negative)
4. The star is not above the plus. (false negative) (p. 483)

As you can see from the picture, sentences 1 and 3 are true statements whereas 2 and 4 are false. Clark and Chase argued that the negative sentences 3 and 4 required the reader to engage in more processing than the affirmative assertions of 1 and 2. Specifically, they argued that the negatives entail both the supposition that the star is above the plus and the assertion that this supposition is false. To expose the additional effort required by the reader, Clark and Chase measured the time required to verify each type of sentence.

If the negative sentences require the reader to presuppose the positive assertion, then the time needed to comprehend this assertion must be factored into total verification time. From the observed times for each of the four sentences, Clark and Chase estimated that comprehension of the simple assertion (the star is above the plus) takes slightly more than 1,450 milliseconds. All four sentences required this amount of time. The researchers further estimated that the time needed to deny the assertion adds roughly another 300 milliseconds. Only sentences 3 and 4 needed this extra time.

Inferences. The memory research from Chapter 4 plainly showed that people falsely remember inferences (e.g., Johnson et al., 1973). If you read this sentence, "Bobby pounded in the nail until the board was safely secured," then you might well recall later that Bobby did some work with a hammer. McKoon and Ratcliff (1980, 1981) provided evidence that readers sometimes draw such inferences during the act of comprehension.

Anaphoric reference provides a revealing case of the dynamics of inference-making during comprehension. Consider this use of anaphora: "Ann predicted that Pam would lose the track race but she came in first very easily." Gernsbacher (1990) contended that activation of words in the mental lexicon takes place during inference-making. She theorized that readers not only enhance the activation of referents (Pam) but suppress the activation of nonreferents (Ann). The results of an elegant experiment revealed these separate effects (Gernsbacher, 1989).

Shown in Table 10.1 are examples of the two-clause sentences that Gernsbacher presented on a computer screen. While reading each sentence, a test name appeared at the top of the screen either 150 milliseconds before or after the anaphoric reference. In the first example, the anaphora was explicit (Pam) whereas in the second example a less explicit pronoun occurred (she). The test name was either the referent name (Pam) or the nonreferent (Ann). The reader had to decide as quickly as possible whether the test name had appeared before in the sentence. Presumably, the more activated the name was in working memory, the faster the person could respond.

The results are shown in Figure 10.5 (from Experiment 2 of Gernsbacher, 1989). The readers actively suppressed the nonreferent name after the occurrence of the explicit anaphora. They needed about 100 milliseconds more time to respond than when given the same test name just

Table 10.1 Example Stimuli in a Study of Inference Making

Sentences	Test Names	
Ann predicted that Pam would lose the track race,[2] but **Pam**[2] came in first very easily.	**Pam** referent name	**Ann** nonreferent name
Ann predicted that Pam would lose the track race,[2] but **she**[2] came in first very easily.	**Pam** referent pronoun	**Ann** nonreferent pronoun
Bill handed John some tickets to a concert,[2] but **Bill**[2] took the tickets back immediately.	**Bill** referent name	**John** nonreferent name
Bill handed John some tickets to a concert,[2] but **he**[2] took the tickets back immediately.	**Bill** referent pronoun	**John** nonreferent pronoun

SOURCE: From Gernsbacher, M. A. (1989). Mechanisms that improve referential access. *Cognition, 32,* 99-156. (Experiment 2). Copyright © 1989 by Elsevier Press. Reprinted by permission.
NOTE: The superscript 2 refers to where in the sentences test names were presented in Experiment 2.

before the anaphora. In contrast, they responded about 100 milliseconds faster to the referent name just after, compared with just before, the explicit anaphora.

Notice that when pronouns were used instead of names, the activation level of both referents and nonreferents remained stable. This outcome means two things. First, the referent (Pam) and nonreferent (Ann) names were both equally active in working memory because they occurred in the first clause of the sentence; this can be seen in the equivalent reaction times in the before-anaphora condition. Second, activation is neither suppressed nor enhanced if the situation poses ambiguity. Because a pronoun could refer to more than one antecedent, readers hold the activation levels steady in building their mental structures.

Metaphors. So far we have talked about comprehension as if each word in a sentence could mean only one thing. The hardest inference considered yet is an ambiguous pronoun such as *she, he,* or *it.* But even here the

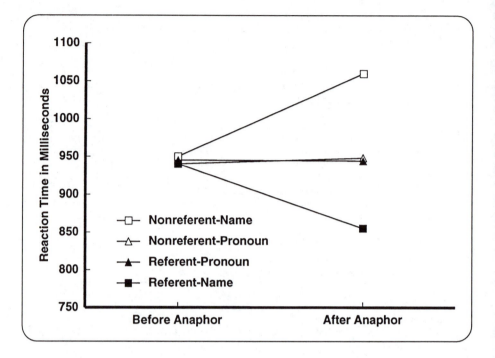

Figure 10.5. Explicit anaphora triggers enhancement and suppression during sentence comprehension.

SOURCE: From Gernsbacher, M. A. (1989). Mechanisms that improve referential access. *Cognition, 32,* 99-156. (Experiment 2). Copyright © 1989 by Elsevier Press. Reprinted by permission.

reader presumably knows that the pronoun is supposed to refer back to a particular concept that has been given earlier in the text. Language is much richer than these cases. Our frequent use of metaphor makes this point most sharply (e.g., "Time flies"). Metaphor lies at the heart of language.

Metaphors are ambiguous because the intended meaning is quite different than the literal meaning. For example, in the above paragraph, were any points literally sharpened or was a beating heart in sight? A word is given a novel, insightful meaning by linking it in a nonliteral fashion with another word in metaphor. Language would be dull indeed without metaphor.

The question arises as to whether we activate the literal meanings of terms used metaphorically. It is possible that readers first try a literal interpretation and then look for nonliteral meanings. Alternatively, they may use the context of the metaphor wisely and immediately capture the nonliteral interpretation. Experiments have shown that with the proper context, the nonliteral meaning of a metaphor is grasped without a first attempt at the literal interpretation (Glucksberg, Gildea, & Bookin, 1982; Inhoff, Lima, & Carroll, 1984).

For example, Inhoff et al. measured how long readers spent looking at and trying to comprehend the sentence with a metaphorical interpretation, such as the meaning of *choked* in the following sentence.

1. The directors mercifully choked smaller companies.

For some readers, this sentence was preceded by an appropriate metaphoric context such as the following:

2. The company used murderous tactics.

For others, the sentence was preceded by a context designed to encourage a literal reading of the term *choked*, such as in this sentence:

3. The company used competitive tactics.

Inhoff et al. found that readers spent less time in comprehending metaphoric sentence 1 when it was preceded by sentence 2 relative to sentence 3. The metaphoric context of sentence 2 primed activation of a nonliteral interpretation of *choked*.

Components of Reading Skill

Having examined the structures that readers build, it would now be useful to gain an overview of the process itself. A fruitful theoretical approach treats reading as a complex cognitive skill, a skill that develops through maturation, practice, and instruction. The model presented in Figure 10.6 captures the component skills and the flow of information during the reading process (Carr, Brown, Vavrus, & Evans, 1990). The solid arrows reflect pathways that are more or less taken for granted in the field. The dotted pathways are more speculative. For example, it is certain that the visual presentation of a word gives rise to phonological processing. We reviewed evidence for this pathway in Chapter 5 in the

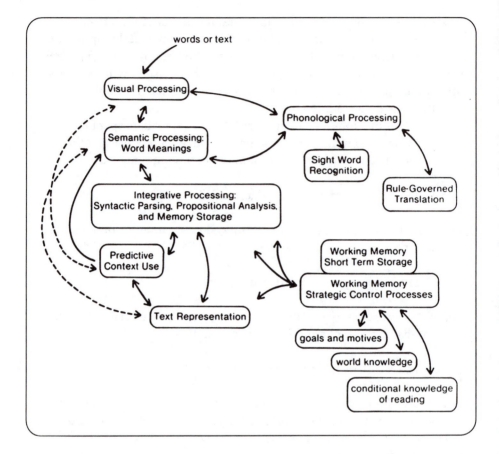

Figure 10.6. Component processes of reading skill.
SOURCE: From Carr, Brown, Vavrus, and Evans (1990). Copyright © 1990 by Academic Press, Inc. Reprinted by permission.

context of acoustic coding in short-term or working memory. Less certain is whether the text representation constructed by the reader directly influences, and conversely is influenced by, the semantic processing of word meanings.

Levy and Hinchley (1990) obtained individual reader profiles on numerous tests of reading ability for 345 children in grades 3 to 6. The testing data clearly separated the readers by their age and, at each point in development, the data separated good readers from poor readers. The younger readers and the poorer readers at a given age shared several common characteristics. These included sensitivity to phonological (or phonemic) differences in words, smaller working memory capacity, slower sight-word recognition, and inability to use the global structure of text to good advantage. The last result meant that good readers showed markedly higher recall for a well-formed story than for a randomly scrambled presentation of the same sentences. Poor readers also did worse on the scrambled story than one that fit a story grammar, but not by much.

My central point in presenting the model of Figure 10.6 is that fluent reading implicates many component skills. Many investigators have shown that the bottom-up or data-driven processes of visual (orthographic), acoustic (phonological), and lexical-semantic analysis are crucial (e.g., Graesser, Hoffman, & Clark, 1980; Perfetti, 1985; Stanovich, Cunningham, & Feeman, 1984). Reading well demands that one handle words effectively and efficiently.

Equally convincing evidence has stressed the role of top-down or conceptually driven processes. By using world knowledge, goals, and semantic context, readers can form hypotheses and make good guesses about the printed words or text (Palmer, MacLeod, Hunt, & Davidson, 1985; Thorndike, 1973-1974). We do not even need to see every letter because the context allows us to guess missing data. Anderson (1990) concocted the following sentence to demonstrate this point (see also Lindsay & Norman, 1977): To xllxstxatx, I cxn rxplxce xvexy txirx lextex of x sextexce xitx an x, anx yox stxll xan xanxge xo rxad xt—wixh sxme xifxicxltx. At the same time, the effective use of working memory plays a crucial role in the process (Baddeley & Hitch, 1974; Daneman & Carpenter, 1980; Just & Carpenter, 1992).

The component model in Figure 10.6 makes clear that a deficit in reading may stem from a breakdown in any one or several of these components. **Dyslexia** is the term used to describe reading disorders. It covers a broad range of specific breakdowns in the components discussed here. For example, visual word recognition fails in individuals suffering from dyslexias based on the visual form of words (McCarthy & Warrington, 1990). In one variant of this, patients attempt to read letter by letter rather than processing the whole word. In another variant, they neglect to read the initial or the terminal portion of a word.

A remarkable study using PET scans has shown that specialized areas in the left hemisphere respond to words and pseudowords, both of which look like words in that they follow the orthographic rules of English (Posner & Raichle, 1994). As shown in Color Plate 3 [and the asso-

BOX 10.2: Fixations in Reading

Just and Carpenter (1980, 1992) have clarified the interaction of perceptual processes and working memory as reading unfolds in real time. They proposed that each fixation of the eyes provides a discrete input to the visual system. Word meanings are identified, syntactic case roles assigned, and sentences integrated through activated representations in working memory. They commented in their 1992 paper that "working memory plays a critical role in storing the immediate and final products of a reader's or listener's computations as she or he constructs and integrates ideas from the stream of successive words in a text or spoken discourse" (p. 122).

The duration of each fixation averages about 200 to 250 milliseconds, although the variability is enormous (Pollatsek & Rayner, 1989). A rapid eye movement, called a saccade, jumps the focus of foveal vision to a new point in between these fixations. In reading a book, a saccadic eye movement typically would advance (or at times regress) foveal vision about seven to nine character spaces in less than 50 milliseconds. The reader in essence gains a series of snapshots of information about the text as the eyes jump across and down the page. The span of each snapshot appears to be biased to the right of the fixation point. The reader extracts information from 4 characters to the left of the point of fixation point and up to 15 characters to the right (McConkie & Rayner, 1975).

Just and Carpenter (1980) made two key assumptions in linking eye fixations to comprehension. The immediacy assumption holds that readers assign an interpretation to each word as it is fixated. Readers sometimes need to revise their interpretations based on a subsequent fixation. For example, in the sentence

Mary loves Jonathan . . .

the reader might initially assign one meaning and then repair it when the final word is encountered—*apples.*

The eye-mind assumption holds that the duration of fixation varies with the amount of information that must be processed in working memory at that instant. In other words, the work of comprehension takes place during the fixation; the next saccadic eye movement is suppressed until the reader is ready to move forward. At times, regressive eye movements are needed so that the reader can go back and reprocess information that was misinterpreted initially. Such a regressive movement would probably take place in reading "Mary loved Jonathon apples." But the reader does not take in several snapshots of data, hold them in memory, and then pause for an extended period of time to comprehend that data.

Just and Carpenter (1980, 1992) have found that the more difficult a section of the text is to read, the longer individuals fixate. Good readers with large working memory capacities take extra time to resolve ambiguities of interpretation. The authors' model and findings are consistent with the idea that reading is a time-consuming, high-level cognitive skill. It is not consistent with claims that, through speed-reading, one can attain full comprehension of a text at three or four times the normal reading rate. Such speed-reading techniques are better thought of as trained skimming.

ciated table at the very end of the book], false fonts and letter strings activate the visual cortex just as do words and pseudowords. All four kinds of stimuli involve a low-level analysis of visual features taken on by the visual cortex at the rear of the brain in both hemispheres. But only the words and pseudowords prompt an analysis by a specialized system in the left hemisphere that analyzes the visual form of words as such.

Central dyslexia results from breakdowns in processing that follow visual analysis of the printed word. In one variant of central dyslexia, patients try to sound out words, reading entirely phonologically. They fail when the spelling-to-sound conversion does not follow the rules (e.g., *yacht*, *ache*, and *sew*) and when they misapply rules (e.g., reading *lace* as *lake*). Another variant ignores phonology altogether, reading entirely by sight vocabulary. Such patients cannot pronounce a nonsense word such as *dar* at all, because they are unable to convert spelling to sound.

▣ SUMMARY ▣

1. Compared with speaking, writing is a recent development for our species, less than 10,000 years old. Writing by hand divides into three stages: the formulation of ideas and sentences, the motor movements of output, and the monitoring of output. All three stages draw on a common pool of cognitive resources, with formulation assuming a higher priority when task demands overload the writer.

2. The formulation of ideas and sentences involves planning ideas (generating and organizing ideas and setting goals), translating

ideas into sentences (semantic, syntactic, and pragmatic operations), and reviewing ideas and text (reading and editing). Planning, translating, and reviewing do not occur in a sequence but are repetitively interwoven throughout all phases of creating a text. Mature writers actively transform their knowledge about a topic through their planning, translating, and reviewing. They juggle numerous demands on attention and devote considerable cognitive effort to writing processes, particularly planning and reviewing. Writers cope with the demands of writing through the use of plans, such as outlining.

3. Text comprehension, reading, has been much more extensively investigated than writing. The theme of cognition as active construction is well illustrated by the processes of reading. Readers build mental structures at the local level of micropropositions expressed in words and sentences and at the global or macropropositional level of paragraphs and discourse. Sentences possess referential coherence when the words and phrases of one sentence refer unambiguously to those of other sentences in the same paragraph. True discourse also demands a global structure. Schemas and macropropositions, story grammars, causal relations, and mental models are four ways of explaining the global structure of discourse.

4. In building mental structures, readers use more than the literal words on the page. They also establish suppositions, draw inferences, and interpret metaphors and other nonliteral language. For example, to comprehend a negative statement, readers first presuppose that a positive statement is true and then take the extra step of denying it. Readers use their knowledge about the world to make plausible inferences during comprehension. Words are activated and suppressed in working memory as inferences are drawn. Words with multiple meanings seem to activate multiple interpretations simultaneously, whereas with metaphors the reader activates only the intended meaning, not the literal meaning.

5. Fluent reading requires a complex orchestration of numerous component processes. Skilled readers handle words effectively through bottom-up processes of visual, phonological, and lexical-semantic analysis. At the same time, such readers work from the top down by using world knowledge, goals, and semantic context. Skilled readers make good use of context to get to the meaning of the text. Dyslexias or reading disorders are varied, reflecting the failure of different component processes.

Key Terms

idiographic writing

phonetic writing

grapheme

orthography

planning

translating

reviewing

content problems

knowledge-telling

knowledge transformation

referential coherence

anaphora

given-new strategy

bridging inferences

micropropositions

leading edge strategy

story grammar

rhetorical problems

dyslexia

Recommended Readings

Gregg and Steinberg's (1980) edited volume titled *Cognitive Processes in Writing* is a classic reference. *The Psychology of Written Composition* by Bereiter and Scardamalia (1987) focuses on the development of writing skills. My own book, *The Psychology of Writing*, offers a recent overview of the field (Kellogg, 1994). Rose's (1984) *Writer's Block: The Cognitive Dimension* gives further information on why people often put off writing projects.

Just and Carpenter (1987) provided an excellent review of reading in their book titled *The Psychology of Reading and Language Comprehension*. I strongly recommend it for information on dyslexia and speed reading. *Language Comprehension as Structure Building* by Gernsbacher (1990) is packed with experimental evidence on the constructive nature of the reading process. Similarly, an edited volume by Graesser and Bower (1990), titled *The Psychology of Learning and Motivation: Inferences and Text Comprehension* (Volume 25), covers contemporary research.

Pollatsek and Rayner's (1989) contribution to *The Foundations of Cognitive Science* and Foss's (1988) chapter in the *Annual Review of Psychology* cover questions about reading. The June 1993 issue of the *Canadian Journal of Experimental Psychology* is also devoted to reading and language processing.

PART V

Thinking Skills and Intelligence

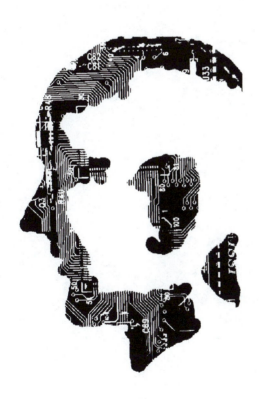

CHAPTER **11**

◉ Problem Solving

The next three chapters concern what cognitive psychologists know about thinking. The term *thinking* traditionally has covered problem solving, reasoning, and decision making. Chapter 13 examines the literature on intelligence as well, for a complete account of the higher cognitive processes can ill afford to ignore it. The study of intelligence traditionally has been rooted in the literature on psychological testing and measurement. But over the years, its core concerns have become increasingly synonymous with the concerns and even the methods of cognitive psychology. This will be readily apparent in our discussions of intelligence as a skill and the information processing components of intelligence.

But first the groundwork must be laid for our discussions of thinking and intelligence with the classic work on problem solving. We will begin this chapter by considering different types of thinking within the context of solving problems. Next, we will turn to the components of representing problems and searching for solutions by means of algorithms and heuristics. We will see that general representation and search procedures are inadequate to explain all aspects of human problem solving. Domain-specific knowledge and metacognition are also critical. We will then examine some of the common obstacles to successful problem solving, before closing with a discussion of creativity, its definition, sources, and stages.

Thinking is a covert set of mental skills that makes use of our knowledge. Thinking draws upon all the basic processes described in the first section of the book—perception, attention, and memory. At times, we think so as to succeed in a task, such as solving a problem or making a decision. At other times, we think merely to bide the time, remembering, imagining, and even dreaming about the world and our life in it. Let us take a concrete example of problem solving to illustrate one kind of thinking.

All of us need food to survive. Whether this is a major or minor problem depends on a host of factors, including where in the world we live, whether we are gainfully employed, whether we have a place to stay where cooking is possible, and so on. To obtain, say, dinner tonight, we must come up with a plan for action. In planning, we might imagine a mental map of a city or town with grocery stores, fast-food chains, and restaurants of various price ranges. Planning stipulates the goal (e.g., eat a grilled steak) and examines the numerous paths that might be taken to reach the goal (e.g., grill at home, find a steak house, "borrow" a steak off the neighbor's grill).

Each such path includes numerous steps along the way, some of which fit together in achieving a specific subgoal. For example, a subgoal for grilling at home might be to fire up some charcoal, assuming that local air quality laws allow it. This would involve several steps: going to the garage, finding the charcoal, putting the charcoal in the grill, applying lighter fluid, lighting the coals, waiting 5 minutes till the coals go cold, reapplying fluid and relighting, and so on. Any one of these steps might send us off on another side path to achieve a new subgoal. For example, it may be necessary to go buy charcoal, to search the house desperately for matches, or to put out a fire on the patio started by all that lighter fluid.

Types of Thinking

The above example illustrates what is called **directed thinking:** It is goal oriented and rational (Gilhooly, 1982). Such thinking requires a clear, well-defined goal. One must then find a path that leads to the goal, with the aim of doing so as directly as possible. The costs of each path are certainly taken into account (e.g., it may be easier to find a steak house but much more affordable to grill at home). In general, directed thinking avoids wandering aimlessly, exploring odd options, and looking for creative solutions. Just such aimless meandering might be necessary to strike upon highly novel solutions (e.g., "borrowing" the neighbor's steak is creative and highly affordable, albeit unscrupulous and possibly dangerous).

Gilhooly's name for wandering thought is **undirected thinking.** Such thought meanders without concern for any goal or purpose. Dreaming and daydreaming are examples. Undirected thinking is anything but rational and goal oriented (Berlyne, 1965). Undirected thinking takes us to destinations that are sometimes murky, sometimes insightful. It seems to play a special role in creativity and the solution of problems that are poorly defined.

Freud (1900) distinguished between dreaming and daydreaming as forms of undirected thought. Dreams in his view reflected primary-process thinking in which our deepest wishes were fulfilled without the bothersome constraints of reality. Daydreaming, in contrast, reflected secondary-process thinking; it conformed to the reality principle that mediates the battles of the ego with the unconscious and superego. Both directed and undirected thinking have a role in solving specific types of problems, as we shall see.

Well-Defined and Ill-Defined Problems

Directed thinking begins with the assumption that the problem at hand is **well defined.** In technical terms, such a problem is said to have a definable **initial state** (e.g., need for dinner), **goal state** (e.g., steak dinner), and one or more paths to obtaining the goal. Each path can be specified as a series of intermediate states, some of which are critical **subgoals** (e.g., burning coals). The way that one moves from one state to the next is defined by a set of rules. Each legal move from the initial state, to intermediate states, to the final goal state is specifically defined by an **operator.** In solving the problem of having a steak dinner, there are many such operators. If theft is not among them, then the creative solution of snatching the neighbor's steak is never even considered. All the states and operators taken together define what is called a **problem space.**

At this point it might help to consider some games and puzzles studied by psychologists in the field of problem solving. Chess is one such game. The initial state is defined by the players lined up on the board for the opening move. The goal state is defined as checkmate. The operators are the legal moves of each game piece (e.g., the bishop may move or

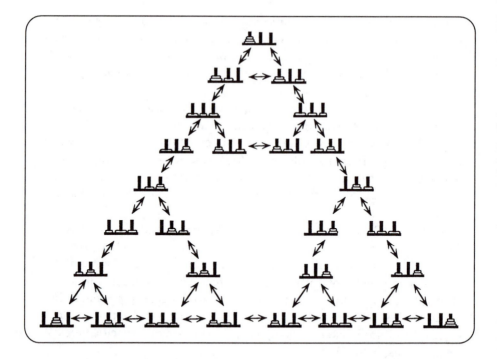

Figure 11.1. Problem space for the Tower of Hanoi. The solution path is shown to the far right.

SOURCE: From Kotovsky, K., & Fallside, D. (1989). Representation and transfer in problem solving. In D. Klahr & K. Kotovsky (Eds.), *Complex information processing: The contributions of Herbert A. Simon* (pp. 69-108). Hillsdale, NJ: Lawrence Erlbaum. Copyright © 1989 by Lawrence Erlbaum Associates. Reprinted by permission.

attack the opponent's pieces in as many spaces as desired, but only along its assigned diagonal on the chessboard). The 64 squares of the game board and the six kinds of pieces yield an immense problem space, one so large that even a supercomputer could not possibly check all possible states before deciding on a move in a game (Simon, 1990).

Part of the problem space of a much simpler puzzle that may be familiar to you is shown in Figure 11.1. It is called the Tower of Hanoi problem. The initial state, at the top of the figures, stacks three disks of different sizes on the first of three pegs as shown. The problem is to move the disks to the third peg so they are stacked as shown in the goal state, on the lower right corner of the figure. The only operator here is to move the top disk from one peg onto another peg with the restriction that it not cover a smaller disk.

Each drawing in Figure 11.1 represents a state of the problem space, a legally possible state that might be reached by applying the operator. From state 1, one can move the smallest disk either to peg 2 or to peg 3, as shown. Moving it to peg 2 allows only one possible next move, namely, putting the middle-sized disk on peg 3. From there, as the reader can see, two possible moves can be made. In solving the Tower of Hanoi, one must find a path through the problem space to progress from the initial to the goal state. The paths on the left in Figure 11.1 lead to states removed from the goal. Directed thinking, when applied flawlessly to the problem, would result in the path on the far right, a stepwise progression through seven moves.

It should be noted that the problem space that exists for a given person may well include errors or omissions. If an operator is misunderstood, such as the rule for moving a knight in chess, then a flawed problem space would be generated. Similarly, an inexperienced chess player who simply never moved the knights would be working within an incomplete problem space.

Of course, many problems encountered in daily life seem quite remote from the problems of having dinner, playing chess, or solving the tower puzzle. Finding a career and succeeding at it is an important problem facing most students reading this book. Although the beginning state of such a problem may be clear enough, the goal state certainly is not. The goal of a successful career could be defined in an infinite variety of ways. One can attempt to structure the problems by deciding in advance exactly what defines success (e.g., becoming the head of General Motors or president of the United States). But a truly well-defined problem specifies all the legal transition states and the operators that generate them. The operators that take one to the head of General Motors or the presidency are difficult if not impossible to enumerate and the ways to get there are many.

Ill-defined problems are those in which the goal state, the initial state, the operators, or possibly all of these are not clearly defined. Writing an essay, painting a picture, or creating a garden are ill-defined problems. That is, their solution cannot be specified in advance, let alone the path for arriving at the eventual solution.

Productive and Reproductive Problem Solving

The Gestalt psychologists distinguished between reproductive and productive thinking (Wertheimer, 1959). **Reproductive thinking** entails the application of tried-and-true paths to solution. The thinker reproduces a series of steps that are known to yield a workable answer by using rote memory. **Productive thinking,** on the other hand, requires insight and creativity. In the view of the Gestalt psychologists, the thinker must see a new way of organizing the problem, a new way of structuring the elements of thought and perception.

Köhler (1925), another Gestalt theorist, distinguished between problem solving based on insight versus trial and error. Trial and error can be regarded as one form of reproductive thinking. The reader may recall that trial and error behavior allowed the cats in Edward Thorndike's (1898) famous puzzle box to discover an escape route. Upon being placed in the box, a cat pawed randomly about the box, obviously irritated by the confinement. Once it chanced upon the escape lever, it learned to associate the lever with a way to escape. In the terms of operant conditioning, the cat learned to escape more and more quickly through negative reinforcement, the avoidance of further confinement.

Köhler spent 7 years studying the problem solving of chimpanzees while stranded on Tenerife, an island in the Atlantic Ocean, during World War I. Köhler designed problems such as the following. A chimpanzee is in a large cage along with several crates. Hanging from the top of the cage, out of reach, is a banana. Köhler reported that in this setting the chimpanzees would appear to be lost in thought and then suddenly the proverbial lightbulb of insight would flash. The animal would suddenly move the crates under the banana, stacking them to form a ladder and to reach the food. In another problem, a chimpanzee insightfully learned to join together two sticks so as to reach a banana lying outside of the cage. Such productive or insightful problem solving differed from the trial and error learning of Thorndike's cats.

Relations Among Terms

Ill-defined problems often demand productive thinking. Undirected thought, as we shall see later in the chapter, is certainly one means for achieving insights. By the same token, well-defined problems often call for reproductive problem solving and directed thought. But it is a mistake to equate the concepts. For instance, in Köhler's experiments, the goal state of reaching a banana was well defined even if the operators for doing so were unclear. The mutilated checkerboard (MC) problem shown in Figure 11.3 also has elements of both a well-defined puzzle and an

BOX 11.1: Problem Solving Constraints

A classic problem calling for productive, insightful thinking is the nine dot problem, shown in Figure 11.2. The task is to connect the nine dots with four straight lines, without lifting your pencil from the paper in drawing the lines. The solution to the problem, as you can see in Panel B of the figure, requires drawing the lines outside the boundaries of the nine dots.

The Gestalt psychologists would have argued that the perceptual organization of the nine dot problem leads one to make an important assumption about the solution. In looking at the square defined by the nine dots, the obvious structure or representation of the problem that comes to mind is that the four lines lie within the square. Although the problem statement says nothing about whether the lines can extend beyond the confines of the square, the Gestalt perception of the problem strongly suggests exactly that. To think productively in this situation, one must restructure the problem, to throw off the unnecessary assumption that the lines must lie within the visual boundaries.

Weisberg and Alba (1981) tested college students' ability to solve the nine dot problem. In the control group, the students made 20 attempts at solution. As expected, not a single participant hit upon the correct solution. In three experimental groups, the researchers allowed the participants 10 attempts before introducing hints designed to generate insight into the problem. One group of students was told to "go outside the square." A second group was told the same, plus was shown the initial diagonal line leading from the lower, right-hand dot to the upper, left-hand dot. A third group was also told to "go outside the square," and was shown the initial line plus the second vertical line extending down the left side of the square and past the lower left dot. In other words, the groups were given more and more explicit direction as to the solution.

Only 20% of the subjects solved the problem with the hint to "go outside the square." This is an improvement but is not as dramatic as one might expect if the only difficulty facing the students was the unwarranted assumption about the lines fitting within the square. Weisberg and Alba contended that another difficulty faced the students; namely, the problem space is too large in that there are too many possible arrangements of lines. By giving one or two of the lines, the researchers expected to reduce the size of the problem space, making the solution more apparent. They succeeded in doing so. With the hint "go outside the square" and one line, about 60% of the students solved it. With two lines given, all students solved it.

Here is another insight problem. See if you can structure or represent the problem in a way that is conducive to solution. With six matches, construct four equilateral triangles. Each side of the triangle is equal in length to a whole match.

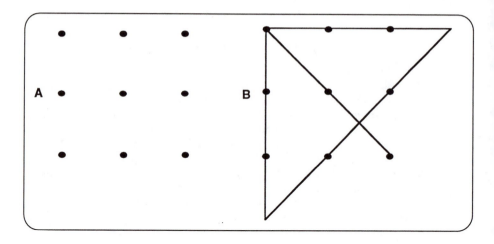

Figure 11.2. The nine dot problem (A) and its solution (B).

ill-defined problem calling for insight (Kaplan & Simon, 1990; Wickelgren, 1974).

In the MC problem, two opposite corners of a standard 8 × 8 checkerboard are removed as shown. The 62 remaining squares are to be covered by 31 dominos. Each domino is large enough to cover exactly two squares, either in a horizontal direction or in a vertical direction. Placing the domino diagonally on adjacent squares is not allowed. The problem is to show how to cover all the remaining squares with 31 dominos or to prove logically that it cannot be done. We will return to this problem later (with the solution), so you might give it a try yourself at this point. For now, take note or, better, warning that the problem seems to be well defined in that the initial and goal states are stated clearly and the rules for placing the dominos are given. Yet, as Kaplan and Simon observed (1990), "the initial representation that problem solvers almost always form fails to solve the problem. . . . Subjects need to change their representation in a nonobvious way" (p. 378).

It is also misleading to assume that the solution to any given problem stems solely from reproduction or recall versus production or insight. Remembering and creating cannot be so neatly severed. In earlier chapters, we saw how recall from long-term memory always involves an element of imagination or creativity. Reconstructive recall taps the creative elements of human thinking in much the same way that problem solving does. Indeed, it is quite appropriate to view the task of trying to remem-

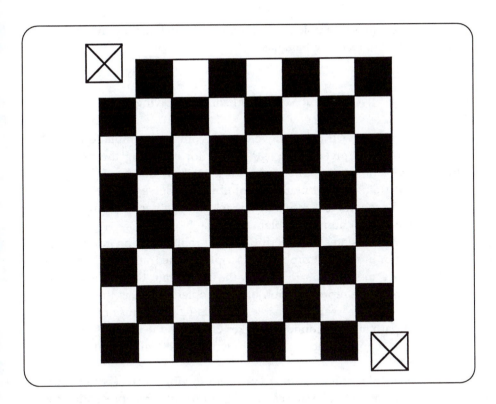

Figure 11.3. The mutilated checkerboard (MC) problem.
SOURCE: From Kaplan and Simon (1990). Copyright © 1990 by Academic Press, Inc.
Reprinted by permission.

ber an event from, say, 5 years ago as a problem to be solved. Both directed
and undirected thinking, and reproductive and productive thinking, enter into the solution of a recall problem as one constructs a mental model,
uses retrieval cues, and so forth.

Similarly, insightful problem solving depends on recollecting past
experience and knowledge as well as creativity. Without drawing on past
knowledge and relating new ideas to old ideas, productive thinking cannot take place. The great creative ideas of Shakespeare, Bach, Picasso, and
Einstein were not given birth in a vacuum, created *ex nihilo*, out of nothing
(Boden, 1992). Rather, their creations played off the accumulated knowledge of others that they had diligently studied. In a much less significant
example in Western civilization, the apes studied by Köhler needed past

experiences with using poles and moving crates before they showed any insights at all in reaching bananas.

A General Model of Problem Solving

Ernst and Newell (1969) developed a computer simulation called General Problem Solver (GPS) as a model for exploring the nature of human problem solving. Their intent was to show that an AI program based on certain general methods could in fact solve a wide range of problems. Psychological research has tested whether GPS provides a good simulation of human problem solving.

GPS first translates the description of a problem into an internal representation or model of a problem description. The translator interprets each sentence and attempts to identify the initial state, the goal state, and the operators. The representation of the problem, then, is the problem space that must be searched using methods or techniques of problem solving. A path must be found that takes GPS from the initial state to the goal state. A representation of this solution path is then generated in the final stage.

It is fruitful to think of human problem solving as proceeding in the same manner as GPS. The two essential components are representing the problem and searching the problem space for a solution. We will examine more about the specifics of GPS and other AI simulations as we look at the research concerning representation and search.

Representing Problems

UNDERSTAND. Coming up with the right way to represent a problem is a crucial step in solving the problem. Another AI program, UNDER-STAND, addressed this issue (Simon & Hayes, 1976). UNDERSTAND used a reading comprehension system to extract the deep structure of the sentences (see Chapter 9) and then it constructed a global description of the problem from these parts. Reading comprehension depended on the interaction of working memory and long-term memory (see Chapter 10). As each sentence of the problem was fed to UNDERSTAND, semantic and syntactic processes in long-term memory derived its meaning. Construction rules stored in long-term memory then operated on these meanings to build the goal state, initial state, and operators of the problem

Table 11.1 The Monster Problem

S1. Three five-handed extraterrestrial monsters were holding three crystal globes.

S2. Because of the quantum-mechanical peculiarities of their neighborhood, both monsters and globes come in exactly three sizes with no others permitted: small, medium, and large.

S3. The medium-sized monster was holding the small globe; the small monster was holding the large globe; and the large monster was holding the medium-sized globe.

S4. Since this situation offended their keenly developed sense of symmetry, they proceeded to transfer globes from one monster to another so that each monster would have a globe proportionate to his own size.

S5. Monster etiquette complicated the solution of the problem since it requires:

S6. (1) that only one globe be transferred at a time,

S7. (2) that if a monster is holding two globes, only the larger of the two may be transferred, and

S8. (3) that a globe may not be transferred to a monster who is holding a larger globe.

S9. By what sequence of transfers could the monsters have solved this problem?

SOURCE: From Simon and Hayes (1976). Copyright © 1976 by Academic Press, Inc. Reprinted with permission.

space in working memory. The resulting problem space was then searched using the procedures of GPS that we will come to shortly.

Let us first see how UNDERSTAND operated by looking at the problem reproduced in Table 11.1 from Simon and Hayes (1976). The construction rules looked for sentences that expressed relations among objects and their features. It especially sought expressions describing the initial state of the problem and the operators that could be used to modify this state. UNDERSTAND assumed that such operators took a primitive form of stating how objects and features should be altered (e.g., "Transfer A from X to Y," or "Exchange X with Y," or "Insert A at X").

Consequently, the meanings of the sentences S1 and S2 in Table 11.1 were ignored by UNDERSTAND. It used S3 to establish the problem representation. It then used S4 plus the three conditions of S6, S7, and S8 to establish the operators. UNDERSTAND interpreted the new information in the context of given information; it knew how to interpret the operators in light of the problem representation already constructed.

Simon and Hayes claimed that human problem solving crucially depends on the representation constructed. To test this, they developed a problem that differs only in its descriptive language from the one shown in Table 11.1. The two problems are said to be **isomorphic** because of this similarity in their fundamental representation. Specifically, the second problem differed from the first only in two sentences:

S4 Since . . . they proceeded to shrink and expand themselves . . .
   S7 that if two monsters are of the size, only the monster holding the larger globe can change.

Although its language is now couched as a change problem, rather than a transfer problem, the underlying structure is still the same. Instead of transferring globes from one fixed monster to another, the globes stayed fixed and the monsters changed in size. The initial state and goal states remained the same.

UNDERSTAND handled the monster isomorphs very much as human beings did in Simon and Hayes's experiments, as revealed by comparisons between simulations and verbal protocol analysis. First, UNDERSTAND constructed a representation of the problem before attempting to solve it. Of the 14 college students who tried to solve these problems, they reread the crucial sentences of S3, S4, and S6-S8 a total of 64 times before making a single move. Most also asked the experimenter questions before beginning to solve the problems. Second, UNDERSTAND constructed a representation for the transfer version of the monster problem in a way that was relatively simple to check for the legality of making a move. In contrast, the change version representation was much more involved and required more time in running the simulation. The students also had a harder time with the change version. More students successfully solved the transfer version and took about 10 minutes less time to do so (17 versus 28 minutes).

Thus the language used to describe a problem powerfully determines how it is represented mentally. If this were not so, then the students in Simon and Hayes's experiments (as well as UNDERSTAND) could have painlessly converted the change version of the problem into a transfer problem. Remember, they are isomorphic. Yet they failed to do so even though the change representation is much harder to manage. It appears that human perception and comprehension of a problem strongly influence the ease with which problems are solved.

The MC problem. Take the MC problem shown earlier (Figure 11.3). How did you represent that problem? Kaplan and Simon (1990) found that most people think in terms of the numbers of squares and dominos and their geometrical arrangement. Perception and comprehension of the problem picture and description would certainly drive one to form exactly such a mental representation. The trouble with this approach is that there are a very large number of possible ways to geometrically arrange the dominos. A computer program tried to prove that 31 dominoes could not cover all the squares by exhaustively trying out alternative placements—it took 758,148 domino placements to succeed. A graduate student in chemical engineering "spent 18 hours and filled 61 pages of a lab notebook with notes, yet still did not solve the problem" (Kaplan & Simon, 1990, p. 379). In addition to drawings of boards and domino placements, the notebook contained many mathematical equations and analyses. Most of us would probably perceive and comprehend the problem in a very similar fashion, to no avail.

The solution to the problem is remarkably simple, assuming that one constructs a manageable representation of the problem. This happens only after an insightful AHA! experience. To help attain this, Kaplan and Simon recommend the following: "If at first you do not succeed, search for a different problem space" (p. 381). The problem space that allows one to solve the MC problem is based on parity, in this case the fixed pattern of alternating black and white squares. Here is the solution:

> Since each of the 31 dominos covers two squares, a covering initially seems possible. To see why a complete covering is actually *impossible* observe that a domino must always cover a black and a white square. But removing two squares of the same color (the diagonal corners) from the 8 × 8 board has left an imbalance between the number of black and white squares that remain. After covering 30 black-white pairs with 30 dominos, the problem solver is always left in the impossible situation of having to cover two same-colored squares with the single remaining domino. (pp. 378-379)

Kaplan and Simon tried to make the parity issue more salient to people by presenting the checkerboard as shown in Figure 11.4. They

butter	bread	butter	bread	butter	bread	butter	bread
bread	butter	bread	butter	bread	butter	bread	butter
butter	bread	butter	bread	butter	bread	butter	bread
bread	butter	bread	butter	bread	butter	bread	butter
butter	bread	butter	bread	butter	bread	butter	bread
bread	butter	bread	butter	bread	butter	bread	butter
butter	bread	butter	bread	butter	bread	butter	bread
bread	butter	bread	butter	bread	butter	bread	butter

Figure 11.4. A checkerboard representation that emphasizes parity.
SOURCE: From Kaplan and Simon (1990). Copyright © 1990 by Academic Press, Inc. Reprinted by permission.

hypothesized that the bread and butter labels would prompt college students to think about opposites that go together (Would male/female have worked still better?). Kaplan and Simon predicted that the bread and butter labels would yield faster solutions than giving a standard red/black checkerboard and their results supported this.

Searching the Problem Space

Two kinds of problem-solving methods must be distinguished: algorithms and heuristics. An **algorithm** is a rule that correctly generates the solution to a problem, given that one can devote sufficient time and effort to applying the rule. For example, an algorithm for solving anagrams is to try every possible letter in every possible position until the word solution appears. This works well for this anagram—atc—but quickly grows tiresome for this one—npisatmisaelndsoi. The costs of using the algorithm are just too great despite its always generating the correct solution. Recall from the opening chapter the important point that cognition is always limited by the costs of computation. A computer could be programmed to play a perfect game of chess using the game-theoretic minimaxing algorithm. The trouble lies in the number of chess positions it would have to examine—a number that exceeds estimates of the known molecules in the universe!

The second type of search method is called a **heuristic,** which refers to a rule of thumb or general strategy that may lead to a solution reasonably quickly. The drawback is that a heuristic, unlike an algorithm, might also fail. One heuristic for solving anagrams is to look for sequences of letters that occur frequently in English (e.g., -tion, dis-, -ism). Another is to eliminate combinations that rarely if ever occur (e.g., np, ii). Still another is to draw on knowledge of how words are put together, such that a syllable often consists of a consonant, vowel, consonant (e.g., pen). Have you solved this one yet: npisatmisaelndsoi? The solution is *dispensationalism.* The next problem—defining it—I leave to you and your dictionary.

In searching a problem space, two general algorithms are trial and error, or random search, and systematic search. For example, trying every letter in every position in an anagram is a type of systematic search. Thorndike's cats seemed to use a trial and error algorithm in trying to find the escape level in his puzzle box. There are also many general-purpose heuristics for problem solving. Here let us consider three of these.

Working backward. Sometimes it is useful to start at the goal state of a problem and attempt to work backward to the initial state. In solving a paper-pencil maze, it may be easier to see the correct path by starting at the end. The reason working backward sometimes helps lies in the subgoals that one begins to see by starting with the final goal. Once the problem solver can envision a string of subgoals projecting backward from the goal state, then going about solving the subgoals in a forward direction can be readily accomplished.

Working backward is only viable when the goal state is uniquely well defined (Wickelgren, 1974). For example, in solving proof problems in geometry, the goal state is precisely stated. It may well help to prune the possible paths of the problem space by starting from the expression to be proved and working backward. Other mathematical problems can be approached in this manner, as students have discovered in solving practice problems in, say, algebra or calculus, where the answer is provided at the end of the text. In contrast, chess illustrates a problem with a well-defined goal that is not uniquely specified. The goal is to checkmate the opponent's king, so that all legal countermoves result in the king still being threatened. However, the precise board positions of the pieces, or even which pieces still remain in the game, are uncertain. Without a specific goal, one can hardly work backward from it.

Analogies. This heuristic looks for similarities between a current problem and one solved in the past. Surely every student has tried this heuristic in geometry, algebra, or calculus courses. Indeed, the noted mathematician Polya (1957) recommended it highly. Science and engineering courses similarly lend themselves well to this strategy. One looks for a problem worked out in the text that is analogous to the one assigned for homework. The same approach is repeated at test time, though now the student must rely on memory for finding a good analogy.

Gick and Holyoak (1980) studied the use of analogy with the problem given in Table 11.2. The Gestalt psychologist Duncker (1935/1945) created this problem to investigate the importance of insight and reorganization of problem elements. Gick and Holyoak replicated Duncker's findings that few people are able to have an AHA! experience and derive an acceptable solution. The problem is nontrivial. Moreover, it is related to a major problem facing AIDS researchers today. Lewis Thomas (1992) explained in his book *The Fragile Species* that researchers must somehow design a virus that will kill the retrovirus that causes AIDS without also killing the body cells that contain it. Try Duncker's radiation problem yourself before reading further.

Gick and Holyoak reasoned that people need to reorganize the problem by drawing an analogy to another situation. To help this occur, they first presented participants with the attack-dispersion problem of

Table 11.2 The Radiation Problem and a Solution Aid

Suppose you are a doctor faced with a patient who has a malignant tumor in his stomach. It is impossible to operate on the patient, but unless the tumor is destroyed the patient will die. There is a kind of ray that can be used to destroy the tumor. If the rays reach the tumor all at once at a sufficiently high intensity, the tumor will be destroyed. Unfortunately, at this intensity the healthy tissue that the rays pass through on the way to the tumor will also be destroyed. At lower intensities the rays are harmless to healthy tissue, but they will not affect the tumor either. What type of procedure might be used to destroy the tumor with the rays, and at the same time avoid destroying the healthy tissue?

Attack-Dispersion Story

A small country was controlled by a dictator. The dictator ruled the country from a strong fortress. The fortress was situated in the middle of the country, surrounded by farms and villages. Many roads radiated outward from the fortress like spokes on a wheel. A general arose who raised a large army and vowed to capture the fortress and free the country of the dictator. The general knew that if his entire army could attack the fortress at once it could be captured. The general's troops were gathered at the head of one of the roads leading to the fortress, ready to attack. However, a spy brought the general a disturbing report. The ruthless dictator had planted mines on each of the roads. The mines were set so that small bodies of men could pass over them safely, since the dictator needed to be able to move troops and workers to and from the fortress. However, any large force would detonate the mines. Not only would this blow up the road and render it impassable, but the dictator would then destroy many villages in retaliation. It therefore seemed impossible to mount full-scale direct attack on the fortress.

SOURCE: From Gick and Holyoak (1980). Copyright © 1980 by Academic Press, Inc. Reprinted by permission.

Table 11.2. They also gave them an explicit hint that the solution to the attack-dispersion problem might be helpful with the radiation problem. Read the attack-dispersion problem and try Duncker's radiation problem once more before reading the solutions to each given in Table 11.3. Gick and Holyoak found only 8% of their participants solved the radiation problem when presented in isolation. This figure jumped to 92% when the hint was given. Clearly, the attack-dispersion problem was used as an analogy, allowing virtually all participants to see a solution.

It is important to note that Gick and Holyoak's participants failed to see the relevance of the attack-dispersion story in the absence of an

Table 11.3 Problem Solutions

Solution to the Radiation Problem:

The ray may be divided into several low-intensity rays, no one of which will destroy the healthy tissue. By positioning these several rays at different locations around the body, and focusing them all on the tumor, their effect will combine, thus being strong enough to destroy the tumor.

Solution to the Attack-Dispersion Story:

The general, however, knew just what to do. He divided his army up into small groups and dispatched each group to the head of a different road. When all was ready he gave the signal, and each group marched down a different road. Each group continued down its road to the fortress, so that the entire army finally arrived together at the fortress at the same time. In this way, the general was able to capture the fortress, and thus overthrow the dictator.

SOURCE: From Gick and Holyoak (1980). Copyright © 1980 by Academic Press, Inc. Reprinted with permission.

explicit hint. Just reading the attack-dispersion story and then tackling the radiation problem led to a poor rate of success. People simply do not readily grasp abstract analogies well, despite their value in helping with the solution of difficult problems.

People do readily see superficial analogies among problems, but these may not be helpful. To illustrate, Ross (1987) taught participants how to solve statistics problems based on a particular principle, such as the algorithm for computing conditional probabilities. The examples used to teach a principle were set in a specific context, such as weather forecasting. When then given a novel problem involving weather forecasting, one that used a different abstract principle of statistics, they mistakenly drew an analogy to the previous examples. They failed to apply the correct principle because of a superficial similarity to examples of the wrong principle. Thus drawing the *right* analogy is a useful heuristic, but one that people do not readily adopt.

Means-end analysis. The means-end heuristic is widely applicable and readily programmable in an AI simulation. This is the search method used by GPS, the simulation discussed earlier. GPS can solve not merely the Tower of Hanoi but also problems in logic, algebra, and calculus

(Ernst & Newell, 1969; Newell & Simon, 1972). Means-end analysis refers to comparing one's current state with the goal state and then finding a means or an operator to reduce the difference. If the analysis turns up that an operator cannot be applied, then the process repeats itself. That is, the heuristic may find that it needs to apply Operator 2 to bring it to a state that allows the application of Operator 1, the thing it set out to do in the first place. The process is therefore recursive. That is, it repeatedly compares states and seeks operators, establishing subgoals and finding ways to reach the subgoals, all on the way to finding a path to the final goal.

Newell and Simon (1972) described the heuristic used by GPS as follows:

1. If an object is given that is not the desired one, differences will be detected between the available object and the desired object.

2. Operators affect some features of their operants and leave others unchanged. Hence operators can be characterized by the changes they produce and can be used to try to eliminate differences between the objects to which they are applied and desired objects.

3. If a desired operator is not applicable, it may be profitable to modify its inputs so that it becomes applicable.

4. Some differences will prove more difficult to affect than others. It is profitable, therefore, to try to eliminate "difficult" differences, even at the cost of introducing new differences of lesser difficulty. This process can be repeated as long as progress is being made toward eliminating the more difficult differences. (p. 416)

To see means-end in action, consider the classic water jar problem first investigated by Luchins (1942). Suppose you have three jars that are different in capacity, as follows:

Jar A = 8 quarts
Jar B = 5 quarts
Jar C = 3 quarts

Assuming that Jar A is full of water, how can you pour out water using the jars so as to arrive at 4 quarts in A and 4 quarts in B? There are no graduated lines on the jars, so you must pour until you either drain the jar or fill up the receiving jar entirely.

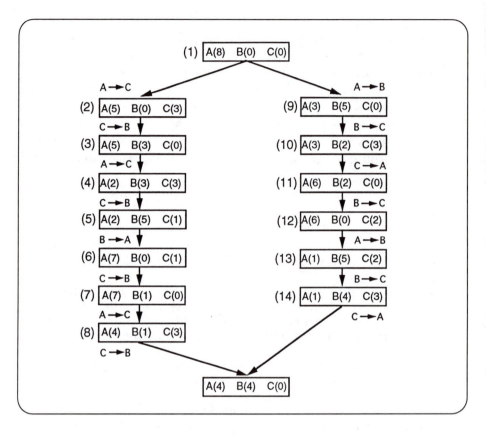

Figure 11.5. Alternative paths to the goal in a water jug problem. Each state shows the contents of Jars A, B, and C. Between each state, the direction of pouring from one jar to another is shown.
SOURCE: From Atwood and Polson (1976). Copyright © 1976 by Academic Press, Inc. Reprinted by permission.

GPS approaches this problem by comparing the amounts in Jars A and B with the amounts that they are supposed to contain in the end, Figure 11.5. It then seeks an operator to reduce the difference between the initial state and the goal state. Consider its opening move, for instance. Two operators are possible. GPS could pour A into B until it fills up. This would result in A with 3 quarts and B with 5 quarts. The total difference after such a transfer would equal 2 quarts. In other words, GPS would still be 1 quart short of the goal for A and 1 quart in excess of the goal for B.

Alternatively, the other legal operator for GPS would be to pour A into C. This would leave 5 quarts in A and fill C with 3 quarts. It would of course leave B empty. The total difference after this transfer therefore would be 5 quarts, with A in excess by 1 quart and B short by 4 quarts. Which move would you make? Because this transfer produces a difference that is greater from the goal than the first possible transfer, the means-end heuristic dictates pouring A into B as an opening move.

Atwood and Polson (1976) investigated this question and found that college students prefer to pour A into B rather than C by a margin of two to one. People overwhelmingly select the same move dictated by means-end analysis, providing evidence that GPS simulates human behavior at least to a degree. Another powerful source of evidence that people rely, unconsciously perhaps, on the means-end heuristic came from a later state in the problem.

One solution path for the problem is shown on the right in Figure 11.5. At state 11, one must pour B into C. This move takes the problem solver away from the goal of having four quarts in Jar B, violating the dictates of means-end analysis. Atwood and Polson found that more than half the time participants stumbled here and tried first to pour A into C as means-end would have it.

Domain-Specific Knowledge and Metacognition

The general model of problem solving considered thus far has attempted to rely exclusively on all-purpose search heuristics and procedures for representing problems. This makes a good deal of sense in that the brain surely has evolved the means for solving problems that crop up in any of a number of specific domains. If a general-purpose cognitive system can handle food gathering, war planning, shelter building, art making, and so on, then it would not be necessary to devise specific procedures for each domain. It also certainly makes sense to hope that an AI model, such as GPS, would prove extremely useful in solving real-world technical problems in computer science, robotics, and engineering. Why build models that can only solve the problems of, say, a robot navigating a natural environment, when a general-purpose program can do the job.

Work over the past two decades has shown that more is needed than a generalist view of human and artificial intelligence, however (Glaser, 1984). First, knowledge about a specific domain must always supplement general procedures. We reviewed this point in detail in the context of studying expertise in Chapter 7 and will only briefly touch on it here. Recall that memory for chess positions is far superior for a master player than for a novice (Chase & Simon, 1973). The master player has no general memory strategy that gives this edge. Rather, it is detailed knowledge of the game itself that allows the master to encode chunks of information in a superior manner.

This has been dramatically demonstrated in Chi's (1978) study of 10-year-old children who played tournament chess and adults who played little chess. In a test of digit span, the adults performed much better than the children. But a test of chess positions yielded precisely the opposite outcome; now the children appeared to be the memory experts solely because of their domain-specific knowledge. Many other studies have further shown that "knowledge is power" when it comes to thinking and problem solving (e.g., Glaser, 1984; Larkin, McDermott, Simon, & Simon, 1980).

Second, with maturation and learning, children begin to acquire more than general heuristics and more than domain-specific knowledge. They also learn to monitor what they are doing as they think and to reflect on what they know. Recall from Chapter 7 that *metacognition* refers to thinking about thinking, the monitoring of cognitive processes, and states of knowledge. Metacognitive skills allow one to monitor progress in solving a problem. Abandoning an unproductive way of representing or searching a problem space and looking for alternatives requires an awareness that things are not going well. Good thinkers are able to evaluate problem-solving efforts as they are under way and to "consolidate gains" at the end of each problem-solving experience (Hayes, 1981). Poor thinkers lack these metacognitive skills.

Obstacles to Problem Solving

The Gestalt psychologists extensively investigated problem solving as well as perception. They saw an intimate link between the two in that both required the proper organization of elements. The reversible figures that we examined in Chapter 2 illustrated how perception changed depending on how the visual features were related to one another in an overall organizational pattern, a Gestalt. The problems we have considered so far in this chapter can be solved only by organizing their elements—the states, operators, indeed, the entire problem space—in a fruitful way. We have seen that problem solving may fail because the

Table 11.4 Luchins' Water Jar Problems

	Jar Sizes			
	A	B	C	Goal
Problem 1	21	127	3	100
Problem 2	14	163	25	99
Problem 3	18	43	10	5
Problem 4	9	42	6	21
Problem 5	20	59	4	31
Problem 6	23	49	3	20

SOURCE: Adapted from Luchins (1942). Used by permission from Abraham S. Luchins.

problem space is not adequately searched or because it is not represented well in the first place. Einstellung and functional fixedness are classic obstacles to both proper representation and search identified by the Gestalt psychologists.

Einstellung

Einstellung is the term used by the Gestaltists to describe the tendency to set the mind into a routine approach to problem solving. Luchins (1942) discovered set or Einstellung effects with a version of the water jar problems described earlier. In this version, you are asked to measure out a desired quantity of water using three jars with different capacities. Here you have a water tap available to fill any jar as often as you like. But as before there are no gradations on the jars. You must fill jars to the top to measure amounts that result in the desired quantity.

For instance, suppose the desired quantity was 5 cups and Jar A held 10 cups, Jar B held 4 cups, and Jar C held 1 cup. The solution would be to fill A first. Next, from A pour into B once, and then pour from B into C once (A-B-C). Try all six problems in Table 11.4 before proceeding.

Luchins found that problem solvers adopt a set in solving these problems. After solving the first two or three, they automatically try the solution B-A-2C without searching the problem space for an alternative solution. Take a look at problem 6 again. Although B-A-2C works fine, it entails much more effort than A-C. Yet because of Einstellung, people typically overlook the obvious, easy solution.

Langer (1989) saw that Einstellung effects are one type of mindless-ness that often characterizes human behavior, particularly in our dealings with other people. All too often we act from a single perspective or rule that has worked in the past. Instead of exploring our environment care-fully to seek out alternative courses of action, we sample just enough features to recognize that our set approach seems to be on track. For example, consider the last time you exchanged greetings, experienced anger over what another person said or did to you, tried as a member of a group to tackle a common problem. In each case, you may well have acted mindlessly, following your set for dealing with each circumstance.

Einstellung also constrains how we represent problems as well as how we search them. This is nicely illustrated by the story of the mathe-matics professor who was given a sequence problem by his students, as recounted by Rubinstein (1986). The professor's task was to provide the next member of the sequence 32, 38, 44, 48, 56, 60. As a hint, the students mentioned that the sequence was familiar to the professor and that the solution was simple. As mathematicians are apt to do, the professor launched into the problem space of polynomial equations and managed to generate a complex solution, not a simple one. Upon giving up, the students informed him that the answer was "Meadowlark." To see the solution, the professor needed to drop one set and adopt another. Every day he rode the subway and every day passed stops at 56th street, 60th street, and then Meadowlark. I have always wondered whether any of the students passed that course.

Functional Fixedness

Duncker (1935/1945) discovered another obstacle to problem solv-ing related to Einstellung. **Functional fixedness** refers to the tendency to see objects as having only a single, typical use. A hammer is for pounding nails and others things, for instance. We categorize objects based on their functional features as well as their features and the prototypical function dominates the way we think. Duncker led an individual into a room with a table holding several small objects. They included three cardboard boxes filled with candles, tacks, and matches, respectively, and an ashtray, paper, paper clips, string, pencils, and tinfoil. The individual was in-structed to mount the candles at eye level on the wall, ostensibly to pre-pare the room for a vision experiment. Can you think of a way to put the candles on the wall using these materials?

Duncker found that only 43% of his participants could develop a solution to the problem. He hypothesized that they fixated on the common function of a box, namely, to serve as a container. To help break their functional fixedness, he repeated the experiment but this time emptied the candles, tacks, and matches on the table, leaving the three boxes empty. Under these circumstances, all participants solved the problem by first mounting the boxes on the wall using the tacks, which then served as platforms for the candles.

Creativity

What can be said about productive thinking or creativity from the perspective of cognitive psychology? Much. Here we restrict our consideration of this fascinating topic to a few key points, but the interested reader should consult the list of recommended readings for more information. Creativity, the creative personality, and the nature of genius take one through large territories of psychology, only portions of which lie within the boundaries of cognitive psychology.

Historical Versus Process Creativity

We begin by defining **historical creativity** as acts of genius that are widely acclaimed by society as meritorious. *Historical creativity* refers to ideas that are novel within the context of the whole of human history (Boden, 1992). The creator produces a product—some visible symbol that embodies her idea—that may be judged by others (Sternberg, 1988). Consider works of art or the equations of physical theory. The Cistine Chapel, the Mona Lisa, the laws of thermodynamics, and the general and special theories of relativity are products that are plainly creative in the historical or product sense.

Hayes (1981) argued that three criteria must be met before a product of the human mind ought to be regarded as creative. First, it must be novel or unique. Certainly this is implicit in our everyday discussions of creative acts as well as in the distinction we encountered earlier between reproductive thinking, on the one hand, and productive, insightful, creative thinking, on the other. Second, a product must be judged as useful in some context. Here many an artist, inventor, scientist, and philosopher has lost in their bid for fame. Their creations may have been novel, but utterly useless. Only when a product somehow connects with the past or finds its niche in a cultural context does it stand a chance of being regarded as creative. This may take time, more time than the creator has. Some have been acclaimed as creative in the historical sense only after their deaths. Third, the product must have demanded some special ability or talent on the part of its creator. Hayes wants to rule out cases of sheer accident or mindless creation, though here the ice begins to get very thin. If I threw paint at a canvas from across the room, no one would mistake it for art, but when Jackson Pollock did so, many saw the work of a genius. Hayes's criteria of novelty, usefulness, and talent give very different answers to the issue of what is creative, depending on one's cultural point of view.

Boden (1992) and Sternberg (1988) dealt with these difficulties by noting that the process of creativity is every bit as important as the product. As long as the process yields a novel idea, then it is important to model how the mind achieved its insight. Whether others judge the idea to be useful or a reflection of genius matters not at all for process creativity. In fact, it makes no difference that the idea even be novel as far as society is concerned. Suppose that two scientists discover a cure for cancer without any contact with each other. Both were creative in the sense of process, yet perhaps only one will enter the history books as creative.

Stages of Creativity

The process of creativity moves through four stages that have been known for some time (Wallas, 1926). The first stage is **preparation**—studying, learning, formulating solutions, and striving to create. As we saw in the chapter on expertise, creating a product that merits the acclaim of society takes years of education, deliberate practice, and continuous attempts to excel in performance. A decade of such preparation appears necessary regardless of the domain. Preparation is no less important in more everyday acts of creativity—figuring out what to write for a term paper assignment, seeing the answer to a personal problem, or coming up with a new arrangement for the annual vegetable garden. But in these cases, the entire process of creativity is briefer, including the preparation stage.

Because of the extensive preparation required in the case of major creative production, individuals need the support and encouragement of family, friends, teachers, and peers (MacKinnon, 1978; Simonton, 1988).

Social, economic, and cultural supports play a role in this cultivation (Hayes, 1981; Ochse, 1990). Without the financial and social supports needed for both formal and informal education and without a cultural setting that values creative work, then creative potential languishes. Because creative potential may be the most critical resource of any nation, it is foolhardy not to adopt policies that nurture the potential of all (Mumford & Gustafson, 1988; Taylor & Sacks, 1981).

Incubation is the second step and it refers to putting the problem aside and doing other things. The incubation phase can again vary widely in duration and form. When working on a major creative project, incubation may take the form of a vacation. When puzzling over a particularly difficult problem in, say, a statistics class, incubation may involve something as simple as taking a shower, jogging, or going out for pizza. In all cases, incubation entails thinking about something, anything, but the problem or project that has been the focus of the preparation stage.

The third stage is **illumination,** when the crucial insight seizes consciousness. It is the AHA! experience that very quickly suggests the solution to the problem at hand. It can reflect the breaking of a mental set that had led the problem solver in the wrong direction. Illumination or insight is a fleeting, sketchy experience, not a protracted, fully detailed solution. It must be followed up by the fourth stage of **verification,** when the outlines of the solution must be filled in and checked carefully. It may turn out that illumination failed to generate an acceptable solution to the problem. Creativity is only complete after verification of the insight through painstaking efforts at writing, calculating, sculpting, painting, drawing, designing, building, and so forth.

You have no doubt enjoyed the AHA! experience during some incubation activity. To the extent that all cognition demands at least minor forms of creativity, insights occur monthly, weekly, or even daily. Boden (1992) recounted some famous flashes of illumination:

> Archimedes leapt from his bath in joy and ran through the streets of Syracuse, crying "Eureka!" as he went. He had solved the problem that had been worrying him for days: how to measure the volume of an irregularly shaped object, such as a golden (or not-so-golden) crown.—Friedrich von Kekulé, dozing by the fire, had a dream suggesting that the structure of the troublesome benzene molecule might be a ring. A whole new branch of science (aromatic chemistry) was founded as a result.—The mathematician Jacques Hadamard, more than once, found a long-sought solution "at the

very moment of sudden awakening".—And Henri Poincaré, as he was boarding a bus to set out on a geological expedition, suddenly glimpsed a fundamental mathematical property of a class of functions he had recently discovered and which had preoccupied him for days. (p. 15)

Incubation and insight are difficult to study in the laboratory. Even when such phenomena are reliably produced, it is difficult to design experiments that distinguish among alternative explanations, as discussed in Box 11.2.

Sources of Creativity

Though few human beings are creative in the historical sense, all of us are creative in the process sense. Indeed, all mental acts can be viewed as creative if one begins with the observation that a person never perceives, recalls, or imagines in *precisely* the same way twice (Weisberg, 1986). As Hericlitus of ancient Greece immortalized, we never enter the same stream twice. The demands of the current situation never *exactly* match past learning. Schemas are flexible and dynamic so as to deal with the need for novel response and adaptation.

That creativity is fundamental in human nature opposes the ancient view that the gods, muses, or inexplicable intuition are somehow responsible for acts of genius. Boden (1992) reviewed this romantic explanation and joined Weisberg in rejecting it:

Plato put it like this: "A poet is holy and never able to compose until he has become inspired, and is beside himself and reason is no longer in him . . . for not by art does he utter these, but by power divine." . . .

Over twenty centuries later, the play *Amadeus* drew a similar contrast between Mozart and his contemporary, Salieri. Mozart was shown as coarse, vulgar, lazy, and undisciplined in every aspect of his life, but apparently informed by a divine spark when composing. The London critic Bernard Levin, in his column in *The Times*, explicitly drew the conclusion that Mozart (like all other great artists) was, literally, divinely inspired. (p. 5)

BOX 11.2: Unconscious Problem Solving?

Three explanations of the incubation effect have been advanced, but to date no one has found a way to distinguish among them empirically. Unconscious problem solving offers one explanation and it is the one favored by many who write on creativity. Because incubation involves thinking about something other than the problem, it seems quite natural to assume that processes are under way at an unconscious level that suddenly, without warning, thrust the solution into consciousness. While eating, bathing, exercising, or sleeping, the mind may be thinking about many things consciously but still carrying on the serious work of problem solving outside awareness. Baars's (1988) theory of consciousness, which we will briefly examine in the final chapter, regards incubation as strong evidence that higher order thinking may take place automatically and unconsciously.

But two other explanations of incubation effects deny any role of unconscious thinking. One alternative suggests that the preparation period results in a buildup of proactive interference for the correct solution. That is, as the individual tries numerous solution attempts and fails to succeed, memory fills up with these wrong approaches and they interfere with retrieval of the right approach. Incubation provides, in effect, a release from PI not unlike that observed in the studies of short-term memory in Chapter 4. The other alternative simply assumes that incubation relieves the fatigue that precludes solution. By restoring the mental energy of problem solvers, they quickly find the solution to the problem once they begin to search for the answer again.

Notice that these alternative hypotheses both assume that the problem once again becomes the subject of conscious thought, perhaps the undirected thought of a daydream, before illumination takes place. It does not, in other words, strike one from out of the blue while the mind is focused elsewhere. The distinction is a subtle one. Perhaps while taking a shower or jogging, the mind turns back to the problem in an active effort to solve it or merely in the form of daydreaming about it. Then, suddenly, the insight occurs. When an insight occurs upon awakening, it is possible that one had been dreaming about the problem. Sometimes the dream might be remembered and other times forgotten. It is troublesome to regard such cases as truly unconscious problem solving, if the altered state of dream consciousness were involved in the incubation phase. In any case, the controversy surrounding the explanation of incubation and insight continues. It may not be resolved any more than the classic dispute over imageless thought was resolved at the turn of the twentieth century by the structuralists (refer to Chapter 1).

As Boden went on to argue, the romantic view fails to even try to explain creativity. It merely sweeps it away under the rug of intuition or into the attic of the muses. As a scientific explanation, it gets us nowhere.

The alternative view assumes that the work on problem solving discussed earlier can tell us much about the process of creativity. It assumes that the problem representations, search heuristics, and diverse forms of knowledge that creators bring to their tasks are all vitally important. Regardless of whether the problem is ill or well defined, the processes discussed throughout this chapter shed light on creativity (Boden, 1992; Weisberg, 1986). Waiting for one's muse is no longer the heuristic of choice.

◙ SUMMARY ◙

1. People think by manipulating mental representations of the world. Through the use of such representations, we can plan courses of action and simulate their effects prior to taking action. The study of problem solving has shed light on how we go about this. Often in solving a problem, one builds a model of the environment with a clear, well-defined goal in mind. One then tries to find a path that leads straight to the goal with little diversion. Such problem solving illustrates directed thinking. Undirected thinking refers to dreaming, daydreaming, and other forms of thought that meander without concern for attaining a goal. Undirected thinking is neither rational nor goal oriented.

2. A well-defined problem is characterized by an initial state, a goal state, and a set of operators. Each legal move from the initial state, to intermediate states, to the goal state is defined by an operator. All the states and operators taken together define the problem space. To solve a well-defined problem, one must select a sequence of operators that follow a path through the problem space to the goal. An ill-defined problem is missing a clear initial state, goal state, known operators, or perhaps all three. An ill-defined problem often calls for insight and creativity, what the Gestalt psychologists called productive thinking. Yet even some well-defined problems demand creative insights for solution.

3. A general model of problem solving entails first representing the problem and then searching the problem space for a path to the goal. Finding a good representation of the problem space is critical and often demands as much insight as the search process itself. Algorithms are rules for searching the problem space that are guaranteed to succeed, though often at prohibitive costs in time and effort. Heuristics are rules of thumb that may or may not lead to success, but they carry fewer costs than algorithms. General Problem Solver (GPS) is one of several AI programs that simulate aspects of human problem solving. It is based on the premise that a general search heuristic called means-end analysis is powerful enough to solve a wide range of problems. Today it is recognized that an adequate simulation of human problem solving must address the effects of domain-specific knowledge and metacognition as well as general heuristics.

4. Gestalt psychologists recognized that both perception and problem solving require the proper organization of elements. They identified two common obstacles to successful problem solving. *Einstellung,* or set, refers to the tendency to set the mind into a routine approach to problem solving. Thinkers who adopt an automatic or mindless approach to problems often overlook ways of representing and searching the problem space that are ideal. *Functional fixedness* refers to the tendency to see objects as having only a single, typical use. Thinkers prematurely categorize the elements of a problem in accordance with their typical use, thus overlooking novel and useful alternatives.

5. *Historical creativity* refers to ideas that are novel within the context of cultural history—few people are recognized as historically creative. Yet, all of us engage in cognitive processes that are creative, even if our creative products are not judged as novel, useful, and extraordinary. The stages of creativity begin with preparation, working with a problem for an extended period of time. Incubation, putting the problem aside, is the next stage. The third stage is illumination, coming up with a crucial insight that leads to the solution of the problem. The fourth stage is verification, when the insight is implemented and tested.

Key Terms

directed thinking	isomorphic
undirected thinking	algorithm
well defined	heuristic
initial state	Einstellung
goal state	functional fixedness
subgoals	historical creativity
operator	preparation
problem space	incubation
reproductive thinking	illumination
productive thinking	verification
ill-defined problems	

Recommended Readings

For an exhaustive treatment of problem spaces and search procedures, there is the classic work by Newell and Simon (1972) titled *Human Problem Solving*. For a briefer introduction to these issues, I recommend Simon's (1978) chapter in the *Handbook of Learning and Cognitive Processes*. Hayes (1981) covers the same topics in an introductory format, as well as other aspects of problem solving, in *The Complete Problem Solver*.

There are numerous books aimed at teaching one how to become a better problem solver. Three in particular are well grounded in theory and research and are well worth reading. One is by Bransford and Stein (1984) and is titled *The IDEAL Problem Solver*. The second is *Effective Problem Solving* by Levine (1988). The third by Wickelgren (1974) is especially helpful in solving problems in mathematics, science, and other technical areas. It is titled *How to Solve Problems: Elements of a Theory of Problems and Problem Solving*.

A classic work on the nature of creativity is Koestler's (1975) *The Act of Creation*. Three excellent books reveal the cognitive processes at work in creativity and debunk the romantic view of the inspired genius. Weisberg's (1986) *Creativity: Genius and Other Myths* is a good place to begin. Weisberg (1993) expanded on many of the themes of his earlier work in *Creativity: Beyond the Myth of Genius*. I also recommend *The Crea-*

tive Mind: Myths and Mechanisms by Boden (1992). For chapters on original research by some of the best scholars in the field, I suggest a volume edited by Sternberg (1988) and titled *The Nature of Creativity: Contemporary Psychological Perspectives.*

Syllogistic Reasoning

Conditional Reasoning

Inductive Reasoning

Decision Making

Summary

Key Terms

Recommended Readings

CHAPTER 12

Reasoning and Decision Making

The ability to reason is a hallmark of the human mind. Both ancient and modern philosophers have identified reasoning and language as the pedestals that lift our species above all others. In Chapter 8, we touched upon the studies of primates seemingly learning languages, findings that, to some scholars, jolted the language pedestal to a degree. We turn now to the pedestal of reasoning and its partner, decision making.

We will begin with a detailed look at reasoning as it has been defined by philosophers. The surprising news is not that other species are just as capable of reasoning as human beings are. Rather, we will encounter evidence that people themselves are poor at reasoning, at least when the task is defined in the classical sense of the philosophers. The same can be said about human decision-making abilities when judged against the decision theories of mathematicians. These findings, too, have generated shock waves, transforming the modern view of human reasoning.

A description of the syllogistic reasoning task will come first. *All men are mortal. Socrates was a man. Therefore Socrates was mortal.* From a major and minor premise, the reasoner must evaluate the conclusion. The rules for doing so correctly are defined by the formal system called the predicate or functional calculus. This comes from a branch of philosophy called symbolic logic. Perhaps the reader has received instruction on the proper way to evaluate syllogisms in a logic course. Our aim here will be to consider some psychological reasons as to why such material may have been a real challenge to learn.

Next, we will take up conditional reasoning. *If p, then q. P is true, therefore q must also be true.* The conditional rule is its own quagmire, as far as human cognition is concerned. It turns out that people have a very difficult time determining how to deduce the proper conclusions.

Syllogisms and conditionals call upon deductive reasoning. In the final sections, we will consider inductive reasoning and decision making. Inductive reasoning lies at the heart of all science. In decision making, the "correct answers" are provided by mathematical decision theories or so-called normative models. As with syllogisms and conditionals, people think differently about matters than normative models would have it. This will not come as a surprise to those of you who struggled at length with statistics, one type of normative model, but the cognitive reasons for the struggle are worth examining. They reveal much about how most people think—excluding perhaps the philosophers and mathematicians.

Syllogistic Reasoning

Syllogistic reasoning involves evaluating whether a conclusion necessarily follows from two premises that are assumed to be true. The two premises are referred to as the major and minor premise. Their truth is taken as certain, regardless of whether the statements make any sense in the real world. For example, consider these three syllogisms.

Syllogism 1
Major Premise: All men are animals.
Minor Premise: Some animals are aggressive.
Conclusion: Some men are aggressive.

Syllogism 2
Major Premise: All men are animals.
Minor Premise: Some animals are female.
Conclusion: Some men are female.

Syllogism 3

Major Premise: All A are B.

Minor Premise: Some B are C.

Conclusion: Some A are C.

Do you accept the conclusion of Syllogism 1 as valid? I suspect that most readers would. After all, it is not difficult to think of at least a few men who certainly appear to be aggressive. The syllogism does not even require that you conclude that all men are aggressive, a conclusion that more than a few readers might also happily accept.

But then, what to do with Syllogism 2? At least if one puts aside sex-change operations, the conclusion does not ring true. The semantics of the conclusion are all wrong. Yet, if you examine the first pair of syllogisms, you will see that their form is identical. This point can be driven home by Syllogism 3. Do you accept the conclusion as more valid in this case than in Syllogism 2, or Syllogism 1?

The task that philosophers set before us is to ignore the semantics or the meaning of the premises altogether. The premises are simply assumed to be true for the sake of the argument. The above examples, then, are really the same syllogism. Because their syntax or structure is identical, their conclusions must be evaluated identically. Either the conclusion is valid in all three or it is invalid in all three.

The meaningfulness of the premises matters not a wit. I could just as well have said: All men are elephants; some elephants are plants; therefore some men are plants. The only matter at hand is whether the conclusion must logically follow from the premises. A **valid conclusion** is one that is *necessarily* true, given that the premises are true. Before reading further, arrive at your evaluation of the validity of our example syllogism(s).

Syllogistic Forms

Presented in Table 12.1 are some of the common syllogistic forms along with the valid conclusion, if any, that follows from the major and minor premises. The conclusion "Can't say" indicates an invalid syllogism—no conclusion *necessarily* follows from the premises. The first on the list corresponds to the famous "All men are mortal" routine, and as you can see, it is correct to conclude that Socrates was indeed a man. That is, the conclusion must be true given the premises. The next on the list

Table 12.1 Examples of Valid and Invalid Syllogisms

Premises	Conclusion	Premises	Conclusion
(1) All A are B All B are C	All A are C	(11) Some A are not B All B are C	Can't say
(2) All A are B Some B are C	Can't say	(12) Some B are A No B are C	Some A are not C
(3) No A are B All C are B	No A are C	(13) All B are A All B are C	Some A are C
(4) Some B are not A All B are C	Can't say	(14) Some A are not B Some B are not C	Can't say
(5) All A are B No C are B	No A are C	(15) Some B are A Some C are not B	Can't say
(6) No B are A Some B are not C	Can't say	(16) All A are B All C are B	Can't say
(7) Some A are B All B are C	Some A are C	(17) No B are A Some B are C	Can't say
(8) All B are A All C are B	Some A are C	(18) Some B are not A Some C are B	Can't say
(9) No A are B No B are C	Can't say	(19) All B are A No B are C	Some A are not C
(10) Some A are B Some B are C	Can't say	(20) All A are B No B are C	No A are C

SOURCE: From Bourne et al., *Cognitive Processes*. Copyright © 1986, Table 9-1. Reprinted by permission of Prentice-Hall, Inc., Englewood Cliffs, NJ.

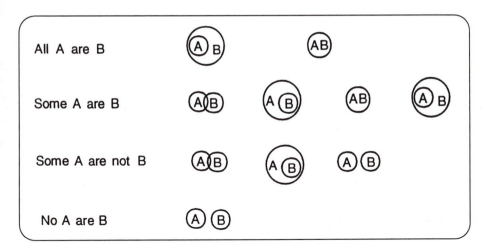

Figure 12.1. Euler circles represent the premises of a categorical syllogism in terms of set relations.
SOURCE: From Bourne et al., *Cognitive Processes*. Copyright © 1986, Fig. 9-1. Reprinted by permission of Prentice-Hall, Inc., Englewood Cliffs, NJ.

corresponds to our example and it might surprise you to learn that no valid conclusion follows from these premises. If you missed this, you are in good company. Only about 10% of college students who have not been trained in logic correctly identify valid and invalid conclusions without error (Dominowski, 1977).

In Figure 12.1, the four types of premises encountered in deductive reasoning are shown. The Euler circles provide a convenient representation of their meanings based on class or set relationships. The universal affirmative—all A are B—has two possible interpretations as shown. Either the reference classes or sets of A and B are identical, or A refers to a subset of B. The universal negative—no A are B—is the only premise that affords a single interpretation! Study the particular affirmative (some A are B) and particular negative (some A are not B) premises for a moment to understand why they allow each of the meanings shown.

Evaluating the conclusion according to the predicate calculus requires three steps. First, one must accurately consider all possible interpretations of the premises and the conclusion. Second, one must consider all possible combinations of meanings of the major and minor premises. That is, one must consider all pairs of meanings that are allowed by the

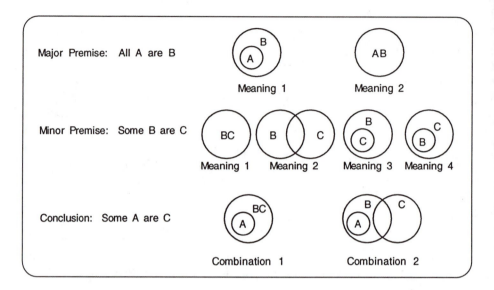

Figure 12.2. All possible meanings of the major and minor premise, followed by two of the eight possible combinations of meanings of these premises. Combination 2 is at odds with the conclusion: Some A are C.

first step. Third, one must then determine whether all possible meanings of the conclusion are consistent with all possible combinations of the premises. If a single interpretation of the conclusion does not follow from a single possible combination of meanings, then no valid conclusion may be drawn. To put this in the form of a question: Is it possible to find one combination of premises that does not fit with one interpretation of the conclusion? If that is so, then the conclusion is invalid. These steps are illustrated in Figure 12.2 for the example syllogism used earlier.

As the reader can see in Figure 12.2, there are two possible meanings of "All A are B," and four possible meanings of "Some B are C." Thus there are eight possible combinations of these meanings of the major and minor premises. To simplify matters, we can hone in on only two of these eight combinations, the two shown next to the conclusion "Some A are C" in the figure. Combination 1 joins Meaning 1 for the major premise (All A are B) and Meaning 1 for the minor premise (Some B are C). Combination 2 joins Meaning 1 for the major premise and Meaning 2 for the minor premise. Note how the relation between B and C expressed in the minor premise is substituted for set B in the major premise.

For Combination 1, note that the conclusion follows: The set labeled A falls within the set labeled BC. For combination 2, however, the conclusion is at odds with the diagram: Set A fails to intersect with set C. There is, then, at least one interpretation of the conclusion at odds with at least one combination of the premises. The conclusion is invalid as a consequence. Try working out the other six combinations of the meanings of the major and minor premises and see how many support the conclusion "Some A are C."

Human Performance

With training, one can learn to evaluate the validity of conclusions without error. The inference rules of the predicate calculus are quite cumbersome (Johnson-Laird & Bara, 1984). So unless one memorizes all the valid forms of syllogisms, correct reasoning can be done most handily with an external representation, such as Euler circles. The load on working memory is greatly alleviated with a diagram. The memory and processing capacity of the central executive of working memory is overloaded by the task of deductive reasoning (Baddeley, 1986).

Ceraso and Provitera (1971) found that people correctly identify a valid conclusion (e.g., cases 1, 3, 5, 7, and 8 in Table 12.1) about three quarters of the time. Bear in mind that there are a total of 64 different syllogisms, obtained by varying the type of premises and the order in which the premises are given. Table 12.1 gives just a sampling of these. Of the total 64, only 19 allow a valid conclusion to be drawn!

People do much worse for the 45 invalid syllogisms, those for which no valid conclusion follows. People often agree that a conclusion is valid when one really cannot say for certain. For instance, Syllogism 3 in our example often elicited a response of valid. Ceraso and Provitera used letters in their syllogisms to remove the possibility that people would evaluate the meaningfulness of the conclusion. Even so, the participants correctly identified invalid conclusions only about a third of the time.

Not only do people perform poorly overall on the invalid syllogisms, the pattern of errors obtained is quite consistent (Dickstein, 1978). When the major premise contains a universal affirmative (all) statement and the minor premise is a particular affirmative (some) statement, then people overwhelming regard a conclusion containing the word *some* as valid. They do the same thing if the major premise is also a particular affirmative or some statement. In contrast, if the major and minor premises are both universal negative statements, people often accept a conclusion that contains the word *no*. As you can see from case 9 in Table 12.1, this is an error.

Explanations

An explanation proposed early on by Woodworth and Sells (1935) presumed that people do not even attempt to evaluate the conclusion logically. Their explanation of the errors was called the **atmosphere hypothesis** and it was restated by Begg and Denny (1969) this way. First, if one or more of the premises is negative (either universal or particular), then the conclusion is generally accepted as negative. Second, if one or more of the premises is a particular or some statement, a particular or some conclusion is accepted. Although this explanation accounts for part of the errors, it misses the mark on others. Moreover, the hypothesis provides no account of why intelligent college students would blindly follow these heuristics instead of trying to reason correctly (Dickstein, 1978).

A second proposal laid the blame for poor performance on the misinterpretation of the premises. **Illicit conversion** refers to people converting "All A are B" into "All B are A," taking the converse of the premise as true in addition to the premise itself. So in the case of "Some A are B," people illicitly convert it into "Some A are not B" (Ceraso & Provitera, 1971; Revlis, 1975). Unlike the atmosphere hypothesis, this hypothesis gives people credit for trying to reason correctly but faults them for starting off on the wrong foot by misinterpreting the premises. Dickstein (1978) noted that people also illicitly convert conclusions. Although a set of premises may allow one to conclude that some A are C (refer to case 13 in Table 12.1), people commit an error when they also conclude that some C are A.

Ceraso and Provitera (1971) showed the importance of illicit conversions with their findings that errors decrease when efforts are made to stop such conversions. The researchers expanded the premises to prevent misinterpretations ("All A are B but there are some B that are not A"). Another way to prevent misinterpretations is to frame the premises in meaningful ways (Revlis, 1975). When told that all men are animals, I sincerely doubt that you would infer that all animals are men. Yet exactly this happens when the meaning is stripped from the premise by saying all A are B.

Illicit conversion must be supplanted with other explanations to account fully for all the observed errors. Because of the heavy demands that syllogistic reasoning places on working memory, it should come as no surprise that people fail to consider all possible combinations of premises. Johnson-Laird and Steedman (1978) reported that reasoners try to simplify the combinations of premises by avoiding those that call for class-inclusion or subset relations. Go back to Figure 12.2 and note that some premise meanings involve a class-inclusion relation (e.g., A is a subset of B). These often will be overlooked in generating combinations of meanings of the major and minor premises. In contrast, simple combinations of meanings (e.g., A, B, C all referring to the same class) are picked up readily.

Similarly, people consider only some of the premise combinations when evaluating the conclusion. If a conclusion fits some but not all of the combinations, then it may well be accepted as valid (Dickstein, 1978). In essence, they simplify the task by not taking to heart the requirement that the conclusion *must absolutely, positively* follow from the premises.

The Importance of Meaning

We have already seen that conversion errors are eliminated when meaningful premises are employed. This fact does not imply that people always reason more logically, as defined by the philosophers, when they can think about meaningful situations. In fact, major errors occur precisely because meaning plays a role.

Belief bias. The phenomenon of *belief bias* refers to people accepting any and all conclusions that happen to fit with their system of beliefs (Henle, 1962). Beliefs and meaning lie at the core of human thinking, not the predicate calculus and other abstract systems invented by philosophers. College students in North America reject valid conclusions if they do not correspond to what they know to be true about the world. The supremacy of meaningful beliefs appears to be universal. In fact, non-Western cultures not exposed to formal schooling find the concept of validity absolutely silly (see Box 12.1).

Belief bias is especially powerful when reasoners ignore the premises altogether and focus on the conclusion (Evans, Barston, & Pollard, 1983). In this case, they accept a believable conclusion (e.g., Some good ice skaters are not professional hockey players) and reject an unbelievable one (Some professional hockey players are not good ice skaters). Using verbal protocols, Barston et al. found that some individuals study the premises and try to reason from them. For these individuals, a serious conflict arises when the conclusion is valid but unbelievable. Politicians and

BOX 12.1: Cross-Cultural Differences

Luria (1976) asked illiterate farmers from Central Asia to reason deductively, giving them syllogisms of the following sort: "In the Far North, where there is snow, all bears are white. Novaga Zemlya is in the Far North. What color are the bears there?" The responses were of this sort: "I don't know; I've seen a black bear, I've never seen any others. . . . Each locality has its own animals; if it's white, they will be white; if it's yellow, they will be yellow." or "How should I know?" (pp. 109-110).

Luria found that the farmers simply ignored or forgot premises that contradicted their own knowledge, and failed to interpret universal statements (e.g., In the Far North, all bears are white) as really universal. They regarded such statements as the view of a particular person. In short, they regarded the reasoning task not as an abstract game but as a question rooted in their own or someone else's real life experience.

Cole and Scribner (1974) found much the same in their work with the Kpelle tribes of Liberia. These people reasoned from their own personal knowledge. They refused to draw conclusions based on premises provided by an experimenter as hypothetical. If pressured by the experimenter to state a conclusion, they justified their answer from personal knowledge, not by drawing valid conclusions from the premises. This may be seen in the following exchange.

> Experimenter (local Kpelle man): At one time spider went to a feast. He was told to answer this question before he could eat any of the food. The question is: Spider and black deer always eat together. Spider is eating. Is black deer eating?
>
> SUBJECT (village elder): Were they in the bush together?
> EXPERIMENTER: Yes.
> SUBJECT: Were they eating together?
> EXPERIMENTER: Spider and black deer always eat together. Spider is eating. Is black deer eating?
> SUBJECT: But I was not there. How can I answer such a question?
> EXPERIMENTER: Can't you answer it? Even if you were not there, you can answer it. (Repeats question)
> SUBJECT: Oh, oh, black deer is eating.
> EXPERIMENTER: What is your reason for saying that black deer is eating?
> SUBJECT: The reason is that black deer always walks about all day eating green leaves in the bush. Then he rests for a while and gets up again to eat. (p. 162)

defense attorneys probably find no surprise in this. Their deductive arguments may be flawlessly valid, but if their conclusions conflict with entrenched beliefs, then voters and juries may not buy them.

Mental models. The overriding importance of meaning in reasoning also should come as no surprise to students of cognitive psychology. Meaningfulness is important in all the tasks studied in this book. Syllogistic reasoning tasks are no exception (Gentner & Stevens, 1983; Johnson-Laird, 1983; Johnson-Laird & Bara, 1984).

For instance, Johnson-Laird proposed that people try to model each premise in working memory, beginning with the first one presented. "All A are B" would be modeled by equating the two terms in working memory and making note that another B may or may not exist. Only two tokens of each class are used to simplify the model and avoid depleting working memory; the zero signifies that other tokens *may exist*, but not with certainty based on the premise as stated. That is to say, some B *may* exist that are not A. Thus

$$a = b$$
$$a = b$$
$$0b$$

If the next premise says that some B are C, then the following would be added to the model:

$$a = b = c$$
$$0a = b \; 0C$$
$$0b$$

The combined model in working memory now represents the information conveyed by both premises. The first line signifies that all A are B and all B are C. The second line signifies that some A may exist that are B and some C may exist that are not B.

With this model in working memory, the reasoner would then evaluate a conclusion such as some A are C. The model plainly supports this conclusion (line 1). It would not support the conclusion that all A are C (line 2). As we learned earlier, many people accept the some-A-are-C conclusion even though it is invalid. According to Johnson-Laird, the difficulty arises because multiple models may be constructed from the same premises. The more alternative models that are possible, the more likely the reasoner will commit an error in syllogistic reasoning. To see the flaw in the conclusion, the reasoner must construct a second model as well:

$$
\begin{array}{c}
a = b \\
0a = b \; 0c \\
b = c \\
0b
\end{array}
$$

In other words, the token of B that is an A (line 1) is different than the one that is a C (line 3).

Johnson-Laird regards mental models as more psychologically plausible than Euler circles or other representations. Mental models of the sort that he proposes are, after all, constructed in working memory for many tasks, such as remembering, comprehending, and solving problems.

And his theory provides a reasonably good accounting of the pattern of errors that people make in abstract reasoning tasks (Johnson-Laird & Bara, 1984). The theory as it stands has problems, though. The procedures for translating premises and combining them into models seem highly abstract for a theory that assumes that models are rooted in concrete experience of the world (Rips, 1990). Further, one would think that having people produce external models with actual tokens would help them to reason more effectively. But this apparently is not the case (Lee & Oakhill, 1984).

Evolutionary considerations. Despite the problems with the theory, it seems clear that mental models or analogies to a single remembered instance play a role in the kind of reasoning needed in real-world situations. A specific model of a specific situation allows one to predict accurately what is true about that situation. Never mind whether the conclusion can be regarded as a logically valid deduction. Accurate predictions would have survival value in the real world independent of their abstract validity. Consider these premises:

All hungry lions are dangerous.

That animal is not a hungry lion.

Is that animal dangerous?

Presumably, those of our ancestors who could draw on concrete experience and construct a usable mental model would have remained in the gene pool. Conclusions must be reached quickly and tell us what we need to know for survival. Knowing whether that animal is in fact a charging elephant or a grazing gnu would have served our ancestors far better than the predicate calculus and Euler circles.

Conditional Reasoning

As noted in discussing concept identification, the conditional rule is expressed as an if-then statement. *Conditional reasoning* refers to the type of deductive reasoning seen in the following examples.

Deduction 1

If the barometer falls today, then it will storm.

The barometer is falling.

Therefore it will storm.

Deduction 2

If P, then Q.

P is true.

Therefore Q is true.

As in our earlier example of syllogistic deduction, these two deductions all convey the same form of conditional reasoning. Given that the first part of the conditional rule is true, then the conclusion reached in each case must be true. It follows as a valid deduction. The abstract form of Deduction 2 removes the meaning from the task and disrupts the typical approach of building a model from concrete experience.

Valid and Invalid Conditional Reasoning

Logicians allow two ways to deduce a valid conclusion from the conditional rule. The first is called *modus ponens* or affirming the antecedent. Deductions 1 and 2 illustrate affirming the antecedent. P is called the antecedent and Q the consequent. **Affirming the antecedent** means that the second premise asserts that P is true. Given that P is true, then Q must also be true. According to the rule as stated, it can never happen that Q is false if P is true.

But what if the premise asserts that the consequent Q is not true. Suppose that you walk outside and see that the weather is balmy. Armed with this knowledge, you could apply the second valid form of conditional reasoning called *modus tollens* or **denying the consequent.** Given that Q is false (it is not storming), then P must also be false. According to the conditional rule, it can never happen that P is true if Q is false.

A moment's reflection on the conditional rule may reveal the other two types of reasoning that might be tried. Logicians recognize that these can lead to faulty conclusions. The first is **denying the antecedent.** Suppose you check your barometer and see that it is rising. Your evidence effectively denies the antecedent, not P. Does it follow from this that it will not storm (not Q)? Well, maybe, but not with any certainty. Does it mean that it will storm (Q)? Again, one cannot tell. The if-then rule describes what we must find to be true *given* that the antecedent is confirmed as true. If the antecedent should turn out to be false, then all bets are off. According to the conditional rule as stated, accurate predictions about the weather can only be made *if* the antecedent is true.

The other faulty form of reasoning is **affirming the consequent.** Suppose you venture outside and find a major storm brewing. Does this tell you with certainty that the barometer was falling? Such a conclusion is certainly possible. But once again, the conditional rule only allows us to make predictions about the weather *given* that the barometer actually is falling. It does *not* make predictions about the barometer *given* that it is storming. In other words, the conditional rule does not claim that it will storm *if and only if* the barometer is falling (although a meteorologist would no doubt prefer this wording).

Human Performance

With training in logic or with the aid of a computer programmed in conditional reasoning, one would never make an error. However, as we saw in syllogistic reasoning, people commit systematic errors (Markus & Rips, 1979; Rips & Marcus, 1977). The eight possible forms of the conditional are shown in Table 12.2. College students were asked whether the conclusion followed from the premises always, sometimes, or never. The correct response is marked with a superscript. Note that the always and never responses are appropriate when one can affirm the antecedent or

Table 12.2 Percentage of the Always, Sometimes, and Never Evaluations of the Eight Forms of the Conditional Syllogism (If P, then Q)

Minor Premise and Conclusion	Evaluation Response		
	Always	Sometimes	Never
1. P is true Therefore Q	100[a]	0	0
2. P is true Therefore not Q	0	0	100[a]
3. P is false Therefore Q	5	79[a]	16
4. P is false Therefore not Q	21	77[a]	2
5. Q is true Therefore P	23	77[a]	0
6. Q is true Therefore not P	4	82[a]	14
7. Q is false Therefore P	0	23	77[a]
8. Q is false Therefore not P	57[a]	39	4

SOURCE: Adapted from Rips, L. J., & Marcus, S. L. (1977), Supposition and the analysis of conditional sentences. In Just, M. A., & Carpenter, P. A. (Eds.), *Cognitive processes in comprehension* (pp. 185-220). Hillsdale, NJ: Lawrence Erlbaum. Copyright © 1980 by Lawrence Erlbaum Associates. Used by permission.
NOTE: a. The correct response.

deny the consequent, the two valid forms of reasoning. The sometimes response is called for in all other cases.

People perform perfectly in applying modus ponens or affirmation of the antecedent (the first two cases in Table 12.2). But errors occur in all other cases. Most striking about these results is the high proportion of errors connected with modus tollens, denial of the consequent. As the last two cases in the table show, about a fourth to a third of the time, people incorrectly give the sometimes response. They seem to be unaware that denying the consequent is just as valid as affirming the antecedent.

The card problem. Wason and Johnson-Laird (1972) undertook a series of experiments to understand further the errors made in conditional reasoning. They provided participants with four cards as shown in Figure 12.3.

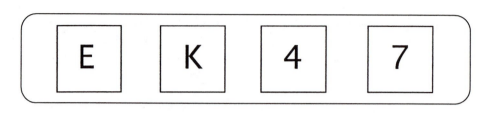

Figure 12.3. The four card selection task of conditional reasoning.

Each card had a letter on one side and a number on the other. They further gave participants this conditional statement:

> If a card has a vowel on one side, then it has an even number on the other side.

The participants' task was to decide which card or cards had to be turned over to prove that the conditional rule was true. They were to avoid turning over cards unnecessarily.

The results of such experiments showed that nearly half of the time participants decided to turn over both E and 4. According to the use of modus ponens or affirming the antecedent, the E card had to be turned over. But the 4 card was an error. Affirming the consequent does not allow one to say for certain whether there will be a vowel or a consonant on the reverse side. In sharp contrast, a mere 4% of the participants decided to turn over E and 7. The 7 card denies the consequent. By applying modus tollens, they could disprove the rule by discovering a vowel on the reverse side. Yet hardly anyone thought to do so in this task.

Confirmation bias. Further research has shown how powerful our misunderstanding of denying the consequent really is. Even after taking a college-level course in logic that covered the issue, performance remained abysmal. In fact, students who had taken the course did no better in applying the logic of denying the consequent to this task than did students who had no formal training (Cheng, Holyoak, Nisbett, & Oliver, 1986).

One explanation for our reluctance to apply modus tollens is that we are predisposed to seek confirming evidence. Evidence that disconfirms our beliefs may well be actively avoided. A confirmation bias certainly accounts for the behavior observed in the card problem and other related versions of the same task (Krauth, 1982). Moreover, the same tendency to seek confirming evidence and to overlook disconfirming evidence has been observed in many other tasks (Klayman & Ha, 1987). It has been observed in testing hypotheses in concept identification (Taplin, 1975). It may help explain why people fail to construct models of premises in syllogistic reasoning that rule out a favored conclusion (Dominowski, 1977). Finally, in social psychology experiments on persuasion, people pay more attention to evidence that confirms their beliefs than evidence that undermines them (Petty & Cacioppo, 1981). We are, it seems, less a thinking species than a believing one.

Meaning and Models Revisited

Cheng and Holyoak (1985) argued that the use of a schema or model that is rooted in practical experience allows one to reason effectively in the conditional task. The Wason card task is a bit abstract, not much more realistic than the if-P-then-Q version of conditional reasoning. By couching the problem in meaningful terms, Cheng and Holyoak stated that people apply denying the consequent every bit as well as affirming the antecedent. Whereas formal training in logic helps little, everyday experience and mental models of that experience help greatly.

For instance, suppose you again have four cards and each card has the age of a person on one side (16 or 22 years of age) and the person's drink on the other side (Coca-Cola or beer). How would you test the following rule? "If the person is drinking beer, then he or she is over 21." As in the other card task, you should turn over as many cards as are necessary to determine whether the conditional applied.

In this situation, you could perhaps draw an analogy to a specific situation encountered in the past. Griggs and Cox (1982) found that college students correctly selected the "drinking beer" and "16 years of age" cards three fourths of time. That is about 18 times the correct response rate found in the Wason and Johnson-Laird experiments with the vowel and digit rule! Griggs and Cox went on to show that to do well in conditional reasoning people must be familiar with the rule and have had actual experience with counterexamples or violations of the rule.

It seems that people construct an interpretation of Wason's vowel and digit rule, not as a conditional but as a biconditional rule. They construe the statement "if P, then Q" to mean if and only if P, then Q (Taplin & Staudenmeyer, 1973). Such an interpretation explains why they so frequently select the 4 card along with the E card. In a biconditional rule, one would find an even number if and only if the reverse side contained a vowel. It makes perfect sense therefore to turn over the 4.

Our everyday experience and uses of language lead us to make such interpretations. Suppose I say: "If you mow the lawn, I will give you ten dollars." This promise strongly suggests that if you do not mow the lawn, I am not about to part with my ten dollars (Geis & Zwicky, 1971). Once again, then, the meanings that we derive from conditional statements depend on our real-world experiences and it is these meanings that determine how well we reason according to the rules of philosophers. But, according to the rules of everyday economics, or should I say common sense, our reasoning may not be flawed at all. If you want the ten dollars, then you had best mow the lawn.

Inductive Reasoning

In the case of valid deductive reasoning, the conclusion is entailed or implied by the premises. The conclusion tells us nothing that we did not already know from the premises. A valid deductive conclusion is a tautology; it must be true if the premises are true.

Inductive reasoning, on the other hand, reaches beyond the evidence of the premises. The reasoner must induce a generalization that explains the evidence observed to date. For example, suppose I observe that every time the University of Missouri plays Kansas in basketball, the University of Kansas wins. If I then conclude that Kansas always beats Missouri in basketball, I have stepped beyond the data to form a general rule. The trouble with inductive reasoning is that a single future observation can prove the rule wrong. Simply by observing a single instance when Missouri beats Kansas in basketball, I can reject the generalization as always true.

We can speak of the validity of a deductive argument, but with inductive reasoning we must speak of our strength of belief. As Rips (1990) put it: "A natural way to think of inductive reasoning is as a process of mutual adjustment to the subjective probability or strengths of beliefs. . . . New evidence triggers an increase or decrease in the strength of related beliefs, where strength is a continuous quantity" (p. 325). Although Rips (1990) questioned whether there is a sound basis for saying that the cognitive processes at work in deductive reasoning differ from those in inductive reasoning, we will retain the classic distinction for purposes of teaching about work in the field.

The generalizations that we formulate become the basis for making decisions. For instance, I may have decided never to attend, or even watch on television, another Kansas-Missouri matchup. As long as the generalization held, this would form a sound basis for policy. I hope it is transparent that all of science and the public policies that we develop on the basis of scientific generalizations depend on inductive reasoning. A scientific law is nothing more or less than a generalization that, at times, has countless observations to back it up. $E = mc^2$ as long and until physicists find a single case to the contrary. The decisions that flow from our science are only as wise as the laws on which they are based. Should we invest in nuclear technology or renewable energy sources such as solar energy? Should we remove asbestos from buildings or leave it alone? Should we spend limited federal dollars on drug interdiction or drug education? The wisdom of the policy decisions hinges on the wisdom of the science underlying them. The final sections of this chapter address the nature of inductive reasoning and decision making.

Hypothesis Testing

Generalizations are formally defined as conditional rules. For example,

If the barometer is falling, then it will storm.

If $E = mc^2$, then a weapon that releases the energy of an atom will be devastatingly powerful.

As we saw in the previous section, one way to refute this rule is to find evidence that denies the consequence. If the bomb is a dud, then the rule is wrong. If, as we know is the case, the bomb works as predicted, then the rule is confirmed. This does not mean that the $E = mc^2$ equation is logically proven. For it is always possible that, one day, a bomb that releases energy from an atom may do nothing. That is, the generalization is never foolproof. It may someday be disconfirmed by negative evidence. But as more and more experimental tests pile up confirming evidence, our belief in the truth of the generalization grows stronger and stronger.

Confirmation Bias Revisited

Philosophers of science have argued that we make progress in our theories by seeking out disconfirming evidence (Popper, 1974). When an experiment produces evidence that denies the consequent, we can be certain through modus tollens that the antecedent is also untrue. The hitch in this strategy is that human beings greatly prefer to confirm their beliefs, hypotheses, and theories, not reject them. We considered this earlier in connection with the card problem and theorists have recognized its importance in our understanding of human reasoning (Klayman & Ha, 1987). Scientists, whose very careers depend on having confirmed theories, are no exception.

Wason (1968) investigated confirmation bias in an inductive reasoning task. The experimenter began by telling participants that they were to discover a general rule that predicts the elements of a sequence. Further, they learned that 2, 4, and 6 fit the rule. To discover the rule, the participants proposed additional elements and the experimenter would tell them whether their series fit the rule also.

An obvious hypothesis, and one often adopted immediately by the participants, was the rule that the numbers must increase in magnitude by two. Armed with such a hypothesis, people set about to test it by suggesting numerous series of numbers that increase by two. For example, they might offer the series 8, 10, 12, 14, 16 and the experimenter would inform them that it fit the rule. Next they might offer 5, 7, 9, 11, 13, 15, 17 and again the experimenter would confirm their hypothesis. With each confirmation, the participant gained greater confidence that the rule was correct and promptly generated another confirming sequence. Some participants became visibly upset when they vocalized their rule and the experimenter told them that they were wrong!

The rule that Wason had in mind was any series of numbers that increased in magnitude. Thus 1, 2, and 3 would also have received the nod from the experimenter. The interesting result of Wason's experiment is in how few participants thought to propose a series that falsified their hypothesis. Typically, all they sought was confirming evidence.

Decision Making

Virtually all fields of human endeavor—economics, politics, law, medicine—revolve around the making of decisions. Decision theory is the branch of mathematics concerned with how to go about the process optimally (Rubinstein, 1975). All decision makers are faced with alternative courses of action. Depending on the states of the environment in which these actions are carried out, there may be one of several outcomes.

Table 12.3 A Decision Payoff Matrix

Alternative Courses of Action	States of Nature		
	Perfect	Fair	Bad
Plant Crop A	10	1	–2
Plant Crop B	8	4	0
Plant Crop C	3	3	3

SOURCE: From Rubinstein and Firstenberg, *Patterns of Problem Solving.* Copyright © 1995, p. 274. Adapted by permission of Prentice-Hall, Inc., Englewood Cliffs, N.J.

Utilities are the values or gains that the decision maker gets with each outcome. Generally, we assume that the objective is to maximize the utilities that are expected.

Shown in Table 12.3 are the courses of action, states of nature, and outcomes for a farmer who must decide what to plant. Rubinstein (1975) explained the model developed by the farmer this way:

> The states of nature (such as rainfall, levels of temperature, winds, etc.) which are relevant to the success of his crops could be described to various degrees of detail. The simplification to three states Perfect, Fair, and Bad constitutes a high level of abstraction. . . . The array of numbers . . . is called a payoff matrix and represents the degree of satisfaction or utility that the farmer believes he will derive. For example, he derives 4 units of utility when he plants crop B and the state of nature is Fair, and he derives no utility when the state of nature is Bad. . . . Normally, you would think of money (say, profit in dollars) as the measure of success in such an enterprise. (pp. 312-313)

Types of Decisions

Some decisions are made under conditions of certainty. That is, we know that a particular course of action will result in a particular outcome for **decisions under certainty.** If the farmer knew for certain that the weather this year was going to be bad, then he would know exactly how to proceed to maximize his profits. **Decisions under risk** refer to the case in which each state of nature is likely to occur with a known probability (e.g., 10% chance of Perfect, 80% chance of Fair, and 10% chance of Bad).

Decisions under uncertainty refer to cases in which the probabilities of states of nature are unknown.

Decision making under uncertainty is the most complicated and realistic situation. To proceed effectively, the farmer must arrive at a subjective probability of the various states of nature. Based on past experience, advice from meteorologists, and perhaps a glance at the *Farmer's Almanac*, the farmer assigns probabilities and then determines the best course of action. Suppose that the farmer reasoned that the chances of Perfect, Fair, and Bad weather were 15%, 60%, and 25%, respectively. He could then compute the expected value of utility for each course of action as follows:

Crop A: .15(10) + .60(1) + .25(–2) = 1.6
Crop B: .15(8) + .60(4) + .25(0) = 3.6
Crop C: .15(3) + .60(3) + .25(3) = 3.0

If the farmer is accurate in his probability estimates, then Crop B should go in the ground to maximize profits.

Reasoning Under Uncertainty

How, then, do people go about arriving at judgments of subjective probability? Are people good or poor intuitive statisticians? An extensive literature exists on this issue. The research aimed at these questions has told us a great deal about the nature of human thinking. But the answers are still not entirely clear. For example, one can marshal evidence that people are good intuitive statisticians (Peterson & Beach, 1967) and other evidence that they are poor at judging probabilities (Kahneman & Tversky, 1982a). Let us turn in this final section to some of the key findings and controversies.

During the 1970s and 1980s, a wide range of cognitive biases and normative fallacies were discovered in tasks calling for decisions under uncertainty. Just as studies of deductive reasoning used a formal normative system to judge how well people performed, human judgments under uncertainty were contrasted with those predicted by statistical theories. Kahneman and Tversky (1973) pioneered these investigations and arrived at the following conclusion in an influential review of the early literature: "In making predictions and judgments under uncertainty, people do not appear to follow the calculus of chance or the statistical theory of prediction. Instead, they rely on a limited number of heuristics which sometimes yield reasonable judgments and sometimes lead to severe and systematic errors" (p. 237).

Representativeness. To illustrate the first important heuristic, consider these two alternative outcomes from tossing a coin six times. Imagine an outcome in which heads turn up three times followed by three tails (HHHTTT). An alternative outcome might be HTTHTH. Is the probability of one of these sequences higher than that of the other? Kahneman and Tversky (1972) found that in this and many related tasks, people generally say that the second, random-appearing outcome is more likely.

For those who have had statistics (and can remember it and use it effectively), the correct answer is apparent. Both outcomes are equally likely. Each toss of the coin is independent of the other. On any given toss, heads or tails has an equal chance of occurring. The total number of possible sequences is 2^6 or 64. The probability of all heads is $\frac{1}{64}$, just as is the probability of any other possible sequence.

Kahneman and Tversky explained that people use a **representativeness heuristic.** This means that events that are representative or typical of a class are assigned a high probability of occurrence. If an event is highly similar to most of the others in a population or class of events, then it is considered representative. Because most of the 64 sequences of coin tosses will necessarily have several alternations of heads and tails, the HHHTTT outcome strikes us as highly unrepresentative and therefore highly unlikely. Also, if an event is highly similar to the process that generates it, then it is considered representative. Tossing a coin is a random process and we expect random-looking outcomes, not "rigged" ones. Never mind that the probability of all heads is as likely as any other outcome.

Over a large sample of, say, 1,000 coin tosses, the likelihood of heads is .50, the same as tails. But for a small sample, such as six tosses, a sequence of even six heads in a row does not imply that a rigged or biased coin is being used. Yet sample size is not a feature that people heed (Bar-Hillel, 1980; Kahneman & Tverksy, 1972). According to the **law of small numbers,** we mistakenly expect even small samples to look random and to mirror the probabilities obtained with large samples (Tversky & Kahneman, 1971).

Gamblers fall prey to this use of the representativeness heuristic. The **gambler's fallacy** refers to the mistaken belief that future tosses of a coin, drops of the ball in roulette, or rolls of the dice in craps are not independent of past events. If you or I see seven rolled on the dice five times in a row, we will have a strong urge to bet against another seven coming up again on the next roll. We expect things to even out in the short run because we know that they must even out in the long run.

Take another quite different illustration of the representativeness heuristic. Kahneman and Tversky (1982a) asked college students to read character sketches and then to make judgments about them: "Linda is 31 years old, single, outspoken, and very bright. She majored in philosophy. As a student, she was deeply concerned with issues of discrimination and social justice, and also participated in anti-nuclear demonstrations" (p. 126). Given this description, would you say that it is more likely that Linda is a bank teller or that she is a bank teller and a feminist? Overwhelmingly, the students selected the latter description.

However, because bank tellers include both feminists and nonfeminists, it must be the case that the bank teller statement is more likely. The conjunctive rule of probability theory informs us that the probability of a conjunction of two events (A and B) cannot be greater than the probability of A or the probability of B. The tendency to judge the conjunction as more likely is called the **conjunctive fallacy.** Of course, the character description sounds more representative of feminists than bank tellers, leading us into the snare of the conjunctive fallacy.

Availability. The second heuristic used to estimate probabilities is based on the ease with which relevant examples come to mind. In deciding whether to buy a car made by Ford or one made by Chevrolet, one might consider the probability that the car will need major repairs within 5 years. If sources such as *Consumer Reports* were not consulted, then one would need to rely on information available in long-term memory. The **availability heuristic** suggests that if relevant examples can readily be retrieved from memory, then the class of events must occur with a high probability. If your Uncle Jack, your sister Alicia, and your cousin Kristin all complained at Christmas about their Fords, then you no doubt assume that they have the worst service records. That Fords are no different or perhaps even better than other makes of cars would be lost on you because of the availability of such examples.

What proportion of nurses are men? What proportion of car mechanics are women? Unless you happened to know several male nurses or female mechanics, both questions would generate low probability estimates. Tversky and Kahneman (1973) experimentally examined how the ease of recall influences our beliefs about the world. They composed four lists of people; each list included 19 names of women and 20 of men; for half the lists, only the men's names were famous (e.g., Richard Nixon), and for the other half, only the women's names were famous (e.g., Elizabeth Taylor). The researchers studied two conditions: recall and estimate. After hearing the lists read to them, the college students in the recall condition wrote down as many names as they could remember. In the estimate condition, they judged whether the list contained more names of men or women.

The results, not surprising, showed that the famous names were easier to recall than the other names on the list. The key result, however, was that the ease of recalling the names had a direct impact on the probability estimates. Specifically, for the lists that included famous females, the students judged that the list contained more female names. The opposite pattern occurred for the lists with the famous males.

Going back to the farmer introduced at the beginning of this section, it is not unlikely that his recollections of the weather in recent years would affect his decision making. If it is easy to recall examples of bad weather, then he would assign a high probability to that state of nature. This may lead the farmer seriously astray. It may be easier to remember bad weather than fair weather, but the latter may be far more likely in reality.

Simulation. As an example of probability heuristics, consider this situation taken from Kahneman and Tversky (1982b):

> Mr. Crane and Mr. Tees were scheduled to leave the airport on different flights, at the same time. They traveled from town in the same limousine, were caught in a traffic jam, and arrived at the airport 30 minutes after the scheduled departure time of their flights. Mr. Crane is told that his flight left on time. Mr. Tees is told that his flight was delayed and just left five minutes ago. Who is more upset, Mr. Crane or Mr. Tees? (p. 203)

Virtually all to whom Kahneman and Tversky posed this question responded Mr. Tees. The investigators noted that both gentlemen are in the same trouble: Both suffered through a traffic jam and both missed their flights. Objectively, both could or even should be equally upset. Why then do we overwhelmingly pity Mr. Tees more?

Kahneman and Tversky proposed that people call upon their knowledge representations or scripts for traveling to the airport. They then simulate the trip themselves and readily imagine alterative scenarios in

BOX 12.2: Evaluating Health Risks

Daily we receive information about the risks of our environment and our behavior. Newspapers, magazines, television, and radio news and other programming provide a constant onslaught of information about the hazards people face in everyday living. We are warned to stay out of the sun because of the thinning of the ozone layer and consequent risk of skin cancer. We are advised to eat a low sodium and low fat diet to combat heart disease, and to eat a high fiber diet rich in certain vitamins and minerals to combat cancer. Virtually everyone has heard about the cancer risks associated with smoking tobacco. But have you heard about the risks of drinking *decaffeinated* coffee? What about the risks of drinking *caffeinated* beverages of any kind? Then there are the risks of drinking too much alcohol, which must be weighed against the benefits to the heart of drinking moderate amounts of alcohol. Recently I learned of the cancer risks of eating too many hot dogs. I expect soon to learn that there may be some other risk associated with eating too few.

If a story receives heavy coverage by the press and media, then it is likely to be available for later recall. The degree of risk publicized may be minuscule compared with the major hazards we face, hazards that receive far less attention and therefore are less available in memory. Because of the availability heuristic, our *perceptions* of risk may be in error. We may be worrying ourselves sick about the wrong risks.

Slovic, Fischhoff, and Lichtenstein (1982) reported on their research in the area of risk perception. People estimate that accidents cause as many deaths as diseases. In fact, diseases, many of which receive little publicity, cause 16 times as many deaths as accidents. People also judge homicides to be as frequent as death by stroke, when in fact the latter is 11 times more deadly. Frequencies of death from botulism and tornados are wildly overestimated. The most underestimated causes of death are smallpox vaccinations, diabetes, and stomach cancer, according to Slovic et al.

In one study, the researchers examined newspaper accounts of death over a period of several months to see if the availability heuristic could account for the observed distortions in risk assessment. As expected, they found that relatively common causes of death, such as diabetes, emphysema, and various types of cancer, were hardly ever reported on by the press. In stark contrast, homicides, car accidents, tornados, fires, drownings, and other violent causes were reported often. Homicides in particular received the heaviest coverage relative to their actual frequency of occurrence. Such findings pose serious challenges to public safety and health programs. People must first know what the real risks are if they are to take sensible steps to avoid them.

which Mr. Tees could have made his flight. If only the driver had gone a bit faster, if only Mr. Tees had left 5 minutes earlier, if only—then things would have worked out differently. But only for Mr. Tees. Mr. Crane missed his flight, plain and simple.

The **simulation heuristic** involves the construction of a mental model of a situation and then "running the model" to predict the course of events. Whereas ease of recall underlies the availability heuristic, ease of construction or imagination underlies the simulation heuristic. As our farmer plans what to plant, he may well imagine possible scenarios and try to assess which is the best course. If it is too difficult to imagine perfect weather, then the farmer could well assign a distorted, low estimate of probability for this state of nature.

The availability and simulation heuristics help us to understand a common phenomenon both in everyday life and in the psychology laboratory (e.g., Fischhoff, 1975, 1977; Hell, Gigerenzer, Gauggel, Mall, & Muller, 1988; Hoch & Lowenstein, 1989). **Hindsight bias** refers to the fact that people confidently judge that they knew an event would occur *after* it had occurred. *Before* the event took place, people may not be able to arrive at a solid prediction. But once history runs its course, we are highly likely to say, "I knew it all along."

For instance, Fischhoff (1975) presented people with historical information about a battle between two armies. Based on this prebattle information, the participants gave before-the-fact judgments about whether one of the armies would win or whether there would be a stalemate. For example, they assigned a probability that Army A would win, at say, 25%. After-the-fact judgments came from participants who were given the same prebattle information but then had also been told how the battle really turned out. Now that they knew Army A actually won, they thought the prebattle information warranted a more confident prediction, say, 50%. On average, participants gave the highest probability estimates of a particular army winning based on the prebattle information when making after-the-fact judgments. The same information warranted stronger predictions given the clear vision of hindsight.

Hindsight effects are to be expected if people rely on ease of recall—the availability heuristic—and ease of imagining—the simulation heuristic. Once the critical information about the outcome is known, people cannot put it aside. Indeed, it dominates our recollection and imagination about the situation at hand, distorting our confidence in our judgments.

Probability or Frequency

The most fundamental question is whether people can mentally represent probabilities at all. It could be that we process the absolute frequency of events. Probability requires more than this; it requires a representation of relative frequencies. Probability ranges from zero to one. It is calculated by knowing the absolute frequency of an event and then dividing it by the maximum number that could have been obtained. In sorting through a deck of cards, you will encounter 13 spades. The probability of a spade is $13/52$ or .25. Which number is processed and stored in human information processing—absolute frequency or relative frequency?

Estes (1976) examined this question in a series of experiments. He gave the participants the results of two opinion polls that compared how popular a product or political candidate was against an alternative. For example, suppose that Candidate A had appeared in 6 polls and won 5 of them. Candidate B, on the other hand, had appeared in 18 polls and won 9 of them. Now, for the first time, Candidates A and B will be tested against each other in the same poll. Which candidate do you expect to win?

Such a test pits absolute frequency against probability. Candidate B has won more polls than Candidate A in terms of frequency, 9 versus 5. But the probability of Candidate A winning a poll is .83 ($5/6$), whereas for Candidate B the probability is only .50 ($9/18$). Estes reported that participants generally selected the candidate with the highest frequency of wins, not the highest probability. People apparently can make decisions on the basis of probability only when there are about the same number of opportunities for both events. In other words, if both candidates had appeared in 18 polls, then participants would select Candidate B, not Candidate A. Of course, in this case, the use of frequency information would make it appear that people could use probabilities effectively.

Numerous other lines of investigation point to the conclusion that people process the frequency with which events occur in the environment. Estes's polling results are by no means the only test that favors frequency over probability. The evidence from an astonishing range of tests confirms the view that frequencies of occurrence, not probabilities, are represented in long-term memory (Gigerenzer, Hoffrage, & Kleinbölting, 1991). Earlier we reviewed evidence that storing of frequency of events information occurs automatically and that use of such frequency information has important influences on memory (e.g., Hasher

& Zacks, 1979; Hintzman & Stern, 1978). Moreover, the frequency of oc-currence of events feature plays an equally central role in concept iden-tification (Bourne et al., 1976).

🔲 SUMMARY 🔲

1. Syllogistic reasoning involves evaluating whether a conclu-sion necessarily follows from two premises that are assumed to be true. A valid deductive conclusion is *necessarily* true, given that the two premises are true. People identify valid conclusions about three quarters of the time. But they perform much worse with invalid con-clusions, recognizing them as invalid only about a third of the time. The pattern of errors is very consistent. When the major premise contains the word *all* and the minor premise the word *some,* people regard a conclusion with the word *some* as valid. When both the major and the minor premises contain the word *no,* then they regard a conclusion with the word *no* as valid.

2. One reason for our poor categorical reasoning performance is illicit conversion. People improperly assume that if all A are B, then all B are A. Another reason is that considering all possible combina-tions of what the premises mean places enormous demands on work-ing memory. Not surprising, people simplify the task by considering only a few combinations and by only considering the combinations that are easily interpreted. In general, people reason in ways that are meaningful by constructing mental models. These models need not mirror the formal systems of logicians. One compelling example is the phenomenon of belief bias, whereby people accept a conclu-sion as valid if it fits their system of beliefs, regardless of the given premises.

3. Conditional reasoning involves deducing a valid conclusion from a rule in the form of "if P, then Q." One way to draw a valid conclusion is affirming the antecedent. By showing that P is true, it follows that Q is also true, according to the conditional rule. The second valid form of reasoning is denying the consequent. By show-ing that Q is false, it follows that P is also false. People reason virtually flawlessly when affirming the consequent. There is a strong tendency toward confirmation bias, seeking evidence that confirms a con-clusion. However, people rarely seek evidence that disconfirms the

conclusion—denial of the consequent. Further, they do not understand that this is a valid form of reasoning.

4. Inductive reasoning involves inferring a general rule from the observation of specific events or evidence. Unlike valid deductive reasoning, the conclusion goes beyond the premises; it is not entailed by them. A generalization is only more or less likely to be true, based on the evidence, rather than necessarily true. Generalizations are formally defined as conditional rules (e.g., If the barometer is falling, then it will rain). Because of confirmation bias, people seek out evidence that proves the rule to be true (the barometer fell and then it rained). They often overlook trying to disprove their beliefs, hypotheses, and theories by seeking disconfirming evidence (the barometer fell and then the sun shined).

5. Making decisions under uncertainty implies that the probability of various scenarios must be estimated subjectively. One does not know for certain what the utility will be for a particular course of action or even what to expect by an objective calculation. In reasoning under uncertainty, people rely on a variety of heuristics for making predictions and judgments. The representativeness heuristic assigns a high probability of occurrence to events that are judged typical of a class. According to the availability heuristic, an event is likely to occur if a specific example of the event can be easily recalled. Similarly, the simulation heuristic assigns a high probability to events that be easily imagined to occur because they fit the sequence of a routine script. Finally, it appears that people encode the frequencies of events, not their relative frequencies or probabilities.

Key Terms

syllogistic reasoning	decisions under risk
valid conclusion	decisions under uncertainty
atmosphere hypothesis	representativeness heuristic
illicit conversion	law of small numbers
affirming the antecedent	gambler's fallacy
denying the consequent	conjunctive fallacy
denying the antecedent	availability heuristic
affirming the consequent	simulation heuristic
decisions under certainty	hindsight bias

Recommended Readings

A classic work on logic is Church's (1956) text titled *Introduction to Mathematical Logic*. Rips's (1983) article in the *Psychological Review* examined how human cognitive processes in reasoning differ from the logician's rules. Johnson-Laird's (1983) book titled *Mental Models: Towards a Cognitive Science of Language, Inference, and Consciousness* provides a wealth of information on the same issue as well as many other topics. For studies on the errors that people make in conditional reasoning, the reader should consult *Psychology of Reasoning: Structure and Content* by Wason and Johnson-Laird (1972).

Rips (1990) discussed the relation between deductive and inductive reasoning in his chapter in the *Annual Review of Psychology*. An excellent book on human failings in inductive reasoning is *Human Inference: Strategies and Shortcomings of Social Judgment* by Nisbett and Ross (1980). Kahneman, Slovic, and Tversky (1982) edited *Judgment Under Uncertainty: Heuristics and Biases*, which contains chapters summarizing the original research in this area.

For a general overview of decision theory, I recommend Rubinstein's (1986) text titled *Tools for Thinking and Problem Solving*. Janis and Mann (1977) cover the topic from the standpoint of real-world decisions in their *Decision Making*. Pitz and Sachs (1984) covered judgment and decision in their contribution to the *Annual Review of Psychology*.

CHAPTER **13**

回　Intelligence and Thinking

I deally, we would begin this chapter with a definition of intelligence. But that is no simple matter. Sternberg and Detterman (1986) reviewed contemporary viewpoints on intelligence and uncovered dozens of definitions. This is by no means a modern dilemma. Psychologists have always offered different answers when asked about the nature of intelligence (Eysenck & Kamin, 1981).

The reader may find such disagreement surprising given that psychological tests for the intelligence quotient or IQ are so widely used. But understand that we psychologists like to measure things, even when we disagree about what those measurements really mean. Some have regarded the psychometric measurement of intelligence as one of psychology's best contributions (Eysenck, 1973), while others have taken a much dimmer view (Gould, 1981; Kamin, 1974).

For some, the biological aspects of intelligence take center stage. Questions arise about its inheritance, relation to neurological development, its variation across species. For others, the cognitive aspects dominate. All the processes considered in this book are relevant to our understanding of intelligence, from perception and attention to problem solving and reasoning. For still others, the motivational, social, and cultural issues surrounding intelligence are most pressing.

The disagreements that engulf the topic may explain why few texts in cognitive psychology even discuss the matter let alone devote a chapter to it. But it is far too interesting to ignore. For example, is it possible to enhance intelligence through training regimens, much as we enhance athletic performance? Programs that try to teach thinking skills aim to do just that. Further, the topic of intelligence serves to integrate much of what you have learned in reading this book. Finally, intelligence provides the entry point into an age-old and still contentious debate. How do men and women differ in thinking abilities?

We shall start by briefly reviewing some common, though not universally agreed upon, definitions of intelligence. We then will examine two distinctly different approaches to the understanding and measuring of intelligence, both proposed by notable cognitive researchers. The triarchic theory and, to a still greater degree, the frames theory fractionate the concept of intelligence into multiple pieces. Next we will take up the question of whether intelligence can be increased at any age through the training of thinking skills or other means. The alternative view is that intelligence is fixed by genetics and early development. We will conclude with a survey of gender differences.

Traditional Views of Intelligence

In the early moments of psychology's history, Sir Francis Galton and Alfred Binet laid out two guiding views of intelligence (Eysenck, 1987). Galton (1892) argued that there is such a thing as **general intelligence** and that it is rooted in biology. Perception, attention, memory, language, problem solving, reasoning, and thinking are all dependent on the power of the nervous system. Galton expected to find some individuals would be good in many cognitive tasks whereas others would not, precisely because intelligence is general. Eysenck noted that "Galton suggested the use of reaction time measures, sensory discrimination, and similar elementary investigations as measures of intelligence" (Eysenck, 1987, p. 24). Today, neurological measures based on EEG recordings would also be added, such as the event related potentials to simple stimuli (Matarazzo, 1992).

Binet (1903) founded the psychometric, as opposed to the biological, view of intelligence. Binet looked to tests of problem solving, learning, and memory—the sort of skills that people use in school. He devised numerous tests of cognitive abilities and administered them to French schoolchildren in an effort to assess their scholastic abilities. American schoolchildren later received these tasks in the form of the well-known Stanford-Binet test of intelligence. Whereas Galton emphasized heredity, Binet argued that the environment determined intelligence. Finally, and somewhat ironically, Binet denied that it made any sense to average across the many tests that he used to derive a general measure of intelligence. The very founder of the **psychometric view** of intelligence thought that cognitive skills, say, memory and language ability, were independent. Doing well at memorizing a string of digits said nothing about verbal abilities, a position diametrically opposite to Galton's.

From the turn of the century to this day, the debate started by Galton and Binet has ended in a draw to the extent it has ended at all. As we shall see later, contemporary cognitive approaches to intelligence have served to broaden the scope of the debate rather than to decide the matter in favor of Galton or Binet. For example, Spearman (1927) argued that the evidence plainly supported the **biological view** of intelligence. He postulated the existence of "g" or general intelligence. Later it became clear that one needed to separate verbal forms of intelligence from motor or performance forms. Distinctions also were needed between the breadth and depth of a person's knowledge, which is called crystallized intelligence, versus their ability to solve novel problems, which is called fluid intelligence (Cattell, 1963).

It turns out that many highly specific cognitive abilities have also been postulated. Visual-spatial, verbal, numerical, and memory abilities may be fundamental cognitive components that need not correlate with one another at all. One might be good at finding one's way through an unfamiliar city, on the way to a job interview, but very poor at conversing with the interviewer. One task demands spatial skill and the other verbal. Similarly, Galton's emphasis on heredity and Binet's on the environment have both found support (Eysenck, 1979). Most psychologists today would argue that individual differences in IQ are roughly half traceable to genetic sources and half to environmental sources.

How to measure intelligence has also never been resolved. Variations in scores on psychometric tests correlate with scores on various reaction-time tests, particular characteristics of brain waves, and even the activity levels of particular neurotransmitters (Eysenck, 1987). Still, there may be much more to human intelligence than either the psychometric or the biological tests attempt to measure. Exactly this point characterizes the contemporary theories of intelligence in cognitive psychology, to which we now turn.

BOX 13.1: Artificial Intelligence

AI or artificial intelligence is the field of programming machines to do tasks that would require intelligence if done by human beings (Minsky, 1968). One branch of AI is wholly concerned with making machines intelligent, without regard for whether the means for doing so shed light on human intelligence. Another branch is closely allied with cognitive psychology and the other cognitive sciences. Procedures developed in AI are intended as simulations of human cognitive processes. At the same time, such AI researchers study how people perform cognitive tasks so as to shed light on how best to program intelligent machines.

The themes of AI echo many if not all of the issues raised in the course of this survey of cognitive psychology. One such theme is knowledge representation. Knowing how—procedural knowledge—and knowing what—declarative knowledge—are fundamental to the success of machine forms of intelligence. The production memory and declarative memory of the ACT* model discussed in Chapter 7 illustrate an approach to knowledge representation that is important in both computer-based and human-based models of intelligence.

A second theme is search. Tasks given to machines are translated into representations of a problem space. Once the initial state, goal state, and operators are specified, the task becomes one of searching for a solution path. The means-end heuristic of GPS and the working backward heuristic of NOAH illustrate two powerful and general search techniques. Delineating the strengths and weaknesses of search procedures is one major thrust of AI research. Another is determining whether solutions to problems are optimal in light of the constraints facing the problem solver. Is the solution a perfect one or merely satisfactory?

A third theme is inference. Expert systems are designed to diagnose problems and make decisions. All such systems have both a knowledge base and an inference engine, a procedure for working from the given pieces of information to diagnosis and decision. The inference engine employs rules stored in the knowledge base to draw new inferences and derive new conclusions. Humans beings, too, make inferences in all forms of reasoning and decision-making tasks. We have seen that human comprehension and memory also heavily involve inference procedures. More than 600 expert systems have been developed (Forsyth, 1989).

The fourth theme is learning. Expert systems, for example, include a knowledge-acquisition component. The system must have some way for adding new procedures and new facts and concepts to its knowledge base. Interest in computers that can learn is intense for several reasons. What kinds of primitive abilities must a computer be given at the outset so as to learn about its world? Are these primitives comparable to the innate mechanisms and knowledge representations of our species? Is it possible for a computer system, armed with only a few primitive abilities, to achieve a high level of intelligence through learning?

One criticism of AI is that the programmer must provide virtually all that the computer knows. A system that can learn on its own would escape such criticism, and may reveal much about cognitive development in people. An impressive demonstration of machine learning is Lenat's (1983) system called EURISKO. It automatically adds new heuristic rules gained from the problems that it solves. EURISKO won a naval war game for three successive years, in spite of attempts to defeat it by redesigning the rules of the game (Forsyth, 1989).

Three Alternatives to Tradition

The Triarchic Theory

Sternberg (1977) initially proposed that the biological and psychometric approaches to intelligence should be replaced by an information processing approach. According to the theory of **componential intelligence,** it would be possible to predict performance on intellectual tasks in a refined manner by identifying and measuring specific components of information processing. A small number of components in theory would account for performance in virtually any task that might turn up on an IQ test.

Componential intelligence. Sternberg distinguished metacomponents, performance components, and knowledge-acquisition components. **Metacomponents** control the course of action in thinking and monitor the success of the selected path. Earlier we considered the notion of a central executive (see Chapter 4) that plans and decides what to do, as well as the notion of metacognitive monitoring (see Chapter 7). **Performance components** actually execute a strategy for thinking. They are lower order processes that encode, combine, and compare sources of information.

In carrying out a routine task, the performance components would largely determine how well one scores. When faced with a novel task, in contrast, the metacomponents would govern one's fate. Finally, the **knowledge-acquisition components** mediate learning and memory. They determine how rapidly a novel task becomes routine. They include acquistion or learning components and retention or memory components. They further include transfer components that generalize knowledge from one thinking task to another. By seeing a connection between a routine task and a novel one, learning can be greatly enhanced by transferring already available knowledge and skills to the problem at hand.

Sternberg (1985) later argued that his componential approach fell short of capturing all there is to intelligence. It did so because it focused exclusively on the mental processes that operate in the same manner no matter what environment people find themselves situated in. It did so because it assumed that the IQ test already captured intelligence well and that all Sternberg needed to do was explain IQ in terms of information processing theory. The triarchic view of intelligence, on the other hand, saw all this as but one subtheory. In addition to the componential subtheory, Sternberg proposed the experiential and contextual subtheories.

Experiential intelligence. An individual with strong componential intelligence would score high on standardized intelligence. But how creative would this individual be? The experiential subtheory addresses the ability of people to cope with novel tasks in a flexible, creative fashion, on the one hand, and the ability to automatize behavior, on the other. **Experiential intelligence** refers to the use of components in responding appropriately to novel and routine tasks. Earlier we noted that metacomponents play a larger role in explaining individual differences in performance when the task is novel. In contrast, performance components play the larger role when the task is routine. Sternberg goes on to assume that we differ from one another in our ability to create—to cope well with new situations—and our ability to respond automatically—to cope well with routine situations. The experiential subtheory attempts to define these differences.

It further suggests the best kinds of tasks for trying to measure intelligent behavior. One can think of tasks as falling along a continuum of the familiar to the novel. If a task is too familiar to everyone, then performance will be solely mediated by automatic performance components. For example, hitting a key as rapidly as possible when a light comes on is no doubt a measure of automatic perceptual encoding and responding, but little else. If a task is far too novel, then everyone might devote all their time to figuring exactly what the task calls for. Such a task would tap metacognitive components but little else. The experiential subtheory aims to specify the optimal level of task novelty for assessing particular types of intelligence.

Contextual intelligence. The contextual subtheory addresses the relation of mental processes to the environment. An individual may not score high on intelligence tests or be regarded as especially creative. Yet the person may be "street smart," knowing how to adapt to variations in the environment. Intelligent behavior involves adaptation to the demands of the environment. It also involves the selection and alteration of environments to suit one's needs. **Contextual intelligence** refers to the use of components in adapting appropriately to different contexts or environments. As the temperature drops in northern climates with the onset of winter, people adapt to the change, for example. Putting on more clothing, building warmer shelters, or heading south to warmer weather are all practical responses to the new demands for survival. Because of the measures taken in our cultural past, human adaptation to cold winter weather is scarcely noticeable today—until a winter storm wipes out the power.

Universality. Different cultures, as with different climates, call for different expressions of intelligent thinking. The mental processes that constitute componential intelligence may be invariant across cultures, but the manner in which these components are used depends wholly on the environment, according to the triarchic theory. As Marr and Sternberg (1987) put the matter:

> Thus, even if a particular mental capacity is a universal component of intelligence, the intelligent expression of that ability may vary from culture to culture (and, within a culture, may vary from environment to environment). Different environments not only give rise to different definitions of intelligence, but also may shape that intelligence in somewhat different ways. Rewards for the exercise and development of particular cognitive abilities will vary from one environment to another, as will opportunities to exercise and develop these abilities. (pp. 275-276)

To conclude, the contextual subtheory tells us how well individuals can relate and adapt to their environment. The experiential subtheory tells us how well they cope with novelty and familiarity. The componential subtheory tells us about the power of basic cognitive processes like encoding and retrieving. These in theory are constant within an individual regardless of his or her physical, social, and cultural environment and regardless of the familiarity or novelty of his or her current task.

The Frames Theory of Multiple Intelligences

Gardner (1983) also regarded the IQ as an entirely too narrow definition of human intelligence. Let us turn to Gardner's own words on why:

> A young girl spends an hour with an examiner. She is asked a number of questions that probe her store of information (Who discovered America? What does the stomach do?), her vocabulary (What does *nonsense* mean? What does *belfry* mean?), her arithmetic skills (At eight cents each, how much will three candy bars cost?), her ability to remember a series of numbers (5,1,7,4,2,3,8), her capacity to grasp the similarity between two elements (elbow and knee, mountain and lake). She may also be asked to carry out certain other tasks—for example, solving a maze or arranging a group of pictures in such a way that they relate a complete story. Some time afterward, the examiner scores the responses and comes up with a single number—the girl's intelligence quotient or IQ. This number (which the little girl may actually be told) is likely to exert appreciable effect upon her future, influencing the way in which her teachers think of her and determining her eligibility for certain privileges. The importance attached to the number is not entirely inappropriate: after all, the score on an intelligence test does predict one's ability to handle school subjects, though it foretells little of success in later life. . . . Many observers are not happy with this state of affairs. There must be more to intelligence than short answers to short questions. (pp. 3-4)

In place of the IQ, Gardner calls for an assessment of the full range of human performances that reflect intelligence. The traditional psychometric approach leaned heavily toward looking at verbal and mathematical aspects of human intelligence. This can also be seen in the achievement testing field in which separate scores are reported for verbal, mathematical, and analytical scales. As Gardner noted, this makes some sense if one wishes to predict performance in the traditional school curricula that also list heavily toward the teaching of verbal, mathematical, and logical skills.

But neither IQ tests nor achievement tests tell us much if anything about performance outside of school settings (McClelland, 1973, 1994). Real-world jobs and adult demands are far too variable for such accurate prediction from limited tests taken early in the life span. Moreover, Gardner wondered why the schools should place so much emphasis on the verbal and mathematical domains of intelligence. A curriculum that seeks to raise all aspects of human intelligence must be much more broadly conceived (see Gardner, 1991).

Gardner recognizes seven independent frames of mind or forms of intelligence. **Linguistic intelligence** is the familiar idea of verbal ability. Language is one of the most, if not the most, important of our cognitive tools. Using this tool, people communicate, socialize, and build cultures through their speaking and writing.

Logical-mathematical intelligence is another such fundamental tool. Logical-mathematical abilities lie at the very core of science, engineering, and architecture. Without geometry, algebra, and calculus, one cannot build skyscrapers. Without integral equations, there is no theory of quantum mechanics. Without differential geometry, there is no theory of relativity. The truly gifted mathematician is rare and characterized by, in Gardner's words, "a love of dealing with the abstract" . . . and "speed and power of abstraction" (pp. 138, 142).

Musical intelligence is yet another frame of mind. Pitch and rhythm are the central elements of this form of intelligence. Timbre or tonal quality is a third element. A good ear for pitch and timbre is important for the development of musical intelligence, but the rhythmic aspect can exist apart from the auditory system altogether. Deaf individuals, Gardner (1983) noted, can learn to experience music through its rhythmic elements. An ability to sense the affective or emotional aspects of music may be critical to musical intelligence.

Spatial intelligence is a fourth frame of mind. It has held a special place in the psychometric tests of IQ because tests of spatial ability eliminated language from the picture. For example, the performance component of the Weschler Adult Intelligence Scale includes spatial tests. An example of a spatial perception test is shown in Figure 13.1. As another example, consider the following tests posed by Gardner (1983):

> Take a square piece of paper, fold it in one half, then fold it twice again in half. How many squares exist after this final fold? Or, consider another test: A man and a girl, walking together, step out with their left feet first. The girl walks three paces in the period when the man walks two. At what point will both lift their right feet from the ground simultaneously? (p. 171)

Intelligence tests that rely heavily if not exclusively on linguistic and mathematical symbol processing are easily criticized as being culturally

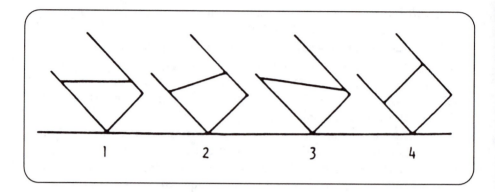

Figure 13.1. Example of a test of spatial perception: Select which tilted bottle has a horizontal water line.
SOURCE: From Linn and Petersen (1985). Copyright © 1985 by the Society for Research in Child Development. Reprinted by permission.

biased. If a person's cultural and educational background failed to provide adequate instruction in formal English and mathematics, then obviously such a person will score poorly. But such an outcome would hardly tell us that the individual lacks the ability to think and act intelligently in other ways, in other environments, and with other symbol systems.

Spatial or visual-spatial thinking is important for practitioners of the visual arts, engineering, and many if not all sciences. Yet it may also be seen in the navigators of the Puluwat, the natives of the Carolina Islands, who can find their way to hundreds of islands over vast stretches of open ocean. Without drawn maps or sextant, and certainly without the satellite-based Global Positioning System of modern navigation, these islanders display uncanny spatial intelligence by a careful reading of geography and the stars. All spatial intelligence includes, in Gardner's (1983) view, "the capacities to perceive the visual world accurately, to perform transformations and modifications upon one's initial perceptions, and to be able to re-create aspects of one's visual experience, even in the absence of relevant physical stimuli" (p. 173).

The next frame of mind represents a departure from any previous theory or test of intelligence. It and the one that follows plainly show that Gardner sees a much wider range of intelligent human performances than do traditionalists. **Bodily-kinesthetic intelligence** refers to skilled motor performance. It may be witnessed in the skilled pianist, typist, gymnast, dancer, diver, sculptor, skater, painter, martial artist, and mime, among others. Gardner (1983) characterized it as the "ability to use one's body in highly differentiated and skilled ways, for expressive as well as goal directed purposes" and as "the capacity to work skillfully with objects, both those that involve the fine motor movements of one's fingers and hands and those that exploit gross motor movements of the body" (p. 206). Despite psychologists' treatment of motor skills as something other than intelligence, Gardner noted that they have been central in our evolution as a species. The flexible use of tools is not found in animals other than primates, and it is likely that bodily-kinesthetic intelligence was selected for through the survival advantages that come with such usage.

In people, the left hemisphere of the brain is generally dominant. As it happens, damage to the areas of the left hemisphere that are dominant for motor behavior produce a dizzying array of disorders called **apraxias.** They are characterized by an inability to perform in proper order a sequence of motor movements, despite the individual being able to comprehend the command and move all the muscles needed for the sequence. For example, a limb-kinetic apraxia means the person cannot carry out a command with either the right hand or the left hand. Because of contralateral control, in which the left hemisphere controls only the right hand, such a bilateral difficulty is especially interesting. With ideomotor apraxia, the patients, noted Gardner (1983), "clumsily execute actions and use the body part itself as an object (for example, when pretending to pound a nail, they will ram a fist against a surface rather than represent the absent implement in their grip" (pp. 212-213). Some apraxias are remarkably specific, as with the dressing apraxia whereby the afflicted individuals cannot put on their clothes.

Finally, there are the two frames of mind called the personal intelligences. The **intrapersonal intelligence** refers to the ability to gain access to one's emotions and to draw upon these emotions in guiding one's thoughts and behaviors. The **interpersonal intelligence** turns outward rather than inward. It refers to the ability to take note of other people's moods, temperaments, motivations, and intentions. As Gardner explained, in their advanced forms, the intrapersonal intelligence "allows one to detect and to symbolize complex and highly differentiated sets of feeling" whereas the interpersonal "permits a skilled adult to read the intentions and desires—even when these have been hidden—of other individuals and, potentially, to act upon this knowledge" (p. 239). The novelist Proust typified the genius of the intrapersonal while the religious leader Mahatma Gandhi or the politician Lyndon Johnson did so for the interpersonal.

Independence of frames. Each of the seven frames of intelligence are independent of the others. For example, linguistic and logical-mathematical intelligence need not covary at all. One might be brilliant in bringing language alive in speaking and writing but incapable of handling calculus. Brilliant mathematicians may find themselves tongue-tied in lecturing to their students. An IQ test or achievement test that lumps these together into a single overall score misses much of interest about individual differences in thinking abilities.

The contrasts are even more dramatic in the cases of the other intelligences. The gifted musician Arthur Rubenstein found mathematics "impossible," whereas the brilliant mathematician Stanislaw Ulam found himself utterly unable to compose a musical tune (Gardner, 1983, p. 143). Just as the apraxic patient can comprehend a verbal command (but not perform it), the aphasic patient retains the ability to perform complicated motor sequences (but cannot understand commands to do them). Recall, too, from earlier chapters the work on implicit learning and memory. Even amnesic patients with no episodic recall can learn and remember complicated procedural skills without difficulty. Perhaps most astonishing are the talents of autistic children who show profound deficits in interpersonal intelligence, yet retain unusual talents in other specific areas. These might be in mathematics, in music, or in bodily activities. Gardner noted the cases of "Earl, who on his own figured out how to make a windmill out of a clock; of Mr. A., who was able to wire his stereo, lights, and television to a single switch; and of another similarly impaired youth who designed and built a functional merry-go-round" (p. 214). Another autistic boy comprehended electronics, navigation, music, and mechanics. He could travel about the city readily with a map and bicycle. Yet he scored an 80 on IQ, far below the average of 100, and worked doing assembly in a Goodwill store.

Conclusions

To summarize, the frames theory of multiple intelligences goes even further than Sternberg in breaking apart the monolith of IQ. It strongly denies that there is anything useful or even meaningful in ranking people along a scale of IQ. A score of 80 may mask remarkable cognitive competencies, while a score of 180 may lead only to an unremarkable lifetime membership in Mensa, the social club for those with high IQ scores.

In place of IQ, tests are needed for specific cognitive competencies. Cognitive theories of intelligence certainly are headed in this direction, despite that most people do not think of intelligence in such a diverse way (Sternberg, Conway, Ketron, & Bernstein, 1981). For example, Hunt (1986) called for researchers to start with a computational theory of cognition and then to develop a taxonomy of tasks that cover the range of relevant competencies. His own work on linguistic or verbal intelligence illustrates the approach (e.g., Hunt, 1987). Guilford's (1967) model of cognitive abilities offers another example, one that distinguishes 120 distinct competencies. Even this large number may not cover all the necessary territory, warned Guilford (1982). Ceci and Liker (1986) demonstrated that the cognitive competencies required in academic settings are not at all the same as those demanded by nonacademic tasks, such as the practical matter of betting on the horses at the race track. Let this serve as a warning to those straight-A students among you who are tempted by gambling.

I hasten to remind the reader that the debate over intelligence is far from over and many distinguished researchers take serious issue with the notion of multiple intelligences and competencies (e.g., Eysenck, 1987; Jensen, 1987; Snow, 1986). Some prefer to limit the concept to cognitive as opposed to emotional proficiencies (e.g., Glaser, 1986). Considering only cognitive proficiencies, Carroll (1993) concluded that there is a hierarchy of abilities. Narrow, domain-specific abilities constitute Stratum I of the hierarchy. But Stratum III consists of a single general ability, the *g* factor discussed earlier. In between, in Stratum II, lies broad abilities such as fluid intelligence (reasoning and problem-solving skills) and crystallized intelligence (knowledge acquired over a lifetime).

Still other scholars contend that the IQ, while missing much in detail, still works well as a holistic score of thinking ability and provides useful guidance for educational decision making (e.g., Detterman, 1986). Certainly IQ scores are in wide use as a diagnostic tool in our educational institutions, particularly in special education programs. So, while cognitive theorists move away from the IQ, it no doubt will survive for many years to come.

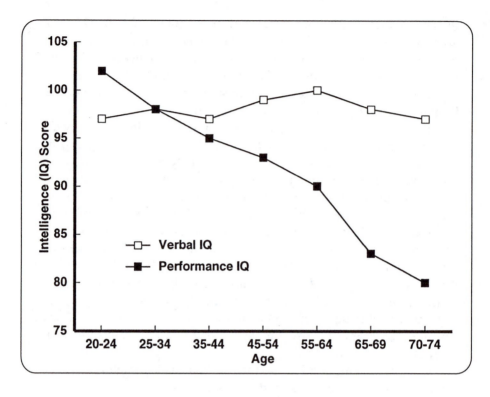

Figure 13.2. Intelligence as measured by the WAIS-R as a function of age.
SOURCE: Adapted from Kaufman, Reynolds, and McLean (1989).

The Enhancement of Thinking Skills

The biological and psychometric approaches assume that intelligence is largely fixed by a combination of genetic fitness and the environment encountered during development. By early adulthood, the major environmental influences on cognitive development and maturation have already had their say. Consistent with such assumptions, IQ either declines steadily past the age of 20, as happens with the performance component of the WIAS-R test, or manages to hold steady until individuals reach their late sixties, as happens with the verbal component. These trends are plotted in Figure 13.2 from a study by Kaufman et al. (1989).

The nonverbal or performance component appears to decline because older adults have greater difficulty in manipulating information in working memory compared with young adults. Specifically, Salthouse and Babcock (1991) concluded that there was a decline in processing efficiency with advancing age. The speed of executing processes in working memory declined with age. Although one can continue to accumulate knowledge throughout the life span, the crystallized intelligence proposed by Cattell (1963), the ability to solve novel, nonverbal puzzles, and other uses of working memory inevitably decline it seems.

If one accepts the biological/psychometric view, then most readers of this book and certainly its author are already on the slippery slope of intellectual decline. But a **competency view** of intelligence offers a much more optimistic prognosis for us all. There is no reason one cannot improve specific cognitive competencies or proficiencies at any age. Working memory may not work as efficiently, but one might well pick up strategies as an older adult that overcome such losses. Cognitive development by no means halts by late childhood or early adulthood, according to the competency view. One can continue to acquire new cognitive procedures as well as new knowledge throughout adulthood. Higher education and lifelong continuing education, both formal and informal, are in essence based on the premise of the competency view.

But the question remains as to whether general thinking skills can be improved or whether gains are limited to a particular domain. For example, by taking a course in college physics, one might learn much about solving physics problems. The question is whether such a skill would generalize to solving problems of other types. Is there a way to enhance general problem-solving ability?

Teaching General Thinking Skills

Alternative programs. A large literature has addressed this question (e.g., Chipman, Segal, & Glaser, 1985; Nickerson, Perkins, & Smith, 1985; Perkins & Salomon, 1989; Segal, Chipman, & Glaser, 1985). With some exceptions, the studies have investigated children or young adults, not the elderly. Broadly speaking, three types of programs have been suggested for the enhancement of teaching skills (Glaser, 1984). First, **process-oriented programs** try to improve metacognitive skills as the route to better overall thinking ability. Presumably, self-monitoring should allow one to select the right representations of problems and the right heuristic for searching the problem space.

One such program uses thinking aloud with a partner as a way of improving metacognition and hence overall problem solving (Whimbey

& Lochhead, 1980). The learner verbalizes his or her thoughts while engaged in a puzzle or other abstract problem of the sort we examined in Chapter 11. The partner, in essence, models good self-monitoring by pointing out errors as the person verbalizes them. For instance, failing to represent the problem clearly or failing to use all known facts would elicit comments from the partner. In theory, the individual doing the thinking aloud internalizes the self-monitoring and uses it in the future when solving problems.

Second, other programs draw upon familiar, everyday situations to teach thinking (de Bono, 1985). Specific problem-solving strategies, including metacognitive skills, are taught in the context of such topics as picking a career, changing jobs, or moving to a new house. The context model directly contrasts with the process-oriented model by avoiding abstract puzzles and games. Instead, the program situates the problem solver in a familiar context. A related program situates the teaching of thinking within the context of the elementary school curriculum (Lipman, Sharp, & Oscanyan, 1980). Teaching the child how to reason and think is best done while teaching reading, writing, and other basic skills, according to this contextually based program.

The third type teaches problem-solving heuristics that apply to well-structured domains; mathematics, physics, or engineering fit this model. For example, Rubinstein (1975) and Hayes (1981) have designed programs for teaching college students how to think effectively. They cover effective communication skills, mnemonic strategies, working backward and hill-climbing strategies for solving mathematical problems, decision-making theory, and probability theory. The learner acquires an assortment of heuristics that may prove useful in their own areas of specialization. Although the heuristics taught come from specific domains, the assumption is that one becomes a better thinker, in a general sense, when armed with many diverse weapons for attacking problems.

Evaluation research. The programs differ in their specifics, but all share in common the idea that thinking skills can be enhanced. No matter the age at which one starts, it should be possible to learn new thinking strategies that are generally useful. Intelligence, then, is hardly a fixed quantity from this point of view. In reviewing the studies evaluating the effectiveness of these approaches, Nickerson et al. (1985) concluded that general thinking skills can indeed be taught. But they warned that only some of the many programs that have been tried have proven effective. Even the same program, when tried with different teachers and different populations in different cultural contexts, has failed to show uniform gains. Moreover, even when a program has proven effective in the aggregate, the degree of improvement in thinking skills has been only modest.

To illustrate these conclusions, Nickerson (1988) cited the many evaluation studies, conducted with pretest-posttest designs, of Feurstein's **Instrumental Enrichment Program.** His program is an example of the process-oriented model. It has been tested in Israel, Venezuela, Canada, and the United States. Nickerson (1988) stated:

> The data from the numerous evaluations were difficult to interpret. Many measures did not show differential gains from the program, and the studies differed from each other with respect to a variety of possibly important characteristics, including the test instruments used, the amount of time spent by subjects in Instrumental Enrichment classes, the amount of training in the program provided to the classroom teachers, the ages and prior intellectual abilities of subjects, and so on. . . . the most commonly reported effects have been obtained with nonverbal measures of intelligence that reflect skill in figural and spatial information processing, and that such effects have been observed primarily with elementary and secondary school students. (p. 41)

In commenting on the same studies, Savell, Twohig, and Rachford (1986) concluded that positive benefits from Feurstein's program can only be obtained by ensuring certain conditions. These include (a) training the teachers for at least 1 week, (b) exposing the students to the program for a minimum of 80 hours over a period of 1 or 2 years, and (c) situating the program in the context of other subjects that are interesting and important to the students.

Bransford, Sherwood, Vye, and Rieser (1986) offered a more encouraging observation about Feurstein's program. Improvements in thinking skills from such a program might well be obtained when observing students in everyday situations outside the classroom. And this, after all, ought to be the primary objective of teaching thinking skills. That these benefits are not observable on IQ tests ought not be a matter of great concern. For the IQ test, as we have already seen, is quite narrow in what it professes to measure. It measures abilities related to academic performance, not everyday practical intelligence (Sternberg & Wagner, 1986).

Theorists agree on one point. It is essential that the thinking skills taught to students transfer from the original learning context to other contexts, both academic and nonacademic. In the words of Perkins and

Salomon (1989), it is imperative that cognitive skills not be bounded by the context in which they were learned so that they fail to transfer to other domains of knowledge. There are, unhappily, many examples of context-bound skills.

Theoretically, learning how to program a computer might conceivably foster the development of logical thinking skills. But training in how to program has no positive benefits in other thinking tasks (Pea & Kurland, 1984). Pressley, Snyder, and Cariglia-Bull (1987) tried six different methods of teaching children how to transfer thinking skills from one setting to another. Yet, all six approaches failed. The cognitive skills gained by the students seemed tightly bound by context. Schoenfeld (1982, 1985) attempted to teach students to apply heuristics to solve a variety of types of mathematics problems. Although they understood a strategy, such as working backward, in one context, they experienced great difficulty in seeing how to apply the strategy within the detailed context of a particular novel problem.

Thus it is not yet possible to draw strong conclusions about the degree to which thinking skills can be enhanced throughout the life span. What is clear at this point is the necessity to do more than just teach thinking skills in a single context. For real improvements to occur that transfer to many domains, it appears that several objectives must be met. First, detailed knowledge about each domain must be available. One cannot be a novice in an area and expect to solve problems by falling back on weak general methods (Glaser, 1984, 1985). Second, when general thinking skills are taught, they must be seen by the student as applicable to many contexts. Using many real-world exercises may help accomplish this objective (Block, 1985). Finally, students must be taught or in some other fashion acquire metacognitive skills. Without the ability to reflect on alternative heuristics that might be used in a given situation and to monitor how well things are going in the course of thinking, then all is lost. In sum, the improvement of thinking requires domain knowledge, general processes, *and* metacognitive skills.

Gender Differences

In this final section, our concern is with differences between the sexes in intelligence or, more precisely, cognitive competencies. Arguments over the differences in abilities of females and males are probably as old as any argument can be. If discussions of religion and politics cause trouble, then discussions of gender differences cause catastrophe. Cognitive psychologists waded into these age-old debates with their batteries of tests and tried to settle the disputes once and for all. Needless to say, the arguments persist. But cognitive research has greatly clarified the matters in two ways. First, as we will soon see, there is far more similarity in the performance of men and women on cognitive tests than there are differences. Second, the data shed some light on the causes of the differences that are observed.

Maccoby and Jacklin (1974) wrote a widely read and widely criticized review of gender differences in cognition. They suggested that the genders differ chiefly in three areas: verbal abilities, visual-spatial abilities, and quantitative or mathematical abilities. Before discussing their conclusions and the more recent updates by other investigators, let us digress to examine how the magnitude of a gender difference is calibrated.

Meta-Analysis

Meta-analysis is a statistical technique for summarizing the results of numerous studies that all examine the same question in roughly the same way. By averaging the difference between males and females in, say, verbal ability, one can draw a much stronger conclusion than is possible from a single or only a handful of studies. Meta-analysis yields an estimate of **effect size,** d, which tells us how large a difference is relative to the variability in the studies. It is defined as the difference in mean scores between males and females in a particular study divided by the standard deviation for the two groups. The larger the value of d, the bigger the effect size. Typically, a d of .20 should be considered a small effect size; .50, a medium; and .80, a large (Cohen, 1969).

In Figure 13.3, three hypothetical differences favoring females over males on a cognitive ability test are shown. The first case (A) is such a small effect that it is equivalent to no difference at all. Both males and females attain the same scores. The second case is a small but reliable difference (B). On average, the females attain a higher score than the males. Note that the distributions overlap so much that there are many males who score higher than many of the females. But the mean difference favors the females. In the third case, the female advantage is large (C). Virtually all females score higher than all males. Notice in these three cases that the shapes of the distributions—their variances—are identical. This is not true in all cases. The variability in scores for males is sometimes

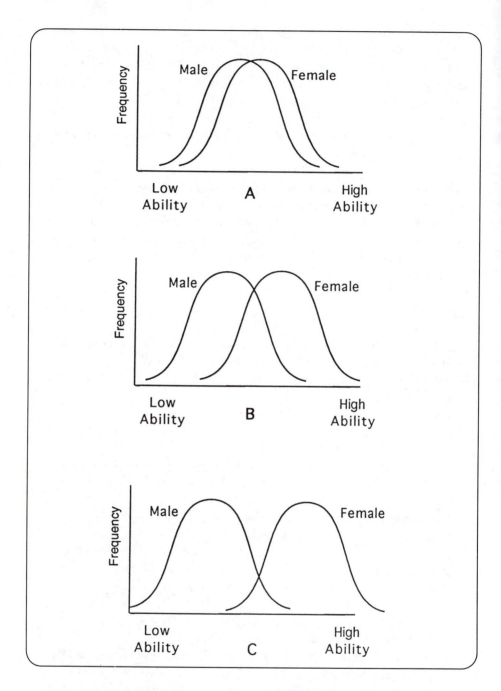

Figure 13.3. Hypothetical frequency distributions illustrating the relative magnitude of gender differences in cognitive ability.

greater than for females even when the mean difference is relatively small. That is, the difference between the lowest and highest scoring male tends to be greater than the same difference calculated for females (Feingold, 1992).

Verbal Differences

By counting the studies that favor females over males on tests of verbal ability, Maccoby and Jacklin suggested that females are more competent in this domain. A later review used meta-analysis to soften this conclusion, however. Hyde and Linn (1988) examined 165 studies and concluded that only a subset of verbal tests revealed any gender difference reliably. These tests measured anagram solution, speech production, and general verbal ability, an amalgam of many tests. The verbal score of the Scholastic Assessment Test (SAT), tests of vocabulary, essay writing, and others showed no differences in the sexes. Moreover, the effect sizes for the three that revealed differences were on the order of .2 or .3. In short, men and women shared far more in common in verbal ability than they showed differences.

As for differences in variability, Maccoby and Jacklin failed to detect any gender effect. Subsequent research confirmed this conclusion (Feingold, 1992).

Visual-Spatial Differences

Maccoby and Jacklin argued that, at least from adolescence onward, males outperform females on visual-spatial tests. They viewed this male advantage as remarkably consistent from study to study and from one type of test to another. With respect to variability, it is quite clear that males show far more variability in visual-spatial skills than do females (Feingold, 1992).

Once again, though, subsequent researchers have questioned Maccoby and Jacklin's conclusions with respect to the differences in means. Linn and Petersen (1985), for example, found that the size of the gender difference varied with the precise test used. For example, the test of spatial perception shown earlier in Figure 13.1 gave different results than the mental rotation test that Shepard and Metzler (1971) used (see Chapter 6).

Their meta-analysis revealed a small to medium effect size on the test of spatial perception ($d = .44$). However, a medium to large effect was obtained when mental rotation was examined ($d = .73$). Furthermore, only the mental rotation effect remained steady no matter what age was studied. For example, the effect size for spatial perception was much greater for older people than younger people. Perhaps this is an effect of cognitive development—with males getting better than females in spatial perception only in later adulthood. A more plausible explanation is that the older females sampled in these studies had much less opportunity to exercise spatial perceptual skills compared with young women and girls today.

Mathematical Differences

Maccoby and Jacklin observed that boys and girls exhibit very similar mathematical abilities throughout elementary school. But then they begin to diverge at adolescence and early adulthood, with males performing better on tests of quantitative ability than females. The males also show much greater variability than females at all ages, according to Maccoby and Jacklin and Feingold.

Hyde (1981) performed the necessary meta-analysis and confirmed that males exhibit superior scores on mathematics tests. The medium effect size in this case equaled .43, which equals nearly a half a standard deviation advantage for males.

Hyde went on to point out the practical meaning of such an effect size. It turns out that an effect size of this magnitude is highly reliable in the statistical sense. But it does not allow one to predict the ability of any given individual with much accuracy. A large number of males score no better than the mean score obtained by females. Remember that males show much greater variability than do females on tests of mathematical and visual-spatial cognition. This can be seen in Figure 13.4. If you had to predict an individual's score on a mathematics test by knowing only his or her gender, you would be able to do so accurately at most 5% of the time. As Feingold (1992) observed: "Boys score only slightly higher than girls on average in mathematics tests but are largely overrepresented among high math scorers" (pp. 62-63).

Explanations

Gender differences in ability, even tiny ones, are fertile ground for the classic debate about nature versus nurture, about biological causes

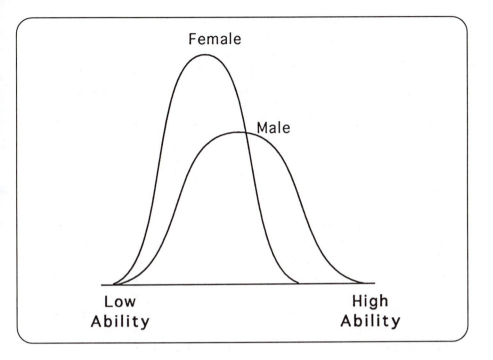

Figure 13.4. Males show greater variability as well as a greater mean score on tests of mathematical ability relative to females.

SOURCE: From Feingold, A. (1992). Sex differences in variability in intellectual abilities: A new look at an old controversy. *Review of Educational Research, 62,* 61-84. Copyright © 1992 by the American Educational Research Association. Reprinted by permission of the publisher.

versus social causes. It should come as no surprise that a mixture of the biological and social appears to underlie the differences discussed earlier.

Social-cultural factors. The social variables are not difficult to discern. The studies upon which Maccoby and Jacklin based their conclusions were conducted when socialization practices for boys and girls were markedly different in North America. Boys were encouraged to play with blocks, Tinkertoys, and erector sets (as well as toy guns). Girls were encouraged to play with dolls, toy tea sets, and dollhouses (but not toy guns). By the onset of adolescence, boys were encouraged to take classes in industrial arts, mathematics, science, and engineering. Girls were steered toward home economics, English, and social studies.

To a lesser extent, these differences in socialization persist today, but there have been marked changes during the past two decades toward more gender-neutral socialization. Once boys were the only ones to receive extensive practice in thinking visually, spatially, and quantitatively as they played with their blocks, erecting castles. Once girls were the only ones to receive extensive practice in talking politely over tea, playing house with a group of friends. These differences were then reinforced after elementary school by the kinds of classes taken by the two sexes. These are plainly generalizations but the exceptions proved the rule. Now the rule is breaking down as our cultural roles for men and women are changing.

One might expect that the gender differences reported by Maccoby and Jacklin would diminish as cultural practices change. Precisely this has been happening. Meta-analytical investigations into the trends in the data collected from adolescents raised at different points have revealed smaller and smaller gender differences (Feingold, 1988). As noted earlier, the gender difference favoring females in verbal ability is gone completely, while those favoring males in mathematical and quantitative abilities are statistically reliable but of little practical significance. It makes no sense at all to tell an adolescent girl to forget a career in engineering because "everyone knows girls can't do math." This is nothing but prejudice, yet today young women are still underrepresented in engineering schools because such nonsense lingers.

Biological factors. What then of biology? Here it is important to bear in mind that our brain structure was shaped by evolutionary forces tens if not hundreds of thousands of years ago. Cultural practices in the twentieth century have nothing to do with ultimate evolutionary causes of brain differences and the cognitive differences that they may force (Goldsmith, 1991). When *Homo sapiens sapiens* survived in the hunter-gatherer culture of the Upper Paleolithic era of archeological time (60,000 to 40,000 years ago), our ancestors began to build hearths, huts, and organized small villages (Stringer & Gamble, 1993). As sociobiologists have pointed out, there may have been selective advantages for male genotypes that supported the visual-spatial skills needed for hunting. Men who could not spot the game and find their way home again did not live to have children. Females by contrast may have been more likely to survive and reproduce by using verbal communication skills. Assuming that women in general stayed near the campsite gathering and preparing food, rather than joining the hunt, verbal skills may have been more important than spatial skills.

Is there any biological evidence to support this evolutionary tale? It is well documented that male brains show greater lateralization than do female brains (Levy & Heller, 1992). This means that the degree of specialization in the two hemispheres, language in the left and spatial skill in the right, is greater in males than in females. Females are more likely to have language skills represented in both hemispheres relative to men. If a stroke causes damage to the left hemisphere, then women are more likely to recover language functioning. The single gender difference that seems to persist even after the changes in socialization is the advantage of males in mental rotation. Conceivably, this ability requires a highly lateralized brain and specialized components in the right hemisphere.

▣ SUMMARY ▣

1. Intelligence has historically been approached from two opposing positions. Galton pioneered the biological view of general intelligence. Individual differences in neural functioning were assumed to affect many cognitive abilities, including perception, attention, memory, problem solving, and reasoning. Heredity was assumed to underlie these individual differences. Spearman later named this "g" for general intelligence. Binet pioneered the opposing psychometric approach to intelligence, which held that cognitive abilities varied independently of one another. Binet assumed that environmental variations caused differences in cognitive abilities. The psychometric approach entailed administering a wide variety of cognitive tests in an effort to predict success in school.

2. The triarchic theory of intelligence assumes, first, that a small number of information processing components account for performance in cognitive tasks (componential subtheory). These include metacomponents, performance components, and knowledge-acquisition components. Second, the triarchic theory addresses the ability of people to cope creatively with novel tasks and, at the same time, to respond automatically to routine tasks (experiential subtheory). Third, it addresses the relation of mental processes to the environment that underlies successful adaptation (contextual subtheory). Selecting and altering the environment to meet human needs

is the third aspect of intelligence. Taken together, intelligence is the use of components to adapt, create, and automatize as needed.

3. The frames of mind approach identifies seven independent modules of intelligence. Linguistic, logical-mathematical, and spatial intelligence have been assessed in various ways on traditional tests of intelligence. Musical, bodily-kinesthetic, intrapersonal, and interpersonal intelligences have traditionally not been viewed as properly included in discussions of intellectual abilities. The frames view holds that human intelligence is much broader than traditionalists contend. It further claims that the seven modules develop independently, thus denying the existence of general intelligence. For example, an individual gifted in logic and mathematics may be incompetent in musical or interpersonal skills.

4. A competency approach assumes that thinking skills can be enhanced by specific training procedures. A key issue in this regard is whether general problem solving and other thinking abilities can be developed. It may be that cognitive skills can be improved in a specific domain, but such improvement does not transfer to other domains. Process-oriented programs regard the enhancement of metacognitive skills as the key to better overall thinking ability. Other programs use everyday situations or well-structured domains (e.g., mathematics) to teach thinking skills. One process-oriented program, Feurstein's Instrumental Enrichment Program, has been extensively evaluated and the results are mixed. It is not yet possible to draw strong conclusions about the degree to which thinking skills can be enhanced throughout the life span. Transfer of thinking skills to many domains is important but difficult to achieve.

5. Gender differences in cognitive competencies have long been of interest. Meta-analyses of large numbers of studies have shown, first, that females perform better than males on some tests of verbal abilities. The effect size takes into account how large a gender difference is relative to the magnitude of variations among individuals. The gender difference in verbal abilities shows a small effect size. On tests of visual-spatial ability, males perform better than females. The size of this effect ranges from small to medium on one test of spatial perception and from medium to large on a standard test of mental rotation. Males also show an advantage on mathematical tests. However, because males show markedly more variability than

do females, it is not possible to predict mathematical ability by knowing gender.

Key Terms

general intelligence	spatial intelligence
psychometric view	bodily-kinesthetic intelligence
biological view	apraxias
componential intelligence	intrapersonal intelligence
metacomponents	interpersonal intelligence
performance components	competency view
knowledge-acquisition components	process-oriented programs
experiential intelligence	Instrumental Enrichment
contextual intelligence	Program
linguistic intelligence	meta-analysis
logical-mathematical intelligence	effect size
musical intelligence	

Recommended Readings

The biological and psychometric approaches to intelligence profoundly shaped the field of psychology. Two books that take opposing views of this influence are Eysenck's (1973) *The Inequality of Man* and Gould's (1981) *The Mismeasure of Man*. For a look at how educational policies have been formulated in light of theories of intelligence, the reader will learn much from Kamin's (1974) *The Science and Politics of IQ* and Linn's (1990) *Intelligence: Measurement, Theory, and Public Policy*.

Three collections of essays elaborate the biological and psychometric approaches. One is Sternberg's (1982) *Handbook of Human Intelligence*. Another is Sternberg and Detterman's (1986) book titled *What Is Intelligence?* and the third is Sternberg and Wagner's (1986) *Practical Intelligence: Nature and Origins of Competence in the Everyday World*. Carroll (1993) undertook a massive reanalysis of over 400 sets of data on cognitive tests in his book *Human Cognitive Abilities: A Survey of Factor-Analytic Studies*.

The teaching of cognitive competencies is covered by Nickerson, Perkins, and Smith's (1985) book titled *The Teaching of Thinking. Thinking and Learning Skills* (Volumes 1 and 2), edited by Segal, Chipman, and Glaser, are standard references in the field. Also of interest is the *Teaching Thinking Skills: Theory and Practice*, edited by Baron and Sternberg (1986). In the *Annual Review of Psychology*, both Resnick (1981) and Glaser and Bassok (1989) covered cognitive process training in the context of instructional psychology. A special issue of the *American Psychologist* (February 1989) also includes several relevant articles.

Deaux (1985) reviewed gender differences in the *Annual Review of Psychology*. In addition to Maccoby and Jacklin's (1974) classic titled *The Psychology of Sex Differences*, the reader should consult the more current *Sex Differences in Cognitive Abilities* by Halpern (1992).

PART VI

The Past and Future

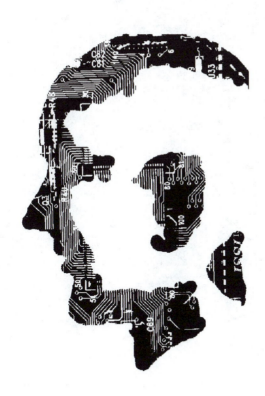

CHAPTER **14**

▣ Consciousness

At the birth of psychology a century ago, consciousness was the focal point of the discipline. Wundt and Titchener set about describing the structure of consciousness using introspective methods. James, Angell, and Thorndike eschewed their efforts in favor of a science based on the uses or functions of consciousness in mental life. Freud turned the field upside down with his insistence that the truly interesting and important aspects of mental life lay buried deep in the unconscious.

But then Watson, Skinner, and other behaviorists turned the field of psychology away from any consideration of consciousness, which they regarded as too subjective to allow a scientific analysis. The objectivism of nineteenth-century physics and biology overtook the young science of psychology almost entirely (Hilgard, 1980). But for the cognitive work of Piaget, Vygotsky, Bartlett, and Tolman in the 1920s, 1930s, and 1940s, psychology became the science of behavior only. The mental processes that intervened between the stimulus and the response were too airy for proper analysis. Consciousness and its psychodynamic partners, the preconscious and unconscious, became pariahs in the science of the day.

As we saw in Chapter 1, this all ended with the cognitive revolution of the 1950s and 1960s. As Bruner (1990) observed: "That revolution was intended to bring 'mind' back into the human sciences after a long cold winter of objectivism" (p. 1). The mind certainly came back to psychology in full force, but, of interest, the troublesome problems of consciousness remained on the fringes of the revolution. Cognitive psychologists peered into the head, looking deeper than the behaviorists preferred or dared, and found the structures and processes that have been chronicled throughout this book. Processes of perception, attentional systems, working memory, long-term encoding, storage, and retrieval processes, sophisticated rules of language and innate devices for their acquistion—all were there for the taking. Yet, curiously, cognitive theorists had little to say directly about consciousness. It was only after an additional 20 to 30 years that Hilgard (1980) could write that consciousness had returned to psychology. The journal titled *Consciousness and Cognition* was founded as recently as 1992.

The reasons for the slow, or perhaps I should say cautious, pace are many. As Hilgard (1980) summarized:

> My reaction is that psychologists and physiologists have to be modest in the face of this problem (consciousness) that has baffled the best philosophical minds for centuries. I do not see that our methods give us any advantage at the ultimate level of metaphysical analysis. A heuristic solution seems to me to be quite appropriate. . . . That is, there are conscious facts and events that can be shared through communication with others like ourselves, and there are physical events that can be observed or recorded on instruments, and the records then observed and reflected upon. Neither of these sets of facts produces infallible data. . . . It is the task of the scientist to use the most available techniques for verification of the data base and for validation of the inferences from these data. (p. 15)

To close our survey of cognitive psychology, it is imperative to look at consciousness directly. It not only brings us full circle, returning us to psychology's roots in the nineteenth century; more important, it takes us to the newest branches of the tree, the sprouts that will become the psychology of the twenty-first century. Consciousness is too central to the enterprise for cognitive psychology to fret that the problem is intractable or, worse, that it is not a problem after all.

We will begin with a discussion of various typologies of consciousness, including a quick glimpse at the controversy over animal consciousness. Then we will turn to the consciousness of dreams and daydreams. The study of these undirected forms of thought is providing interesting insights in the broader concerns of cognitive psychology. We will then address a few of the key properties of waking consciousness and relate these to illustrative theoretical models. We will end with the problem that no doubt bedeviled the protophilosophers of our early ancestors. The mind-body problem, as Hilgard (1980) warned, will not evaporate under the scrutiny of cognitive scientists. Yet many hope that cognitive psychology will bring us to a deeper understanding of the human condition than ever before. The cognitive revolution, whose fruits you have studied in this book, may one day be regarded as significant for humankind as have the Copernican and Darwinian revolutions (Sperry, 1993).

Varieties of Waking Consciousness

Anoetic, Noetic, and Autonoetic Consciousness

Tulving (1985) differentiated three types of consciousness in the context of his proposal for multiple memory systems. Shown in Figure 14.1 are the familiar types of memory and their associated forms of consciousness. Tulving suggested a monohierarchical arrangement of the memory systems, such that episodic memory is a subsystem of semantic memory, which is in turn a subsystem of procedural memory. The descending arrows in Figure 14.1 are meant to denote these nested relations among memory systems. Each memory subsystem depends on, and shows properties different than, those below it in the hierarchy. Tulving further suggested parallel relations for the types of consciousness.

Starting at the bottom, Tulving (1985) proposed **anoetic consciousness** for procedural memory. It means not knowing. Let us look to Tulving for a precise definition of the term:

> It refers to an organism's capability to sense and to react to external and internal stimulation, including complex stimulus patterns. Plants and very simple animals possess anoetic consciousness as do computers and learning machines that have knowledge and that can improve it. (p. 388)

Noetic (or knowing) **consciousness** is associated with semantic memory, the schemas and models about which much has been said in our journey through cognitive psychology. Tulving (1985) defined it thus:

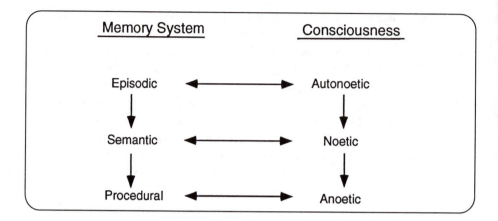

Figure 14.1. The types of consciousness associated with procedural, semantic, and episodic memory systems.

SOURCE: From Tulving, E. (1985). How many memory systems are there? *American Psychologist, 40,* 385-398. Copyright © 1985 by the American Psychological Association. Reprinted by permission.

It makes possible introspective awareness of the internal and external world. We can say that the object of noetic consciousness is the organism's knowledge of its world. Noetic consciousness is to such knowledge as the knowledge is to the world. Lower animals, very young children, and people suffering from brain damage may lack episodic memory and autonoetic consciousness but may have fully developed noetic consciousness. (p. 388)

Autonoetic (or self-knowing) **consciousness,** then, is found only when an individual can recall episodes of past experience.

It allows an individual to become aware of his or her own identity and existence in subjective time that extends from the past through the present to the future. It provides the familiar phenomenal flavor of recollective experience characterized by "pastness" and subjective veridicality. It can be impaired or lost without the impairment or loss of other forms of consciousness. (p. 388)

As we reviewed in Chapter 4, there is abundant evidence that people store implicit memories that influence their behavior in the absence of any conscious experience of knowing. To take but one example, prosopagnosic patients report not knowing the faces of even their family and friends. Yet, when tested carefully for signs of anoetic, procedural knowing, they clearly can discriminate familiar from unfamiliar faces, as evidenced by differences in galvanic skin conductance to the two types of stimuli (Tranel & Damasio, 1985). Furthermore, it is reasonable to attribute different kinds of consciousness to different living organisms. The family dog is probably noetically conscious in the sense that it can perceive and model its environment. But the dog probably lacks autonoetic consciousness, precluding it from reflecting on its past or anticipating its future.

Tulving's distinctions appear useful and perhaps even necessary for a full accounting of consciousness, but others take pains to separate conscious awareness from any particular memory system (Jacoby, 1984; Johnson, 1983; Schacter, 1989). For example, Schacter anticipated problems with equating episodic recall with autonoetic consciousness. Because episodic information can lead to implicit priming effects that occur without awareness, Schacter posited a **conscious awareness system (CAS)** that stands apart from procedural memory and declarative/episodic memory. Consciousness, in Schacter's view, is not a property of any memory system at all.

Normal Versus Dissociated Consciousness

James's theory. To grasp the next topic, we must return to James's early descriptions of consciousness. The states that flow together in the stream of consciousness could be characterized by four properties in James's (1962) view:

(1) Every "state" tends to be part of a personal consciousness.
(2) Within each personal consciousness, states are always changing.
(3) Each personal consciousness is sensibly continuous.
(4) It is interested in some parts of its object to the exclusion of others, and welcomes or rejects—*chooses* from among them, in a word—all the while. (p. 167)

Properties 2 and 3 are needed here. James observed that thoughts are owned, like property. But unlike property there are no public territories. Consciousness is ruthlessly personal or private. Two people can share their states of consciousness only by translating them into symbols that both can perceive and understand, such as oral or written language. The

BOX 14.1: Animal Consciousness

The nature of animal consciousness has always been a source of speculation. As Roitblat and von Fersen (1992) observed:

> For much of scientific history, animals were seen as passive mechanistic entities with few, if any, mental processes. Animals were viewed as mere passive stimulus-response devices, controlled by characteristics of their immediate environment and their history in it. To the extent that they formed and used representations of the events and environments around them they did so by passively recording traces of the neural activity recorded by their senses. In contrast to this passive view, a more active perspective on animal representations has been emerging in recent years. This view sees animals as active information processors that seek information in their environment, encode it, and use it for their benefit in flexible and intelligent ways. (p. 672)

Griffin (1984) has championed the view that consciousness of some sort is pervasive throughout the animal kingdom. His thesis rests on evidence that animals can think in a variety of interesting ways. Evidence of animal thinking can be found in the shelters they build, for instance. Termites, wasps, ants, and bees all build a variety of complex structures to house their eggs and developing young. As Griffin (1984) noted: "Among some species of solitary bees and wasps a single female that is ready to lay her eggs goes to great trouble to gather suitable materials from a considerable distance and prepare a place in which the egg has a good chance of developing" (p. 101). Such insects modify their behavior in the face of unforeseen circumstances and repair damage to their nests. Griffin argues that such behavior is less likely to be the result of instinctive programming and more likely the result of simple conscious thinking.

Tool use also provides intriguing evidence in both birds and mammals. Birds protect their young by defecating on and pecking at intruders to the nest. Ravens, however, take this a step further by picking up, or even burrowing for, small rocks and then dropping them on human intruders. Polar bears have been observed to throw chunks of ice and other objects at seals to injure or kill them. Sea otters make use of small stones to open shellfish. Among the primates, the most widely known example of apparent thought through tool use is fishing for termites by chimpanzees. The chimpanzee will select a branch, strip it of its leaves, break it to the proper length, and then skillfully lower it into a mound of termites. With luck, the chimpanzee can retrieve a swarm of termites by carefully pulling the tool from the hole. Human beings have found it difficult to match the chimpanzee's skill at termite fishing.

These illustrations may not convince skeptics that animals possess some form of consciousness. But the direction of the field is clearly toward a greater appreciation of the diversity of consciousness. Research with animals is demonstrating that other species also possess representations in working memory, imagery and cognitive maps, and abstract and natural concepts (Roitblat & von Fersen, 1992). The key now is to describe the important similarities and differences that are found among different phylogenies, classes, orders, families, and species.

personal symbols of consciousness apparently cannot be communicated directly (but see Box 2.1).

The changing states of consciousness are "sensibly continuous," meaning one state associates plainly with the next state. Again, in James's words:

> When Peter and Paul wake up in the same bed, and recognize that they have been asleep, each one of them mentally reaches back and makes connection with but *one* of the two streams of thought which were broken by the sleeping hours. . . . Peter's present instantly finds out Peter's past, and never by mistake knits itself on to that of Paul. Paul's thought in turn is as little liable to go astray. The past thought of Peter is appropriated by the present Peter alone. (pp. 172-173)

Although James characterized normal consciousness as personal and sensibly continuous, he recognized that "dissociated" states of consciousness occurred. The most benign form of this came through amnesia. An individual might not feel like himself after losing significant memories. In more extreme cases of dissociative consciousness, James identified three types: "insane delusions," "alternating selves," or "possessions" (p. 218). Today we refer to most dissociative states as forms of mental disorder under the DSM-IV, the diagnostic manual of the American Psychiatric Association. These include amnesia, fugue, and multiple personalities.

Hypnosis. Hilgard (1986) noted that interest in dissociated forms of consciousness peaked during the heyday of Pierre Janet's work at the beginning of the twentieth century. Janet pioneered the study of multiple personalities and hysterical conditions, such as functional blindness. Janet believed that dissociated states of consciousness became severed from the states making up the primary personality or self. These states could coexist as a separate personality that remains hidden in the unconscious, until brought into the light of day under hypnosis. Janet proposed the term *subconscious* to avoid the mysterious qualities that were already associated with Freud's use of the term *unconscious*. On its way to present usage, Morton Prince characterized dissociated states as *coconscious* to, in Hilgard's (1986) words, "emphasize the splitting of a normal consciousness into separate parts" (p. 5). The key ingredient for dissociated consciousness is an "amnesic barrier that prevents integration of the dissociated systems."

Hilgard explored dissociated consciousness in people who are highly hypnotizable. He suspected that dissociated consciousness could be observed in people who would not be characterized as abnormal. Fugues, multiple personalities, and possession states certainly epitomize the phenomenon, but Hilgard argued that minor dissociations occur in everyday experience and in hypnosis. Compulsive behavior or recurrent, obsessive thoughts are examples, and these are readily induced under hypnosis.

Hilgard used two experimental methods to get at these minor dissociations. Under hypnosis, certain individuals carry out suggestions to feel no pain in a portion of the body so well that normally painful procedures can be performed in dentistry and medicine without the administration of anesthetics. Only highly hypnotizable individuals are capable of this feat. Hilgard used the cold pressor method to induce pain by asking a person to leave his or her arm in a bucket of ice water for as long as he or she could tolerate. Shown in Figure 14.2 are the verbal pain reports of these individuals in the normal waking state (upper curve); after 20 to 30 seconds in the ice water, the pain is immense. But under deep hypnosis, the same individuals can tolerate the pain without difficulty, as shown by the lower curve in Figure 14.2.

The second method Hilgard called the "hidden observer." He asked the participant to go deeper in hypnosis and find the part of the mind that is aware of the true level of pain. The so-called **hidden observer,** then, theoretically represents a dissociated part of consciousness that can be tapped through hypnosis. In the study plotted in Figure 14.2, the hidden observer was prompted to press a key that represents the covert or real level of pain. As can be seen, the hidden observer experienced much greater discomfort than the hypnotized self, though still less than the waking self.

In examining these curves, bear in mind that these are the same individuals in all three. Only under hypnosis does the individual not feel

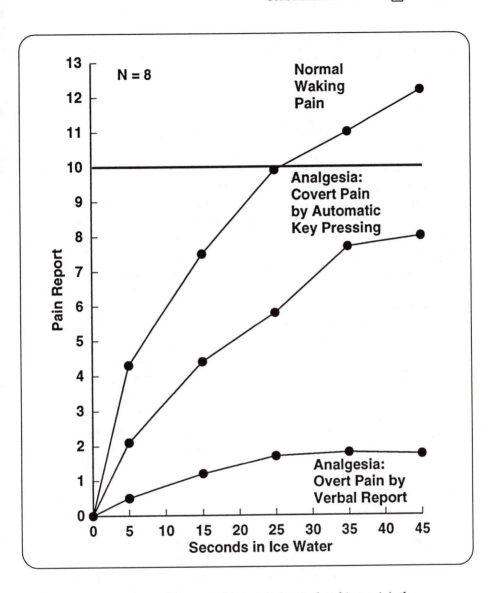

Figure 14.2. Pain reports from a waking state (normal waking pain), the hidden observer (covert pain), and a hypnotized state (overt pain).
SOURCE: From Hilgard (1986). Copyright © 1986 by John Wiley & Sons. Reprinted by permission.

the pain (as reported through introspection, just as in the waking condition), but at another level of awareness the pain nonetheless registered.

The hidden observer therefore seems to reveal dissociated consciousness much like that observed by clinical psychologists in the realm of mental disorders.

Dreaming and Daydreaming

Other researchers have investigated the differences between waking and dreaming consciousness. As pointed out earlier in the book, waking consciousness reflects either directed or undirected thoughts. The undirected thoughts of daydreaming take us only partway into the dreams of **rapid eye movement (REM) sleep.** When we daydream, the imagination takes hold and sends us into the past or the future. But for most of us the daydream shares more in common with the consciousness of directed thought than it does with REM dreaming. Highly hypnotizable individuals, between 1% and 5% of the population (Hilgard, 1986), experience the vividness of imagination that characterizes our dreams, but the vast majority do not. The **hypnogogic images** that float through consciousness as we fall asleep, and the **hypnopompic images** that bid us as we awake, come closer to dreams, but even they fall short. Consciousness assumes different appearances depending on whether we are awake (and, if so, how much) or whether we are asleep (and, if so, in what stage). The paradoxical sleep of REM brings to us an entirely different world, one that in Freud's view held the secrets of the unconscious and human personality.

Dreaming

Characteristics of dreaming. Aserinsky and Kleitman (1953) discovered over four decades ago that REM or paradoxical sleep often yields a report of dreaming if the person is aroused and asked to describe what has just occurred. It is called paradoxical sleep because some signs indicate the person is awakening while others show the opposite. The EEG pattern reveals the high-frequency, low-amplitude beta waves characteristic of Stage 1 sleep. Autonomic arousal, such as increased heartbeat and respiration, is also observed together with the rapid movement of the eyes. It is as if the person is on the verge of awakening, yet it is difficult to arouse a person from REM sleep and the muscle system is relaxed, virtually paralyzed. It is as if the eyes are scanning an internal drama while the body remains immobile, unable to physically act out the scenes.

When aroused during non-REM (NREM) sleep, people also report mental activity. But NREM thoughts lack the intensely visual, almost hallucinatory, narratives of dreaming (Antrobus, 1983). A story unfolds for the dreamer as if it were really happening, though at times the scenes and events are so jumbled and bizarre that they lack any contact with reality. Dreaming, then, is an altered state of consciousness that all of us experience, without the use of drugs, hypnosis, or meditation techniques (Tart, 1969). Even individuals who rarely if ever remember their dreams have them virtually every night; so-called nondreamers are just as likely as others to report dreams when aroused during REM sleep in the sleep laboratory (Dement, 1978).

Sources of dreams. Whereas Freud looked to psychological conflicts in the unconscious for the source of dreams, cognitive scientists have looked at a combination of psychological and neural factors. To begin, several theorists suggested that dreaming originates in the right hemisphere (Broughton, 1975; Galin, 1974; Ornstein, 1972). This proposal followed Gazzaniga's (1970) discovery that the right hemisphere specialized to a degree in visual-spatial processing, judging from his work with split-brain patients. It should follow that the right hemisphere is differentially activated during REM sleep.

Antrobus (1987) failed to find any such thing in his review of the relevant literature. He concluded in fact that the left hemisphere was more essential for dreaming than the right. More specifically, Antrobus argued that a dream is much more than visual imagery. It also contains a story line that emerges from the interpretations the dreamer assigns to visual images. Because the perceptual and cognitive systems of the brain receive no environmental input during dreaming, they are left to generate it on their own. Under these conditions, Antrobus suggested, the right and the left hemispheres generate images with abandon, some of which are completely out of the context of the narrative occurring in a given dream. The left hemisphere, however, is given the task of interpreting the images generated by both hemispheres. If an out-of-context image pops up, then the left hemisphere alters the story sequence and attempts to accommodate the image in as realistic a scene as possible.

For example, one participant in Antrobus's (1978) research reported, when awakened from REM sleep, that she had noticed the fingernail of

BOX 14.2: Altered Consciousness

Since the dawn of recorded history, people have ingested psychoactive chemicals to alter their state of consciousness (Brecher, 1972). Drugs have been used in America since the colonial period for purposes of recreation and self-medication. Today is certainly no exception. According to a 1990 national survey, 5% of high school seniors in America reported the use of cocaine and 2% admitted use of crack, a particularly powerful form of the drug (Johnston, O'Malley, & Bachman, 1991). The same survey showed fully one third of the students trying one or more illicit drugs during the past year. More than 100 million Americans drink alcohol (Engs, Slawinska, & Hanson, 1991).

The manner and degree to which a psychoactive substance alters normal consciousness depends on several factors (Tart, 1975). Obviously, the chemical composition, dosage, and method of administration are important. Less obvious are the immediate psychological factors of mood, expectations, and desires of the drug taker. The same drug dosage, taken in the same manner, can produce pleasurable or adverse alterations of consciousness, depending on, for example, the user's expectations. Long-term psychological factors also affect the experience, such as the individual's culture, personality, physiology, and previous drug experience. The physical and social environment in which drugs are taken also mediates their effects, as powerfully shown by placebo effects. If people are led to believe they have consumed alcohol and the social environment is conducive to an altered state of consciousness, then they may act and feel intoxicated right along with those who drank the real thing (Marlatt, 1978).

One reason for such drug use is thrill seeking (Shedler & Block, 1990). Some individuals alter their consciousness on an occasional basis simply for the fun of it. Another reason lies in attempts to enrich inner experiences that normally are impoverished. Segal et al. (1980) observed that "individuals who lack a well-developed capacity for self-entertainment through fantasy or for shifting from unpleasant thoughts to playful positive images may be especially susceptible to resorting to drugs or alcohol on a regular basis to reduce negative affect" (p. 221).

Social factors also play a role. Individuals with no direction, meaning, or hope in their lives, a common pattern among high school dropouts without job skills, are susceptible to heavy substance use (Newcomb & Harlow, 1986). Further, among teenagers at least, peer pressure to use alcohol and other drugs is an extremely powerful influence (Oetting & Beauvais, 1987). An individual is likely to be a user if his or her friends are users. There is also clearly a genetic predisposition to abuse alcohol and possibly other drugs. For example, adopted children are more susceptible to alcohol abuse if their biological parents were also abusers (Mirin & Weiss, 1989).

a person in her dream "was flatter than the others." Immediately, the story line of her dream shifted to deal with this strange image. The characters suddenly talked the matter over and concluded "that probably she hit herself and that was the reason" (p. 577). Antrobus (1987) described another unpublished study in which participants were reinforced while awake to find images, from a variety of pictures at their disposal, of running scenes whenever a high-pitched tone occurred. Alternatively, they found cutting scenes when a low tone occurred. Later, when participants were asleep, these images were cued by sounding either a high- or a low-pitched tone. The intriguing results were described as follows:

> Presentation of the high tone in REM sleep typically elicited mentation reports in which a character was running; cutting was observed with the low tone (Kute, 1982). The ingenuity with which sleeping subjects incorporated the externally signaled features into their ongoing mentation was truly astounding. . . . the sleeper in Stage 1 REM produces mentation in such a way as to make sense of the currently active goals and meanings. Some sleep mentation may, indeed, be interpretations of external stimuli, as Maury (cited in MacKenzie, 1965) suggested when, during the French Revolution, his bed rail fell on his neck and he awakened with the dream that he had just been guillotined. Incorporated stimuli need not awaken the subject, as illustrated by the Dement and Wolpert (1958) study where subjects reported dreams of being "squirted" by someone, sudden rainfall, or leaking roofs, after being gently sprayed with water by the experimenter and awakened 30 seconds later. (Antrobus, 1987, p. 365)

In a related vein, Hobson and McCarley (1977) proposed an activation-synthesis theory of dreaming. They described in detail the neurological structures that bring eye movement information from the brain stem up to the cortex. This information serves as input to activate the cortex. Specifically, the pontine brain stem originates the information that produces bursts of activity in the visual areas of the cortex. These are called pontine-lateral geniculate-occipital (PGO) spike bursts. They assumed the PGO bursts come spontaneously to the cortex. The bizarreness of the resulting dream, then, stems from the difficulty experienced in synthesizing this eye movement information within the context of the ongoing mentation in the cortex.

Seligman and Yellen (1987) further suggested that the difficulties in synthesis involved more than trying to integrate visual images into a coherent story. At the same time that spontaneous eye movement information reaches the cortex, powerful emotions are also being generated from elsewhere in the brain. The task is thus one of integrating unrelated visual images, on the one hand, and often unrelated emotional episodes, on the other. The dreamer synthesizes, integrates, or interprets the visual and emotional streams in perhaps the only manner possible, as a loosely structured, surprising story.

Antrobus (1991) concluded that input to the cortex is not only visual and emotional, but essentially duplicates the normal input of waking consciousness. Antrobus's connectionist model, DREAMIT:BP, highlights the links between normal imaginative processes and dreaming. As Antrobus (1991) observed:

> The imagery and thought of sleep occur periodically when in Stage 1 REM, subcortical processes activate in a distributed manner a large portion of the cortical processes that, in the waking state, compute perceptual, cognitive, and motor responses to external stimuli. Sleep imagery and thought, therefore, share many of the characteristics of waking responses to sensory stimuli. These responses include the creation of perceptual features that are predominately visual in character but also include the auditory and haptic modalities. Also included are most of the cognitive responses of identification or recognition, the interpretation of relationships among the perceptual features, the interpretation of the meaning of objects and event sequences, problem solving, and the cognitive and premotor processes of motor response. (p. 107)

But REM sleep shows additional characteristics not found in waking cognition. The first is that sensory input and motor output are strongly inhibited for prolonged periods of time. The lack of external input and proprioceptive feedback leads the dreamer to believe that the imagined story is every bit as real as waking perception. Antrobus (1991) noted: "It is this belief in the reality of imagined events that earns the REM experience the label *hallucinatory*" (p. 107). As noted earlier, the dreamer must then interpret bizarre images by modifying the story for they cannot be simply dismissed as "fanciful." Suddenly finding oneself before a hissing three-headed snake leaves but two options: fight or flee. Ignoring it and hoping a better image will come along just will not do. The lack of any constraints on what might pop up next and the constant need to adjust the story to these images give dreams a bizarre quality not seen in waking, unaltered cognition.

Daydreaming

IPI data. Singer and Antrobus (1963, 1972) investigated daydreaming through a questionnaire called the **Imaginal Processes Inventory (IPI)**. It consists of a series of self-descriptions such as "I am aroused and excited by a daydream" or "I daydream about what I would like to see happen in the future." People indicate the degree to which the statement applies to them. The 28 scales of the IPI measure individuals' thinking style (e.g., distractibility, rate of thinking, and imagery), attitudes about daydreaming (e.g., acceptance of daydreaming as a normal activity for adults), and daydream contents (e.g., hostile daydreams versus guilt daydreams).

By analyzing the correlations of the scales that make up the IPI, Singer and Antrobus concluded that three factors independently operate in daydreaming. They described these as the factors of Positive-Vivid Daydreaming, Anxious-Distractible Daydreaming or Mindwandering, and Guilty-Dysphoric Daydreaming. We differ in the extent to which our daydreams are vivid and positive in outlook, for example. Armed with a well-defined measurement scale, researchers have probed into how our daydreams differ across the life span and among groups. It appears that we daydream regardless of age, though sexual and heroic daydreams decline with advanced age (Giambra, 1974).

Thought sampling. Pope (1977) reported that when thinking aloud, people shift their thoughts to a new topic every 30 seconds or so. When asked to press a key each time their thoughts wandered to a new topic while thinking silently, these shifts occurred much more frequently, on the order of every 5 or 6 seconds. Klinger (1978), based on his work with thought sampling, contended that the normal stream of consciousness fluctuates in topic very close to these shorter time estimates.

Klinger sampled thoughts at random intervals by interrupting participants with a beeper. They were to report whatever they were thinking when the beeper sounded (and they were permitted to turn the beeper off during activities that would prove too embarrassing to report). The beeper sounded about every 40 minutes on average and the participants carried it, whenever awake, for 24 hours a day for many days. Upon hearing the beeper, they reported their inner experiences using a Thought-Sampling Questionnaire. The participants also reported on their thoughts while in a laboratory setting. While listening to two simultaneous prose narratives through headphones, they were interrupted roughly once every minute on average by a tone. They then reported on the contents of their thoughts as they did in the out-of-lab setting.

First, Klinger found that people estimated the length of their thoughts in the lab setting at nearly 9 seconds, compared with nearly 15 seconds outside the lab. The nature of their thoughts are shown in Table 14.1. It may be seen that directed thoughts were more common outside the lab than in the lab, and that these directed thoughts took on a more specific as opposed to vague character. Paying attention to external cues and recalling those cues later were two to three times more likely outside the lab. People found the natural environment more interesting than the lab.

Similarities Among Modes of Consciousness

Shepard (1984) suggested that perceiving, imagining, thinking, and dreaming are governed by the same laws of mental representation. He argued that our species has acquired, over our evolutionary history, a set of constraints on how mental representations are structured. The Euclidean space of the external environment and the way objects and events change in the environment (i.e., the laws of kinematic geometry) provide the source of these constraints.

Our mental representations are activated in different ways and in different degrees under various modes of consciousness. In Figure 14.3, we can see Shepard's portrayal of four modes, with the arrow at the top of the rectangle reflecting conceptually driven processes, those that are most abstract. The arrows at the bottom represent the data-driven processes, those that are most concrete or sensory in nature. The direction and length of the arrows represent distinctions among perceiving, imagining or remembering, dreaming or hallucinating, and thinking.

For example, perceiving under ideal circumstances Shepard sees as data driven, whereas under reduced or ambiguous circumstances, it is a mixture of conceptual and data-driven processing. Notice that the only difference in dreaming or hallucinating, on the one hand, and imagining or remembering, on the other, is in the degree of top-down activation.

Table 14.1 Qualities of Thought and Imagery

Quality	In Lab (N = 936 thoughts) %	Out of Lab (N = 285 thoughts) %	Significance: Level of Difference[a]
Specific (versus vague)	60	70	$p < .02$
Directed (all or mainly)	36	56	$p < .02$
Undirected (all or mainly)	43	27	$p < .01$
Detailed (greatly or moderately)	66	48	n.s.
Number of things at one time (more than one)	46	61	n.s.
Visual (very or moderately)	61	64	n.s.
Auditory (very or moderately)	20	38	n.s.
Attentiveness to external cues (great or fair amount)	32	66	$p < .02$
Recall for external cues (at least moderate)	21	77	$p < .005$
Controllability (complete or moderate)	56	77	n.s.
Trust in memory of thought (complete or moderate)	89	91	n.s.
Familiarity (similar to normal daily experience)	87	—	—
Usualness (at least fair)	—	96	—
Strangeness/distortedness (very or somewhat)	—	22	—
Time of life (present)	50	75	$p < .05$
(past)	17	5	$p < .01$
(future)	5	6	n.s.
(no special time)	28	14	n.s.

SOURCE: From Klinger (1978). Copyright © 1978 by Plenum Press. Reprinted by permission.
NOTE: a. p less than .05 or smaller implies the difference between the in-lab and out-of-lab percentages was statistically reliable.

Note, too, that these two modes differ from thinking only in the degree to which the internal representations are activated. Thinking therefore shares much in common with having sensations; only the former comes entirely from the top down, and the latter from the bottom up.

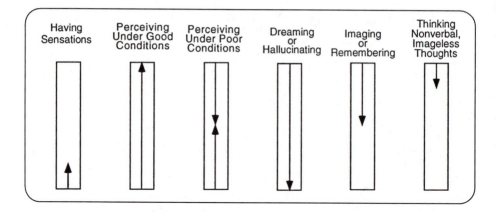

Figure 14.3. Modes of excitation in a system of perception and representation when it is activated from without (arrow pointing up) and from within (arrow pointing down). The arrow in the lower half of each rectangle corresponds to relatively more concrete, sensory excitation; the arrow in the upper half of each rectangle corresponds to relatively more abstract, conceptual excitation.

SOURCE: From *Images of Mind* by Posner and Raichle. Copyright © 1994 by Scientific American Library. Used with permission of W. H. Freeman and Company.

Properties of Waking Consciousness

Narration

Consciousness is characterized, first of all, by a running narrative or interpretation of our environment, our perceptions, our thoughts, and our beliefs. Jaynes (1976) characterized the narrative nature of consciousness in the following way:

> Seated where I am, I am writing a book and this fact is imbedded more or less in the center of the story of my life, time being spatialized into a journey of my days and years. New situations are selectively perceived as part of this ongoing story, perceptions that do not fit into it being unnoticed or at least not remembered. More important, situations are chosen which are congruent to this ongoing story, until the picture I have of myself in my life story determines how I am to act and choose in novel situations as they arise. (pp. 63-64)

Klinger (1990) found with thought-sampling techniques that the stream of everyday thinking and daydreaming are characterized by an incessant self-narratization. When outside the lab, we talk to ourselves 75% of the time, judging from the reports of people at the moments when the beeper sounded. In fact, about 50% of the probes yielded fairly complete statements of running commentaries and the remaining 25% produced only a few words. Klinger summarized these findings as follows:

> We talk to ourselves continually, even when we seem to be quiet. Even the reputedly taciturn Scandinavian-American Minnesotans who made up a large part of our beeper sample chattered away to themselves most of the time. . . . The single most common feature of daydreams and other thoughts is self-talk. We hear an unexpected sound and say to ourselves, "What the heck was that?" We walk along appreciating the nice weather, and comment to ourselves, "What a nice day!" We play through our minds an image of a friend. We see him in our daydreams smiling and talking and we think in nearly so many words, "I wonder if he'll visit. I wonder if he really cares about me." (p. 68)

As we saw earlier with dreaming, waking consciousness tries to interpret the events that pass through it. The most striking demonstration of this fact comes from Gazzaniga's (1985, 1992) work with split-brain patients. One such patient was presented with the word *walk* in the left visual field, meaning that it was processed solely by the right hemisphere. The individual could not report the word because, being left hemisphere dominant, the language centers failed to register the word. The person had no conscious awareness of having seen *walk*. Yet, the individual arose from the chair and started to walk out of the mobile laboratory, a van parked next to the patient's house. When the experimenter asked, "Where are you going?" the patient responded, "I'm going into the house to get a Coke." This incident was but one of many observed by Gazzaniga in which the left hemisphere tried to interpret behavior initiated unconsciously by the right hemisphere. Although the individual had no awareness or recollection of the word *walk*, interpretative systems of the left hemisphere took control of the situation and generated an appropriate narrative to explain his behavior.

Gazzaniga labeled the brain mechanisms responsible for these explanations of behavior, the "interpreter." He suggested that its primary function is to interpret the actions of other automatic modules of the brain that elicit thoughts, emotions, and behaviors. Calvin (1990) similarly referred to this function as the "narrator" of consciousness, but he stressed that it need not be associated with a particular neural circuit or even be localized in the left hemisphere. Although the specific neural circuits for the "interpreter" or "narrator" of consciousness are unclear, there seems little doubt that a major function of consciousness is to provide coherent causal explanations of ongoing events.

Sequential Construction

Matters of timing. A second property of consciousness is its sequential, constructive nature (Baars, 1988). From the moment that a stimulus occurs, there is a lag of 500 milliseconds before a conscious experience enters awareness (Libet, 1981). During this time, perceptual processes construct or, in Gibson's direct perception wording, pick up the stimulus information. As the sensory and conceptual features of the stimulus are processed, information "snowballs" until entry into consciousness becomes possible (Baars, 1988). The information then remains in consciousness for a minimum of 50 and a maximum of 200 milliseconds (Blumenthal, 1977). Typically, the duration of a conscious moment is about 100 milliseconds. In Chapters 2 and 3, we reviewed the nature of perceptual and attentional processes at work here.

No one doubts that people can apprehend many events in the environment over the course of several seconds. As Baars noted, a stimulus remains available in short-term memory at least 10 seconds and can be readily brought back into the focus of attention, the gateway to consciousness. But within the narrow window of 100 milliseconds, sequential processing appears to be the rule.

The global workspace. Baars placed these and many other facts about perception, attention, memory, comprehension, problem solving, reasoning, and thinking into a **global workspace theory** of consciousness. His theory contains three elements: a global workspace, specialized unconscious processors, and contexts (see Figure 14.4). Consciousness is defined as a central information exchange, the global workspace, in which specialized processors broadcast messages to the entire cognitive system. Metaphorically, consciousness is similar to a blackboard information system that acts as a central exchange for messages that must reach many recipients. Each message, an unconscious specialized processor, competes for entry into the global workspace. Its output becomes conscious, in the form of a percept, an image, or a thought, once it "snowballs" sufficiently and powerfully relative to all competitors.

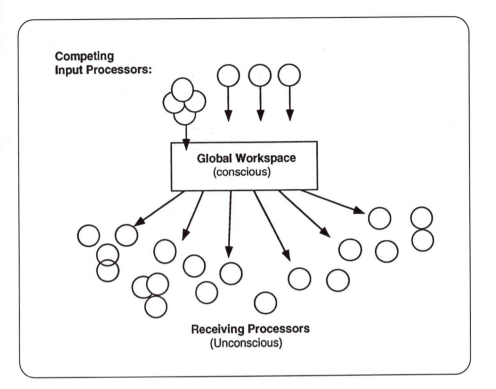

Figure 14.4. The global work space theory of consciousness.
SOURCE: From Baars, B. J. (1988). *A cognitive theory of consciousness.* Cambridge: Cambridge University Press. Copyright © 1988 by Cambridge University Press. Reprinted with the permission of Cambridge University Press.

Once a message enters the global workspace, it is broadcast everywhere in the nervous system. This provides feedback to the specialized processors initiating messages. It also alerts all processors of news of global importance, so important that it made entry to the broadcast station of the global workspace. If the receivers of these feedback signals start to originate messages related to the current occupant of consciousness, then one of them will gain entry next.

Remember that entry is sequential and each message persists only 100 milliseconds. To sustain a train of thought for 15 to 20 seconds, it is necessary for a lengthy sequence of related messages to enter the workspace, one at a time. If the global message is not very popular with the receiving processors, then they will send back different messages, unrelated to the current occupant of the workspace. The result is that the thought of the moment quickly loses access to the workspace, and a new thought arises.

A specialized processor is defined as "a relatively unitary, organized set of processes that work together in the service of a particular function" (Baars, 1988, p. 50). Each processor can be viewed as a special skill that is highly practiced, automatic, and unconscious. The theory illustrates **modularity** (Fodor, 1983), wherein each specialized processor or module works quickly and automatically within a narrow domain. For example, one might be dedicated to face recognition, whereas another handles speech recognition. Although they serve us well most of the time, they fail whenever we are confronted with a novel, degraded, or ambiguous stimulus. No single processor can cope with these troublesome situations, according to Baars.

Contexts, the third element of Baars's theory, are really just clusters of unconscious processors. Whenever these processors work together to cope with a troublesome situation, they strengthen their likelihood of being called upon again in the future. Contexts govern the way information is processed and bias entry into the global workspace.

Executive Control

Another property often attributed to consciousness is a central role in controlling the cognitive system. Recall that Baddeley's (1986) model of working memory placed the central executive at the heart of things. Shallice (1988) refers to this property as the **supervisory attentional system (SAS).** The defining feature of the central executive or SAS is its decision-making power. As we have seen, schemas can operate automatically in certain well-learned tasks, such as driving a car or carrying on a conversation. At times, however, such schemas may conflict with each other, as when traffic suddenly becomes congested while one is driving on a highway. To continue a conversation with a partner in the car would be hazardous in dense traffic. The central executive or SAS sets priorities in such a case, inhibiting the conversation schemas and allocating greater attention to the driving schemas.

Damage to the frontal lobes of the brain disrupts the normal functioning of executive control, a disorder termed the *dysexecutive syndrome* by Baddeley (1986). Patients with frontal lobe damage repeatedly say or do the same thing over and over again. They also will repeatedly pick up objects within reach, regardless of whether it is socially appropriate to do so. It appears that they lack control over schemas that are running amuck automatically. It is as if SAS or the central executive fails to inhibit some schemas and activate others to maintain control over behavior (Shallice, 1988).

Other models, such as Baars's theory (1988), deny the need for a central executive. Each specialized processor acts as its own executive; control is wholly decentralized. As Baars (1988) noted: "The processors themselves decide what to take on and what to ignore" (p. 87). Consciousness still serves in a centralized capacity, however. It does so by serving as a global blackboard or message exchange center, as described earlier. The value of this central facility is not in controlling the flow of information but in providing all the specialized processors with the information they need to make proper decisions in a decentralized fashion. Baars (1988) illustrates the idea by asking us to imagine an assembly of many experts:

> Suppose this assembly were called upon to solve a series of problems that could not be handled by any one expert alone. Various experts could agree or disagree on different parts of the problem, but there would be a problem of communication: Each expert can best understand and express what he or she means to say by using a technical jargon that may not be fully understood by all the other experts. One helpful step in solving this communication problem is to make public a *global* message on a large blackboard in front of the auditorium, so that in principle anyone can read the message and react. In fact, it would only be read by experts who could understand it or parts of it, but one cannot know ahead of time who those experts are, so that it is necessary to make it potentially available to anyone in the audience. (pp. 87-88)

Through the global workspace, then, decisions are made locally, not centrally, but their results are communicated to all.

Schacter (1989) also separated the conscious awareness system (CAS) from the executive system, as shown in Figure 14.5. The CAS is activated by specialized knowledge modules, similar to those in Baars's model. It then sends outputs to an executive system that regulates what to attend to next and initiates all voluntary acts of cognition, such as memory search, planning, decision making, and voluntary motor behavior. The key point to make about Schacter's model is that the CAS and executive system are separate, a view that several neuropsychological studies validate.

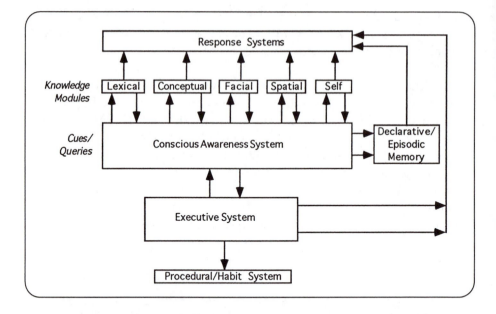

Figure 14.5. The conscious awareness system (CAS) versus executive control.
SOURCE: From Schacter, D. L. (1989). On the relation between memory and consciousness: Dissociable interactions and conscious experience. In H. L. Roediger III & F. I. M. Craik (Eds.), *Varieties of memory and consciousness: Essays in honour of Endel Tulving* (pp. 355-389). Hillsdale, NJ: Lawrence Erlbaum. Copyright © 1989 by Lawrence Erlbaum Associates. Reprinted by permission.

Some neuropsychological evidence suggests that consciousness, the CAS of Schacter's model, is localized in only a few components of the brain (Diamond, 1976). These include the posterior region of the cortex along with the parietal lobes on each side of the brain. Another key component is the posterior regions of the corpus callosum, the structure that connects the two hemispheres. In the split-brain procedure, Gordon, Bogen, and Sperry (1971) found that severing the posterior third of the corpus callosum produced a disturbance in conscious awareness. Cutting the remaining portions had no such effect. Similarly, patients with lesions in this critical area cannot attend selectively and experience confusion and disorientation (Whitty & Lewin, 1960). Parietal lesions also produce confusional states (Geschwind, 1982).

The final piece of evidence comes from the disorder of **anosognosia,** which entails a lack of awareness of cognitive deficits. The anosognosic patient may suffer from severe motor or perceptual deficits yet lack any awareness of the loss. A particularly striking example occurs in the case of total blindness, with vision lost in adulthood. Despite losing all visual ability, the patients show no signs of panic or any other indicator that they are aware of their loss. Lesions in the critical parietal lobes have been detected in anosognosic patients (Schacter, 1989).

It must be noted that other theorists question whether consciousness can be localized in a particular area of the brain (Calvin, 1990; Dennett, 1991; Sperry, 1969). Alternatively, consciousness might be best viewed as a property of many, if not all, neural systems acting in concert. A related idea that will be returned to in the final section is to view consciousness as an emergent property of neural activity throughout the brain. In understanding the brain correlates of consciousness, it would help to differentiate noetic consciousness from autonoetic. It may be that the self-consciousness associated with reflections on autobiographical information is handled differently by the brain than the consciousness involved in knowing the internal and external environment.

The Mind-Body Problem

This is not an ideal place to review the philosophical disputes that have raged over the relationship of the mind to the brain. The territory is too vast to even begin to do it justice. Nevertheless, a chapter on consciousness can scarcely ignore the matter altogether.

Classic Viewpoints

Simply put, there have been two traditional ways of characterizing the relations between the nervous system, principally the brain, and the subjective experience of consciousness, the mind. First, **dualism** holds that the two are separate entities. The identity version of dualism further argues that each state in the brain is associated with a unique state of mind—the two are perfectly correlated. The second view, **monism,** holds that one can reduce the mind to the brain or, alternatively, that one can reduce the brain to mind. The second reading of this—that all is mind—has had significant success in Eastern mysticism but is not taken as a serious, working hypothesis of Western science. So we will restrict our attention to the materialistic version of monism. **Materialism** holds that all mind is nothing but matter, neural matter to be precise.

Hilgard (1980), in the passage quoted at the beginning of the chapter, essentially argued the dualist position as a useful heuristic for psychological research. Instead of trying to reduce the mind to the brain, or otherwise speculating on their relationship, cognitive psychologists might be best served by not taking a stand at all. As Hilgard (1980) stated: "The position here recommended is sometimes called a double-language theory that need not commit itself regarding ultimates" (p. 15). On the one hand, there is a language for describing subjective conscious states of mind (e.g., verbal protocols or related forms of introspection) and, on the other, a language for describing physical brain activities (e.g., EEG or PET scans).

The materialistic road to reducing the mind to brain states also has advocates (Crick, 1994; Dennett, 1991). This position is obviously appealing from the standpoint of neuroscientists. By understanding the brain and the rest of the nervous system in sufficient detail, it will be possible to dispense with discussions of the mind altogether. Let us turn here to Dennett's (1991) wording of the materialistic and monistic position:

> The prevailing wisdom, variously expressed and argued for, is *materialism:* there is only one sort of stuff, namely *matter*—the physical stuff of physics, chemistry, and physiology—and the mind is somehow nothing but a physical phenomenon. According to the materialists, we can (in principle!) account for every mental phenomenon using the same physical principles, laws, and raw materials that suffice to explain radioactivity, continental drift, photosynthesis, reproduction, nutrition, and growth. (p. 33)

Although neuroscientists, philosophers, and members of other disciplines of cognitive science hope someday to reduce the mind to a mechanism, materialism is often dismissed by cognitive psychologists. For example, Gibson (1994) argued strongly against reductionism as an agenda for cognitive psychologists. The field should not look for "reductionistic theories, at some other level, be it neural, genetic, nuclear, or especially artificial" (p. 69). She further stated:

> However impressed I am by recent progress in neuroscience (and I am—who would not be excited by the imaging techniques that now exist?), we must not let our own science be driven by that field. . . . We are badly needed as the scientists who know how to study behavior, who can describe the intricate intertwining of perceiving and acting in the adaptive life of a human animal. (pp. 70-71)

An Interactive Synthesis

An interactive synthesis, sharing features of both classical dualism and materialism, has emerged in the wake of the cognitive revolution (Hilgard, 1980). Eccles (1966), Sperry (1969, 1980), and Pribram (1971, 1976, 1986), three of the world's most widely esteemed neuropsychologists, have all proposed variations on a theme that consciousness cannot be reduced to brain states (also see Popper & Eccles, 1977). Nor must we maintain the double language of dualism, as if mind and matter were entirely separate entities. All these theorists suggest, in various forms, that consciousness is an emergent property of neural matter that then interacts with the very same neural matter from which it came.

The mind takes on a life of its own; it cannot be reduced to matter. Further, it cannot be seen as some separate stuff that has no connection with matter. Rather, the mind, or consciousness, is an emergent property of the brain. Consciousness emerges from the workings of the brain; it then can interact with the brain, the very organ from which it presumably arose, a hypothesis called **interactionism.** Consciousness can directly affect the ongoing activities of the brain, according to this nondualistic theory. How all this happens is still disputed by those who subscribe to interactionism (Pribram, 1986).

Neither materialistic monism nor dualism captures the true nature of consciousness, if it indeed is an emergent property of neural matter. Sperry (1993) put the matter well:

> The new position is mentalistic, holding that behavior is mentally and subjectively driven. This, however, does not mean that it is dualistic. In the new synthesis, mental states, as dynamic emergent properties of brain activity, become inseparably interfused with and tied to the brain activity of which they are an emergent property. Consciousness in this view cannot exist apart from the functioning brain. (p. 879)

The emergent property position of interactionism is a complicated stand to take. But it must be remembered that the brain may well be the most complex object in the known universe. Given this complexity, the emergent property view deserves consideration, for although it seems at odds with what we regard as the physical laws of the universe, the brain may well be unlike other objects in certain respects. Remember that the human cerebral cortex alone involves 55,000,000,000 neurons with as many as 10,000 connections branching from a single neuron (Baars, 1988;

Mountcastle, 1979). Add in the other areas of the brain plus a complicated biochemical factory of neurotransmitters and one can only stand back in awe.

Here in the 1990s, the Decade of the Brain, we may be reaching for a prize beyond our grasp: an ultimate explanation of consciousness. Is the human brain too complicated to understand itself in full detail?

The Future of Cognitive Psychology

Regardless of the answer to this question, the research will proceed. These are exciting times for cognitive psychology and the other cognitive sciences. It is not an idle wish to expect that the physical, biological, and psychological sciences will begin to converge in the foreseeable future (Pribram, 1986). In 1991 at the 99th Annual Convention of the American Psychological Association, Sperry (1993) speculated that psychology may well be taking the lead in advancing such a convergence as a result of work on consciousness.

As Sperry (1993) put it: "In the cognitive revolution psychology is leading the way among the sciences to a new and improved, that is, a more comprehensive, adequate, and valid conceptual foundation for scientific as well as for all causal explanation and understanding" (p. 878). Developments in brain theory, evolutionary theory, and quantum theory are all leading us to reject the "traditional reductive (or microdeterminist) physicalism, heretofore accepted as a seemingly incontestable, complete, and coherent working paradigm for science, time tested over centuries" (p. 882).

As exciting as this all will be for scientists, what will it do for humanity as a whole? On this point, Sperry gave an even more stunning forecast. He wondered, along with B. F. Skinner, whether the American Psychological Association or any human organization could count on another century of existence, given the threats our species has created for its own survival. Thermonuclear war, overpopulation, destruction of the rain forests, ozone depletion—the list is a familiar one that need not be fully recounted here. Skinner, late in his life, became less optimistic about our chances as he learned more and more about the nature of human behavior. Sperry, in contrast, sees hope as we learn more and more about human cognition. Let us close, optimistically, with Sperry's (1993) forecast:

Nothing in science today is of more basic importance than the effort to save science and all the other hard-won legacies of eons of evolution. . . . What is needed to remedy our present self-destructive course is going to involve major changes worldwide in human thinking and behavior. . . . For the first time, the cognitive-mentalist paradigm now makes possible a science-based approach to Global Forum type questions, such as "What kind of world do we want and what must we do to get there?" A new approach can be seen to ultimate moral issues, such as "What ideals best guide existence on planet Earth?" and "What constitutes the highest measure for right and wrong and social justice?" . . . what is needed is a basic revision worldwide in human life-styles, aims, and attitudes, with redirection of social values and policy toward more long-term priorities that will preserve an evolving quality of life for future generations. A major reconception of the human venture is called for, a higher overarching perspective including ultimate goals and values, or as Einstein put it in reference to atomic power, "We need a new way of thinking if mankind is to survive." (p. 883)

▣ SUMMARY ▣

1. Multiple systems of memory may be associated with different varieties of consciousness. *Anoetic* or nonknowing *consciousness* refers to the ability to sense and react to stimuli from the external and internal environments, and is associated with procedural memory. *Noetic* or knowing *consciousness* is associated with semantic memory and takes as its object knowledge of the world. It enables one to be introspectively aware of external and internal stimuli. *Autonoetic* or self-knowing *consciousness* enables one to be aware of his or her own identity. Associated with episodic memory, it is consciousness of the personal events of the past, present, and future.

2. Normal consciousness is both personal and sensibly continuous. It is not disconnected from the individual's sense of identity, nor is it split or disconnected from moment to moment. However, dissociative states of consciousness also exist that are characterized by their impersonal and discontinuous nature. Dissociative states include psychiatric disorders such as amnesia, fugue, and multiple personalities. Dissociated states may also be observed in highly hypnotizable individuals using a method called the hidden observer. Under

hypnosis, some people experience profound analgesia, reporting verbally little if any pain to stimuli that cause excruciating pain under waking conditions. Yet, at another dissociated level of consciousness that may be tapped by the hidden observer method, these individuals report that they are indeed aware of the pain.

3. The qualities of consciousness vary depending on whether a person is awake and attentive to the environment, daydreaming, drowsy upon awakening or preparing to fall asleep, or in various stages of sleep. During NREM sleep, people report mental activity if aroused, but it lacks the hallucinatory and narrative qualities of REM dreaming. Contemporary theories of dreaming contend that the brain generates images and emotions spontaneously that the dreamer then weaves into a story. The dreamer attempts, at times unsuccessfully, to incorporate the images and feelings into a coherent story line.

4. Daydreaming or undirected thinking while awake is a common experience. Thought-sampling studies indicate that on average about every 15 seconds (less in the laboratory) our thinking shifts in a new direction and that about a third of our thoughts outside of the laboratory are daydreams. The content of daydreams varies along three dimensions. There are individual differences in the degree to which daydreams are positive and vivid, the degree to which they exhibit "mindwandering" or distractibility, and the degree to which they express guilt and dysphoria.

5. Waking consciousness is characterized by a running narration or interpretation of our external and internal environment. Both directed and undirected thinking exhibits this property of self-narratization. Its purpose is apparently to interpret the meaning of our perceptions, thoughts, and emotions. A second property of consciousness is its sequential, constructive nature. A single event enters into consciousness after about 500 milliseconds of cognitive processing and remains there for a minimum of 50 and a maximum of 200 milliseconds. Another property sometimes assigned to consciousness is executive or supervisory control. This entails deciding which schemas should control behavior at a given moment. An alternative view regards consciousness as a global workspace; it merely receives and broadcasts the results of decisions and control that are executed locally, in a decentralized manner.

6. Two traditional explanations of the relationship between mind and body are dualism and materialism. Dualism views the two as separate entities. Each state of the brain is associated with a state of mind; the two sets of states are correlated with each other. Materialism or reductionism argues that the mind is not separate from the brain at all. Rather, the mind is nothing but the workings of the brain and other neural structures and possesses no independent existence. An interactive synthesis of these positions, stemming from cognitive psychology and neuropsychology, is interactionism. It regards the mind as an emergent property of brain functioning. The mind cannot be reduced to the brain in this view, because it is an emergent property with a separate existence. Nor is dualism a satisfactory explanation, because the mind is seen as exerting direct influence over states of the brain.

Key Terms

anoetic consciousness	global workspace theory
noetic consciousness	modularity
autonoetic consciousness	supervisory attentional
conscious awareness system (CAS)	system (SAS)
hidden observer	anosognosia
rapid eye movement (REM) sleep	dualism
hypnogogic images	monism
hypnopompic images	materialism
Imaginal Processes Inventory (IPI)	interactionism

Recommended Readings

A classic overview of human consciousness is Ornstein's (1968) collection titled *The Nature of Human Consciousness: A Book of Readings.* Hilgard's (1986) book titled *Divided Consciousness: Multiple Controls in Human Thought and Action* covers not only his pioneering research on hypnosis but all dissociative states, including possession states, fugues, amnesia, and multiple personalities. *Consciousness Reconsidered* written by Flanagan (1992) and *Consciousness: Psychological and Philosophical Essays* edited by Davies and Humphreys (1993) provide contemporary perspectives on the topic.

Two well-known works on altered states of consciousness are *States of Consciousness* by Tart (1975) and his edited collection *Altered States of Consciousness* (1969). Also of interest is Segal, Huba, and Singer's (1980) monograph titled *Drugs, Daydreaming, and Personality: A Study of College Youth.* Marlatt, Baer, Donovan, and Kivlahan (1988) treated the subject of substance abuse and Hilgard (1980) covered consciousness in all its varieties in the *Annual Review of Psychology.*

Pribram's (1971) *Languages of the Brain: Experimental Paradoxes and Principles in Neuropsychology,* Sperry's (1969) article in the *Psychological Review,* Popper and Eccles's (1977) *The Self and Its Brain,* and Eccles (1994) *How the Self Controls the Brain* are essential reading on the topic of mind-body interactionism. For a readable account of the materialistic viewpoint, I recommend Crick's (1994) *The Astonishing Hypothesis: The Scientific Search for the Soul.* Crick, the codiscoverer of the molecular structure of DNA, has turned to the neurobiology of vision in his efforts to understand consciousness. For other contemporary readings on the mind-body problem, I recommend Dennett's (1991) *Consciousness Explained* and Hill's (1991) *Sensations: A Defense of Type Materialism.*

◙ References

Abelson, R. P. (1981). Psychological status of the script concept. *American Psychologist, 36,* 715-729.

Adelson, B. (1984). When novices surpass experts: The difficulty of a task may increase with expertise. *Journal of Experimental Psychology: Learning, Memory, and Cognition, 10,* 483-495.

Akmajian, A., Demers, R. A., & Harnish, R. M. (1984). *Linguistics: An introduction to language and communication* (2nd ed.). Cambridge: MIT Press.

Alba, J. W., & Hasher, L. (1983). Is memory schematic? *Psychological Bulletin, 93,* 203-231.

Allport, D. A., Antonis, B., & Reynolds, P. (1972). On the division of attention: A disproof of the single channel hypothesis. *Quarterly Journal of Experimental Psychology, 24,* 225-235.

Anderson, J. R. (1978). Arguments concerning representations for mental imagery. *Psychological Review, 85,* 249-277.

Anderson, J. R. (Ed.). (1981). *Cognitive skills and their acquisition.* Hillsdale, NJ: Lawrence Erlbaum.

Anderson, J. R. (1983). *The architecture of cognition.* Cambridge, MA: Harvard University Press.

Anderson, J. R. (1987). Skill acquisition: Compilation of weak method problem solutions. *Psychological Review, 94,* 192-210.

Anderson, J. R. (1990). *Cognitive psychology and its implications* (3rd ed.). New York: Freeman.

Antrobus, J. S. (1978). Dreaming for cognition. In A. M. Arkin, J. S. Antrobus, & S. Ellman (Eds.), *The mind in sleep* (pp. 569-581). Hillsdale, NJ: Lawrence Erlbaum.

Antrobus, J. S. (1983). REM and NREM sleep reports: Comparison of word frequencies by cognitive classes. *Psychophysiology, 20*, 562-568.

Antrobus, J. S. (1987). Cortical hemisphere asymmetry and sleep mentation. *Psychological Review, 94,* 359-368.

Antrobus, J. S. (1991). Dreaming: Cognitive processes during cortical activation and high afferent thresholds. *Psychological Review, 98*, 96-121.

Arnheim, R. (1986). *New essays on the psychology of art.* Los Angeles: University of California Press.

Aserinsky, E., & Kleitman, N. (1953). Regularly occurring periods of ocular motility and concomitant phenomena during sleep. *Science, 118,* 361-375.

Atkinson, R. C., & Shiffrin, R. M. (1968). Human memory: A proposed system and its control processes. In K. W. Spence & J. T. Spence (Eds.), *The psychology of learning and motivation* (Vol. 2, pp. 89-195). Orlando, FL: Academic Press.

Atkinson, R. C., & Shiffrin, R. M. (1971). The control of short-term memory. *Scientific American, 225*, 82-90.

Attneave, F. (1957). Transfer of experience with a class schema to identification of patterns and shapes. *Journal of Experimental Psychology, 54*, 81-88.

Atwood, M. E., & Polson, P. G. (1976). A process model for water jar problems. *Cognitive Psychology, 8,* 191-216.

Averbach, E., & Coriell, A. S. (1961). Short-term memory in vision. *Bell System Technical Journal, 40*, 309-328.

Ayres, T. J., Jonides, J., Reitman, J. S., Egan, J. C., & Howard, D. A. (1979). Differing suffix effects for the same physical stimulus. *Journal of Experimental Psychology: Human Learning and Memory, 5*, 315-321.

Baars, B. J. (1986). *The cognitive revolution in psychology.* New York: Guilford.

Baars, B. J. (1988). *A cognitive theory of consciousness.* Cambridge: Cambridge University Press.

Baddeley, A. D. (1982). *Your memory: A user's guide.* New York: Macmillan.

Baddeley, A. D. (1986). *Working memory.* New York: Oxford University Press.

Baddeley, A. D., & Hitch, G. (1974). Working memory. In G. H. Bower (Ed.), *The psychology of learning and motivation* (Vol. 8, pp. 47-89). New York: Academic Press.

Baddeley, A. D., & Scott, D. (1971). Short-term forgetting in the absences of proactive interference. *Quarterly Journal of Experimental Psychology, 23,* 275-283.

Baddeley, A. D., & Warrington, E. K. (1970). Amnesia and the distinction between long-term and short-term memory. *Journal of Verbal Learning and Verbal Behavior, 9*, 176-189.

Badecker, W., Hillis, A., & Caramazza, A. (1990). Lexical morphology and its role in the writing process: Evidence from a case of acquired dysgraphia. *Cognition, 35*, 205-243.

Bahrick, H. P. (1983). The cognitive map of a city: 50 years of learning and memory. In G. H. Bower (Ed.), *The psychology of learning and motivation: Advances in research and theory* (Vol. 17, pp. 125-163). New York: Academic Press.

Bahrick, H. P. (1984). Semantic memory content in permastore: Fifty years of memory for Spanish learned in school. *Journal of Experimental Psychology: General, 113,* 1-29.

Bahrick, H. P., Bahrick, P. C., & Wittlinger, R. P. (1975). Fifty years of memories for names and faces: A cross-sectional approach. *Journal of Experimental Psychology: General, 104,* 54-75.

Banaji, M. R., & Crowder, R. G. (1989). The bankruptcy of everyday memory. *American Psychologist, 44,* 1185-1193.

Banks, W. P., & Krajicek, D. (1991). Perception. *Annual Review of Psychology, 42,* 305-331.

Bargh, J. A. (1989). Conditional automaticity: Varieties of automatic influence in social perception and cognition. In J. S. Uleman & J. A. Bargh (Eds.), *Unintended thought* (pp. 3-51). New York: Guilford.

Bar-Hillel, M. (1980). What features make samples seem representative? *Journal of Experimental Psychology: Human Perception and Performance, 6,* 578-589.

Baron, J., & Sternberg, R. S. (Eds.). (1986). *Teaching thinking skills: Theory and practice.* New York: Freeman.

Baron, J., & Thurston, I. (1973). An analysis of the word superiority effect. *Cognitive Psychology, 4,* 207-228.

Barsalou, L. W. (1983). Ad hoc categories. *Memory & Cognition, 11,* 211-227.

Barsalou, L. W. (1987). The instability of graded structure: Implications for the nature of concepts. In U. Neisser (Ed.), *Concepts and conceptual development: Ecological and intellectual factors in categorization* (pp. 101-140). New York: Cambridge University Press.

Barsalou, L. W., & Sewell, D. R. (1985). Contrasting the representation of scripts and categories. *Journal of Memory and Language, 24,* 646-665.

Bartlett, F. C. (1932). *Remembering: A study in experimental and social psychology.* London: Cambridge University Press.

Bartlett, J. C., & Searcy, J. (1993). Inversion and configuration of faces. *Cognitive Psychology, 25,* 281-316.

Beauvois, M. F., & Dérouesné, J. (1981). Lexical or orthographic agraphia. *Brain, 104,* 21-49.

Begg, I., & Denny, J. P. (1969). Empirical reconciliation of atmosphere and conversion interpretations of syllogistic reasoning errors. *Journal of Experimental Psychology, 81,* 351-354.

Begg, I., & White, P. (1985). Encoding specificity in interpersonal communication. *Canadian Journal of Psychology, 39,* 70-87.

Bellezza, F. S. (1986). A mnemonic based on arranging words on visual patterns. *Journal of Educational Psychology, 78,* 217-224.

Bem, D. J., & Honorton, C. (1994). Does psi exist? Replicable evidence for an anomalous process of information transfer. *Psychological Bulletin, 115,* 4-18.

Bereiter, C., & Scardamalia, M. (1987). *The psychology of written composition.* Hillsdale, NJ: Lawrence Erlbaum.

Berlyne, D. E. (1965). *Structure and direction in thinking.* New York: John Wiley.

Bernstein, J. (1993, October). In many tongues. *Atlantic Monthly,* pp. 92-102.

Bertoncini, J., Bijeljac-Babic, R., Jusczyk, P. W., Kennedy, L. J., & Mehler, J. (1988). An investigation of young infants' perceptual representations of speech sounds. *Journal of Experimental Psychology: General, 117*, 21-33.

Biederman, I. (1985). Human image understanding: Recent research and a theory. *Computer Vision, Graphics, and Image Processing, 32*, 29-73.

Biederman, I. (1987). Recognition-by-components: A theory of human understanding. *Psychological Review, 94*, 115-147.

Biederman, I., Glass, A. L., & Stacy, E. W. (1973). Searching for objects in real world scenes. *Journal of Experimental Psychology, 97*, 22-27.

Biederman, I., & Ju, G. (1988). Surface vs. edge-based determinants of visual recognition. *Cognitive Psychology, 20*, 38-64.

Binet, A. (1903). *L'Etude experimentale de l'intelligence.* Paris, France: Schleicher, Frencs.

Bjork, R. A., & Whitten, W. B. (1974). Recency-sensitive retrieval processes in long-term free recall. *Cognitive Psychology, 6*, 173-189.

Black, J. B., & Bower, G. H. (1979). Episodes as chunks in narrative memory. *Journal of Verbal Learning and Verbal Behavior, 18*, 187-198.

Blackmer, E. R., & Mitton, J. L. (1991). Theories of monitoring and the timing of repairs in spontaneous speech. *Cognition, 39*, 173-194.

Blaney, P. H. (1986). Affect and memory: A review. *Psychological Bulletin, 99*, 229-246.

Block, R. A. (1985). Education and thinking skills reconsidered. *American Psychologist, 40*, 574-575.

Blum, G. S., & Barbour, J. S. (1979). Selective inattention to anxiety-linked stimuli. *Journal of Experimental Psychology: General, 108*, 182-224.

Blumenthal, A. L. (1967). Prompted recall of sentences. *Journal of Verbal Learning and Verbal Behavior, 6*, 203-206.

Blumenthal, A. L. (1977). *The process of cognition.* Englewood Cliffs, NJ: Prentice-Hall.

Bock, J. K. (1982). Toward a cognitive psychology of syntax: Information processing contributions to sentence formulation. *Psychological Review, 89*, 1-47.

Boden, M. (1992). *The creative mind: Myths and mechanisms.* New York: Basic Books.

Bond, C. F., & Omar, A. S. (1990). Social anxiety, state dependence, and the next-in-line effect. *Journal of Experimental Social Psychology, 26*, 185-198.

Bonke, B., Fitch, W., & Millar, K. (Eds.). (1990). *Memory and awareness in anaesthesia.* Amsterdam: Swets & Zeitlinger.

Boring, E. G. (1957). *A history of experimental psychology.* Englewood Cliffs, NJ: Prentice-Hall.

Bourne, L. E., Jr. (1966). *Human conceptual behavior.* Boston: Allyn & Bacon.

Bourne, L. E., Jr. (1970). Knowing and using concepts. *Psychological Review, 77*, 546-556.

Bourne, L. E., Jr. (1982). Typicality effects in logically defined categories. *Memory & Cognition, 10*, 3-9.

Bourne, L. E., Jr., Dominowski, R. L., Loftus, E. F., & Healy, A. F. (1986). *Cognitive processes* (2nd ed.). Englewood Cliffs, NJ: Prentice-Hall.

Bourne, L. E., Ekstrand, B. R., Lovallo, W. R., Kellogg, R. T., Hiew, C. C., &

Yaroush, R. A. (1976). Frequency analysis of attribute identification. *Journal of Experimental Psychology: General, 105,* 294-312.

Bourne, L. E., Jr., & Restle, F. (1959). A mathematical theory of concept identification. *Psychological Review, 66,* 278-296.

Bousfield, W. A. (1953). The occurrence of clustering in the recall of randomly arranged associates. *Journal of General Psychology, 49,* 229-240.

Bower, G. H. (1970). Analysis of a mnemonic device. *American Psychologist, 36,* 129-148.

Bower, G. H. (1972). Mental imagery and associative learning. In L. W. Gregg (Ed.), *Cognition in learning and memory* (pp. 51-88). New York: John Wiley.

Bower, G. H. (1981). Mood and memory. *American Psychologist, 36,* 129-148.

Bower, G. H., Black, J. B., & Turner, T. J. (1979). Scripts in memory for text. *Cognitive Psychology, 11,* 177-220.

Bower, G. H., & Gilligan, S. G. (1979). Remembering information related to one's self. *Journal of Research in Personality, 13,* 420-432.

Bower, G. H., & Hilgard, E. R. (1981). *Theories of learning* (5th ed.). Englewood Cliffs, NJ: Prentice-Hall.

Bransford, J. D., & Franks, J. J. (1971). Abstraction of linguistic ideas. *Cognitive Psychology, 2,* 331-350.

Bransford, J. D., & Johnson, M. K. (1972). Contextual prerequisites for understanding: Some investigations of comprehension and recall. *Journal of Verbal Learning and Verbal Behavior, 11,* 717-726.

Bransford, J. D., Sherwood, R., Vye, N., & Rieser, J. (1986). Teaching thinking and problem solving. *American Psychologist, 41,* 1078-1089.

Bransford, J. D., & Stein, B. S. (1984). *The IDEAL problem solver.* New York: Freeman.

Brecher, E. M. (1972). *Licit & illicit drugs.* Boston: Little, Brown.

Brewer, W. F., & Treyens, J. C. (1981). Role of schemata in memory for places. *Cognitive Psychology, 13,* 207-230.

Broadbent, D. E. (1957). A mechanical model for human attention and immediate memory. *Psychological Review, 64,* 205-215.

Broadbent, D. E. (1958). *Perception and communication.* New York: Pergamon.

Broadbent, D. E. (1975). The magic number seven after fifteen years. In A. Kennedy & A. Wilkes (Eds.), *Studies in long-term memory* (pp. 3-18). London: John Wiley.

Broca, P. (1861). Remarques sur le siège de la faculté du langage atticulé suivie d'une observation d'aphémie. *Bulletin de la Société Anathropologique, Paris, 6,* 330. (Translation in R. Hernstein & E. G. Boring, 1965, *A source book in the history of psychology,* Cambridge, MA: Harvard University Press)

Brooks, L. R. (1968). Spatial and verbal components of the act of recall. *Canadian Journal of Psychology, 22,* 349-368.

Broughton, R. (1975). Biorhythmic variation in consciousness and psychological functions. *Canadian Psychological Review, 16,* 217-239.

Brown, A. L., Bransford, J. D., Ferrara, R. A., & Campione, J. C. (1983). Learning, remembering, and understanding. In J. H. Flavell & E. M. Markman (Eds.), *Handbook of child* psychology: Cognitive development (Vol. 3, pp. 77-176; P. H. Mussen, General Ed.). New York: John Wiley.

Brown, A. S. (1991). A review of the tip-of-the-tongue experience. Psychological Bulletin, 109, 204-223.

Brown, J. A. (1958). Some tests of the decay theory of immediate memory. Quarterly Journal of Experimental Psychology, 10, 12-21.

Brown, J. S., McDonald, J. L., Brown, T. L., & Carr, T. H. (1988). Adapting to processing demands in discourse production: The case of handwriting. Journal of Experimental Psychology: Human Perception and Performance, 14, 45-59.

Brown, R. W. (1976). Reference in memorial tribute to Eric Lenneberg. Cognition, 4, 125-153.

Brown, R. W., & Kulik, J. (1977). Flashbulb memories. Cognition, 5, 73-99.

Brown, R. W., & Lenneberg, E. H. (1954). A study in language and cognition. Journal of Abnormal and Social Psychology, 49, 454-462.

Brown, R., & McNeill, D. (1966). The "tip-of-the-tongue" phenomenon. Journal of Verbal Learning, 5, 325-337.

Bruner, J. S. (1990). Acts of meaning. Cambridge, MA: Harvard University Press.

Bruner, J. S., Goodnow, J. J., & Austin, G. A. (1956). A study of thinking. New York: John Wiley.

Buckhout, R. (1974). Eyewitness testimony. Scientific American, 231, 23-31.

Calvin, W. H. (1990). The cerebral symphony: Seashore reflections on the structure of consciousness. New York: Bantam.

Camerer, C. F., & Johnson, E. J. (1991). The process-performance paradox in expert judgment: How can experts know so much and predict so badly? In K. A. Ericsson & J. Smith (Eds.), Toward a general theory of expertise (pp. 195-217). Cambridge, UK: Cambridge University Press.

Cantor, N., Mischel, W., & Schwartz, J. C. (1982). A prototype analysis of psychological situations. Cognitive Psychology, 14, 45-77.

Caramazza, A. (1991). Issues in reading, writing and speaking: A neuropsychological perspective. Dordrecht, the Netherlands: Kluwer Academic.

Carlson, R. A., & Dulany, D. E. (1985). Conscious attention and abstraction in concept learning. Journal of Experimental Psychology: Learning, Memory, and Cognition, 11, 45-58.

Carr, T. H., Brown, T. L., Vavrus, L. G., & Evans, M. A. (1990). Cognitive skill maps and cognitive skill profiles: Componential analysis of individual differences in children's reading efficiency. In T. H. Carr & B. A. Levy (Eds.), Reading and its development: Component skills approaches (pp. 1-55). San Diego, CA: Academic Press.

Carr, T. H., Davidson, B. J., & Hawkins, H. L. (1978). Perceptual flexibility in word recognition: Strategies affect orthographic computation but not lexical access. Journal of Experimental Psychology: Human Perception and Performance, 4, 674-690.

Carroll, D. W. (1994). Psychology of language (2nd ed.). Pacific Grove, CA: Brooks/Cole.

Carroll, J. B. (1993). Human cognitive abilities: A survey of factor-analytic studies. Cambridge, UK: Cambridge University Press.

Cattell, R. B. (1963). Theory of fluid and crystallized intelligence: A critical experiment. *Journal of Educational Psychology, 54*, 1-22.

Cavanagh, J. P. (1972). Relation between the immediate memory span and the memory search rate. *Psychological Review, 79*, 525-530.

Ceci, S. J., & Bruck, M. (1993). Suggestibility of the child witness: A historical review and synthesis. *Psychological Bulletin, 113*, 403-439.

Ceci, S. J., Leichtman, M., Putnick, M., & Nightingale, N. (1993). Age differences in suggestibility. In D. Cicchetti & S. Toth (Eds.), *Child abuse, child development, and social policy* (pp. 117-137). Norwood, NJ: Ablex.

Ceci, S. J., & Liker, J. K. (1986). A day at the races: A study of IQ, expertise, and cognitive complexity. *Journal of Experimental Psychology: General, 115*, 255-266.

Ceci, S. J., Ross, D. F., & Toglia, M. P. (Eds.). (1989). *Perspectives on children's testimony.* New York: Springer-Verlag.

Ceraso, J., & Provitera, A. (1971). Sources of error in syllogistic reasoning. *Cognitive Psychology, 2*, 400-410.

Cermak, L. S., & Craik, F. I. M. (Eds.). (1979). *Levels of processing in human memory.* Hillsdale, NJ: Lawrence Erlbaum.

Chafe, W. L. (1990). Some things that narratives tell us about the mind. In B. K. Britton & A. D. Pellegrini (Eds.), *Narrative thought and narrative language* (pp. 79-98). Hillsdale, NJ: Lawrence Erlbaum.

Chance, J. E., & Goldstein, A. G. (1981). Depth of processing in response to own and other-race faces. *Personality and Social Psychology Bulletin, 7*, 475-480.

Chang, T. M. (1986). Semantic memory: Facts and models. *Psychological Bulletin, 99*, 199-220.

Charness, N. (1976). Memory for chess positions: Resistance to interference. *Journal of Experimental Psychology: Human Learning and Memory, 2*, 641-653.

Charness, N. (1979). Components of skill in bridge. *Canadian Journal of Psychology, 33*, 1-16.

Chase, W. G. (Ed.). (1973). *Visual information processing.* New York: Academic Press.

Chase, W. G., & Ericsson, K. A. (1981). Skilled memory. In J. R. Anderson (Ed.), *Cognitive skills and their acquisition* (pp. 141-189). Hillsdale, NJ: Lawrence Erlbaum.

Chase, W. G., & Ericsson, K. A. (1982). Skill and working memory. In G. H. Bower (Ed.), *The psychology of learning and motivation* (pp. 1-58). New York: Academic Press.

Chase, W. G., & Simon, H. A. (1973). Perception in chess. *Cognitive Psychology, 4*, 55-81.

Cheesman, I., & Merikle, P. M. (1984). Priming with and without awareness. *Perception & Psychophysics, 36*, 387-395.

Cheng, P. W., & Holyoak, K. J. (1985). Pragmatic reasoning schemas. *Cognitive Psychology, 17*, 391-416.

Cheng, P. W., Holyoak, K. J., Nisbett, R. E., & Oliver, L. M. (1986). Pragmatic versus syntactic approaches to training deductive reasoning. *Cognitive Psychology, 18*, 293-328.

Cherry, C. (1953). Some experiments on the recognition of speech with one and with two ears. *Journal of the Acoustical Society of America, 25,* 975-979.

Chi, M. T. H. (1978). Knowledge structures and memory development. In R. S. Siegler (Ed.), *Children's thinking: What develops?* (pp. 73-96). Hillsdale, NJ: Lawrence Erlbaum.

Chi, M. T. H., Bassok, M., Lewis, M., Reimann, P., & Glaser, R. (1989). Self-explanations: How students study and use examples in learning to solve problems. *Cognitive Science, 13,* 145-182.

Chi, M. T. H., Feltovich, P. J., & Glaser, R. (1981). Categorization and representation of physics problems by experts and novices. *Cognitive Science, 5,* 121-152.

Chi, M. T. H., Glaser, R., & Farr, M. J. (Eds.). (1988). *The nature of expertise.* Hillsdale, NJ: Lawrence Erlbaum.

Chipman, S. F., Segal, J. W., & Glaser, R. (Eds.). (1985). *Thinking and learning skills: Current research and open questions.* Hillsdale, NJ: Lawrence Erlbaum.

Christiaansen, R. E., & Ochalek, K. (1983). Editing misleading information from memory: Evidence for the coexistence of original and postevent information. *Memory & Cognition, 11,* 467-475.

Christianson, S. A. (1992). Emotional stress and eyewitness memory: A critical review. *Psychological Bulletin, 112,* 284-309.

Chomsky, N. (1959). Review of *Verbal Behavior* by B. F. Skinner. *Language, 35,* 26-58.

Chomsky, N. (1965). *Aspects of the theory of syntax.* Cambridge: MIT Press.

Chomsky, N. (1968). *Language and mind.* New York: Harcourt Brace Jovanovich.

Chomsky, N. (1986). *Knowledge of language: Its nature, origin, and use.* New York: Praeger.

Church, A. (1956). *Introduction to mathematical logic.* Princeton, NJ: Princeton University Press.

Cirilo, R. K. (1981). Referential coherence and text structure in story comprehension. *Journal of Verbal Learning and Verbal Behavior, 20,* 358-367.

Cirilo, R. K., & Foss, D. J. (1980). Text structure and reading time for sentences. *Journal of Verbal Learning and Verbal Behavior, 19,* 96-109.

Clark, H. H. (1977). Inferences in comprehension. In D. LaBerge & S. J. Samuels (Eds.), *Basic processes in reading: Perception and comprehension* (pp. 243-263). Hillsdale, NJ: Lawrence Erlbaum.

Clark, H. H., & Chase, W. G. (1972). On the process of comparing sentences against pictures. *Cognitive Psychology, 3,* 472-517.

Clark, H. H., & Clark, E. V. (1977). *Psychology and language.* New York: Harcourt Brace Jovanovich.

Clark, H. H., & Wilkes-Gibbs, D. (1986). Referring as a collaborative process. *Cognition, 22,* 1-39.

Cleary, L. M. (1991). Affect and cognition in the writing processes of eleventh graders: A study of concentration and emotion. *Written Communication, 8,* 473-507.

Cohen, J. (1969). *Statistical power and analysis for the behavioral sciences.* New York: Academic Press.

Cole, M., & Scribner, S. (1974). *Culture and thought: A psychological introduction.* New York: John Wiley.

Cole, R. A., & Jakimik, J. (1980). A model of speech perception. In R. A. Cole (Ed.), *Perception and production of fluent speech* (pp. 133-163). Hillsdale, NJ: Lawrence Erlbaum.

Collins, A. M., & Loftus, E. F. (1975). A spreading activation theory of semantic processing. *Psychological Review, 82,* 407-428.

Collins, A. M., & Quillian, M. R. (1969). Retrieval time from semantic memory. *Journal of Verbal Learning and Verbal Behavior, 8,* 240-247.

Coltheart, M. (1980). Iconic memory and visible persistence. *Perception and Psychophysics, 27,* 183-228.

Conrad, C. (1972). Cognitive economy in semantic memory. *Journal of Experimental Psychology, 92,* 49-54.

Conrad, R. (1964). Acoustic confusions in immediate memory. *British Journal of Psychology, 55,* 77-84.

Conway, M. A., Anderson, S. J., Larsen, S. F., Donnelly, C. M., McDaniel, M. A., McClelland, A. G. R., Rawles, R. E., & Logic, R. H. (1994). The formation of flashbulb memories. *Memory & Cognition, 22,* 326-343.

Conway, M. A., Cohen, G., & Stanhope, N. (1991). On the very long-term retention of knowledge acquired through formal education: Twelve years of cognitive psychology. *Journal of Experimental Psychology: General, 120,* 395-409.

Cook, M. (1977). Gaze and mutual gaze in social encounters. *American Scientist, 65,* 328-333.

Cooper, W. E. (1979). *Speech perception and production: Studies in selective adaptation.* Norwood, NJ: Ablex.

Corballis, M. C. (1989). Laterality and human evolution. *Psychological Review, 96,* 492-505.

Coren, S. (1984). Subliminal perception. In R. J. Corsini (Ed.), *Encyclopedia of psychology* (Vol. 3, p. 382). New York: John Wiley.

Cornsweet, T. N. (1970). *Visual perception.* New York: Academic Press.

Cowan, N. (1988). Evolving conceptions of memory storage, selective attention, and their mutual constraints within the human information-processing system. *Psychological Bulletin, 104,* 163-191.

Cowan, N. (1993). Activation, attention, and short-term memory. *Memory & Cognition, 21,* 162-167.

Cowan, N., Lichty, W., & Grove, T. R. (1990). Properties of memory for unattended spoken syllables. *Journal of Experimental Psychology: Learning, Memory, and Cognition, 16,* 258-269.

Cowan, N., Wood, N. L., & Bourne, D. N. (1994). Reaffirmation of the short-term storage concept. *Psychological Science, 5,* 103-106.

Craik, F. I. M., & Lockhart, R. S. (1972). CHARM is not enough: Comments on Eich's model of cued recall. *Psychological Review, 93,* 360-364.

Craik, F. I. M., & Tulving, E. (1975). Depth of processing and the retention of words of episodic memory. *Journal of Experimental Psychology: General, 104,* 268-294.

Craik, F. I. M., & Watkins, M. J. (1973). The role of rehearsal in short-term memory. *Journal of Verbal Learning and Verbal Behavior, 12,* 599-607.

Crick, F. H. C. (1994). *The astonishing hypothesis: The scientific search for the soul.* New York: Scribner.

Crowder, R. G. (1978). Mechanisms of auditory backward masking in the stimulus suffix effect. *Psychological Review, 85,* 502-524.

Crowder, R. G. (1982a). Decay of auditory memory in vowel discrimination. *Journal of Experimental Psychology: Learning, Memory, and Cognition, 8,* 153-162.

Crowder, R. G. (1982b). The demise of short-term memory. *Acta Psychologica, 50,* 291-323.

Crowder, R. G. (1989). Modularity and dissociations in memory systems. In H. L. Roediger III & F. I. M. Craik (Eds.), *Varieties of memory and consciousness: Essays in honour of Endel Tulving* (pp. 271-294). Hillsdale, NJ: Lawrence Erlbaum.

Crowder, R. G. (1993). Short-term memory: Where do we stand? *Memory & Cognition, 21,* 142-146.

Crowder, R. G., & Morton, J. (1969). Precategorical acoustic storage (PAS). *Perception Psychophysics, 5,* 365-373.

Csikszentmihalyi, M. (1990). *Flow: The psychology of optimal experience.* New York: Harper & Row.

Curran, T., & Keele, S. W. (1993). Attentional and nonattentional forms of sequence learning. *Journal of Experimental Psychology: Learning, Memory, and Cognition, 19,* 189-202.

Dale, R. S. (1976). *Language development: Structure and function* (2nd ed.). New York: Holt, Rinehart & Winston.

Daneman, M., & Carpenter, P. A. (1980). Individual differences in working memory and reading. *Journal of Verbal Learning and Verbal Behavior, 18,* 450-466.

Darley, C. F., & Glass, A. L. (1975). Effects of rehearsal and serial list position on recall. *Journal of Experimental Psychology: Learning, Memory, and Cognition, 104,* 453-458.

Darwin, C. J., Turvey, M. T., & Crowder, R. G. (1972). An auditory analogue of the Sperling partial report procedure: Evidence for brief auditory storage. *Cognitive Psychology, 3,* 255-267.

David, A. S. (1993). Spatial and selective attention in the cerebral hemispheres in depression, mania, and schizophrenia. *Brain & Cognition, 23,* 166-180.

Davies, M., & Humphreys, G. W. (Ed.). (1993). *Consciousness: Psychological and philosophical essays.* Cambridge: Blackwell.

Deaux, K. (1985). Sex and gender. *Annual Review of Psychology, 36,* 49-81.

Debner, J. A., & Jacoby, L. L. (1994). Unconscious perception: Attention, awareness, and control. *Journal of Experimental Psychology: Learning, Memory, and Cognition, 20,* 304-317.

de Bono, E. (1985). The CoRT thinking program. In J. W. Segal, S. F. Chipman, & R. Glaser (Eds.), *Thinking and learning skills: Relating instruction to basic research* (Vol. 1, pp. 363-388). Hillsdale, NJ: Lawrence Erlbaum.

de Groot, A. D. (1965). *Thought and choice in chess.* The Hague, the Netherlands: Mouton.

Dement, W. C. (1978). *Some must watch while some must sleep.* New York: Norton.

Dement, W. C., & Wolpert, E. (1958). The relation of eye movements, body motility, and external stimuli to dream content. *Journal of Experimental Psychology, 55,* 543-553.

Dennett, D. C. (1991). *Consciousness explained.* Boston: Little, Brown.

Detterman, R. (1986). Human intelligence is a complex system of separate processes. In R. J. Sternberg & D. K. Detterman (Eds.), *What is intelligence? Contemporary viewpoints on its nature and definition* (pp. 57-61). Norwood, NJ: Ablex.

Deutsch, D. (1982). *The psychology of music.* New York: Academic Press.

Deutsch, J. A., & Deutsch, D. (1963). Attention: Some theoretical considerations. *Psychological Review, 70,* 80-90.

de Valois, R. L., & Jacobs, G. H. (1968). Primate color vision. *Science, 162,* 533-540.

de Villiers, J. G., & de Villiers, P. A. (1978). *Language acquisition.* Cambridge, MA: Harvard University Press.

Diamond, S. J. (1976). Brain circuits for consciousness. *Brain, Behaviour and Evolution, 13,* 376-395.

Dickstein, L. S. (1978). Error processes in syllogistic reasoning. *Memory & Cognition, 6,* 537-543.

Dolnick, E. (1993, September). Deafness as a culture. *Atlantic Monthly,* pp. 37-51.

Dominowski, R. L. (1977). Reasoning. *Interamerican Journal of Psychology, 11,* 68-77.

Dooling, D. J., & Christiaansen, R. E. (1977). Episodic and semantic aspects of memory for prose. *Journal of Experimental Psychology: Human Learning and Memory, 3,* 428-436.

Dowling, W. J., & Harwood, D. L. (1986). *Music cognition.* Orlando, FL: Academic Press.

Druckman, D., & Bjork, R. A. (Eds.). (1991). *In the mind's eye: Enhancing human performance.* Washington, DC: National Academy Press.

Dulany, D. E., Carlson, R. A., & Dewey, G. I. (1984). A case of syntactical learning and judgement: How conscious and how abstract? *Journal of Experimental Psychology: General, 113,* 541-555.

Duncker, K. (1945). On problem-solving (L. S. Lees, Trans.). *Psychological Monographs, 58*(Whole No. 270). (Original work published 1935)

D'Ydewalle, G., Delhaye, P., & Goessens, L. (1985). Structural, semantic, and self-reference processing of pictorial advertisements. *Human Learning, 4,* 29-38.

Ebbinghaus, H. (1885). *Uber das Gedächtnis: Intersuchungen zur experimentellen psychologie.* Leipzig: Duncker and Humboldt. (H. A. Ruger & C. D. Bussenius, Trans., 1913; reissued by Dover, 1964)

Eccles, J. C. (Ed.). (1966). *Brain and conscious experience.* New York: Springer.

Eccles, J. C. (1994). *How the self controls the brain.* Berlin: Springer-Verlag.

Egan, D. E., & Schwartz, B. J. (1979). Chunking in recall of symbolic drawings. *Memory & Cognition, 7,* 149-158.

Eich, J. E. (1980). The cue-dependent nature of state-dependent retrieval. *Memory & Cognition, 8,* 157-173.

Eich, J. E. (1989). Theoretical issues in state-dependent memory. In H. L. Roediger III & F. I. M. Craik (Eds.), *Varieties of memory and consciousness: Essays in honour of Endel Tulving* (pp.

331-354). Hillsdale, NJ: Lawrence Erlbaum.

Eich, J. M. (1982). A composite holographic associative recall model. *Psychological Review, 89,* 627-661.

Eimas, P. D. (1974). Auditory and linguistic processing of cues for place of articulation by infants. *Perception & Psychophysics, 16,* 521-531.

Eimas, P. D. (1975). Speech perception in early infancy. In L. B. Cohen & P. Salapatek (Eds.), *Infant perception* (pp. 193-231). New York: Academic Press.

Eimas, P. D., & Miller, J. L. (Eds.). (1981). *Perspectives on the study of speech.* Hillsdale, NJ: Lawrence Erlbaum.

Eimas, P. D., & Miller, J. L. (1992). Organization in the perception of speech by young infants. *Psychological Science, 3,* 340-344.

Eimas, P. D., Miller, J. L., & Jusczyk, P. W. (1987). On infant speech perception and the acquisition of language. In S. Harnad (Ed.), *Categorical perception* (pp. 161-195). New York: Cambridge University Press.

Ellenberger, H. (1970). *Discovery of the unconscious.* New York: Basic Books.

Ellis, A. W. (1980). On the Freudian theory of speech errors. In V. A. Fromkin (Ed.), *Errors in linguistic performance* (pp. 123-131). New York: Academic Press.

Ellis, A. W. (Ed.). (1982). *Normality and pathology in cognitive functions.* London: Academic Press.

Ellis, H. C., Thomas, R. L., & Rodriguez, I. A. (1984). Emotional mood states and memory: Elaborative encoding, semantic processing, and cognitive effort. *Journal of Experimen-* *tal Psychology: Learning, Memory, and Cognition, 10,* 470-482.

Engs, R. C., Slawinska, J. B., & Hanson, D. J. (1991). The drinking patterns of American and Polish university students: A cross-nation study. *Drug and Alcohol Dependence, 27,* 167-175.

Erdelyi, M. H. (1974). A new look at the new look: Perceptual defense and vigilance. *Psychological Review, 81,* 1-25.

Erdelyi, M. H., & Becker, J. (1974). Hypermnesia for pictures: Incremental memory for pictures but not for words in multiple recall trials. *Cognitive Psychology, 6,* 159-171.

Erdelyi, M. H., & Goldberg, B. (1979). Let's not sweep repression under the rug: Toward a cognitive psychology of repression. In J. F. Kihlstrom & F. J. Evans (Eds.), *Functional disorders of memory* (pp. 355-402). Hillsdale, NJ: Lawrence Erlbaum.

Ericsson, K. A., & Chase, W. G. (1982). Exceptional memory. *American Scientist, 70,* 607-615.

Ericsson, K. A., & Kintsch, W. (1995). Long-term working memory. *Psychological Review, 102,* 211-245.

Ericsson, K. A., Krampé, R. T., & Tesch-Römer, C. (1993). The role of deliberate practice in the acquisition of expert performance. *Psychological Review, 100,* 363-406.

Ericsson, K. A., & Polson, P. G. (1988). An experimental analysis of the mechanisms of a memory skill. *Journal of Experimental Psychology: Learning, Memory, and Cognition, 14,* 305-316.

Ericsson, K. A., & Smith, J. (1991). *Toward a general theory of expertise: Prospects and limits.* New York: Cambridge University Press.

Ernst, G. W., & Newell, A. (1969). *GPS: A case study in generality and problem solving.* Orlando, FL: Academic Press.

Estes, W. K. (1976). The cognitive side of probability learning. *Psychological Review, 83,* 37-64.

Estes, W. K. (1988). Human learning and memory. In R. C. Atkinson, R. J. Herrnstein, G. Lindsay, & R. D. Luce (Eds.), *Stevens' handbook of experimental psychology* (Vol. 2, 2nd ed., pp. 351-415). New York: John Wiley.

Evans, J. St. B. T., Barston, J. L., & Pollard, P. (1983). On the conflict between logic and belief in syllogistic reasoning. *Memory & Cognition, 11,* 295-306.

Eysenck, H. J. (1973). *The inequality of man.* London: Temple Smith.

Eysenck, H. J. (1979). *The structure and measurement of intelligence.* New York: Springer.

Eysenck, H. J. (1987). Speed of information processing, reaction time, and the theory of intelligence. In P. A. Vernon (Ed.), *Speed of information processing and intelligence* (pp. 21-67). Norwood, NJ: Ablex.

Eysenck, H. J., & Kamin, L. (1981). *The intelligence controversy: H. J. Eysenck vs. Leon Kamin.* New York: John Wiley.

Farah, M. J. (1988). Is visual imagery really visual? Overlooked evidence from neuropsychology. *Psychological Review, 95,* 307-317.

Feingold, A. (1988). Cognitive gender differences are disappearing. *American Psychologist, 43,* 95-103.

Feingold, A. (1992). Sex differences in variability in intellectual abilities: A new look at an old controversy. *Review of Educational Research, 62,* 61-84.

Fillmore, C. J. (1968). The case for case. In E. Bach & R. T. Harms (Eds.), *Universals in linguistic theory* (pp. 1-88). New York: Holt, Rinehart & Winston.

Finke, R. A. (1980). Levels of equivalence in imagery and perception. *Psychological Review, 87,* 113-132.

Fischhoff, B. (1975). Hindsight = foresight: The effect of outcome knowledge on judgment under uncertainty. *Journal of Experimental Psychology: Human Perception and Performance, 1,* 288-299.

Fischhoff, B. (1977). Perceived informativeness of facts. *Journal of Experimental Psychology: Human Perception and Performance, 3,* 349-358.

Fisk, A. D., & Schneider, W. (1984). Memory as a function of attention, level of processing, and automatization. *Journal of Experimental Psychology: Learning, Memory, and Cognition, 10,* 181-197.

Fiske, S. T., & Taylor, S. E. (1991). *Social cognition* (2nd ed.). New York: McGraw-Hill.

Fivush, R., Gray, J. T., & Fromhoff, F. A. (1987). Two-year-olds talk about the past. *Cognitive Development, 2,* 393-409.

Flanagan, O. J. (1992). *Consciousness reconsidered.* Cambridge: MIT Press.

Flavell, J. H., Miller, P. H., & Miller, S. A. (1993). *Cognitive development* (2nd ed.). Englewood Cliffs, NJ: Prentice-Hall.

Flower, L. S., & Hayes, J. R. (1980). The dynamics of composing: Making plans and juggling constraints. In L. W. Gregg & E. R. Steinberg (Eds.), *Cognitive processes in writing* (pp. 31-50). Hillsdale, NJ: Lawrence Erlbaum.

Flower, L. S., & Hayes, J. R. (1984). Images, plans and prose: The representation of meaning in writing. *Written Communication, 1,* 120-160.

Fodor, J. A. (1983). *The modularity of mind.* Cambridge: MIT Press.

Forsyth, R. (Ed.). (1989). *Expert systems: Principles and case studies.* London: Chapman & Hall Computing.

Foss, D. J. (1988). Experimental psycholinguistics. *Annual Review of Psychology, 39,* 301-348.

Foss, D. J., & Hakes, D. T. (1978). *Psycholinguistics: An introduction to the psychology of language.* Englewood Cliffs, NJ: Prentice-Hall.

Foulke, E., & Sticht, T. (1969). Review of research on the intelligibility and comprehension of accelerated speech. *Psychological Bulletin, 72,* 50-62.

Franks, J. J., & Bransford, J. D. (1971). Abstraction of visual patterns. *Journal of Experimental Psychology, 90,* 65-74.

Freedman, S. W. (1983). Student characteristics and essay test writing performance. *Research in the Teaching of College English, 17,* 313-325.

Freud, S. (1953a). The interpretation of dreams. In J. Strachey (Ed.), *The standard edition of the complete psychological works of Sigmund Freud* (Vols. 4-5). London: Hogarth. (Original work published 1900)

Freud, S. (1953b). Three essays on the theory of sexuality. In J. Strachey (Ed.), *The standard edition of the complete psychological works of Sigmund Freud* (Vol. 7). London: Hogarth. (Original work published 1905)

Friedman, A. (1979). Framing pictures: The role of knowledge in automized encoding and memory for gist. *Journal of Experimental Psychology: General, 108,* 316-355.

Friedman, A., & Polson, M. C. (1981). Hemispheres as independent resources systems: Limited-capacity processing and cerebral specialization. *Journal of Experimental Psychology, 7,* 1031-1058.

Fromkin, V. A. (Ed.). (1973). *Speech errors as linguistic evidence.* The Hague, the Netherlands: Mouton.

Galin, D. (1974). Implications for psychiatry of left and right cerebral specialization: A neurophysiological context for unconscious processes. *Archives of General Psychiatry, 31,* 572-583.

Gallahue, D. L. (1989). *Understanding motor development: Infants, children, adolescents* (2nd ed.). Indianapolis: Benchmark.

Galton, F. (1892). *Hereditary genius: An enquiry into its laws and consequences.* London: Macmillan.

Gardner, B. T., & Gardner, R. A. (1975). Evidence for sentence constituents in the early utterances of child and chimpanzee. *Journal of Experimental Psychology: General, 104,* 244-267.

Gardner, H. (1983). *Frames of mind: The theory of multiple intelligences.* New York: Basic Books.

Gardner, H. (1985). *The mind's new science: A history of the cognitive revolution.* New York: Basic Books.

Gardner, H. (1991). *The unschooled mind: How children think and how schools should teach.* New York: Basic Books.

Gardner, R. A., & Gardner, B. T. (1969). Teaching sign language to a chimpanzee. *Science, 165,* 644-672.

Garrett, M. F. (1988). Processes in language production. In F. J. Newmeyer

(Ed.), *Linguistics: The Cambridge Survey: Vol. 3. Language: Psychological and biological aspects* (pp. 69-96). Cambridge: Cambridge University Press.

Garrett, M. F. (1990). Sentence processing. In D. N. Osherson & H. Lasnik (Eds.), *An invitation to cognitive science: Vol. 1. Language* (pp. 133-175). Cambridge: MIT Press.

Garrett, M., Bever, T., & Fodor, J. (1966). The active use of grammar in speech perception. *Perception & Psychophysics, 1,* 30-32.

Gazzaniga, M. S. (1970). *The bisected brain.* New York: Appleton-Century-Crofts.

Gazzaniga, M. S. (1985). *The social brain: Discovering the networks of the mind.* New York: Basic Books.

Gazzaniga, M. S. (1992). *Nature's mind: The biological roots of thinking, emotions, sexuality, language, and intelligence.* New York: Basic Books.

Gazzaniga, M. S., Bogen, J. E., & Sperry, R. W. (1965). Observations on visual perception after disconnection of the cerebral hemispheres on man. *Brain, 88,* 221-236.

Geis, M. L., & Zwicky, A. M. (1971). On invited inferences. *Linguistic Inquiry, 2,* 561-566.

Gentner, D., & Stevens, A. L. (1983). *Mental models.* Hillsdale, NJ: Lawrence Erlbaum.

Gernsbacher, M. A. (1989). Mechanisms that improve referential access. *Cognition, 32,* 99-156.

Gernsbacher, M. A. (1990). *Language comprehension as structure building.* Hillsdale, NJ: Lawrence Erlbaum.

Geschwind, N. (1970). The organisation of language and the brain. *Science, 170,* 940-944.

Geschwind, N. (1982). Disorders of attention: A frontier in neuropsychology. *Philosophical Transactions of the Royal Society of London, B298,* 173-185.

Ghiselli, E. (1966). *The validity of occupational aptitude tests.* New York: John Wiley.

Giambra, L. M. (1974). Daydreaming across the life span: Late adolescent to senior citizen. *Aging and Human Development, 5,* 118-135.

Gibson, E. J. (1969). *Principles of perceptual learning and development.* New York: Prentice-Hall.

Gibson, E. J. (1994). Has psychology a future? *Psychological Science, 5,* 69-76.

Gibson, J. J. (1966). *The senses considered as perceptual systems.* Boston: Houghton.

Gibson, J. J. (1979). *The ecological approach to visual perception.* Boston: Houghton Mifflin.

Gick, M. L., & Holyoak, K. J. (1980). Analogical problem solving. *Cognitive Psychology, 12,* 306-355.

Gigerenzer, G., Hoffrage, U., & Kleinbölting, H. (1991). Probabilistic mental models: A Brunswikean theory of confidence. *Psychological Review, 98,* 506-528.

Gilhooly, J. J. (1982). *Thinking: Directed, undirected, and creative.* London: Academic Press.

Glanzer, M., & Cunitz, A. R. (1966). Two storage mechanisms in free recall. *Journal of Verbal Learning and Verbal Behavior, 5,* 351-360.

Glaser, R. (1984). Education and thinking: The role of knowledge. *American Psychologist, 39,* 93-104.

Glaser, R. (1985). All's well that begins and ends with both knowledge and process: A reply to Sternberg. *American Psychologist, 40,* 573-574.

Glaser, R. (1986). Intelligence as acquired proficiency. In R. J. Sternberg & D. K. Detterman (Eds.), *What is intelligence? Contemporary viewpoints on its nature and definition* (pp. 77-83). Norwood, NJ: Ablex.

Glaser, R., & Bassok, M. (1989). Learning theory and the study of instruction. *Annual Review of Psychology, 40,* 631-666.

Glaser, R., & Chi, M. T. H. (1988). Overview. In M. T. H. Chi, R. Glaser, & M. J. Farr (Eds.), *The nature of expertise* (pp. xv-xxxvi). Hillsdale, NJ: Lawrence Erlbaum.

Glass, A. L., & Holyoak, K. J. (1975). Alternative conceptions of semantic memory. *Cognition, 3,* 313-339.

Glenberg, A. M. (1987). Temporal context and memory. In D. S. Gorfein & R. R. Hoffman (Eds.), *Memory and learning: The Ebbinghaus centennial conference* (pp. 173-190). Hillsdale, NJ: Lawrence Erlbaum.

Glenberg, A. M., Bradley, M. M., Stevenson, J. A., Kraus, T. A., Tkachuk, M. J., Gretz, A. L., Fish, J. F., & Turpin, B. A. M. (1980). A two-process account of long-term serial position effects. *Journal of Experimental Psychology: Human Learning and Memory, 6,* 355-369.

Glucksberg, S., & Danks, J. H. (1975). *Experimental psycholinguistics: An introduction.* Hillsdale, NJ: Lawrence Erlbaum.

Glucksberg, S., Gildea, P., & Bookin, H. B. (1982). On understanding nonliteral speech: Can people ignore metaphors? *Journal of Verbal Learning & Verbal Behavior, 21,* 85-98.

Goldin-Meadow, S., & Mylander, C. (1990). Beyond the input given: The child's role in the acquisition of language. *Language, 66,* 323-355.

Goldman-Eisler, F. (1968). *Psycholinguistics: Experiments in spontaneous speech.* New York: Academic Press.

Goldsmith, T. H. (1991). *The biological roots of human nature: Forging links between evolution and behavior.* New York: Oxford University Press.

Goldstein, E. B. (1989). *Sensation and perception* (3rd ed.). Belmont, CA: Wadsworth.

Goodman, G., & Aman, C. (1990). Children's use of anatomically detailed dolls to recount an event. *Child Development, 61,* 1859-1871.

Goodman, R., & Caramazza, A. (1986). Aspects of the spelling process: Evidence from a case of acquired dysgraphia. *Language and Cognitive Processes, 1,* 263-296.

Gordon, H. W., Bogen, J. E., & Sperry, R. W. (1971). Absence of deconnexion syndromes in two patients with partial section of the neocommissures. *Brain, 94,* 327-336.

Gould, S. (1981). *The mismeasure of man.* New York: Norton.

Graesser, A. C. (1981). *Prose comprehension beyond the word.* New York: Springer-Verlag.

Graesser, A. C., & Bower, G. H. (Eds.). (1990). *The psychology of learning and motivation: Vol. 25. Inferences and text comprehension.* New York: Academic Press.

Graesser, A. C., Hoffman, N., & Clark, L. F. (1980). Structural components of reading time. *Journal of Verbal Learning and Verbal Behavior, 19,* 135-151.

Graf, P., Squire, L. R., & Mandler, G. (1984). The information that amnesic patients do not forget. *Journal of Experimental Psychology: Learning, Memory, and Cognition, 10,* 164-178.

Green, D. M., & Swets, J. A. (1966). *Signal detection theory and psychophysics.* New York: John Wiley.

Green, E., & Howes, D. H. (1977). The nature of conduction aphasia: A study of anatomic and clinical features and underlying mechanisms. In H. Whitaker & H. A. Whitaker (Eds.), *Studies in neurolinguistics* (Vol. 3, pp. 123-156). New York: Academic Press.

Greenberg, J. H. (1966). *Language universals.* The Hague, the Netherlands: Mouton.

Greene, R. L. (1986). Sources of recency effects in free recall. *Psychological Bulletin, 99,* 221-228.

Greene, R. L. (1987). Effects of maintenance rehearsal on human memory. *Psychological Bulletin, 102,* 403-413.

Gregg, L. W., & Steinberg, E. R. (Eds.). (1980). *Cognitive processes in writing.* Hillsdale, NJ: Lawrence Erlbaum.

Grice, H. P. (1975). Logic and conversation. In P. Cole & J. L. Morgan (Eds.), *Syntax and semantics: Vol. 3. Speech acts* (pp. 41-48). New York: Seminar Press.

Griffin, D. R. (1984). *Animal thinking.* Cambridge, MA: Harvard University Press.

Griggs, R. A., & Cox, J. R. (1982). The elusive thematic-materials effect in Wason's selection task. *British Journal of Psychology, 73,* 407-420.

Guilford, J. P. (1967). *The nature of human intelligence.* New York: McGraw-Hill.

Guilford, J. P. (1982). Cognitive psychology's ambiguities: Some suggested remedies. *Psychological Review, 89,* 48-59.

Gulick, W. L. (1971). *Hearing: Physiology and psychophysics.* New York: Oxford University Press.

Gummerman, K., & Gray, C. R. (1982). An uncommon case of visual memory. In U. Neisser (Ed.), *Memory observed: Remembering in natural contexts* (pp. 405-411). San Francisco: Freeman.

Haber, R. N. (1979). Twenty years of haunting eidetic images: Where's the ghost? *Behavioral and Brain Sciences, 2,* 583-594.

Halliday, M. A. K., & Hasan, R. (1976). *Cohesion in English.* London: Longman.

Halpern, D. F. (1992). *Sex differences in cognitive abilities* (2nd ed.). Hillsdale, NJ: Lawrence Erlbaum.

Hampton, J. A. (1982). An investigation of the nature of abstract concepts. *Memory & Cognition, 9,* 149-156.

Harnad, S. (Ed.). (1987). *Categorical perception: The groundwork of cognition.* Cambridge: Cambridge University Press.

Hasher, L., & Zacks, R. T. (1979). Automatic and effortful processes in memory. *Journal of Experimental Psychology: General, 108,* 356-388.

Hasher, L., & Zacks, R. T. (1984). Automatic processing of fundamental information: The case of frequency of occurrence. *American Psychologist, 39,* 1372-1388.

Hashtroudi, S., Parker, E. S., DeLisi, L. E., Wyatt, R. J., & Mutter, S. A. (1984). Intact retention in acute alcohol amnesia. *Journal of Experimental Psychology: Learning, Memory, and Cognition, 10,* 156-163.

Haviland, S. E., & Clark, H. H. (1974). What's new? Acquiring new information as a process in comprehension. *Journal of Verbal Learning and Verbal Behavior, 13,* 512-521.

Hayes, J. R. (1981). *The complete problem solver.* Philadelphia: Franklin Institute Press.

Hayes, J. R., & Flower, L. S. (1980). Identifying the organization of writing processes. In L. W. Gregg & E. R. Steinberg (Eds.), *Cognitive processes in writing* (pp. 3-30). Hillsdale, NJ: Lawrence Erlbaum.

Hayes, N. A., & Broadbent, D. E. (1988). Two modes of learning for interactive tasks. *Cognition, 28,* 249-276.

Haygood, R. C., & Bourne, L. E., Jr. (1965). Attribute and rule-learning aspects of conceptual mail. *Psychological Review, 72,* 175-195.

Hayman, C. A., & Tulving, E. (1989). Contingent dissociation between recognition and fragment completion: The method of triangulation. *Journal of Experimental Psychology: Learning, Memory, and Cognition, 15,* 228-240.

Healy, A. F., & Levitt, A. G. (1978). The relative accessibility of semantic and deep syntactic concepts. *Memory & Cognition, 6,* 518-526.

Hecht, S., Schlaer, S., & Pirenne, M. H. (1942). Energy, quanta, and vision. *Journal of General Physiology, 25,* 819-840.

Heider, E. R. (1972). Universals in color naming and memory. *Journal of Experimental Psychology, 93,* 10-20.

Hell, W., Gigerenzer, G., Gauggel, S., Mall, M., & Muller, M. (1988). Hindsight bias: An interaction of automatic and motivational factors? *Memory & Cognition, 16,* 533-538.

Henle, M. (1962). On the relation between logic and thinking. *Psychological Review, 69,* 366-378.

Hertel, P. T., & Hardin, T. S. (1990). Remembering with and without awareness in a depressed mood: Evidence of deficits in initiative. *Journal of Experimental Psychology: General, 119,* 45-59.

Hilgard, E. R. (1980). Consciousness in contemporary psychology. *Annual Review of Psychology, 31,* 1-26.

Hilgard, E. R. (1986). *Divided consciousness: Multiple controls in human thought and action.* New York: John Wiley.

Hilgard, E. R. (1987). *Psychology in America: A historical survey.* San Diego: Harcourt Brace Jovanovich.

Hill, C. S. (1991). *Sensations: A defense of type materialism.* New York: Cambridge University Press.

Hintzman, D. L. (1986). "Schema abstraction" in a multiple-trace memory model. *Psychological Review, 93,* 411-428.

Hintzman, D. L. (1990). Human learning and memory: Connections and dissociations. *Annual Review of Psychology, 41,* 109-139.

Hintzman, D. L., & Stern, L. D. (1978). Contextual variability and memory for frequency. *Journal of Experimental Psychology: Human Learning and Memory, 4,* 539-549.

Hobson, J. A., & McCarley, R. W. (1977). The brain as a dream state generator: An activation-synthesis hypothesis of the dream process. *American Journal of Psychiatry, 134,* 1335-1348.

Hoch, S. J., & Loewenstein, G. F. (1989). Outcome feedback: Hindsight and information. *Journal of Experimental*

Psychology: Learning, Memory, and Cognition, 15, 605-619.

Hockett, C. F. (1966). The problems of universals in language. In J. H. Greenberg (Ed.), *Universals of language* (2nd ed., pp. 1-29). Cambridge: MIT Press.

Holender, D. (1986). Semantic activation without conscious identification in dichotic listening, parafoveal vision, and visual masking: A survey and appraisal. *Behavioral and Brain Sciences, 9,* 1-23.

Holyoak, K. J. (1991). Symbolic connectionism: Toward third-generation theories of expertise. In K. A. Ericsson & J. Smith (Eds.), *Toward a general theory of expertise* (pp. 301-336). Cambridge, UK: Cambridge University Press.

Howe, M. L., & Courage, M. L. (1993). On resolving the enigma of infantile amnesia. *Psychological Bulletin, 113,* 305-326.

Hubel, D. H. (1963). The visual cortex of the brain. *Scientific American, 209,* 54-62.

Hubel, D. H., & Wiesel, T. N. (1959). Receptive fields of single neurones in the cat's striate cortex. *Journal of Physiology, 148,* 574-591.

Hubel, D. H., & Wiesel, T. N. (1963). Receptive fields of cells in the striate cortex of very young, visually inexperienced kittens. *Journal of Neurophysiology, 26,* 994-1002.

Hull, C. L. (1920). Quantitative aspects of the evolution of concepts: An experimental study. *Psychological Monographs, 28*(Whole No. 123).

Hummel, J. E., & Biederman, I. (1992). Dynamic binding in a neural network for shape recognition. *Psychological Review, 99,* 480-517.

Hunt, E. B. (1975). *Artificial intelligence.* New York: Academic Press.

Hunt, E. B. (1986). The Heffalump of intelligence. In R. J. Sternbery & D. K. Detterman (Eds.), *What is intelligence: Contemporary viewpoints of its nature and definitions* (pp. 101-107). Norwood, NJ: Ablex.

Hunt, E. B. (1987). The next word on verbal ability. In P. A. Vernon (Ed.), *Speed of information processing and intelligence* (pp. 347-392). Norwood, NJ: Ablex.

Hunt, E. B. (1989). Cognitive science: Definition, status and questions. *Annual Review of Psychology, 40,* 603-629.

Hunt, E. B., & Agnoli, F. (1991). The Whorfian hypothesis: A cognitive psychology perspective. *Psychological Review, 98,* 377-389.

Hunt, E. B., & Love, T. (1982). The second mnemonist. In U. Neisser (Ed.), *Memory observed: Remembering in natural contexts* (pp. 390-398). San Francisco: Freeman.

Hunt, M. (1982). *The universe within.* New York: Simon & Schuster.

Hunt, R. R., & Einstein, G. O. (1981). Relational item-specific information in memory. *Journal of Verbal Learning and Verbal Behavior, 19,* 497-514.

Hunt, R. R., & McDaniel, M. A. (1993). The enigma of organization and distinctiveness. *Journal of Memory and Language, 32,* 421-445.

Hunter, I. M. L. (1957). *Memory: Facts and fallacies.* Harmondsworth, Middlesex, England: Penguin.

Hunter, I. M. L. (1962). An exceptional talent for calculative thinking. *British Journal of Psychology, 53,* 243-258.

Hunter, I. M. L. (1964). *Memory*. Harmondsworth, Middlesex, England: Penguin.

Hyde, J. S. (1981). How large are cognitive gender differences? *American Psychologist, 36,* 892-901.

Hyde, J. S., & Linn, M. C. (1988). Gender differences in verbal ability: A meta-analysis. *Psychological Bulletin, 104,* 53-69.

Hyman, R. (1985). The Ganzfeld psi experiment: A critical appraisal. *Journal of Parapsychology, 49,* 3-49.

Hyman, R. (1994). Anomaly or artifact? Comments on Bem and Honorton. *Psychological Bulletin, 115,* 19-24.

Inhoff, A. W., Lima, S. D., & Carroll, P. J. (1984). Contextual effects on metaphor comprehension in reading. *Memory & Cognition, 12,* 558-567.

Jacoby, L. L. (1974). The role of mental contiguity in memory: Registration and retrieval effects. *Journal of Verbal Learning and Verbal Behavior, 13,* 483-496.

Jacoby, L. L. (1983a). Perceptual enhancement: Persistent effects of an experience. *Journal of Experimental Psychology: Learning, Memory, and Cognition, 9,* 21-38.

Jacoby, L. L. (1983b). Remembering the data: Analyzing interactive processes in reading. *Journal of Verbal Learning and Verbal Behavior, 22,* 458-508.

Jacoby, L. L. (1984). Incidental versus intentional retrieval: Remembering and awareness as separate issues. In L. R. Squire & N. Butters (Eds.), *Neuropsychology of memory* (pp. 145-156). New York: Guilford.

Jacoby, L. L., & Dallas, M. (1981). On the relationship between autobiographical memory and perceptual learning. *Journal of Experimental Psychology: General, 110,* 306-340.

Jacoby, L. L., & Whitehouse, K. (1989). An illusion of memory: False recognition influenced by unconscious perception. *Journal of Experimental Psychology: General, 118,* 126-135.

Jaffe, J., & Feldstein, S. (1970). *Rhythms of dialogue*. New York: Academic Press.

James, W. (1890). *The principles of psychology* (Vol. 1). New York: Holt.

James, W. (1962). *Psychology: Briefer course* (1st Collier Books ed.). New York: Collier.

Janis, I. L., & Mann, L. (1977). *Decision making*. New York: Free Press.

Jaynes, J. (1976). *The origin of consciousness in the breakdown of the bicameral mind*. Boston: Houghton Mifflin.

Jenkins, J. J. (1969). Language and thought. In J. F. Voss (Ed.), *Approaches to thought* (pp. 211-236). Columbia, OH: Merrill.

Jenkins, J. J. (1974). Remember that old theory of memory? Well, forget it! *American Psychologist, 29,* 785-795.

Jensen, A. R. (1987). Individual differences in the Hick paradigm. In P. A. Vernon (Ed.), *Speed of information-processing and intelligence* (pp. 101-175). Norwood, NJ: Ablex.

Johnson, M. (1983). A multiple-entry, modular memory system. In G. H. Bower (Ed.), *The psychology of learning and motivation* (Vol. 17, pp. 81-123). New York: Academic Press.

Johnson, M. H., & Magaro, P. A. (1987). Effects of mood and severity on memory processes in depression and mania. *Psychological Bulletin, 101,* 28-40.

Johnson, M. H., Posner, M. I., & Rothbart, M. K. (1994). Facilitation of saccades toward a covertly attended location in early infancy. *Psychological Science, 5,* 90-93.

Johnson, M. K. (1988). Discriminating the origin of information. In T. F. Oltmans & B. A. Maher (Eds.), *Delusional beliefs: Interdisciplinary perspectives* (pp. 34-65). New York: John Wiley.

Johnson, M. K., Bransford, J. D., & Solomon, S. K. (1973). Memory for tacit implications of sentences. *Journal of Experimental Psychology, 98,* 203-205.

Johnson, M. K., & Hasher, L. (1987). Human learning and memory. *Annual Review of Psychology, 38,* 631-668.

Johnson-Laird, P. N. (1983). *Mental models: Towards a cognitive science of language, inference, and consciousness.* Cambridge, MA: Harvard University Press.

Johnson-Laird, P. N., & Bara, B. G. (1984). Syllogistic inference. *Cognition, 16,* 1-61.

Johnson-Laird, P. N., & Steedman, M. (1978). The psychology of syllogisms. *Cognitive Psychology, 10,* 64-99.

John-Steiner, V. (1985). *Notebooks of the mind: Explorations of thinking.* Albuquerque: University of New Mexico Press.

Johnston, L. D., O'Malley, P. M., & Bachman, J. G. (1991). *Drug use among American high school seniors, college students and young adults, 1975-1990* (Vol. 1, DHHS Pub. No. [ADM] 91-1813). Washington, DC: Government Printing Office.

Johnston, W. A., & Heinz, S. P. (1978). Flexibility and capacity demands of attention. *Journal of Experimental Psychology: General, 107,* 420-435.

Jolicoeur, P. (1988). Mental rotation and the identification of disoriented objects. *Canadian Journal of Psychology, 42,* 461-478.

Just, M. A., & Carpenter, P. A. (1980). A theory of reading: From eye fixations to comprehension. *Psychological Review, 87,* 329-354.

Just, M. A., & Carpenter, P. A. (1987). *The psychology of reading and language comprehension.* Newton, MA: Allyn & Bacon.

Just, M. A., & Carpenter, P. A. (1992). A capacity theory of comprehension: Individual differences in working memory. *Psychological Review, 99,* 122-149.

Kahneman, D. (1973). *Attention and effort.* Englewood Cliffs, NJ: Prentice-Hall.

Kahneman, D., Slovic, P., & Tversky, A. (Eds.). (1982). *Judgment under uncertainty: Heuristics and biases.* Cambridge: Cambridge University Press.

Kahneman, D., & Tversky, A. (1972). Subjective probability: A judgment of representativeness. *Cognitive Psychology, 3,* 430-454.

Kahneman, D., & Tversky, A. (1973). On the psychology of prediction. *Psychological Review, 80,* 237-251.

Kahneman, D., & Tversky, A. (1982a). On the study of statistical intuitions. *Cognition, 11,* 123-141.

Kahneman, D., & Tversky, A. (1982b). The simulation heuristic. In D. Kahneman, P. Slovic, & A. Tversky (Eds.), *Judgment under uncertainty: Heuristics and biases* (pp. 201-208). Cambridge: Cambridge University Press.

Kail, R. (1984). *The development of memory in children* (2nd ed.). New York: Freeman.

Kalick, S. M. (1988). Physical attractiveness as a status cue. *Journal of Experimental Social Psychology, 24,* 469-489.

Kamin, L. (1974). *The science and politics of IQ.* Hillsdale, NJ: Lawrence Erlbaum.

Kaplan, G. A., & Simon, H. A. (1990). In search of insight. *Cognitive Psychology, 22,* 374-419.

Kaufman, A. S., Reynolds, C. R., & McLean, J. E. (1989). Age and WAIS-R intelligence in a national sample of adults in the 20 to 74 year age range: A cross-sectional analysis with educational level controlled. *Intelligence, 13,* 235-253.

Kay, P., & Kempton, W. (1984). What is the Sapir-Wharf hypothesis? *American Anthropologist, 86,* 65-79.

Keil, F. C. (1989). *Concepts, kinds, and cognitive development.* Cambridge: MIT Press.

Kellogg, R. T. (1980). Is conscious attention necessary for long-term storage? *Journal of Experimental Psychology: Human Learning and Memory, 6,* 379-390.

Kellogg, R. T. (1988). Attentional overload and writing performance: Effects of rough draft and outline strategies. *Journal of Experimental Psychology: Learning, Memory, and Cognition, 14,* 355-365.

Kellogg, R. T. (1994). *The psychology of writing.* New York: Oxford University Press.

Kellogg, R. T., Robbins, D. W., & Bourne, L. E., Jr. (1978). Memory for intratrial events in feature identification. *Journal of Experimental Psychology: Human Learning and Memory, 4,* 256-265.

Kemper, S., & Thissen, D. (1981). Memory for the dimensions of requests. *Journal of Verbal Learning and Verbal Behavior, 20,* 552-563.

Keppel, G., & Underwood, B. J. (1962). Proactive inhibition in short-term retention of single items. *Journal of Verbal Learning and Verbal Behavior, 1,* 153-161.

Kieras, D. E. (1978). Good and bad structure in simple paragraphs: Effects on apparent theme, reading time, and recall. *Journal of Verbal Learning and Verbal Behavior, 17,* 13-28.

Kihlstrom, J. F., & Evans, F. J. (Eds.). (1979). *Functional disorders of memory.* Hillsdale, NJ: Lawrence Erlbaum.

Kihlstrom, J. F., Schacter, D. L., Cork, R. C., Hunt, L. A., & Bahr, S. E. (1990). Implicit and explicit memory following surgical anesthesia. *Psychological Science, 1,* 303-306.

Kinchla, R. A. (1992). Attention. *Annual Review of Psychology, 43,* 711-742.

Kintsch, W. (1970). *Learning, memory, and conceptual processes.* New York: John Wiley.

Kintsch, W. (1974). *The representation of meaning in memory.* Hillsdale, NJ: Lawrence Erlbaum.

Kintsch, W. (1980). Semantic memory: A tutorial. In R. S. Nickerson (Ed.), *Attention and performance VIII* (pp. 595-620). Hillsdale, NJ: Lawrence Erlbaum.

Kintsch, W. (1988). The role of knowledge in discourse comprehension: A construction-integration model. *Psychological Review, 95,* 163-182.

Kintsch, W., & Keenan, J. M. (1973). Reading rate as a function of the number of propositions in the base structure of sentences. *Cognitive Psychology, 5,* 257-274.

Kintsch, W., & van Dijk, T. A. (1978). Toward a model of text comprehension and production. *Psychological Review, 85,* 363-394.

Klahr, D., Langley, P., & Neches, R. (Eds.). (1987). *Production system models of learning and development.* Cambridge: MIT Press.

Klayman, J., & Ha, Y. W. (1987). Confirmation, disconfirmation, and information in hypothesis testing. *Psychological Review, 94,* 211-228.

Klinger, E. (1978). Modes of normal conscious flow. In K. S. Pope & J. L. Singer (Eds.), *The stream of consciousness: Scientific investigations into the flow of human experience* (pp. 225-258). New York: Plenum.

Klinger, E. (1990). *Daydreaming: Using waking fantasy and imagery for self-knowledge and creativity.* Los Angeles: Jeremy P. Tarcher.

Knowlton, B. J., Ramus, S. J., & Squire, L. R. (1992). Intact artificial grammar learning in amnesia: Dissociation of classification learning and explicit memory for specific instances. *Psychological Science, 3,* 172-179.

Koestler, A. (1975). *The act of creation.* London: Picador.

Koffka, K. (1935). *Principles of Gestalt psychology.* New York: Harcourt, Brace.

Köhler, W. (1925). *The mentality of apes.* London: Routledge & Kegan-Paul.

Kolers, P. A. (1983). Perception and representation. *Annual Review of Psychology, 34,* 129-166.

Komatsu, L. K. (1992). Recent views of conceptual structure. *Psychological Bulletin, 112,* 500-526.

Kosslyn, S. M. (1973). Scanning visual images: Some structural implications. *Perception and Psychophysics, 14,* 90-94.

Kosslyn, S. M. (1975). Information representation in visual images. *Cognitive Psychology, 7,* 341-370.

Kosslyn, S. M. (1980). *Image and mind.* Cambridge, MA: Harvard University Press.

Kosslyn, S. M. (1981). The medium and the message in mental imagery. *Psychological Review, 88,* 46-66.

Kosslyn, S. M. (1983). *Ghosts in the mind's machine.* New York: Norton.

Kosslyn, S. M., & Pomerantz, J. R. (1977). Imagery, propositions, and the form of internal representations. *Cognitive Psychology, 9,* 52-76.

Kotovsky, K., & Fallside, D. (1989). Representation and transfer in problem solving. In D. Klahr & K. Kotovsky (Eds.), *Complex information processing: The contributions of Herbert A. Simon* (pp. 69-108). Hillsdale, NJ: Lawrence Erlbaum.

Krauth, J. (1982). Formulation and experimental verification of models in propositional reasoning. *Quarterly Journal of Experimental Psychology, 34,* 285-298.

Kucera, H., & Francis, W. N. (1967). *A computational analysis of present day American English.* Providence, RI: Brown University Press.

Kunst-Wilson, W. R., & Zajonc, R. B. (1980). Affective discrimination of stimuli that cannot be recognized. *Science, 207,* 557-558.

Kutas, M., & Hillyard, S. A. (1980). Reading senseless sentences: Brain potentials reflect semantic incongruity. *Science, 207,* 203-205.

Kutas, M., Van Petten, C., & Besson, M. (1988). Event-related potential asymmetries during the reading of sentences. *Electroencephalography and Clinical Neurophysiology, 69,* 218-233.

Kute, S. (1982). *Incorporation of conditioned stimuli during REM sleep.* Unpublished doctoral dissertation, City University of New York.

LaBerge, D. L. (1990). Attention. *Psychological Science, 1,* 156-162.

LaBerge, D., Brown, V., Carter, M., Bash, D., & Hartley, A. (1991). Reducing the effects of adjacent distractions by narrowing attention. *Journal of Experimental Psychology: Human Perception and Performance, 17,* 90-95.

LaBerge, D., & Buchsbaum, M. S. (1990). Positron emission tomographic measurements of pulvinar activity during an attention task. *Journal of Neuroscience, 10,* 613-619.

Labov, W. (1973). The boundaries of words and their meanings. In C. J. N. Bailey & R. W. Shuy (Eds.), *New ways of analyzing variations in English* (pp. 340-373). Washington, DC: Georgetown University Press.

Lackner, J. R. (1974). Speech production: Evidence for corollary discharge stabilization of perceptual mechanisms. *Perceptual and Motor Skills, 39,* 899-902.

Ladefoged, P. (1975). *A course in phonetics.* New York: Harcourt Brace Jovanovich.

Lakoff, G. (1987). *Women, fire, and dangerous things.* Chicago: University of Chicago Press.

Langer, E. J. (1989). *Mindfulness.* Reading, MA: Addison-Wesley.

Larkin, J. H., McDermott, J., Simon, D. P., & Simon, H. A. (1980). Expert and novice performance in solving physics problems. *Science, 208,* 1335-1342.

Lashley, K. S. (1951). The problem of serial order in behavior. In L. A. Jeffress (Ed.), *Cerebral mechanisms in behavior* (pp. 112-136). New York: John Wiley.

Leahey, T. H. (1987). *A history of psychology: Main currents in psychological thought.* Englewood Cliffs, NJ: Prentice-Hall.

Lee, G., & Oakhill, J. (1984). The effects of externalization on syllogistic reasoning. *Quarterly Journal of Experimental Psychology, 36A,* 519-530.

Lenat, D. (1983). Eurisko: A program that learns new heuristics and domain concepts. *Artificial Intelligence, 21*(1-2), 61-98.

Levelt, W. J. M. (1989). *Speaking: From intention to articulation.* Cambridge: MIT Press.

Levine, M. A. (1966). Hypothesis behavior by humans during discrimination learning. *Journal of Experimental Psychology, 71,* 331-338.

Levine, M. A. (1975). *A cognitive theory of learning.* Hillsdale, NJ: Lawrence Erlbaum.

Levine, M. A. (1988). *Effective problem solving.* Englewood Cliffs, NJ: Prentice-Hall.

Levine, M. W., & Shefner, J. M. (1981). *Fundamentals of sensation and perception.* Reading, MA: Addison-Wesley.

Levy, B. A., & Hinchley, J. (1990). Individual and developmental differences in the acquisition of reading skills. In T. H. Carr & B. A. Levy (Eds.), *Reading and its development: Component skills approaches* (pp. 81-128). San Diego, CA: Academic Press.

Levy, J., & Heller, W. (1992). Gender differences in human neuropsychological function. In A. A. Gerall, H. Moltz, & I. L. Ward (Eds.), *Handbook of behavioral neurobiology* (Vol. 11, pp. 245-274). New York: Plenum.

Lewandowsky, S., Dunn, J. C., & Kirsner, K. (Eds.). (1989). *Implicit memory: Theoretical issues*. Hillsdale, NJ: Lawrence Erlbaum.

Lewicki, P., Czyzewska, M., & Hoffman, H. (1987). Unconscious acquisition of complex procedural knowledge. *Journal of Experimental Psychology: Learning, Memory, and Cognition, 13*, 523-530.

Liberman, A. M., Cooper, F., Shankweiler, D., & Studdert-Kennedy, M. (1967). Perception of the speech code. *Psychological Review, 74*, 431-459.

Libet, B. (1978). Neuronal versus subjective timing for a conscious sensory experience. In P. A. Buser & A. Rougeul-Buser (Eds.), *Cerebral correlates of conscious experience* (pp. 69-82, INSERM Symposium No. 6). Amsterdam: North Holland/Elsevier.

Libet, B. (1981). Timing of cerebral processes relative to concomitant conscious experiences in man. In G. Adam, I. Meszaros, & R. E. I. Banyai (Eds.), *Advances in physiological science* (Vol. 17, pp. 313-317). Elmsford, NY: Pergamon.

Lieberman, P. (1967). *Intonation, perception, and language*. Cambridge: MIT Press.

Lieberman, P. (1984). *The biology and evolution of language*. Cambridge, MA: Harvard University Press.

Light, L. L., & Carter-Sobell, L. (1970). Effects of changed semantic context on recognition memory. *Journal of Verbal Learning and Verbal Behavior, 9*, 1-11.

Lindsay, P. H., & Norman, D. A. (1977). *Human information processing: An introduction to psychology* (2nd ed.). New York: Academic Press.

Linn, M. C., & Petersen, A. C. (1985). Emergence and characterization of sex differences in spatial ability: A meta-analysis. *Child Development, 56*, 1479-1498.

Linn, R. L. (Ed.). (1990). *Intelligence: Measurement, theory, and public policy: Proceedings of a symposium in honor of Lloyd G. Humphreys*. Urbana: University of Illinois Press.

Lipman, M., Sharp, A. M., & Oscanyan, F. S. (1980). *Philosophy in the classroom* (2nd ed.). Philadelphia: Temple University Press.

Lisker, L. (1986). "Voicing" in English: A catalog of acoustic features signalling /b/ versus /p/ in trochees. *Language and Speech, 29*, 3-11.

Lisker, L., & Abramson, A. (1970). The voicing dimension: Some experiments in comparative phonetics. In *Proceedings of Sixth International Congress of Phonetic Sciences, Prague, 1967* (pp. 563-567). Prague: Academia.

Livingston, M. S., & Hubel, D. H. (1987). Psychological evidence for separate channels for the perception of form, color, movement and depth. *Journal of Neuroscience, 7*, 3416-3468.

Loftus, E. F. (1979). *Eyewitness testimony*. Cambridge, MA: Harvard University Press.

Loftus, E. F. (1986). Ten years in the life of an expert witness. *Law and Human Behavior, 10*, 241-263.

Loftus, E. F. (1993). The reality of repressed memories. *American Psychologist, 48,* 518-537.

Loftus, E. F. (1994). The repressed memory controversy. *American Psychologist, 49,* 443-445.

Loftus, E. F., & Loftus, G. R. (1980). On the permanence of stored information in the human brain. *American Psychologist, 35,* 409-420.

Loftus, E. F., Miller, D. G., & Burns, H. J. (1978). Semantic integration of verbal information into a visual memory. *Journal of Experimental Psychology: Human Learning and Memory, 4,* 19-31.

Loftus, E. F., & Palmer, J. C. (1974). Reconstruction of automobile destruction: An example of the interaction between language and memory. *Journal of Verbal Learning and Verbal Behavior, 13,* 585-589.

Loftus, E. F., Schooler, J. W., & Wagenaar, W. A. (1985). The fate of memory: Comment on McCloskey and Zaragoza. *Journal of Experimental Psychology: General, 114,* 375-380.

Logan, G. D. (1988). Toward an instance theory of automatization. *Psychological Review, 95,* 492-527.

Logan, R. K. (1986). *The alphabet effect: The impact of the phonetic alphabet on the development of Western civilization.* New York: William Morrow.

Luchins, A. S. (1942). Mechanization in problem solving: The effect of Einstellung. *Psychological Monographs, 4*(6, Whole No. 248).

Luria, A. R. (1968). *The mind of a mnemonist.* New York: Basic Books.

Luria, A. R. (1976). *Cognitive development: Its cultural and social foundations* (M. Cole, Ed.; M. Lopez-Morillas & L. Solotaroff, Trans.). Cambridge, MA: Harvard University Press.

Maccoby, E. E., & Jacklin, C. N. (1974). *The psychology of sex differences.* Stanford, CA: Stanford University Press.

MacGregor, J. N. (1987). Short-term memory capacity: Limitation or optimization? *Psychological Review, 94,* 107-108.

MacKay, D. G. (1973). Aspects of the theory of comprehension, memory and attention. *Quarterly Journal of Experimental Psychology, 25,* 22-40.

MacKay, D. G. (1987). *The organization of perception and action: A theory for language and other cognitive skills.* New York: Springer-Verlag.

MacKay, D. G., Wulf, G., Yin, C., & Abrams, L. (1993). Relations between word perception and production: New theory and data on the verbal transformation effect. *Journal of Memory and Language, 32,* 624-646.

MacKenzie, N. (1965). *Dreams and dreaming.* London: Aldus.

MacKinnon, D. W. (1978). *In search of human effectiveness.* New York: Creative Education Foundation.

MacLean, H. N. (1993). *Once upon a time: A true story of memory, murder, and the law.* New York: HarperCollins.

MacLeod, C. M. (1991). Half a century of research on the Stroop effect: An integrative review. *Psychological Bulletin, 109,* 163-203.

Mandler, G. (1979). Organization and repetition: Organizational principles with special reference to rote learning. In L. G. Nilsson (Ed.), *Perspectives on memory research: Essays in honor of Uppsala University's 500th Anniversary* (pp. 293-328). Hillsdale, NJ: Lawrence Erlbaum.

Mandler, G. (1980). Recognizing: The judgment of previous occurrence. *Psychological Review, 87,* 252-271.

Mandler, G. (1985). *Cognitive psychology: An essay in cognitive science.* Hillsdale, NJ: Lawrence Erlbaum.

Mandler, G., Pearlstone, Z., & Koopmans, H. J. (1969). Effects of organization and semantic similarity on recall and recognition. *Journal of Verbal Learning and Verbal Behavior, 8,* 410-423.

Mandler, J. M. (1979). Categorical and schematic organization in memory. In C. R. Puff (Ed.), *Memory organization and structure* (pp. 259-299). New York: Academic Press.

Mandler, J. M. (1984). *Stories, scripts, and scenes: Aspects of schema theory.* Hillsdale, NJ: Lawrence Erlbaum.

Mandler, J. M., & Johnson, N. S. (1977). Remembrance of things parsed: Story structure and recall. *Cognitive Psychology, 9,* 111-151.

Mandler, J. M., & Ritchey, G. H. (1977). Long-term memory for pictures. *Journal of Experimental Psychology: Human Learning and Memory, 3,* 386-396.

Mandler, J. M., Scribner, S., Cole, M., & DeForest, M. (1980). Cross-cultural invariance in story recall. *Child Development, 51,* 19-26.

Mantyla, T. (1986). Optimizing cue effectiveness: Recall of 500 and 600 incidentally learned words. *Journal of Experimental Psychology: Learning, Memory, and Cognition, 12,* 66-71.

Marcel, A. J. (1983). Conscious and unconscious perception: Experiments on visual masking and word recognition. *Cognitive Psychology, 15,* 197-237.

Marcus, S. L., & Rips, L. J. (1979). Conditional reasoning. *Journal of Verbal Learning and Verbal Behavior, 18,* 199-223.

Markman, E. M. (1977). Realizing that you don't understand. *Child Development, 48,* 986-992.

Marks, L. E. (1987). On cross-modal similarity: Auditory-visual interactions in speeded discrimination. *Journal of Experimental Psychology: Human Perception and Performance, 13,* 384-394.

Markus, H., & Wurf, E. (1987). The dynamic self-concept: A social psychological perspective. *Annual Review of Psychology, 38,* 299-337.

Marlatt, G. A. (1978). Behavioral assessment of social drinking and alcoholism. In G. A. Marlatt & P. E. Nathan (Eds.), *Behavioral approaches to alcoholism* (pp. 35-57). New Brunswick, NJ: Rutger's Center for Alcohol Studies.

Marlatt, G. A., Baer, J. S., Donovan, D. M., & Kivlahan, D. R. (1988). Addictive behaviors: Etiology and treatment. *Annual Review of Psychology, 39,* 223-252.

Marr, D. (1982). *Vision: A computational investigation into the representation and processing of visual information.* San Francisco: Freeman.

Marr, D. B., & Sternberg, R. J. (1987). The role of mental speed in intelligence: A triarchic perspective. In P. A. Vernon (Ed.), *Speed of information processing and intelligence* (pp. 271-294). Norwood, NJ: Ablex.

Marschark, M., Richman, C. L., Yuille, J. C., & Hunt, R. R. (1987). The role of imagery in memory: On shared and distinctive information. *Psychological Bulletin, 102,* 28-41.

Massaro, D. W. (1970). Preperceptual auditory images. *Journal of Experimental Psychology, 85,* 411-417.

Massaro, D. W., & Cowan, N. (1993). Information processing models: Microscopes of the mind. *Annual Review of Psychology, 44,* 383-425.

Matarazzo, J. D. (1992). Psychological testing and measurement in the 21st century. *American Psychologist, 47,* 1007-1018.

McCarthy, R. A., & Warrington, E. K. (1990). *Cognitive neuropsychology: A clinical introduction.* New York: Academic Press.

McClelland, D. C. (1973). Testing for competence rather than for "intelligence." *American Psychologist, 28,* 1-14.

McClelland, D. C. (1994). The knowledge-testing-educational complex strikes back. *American Psychologist, 49,* 66-69.

McClelland, J. L., & Elman, J. L. (1986). The TRACE model of speech perception. *Cognitive Psychology, 18,* 1-86.

McCloskey, M., Wible, C. G., & Cohen, N. J. (1988). Is there a special flashbulb-memory mechanism? *Journal of Experimental Psychology: General, 117,* 171-181.

McCloskey, M., & Zaragoza, M. (1985). Misleading postevent information and memory for events: Arguments and evidence against memory impairment hypotheses. *Journal of Experimental Psychology: General, 114,* 1-16.

McConkie, G. W., & Rayner, K. (1975). The effective stimulus during a fixation in reading. *Perception and Psychophysics, 17,* 578-586.

McDaniel, M. A., & Einstein, G. O. (1986). Bizarre imagery as an effective memory aid: The importance of distinctiveness. *Journal of Experimental Psychology: Learning, Memory, and Cognition, 12,* 54-65.

McDaniel, M. A., & Pressley, M. (Eds.). (1987). *Imagery and related mnemonic processes.* New York: Springer-Verlag.

McGeoch, J. A. (1942). *The psychology of human learning: An introduction.* New York: Longmans, Green.

McGraw, K. L., & Harbison-Briggs, K. (1989). *Knowledge acquisition: Principles and guidelines.* Englewood Cliffs, NJ: Prentice-Hall.

McKoon, G., & Ratcliff, R. (1980). The comprehension processes and memory structures involved in anaphoric reference. *Journal of Verbal Learning and Verbal Behavior, 19,* 668-682.

McKoon, G., & Ratcliff, R. (1981). The comprehension processes and memory structures involved in instrumental inference. *Journal of Verbal Learning and Verbal Behavior, 20,* 671-682.

McLaughlin, B. (1978). *Second-language acquisition in childhood.* Hillsdale, NJ: Lawrence Erlbaum.

Medin, D. L., & Schaffer, M. M. (1978). Context theory of classification. *Psychological Review, 85,* 207-238.

Medin, D. L., & Smith, E. E. (1984). Concepts and concept formation. *Annual Review of Psychology, 35,* 113-138.

Melton, A. W. (1970). The situation with respect to the spacing of repetitions and memory. *Journal of Verbal Learning and Verbal Behavior, 9,* 596-606.

Merikle, P. M. (1980). Selection from visual persistence by perceptual groups and category membership. *Journal of*

Experimental Psychology: General, 109, 279-295.

Merikle, P. M., & Reingold, E. M. (1992). Measuring unconscious perceptual processes. In R. F. Bornstein & T. S. Pittman (Eds.), *Perception without awareness: Cognitive, clinical, and social perspectives* (pp. 55-80). New York: Guilford.

Metzler, J., & Shepard, R. N. (1974). Transformational studies of the internal representations of three dimensional objects. In R. L. Solso (Ed.), *Information processing and cognition: The Loyola Symposium* (pp. 147-201). Hillsdale, NJ: Lawrence Erlbaum.

Meyer, B. J. F. (1975). *The organization of prose and its effect on memory.* Amsterdam: North-Holland.

Meyer, D. E. (1970). On the representation and retrieval of stored semantic information. *Cognitive Psychology, 1,* 242-300.

Miller, G. A. (1956). The magical number seven, plus or minus two: Some limits on our capacity for processing information. *Psychological Review, 63,* 81-97.

Miller, G. A., Heise, G., & Lichten, W. (1951). The intelligibility of speech as a function of the context of the test materials. *Journal of Experimental Psychology, 41,* 329-335.

Miller, G. A., & Isard, S. (1963). Some perceptual consequences of linguistic rules. *Journal of Verbal Learning and Verbal Behavior, 2,* 217-228.

Miller, J. L. (1990). Speech perception. In D. N. Osherson & H. Lasnik (Eds.), *An invitation to cognitive science: Vol 1. Language* (pp. 69-93). Cambridge: MIT Press.

Miller, J. L., & Eimas, P. D. (1983). Studies on the categorization of speech by infants. *Cognition, 13,* 135-165.

Miller, J. L., & Volaitis, L. E. (1989). Effect of speaking rate on the perceptual structure of a phonetic category. *Perception and Psychophysics, 46,* 505-512.

Miller, J. R., & Kintsch, W. (1980). Readability and recall of short prose passages: A theoretical analysis. *Journal of Experimental Psychology: Human Learning and Memory, 6,* 335-354.

Milner, B. (1965). Visually-guided maze learning in man: Effects of bilateral hippocampal, bilateral frontal, and unilateral cerebral lesions. *Neuropsychologica, 3,* 317-338.

Milner, B. (1966). Amnesia following operations on the temporal lobes. In C. W. M. Whitney & O. L. Zangwill (Eds.), *Amnesia* (pp. 109-133). London: Butterworth.

Milner, B. (1975). Psychological aspects of focal epilepsy and its neurosurgical management. *Advances in Neurology, 8,* 299-321.

Minsky, M. L. (Ed.). (1968). *Semantic information processing.* Cambridge: MIT Press.

Minsky, M. L. (1977). Frame-system theory. In P. N. Johnson-Laird & P. C. Wason (Eds.), *Thinking: Readings in cognitive science* (pp. 355-376). Cambridge: Cambridge University Press.

Mirin, S. M., & Weiss, R. D. (1989). Genetic factors in the development of alcoholism. *Psychiatric Annuals, 19,* 239-242.

Mishkoff, H. (1985). *Understanding artificial intelligence.* Dallas: Texas Instruments Inc.

Moran, J., & Desimone, R. (1985). Selective attention gates visual processing in the extrastriate cortex. *Science, 229,* 782-784.

Moray, N. (1959). Attention in dichotic listening: Affective cues and the influence of instructions. *Quarterly Journal of Experimental Psychology, 11,* 56-60.

Moray, N., Bates, A., & Barnett, T. (1965). Experiments on the four-eared man. *Journal of Acoustical Society of America, 42,* 196-201.

Morris, C. D., Bransford, J. D., & Franks, J. J. (1977). Levels of processing versus transfer appropriate processing. *Journal of Verbal Learning and Verbal Behavior, 16,* 519-533.

Morton, E. S., & Page, J. (1992). *Animal talk: Science and voices of nature.* New York: Random House.

Moscovitch, M. (1982). Multiple dissociations of function in amnesia. In L. S. Cermak (Ed.), *Human memory and amnesia* (pp. 337-370). Hillsdale, NJ: Lawrence Erlbaum.

Mountcastle, V. B. (1979). An organizing principle for cerebral function: The unit module and the distributed system. In F. O. Schmitt & F. G. Worden (Eds.), *The neurosciences* (pp. 21-42). Cambridge: MIT Press.

Mumford, M. D., & Gustafson, S. B. (1988). Creativity syndrome: Integration, application, and innovation. *Psychological Bulletin, 103,* 27-43.

Murdock, B. B. (1974). *Human memory: Theory and data.* Potomac, MD: Lawrence Erlbaum.

Murdock, B. B. (1982). A theory for the storage and retrieval of item and associative information. *Psychological Review, 89,* 609-626.

Murphy, G. L., & Medin, D. L. (1985). The role of theories in conceptual coherence. *Psychological Review, 92,* 289-316.

Murphy, G. L., & Smith, E. E. (1982). Basic level superiority in picture categorization. *Journal of Verbal Learning and Verbal Behavior, 21,* 1-20.

Murphy, T. D., & Eriksen, C. W. (1987). Temporal changes in the distribution of attention in the visual field in response to precues. *Perceptions & Psychophysics, 42,* 576-586.

Murray, D. M. (1982). *Learning by teaching: Selected articles on writing and teaching.* Montclair, NJ: Boynton/Cook.

Myers, H. F. (1991, November 25). Das kapital. *Wall Street Journal,* pp. 1, 10.

Näätänen, R. (1992). *Attention and brain function.* Hillsdale, NJ: Lawrence Erlbaum.

Nash, M. (1987). What, if anything, is regressed about hypnotic age regression? A review of the empirical literature. *Psychological Bulletin, 102,* 42-52.

Navon, D., & Gopher, D. (1979). On the economy of the human-processing system. *Psychological Review, 86,* 214-255.

Neath, I., Surprenant, A. M., & Crowder, R. G. (1993). The context-dependent stimulus suffix effect. *Journal of Experimental Psychology: Learning, Memory, and Cognition, 19,* 698-703.

Neisser, U. (1963). Decision time without reaction time: Experiments in visual scanning. *American Journal of Psychology, 76,* 376-385.

Neisser, U. (1967). *Cognitive psychology.* New York: Appleton.

Neisser, U. (1976). *Cognition and reality.* San Francisco: Freeman.

Neisser, U. (1981). John Dean's memory: A case study. *Cognition, 9,* 1-22.

Neisser, U. (1982). *Memory observed: Remembering in natural contexts.* San Francisco: Freeman.

Neisser, U., & Harsch, N. (1992). Phantom flashbulbs: False recollections of hearing the news about Challenger. In E. Winograd & U. Neisser (Eds.), *Affect and accuracy in recall: Studies of "flashbulb memories"* (pp. 9-31). Cambridge: Cambridge University Press.

Nelson, K. (1990). Remembering, forgetting, and childhood amnesia. In R. Fivush & J. A. Hudson (Eds.), *Knowing and remembering in young children* (pp. 301-316). New York: Cambridge University Press.

Neves, D. M., & Anderson, J. R. (1981). Knowledge compilation: Mechanisms for the automatization of cognitive skills. In J. R. Anderson (Ed.), *Cognitive skills and their acquisition* (pp. 57-84). Hillsdale, NJ: Lawrence Erlbaum.

Newcomb, M. D., & Harlow, L. L. (1986). Life events and substance use among adolescents: Mediating effects of perceived loss of control and meaninglessness in life. *Journal of Personality and Social Psychology, 51,* 564-577.

Newell, A., & Simon, H. A. (1972). *Human problem solving.* Englewood Cliffs, NJ: Prentice-Hall.

Nezworski, T., Stein, N. L., & Trabasso, T. (1981). Story structure versus content in children's recall. *Journal of Verbal Learning and Verbal Behavior, 21,* 196-201.

Nickerson, R. S. (1988). On improving thinking through instruction. In E. Z. Rothkopf (Ed.), *Review of research in education* (pp. 3-57). Washington, DC: American Educational Research Association.

Nickerson, R. S., & Adams, M. J. (1979). Long-term memory for a common object. *Cognitive Psychology, 11,* 287-307.

Nickerson, R. S., Perkins, D. N., & Smith, E. E. (1985). *The teaching of thinking.* Hillsdale, NJ: Lawrence Erlbaum.

Nisbett, R. E., & Ross, L. (1980). *Human inference: Strategies and shortcomings of social judgment.* Englewood Cliffs, NJ: Prentice-Hall.

Nissen, M. J., & Bullemer, P. (1987). Attentional requirements of learning: Evidence from performance measures. *Cognitive Psychology, 19,* 1-32.

Nissen, M. J., Knopman, D., & Schacter, D. L. (1987). Neurochemical dissociation of memory systems. *Neurology, 37,* 789-794.

Norman, D. A. (1968). Toward a theory of memory and attention. *Psychological Review, 75,* 522-536.

Norman, D. A. (1969). Memory while shadowing. *Quarterly Journal of Experimental Psychology, 21,* 85-93.

Norman, D. A. (1981). Categorization of action slips. *Psychological Review, 88,* 1-15.

Nystrand, M. (1989). A social-interactive model of writing. *Written Communication, 6,* 66-85.

Ochse, R. (1990). *Before the gates of excellence.* New York: Cambridge University Press.

Oden, G. C. (1987). Concept, knowledge, and thought. *Annual Review of Psychology, 38,* 203-227.

Oetting, E. R., & Beauvais, F. (1987). Peer cluster theory, socialization characteristics, and adolescent drug use: A path analysis. *Journal of Counseling Psychology, 34,* 205-213.

Olio, K. A. (1989). Memory retrieval in the treatment of adult survivors of sexual abuse. *Transactional Analysis Journal, 19,* 93-100.

Olio, K. A. (1994). Truth in memory. *American Psychologist, 49,* 442-443.

Omanson, R. C. (1982). The relation between centrality and story category variation. *Journal of Verbal Learning and Verbal Behavior, 21,* 326-337.

Ornstein, R. E. (Ed.). (1968). *The nature of human consciousness: A book of readings.* San Francisco: Freeman.

Ornstein, R. E. (1972). *The psychology of consciousness.* San Francisco: Freeman.

Osherson, D. H., & Smith, E. E. (Eds.). (1990). *An invitation to cognitive science: Vol. 3. Thinking.* Cambridge: MIT Press.

Overton, D. A. (1971). State-dependent learning produced by alcohol and its relevance to alcoholism. In B. Kissin & H. Begleiter (Eds.), *The biology of alcoholism: Vol. 2. Physiology and behavior* (pp. 193-217). New York: Plenum.

Paivio, A. (1971). *Imagery and verbal processes.* New York: Holt, Rinehart & Winston.

Paivio, A. (1983). The empirical case for dual coding. In J. Yuille (Ed.), *Imagery, memory, and cognition: Essays in honor of Allen Paivio* (pp. 307-332). Hillsdale, NJ: Lawrence Erlbaum.

Palmer, J., MacLeod, C. M., Hunt, E., & Davidson, J. E. (1985). Information processing correlates of reading. *Journal of Memory and Language, 24,* 59-88.

Palmer, S. E. (1975). The effects of contextual scenes on the identification of objects. *Memory & Cognition, 3,* 519-526.

Parasuraman, R., & Davies, D. R. (1984). *Varieties of attention.* Orlando, FL: Academic Press.

Parker, S. T., & Gibson, K. R. (1990). *"Language" and intelligence in monkeys and apes: Comparative developmental perspectives.* New York: Cambridge University Press.

Parkin, A. J. (1993). *Memory: Phenomena, experiment, and theory.* Oxford: Blackwell.

Patel, V. L., & Groen, G. J. (1991). The general and specific nature of medical expertise: A critical look. In K. A. Ericsson & J. Smith (Eds.), *Toward a general theory of expertise* (pp. 93-125). Cambridge: Cambridge University Press.

Payne, D. G. (1987). Hypermnesia and reminiscence in recall: A historical and empirical review. *Psychological Bulletin, 101,* 5-27.

Payne, D. G., & Wenger, M. J. (1992). Improving memory through practice. In D. J. Hermann, H. Weingartner, A. Searlman, & C. L. McEvoy (Eds.), *Memory improvement: Implications for memory theory* (pp. 187-209). New York: Springer-Verlag.

Pea, R. D., & Kurland, D. M. (1984). On the cognitive effects of learning computer programming: A critical look. *New Ideas in Psychology, 2,* 137-168.

Penfield, W. (1959). The interpretive cortex. *Science, 129,* 1719-1725.

Penney, C. G. (1975). Modality effects in short-term verbal memory. *Psychological Bulletin, 82,* 68-84.

Penney, C. G. (1989). Modality effects and the structure of short-term verbal memory. *Memory & Cognition, 17,* 398-422.

Perfetti, C. A. (1985). *Reading ability.* New York: Oxford University Press.

Perkins, D. N., & Salomon, G. (1989). Are cognitive skills context-bound? *Educational Researcher, 18,* 16-25.

Perris, E. E., Myers, N. A., & Clifton, R. K. (1990). Long-term memory for a single infancy experience. *Child Development, 61,* 1796-1807.

Perruchet, P., & Pacteau, C. (1990). Synthetic grammar learning: Implicit rule abstraction or fragmentary knowledge? *Journal of Experimental Psychology: General, 119,* 264-275.

Peterson, C. R., & Beach, L. R. (1967). Man as an intuitive statistician. *Psychological Bulletin, 68,* 29-46.

Peterson, L. R., & Peterson, M. J. (1959). Short-term retention of individual verbal items. *Journal of Experimental Psychology, 58,* 193-198.

Peterson, S. E., Fox, P. T., Posner, M. I., Mintun, M., & Raichle, M. E. (1989). Positron emission tomographic studies of the processing of single words. *Journal of Cognitive Neuroscience, 1,* 153-170.

Petty, R. E., & Cacioppo, J. T. (1981). *Attitudes and persuasion: Classic and contemporary approaches.* Dubuque, IA: William C. Brown.

Pillemer, D. B. (1984). Flashbulb memories of the assassination attempt on President Reagan. *Cognition, 16,* 63-80.

Pinker, S. (1984a). *Language learnability and language development.* Cambridge, MA: Harvard University Press.

Pinker, S. (1984b). Visual cognition: An introduction. *Cognition, 18,* 1-63.

Pinker, S. (1985). *Visual cognition.* Cambridge: MIT Press.

Pinker, S. (1990). Language acquisition. In D. N. Osherson & H. Lasaik (Eds.), *An invitation to cognitive science: Vol. 1. Language* (pp. 199-241). Cambridge: MIT Press.

Pitz, G. F., & Sachs, N. J. (1984). Judgment and decision: Theory and application. *Annual Review of Psychology, 35,* 139-163.

Place, E. J. S., & Gilmore, G. C. (1980). Perceptual organization in schizophrenia. *Journal of Abnormal Psychology, 89,* 125-144.

Plomin, R., DeFries, J. C., & McClearn, G. E. (1990). *Behavioral genetics: A primer* (2nd ed.). New York: Freeman.

Pollack, I., & Pickett, J. M. (1964). Intelligibility of excerpts from fluent speech: Auditory vs. structural context. *Journal of Verbal Learning and Verbal Behavior, 3,* 79-84.

Pollatsek, A., & Rayner, K. (1989). Reading. In M. I. Posner (Ed.), *The foundations of cognitive science* (pp. 401-436). Cambridge: MIT Press.

Polson, M. C., & Friedman, A. (1988). Task-sharing within and between hemispheres: A multiple-resources approach. *Human Factors, 30,* 633-643.

Polya, G. (1957). *How to solve it: A new aspect of mathematical method* (2nd ed.). Garden City, NY: Doubleday.

Pope, K. S. (1977). *The stream of consciousness.* Unpublished doctoral dissertation, Yale University.

Popper, K. R. (1974). *Conjectures and refutations: The growth of scientific knowl-*

edge. London: Routledge & Kegan Paul.

Popper, K. R., & Eccles, J. C. (1977). *The self and its brain.* Berlin: Springer-Verlag.

Posner, M. I. (1980). Orienting of attention. *Quarterly Journal of Experimental Psychology, 32,* 3-25.

Posner, M. I. (Ed.). (1989). *Foundations of cognitive science.* Cambridge: MIT Press.

Posner, M. I., & Cohen, Y. (1984). Components of visual orienting. In H. Bouma & D. G. Bouwhuis (Eds.), *Attention and performance X: Control of language processes* (pp. 531-554). Hillsdale, NJ: Lawrence Erlbaum.

Posner, M. I., Cohen, Y., & Rafal, R. D. (1982). Neural systems control of spatial orienting. *Philosophical Transactions of the Royal Society of London, 298B,* 187-198.

Posner, M. I., & Peterson, S. E. (1990). The attention system of the human brain. *Annual Review of Neuroscience, 13,* 25-42.

Posner, M. I., & Raichle, M. E. (1994). *Images of mind.* New York: Scientific American Library.

Posner, M. I., & Snyder, C. R. R. (1974). Attention and cognitive control. In R. L. Solso (Ed.), *Information processing and cognition: The Loyola Symposium* (pp. 55-85). Hillsdale, NJ: Lawrence Erlbaum.

Posner, M. I., & Snyder, C. R. R. (1975). Facilitation and inhibition in the processing of signals. In P. M. A. Rabbit & S. Dornic (Eds.), *Attention and performance V* (pp. 669-682). London: Academic Press.

Potter, M. C. (1990). Remembering. In D. N. Osherson & E. E. Smith (Eds.),

Thinking: An invitation to cognitive science (Vol. 3, pp. 3-32). Cambridge: MIT Press.

Pressley, M., Snyder, B. L., & Cariglia-Bull, T. (1987). How can good strategy use be taught to children? Evaluation of six alternative approaches. In S. M. Cormier & J. D. Hagman (Eds.), *Transfer of learning* (pp. 81-120). New York: Academic Press.

Pribram, K. H. (1971). *Languages of the brain: Experimental paradoxes and principles in neuropsychology* (3rd ed.). New York: Brandon House.

Pribram, K. H. (1976). Problems concerning the structure of consciousness. In G. G. Globus, G. Maxwell, & I. Savodnik (Eds.), *Consciousness and the brain: A scientific and philosophical inquiry* (pp. 798-809). New York: Plenum.

Pribram, K. H. (1986). The cognitive revolution and mind/brain issues. *American Psychologist, 41,* 507-520.

Pylyshyn, Z. W. (1973). What the mind's eye tells the mind's brain: A critique of mental imagery. *Psychological Bulletin, 80,* 1-24.

Pylyshyn, Z. W. (1981). The imagery debate: Analogue media versus tacit knowledge. *Psychological Review, 88,* 16-45.

Raaijmakers, G. W., & Shiffrin, R. M. (1981). Search of associative memory. *Psychological Review, 88,* 93-134.

Radford, A. (1988). *Transformational grammar: A first course.* New York: Cambridge University Press.

Rafal, R. D., & Posner, M. I. (1987). Deficits in human visual spatial attention following thalamic lesions. *Proceedings of the National Academy of Science USA, 84,* 7349-7353.

Reber, A. S. (1989). Implicit learning and tacit knowledge. *Journal of Experimental Psychology: General, 118*, 219-235.

Reber, A. S. (1993). *Implicit learning and tacit knowledge: An essay on the cognitive unconscious.* New York: Oxford University Press.

Reber, A. S., & Allen, R. (1978). Analogical and abstraction strategies in synthetic grammar learning: A functionalist interpretation. *Cognition, 6*, 189-221.

Reber, A. S., Kassin, S. M., Lewis, S., & Cantor, G. (1980). On the relationship between implicit and explicit modes in the learning of complex rule structure. *Journal of Experimental Psychology: Human Learning and Memory, 6*, 492-502.

Reed, S. K. (1972). Pattern recognition and categorization. *Cognitive Psychology, 3*, 383-407.

Reed, S. K. (1973). *Psychological processes in pattern recognition.* New York: Academic Press.

Reed, S. K. (1974). Structural descriptions and the limitations of visual images. *Memory & Cognition, 2*, 329-336.

Reed, S. K., & Johnsen, J. A. (1975). Detection of parts in patterns and images. *Memory & Cognition, 3*, 569-575.

Reeves, A., & Sperling, G. (1986). Attention gating in short-term visual memory. *Psychological Review, 93*, 180-206.

Reicher, G. M. (1969). Perceptual recognition as a function of meaningfulness of stimulus material. *Journal of Experimental Psychology, 81*, 275-280.

Reitman, J. S. (1974). Without surreptitious rehearsal, information in short-term memory decays. *Journal of Verbal Learning and Verbal Behavior, 13*, 365-377.

Reitman, J. S. (1976). Skilled perception in GO: Deducing memory structures from interresponse times. *Cognitive Psychology, 8*, 336-356.

Repp, B. H., & Liberman, A. M. (1987). Phonetic boundaries are flexible. In S. Harnad (Ed.), *Categorical perception: The groundwork of cognition* (pp. 89-112). Cambridge: Cambridge University Press.

Resnick, L. B. (1981). Instructional psychology. *Annual Review of Psychology, 32*, 659-704.

Revlis, R. (1975). Two models of syllogistic reasoning: Feature selection and conversion. *Journal of Verbal Learning and Verbal Behavior, 14*, 180-195.

Richardson-Klavehn, A., & Bjork, R. A. (1988). Measures of memory. *Annual Review of Psychology, 39*, 475-543.

Rips, L. J. (1983). Cognitive processes in propositional reasoning. *Psychological Review, 90*, 38-71.

Rips, L. J. (1990). Reasoning. *Annual Review of Psychology, 41*, 321-353.

Rips, L. J., & Marcus, S. L. (1977). Supposition and the analysis of conditional sentences. In M. A. Just & P. A. Carpenter (Eds.), *Cognitive processes in comprehension* (pp. 185-220). Hillsdale, NJ: Lawrence Erlbaum.

Rips, L. J., Shoben, E. J., & Smith, E. E. (1973). Semantic distance and the verification of semantic relations. *Journal of Verbal Learning and Verbal Behavior, 12*, 1-20.

Roediger, H. L. (1984). Does current evidence from dissociation experiments favor the episodic/semantic distinction? *Behavioral and Brain Sciences, 7*, 252-254.

Roediger, H. L. (1991). They read an article? A commentary on the everyday memory controversy. *American Psychologist, 46*, 37-40.

Roediger, H. L., & Blaxton, T. A. (1987). Retrieval modes produce dissociations in memory for surface information. In D. S. Gorfein & R. R. Hoffman (Eds.), *Memory and cognitive processes: The Ebbinghaus centennial conference* (pp. 349-379). Hillsdale, NJ: Lawrence Erlbaum.

Roediger, H. L., & Craik, F. I. M. (1989). *Varieties of memory and consciousness: Essays in honour of Endel Tulving.* Hillsdale, NJ: Lawrence Erlbaum.

Roediger, H. L., & Crowder, R. G. (1976). A serial position effect in recall of United States presidents. *Bulletin of the Psychonomic Society, 8*, 275-278.

Roediger, H. L., & Payne, D. G. (1982). Hypermnesia: The role of repeated testing. *Journal of Experimental Psychology: Learning, Memory, and Cognition, 8*, 66-72.

Rogers, T. B., Kuiper, N. A., & Kirker, W. S. (1977). Self-reference and the encoding of personal information. *Journal of Personality and Social Psychology, 35*, 677-688.

Roitblat, H. L., & von Fersen, L. (1992). Comparative cognition: Representations and processes in learning and memory. *Annual Review of Psychology, 43*, 671-710.

Romney, A. K., & D'Andrade, R. G. (1964). Cognitive aspects of English kin terms. In A. K. Romney & R. G. D'Andrade (Eds.), Transcultural studies in cognition [Special issue]. *American Anthropologist, 66*(3, Pt. 2), 146-170.

Rosch, E. H. (1973). Natural categories. *Cognitive Psychology, 4*, 328-350.

Rosch, E. H. (1975). Cognitive representations of semantic categories. *Journal of Experimental Psychology: General, 104*, 192-233.

Rosch, E. H., & Lloyd, B. B. (1978). *Cognition and categorization.* Hillsdale, NJ: Lawrence Erlbaum.

Rosch, E. H., & Mervis, C. B. (1975). Family resemblances: Studies in the internal structure of categories. *Cognitive Psychology, 7*, 573-605.

Rosch, E. H., Mervis, C. B., Gray, W. D., Johnson, D. M., & Boyes-Braem, P. (1976). Basic objects in natural categories. *Cognitive Psychology, 8*, 382-439.

Rose, M. (1984). *Writer's block: The cognitive dimension.* Carbondale: Southern Illinois University Press.

Rosenbloom, P. S., Laird, J. E., & Newell, A. (1993). *The Soar papers: Research on integrated intelligence.* Cambridge: MIT Press.

Ross, B. H. (1987). This is like that: The use of earlier problems and the separation of similarity effects. *Journal of Experimental Psychology: Learning, Memory, and Cognition, 13*, 629-639.

Ross, D. F., Read, J. D., & Toglia, M. P. (1994). *Adult eyewitness testimony: Current trends and developments.* Cambridge: Press Syndicate of the University of Cambridge.

Ross, M. (1989). Relation of implicit theories to the construction of personal histories. *Psychological Review, 96*, 341-357.

Rubinstein, M. F. (1975). *Patterns of problem solving.* Englewood Cliffs, NJ: Prentice-Hall.

Rubinstein, M. F. (1986). *Tools for thinking and problem solving.* Englewood Cliffs, NJ: Prentice-Hall.

Rubinstein, M. F., & Firstenberg, J. (1995). *Patterns of problem solving* (2nd. ed.). Englewood Cliffs, NJ: Prentice-Hall.

Rumelhart, D. E., & McClelland, J. L. (Eds.). (1986). *Parallel distributed processing: Explorations in the microstructure of cognition* (Vol. 1). Cambridge: MIT Press/Bradford Books.

Rumelhart, D. E., & Norman, D. A. (1978). Accretion, tuning, and restructuring: Three models of learning. In J. W. Cotton & R. Klatzky (Eds.), *Semantic factors in cognition* (pp. 37-53). Hillsdale, NJ: Lawrence Erlbaum.

Rundus, D. (1971). Analysis of rehearsal processes in free recall. *Journal of Experimental Psychology, 89*, 63-77.

Sacks, H., Schegloff, E. A., & Jefferson, G. (1974). A simplest systematics for the organization of turn-taking for conversation. *Language, 50*, 696-735.

Sacks, O. (1970). *The man who mistook his wife for a hat and other clinical tales*. New York: HarperCollins.

Sakitt, B. (1976). Iconic memory. *Psychological Review, 83*, 257-276.

Salasoo, A., & Pisoni, D. (1985). Interaction of knowledge sources in spoken word identification. *Journal of Memory and Language, 24*, 210-231.

Salthouse, T. A., & Babcock, R. I. (1991). Decomposing adult age differences in working memory. *Developmental Psychology, 27*, 763-776.

Sanders, M. S., & McCormick, E. J. (1993). *Human factors in engineering and design* (7th ed.). New York: McGraw-Hill.

Sanders, R. E., Gonzalez, E. G., Murphy, M. D., Liddle, C. L., & Vitina, J. R. (1987). Frequency of occurrence and the criteria for automatic processing. *Journal of Experimental Psychology: Learning, Memory, and Cognition, 13*, 241-250.

Sarbin, T. (1986). The narrative as a root metaphor for psychology. In T. Sarbin (Ed.), *Narrative psychology: The storied nature of human conduct* (pp. 3-21). New York: Praeger.

Savell, J. M., Twohig, P. T., & Rachford, D. L. (1986). Empirical status of Feurstein's "Instrumental Enrichment" (FEI) technique as a method of teaching thinking skills. *Review of Educational Research, 56*, 381-409.

Scardamalia, M., & Bereiter, C. (1991). Literate expertise. In K. A. Ericsson & J. Smith (Eds.), *Toward a general theory of expertise* (pp. 172-194). Cambridge: Cambridge University Press.

Schacter, D. L. (1987). Implicit memory: History and current status. *Journal of Experimental Psychology: Learning, Memory, and Cognition, 13*, 501-518.

Schacter, D. L. (1989). On the relation between memory and consciousness: Dissociable interactions and conscious experience. In H. L. Roediger III & F. I. M. Craik (Eds.), *Varieties of memory and consciousness: Essays in honour of Endel Tulving* (pp. 355-389). Hillsdale, NJ: Lawrence Erlbaum.

Schacter, D. L., & Graf, P. (1986). Effects of elaborative processing on implicit and explicit memory for new associations. *Journal of Experimental Psychology: Learning, Memory, and Cognition, 12*, 432-444.

Schank, R. C. (1975). *Conceptual information processing*. Amsterdam: North-Holland.

Schank, R. C. (1982). *Dynamic memory: A theory of reminding and learning in computers and people.* New York: Cambridge University Press.

Schank, R. C., & Abelson, R. (1977). *Scripts, plans, goals, and understanding.* Hillsdale, NJ: Lawrence Erlbaum.

Schmandt-Besserat, D. (1988). From accounting to written language. In B. A. Rafoth & D. L. Rubin (Eds.), *The social construction of written communication* (pp. 119-130). Norwood, NJ: Ablex.

Schmidt, S. R., & Bohannon, J. N., III. (1988). In defense of the flashbulb-memory hypothesis: A comment on McCloskey, Wible, and Cohen (1988). *Journal of Experimental Psychology: General, 117,* 332-335.

Schneider, W., & Detweiler, M. (1987). A connectionist/control architecture for working memory. In G. H. Bower (Ed.), *The psychology of learning and motivation* (Vol. 21, pp. 54-119). New York: Academic Press.

Schneider, W., & Shiffrin, R. M. (1977). Controlled and automatic human information processing: Detection, search, and attention. *Psychological Review, 84,* 1-66.

Schneiderman, B. (1976). Exploratory experiments in programmer behavior. *International Journal of Computer and Information Sciences, 5,* 123-143.

Schoenfeld, A. H. (1982). Measures of problem-solving performance and of problem-solving instruction. *Journal for Research in Mathematics Education, 13,* 31-49.

Schoenfeld, A. H. (1985). *Mathematical problem solving.* New York: Academic Press.

Schultz, D. P., & Schultz, S. E. (1992). *A history of modern psychology* (5th ed.).

New York: Harcourt Brace Jovanovich.

Seamon, J. G., Marsh, R. L., & Brody, N. (1984). Critical importance of exposure duration for affective discrimination of stimuli that are not recognized. *Journal of Experimental Psychology: Learning, Memory, and Cognition, 10,* 465-469.

Segal, B., Huba, G. J., & Singer, J. L. (1980). *Drugs, daydreaming, and personality: A study of college youth.* Hillsdale, NJ: Lawrence Erlbaum.

Segal, J. W., Chipman, S. F., & Glaser, R. (Eds.). (1985). *Thinking and learning skills: Relating instruction to basic research* (Vols. 1, 2). Hillsdale, NJ: Lawrence Erlbaum.

Seger, C. A. (1994). Implicit learning. *Psychological Bulletin, 115,* 163-196.

Seifert, C. M., McKoon, G., Abelson, R. P., & Ratcliff, R. (1986). Memory connections between thematically similar episodes. *Journal of Experimental Psychology: Learning, Memory, and Cognition, 12,* 220-231.

Seligman, M. E. P., & Yellen, A. (1987). What is a dream? *Behavior Research Therapy, 25,* 1-24.

Shallice, T. (1988). *From neuropsychology to mental structure.* Cambridge: Cambridge University Press.

Shapiro, A. M., & Murphy, G. L. (1993). Can you answer a question for me? Processing indirect speech acts. *Journal of Memory and Language, 32,* 211-229.

Shaw, R., & Pittenger, J. (1977). Perceiving the face of change in changing faces: Implications for a theory of object perception. In R. Shaw & J. Bransford (Eds.), *Perceiving, acting and knowing: Toward an ecological psy-*

chology (pp. 103-132). Hillsdale, NJ: Lawrence Erlbaum.

Shedler, J., & Block, J. (1990). Adolescent drug use and psychological health: A longitudinal inquiry. *American Psychologist, 45,* 612-630.

Shepard, R. N. (1967). Recognition memory for words, sentences, and pictures. *Journal of Verbal Learning and Verbal Behavior, 6,* 156-163.

Shepard, R. N. (1984). Ecological constraints on internal representation: Resonant kinematics of perceiving, imagining, thinking, and dreaming. *Psychological Review, 91,* 417-447.

Shepard, R. N. (1990). *Mind sights.* New York: Freeman.

Shepard, R. N. (1994). Perceptual-cognitive universals as reflections of the world. *Psychonomic Bulletin & Review, 1,* 2-28.

Shepard, R. N., & Chipman, S. (1970). Second-order isomorphism of internal representations: Shapes of states. *Cognitive Psychology, 1,* 1-17.

Shepard, R. N., & Cooper, L. A. (1983). *Mental images and their transformations.* Cambridge: MIT Press.

Shepard, R. N., & Metzler, J. (1971). Mental rotation of three-dimensional objects. *Science, 171,* 701-703.

Sherry, D. F., & Schacter, D. L. (1987). The evolution of multiple memory systems. *Psychological Review, 94,* 439-454.

Shiffrin, R. M. (1993). Short-term memory: A brief commentary. *Memory & Cognition, 21,* 193-197.

Shiffrin, R., & Schneider, W. (1977). Controlled and automatic human information processing: II. Perceptual learning, automatic attending, and a general theory. *Psychological Review, 84,* 127-190.

Shimamura, A. P. (1986). Priming effects in amnesia: Evidence for dissociable memory function. *Quarterly Journal of Experimental Psychology, 38A,* 619-644.

Shortliffe, E. (1976). *Computer based medical consultations: MYCIN.* New York: American Elsevier.

Simon, H. A. (1969). *The sciences of the artificial.* Cambridge: MIT Press.

Simon, H. A. (1978). Information processing theory of human problem solving. In W. K. Estes (Ed.), *Handbook of learning and cognitive processes* (Vol. 5, pp. 271-295). Hillsdale, NJ: Lawrence Erlbaum.

Simon, H. A. (1990). Invariants of human behavior. *Annual Review of Psychology, 41,* 1-19.

Simon, H. A., & Gilmartin, K. (1973). A simulation of memory for chess positions. *Cognitive Psychology, 5,* 29-46.

Simon, H. A., & Hayes, J. R. (1976). The understanding process: Problem isomorphs. *Cognitive Psychology, 8,* 165-190.

Simonton, D. K. (1988). *Scientific genius: A psychology of science.* Cambridge: Cambridge University Press.

Singer, J. L., & Antrobus, J. S. (1963). A factor analytic study of daydreaming and conceptually-related cognitive and personality variables. *Perceptual and Motor Skills, 17,* 187-209.

Singer, J. L., & Antrobus, J. S. (1972). Daydreaming, imaginal processes, and personality: A normative study. In P. W. Sheehan (Ed.), *The function and nature of imagery* (pp. 175-202). New York: Academic Press.

Skinner, B. F. (1938). *The behavior of organisms.* New York: Appleton-Century-Crofts.

Skinner, B. F. (1957). *Verbal behavior.* New York: Appleton-Century-Crofts.

Skinner, B. F. (1971). *Beyond freedom and dignity.* New York: Knopf.

Slovic, P., Fischhoff, B., & Lichtenstein, S. (1982). Facts versus fears: Understanding perceived risk. In D. Kahneman, P. Slovic, & A. Tversky (Eds.), *Judgment under uncertainty: Heuristics and biases* (pp. 463-489). New York: Cambridge University Press.

Smith, E. E. (1978). Theories of semantic memory. In W. K. Estes (Ed.), *Handbook of learning and cognitive processes* (Vol. 6, pp. 1-56). Hillsdale, NJ: Lawrence Erlbaum.

Smith, E. E., & Medin, D. L. (1981). *Categories and concepts.* Cambridge, MA: Harvard University Press.

Smith, E. E., Shoben, E. J., & Rips, L. J. (1974). Structure and process in semantic memory: A featural model for semantic decisions. *Psychological Review, 81,* 214-241.

Smith, S. B. (1983). *The great mental calculators: The psychology, methods and lives of calculating prodigies, past and present.* New York: Columbia University Press.

Smith, S. M., Brown, H. O., Toman, J. E. P., & Goodman, L. S. (1947). The lack of cerebral effects of d-Tubercurarine. *Anesthesiology, 8,* 1-14.

Smith, S. M., Glenberg, A., & Bjork, R. A. (1978). Environmental context and human memory. *Memory & Cognition, 6,* 342-353.

Snow, R. E. (1986). On intelligence. In R. J. Sternberg & D. K. Detterman (Eds.), *What is intelligence? Contempo-*

rary viewpoints on its nature and definition (pp. 133-139). Norwood, NJ: Ablex.

Solomans, L., & Stein, G. (1896). Normal motor automatism. *Psychological Review, 3,* 492-512.

Spear, N. E. (1979). Experimental analysis of infantile amnesia. In J. F. Kihlstrom & F. J. Evans (Eds.), *Functional disorders of memory* (pp. 75-102). Hillsdale, NJ: Lawrence Erlbaum.

Spearman, C. (1927). *The ability of man.* London: Macmillan.

Spelke, E. S. (1990). Principles of object perception. *Cognitive Science, 14,* 29-56.

Spelke, E., Hirst, W., & Neisser, U. (1976). Skills of divided attention. *Cognition, 4,* 215-230.

Sperling, G. (1960). The information available in brief visual presentations. *Psychological Monographs, 74*(Whole No. 498).

Sperry, R. W. (1969). A modified concept of consciousness. *Psychological Review, 76,* 532-536.

Sperry, R. W. (1980). Mind/brain interaction: Mentalism, yes—Dualism, no. *Neuroscience, 2,* 195-206.

Sperry, R. W. (1993). The impact and promise of the cognitive revolution. *American Psychologist, 48,* 878-885.

Spiro, R. J. (1980). Accommodative reconstruction in prose recall. *Journal of Verbal Learning and Verbal Behavior, 19,* 84-95.

Spitzer, H., Desimone, R., & Moran, J. (1988). Increased attention enhances both behavioral and neuronal performance. *Science, 240,* 338-340.

Squire, L. R. (1992). Memory and the hippocampus: A synthesis from findings with rats, monkeys, and humans. *Psychological Review, 99,* 195-231.

Squire, L. R., Amaral, D. G., & Press, G. A. (1990). Magnetic resonance measurements of hippocampal formation and mammillary nuclei distinguish medial temporal lobe and diencephalic amnesia. *Journal of Neuroscience, 10,* 3106-3117.

Squire, L. R., & Cohen, N. J. (1984). Human memory and amnesia. In J. McGaugh, G. Lynch, & N. Weinberger (Eds.), *Proceedings of the conference on the neurobiology of learning and memory* (pp. 3-64). New York: Guilford.

Squire, L. R., Knowlton, B., & Musen, G. (1993). The structure and organization of memory. *Annual Review of Psychology, 44,* 453-495.

Squire, L. R., & Zola-Morgan, S. (1991). The medial temporal lobe memory system. *Science, 253,* 1380-1386.

Stadler, M. A. (1993). Implicit serial learning: Questions inspired by Hebb (1961). *Memory & Cognition, 21,* 819-827.

Standing, L. (1973). Learning 10,000 pictures. *Quarterly Journal of Experimental Psychology, 25,* 207-222.

Stanovich, K. E., Cunningham, A. E., & Feeman, D. J. (1984). Intelligence, cognitive skills, and early reading progress. *Reading Research Quarterly, 19,* 278-303.

Stanzel, F. K. (1984). *A theory of narrative.* Cambridge: Cambridge University Press.

Staszewski, J. J. (1988). Skilled memory and expert mental calculation. In M. T. H. Chi, R. Glaser, & M. J. Farr (Eds.), *The nature of expertise* (pp. 71-128). Hillsdale, NJ: Lawrence Erlbaum.

Stein, N. L., & Glenn, C. G. (1979). An analysis of story comprehension in elementary school children. In R. O. Freedle (Ed.), *New directions in discourse processing* (pp. 53-120). Hillsdale, NJ: Lawrence Erlbaum.

Stemberger, J. P. (1985). An interactive activation model of language production. In A. W. Ellis (Ed.), *Progress in the psychology of language* (Vol. 1, pp. 143-186). Hillsdale, NJ: Lawrence Erlbaum.

Sternberg, R. J. (1977). *Intelligence, information processing, and analogical reasoning: The componential analysis of human abilities.* Hillsdale, NJ: Lawrence Erlbaum.

Sternberg, R. J. (1982). *Handbook of human intelligence.* New York: Cambridge University Press.

Sternberg, R. J. (1985). *Beyond IQ: A triarchic theory of human intelligence.* New York: Cambridge University Press.

Sternberg, R. J. (1988). *The nature of creativity: Contemporary psychological perspectives.* Cambridge: Cambridge University Press.

Sternberg, R. J., Conway, B. E., Ketron, J. L., & Bernstein, M. (1981). People's conceptions of intelligence. *Journal of Personality and Social Psychology, 41,* 37-55.

Sternberg, R. J., & Detterman, D. K. (1986). *What is intelligence? Contemporary viewpoints on its nature and definition.* Norwood, NJ: Ablex.

Sternberg, R. J., & Kolligian, J., Jr. (Ed.). (1990). *Competence considered.* New Haven, CT: Yale University Press.

Sternberg, R. J., & Wagner, R. K. (Eds.). (1986). *Practical Intelligence: Nature and origins of competence in the everyday world.* New York: Cambridge University Press.

Sternberg, S. (1966). High-speed scanning in human memory. *Science, 153,* 652-654.

Stevens, A., & Coupe, P. (1978). Distortions in judged spatial relations. *Cognitive Psychology, 10,* 422-437.

Stillings, N. A., Feinstein, M. H., Garfield, J. L., Rissland, E. L., Rosenbaum, D. A., Wiesler, S. E., & Baker-Ward, L. (1987). *Cognitive science: An introduction.* Cambridge: MIT Press.

Stokoe, W. C., Jr., Casterline, D. C., & Croneberg, C. G. (1965). *A dictionary of American Sign Language.* Washington, DC: Gallaudet College Press.

Stringer, C., & Gamble, C. (1993). *In search of the Neanderthals.* New York: Thames and Hudson.

Stromeyer, C. F. (1982). An adult eideticker. In U. Neisser (Ed.), *Memory observed: Remembering in natural contexts* (pp. 399-404). San Francisco: Freeman.

Stromeyer, C. F., & Psotka, J. (1970). The detailed texture of eidetic images. *Nature, 225,* 346-349.

Stroop, J. R. (1935). Studies of interference in serial verbal reactions. *Psychological Monographs, 50,* 38-48.

Sutherland, N. S. (1968). Outlines of a theory of visual pattern recognition in animals and man. *Proceedings of the Royal Society, 171,* 297-317.

Taplin, J. E. (1975). Evaluation of hypotheses in concept identification. *Memory & Cognition, 3,* 85-96.

Taplin, J. E., & Staudenmeyer, H. (1973). Interpretation of abstract conditional

sentences in deductive reasoning. *Journal of Verbal Learning and Verbal Behavior, 12,* 530-542.

Tart, C. T. (Ed.). (1969). *Altered states of consciousness.* New York: John Wiley.

Tart, C. T. (1975). *States of consciousness.* New York: E. P. Dutton.

Tartter, V. C. (1986). *Language processes.* New York: Holt, Rinehart & Winston.

Taylor, C. W., & Sacks, D. (1981). Facilitating lifetime creative processes: A think piece. *Gifted Child Quarterly, 25,* 116-118.

Terrace, H. S., Petitto, L. A., Sanders, R. J., & Bever, T. G. (1979). Can an ape create a sentence? *Science, 206,* 891-902.

Thomas, L. (1992). *The fragile species.* New York: Maxwell Macmillan International.

Thorndike, E. L. (1898). Animal intelligence: An experimental study of the associative processes in animals. *Psychological Review, Monograph Supplements, 2*(Serial No. 8).

Thorndike, R. L. (1973-1974). Reading as reasoning. *Reading Research Quarterly, 9,* 135-147.

Thorndyke, P. W. (1977). Cognitive structures in comprehension and memory of narrative discourse. *Cognitive Psychology, 9,* 77-110.

Tiffany, S. T. (1990). A cognitive model of drug urges and drug-use behavior: Role of automatic and nonautomatic processes. *Psychological Review, 97,* 147-168.

Tobias, P. V. (1987). The brain of *Homo habilis:* A new level of organization in cerebral evolution. *Journal of Human Evolution, 16,* 741-761.

Trabasso, T., & van den Broek, P. (1985). Causal thinking and the representation of narrative events. *Journal of Memory and Language, 24,* 612-630.

Tranel, D., & Damasio, A. R. (1985). Knowledge without awareness: An autonomic index of facial recognition by prosopagnosics. *Science, 228,* 1453-1454.

Treisman, A. M. (1960). Contextual cues in encoding listening. *Quarterly Journal of Experimental Psychology, 12,* 242-248.

Treisman, A. M. (1970). Contextual cues in selective listening. *Quarterly Journal of Experimental Psychology, 12,* 242-248.

Treisman, A. M. (1987). Properties, parts, and objects. In K. Boff, L. Kaufman, & J. Thomas (Eds.), *Handbook of perception and performance* (pp. 159-198). New York: John Wiley.

Treisman, A. M., & Gelade, G. (1980). A feature-integration theory of attention. *Cognitive Psychology, 12,* 97-136.

Treisman, A. M., & Sato, S. (1990). Conjunction search revisited. *Journal of Experimental Psychology: Human Perceptual Performance, 16,* 459-478.

Tulving, E. (1962). Subjective organization in free recall of "unrelated" words. *Psychological Review, 69,* 344-354.

Tulving, E. (1972). Episodic and semantic memory. In E. Tulving & W. Donaldson (Eds.), *Organization of memory* (pp. 381-403). New York: Academic Press.

Tulving, E. (1983). *Elements of episodic memory.* New York: Oxford University Press.

Tulving, E. (1985). How many memory systems are there? *American Psychologist, 40,* 385-398.

Tulving, E., Mandler, G., & Baumel, R. (1964). Interaction of two sources of information in tachistoscopic word recognition. *Canadian Journal of Psychology, 18,* 62-71.

Tulving, E., & Pearlstone, Z. (1966). Availability versus accessibility of information in memory for words. *Journal of Verbal Learning and Verbal Behavior, 5,* 381-391.

Tulving, E., & Schacter, D. L. (1990). Priming and human memory systems. *Science, 247,* 301-306.

Tulving, E., & Thomson, D. M. (1973). Encoding specificity and retrieval processes in episodic memory. *Psychological Review, 80,* 352-373.

Turing, A. M. (1950). Computing machinery and the mind. *Mind, 59,* 433-460.

Tversky, A., & Kahneman, D. (1971). Belief in the law of small numbers. *Psychological Bulletin, 76,* 105-110.

Tversky, A., & Kahneman, D. (1973). Availability: A heuristic for judging frequency and probability. *Cognitive Psychology, 5,* 207-232.

Tversky, B. (1981). Distortions in memory for maps. *Cognitive Psychology, 13,* 407-433.

Tversky, B. (1991). Spatial mental models. *Psychology of Learning and Motivation, 27,* 109-145.

Ullman, S. (1989). Aligning pictorial descriptions: An approach to object recognition. *Cognitive Psychology, 32,* 193-254.

Valentine, T. (1988). Upside-down faces: A review of the effect of inversion upon face recognition. *British Journal of Psychology, 79,* 471-491.

Van Petten, C., & Kutas, M. (1987). Ambiguous words in context: An event-related potential analysis of the time course of meaning activation. *Journal of Memory and Language, 26,* 188-208.

Vokey, J. R., & Read, J. D. (1985). Subliminal messages: Between the devil and the media. *American Psychologist, 40,* 1231-1239.

von Frisch, K. (1950). *Bees: Their vision, chemical senses, and language.* Ithaca, NY: Cornell University Press.

von Restorff, H. (1933). Über die Wirkung von Bereichsbildungen in Spurenfeld. *Psychologische Forshung, 18,* 299-342.

Vygotsky, L. S. (1962). *Thought and language* (E. Haufmann & G. Vakar, Eds. and Trans.). Cambridge: MIT Press.

Wada, J., & Rasmussen, T. (1960). Intracarotid injection of sodium amytal for lateralisation of cerebral speech dominance. *Journal of Neurosurgery, 17,* 266-282.

Wagner, M. W., & Monnet, M. (1979). Attitudes of college professors toward extrasensory perception. *Zetetic Scholar, 5,* 7-17.

Wallas, G. (1926). *The art of thought.* New York: Harcourt Brace.

Warren, R. M. (1968). Verbal transformation effect and auditory perceptual mechanisms. *Psychological Bulletin, 70,* 261-270.

Warren, R. M. (1970). Perceptual restoration of missing speech sounds. *Science, 167,* 392-393.

Warren, R. M., & Meyers, M. D. (1987). Effects of listening to repeated syllables: Category boundary shifts versus verbal transformations. *Journal of Phonetics, 15,* 169-181.

Warrington, E. K., & Shallice, T. (1972). Neuropsychological evidence of visual storage in short-term memory tasks. *Quarterly Journal of Experimental Psychology, 24,* 30-40.

Warrington, E. K., & Weiskrantz, L. (1970). Amnesia: Consolidation or retrieval? *Nature, 228,* 628-630.

Wason, P. C. (1968). On the failure to eliminate hypotheses: A second look. In P. C. Wason & P. N. Johnson-Laird (Eds.), *Thinking and reasoning* (pp. 44-75). Baltimore, MD: Penguin.

Wason, P. C., & Johnson-Laird, P. N. (1972). *Psychology of reasoning: Structure and content.* Cambridge, MA: Harvard University Press.

Watkins, O. C., & Watkins, M. J. (1980). The modality effect and echoic persistence. *Journal of Experimental Psychology: General, 109,* 251-278.

Watson, J. B. (1913). Psychology as the behaviorist views it. *Psychological Review, 20,* 158-177.

Watson, J. B. (1930). *Behaviorism* (2nd ed.). New York: Norton. (Original work published 1924)

Waugh, N. C., & Norman, D. A. (1965). Primary memory. *Psychological Review, 72,* 89-104.

Weisberg, R. W. (1986). *Creativity: Genius and other myths.* New York: Freeman.

Weisberg, R. W. (1993). *Creativity: Beyond the myth of genius.* New York: Freeman.

Weisberg, R. W., & Alba, J. W. (1981). An examination of the alleged role of "fixation" in the solution of several "insight" problems. *Journal of Experi-*

mental Psychology: General, 110, 169-192.

Weiskrantz, L., & Warrington, E. K. (1979). Conditioning in amnesic patients. *Neuropsychologia, 17*, 187-194.

Wellman, H. M., & Gelman, S. A. (1992). Cognitive development: Foundational theories of core domains. *Annual Review of Psychology, 43*, 337-375.

Wertheimer, M. (1912). Experimentelle Studien über das Sehen von Bewegung. *Zeitschrift für Psychologie, 61*, 121-165.

Wertheimer, M. (1959). *Productive thinking*. New York: Harper & Row.

Wheeler, D. D. (1970). Processes in word recognition. *Cognitive Psychology, 1*, 59-85.

Whimbey, A., & Lochhead, J. (1980). *Problem solving and comprehension: A short course in analytical reasoning* (2nd ed.). Philadelphia: Franklin Institute Press.

Whitty, C. W. M., & Lewin, W. (1960). A Korsakoff syndrome in the postcingulectomy confusional state. *Brain, 83*, 648-653.

Wickelgren, W. A. (1974). *How to solve problems: Elements of a theory of problems and problem solving*. San Francisco: Freeman.

Wickens, C. D. (1980). The structure of attentional resources. In R. Nickerson (Ed.), *Attention and performance VIII* (pp. 239-257). Hillsdale, NJ: Lawrence Erlbaum.

Wickens, D. D. (1972). Characteristics of word encoding. In A. W. Melton & E. Martin (Eds.), *Coding processes in human memory* (pp. 191-215). New York: Winston.

Wickens, D. D., Dalezman, R. E., & Eggemeier, F. T. (1976). Multiple encoding of word attributes in memory. *Memory & Cognition, 4*, 307-310.

Wierzbicka, A. (1985). The double life of a bilingual. In R. Sussex & J. Zubrzycki (Eds.), *Polish people and culture in Australia* (pp. 187-223). Canberra: Australian National University.

Winograd, E., & Neisser, U. (Eds.). (1992). *Affect and accuracy in recall: Studies of "flashbulb" memories*. New York: Cambridge University Press.

Winograd, T. (1983). *Language as a cognitive process*. Reading, MA: Addison-Wesley.

Woodworth, R., & Sells, S. (1935). An atmosphere effect in formal syllogistic reasoning. *Journal of Experimental Psychology, 18*, 451-460.

Yarbus, A. L. (1967). *Eye movements and vision* (B. Haigh, Trans.). New York: Plenum.

Yates, F. A. (1966). *The art of memory*. Chicago: University of Chicago Press.

Yerkes, R. M., & Dodson, J. D. (1908). The relation of strength of stimulus to rapidity of habit-formation. *Journal of Comparative Neurology of Psychology, 18*, 459-482.

Zaragoza, M. S., McCloskey, M., & Jamis, M. (1987). Misleading post event information and recall of the original event: Further evidence against the memory impairment hypothesis. *Journal of Experimental Psychology: Learning, Memory, and Cognition, 13*, 36-44.

Zbrodoff, N. J. (1985). Writing stories under time and length constraints. *Dissertation Abstracts International, 46*, 1219A.

Zola-Morgan, S., & Squire, L. R. (1990). Neurophysiological investigations of memory and amnesia: Findings from humans and nonhuman primates. In A. Diamond (Ed.), *The development and neural bases of higher cognitive functions* (pp. 434-456). New York: New York Academy of Sciences.

Zola-Morgan, S., Squire, L. R., & Amaral, D. G. (1986). Human amnesia and the medial temporal region: Enduring memory impairment following a bilateral lesion limited to field CA1 of the hippocampus. *Journal of Neuroscience, 6,* 2950-2967.

Author Index

Subject Index

Verbal transformation
    effect, 290, 482, 500
Verification, 192, 194, 316,
    355, 359, 360, 426
Vision, 32, 38, 42, 44, 47, 48,
    53-55, 67, 90, 96, 183,
    322, 352, 389, 449
Visual agnosia, 63
Visual attention, 70, 90, 92,
    94, 96
Visual field, 41, 90, 92, 93,
    443
Visual imagery. *See* Imagery
Visual sensory memory. *See*
    Iconic memory
Visual search, 55
Voice onset time, 270, 282,
    283, 293

Voicing, 236, 268, 270, 281,
    282, 293
Von Restorff effect, 139

Weber, 36, 37, 66
Weber-Fechner Law, 36, 66
Well-defined problem, 333,
    358
Wernicke's area, 243, 244,
    272, 273
Whole report, 43, 45, 46
Whorf, 258
Whorfian hypothesis, 258-
    262
Word order, 260
Word superiority effect, 51,
    66

Working memory, 18, 20,
    21, 100, 121, 129, 130,
    197, 267, 268, 297, 300,
    339, 391, 408, 409, 426,
    427, 446
in concept learning, 177-
    179, 181
in expertise, 203, 204,
    218, 224, 225
in reading, 305, 308-310,
    316, 317, 320-324
in reasoning, 369, 370,
    373, 374
in writing, 297, 300
Writing, 295-304